AF709537

Terrorism and Asylum

International Refugee Law Series

Editor-in-Chief

Professor David James Cantor

Editorial Board

Professor Deborah Anker
Professor Bhupinder Chimni
Professor Geoff Gilbert
Professor Guy S. Goodwin-Gill
Professor Liliana Jubilut
Professor Susan Kneebone
Professor Hélène Lambert
Professor Bonaventure Rutinwa
Dr. Volker Türk

VOLUME 17

The titles published in this series are listed at *brill.com/irls*

Terrorism and Asylum

Edited by

James C. Simeon

BRILL
NIJHOFF

LEIDEN | BOSTON

Library of Congress Cataloging-in-Publication Data

Names: Simeon, James C., editor.
Title: Terrorism and asylum / edited by James C. Simeon.
Description: Leiden, the Netherlands ; Boston : Koninklijke Brill NV, [2020] | Series: International refugee law series, 2213-3836 ; volume17 | Includes index. | Summary: "Terrorism and Asylum, edited by James C. Simeon, explores terrorism and asylum in all its interrelated and variable aspects, and permutations. The critical role terrorism plays as a driver in forced displacement, within the context of protracted armed conflict and extreme political violence, is analyzed. Exclusion from refugee protection for the alleged commission of terrorist activities is thoroughly interrogated. Populist politicians' blatant use of the "fear of terrorism" to further their public policy security agenda and to limit access to refugee protection is scrutinized. The principal issues and concerns regarding terrorism and asylum and how these might be addressed, in the public interest while, at the same time, protecting and advancing the human rights and dignity of everyone are offered"-- Provided by publisher.
Identifiers: LCCN 2020018045 (print) | LCCN 2020018046 (ebook) | ISBN 9789004273696 (hardback) | ISBN 9789004295995 (ebook)
Subjects: LCSH: Refugees--Legal status, laws, etc. | Political refugees--Legal status, laws, etc. | Asylum, Right of. | Convention Relating to the Status of Refugees (1951 July 28) | Freedom of movement (International law) | Terrorism (International law) | Terrorism--Prevention--Law and legislation.
Classification: LCC KZ6530 .T47 2020 (print) | LCC KZ6530 (ebook) | DDC 341.4/86--dc23
LC record available at https://lccn.loc.gov/2020018045
LC ebook record available at https://lccn.loc.gov/2020018046

Typeface for the Latin, Greek, and Cyrillic scripts: "Brill". See and download: brill.com/brill-typeface.

ISSN 2213-3836
ISBN 978-90-04-27369-6 (hardback)
ISBN 978-90-04-29599-5 (e-book)

Copyright 2020 by Koninklijke Brill NV, Leiden, The Netherlands.
Koninklijke Brill NV incorporates the imprints Brill, Brill Hes & De Graaf, Brill Nijhoff, Brill Rodopi, Brill Sense, Hotei Publishing, mentis Verlag, Verlag Ferdinand Schöningh and Wilhelm Fink Verlag.
All rights reserved. No part of this publication may be reproduced, translated, stored in a retrieval system, or transmitted in any form or by any means, electronic, mechanical, photocopying, recording or otherwise, without prior written permission from the publisher.
Authorization to photocopy items for internal or personal use is granted by Koninklijke Brill NV provided that the appropriate fees are paid directly to The Copyright Clearance Center, 222 Rosewood Drive, Suite 910, Danvers, MA 01923, USA. Fees are subject to change.

This book is printed on acid-free paper and produced in a sustainable manner.

Contents

Foreword

Terrorism and asylum dominate the agendas of states, regional and global organizations such as the EU, African Union, Organization of American States, and the UN. Whilst often addressed as separate issues they ought to be viewed *in tandem.*

It is impossible to deny the destabilizing effect of forced displacement fuelled by conflict, violence and human rights violations. In 2018, the UNHCR reported the global population of forcibly displaced people grew substantially from 43.3 million in 2009 to 70.8 million in 2018, reaching a record high (UNHCR, Global Trends 2018). Most of this increase was driven by the Syrian conflict. Conflicts in other areas contributed to this rise, including in Iraq and Yemen, the Democratic Republic of the Congo (DRC) and South Sudan, as well as the flow of Rohingya refugees to Bangladesh at the end of 2017. The refugee population under UNHCR's mandate is currently 20.4 million. This means that it has nearly doubled since 2012 when it stood at 10.5 million.

According to terrorism expert Alex Schmid, the study of terrorism and the study of migration have for too long been two separate fields. He advocates research on the intersection of the two phenomena (ICCT Research paper, May 2016). Whilst there are multiple causal relations between (forced/irregular) migration and terrorism, it is clear that a major driver of forced migration is severe state repression involving attacks on civilian populations that, in cases of (civil) war, often also amount to war crimes or war-time terrorism. Terrorism by non-state actors with deliberate attacks on civilians is another major driver of forced migration.

Linking terrorism to forced displacement has its own dimension and challenges when it comes to refugee protection and the concomitant exclusion of those who are 'underserving' of such protection. The exclusion clauses of the Refugee Convention of 1951 are increasingly used to exclude those against whom there are "serious reasons for considering" they have engaged in (wartime) terrorism. Exclusion has become a way for states to counter terrorism, which erodes the protection of asylum seekers. We are reminded of the fact that there is no clear and universally adopted definition of terrorism and the concept is prone to expansion and abuse.

In my own area of research, international criminal law, refugee exclusion generates a group of 'outlaws'. For instance, in the Netherlands hundreds of asylum claimants, mainly from Afghanistan and Iraq, are excluded for (allegedly) having engaged in war crimes. Exclusion is not followed by prosecution. Courts lack jurisdiction or there is a lack of resources, or even evidence to meet the threshold of a *prima facie* case. Most excluded persons cannot be sent back to their country of origin where they will face ill-treatment. They end up in a 'legal limbo' with no right to reside or work and rely on support of family and civil society. A similar situation exists in other European countries[1], Canada, Australia, and New Zealand. The exclusion clause of the Refugee Convention and the policy to end impunity of those who are considered the enemy of mankind, *hostis humanis*, generates a growing group of unwanted and undesirable individuals.

The enemy of mankind narrative is reflected in recent debates on foreign fighters and their brides. These people are regarded as having forfeited their right of protection *via* citizenship. The link with international criminal law *via* terrorism and war crimes, enables lawmakers and politicians to argue in favour of a justice system outside the regular court system, preferably outside the country; in a jurisdictional bubble – a space beyond sovereignty.

This work, linking conflict, terrorism, forced displacement and asylum, is a timely publication. The authors and its editor deserve praise for linking the two fields of terrorism and asylum; for unpacking the complex relationship between two phenomena that are connected in such a complex and multidimensional way. This book is a must-read for academics, policy makers, legal practitioners and anyone interested in the area of terrorism and asylum studies. I congratulate the editor and authors with producing such a fine collection of essays.

Elies van Sliedregt
Leeds, October 2019

1 M.P. Bolhuis and J. van Wijk, *Study on the Exchange of Information between European countries regarding persons excluded from refugee status in accordance with Article 1F Refugee Convention*, 2015, 14–22; M.P. Bolhuis, H. Battjes, J. van Wijk, 'Undesirable but Unreturnable Migrants in the Netherlands', *Refugee Survey Quarterly*, 2017, 61–84

Preface

Two of the most pressing issues confronting the international community today are "terrorism" and "asylum." Since 9/11, the worst terrorist attack in modern history, States and, in particular, the United States of America, have been preoccupied with national security and the prevention of another unprecedented devastating terrorist attack on their soil.[1] Likewise, the so-called, "refugee crises"[2] appear to be ever escalating and reaching unprecedented levels with some 70.8 million people who were forcibly displaced worldwide at the end of 2018.[3] The UNHCR states that in every minute of 2018, 25 people were forced to flee their homes.[4] In fact, the overall general trend for both "terrorism" and "asylum" appears to be upward, despite the apparent best efforts of the United Nations, other international organizations, and States to try to address fundamentally both of these global issues, with their most disturbing growing trends. Accordingly, a volume that is dedicated to examining critically and assessing these two subjects from several theoretical approaches and different perspectives is long overdue.

What is a most troubling aspect with respect to "terrorism" and "asylum" is how these two concepts are so different and misunderstood. The first, "terrorism," is premised on the purposive wanton random killing of people and the destruction of property in order to incite extreme fear, indeed, terror, in order to persuade public policy makers to their political cause. The second, "asylum" is premised on those who are fleeing their countries of nationality or former

1 United Nations Office on Drugs and Crime, UNODC, "The United Nations Office of Drugs and Crime and Terrorism Prevention," https://www.unodc.org/unodc/en/terrorism/index.html. (accessed November 3, 2019); Ivo H. Daalder and James M. Lindsay, "Nasty, Brutish, and Long: America's War on Terrorism," December 1, 2001, Brookings, https://www.brookings.edu/articles/nasty-brutish-and-long-americas-war-on-terrorism/. (accessed November 3, 2019); Leon E. Panetta, "The fight against terrorism is far from over," *The Washington Post, Democracy Dies in Darkness*, August 23, 2019. https://www.washingtonpost.com/opinions/the-fight-against-terrorism-is-far-from-over/2019/08/23/703e5bc2-c532-11e9-b72f-b31dfaa77212_story.html. (accessed November 3, 2019).

2 Humanitarian Coalition, "Conflicts and Refugee Crises," https://www.humanitariancoalition.ca/conflicts-and-refugee-crises. (accessed November 3, 2019) Wherein at least a dozen refugee crises are identified that are all as a result of protracted armed conflicts.

3 UNHCR, Global Trends, Forced Displacement in 2018, Geneva: UNHCR, 2019, https://www.unhcr.org/5d08d7ee7.pdf. (accessed November 3, 2019).

4 UNHCR, Global Trends, Forced Displacement in 2018, "2018 in Review, Trends at a Glance," https://www.unhcr.org/globaltrends2018/. (accessed November 3, 2019).

habitual residence in order to save their lives, liberty, and security, and, most importantly, their human dignity. Yet, both terms are rooted in the same conditions. Sadly, statistics clearly show that they are each rooted primarily in extreme organized violence such as war, armed conflict, and repressive authoritarian political regimes.[5] Terrorism occurs most frequently in areas where armed conflict is taking place or wherever severe political oppression occurs. Put simply, "violence breeds further violence."[6]

The genesis for this edited collection lies in the University of London's School of Advanced Study's Refugee Law Initiative's Workshop on "Terrorism and Asylum," that was held on December 8, 2017.[7] This was followed by the publication of a "Terrorism and Asylum Working Paper Series Mini-Volume."[8] What evolved from there was a broader publication project with Brill Nijhoff Publishers.

A publication project of this nature depends, of course, on the dedication and commitment of its contributing authors, but, equally importantly, on those who supported and sustained this initiative from the very outset to its conclusion. In this regard, a special note of thanks goes to Professor David James Cantor, and, Senior Lecturer, Dr. Sara Singer, for their support of this initiative from the beginning. But special thanks are also in order for the Refugee Law Initiative (RLI), as a whole, for their support and commitment of this project, including, most especially, Susan Reardon-Smith. The RLI's guidance and assistance throughout has been essential. I should like to thank the RLI for seeing this research project through to its completion and for the publication

5 James C. Simeon, "Terrorism and Asylum: Unravelling the Myths," *RLI Blog on Refugee Law and Forced Migration*, January 25, 2018, https://rli.blogs.sas.ac.uk/2018/01/25/terrorism-and-asylum-unravelling-the-myths/. (accessed November 3, 2019).

6 Isabel Bramsen, "How Violence Breeds Violence: Micro-dynamics and Reciprocity of Violent Interaction in the Arab Uprisings," *International Journal of Conflict and Violence*, Vol. 11, 2017, 1-11. doi: 10.4119/UNIBI/ijcv.625. file:///C:/Users/jcsimeon/Downloads/625-2967-1-PB.pdf. (accessed November 4, 2019); Laurie Calhoun, "How Violence Breeds Violence: Some Utilitarian Considerations," *Politics*, 2002, Vol. 22(2), 95-108, https://onlinelibrary.wiley.com/doi/pdf/10.1111/1467-9256.00164. (accessed November 4, 2019); Martin Luther King Program, Washington State University, Famous Quotes, On Nonviolence, "Hate begets hate; violence begets violence; toughness begets a greater toughness. We must meet the forces of hate with the power of love." (1958) https://mlk.wsu.edu/about-dr-king/famous-quotes/. (accessed November 4, 2019).

7 Refugee Law Initiative, School of Advanced Study, University of London, "RLI 'Terrorism and Asylum' Workshop: Report Published," Tuesday 23 January 2018, https://rli.sas.ac.uk/about-us/news/rli-terrorism-and-asylum-workshop-report-published. (accessed November 3, 2019).

8 James C. Simeon, ed., *Terrorism and Asylum* (*RLI Working Paper Series Mini-Volume*), No. 31-36, May, 2019, https://sas-space.sas.ac.uk/9204/. (accessed November 3, 2019).

of this volume. Without the Refugee Law Initiative's support and backing this project would not have been possible.

I am also very grateful, of course, to all of our contributors to this volume and, above all, for their patience, understanding, and dedication to this publication project. The chapters for this edited volume went through multiple drafts and revisions before their final publication. Some of the chapters appeared in the RLI Working Papers Series Mini-Volume and went through major changes, amendments, and updates, before appearing as new contributions for this volume.

I should also like to thank Brill Nijhoff Publishers for their support for this publication project. Especially, Lindy Melman, for all her assistance throughout this publication project. Her very good humour and mild temperament were very much appreciated.

Much of the work that was done on this research and publication project took place while I was on my Sabbatical Leave at the University of Cambridge, where I was affiliated with Clare Hall and the Lauterpacht Centre for International Law. Both Clare Hall and the Lauterpacht Centre for International Law provided a conducive and rich intellectual environment for undertaking such a demanding and challenging research project. I should like to thank, especially, Professor David J. Ibbeston, President of Clare Hall, and Professor Eyal Benvenisti, Director of the Lauterpacht Centre for International Law, for allowing me to conduct my research for this project at two of the most stimulating, interesting, and the finest learning communities and research centres of their kind in the world today.

I should also like to thank York University, my Faculty of Liberal Arts and Professional Studies, my School of Public Policy and Administration, and, of course, McLaughlin College, and all those who are affiliated with these distinct higher educational entities, for their support and assistance, while I was on my Sabbatical Leave, and, subsequently, upon my return to York University, for the completion this publication project. My colleagues at York University have supported and sustained my research efforts and scholarship throughout my time as a faculty member there.

I should also like to thank my colleagues at the Canadian Association for Refugees and Forced Migration Studies (CARFMS) for their support of my research efforts in this regard and for publishing my piece on "Exposing Terrorism's False Association with Asylum" in the *CARFMS Newsletter*, Winter 2018, Issue 9.[9] All of my colleagues in CARFMS, and those who are affiliated with the

9 James C. Simeon, "Exposing Terrorism's False Association with Asylum," *CARFMS Newsletter*, Winter 2018, Issue 9, pp. 13-19, http://carfms.org/wp-content/uploads/2018/01/CARFMS-newsletter-winter-2018.pdf. (accessed November 3, 2019).

Centre for Refugee Studies and the Jack and Mae Nathanson Centre on Transnational Human Rights, Crime and Security, Osgoode Hall Law School, at York University, have encouraged and supported my scholarship in the field of refugee and forced migration studies throughout my tenure at York University.

It takes the capable and sustained efforts of many people, over an extended period, to produce an edited collection. I am very grateful and appreciative of all the support and assistance of so many people to get this volume into print. Thank you all for your support throughout this enterprise in scholarship!

My hope is that this edited volume will further the work that is being done on both of these highly significant and challenging subject areas that are preoccupying the international community, including civil society, and States in the world today.

Dr. James C. Simeon, Associate Professor
Head of McLaughlin College, 224 McLaughlin College
School of Public Policy and Administration
Faculty of Liberal Arts and Professional Studies
York University
4700 Keele Street North Toronto, Ontario, Canada
M3J 1P3
jcsimeon@yorku.ca

Notes on Contributors

Dr. Rebecca Ananian-Welsh

is a Senior Lecturer at The School of Law, The University of Queensland. Her research focuses primarily on judges and courts, as well as concerning human rights and national security law and policy. Dr. Ananian-Welsh has co-edited two books as well as publishing book chapters, articles in leading journals and has spoken widely at Australian and international events on these topics. Prior to joining The School of Law, Dr. Ananian-Welsh was an academic member of the Laureate Fellowship Project 'Anti-Terror Laws and the Democratic Challenge'.

Dr. Peter Billings

is a Professor at The School of Law, The University of Queensland. His research interests are in administrative law, immigration and refugee law, human rights law and crimmigration. He has published over thirty peer reviewed journal articles, and book chapters in edited collections, in Australia, the US, and Europe. Prior to working in Australia, he lectured Public Law and Refugee Law, respectively, in the United Kingdom from 1995–2007.

Dr. John R. Campbell

is a Emeritus Reader in the Anthropology of Africa and Law. He currently teaches anthropology at the School of Oriental and African Studies (SOAS), London, and has conducted fieldwork in Ghana, Tanzania and the UK and has spent 10 years as a development consultant for international development agencies (evaluating or working on projects in Ethiopia, Kenya and Botswana) He has written about development, refugees and refugee and criminal law. John's most recent publications include: *Nationalism, Law and Statelessness. Grand Illusions in the Horn of Africa* (Routledge, 2014), *Bureaucracy, Law and Dystopia in the United Kingdom's Asylum System* (Routledge, 2017) In 2016–2017 he conducted fieldwork in London's magistrates' courts and will soon be published as *Entanglements of Life with the Law: Precarity and Justice in London's Magistrates' Courts* by Cambridge Scholars Publishing.

Dr. Nula Frei

is a senior researcher and lecturer at the Institute of European Law, University of Fribourg, Switzerland. She wrote her Ph.D. thesis on the protection of victims of human trafficking in asylum law. Nula has also worked at the Centre for Migration Law of the University of Bern, the Swiss Centre for Expertise in Human Rights and the UNHCR Office for Switzerland and Liechtenstein.

Dr. Constantin Hruschka

has worked as a Senior Research Fellow at the Max Planck Institute for Social Law and Social Policy in Munich since November 2017. Before that he worked as head of the protection department at the Swiss Refugee Council (2014–2017) and as a lawyer for UNHCR, the UN Refugee Agency (2004–2014). Dr. Hruschka studied law, history and philosophy in Würzburg, Poitiers and Paris. In addition to his work at the Max-Planck-Institute he is teaching European Law and European Asylum Law as well as Human Rights Law mainly at the Universities of Bielefeld, Munich, Erlangen-Nuremberg and Fribourg. He is a part of the pool of experts of the European Asylum Support Office (EASO) and was appointed as a member of the Swiss Federal Commission on Migration in December 2015. He has written (mostly in German) articles on the Swiss and the European Asylum system with a focus on the Dublin system.

The most recent articles in English are: "Access to Asylum Procedures for Victims of Trafficking under a Human Rights-based Approach," in: Maria O'Sullivan/Dallal Stevens, editors, *States, the Law and Access to Refugee Protection: Fortresses and Fairness.* Hart Publishing, 2017, "Toward better Integration of People in Need of Protection," in: National Centre of Competence in Research (NCCR) (ed.), *From Temporary to Durable Stay: Integration in the Field of Asylum*, Highlights #2, 2017, pp. 41–45 and "Enhancing Efficiency and Fairness? The Commission Proposal for a Dublin IV Regulation," in: *ERA Forum*, Vol. 17, 2017, pp. 521–534. He has also commented alongside with Francesco Maiani on the Dublin III Regulation in: Kay Hailbronner/Daniel Thym, *EU Immigration and Asylum Law. A Commentary*, 2nd edition, C.H. Beck, 2016.

Julia Kienast

in 2014, Mag.a Julia Kienast graduated from the University of Vienna with a general law degree and a specialization in Criminal Law and Criminology as well as European Human Rights. After volunteering in the City of Huaraz, Peru and working at the Viennese Criminal Court, she returned to the University of Vienna in 2015, where she is working as a research and teaching assistant at the Department of Constitutional and Administrative Law. Ms. Kienast has published in the area of migration, asylum and human trafficking and edited two handbooks on pre-trial detention standards for juveniles and the radicalization of juveniles in detention. In the course of her Ph.D. studies, Ms. Kienast is researching sustainable and adequate instruments for the management of mass migration in Austria and Europe. Her work has been recognized through several grants and scholarships, most recently by the Fulbright Program. Ms. Kienast is, amongst others, an active member of the German *Netzwerk Migrationsrecht*, the Viennese Refugee Law Clinic (VLC) and the Academic Council on the United Nations System (ACUNS).

Barbara Kőhalmi
is a practicing human rights lawyer. She obtained an LL.M. in human rights with special focus on the European framework of human rights protection. Her main field of expertise and interest is migration and its human rights aspects. She has a good knowledge of international and the Hungarian legal framework of migration gained through working in the Hungarian central public administration for six years. Now she does research on the nexus between migration and statelessness.

Selina March
holds an MA in Refugee Protection and Forced Migration Studies from the University of London, and a BA (Honours) Development Studies and International Relations from the University of Westminster. She has a keen interest in the way language and communication impact the way we view the world, which has driven her previous work on the impact of charity marketing methods and social media on global stratification. Her research is interdisciplinary in nature, with recent work drawing on policy analysis, critical legal studies, refugee studies, criminology, and sociology. Her research interests within and beyond the study of forced migration include tools and impacts of political discourse, critical race theory and the sociology of law, and the impact of criminalisation and securitisation on targeted populations.

Dr. Christopher McDowell
is a political anthropologist and Reader in International Politics at City, University of London. He conducts research on forced migration and involuntary resettlement in the context of conflict and violence, development interventions and environmental change with a geographical focus on South Asia and East and Central Africa. Christopher is an international resettlement specialist advising international agencies including the World Bank and UNHCR.

Anita Nagy-Nádasdi
is a lawyer who worked for eight years in various governmental and non-governmental organisations that helped the integration of refugees in Hungary. Currently, she is a Ph.D. student at Eötvös Lóránd University in Budapest. Her main research focus is to connect international refugee law, children's rights, and humanitarian law in order to highlight national obligations for protecting children involved in armed conflict. She has also participated in a migration

research project with the National University of Public Service and a research project with the Eötvös Lóránd University Faculty of Law on sovereignty and statehood in 2017.

Dr. Joseph Rikhof

is an adjunct professor at the Faculty of Common Law at the University of Ottawa where he teaches the course on International Criminal Law. His expertise lies with the law related to genocide, war crimes and crimes against humanity, especially, as practised at the domestic level and in the context of immigration and refugee law. He has lectured on the same topics on all continents. He has also published over 50 articles as well as several books: *The Criminal Refugee: The Treatment of Asylum Seekers with a Criminal Background in International and Domestic Law* (2012); as co-author with Terje Einarsen, *A Theory of Punishable Participation in Universal Crimes,* (2018) and as co-author with Robert Currie, *International and Transnational Criminal Law, Third Edition* (2020).

Dr. James C. Simeon

is the Head of McLaughlin College and an Associate Professor in the School of Public Policy and Administration (SPPA), Faculty of Liberal Arts and Professional Studies, York University, Toronto, Canada. He is a Member-at-Large of the Executive of the Canadian Association for Refugee and Forced Migration Studies (CARFMS) and a past President of CARFMS. He also serves as the Coordinator of the International Association of Refugee and Migration Judges' (IARMJ) Inter-Conference Working Party Process. His primary areas of research are international refugee law, international human rights law, international humanitarian law, international criminal law, and public policy and public administration. He has published widely in these areas of research and he has organized and led many highly successful academic and professional conferences, symposia and workshops. Before joining the faculty at York University he served as the IARMJ's first Executive Director and prior to that he was a Member and Coordinating Member of the Immigration and Refugee Board of Canada (IRB). He has also worked as a Special Assistant on Parliament Hill and as a Researcher and Policy Analyst in the Communications Division of the former Ministry of Transportation and Communications in the Ontario Public Service.

Dr. Elies van Sliedregt

is currently the Professor of International and Comparative Criminal Justice, School of Law, University of Leeds. From 2011–2015 she was the Professor of Criminal Law at Vrije Universiteit Amsterdam and Dean of the Faculty of Law. She has also taught at the Universities in Leiden and Utrecht. She has held visiting fellowships at the universities in Cambridge, Oxford, Bologna, and at the University of New South Wales, Sydney, Australia. In 2015, she was Holding Redlich fellow at the Castan Center for Human Rights at Monash University, Melbourne. In 2010, she was a visiting professional at the International Criminal Court. She is a member of the Royal Holland Society of Sciences and Humanities and the senior editor of the *Leiden Journal of International Law* and she is a member of the editorial board of the *Journal of Conflict and Security Law*. She is an author-contributor to the *Oxford Bibliographies in International Law* (on joint enterprise liability and conspiracy).

Mark Symes
is a Barrister who practices out of the Garden Court Chambers in London, United Kingdom. He provides advice and representation in all areas of immigration, asylum, and human rights law, including European Union free movement law. He has represented clients in every court from the Tribunal to the Supreme Court and European Court of Human Rights. Mark sits as a judge of the Upper Tribunal and First-tier Tribunal which gives him great insight into the way a case should be presented. He has particular expertise in higher appeals having spent many years specializing in test-case litigation both with the Refugee Legal Centre and since arriving in private practice; he is very well known to the Senior Immigration Judiciary at Field House - see for example the Foreword to his new book with Peter Jorro *Immigration Appeals and Remedies Handbook* ("invaluable ... to the armoury of all ... a compulsory addition to the library of every immigration judge and practitioner": President of the Upper Tribunal Mr Justice McCloskey).

Patricia Tuitt
is a legal academic and author of numerous publications in the field of refugee law, including the monograph, *False Images: Law's Construction of the Refugee* (1996) and the article "Transitions: Refugees and Natives" (2013). Formerly Professor and Dean of the School of Law at Birkbeck, University of London (2009–2017), she now directs an online academic resource in her name (patriciatuitt, com). Recent open access publications include: "The UK's General Strike: Brexit and Critiques of Violence" (2017) and "Academic Judgement and the Force of Law" (2018).

INTRODUCTION

Terrorism, Asylum, and Exclusion from International Protection

James C. Simeon

1 Introduction

Terrorism and asylum have been two of the most pressing issues of our time. They have preoccupied public international law and, specifically, international humanitarian law and international criminal law as well as international human rights and international refugee law. Not to mention the United Nations, regional organizations, and, of course, nation-states, for decades, but, obviously, most decidedly since September 11, 2001 or 9/11, that forever changed the course of modern history and everyone's life.[1] This edited collection seeks to examine both of these concepts and how they are inter-related and have impacted the course of public policy and, especially, migration policy, that is, asylum and refugee law and practice, across a number of Western liberal democracies, principally, in Europe and North America.

What follows in this introduction is a review of the background and context of these two highly charged and emotive terms. It considers the direct and indirect relationship between these two terms through their predominately common origins in protracted armed conflict, particularly of a non-international character or intrastate conflict. It goes on to analyse briefly the relationship between these two terms. It then provides a brief summary of some of the main arguments presented in each of the contributions to this edited volume and offers a number of conclusions.

The purpose of this edited collection is to make a contribution to the literature that covers both terrorism and asylum, that are largely quite separate and

1 Jon Henley, "Was 9/11 the day that changed the world forever?" *The Guardian*, September 9, 2011, https://www.theguardian.com/world/2011/sep/09/9-11-changed-world-forever. (accessed July 31, 2019); Laura Santhanam and Larisa Epatko, "9/11 to today: Ways we have changed," *PBS News Hour*, September 11, 2018, https://www.pbs.org/newshour/nation/9-11-to-today-ways-we-have-changed. (accessed July 31, 2019); Jennie Wood, "How We've Changed Since 9/11," *Infoplease*, undated, https://www.infoplease.com/us/government/how-weve-changed-since-911. (accessed July 31, 2019); Kent Roach, *The 9/11 Effect: Comparative Counter-Terrorism*. (Cambridge: Cambridge University Press, 2011).

© KONINKLIJKE BRILL NV, LEIDEN, 2020 | DOI:10.1163/9789004295995_002

distinct. Despite the overwhelming evidence that indicates that they have common origins in organized extreme political violence. Protracted armed conflict and severe political oppression produce terrorism and refugees and until and unless we address these "root causes" both terrorism and refugees will remain at the forefront of all our public international concerns.

2 Background and Context

Since the horrific events of September 11, 2001, the international community and the United States, specifically, have been preoccupied with the issue of terrorism. The events of 9/11 will forever be etched indelibly in the minds of all those who experienced that day.[2] It was the worst terrorist attack in modern history.[3] The aftermath of these four coordinated terrorist attacks that felled the Twin Towers of the World Trade Centre in New York City; destroyed a whole section of the Pentagon in Washington, DC; and, through the heroic actions of the passengers of United Airlines 93, brought down their hijacked airliner in Shanksville, Pennsylvania, killing all those on board, that was targeted, ostensibly, to strike the US Capitol Building, in Washington, DC, was to change inconvertibly the world forever.[4]

A shocked and terrorized world responded through the United Nations calling on all states to bring the perpetrators of 9/11 to justice, while the United

2 Dana Rose Garfin, "How the pain of 9/11 still stays with a generation," *The Conversation*, September 9, 2016, updated September 11, 2016, https://theconversation.com/how-the-pain-of-9-11-still-stays-with-a-generation-64725. (accessed September 15, 2018); Carlin Crisanti and Jennifer Merolla, "The Effects of the 9/11 Terrorist Attacks on American Public Opinion and Behavior," *Oxford Bibliographies*, last modified 27 February 2019, http://www.oxfordbibliographies.com/abstract/document/obo-9780199756223/obo-9780199756223-0270.xml?rskey=mDrMWf&result=5&q=Counterterrorism#firstMatch. (accessed March 24, 2019)

3 Benjamin Elisha Sawe, "Worst Terrorist Attacks in World History," *worldatlas*, April 25, 2017, https://www.worldatlas.com/articles/worst-terrorist-attacks-in-history.html. (accessed March 16, 2019)

4 Helaina Hovitz, "I was 12 years old and blocks away from the World Trade Centre on 9/11 – here's how I saw the world change around me forever," *Business Insider*, September 11, 2018, https://www.businessinsider.com/911-completely-changed-the-world-as-we-knew-it-heres-how-2018-9. (accessed September 15, 2018); Meagan Smith, Sean M. Zeigler, "Terrorism before and after 9/11 – a more dangerous world?" *Research & Politics*, November 10, 2017, pp. 1–8, http://journals.sagepub.com/doi/pdf/10.1177/2053168017739757. (accessed September 15, 2018); Satvinder S. Juss, ed., *Beyond Human Rights and the War on Terror*. (London: Routledge, 2019). Manfred Nowak and Anne Charbord, eds., *Using Human Rights to Counter Terrorism*. (Cheltenham, UK: Edward Elgar Publishing, 2018)

States announced it would undertake a "War on Terror."[5] Within a month, the United States and its coalition partners invaded Afghanistan to dismantle Al Qaeda and to deny it a safe base of operations under the radical fundamentalist Taliban regime. Sadly, the "War in Afghanistan" that commenced on October 7, 2001, is still ongoing today. Contentious from the very outset, the "War on Terror," has undergone various permutations and has been renamed the "Overseas Contingency Operations."[6] What has also endured is the heightened state of security and the resolve that no other terrorist attack like 9/11 will ever occur again. This has often been described as "securitization."[7] The preoccupation with national security concerns and, more specifically, the prevention of terrorism, that has resulted in an increase in monitoring and surveillance and intelligence gathering with, ineluctably, a commensurate diminution in individual privacy and liberty.[8]

Despite all of the efforts on the part of the United Nations and its member states, terrorism has not decreased since 9/11, but, on the contrary and counter intuitively, it has increased over time even though there has been yearly ebbs and flows in the number of terrorist incidents and deaths due to terrorist attacks.[9]

> When examining the drivers of terrorism the presence of armed conflict, political violence by governments, political exclusion and group grievances remain critical factors. The analysis finds that 99 per cent of all deaths over the last 17 years has been in countries that are either in

5 United Nations Security Council Resolution 1368, 12 September 2001, http://www.un.org/en/ga/search/view_doc.asp?symbol=S/RES/1368%282001%29. (accessed September 15, 2018); United Nations Security Council Resolution 1373, 28 September 2001, https://www.unodc.org/pdf/crime/terrorism/res_1373_english.pdf. (accessed September 15, 2018)

6 Overseas Contingency Operations, Department of Defense – Military Programs, https://www.whitehouse.gov/wp-content/uploads/2018/02/08_OCO_508.pdf. (accessed September 9, 2018) GAO, US Government Accountability Office, Overseas Contingency Operations: Alternatives Identified to the Approach to Fund War-Related Activities, GAO-19-211, January 28, 2019, https://www.gao.gov/products/GAO-19-211. (accessed April 20, 2020)

7 Rens van Munster, "Securitization," *Oxford Bibliographies,* last reviewed 19 September 2014, http://www.oxfordbibliographies.com/view/document/obo-9780199743292/obo-9780199743292-0091.xml. (accessed March 24, 2019)

8 Matt McDonald, "Securitization and the Construction of Security," *European Journal of International Relations*, 14:4 (2008), http://wrap.warwick.ac.uk/1232/1/WRAP_McDonald_0671572-pais-270709-mcdonald_securitisation_and_construction_of_security_ejir_forthcoming_2008.pdf. (accessed September 15, 2018); Guy S. Goodwin-Gil, "Forced Migration: Refugees, Rights and Security," in *Forced Migration, Human Rights and Security*. Ed., Jane McAdam (Oxford: Hart Publishing, 2008).

9 *Global Terrorism Index 2017, Measuring and understanding the impact of terrorism*, Institute for Economics and Peace (IEP), November 2017, IEP Report 55, p. 3. http://visionofhumanity.org/app/uploads/2017/11/Global-Terrorism-Index-2017.pdf. (accessed March 18, 2019)

conflict or have high levels of political terror. Political terror involves extrajudicial killings, torture and imprisonment without trial. This shows that the great majority of terrorism is used as a tactic within an armed conflict or against repressive political regimes. It also demonstrates the risks of political crackdowns and counterterrorism actions that can exacerbate existing grievances and the drivers of extremism and terrorism. Both Egypt and Turkey recorded substantially higher levels of terrorism following government crackdowns.[10]

2.1 *Terrorism*

The impact of terrorism in the modern world should never be underestimated.[11] According to the Institute of Economics and Peace, the global economic cost of terrorism in 2016 was US $84 billion, and, while this was substantial it was only a small fraction of the global economic impact of violence that was $14.3 trillion in 2016.[12] What is important to note here is that terrorism is one of the few categories of violence where costs associated with containment probably exceed its consequential costs. But, it is argued, that while the estimated economic impact of terrorism may be small it is still critical to contain it, because, terrorism has the potential to spread quickly and with significant social ramifications.[13]

The random use of extreme violence "to terrorize" or to strike paralyzing fear on a population, and, especially, its opinion leaders and policy makers, and, thereby, influence decision-making, in favour of the terrorist cause, research has shown to be highly ineffective as a means of realizing societal change in keeping with the terrorists' preferences.[14]

---

10 Ibid.

11 Hall Gardner, "Terrorism," *Oxford Bibliographies*, last reviewed 15 November 2016, http://www.oxfordbibliographies.com/abstract/document/obo-9780199743292/obo-9780199743292-0055.xml?rskey=mDrMWf&result=10&q=Counterterrorism#firstMatch. (accessed March 24, 2019)

12 *Global Terrorism Index 2017, Measuring and understanding the impact of terrorism*, Institute for Economics and Peace (IEP), November 2017, IEP Report 55, p. 3. http://visionofhumanity.org/app/uploads/2017/11/Global-Terrorism-Index-2017.pdf. (accessed March 18, 2019)

13 Ibid.

14 Max Abrahms, "The Political Effectiveness of Terrorism Revisited," *Comparative Political Studies*, 2012, 45(3): 366–393, https://www.gwern.net/docs/terrorism/2012-abrahms.pdf. (accessed March 23, 2019); "Terrorism is not effective," created 14 April 2009, modified 7 March 2019, What's the value of x? triplebite, *Gwern Branwen*, https://www.gwern.net/Terrorism-is-not-Effective. (accessed March 23, 2019)

Refugees and other forced migrants, like everything else, has been adversely affected by 9/11 and its aftermath. The preoccupation with national security and the prevention of terrorist attacks has made refugees and other forced migrants suspected security threats. All legitimate channels for entering the territory of a state have been "securitized" or "sealed," in an effort to prevent terrorists from exploiting their potential host states, for their own benefit, including, the use of the asylum systems of states to gain access and admission to their territory.[15] Whether these concerns are legitimate and well-founded is another matter entirely.[16]

With Donald J. Trump assuming the Office of the President of the United States in January 2017, not surprisingly,[17] there was a dramatic change in immigration and refugee policy. There was a suspension of immigration from what Trump called "terror-prone regions."[18] Presidential Proclamation No. 9645 placed entry restrictions on the nationals of eight countries, including refugee claimants without valid travel documents: Chad, Iran, Libya, North

15 Todd Bensman, "What Migration Over European Borders can Teach about American Border Security," Centre for Immigration Studies, November 6, 2019, https://cis.org/Report/Terrorist-Migration-Over-European-Borders. (accessed April 20, 2020) Jane McAdam, ed. *Forced Migration, Human Rights and Security*. Oxford: Hart Publishing, 2008.

16 Polly Toynbee, "Our borders are porous. Why can't our politicians admit the problems of immigration?" *The Guardian*, Opinion, Immigration and Asylum, 27 February 2010, https://www.theguardian.com/commentisfree/2010/feb/27/our-borders-are-porous. (accessed September 16, 2018); Sian Elin Dafydd, "Slavery and human trafficking aided by 'porous borders.'" *BBC News*, 16 May 2017, https://www.bbc.com/news/uk-wales-39924457. (accessed September 16, 2018)

17 Jenna Johnson, "Trump calls for a 'total and complete shutdown of Muslims entering the United States,'" *The Washington Post*, December 7, 2015, https://www.washingtonpost.com/news/post-politics/wp/2015/12/07/donald-trump-calls-for-total-and-complete-shutdown-of-muslims-entering-the-united-states/?noredirect=on&utm_term=.cdf5d46da14e. (accessed March 17, 2019); Gregory Krieg, "Trump's history of anti-Muslim rhetoric hits dangerous new low," *CNN politics*, November 30, 2017, https://www.cnn.com/2017/11/29/politics/donald-trump-muslim-attacks/index.html. (accessed March 17, 2019)

18 Josh Keller, Adam Pearce, Wilson Andrews, "Tracking Trumps Agenda, Step by Step," *The New York Times*, October 1, 2018, https://www.nytimes.com/interactive/2017/us/politics/trump-agenda-tracker.html. (accessed March 16, 2019); Adam Liptak and Michael D. Shear, "Trump Travel Ban is Upheld by Supreme Court," *The New York Times*, June 26, 2018, https://www.nytimes.com/2018/06/26/us/politics/supreme-court-trump-travel-ban.html. (accessed March 16, 2019); Presidential Proclamation No. 9645, *Presidential Proclamation Enhancing Vetting Capabilities and Processes for Detecting Attempted Entry into the United States by Terrorists or Other Public-Safety Threats*, September 24, 2017, Donald J. Trump, https://www.whitehouse.gov/presidential-actions/presidential-proclamation-enhancing-vetting-capabilities-processes-detecting-attempted-entry-united-states-terrorists-public-safety-threats/. (accessed March 16, 2019); *Trump v. Hawaii*, No. 17-965, 585 U.S. (2018), https://www.supremecourt.gov/opinions/17pdf/17-965_h315.pdf. (accessed March 17, 2019)

Korea, Somalia, Syria, Venezuela, and Yemen.[19] Following a series of court rulings, the US Supreme Court in the *2018 Trump v. Hawaii* landmark ruling, in a 5 to 4 judgement with the majority opinion written by Chief Justice John Roberts, concluded that the Presidential Proclamation was valid.[20]

An equally contentious Trump Administration campaign promise and policy initiative has been the construction of a wall on its southern border with Mexico.[21] Moreover, the Trump Administration has deployed active-duty troops to the southern border to support US Customs and Border Protection officials in "hardening the southern border."[22] The impetus for the construction of the wall is, in part, "to stop illegal immigrants spreading crime and drugs."[23] Nonetheless, it has been argued persuasively that, "President Trump's wall would be a mammoth expenditure that would have little impact on illegal immigration."[24] In essence, the wall has become a symbol for the Trump's Administration efforts to protect the U.S. homeland from, what he has described as a foreign "invasion."[25] The Trump Administration has been imposing restriction on those seeking asylum at its southern border, the Migrant Protection Protocols (MPP) or what are better known as the "Remain in Mexico."[26]

19 Presidential Proclamation No. 9645.

20 *Trump v. Hawaii*, No. 17-965, 585 U.S. (2018); Harvard Law Review, "Establishment Clause, Trump v. Hawaii, Leading Case: 138 S. Ct. 2392 (2018)" March 17, 2019, 132 Harv. L. Rev. 327, https://harvardlawreview.org/2018/11/trump-v-hawaii// (accessed March 17, 2019)

21 Amanda Holpuch, "Trump re-ups controversial Muslim ban and Mexico wall in first campaign ad," *The Guardian,* January 4, 2016, https://www.theguardian.com/us-news/2016/jan/04/donald-trump-great-again-first-campaign-ad-isis-mexico-wall-muslim-ban. (accessed March 17, 2019) Astonishingly, Trump claimed that if elected President that he would build the wall to prevent immigrants from illegally crossing into the United States from its southern border and that Mexico would pay for the wall.

22 Claire Felter and Zachery Laub, "Who Secures the U.S. Border?" *Council on Foreign Relations*, February 15, 2019, https://www.cfr.org/backgrounder/us-mexico-border-woes?gclid=CjwKCAjw4LfkBRBDEiwAc2DSlEkqNJCoGIJhZo5LeXX6zxZwWEjEAt9D-C2AJ7SdrGig-NfSE-skWfhoCPJEQAvD_BwE. (accessed March 17, 2019)

23 David Smith, "Trump declares national emergency to build US-Mexico border wall," *The Guardian*, February 15, 2019, https://www.theguardian.com/us-news/2019/feb/15/national-emergency-border-wall-trump-latest-news. (accessed March 17, 2019)

24 David Bier, "Why the Wall Won't Work," *CATO Institute*, Commentary, this article appeared in the May 2017 issue of *Reason*, https://www.cato.org/publications/commentary/why-wall-wont-work. (accessed March 17, 2019)

25 David Smith, "Trump declares national emergency to build US-Mexico border wall," *The Guardian*, February 15, 2019, https://www.theguardian.com/us-news/2019/feb/15/national-emergency-border-wall-trump-latest-news. (accessed March 17, 2019). Wherein, Trump is quoted as saying, "We're talking about an invasion of our country, with drugs, with human traffickers, with all types of criminals and gangs."

26 Isaac Bloch and Anne Dutton, "Border Purgatory: Trump Administration's Latest Efforts to Deter Refugees," *Refugees Deeply*, February 22, 2019, https://www.newsdeeply.com/

The election of Donald Trump, as President of the United States, and his agenda of limiting the number of migrants entering the United States is due, at least in some part, to the traumatizing effects of terrorist actions within the United States but also elsewhere in the world today. Like other populist leaders, he has played on the public's insecurity and fear of terrorism following the traumatizing effects of 9/11.[27]

2.2 *Refugees*

The other great concern of our time is the seemingly endlessly increasing numbers of refugees and other forced migrants. Indeed, the so-called, "refugee crisis," shows no signs of abetting. The number of forcibly displaced persons has been escalating for the past decade. The UNHCR has underscored that there are now over 70 million people who have been forcibly displaced in the world today. What is perhaps most astonishing is that more than two-thirds of the world's forcibly displaced people (67%) come from only five countries: the Syrian Arab Republic; Afghanistan; South Sudan, Myanmar, and Somalia. And, sadly, about half of the world's refugees are children under the age of 18 years of age.[28] These statistics underscore that the "root cause" of the vast majority of the world's refugees come from states that have been embroiled in armed conflict for years. The nature of the armed conflict is nearly entirely non-international armed conflict that, frequently, has been internationalized.[29]

refugees/community/2019/02/22/border-purgatory-trump-administrations-latest-effort-to-deter-refugees. (accessed March 18, 2019)

27 Molly Ball, "Donald Trump and the Politics of Fear," *The Atlantic*, September 2, 2016, https://www.theatlantic.com/politics/archive/2016/09/donald-trump-and-the-politics-of-fear/498116/. (accessed July 17, 2019); Julie Hirschfeld Davis, "Obama Accuses Trump of Exploiting Working-Class Fears," *The New York Times*, December 21, 2015, https://www.nytimes.com/2015/12/22/us/politics/president-obama-accuses-donald-trump-of-exploiting-working-class-fears.html. (accessed July 17, 2019); David Remnick, "Donald Trump's Exploitation of Orlando," *The New Yorker*, June 12, 2016, https://www.newyorker.com/news/daily-comment/donald-trumps-exploitation-of-orlando. (accessed July 17, 2019); Uri Friedman, "Where America's Terrorists Actually Come From: Syrian refugees have committed zero attacks in the United States," *The Atlantic*, January 30, 2017. https://www.theatlantic.com/international/archive/2017/01/trump-immigration-ban-terrorism/514361/. (accessed April 22, 2020); Tamara Khandaker, "Most Terrorists are Homegrown, Not Refugees," *Vice*, October 2, 2017, https://www.vice.com/en_ca/article/bjvpw8/most-terrorists-are-homegrown-not-refugees. (accessed April 22, 2020)

28 United Nations High Commissioner for Refugees, UNHCR, *Global Trends: Forced Displacement 2018*. Geneva: UNHCR, 2019. https://www.unhcr.org/5d08d7ee7.pdf. (accessed June 30, 2019)

29 International Institute for Strategic Studies (IISS), *Armed Conflict Survey, 2018*, July 2018, Editor's Introduction, https://www.iiss.org/publications/armed-conflict-survey/2018/armed-conflict-survey-2018/acs2018-02-introduction. (accessed March 23, 2019)

In a fascinating paper by Barbara F. Walter, titled, "Conflict Relapse and the Sustainability of Post-Conflict Peace," she points out the "three disturbing patterns of regarding civil wars" or non-international armed conflicts and their reoccurrence.[30] First, she notes that civil wars have a high recidivism rate.[31] Of the 103 countries that experienced civil war in the period 1945–2009, only 44 did not experience a subsequent civil war. Thus, 56 percent of the countries that had one civil war experienced another. This has been described in the literature as the "conflict trap."[32] Her second point is that "recurring civil wars have become the dominant form of armed conflict in the world today."[33] This is underscored by the fact that every civil war since 2003 has been a continuation of a previous civil war.[34] She states that "90 percent of the conflicts initiated in the 21st century were in countries that had already experienced a civil war."[35] Hence, she argues that "the problem of civil wars is not of preventing new conflicts from arising, but of permanently ending the ones that have already started."[36] Thirdly, "civil wars are increasingly concentrated in a few regions of the world."[37] She makes the point that in the first decade of the 21st century that 35 percent of all civil wars occurred in Sub-Saharan Africa.[38] The observation she makes here is that "civil wars are increasingly being ghettoized in the world's poorest and weakest states."[39] Walter's findings reinforce the UNHCR's statistics with respect to the fact that more than two-thirds of the world's refugees come from only five protracted, and seemingly unending, civil wars or non-international armed conflicts.

3 Protracted Armed Conflict, Extreme Political Violence, Terrorism and Asylum

One truism of modern warfare is that it intentionally kills people, civilian noncombatants more so than armed combatants, and destroys property on a

30 Barbara F. Walter, "Conflict Relapse and the Sustainability of Post-Conflict Peace," *World Development Report 2011*, Background Paper, September 13, 2010, World Bank, p. 1, http://documents.worldbank.org/curated/en/128031468182669586/Conflict-relapse-and-the-sustainability-of-post-conflict-peace. (accessed March 23, 2019)

31 Ibid.

32 Ibid.

33 Ibid.

34 Ibid.

35 Ibid.

36 Ibid., p. 2.

37 Ibid.

38 Ibid.

39 Ibid.

massive scale. Another truism of modern warfare is that it produces refugees and other forced migrants on a massive scale.[40] No one should be expected to have to try to live in a war zone or an armed conflict zone, where you might be subject to "cross fire" or be a victim of "collateral damage" or to have to suffer the lack of the bare necessities of life such as water, food, medicine, and, the right to earn a livelihood or a living. No one should be expected to have to try to live in a war zone or armed conflict zone and be subjected to the threat of dehydration, starvation, disease or the fear of personal insecurity that could singly or in combination prove to be fatal. In fact, modern warfare is characterized by the death of significantly more civilian non-combatants than armed combatants, with the majority of deaths being attributed to starvation and disease than deliberate targeting or collateral damage.[41] Hence, it is entirely understandable that citizens would be motivated to flee the uninhabitable and the insufferable conditions of a protracted war or armed conflict.

Two points are worth emphasizing. The first is the overwhelming type of armed conflict that takes place in the world today is non-international armed conflict or intrastate conflict or civil war. The other significant point is that a number of these non-international armed conflicts have been internationalized with the participation of other states supporting one side or the other in the civil war. The "internationalization" of a civil war or internal armed conflict is what makes it a far more vicious and deadly affair that is extremely difficult to resolve and, as a consequence, tends to last much longer.[42]

The second point is that most of the world's terrorism occurs in situations of armed conflict or extreme political violence where, for example, a state is oppressing its own citizens. Terrorism is concentrated geographically to those regions of the world that experience protracted armed conflict and/or extreme political violence. It is important to emphasize that terrorism can take place

40 Mary Kaldor, *New and Old Wars: Organized Violence in a Global Era*. 3rd Edition. Cambridge: Polity Press, 2012.

41 Valerie Epps, "Civilian Casualties in Modern Warfare: The Death of the Collateral Damage Rule," *Georgia Journal of International and Comparative Law*, 2013, Vol. 41, 307–355, https://digitalcommons.law.uga.edu/cgi/viewcontent.cgi?article=1036&context=gjicl. (accessed March 23, 2019); Neta C. Crawford, "Costs of War, Human Costs of the Post-9/11 Wars: Lethality and the Need for Transparency," *Watson Institute, International and Public Affairs*, Brown University, November 2018, https://watson.brown.edu/costsofwar/files/cow/imce/papers/2018/Human%20Costs%2C%20Nov%208%202018%20CoW.pdf. (accessed March 23, 2019)

42 Kendra Dupuy, Scott Gates, Håvard M Nygård, Ida Rudolfsen, Siri Aas Rustad, Håvard Strand and Henrik Urdal, "Trends in Armed Conflict 1946–2016," Peace Research Institute Oslo (PRIO), 22 June 2017. *ETH Zurich, Centre for Strategic Studies*, http://www.css.ethz.ch/en/services/digital-library/articles/article.html/a7992888-34fc-44e6-8176-2fcb3aada995/pdf. (accessed September 15, 2018)

both in armed conflict situations or non-armed conflict situations, that is, both in times of war and in peace. The essential aspect is that organized extreme violence is the fundamental characteristic under circumstances of either protracted armed conflict or extreme political violence such as under a totalitarian regime.[43]

The pertinent point here with respect to forced displacement is that terrorism can serve as an accelerator of mass forced displacement in situations of armed conflict or political violence. The fear that terrorism imposes on civilians and the public at large in situations of armed conflict and extreme political violence can trigger and result in widespread mass forced displacement. In short, terrorism accelerates mass forced displacement in a war setting or situation of extreme political violence.[44]

If war and armed conflict are synonymous with the mass production of refugees, then, terrorism is its catalyst. Consequently, these four terms are intimately related: protracted armed conflict; extreme political violence; terrorism; and, forced displacement. From this, it is obvious that to resolve the so-called "refugee crisis" in the world today it is necessary to address the problem of terrorism within the context of protracted armed conflict and/or extreme political violence.

4 Analyzing the Relationship between Terrorism and Asylum

The purpose of this edited volume is to explore in detail the relationship between terrorism and asylum in all its interrelated and variable aspects, variants, and permutations. It considers the role that terrorism plays as a driver in forced displacement within the context of protracted armed conflict and extreme political violence. It also considers the role that terrorism plays in the refugee status determination process, both as a basis for a well-founded fear of persecution within the context of a state that is not willing or able to

43 START, National Consortium for the Study of Terrorism and Responses to Terrorism, Background Report, Global Terrorism 2017, University of Maryland, August 2018, https://www.start.umd.edu/pubs/START_GTD_Overview2017_July2018.pdf. (accessed September 15, 2018)

44 Phil Orchard, "Making States Accountable for Deliberate Forced Displacement," World Refugee Council Research Paper No. 17 -- June 25, 2019, https://www.cigionline.org/publications/making-states-accountable-deliberate-forced-displacement. (accessed April 20, 2020) James C. Simeon, "Enhancing Refugee Protection Through the Criminalization of 'Mass Forced Displacement.'" *RLI Blog on Refugee Law and Forced Migration*, August 2, 2018, https://rli.blogs.sas.ac.uk/2018/08/02/enhancing-refugee-protection-through-the-criminalization-of-mass-forced-displacement/. (accessed September 15, 2018)

provide the refugee applicant adequate state protection from the alleged perpetrators of terrorism and the alleged persecutors. It will also consider the exclusion from refugee protection of all those who have been involved in terrorist activities. It will also consider how terrorism has been driving the public policy agenda regarding refugees and other forced migrants in a number of different jurisdictions. Politicians have been using the fear generated by the risk of terrorist attacks to further their public policy agenda to limit and to restrict refugees' access to refugee protection within their respective countries. The edited collection concludes by identifying the major issues and concerns related to refugees and terrorism and how these might be addressed in the broader public interest while, at the same time, protecting and advancing the human rights and dignity of everyone.

This edited volume on "Terrorism and Asylum" brings together a number of senior legal scholars, researchers and academics to provide their original work on a very important topic that has pre-occupied States, in a very serious way, for close to the last two decades, if not more. The edited volume fills a very important existing gap in the literature on public international law, dealing with both international criminal law and, specifically, with the "crime of terrorism," and international refugee law, and, in particular, the exclusion from asylum under Article 1F for being involved in terrorism or terrorist activities. This edited volume provides an innovative, detailed, and thorough legal analysis, from a number of different levels and perspectives, of "terrorism and asylum" in international, transnational, and national law, with the aim of providing new insights, analyses, findings, and recommendations for how to address these modern challenges confronting the world community today, within and across States – as well as regionally and internationally, in the seemingly ever escalating 'wicked public policy problems' of terrorism,[45] and, the ongoing, and seemingly ever rising, unprecedented "refugee crisis."[46]

---

45 Brian Head, "Understanding 'Wicked' Policy Problems," *Policy Options*, January 9, 2018, https://policyoptions.irpp.org/magazines/january-2018/understanding-wicked-policy-problems/. (accessed April 20, 2020). Fact Sheet, For up-to-date knowledge relating to healthy public policy, "Wicked Problems and Public Policy," June 2013, National Collaborating Centre for Healthy Public Policy, Institut National de sante publique, Quebec, https://www.inspq.qc.ca/pdf/publications/1841_Wicked_Problems_Policy.pdf. (accessed September 16, 2018)

46 Centre for International Governance Innovation, Transforming the Global Refugee System, https://www.cigionline.org/interactives/2017annualreport/index.html?gclid=CjoKCQjw_vfcBRDJARIsAJafEnFMjHGBlZh12ppghrm9chjMjKgdqh91IraSUpLszbPhfKSYcoMxlL-gaAmVnEALw_wcB#/?slide=11. (accessed September 16, 2018); World Refugee Council, https://www.worldrefugeecouncil.org/?source=ar2017. (accessed September 16, 2018). Wherein it states, "Bold and creative thinking is required to address the global refugee crisis."

What follows is further background and contextual information for this edited collection and it continues with an outline and explanation of the relationship and interdependence, among and between, these four key concepts: protracted armed conflict, extreme political violence, terrorism and forced displacement. It further makes reference to the concept of "securitization" and how this has impacted those seeking asylum with a well-founded fear of persecution. It then goes on to indicate how this edited collection fits into the existing literature on terrorism and on asylum. Moreover, it presents the rationale for why this volume is necessary, how it is structured, who this book is intended for, and, it finishes with some final thoughts and justifications for the volume, in light of the fact that it came out of a "Terrorism and Asylum" Workshop that was sponsored and held at the Refugee Law Initiative (RLI), School of Advanced Study, University of London, in December 2017 and has resulted in a number of important contributions to this critical topic in international refugee, criminal, and humanitarian law and to the field of refugees and forced migration studies in general.

4.1 *How This Edited Volume Fits into the Existing Literature on Terrorism and Asylum*

Although there is an extensive literature on terrorism and on asylum, the literature examining 'terrorism *and* asylum' is scant. I have included some of the following sources available in the literature that demonstrates this basic point. Some of these works cover the topic of "terrorism and asylum" but often times not directly. There are a number of exceptions that are worth noting. Some of the notable exceptions, include: Sarah Singer's book, *Terrorism and Exclusion from Refugee Status in the UK: Asylum Seekers Suspected of Serious Criminality;*[47] Alex P. Schmid, "Links Between Terrorism and Migration: An Exploration";[48] Alex Nowrasteh, "Terrorism and Immigration: A Risk Analysis";[49] Swetha Sridharan, "Material Support to Terrorism – Consequences for Refugees and Asylum Seekers in the United States";[50] Won Kidane, "The Terrorism Bar to Asylum

47 Sarah Singer, *Terrorism and Exclusion from Refugee Status in the UK: Asylum Seekers Suspected of Serious Criminality.* Leiden, The Netherlands: Koninklijke Brill, 2015.

48 Alex P. Schmid, "Links Between Terrorism and Migration: An Exploration," International Centre for Counter-Terrorism, The Hague, ICCT Research Paper, May 2016, https://www.icct.nl/wp-content/uploads/2016/05/Alex-P.-Schmid-Links-between-Terrorism-and-Migration-1.pdf. (accessed September 13, 2018)

49 Alex Nowrasteh, *Terrorism and Immigration: A Risk Analysis.* CATO Institute, September 13, 2016. https://www.cato.org/publications/policy-analysis/terrorism-immigration-risk-analysis. (accessed September 13, 2018)

50 Swetha Sridharan, "Material Support to Terrorism – Consequences for Refugees and Asylum Seekers in the United States," Migration Information Source, Migration Policy

in Australia, Canada, the United Kingdom, and the United States: Transporting Best Practices";[51] and, Maria Paz, "Asylum and Terrorism: The Death of Human Rights Law?"[52] among some others. And, of course, the extensive work that has been done on this subject by Ben Saul, that includes: "Exclusion of Suspected Terrorists from Asylum: Trends in International and European Refugee Law," *Research Handbook on International Law and Terrorism; Defining Terrorism in International Law*.[53]

However, this edited collection is unique in that it covers the topic of "terrorism and asylum" directly and from the perspective of a number of essential aspects: normative; international and transnational law; and, national law and practice. It is the only book of its kind that features the work of a number of highly established international refugee law scholars as well as a number of promising new legal scholars in the early stages of their careers. Accordingly, this volume seeks to make an important contribution to the literature on this critical subject matter that explores the complex, complicated and convoluted relationship between "Terrorism and Asylum."[54]

This edited collection, thus, aims to fill an important gap in the existing literature on the connections between two crucial concepts in the world today, terrorism and asylum. The volume is comprised of 11 original chapters, and with an introductory and a concluding chapter. The chapters are arrayed in

Institute, January 30, 2008, https://www.migrationpolicy.org/article/material-support-terrorism-%E2%80%94-consequences-refugees-and-asylum-seekers-united-states. (accessed September 13, 2018)

51 Won Kidane, "The Terrorism Bar to Asylum in Australia, Canada, the United Kingdom, and the United States: Transporting Best Practices," *Fordham International Law Journal*, 2009–2010, Vol. 33, pp. 300–371. https://digitalcommons.law.seattleu.edu/cgi/viewcontent.cgi?article=1068&context=faculty. (accessed September 15, 2018)

52 Maria Paz, "Asylum and Terrorism: The Death of Human Rights Law?" *Iowa Law Review Online*, 102, 41 (2016), https://ilr.law.uiowa.edu/online/volume-102/asylum-and-terrorism-the-death-of-human-rights-law/. (accessed September 15, 2018)

53 Ben Saul, "Exclusion of Suspected Terrorists from Asylum: Trends in International and European Refugee Law," IIIS Discussion Paper No. 26, June 2005. https://papers.ssrn.com/sol3/papers.cfm?abstract_id=735265. (accessed September 15, 2018); Ben Saul, ed. *Research Handbook on International Law and Terrorism*. Cheltenham: Edward Elgar Publishing Inc., 2014; Ben Saul, *Defining Terrorism in International Law*. Oxford: Oxford University Press, 2006.

54 Juan Carlos Antunez, "Refugees and Terrorism: The Real Threat," GESI, International Securities Studies Group, Universidad De Granada, October 21, 2019, https://www.seguridadinternacional.es/?q=en/content/refugees-and-terrorism-real-threat. (accessed April 22, 2020) James C. Simeon, "Exposing Terrorism False Association with Asylum," *Canadian Association for Refugees and Forced Migration Studies* (CARFMS) *Newsletter*, Winter 2018, Issue 9, pp. 13–19. http://carfms.org/wp-content/uploads/2018/01/CARFMS-newsletter-winter-2018.pdf. (accessed September 15, 2018)

three parts: (1) the normative constructions of exclusion from asylum for terrorist activities; (2) international, transnational, and national perspectives on the crime of terrorism; and, (3) the national dimensions and dynamics of terrorism and exclusion from asylum. Each of the parts of the collection builds upon the other to allow the reader to develop their knowledge and understanding of the subject matter in logical and discreet portions. To acquire a fuller and a deeper understanding of the subject matter it is best to read the chapters sequentially. Nonetheless, each of the chapters can stand on their own and can allow the reader to gain a deeper appreciation of the subject matter and the contents that are addressed in each of the individual contributions.

The logic of the three parts of the collection should be self-evident. Starting from the normative basis of the concepts of "terrorism" and "asylum," the collection then moves on, in the second part, to an examination and consideration of the international, transnational and national crime of terrorism and its relation to asylum. The third part deals with the national dimensions and dynamics of terrorism and exclusion from asylum. Organized on this basis, all three levels of legal analysis are covered: international, transnational, and national. The structure of the text helps to ensure that the edited collection provides a thorough and comprehensive coverage of the subject matter. It also provides a familiar framework for providing a detailed and in depth analysis of a highly complex and complicated phenomenon: the interplay between terrorism and asylum and its ever shifting contours and dynamics, within the international, transnational and national contexts.

One of the important and innovative contributions of this edited volume is the manner that it approaches the topic of "terrorism and asylum." There is nothing in the literature to date that takes this multi-layered legal analysis on this subject matter. In this way, it is breaking new ground and will, therefore, make, hopefully, a significant contribution to this area of research, study, and analysis. In addition, it will hopefully also generate new insights, findings, and policy relevant recommendations for how to address these critical areas of international, transnational and national law and to public policy and administration. It should, equally, it is hoped, make an important contribution to public international law and, hopefully, international refugee and criminal law.

An edited volume of this nature will be of interest to a broad cross section of a segment of the public and, especially, anyone who may have an interest in international law, terrorism, refugees, and forced migration issues and concerns. Further, a volume of this nature on a topic of such vital public importance as this is long overdue.

To reiterate, the edited volume covers two of the most significant legal and public policy issues and concerns of our time. Its policy relevance should be obvious, and, its impact over time will likely prove to be important and far reaching.

As noted, the idea for this edited volume came out of the "Terrorism and Asylum" Workshop that was held at the Refugee Law Initiative, School of Advanced Study, University of London, London, UK, on December 8, 2017.[55] The Workshop was a success and produced a Report[56] and a Special Issue of the RLI Working Paper Series of some of the papers that were presented at the Workshop.[57] Only five of the contributors to this edited collection were part of the RLI Working Papers Series publication and their chapter contributions have all been updated and revised extensively and differ quite substantially from their published RLI Working Papers. All of the other contributions, six new ones, are original contributions that also include, this introductory chapter and a concluding chapter that are all entirely new contributions for this volume.

It is important and worth emphasizing here that the "Terrorism and Asylum" Workshop was also a success in providing researchers, practitioners and graduate students with an opportunity to present their work on this topic, obtain expert feedback, and continue working on their papers for publication. This edited volume is a continuation of this previous work, in part, but, with the addition of a number of other outstanding legal scholars, researchers and academics in the field of international and national law who have also done work on terrorism and asylum.

In short, this edited collection should prove valuable to those who are working directly in the field of refugee law writ large. The work being done on this subject matter is of great interest and of need to everyone who is interested and concerned with these two overriding issues and concerns. We fully anticipate, and very much hope, that an edited volume of this nature will be of great interest and will make an important contribution to the literature in this

55 "RLI, 'Terrorism and Asylum' Workshop: Report Published," Refugee Law Initiative, School of Advanced Study, University of London, January 23, 2018. https://rli.sas.ac.uk/about-us/news/rli-terrorism-and-asylum-workshop-report-published. (accessed September 15, 2018)

56 James C. Simeon, "'Terrorism and Asylum' Workshop Report," Refugee Law Initiative, School of Advanced Study, University of London, January 23, 2018, https://rli.sas.ac.uk/sites/default/files/files/Terrorism%20and%20Asylum%20Workshop%20Report_RLI.pdf. (accessed September 15, 2018)

57 Refugee Law Initiative, *Terrorism and Asylum* (*RLI Working Paper Series Mini-Volume*), January 2019, https://sas-space.sas.ac.uk/9204/. (accessed March 23, 2019)

subject area, but, also to the knowledge and understanding that will be generated on the crucial subject of "Terrorism and Asylum."

4.2 *The Chapter Contributions*

4.2.1 Part One

Part one of this edited collection covers the normative constructions of asylum and exclusion from asylum for terrorist activities and includes four chapters. The first of these is by Patricia Tuitt who addresses the subject, "The construction of a terrorist under Article 1 of the *Convention relating to the Status of Refugees*"; this is followed by Selina March, who's chapter is entitled, "Manufacturing Fear: Examining the Social Components of Anti-Immigration Policies within Counter-Terrorism Discourse." The third by John R. Campbell, takes an anthropological approach to understanding the law of terrorism and the "secret trials" of terrorists. His chapter is titled, "Guilty by Association: Contrasting Views on the Fairness of the "Secret Trials" of "Terrorists." And, Christopher McDowell presents his chapter on "Forced Migration, Diaspora Politics and Extremism: Conceptual, Policy and Operational Implications with a Focus on the United Kingdom." Together they examine the normative constructions of asylum and exclusion from asylum for terrorist activities and so much more.

Patricia Tuitt's philosophy of law approach challenges the very basis of the *1951 Convention relating to the Status of Refugees* in her broad sweeping examination of the very legitimacy of law itself that is based on the foundations of the exercise of violence. Drawing on the works of Walter Benjamin, she articulates that the essence of violence, from a historical philosophical reading, is its dualist distinction between sanctioned versus unsanctioned violence. Tuitt argues that "it is violence that preserves the law against the forces that would threaten its stability." Likewise, she incorporates the work of Nisha Kapoor who provides the insight that the justification for the use of excessive levels of state power as both necessary and legitimate in the policing of the "terrorist suspect." This begs the question, then, of how the nature and degree of state force can be legally sanctioned within the parameters of a humanitarian framework. The ready reply here is that there are certain acts of violence – the indiscriminate and random killing of innocent civilians – that are deemed to be simply "evil." But, Tuitt also recognizes that within the 1951 Refugee Convention is the legal right that undermines, in a way, the state monopoly of violence but that this is curtailed immediately by the construction of the "refugee terrorist" who poses a threat to the state. The very foundation of the state is premised on its ability to maintain its territorial integrity, the security of its population, and the exercise of its legitimate authority. Volker Turk, among others, has argued that the framework of international refugee law is based on the security of the refugee and the security of the state. Tuitt questions whether states have, indeed, achieved the right balance between "legitimate self-preservation and humanitarianism." Nonetheless, Tuitt emphasizes Article 1F's central place in the 1951 Refugee Convention.

With respect to the UK, Tuitt, reviews the Special Immigration Appeals Commission (SIAC) and its statutory framework that allows for the appellant not to be given all of the particulars of their reasons for their decision and any appeals against their decisions must be filed within ten days for those still in the UK and 28 days if outside the UK. One of the great criticisms of the SIAC process, Tuitt emphasizes, is that it can hold hearings in private and in the absence of either the appellant or his or her legal representative. The critics of the SIAC process have noted that it breaches the principles of fundamental justice by holding secret trials, the appellant and their lawyer have restricted access to information, and do not have the right to know the case against them, despite the fact that there is a special counsel assigned to the case who can review the evidence against the appellant, but, once the trial starts can no longer have any contact with the appellant or their counsel. Critics such as Nisha Kapoor argue that the standard of proof in terrorism cases is unacceptably low. Tuitt concludes her chapter by noting that the treatment of terror suspects in the UK legal system, especially those that are made in secret 'closed court', has the effect of a denial of justice.

Selina March's chapter seeks to untangle the complex intertwined relationship of terrorism and asylum. March focuses on the social component of the terrorism and asylum nexus. She argues that a securitization narrative, within a counter-terrorism discourse, allows politicians to dampen any sympathetic reactions to the plight of refugees while rationalizing the restrictive response to national security concerns. In short, she contends that politicians' resort to immigration as a "hot button" issue to gather political support and votes when they pit national security concerns against the safety of asylum seekers. The chapter examines the rise of anti-immigrant sentiment and policy in the United States with the surprise election of Donald Trump as US President. Using critical race theory, March asserts that racism is deeply engrained in US society and that law is not neutral but, rather, reinforces racial hierarchies. In this regard, the Trump Presidency has been characterized by "fearmongering tactics and policy positions" that have advanced anti-immigrant policies through the guise of "making America great again." The advancement of a narrative that characterizes immigrants and refugees as a national security threat, March argues, further codifies nativist sentiment. What is evident is that Trump is the figurehead of the current US anti-immigrant policies and what is critical is that a number of social components are driving these policies consisting of existing biases, insecurities and fears and increased social and political polarisation, among others, that can be classified as the worldview of the American populace. March identifies two key strategies to legitimize this worldview. The first stratagem is to group refugees with other migrants and, the second, is to normalize a factual, but, unwarranted link between refugees and Muslim-majority countries and terrorism. The 'fear of terrorism' is employed to influence the worldview of wide sections of the American public in order to manufacture the 'cultural racism' necessary to push through policies for banning or significantly curtailing the number of refugees resettling in the United States. In addition, March points out, that the rhetoric surrounding the 'zero-tolerance policy' and the 'migrant caravan' is riddled with criminalization and dehumanization narratives that are intended to distance the general public from the asylum seekers. The use of labels such as "aliens" and "illegals" furthers the objectification and "othering" of asylum seekers, a process that is consistent with fostering 'cultural racism'. The current anti-immigrant and nativist rhetoric goes well beyond the individual racism of Trump and his supporters, March argues, and it is essential to be able to understand the deeper cultural and institutional narratives to get a full appreciation of the extent of the problem and the challenge of addressing it. Consequently, a critical assessment of current immigration and refugee policies is absolutely necessary in order to understand and untangle convoluted negative and deliberately exploited inter-relationships between terrorism and asylum, if we ever hope to address properly these two central concerns of our time.

John R. Campbell examines the "secret trials" of terrorists by contrasting the normative judgements of the law with the anthropological requirements of situating the cases in the wider social context of society to understand the complex legal processes and the roles played by the state, the courts, judges, lawyers, and defendants. Campbell argues that terrorist attacks since 9/11 have given legislators the authority to reshape, fundamentally, the quality of justice and the work of the law in Europe and North America. Campbell notes that this is especially evident in the immigration policy field where strategic preoccupations about national security and terrorism have been used to rewrite the law, pass new legislation, and reinforce the discretionary power of the political executive in ways that would not have been possible prior to 9/11. The argument is made that "counter-terrorism" measures have shifted from investigation, criminalization and the proscription of individuals and organizations to preemptive, anticipatory, and preventative strategies. This chapter focuses specifically on the "Closed Material Proceedings" (CMP) or "secret trials." These types of trials have serious implications for the defendant's right to have a fair trial; including: (a) the right to be tried by an independent and impartial tribunal; (b) the right to have one's case defended on the basis of established facts and the law; and, (c) the right to know the case you have to meet and the right to respond to that case in an open court. "Secret trials," Campbell points out, need to be understood as uneven contests between the defendant and the state whose outcomes are influenced by many inter-related factors such as an ever changing legislative agenda; lobbying in Parliament and the House of Lords; efforts by the Home Office to create primary legislation, and so on. What is thoroughly examined here is the case of O2, a person who was charged and tried under the CMP. Campbell served as an "expert witness" in his trial. Such trials are conducted by the Special Immigration Appeals Commission (SIAC) and the appellants are represented by a Special Advocate (SA), a lawyer who is vetted by the Security Service, and who gets access to secret evidence, that only the judges and SAs are privy to. The role of the SA is to protect the human rights of the accused, but, they are barred from communicating with the accused or their counsel after they have been given access to the secret evidence. Campbell reviews the testimony of the appellant in this "secret trial" at SIAC, where he presented two "expert witness" reports, and finds the judgements in this case, of both the presiding Justice at SIAC and at the Court of Appeal, to be wanting. Obtaining a conviction under the *Prevention of Terrorism Act* based on a mere "reasonable suspicion" of being involved in terrorist related acts is hardly a high standard of proof. Campbell concludes by noting that "secret trials," that rely on the use of SA, undermine some of the most fundamental principles of procedural fairness and, consequently, are unlike to produce just outcomes.

Christopher McDowell's chapter focuses on the displacement and security threat nexus and the response to conflict induced displacement and refugee resettlement. McDowell's chapter is concerned with the aggressive recruitment and the radicalization of vulnerable persons, whether they are asylum seekers or nationals. He argues that extremist networks are exploiting the spaces created by the failures of refugee protection and integration in host societies. Inevitably, inherent in the internationalization of contemporary conflict are at least four interrelated elements: large scale population displacement, dispersal, encampment, and the refugee journey; the process and experience of settlement and integration in the country of asylum; diaspora politics that links the movement and settlement; and, the growing involvement of organized criminality in asylum migration. McDowell's chapter is based on the Centre for Research and Evidence on Security Threats (CREST) funded research conducted in the United Kingdom, Europe, and Canada that examined diaspora refugee politics and on McDowell's commissioned research on Syrian resettlement in the UK. The CREST project examined the internationalization of the Sri Lankan civil war, between 1983 to 2009, and Tamil diaspora politics and the strategies of the Liberation Tigers of Tamil Eelam (LTTE) to further their political and military objectives through the mobilization of Tamil asylum seekers and refugees in

Western States. McDowell argues that the LTTE provided a model for international Jihadists and Salafi political activists among Europe-bound migrants and refugees fleeing the protracted armed conflicts in the Middle East. Drawing on the diaspora, conflict and refugee studies literature and the extremism and radicalization literature, McDowell points out that diasporic associations and their elites play a central role in the mobilization of their communities by seizing specific events and framing the issues and defining grievances and claims to legitimate political action. The prevalence of terrorist attacks in Europe since 2016 has raised questions about what may be specific with respect to refugee diaspora politics, asylum seeking, and integration that increase the risk to radicalization. With respect to the triggers of radicalization among migrants and refugees, McDowell identifies the following: identity crises; social alienation; discrimination and/or social exclusion; racism; and, poverty. His own research on the subject has demonstrated how the direct engagement of extremist networks in displacement and the onward refugee journey creates opportunities to keep the conflict 'alive' with overseas populations. McDowell argues that the exploitation of asylum migration and settlement allows for the building of networks and dependent relationships with the displaced, that may be mobilized at some later date for either a benign or maligned purpose. In the case of the LTTE, it had a highly sophisticated transnational network that coordinated the flow of information and propaganda and oversaw the collection of "donations" that were vital to the struggle for an independent Tamil homeland. In addition, the LTTE used the asylum system of States to pension off their fighters who could no longer serve on the front lines. The LTTE provided their diaspora communities with the kind of social support they needed to settle abroad, but in the process became dependent on them and, especially, among those who still had family members living in Sri Lanka. McDowell also points to evidence that shows that Jihadists and Safalist extremist networks are applying the LTTE's strategy for harnessing its diaspora into serving its needs. There is evidence that these extremist groups are recruiting among refugees in Lebanon, Jordan and Turkey. McDowell's own research among the Syrian refugees in the UK found that, among those on the move, the highest risk group was young men, 16–30 years old. What the data demonstrated was that engagement in extremist politics is more likely when there are 'opportunities to engage'. It was further discerned that among those who were convicted of terrorist offenses were people who migrated to the UK with their families as children or people who migrated alone as teenagers or young adults. The typical radicalized profile appears to be young men who are disaffected with the state and their host communities.

The chapter also considers the 2018 UK Parliament's Intelligence and Security Committee of Parliament's Report and the 2017 Anderson Operational Improvement Review and the 2018 UK counter terrorism strategy, CONTEST. McDowell focuses on the weaknesses of CONTEST by noting that it fails to connect the national to the international dimensions of terrorism and the commonality of the "internationalization of conflict." This is the central weakness of current counter terrorism strategies and practices in the UK and, most likely, on a transnational basis as well.

4.2.2 Part Two

Part two of the edited collection covers the topic of "International, Transnational, and National Perspectives on the Crime of Terrorism and Asylum." It includes three chapters by the following authors and their titles: Joseph Ripkof covers the subject of "Complicity in Exclusion for Terrorist Crimes" while, Peter Billings and Rebecca Ananian-Welsh deal with the subject of "Counter-Terrorism and the Exclusion of Refugees and Refugee-Citizens from Australia"; and, James C. Simeon, the editor of this volume, who covers the subject of "Prosecution and Exclusion for Terrorism in International and National Law."

Joseph Rikhof's contribution considers the parameters of complicity in exclusion from refugee protection for terrorist crimes. Rikhof begins by stating that even though it is possible to exclude those who are involved in terrorist activities under all the subsections of Article 1F, in practice states have relied on Articles 1F(b) and 1F(c) to do so. While the vast majority of those who are excluded for their complicity in serious international crimes come under Article 1F(a), the situation for exclusion under Articles 1F(b) and 1F(c) cover a broad spectrum from personal participation to complicity and, consequently, are not as clear cut. Rikhof examines the jurisprudence with respect to Article 1F(a), (b), and (c) to discern the methodology that was used to determine the appropriate test for complicity within each subsection of Article 1F. Keeping in mind, however, that Article 1F(a) differs as it imports International Criminal Law (ICL) within its provisions. The status of terrorism in international law, Rikhof underscores, is the subject of some debate. It is part of Transnational Criminal Law (TCL), as found in various treaties dealing with the suppression of terrorism, and since several states have used universal jurisdiction for the prosecution of terrorism makes it part of International Criminal Law (ICL) as well.

Turning to the *1937 Convention for the Prevention and the Punishment of Terrorism* that lists an array of extended liability concepts that include:

1) Conspiracy to commit any such act;
2) Any incitement to any such act, if successful;

3) Direct public incitement to any acts mentioned under heads (1), (2) or (3) of Article 2, whether the incitement be successful or not;
4) Wilful participation in any such act;
5) Assistance, knowingly given, towards the commission of any such act.

Rikhof compiles a list of all the forms of complicity found in the post-World War II terrorism treaties, eight in total, that include the following:

- attempt
- organizes
- directs
- participates as an accomplice
- assisting after the fact
- conspiracy
- common purpose
- threat.

He also notes that the *1998 Rome Statute* of the International Criminal Court includes the following types of involvement:

- ordering,
- soliciting,
- inducing,
- aiding and abetting,
- common purpose,
- incitement,
- attempt,
- command/superior responsibility.

Rikhof concentrates on ten Western liberal democracies: Australia; Belgium; Canada; France; Germany; The Netherlands; New Zealand; Sweden; UK; and USA, that have contributed the most on exclusion. In terms of methodology, he examines the terrorism legislation with respected to extended liability in these ten countries. These countries seem to apply similar conceptual notions of extended liability with respect to personal liability. However, the precise parameters of liability vary from country to country. For half of these countries, Australia, Canada, New Zealand, UK, and the US, use more inchoate liability such as attempt, conspiracy, and incitement. In the common law jurisdictions, common purpose and common intention are used to delineate forms of group liability. Rikhof considers the *Criminal Code* provisions of these ten countries to analyze comparatively the different forms of extended liability. He concludes that there is wide variation amongst these ten countries of the different forms of extended liability with 25 forms of assistance to terrorist offences or individuals involved in such offences. And, there are 16 forms of assistance to terrorist organizations, groups or associations. Two questions are raised among the 41 forms of extended liability for terrorist activities: Are the 41 forms of extended liability unique descriptions or are they further clarifications of the general forms of complicity that are set out in criminal law?; and, If these are unique forms of liability do they add to the regular forms of liability and are they already within the parameters and overarching tests of *JS* (*Sri Lanka*) and *Ezokola*? With respect to the first question, Rikhof states, that several forms of extended liability are related to aiding and abetting and in this regard recommends considering the Charles Taylor case that was before the Sierra Leone Special Court. Rikhof concludes by stating, the "number of types of extended liability in national criminal legislation now go beyond the extended liability in refugee law in 1F(a) with the recent contractions in the area of membership." He argues that for Articles 1F(a) and 1F(b) all forms of extended liability should apply to both of these provisions of the exclusion clauses. What follows then is that International Criminal Law can be imported into Article 1F(b). Transnational Criminal Law could also be applied to Article 1F(b). Equally, it is argued, these extended forms of liability would also be applicable to Article 1F(c). Hence, International Criminal Law is very much part of all of the subsections of Article 1F and not simply 1F(a).

Peter Billings and Rebecca Ananian-Welsh note that the securitization of migration, and particularly those that are identified as risky, epitomizes the "growing culture of exclusion" from asylum. Focusing on Australia, they point out that their "crimmigration" laws have essentially outlawed seeking asylum by boat. The Australian Government has also introduced national security grounds for revocation of Australian citizenship to dual nationals, so that they can be rendered alien and subjected to the Australian securitized migration system. Billings and Ananian-Welsh point out that the Howard Government in Australia, from October 2001 to November 2003, used military interdiction at sea with regional offshore processing and temporary protection visas as a response to asylum seekers that became known as the "Pacific Solution." They note that, "The Howard Government justified these policies by constructing asylum seekers as potential terrorists, which had significant political impact in the wake of the notorious *MV Tampa* affair and 9/11." In 2013, the Australian government returned to its practice of offshore processing, the detention of asylum seekers, and maritime interdiction, through a military-led, "Operation Sovereign Borders." These policies are intended to deter and to disrupt irregular migration at sea for the purpose of preventing people smuggling, a serious transnational crime, and promoting human security by preventing hazardous journeys on unseaworthy vessels, and restoring integrity to the immigration system and, thus, facilitating an orderly and controlled humanitarian intake.

Billings and Ananian-Welsh indicate that the exclusion provisions under Article 1F of the 1951 Refugee Convention are of secondary and minor importance in comparison to the Australian *Migration Act*'s call for exclusion for refugee protection: (1) on national security grounds; (2) because they are a danger to the community; and, (3) by failing public interest criteria. And, since 2014, importantly, the statutory power of removal is no longer conditional on the legal requirement to consider the fundamental principle of *non-refoulement* before administrative action is taken. Consequently, Billings and Ananian-Welsh state that the Australian Government purports to meet its *non-refoulement* treaty obligations through policy and practice and not the rule of law. The *1979 Australian Security Intelligence Organization Act* (ASIO) allows for security officials to determine whether the person is a security threat, and, if they do, then, the person is removable and cannot be determined in need of refugee protection and may be held in detention. Indefinite detention is constitutionally permissible in Australia. This could result in those who are perceived to be a national security threat with protracted detention if they are not removable.

The Australian *1995 Criminal Code* defines a 'terrorist act' as "an action or threat necessarily undertaken with the intention of advancing a *political*, or religious, or ideological cause, and either coercing or influencing by intimidation a government, or intimidating the public or a section of the public."[58] Defining what constitutes a political intent is a matter of some contention, Billings and Ananian-Welsh, outline that "a political motivation must be more than a significant factor, it must be the primary motivation."

Article 1F is rarely invoked in Australia for at least two reasons: there are many alternative grounds for excluding someone such as an adverse security assessment and the character test; and, Article 1F entails greater transparency, procedural justice and independent review rights attendant to these decisions compared to the adverse security assessments and adverse character test. The broad-based discretionary powers of the Minister to determine under "reasonable suspicion" of mere membership of a relevant group. Membership in a terrorist organization is subject to a ten-year imprisonment in Australia. Terrorist organisation offences further extend, to directing, recruiting, training, funding and supporting these groups, with these offences attracting up to 25 years imprisonment if the person knows the group is a terrorist organisation, and up to 15 years if the person is reckless as to this fact.

58 This definition is similar to what is found in the United Kingdom and Canada. See James C. Simeon, "The Evolving Common Law Jurisprudence Combatting the Threat of Terrorism in the United Kingdom, United States, and Canada." *Laws*, 2019, *8*, 5. https://www.mdpi.com/2075-471X/8/1/5. (accessed April 19, 2019)

The revoking of the Australian citizenship of dual nationals is also a major concern as it may leave the person stateless, contrary to international law, and/or leave them in "legal limbo" with the potential risk of *refoulement* and possibly indefinite administrative detention. Dual nationals who are members of or are instructed by, or are cooperating with, a listed terrorist organization have satisfied the "renunciation by conduct" ground for loss of citizenship. The revoking of Australian citizenship of dual nationals is automatic when a person serves in the armed forces of a country at war with Australia or serves or fights for a listed terrorist organization. The third way in which a dual national can lose their Australian citizenship is by being convicted of one or more terrorist offences or foreign incursion offences and is sentenced to six or more years of imprisonment. Billings and Ananian-Welsh conclude by observing that Australian Governments have repeatedly redefined and limited their responsibilities of providing asylum seekers protection under municipal law and have concentrated instead on broad and effectively non-reviewable decision-making power in security officials and politicians and, thereby, the appropriate application of the rule of law. The purported connection between asylum seekers and refugees with terrorism has been the justification for the securitization of immigration and asylum laws. While, at the same time, this approach risks alienating minority groups and those seeking protection, coupled with the failure to respect human rights and the rule of law, it lowers Australia's domestic and global status and, arguably, risks making individuals more vulnerable to radicalization and recruitment. Billings and Ananian-Welsh conclude that the Australian approach to counterterrorism, as it impacts immigration, is "secretive and largely unreviewable" with "the focus on securitization and exclusion."

James C. Simeon examines the prosecution of the "crime of terrorism" in international criminal law, based on three infamous cases at the International Criminal Tribunal of the Former Yugoslavia (ICTY), and exclusion from asylum of those who are responsible for terrorism, based on three Supreme Court judgements in Canada, United States, and the United Kingdom. Clearly, international criminal law and international humanitarian law have prohibited terrorism in situations of international and non-international armed conflict. Despite the fact there is a clear prohibition of terrorism in international humanitarian law, both in terms of customary international law and treaty law, but, no universally accepted definition of terrorism or, in fact, a comprehensive convention on terrorism, and, because states have failed to agree on a common definition of what constitutes terrorism, this results in varying definitions in terms of what constitutes terrorism.

However, there is a highly contentious judgement of the Appeals Chamber of the Special Tribunal of Lebanon that has issued a landmark ruling that a definition of terrorism has emerged in international customary law consisting of three elements:

1. the perpetration of a criminal act (such as murder, kidnapping, hostage-taking, arson, and so on), or threatening such an act;
2. the intent to spread fear among the population (which would generally entail the creation of public danger) or directly or indirectly coerce a national or international authority to take some action, or to refrain from taking it;
3. when the act involves a transnational element.[59]

Interestingly, the joint Appeals Chamber of the ICTY and the International Criminal Tribunal for Rwanda (ICTR), essentially, came to the same judgement earlier in the *2006 Galic* case; that is, that the prohibition of the use of terrorism against a civilian population was part of international customary law well before the Geneva Conventions were negotiated and ratified. This was confirmed by the ICTY through a number of cases; including: the *2001 Krstic* case, and as mentioned, the *2006 Galic* judgement, and the *2017 Mladic* case, that there is a "crime of terror" and a "crime of persecution" which encompasses, terrorizing civilians. These judgements have marked a significant step forward with respect to defining the legal term "terrorism" in international criminal law. For instance, in the *2001 Krstic* judgement, the ICTY ruled that the "crime of persecution" includes the "terrorizing of civilians." In the Stanislav Galic case, the defendant was specifically indicted on the charge of the "infliction of terror." In fact, Stanislav Galic, commander of the Bosnian Serb forces, became the first person to be convicted of the spreading of terror among the civilian population. In fact, the *2006 Galic* case was the first case in which terrorism was considered as an autonomous war crime.

Ratko Mladic was the Chief of Staff of the Army of the Republika Srpska and was labelled the "Butcher of Bosnia" by the media. Among the many crimes that he was indicted for was the "Crimes Committed to Spread Terror among the Civilian Population of Sarajevo through a Campaign of Sniping and Shelling." Further, the Trial Chamber ruled that the "crime of terror" required the proof of the following three elements:

a) acts or threats of violence directed against the civilian population or individual civilians not taking direct part in hostilities causing the victims to suffer grave consequences;

---

59 Interlocutory Decision on the Applicable Law: Terrorism, Conspiracy, Homicide, Perpetration, Cumulative Charging, Case No. STL-11-01/I (Feb. 16, 2011), https://www.stl-tsl.org/en/the-cases/stl-11-01/main/filings/orders-and-decisions/appeals-chamber/534-f0936. (accessed February 11, 2018)

b) the offender willfully made the civilian population or individual civilians not taking direct part in hostilities the object of those acts or threats of violence; and
c) the above acts or threats of violence were committed with the primary purpose of spreading terror among the civilian population.[60]

The Trial Chamber of the ICTY further ruled that the "crime of terror" was a violation of the laws and customs of war.

Simeon also considers three famous Supreme Court rulings on terrorism: the Canadian *2002 Suresh* judgement; the UK, *2010 JS* (*Sri Lanka*) case; the US, *2010 Holder v. Humanitarian Law Project*. All three cases deal with Sri Lankan appellants, at least in some part, and involve the Liberation Tigers of Tamil Eelam (LTTE), that are listed as a terrorist organization in each of these three countries. The respective Supreme Courts in these three jurisdictions upheld their governments' impugned legislation that were all challenged, in part, on substantive human rights and on procedural grounds.

The Supreme Court of Canada's *Suresh* judgement came to the conclusion that if a person who was determined to be refugee was properly found to be a "danger to Canada," then, they could be sent back, in exceptional circumstances, to a risk of torture and/or even death. This was an extraordinary judgement that came under heavy criticism internationally for apparently violating the international customary law principle of *non-refoulement*. In the *JS* (*Sri Lanka*) judgement of the UK Supreme Court, the LTTE was not accepted to be "predominantly a terrorist organization" and the focus was on the personal liability of the applicant and in order for the person to be excluded from refugee protection, the applicant had to have made a "voluntary" and a "significant contribution" to a terrorist action and activities. The US Supreme Court found the material support bar in the *Holder v. Humanitarian Law Project* to be constitutional and that it did not infringe on either the First or the Fifth amendments of the US Constitutional Bill of the Rights. The material support bar is, undoubtedly, one of the lowest standards for barring a refugee applicant from asylum in any jurisdiction.

Simeon concludes by calling upon the international community to address the gaps and shortcomings in international criminal law by ensuring that there is a universal standard for what constitutes terrorism in a non-war setting, consistent with what has emerged in international humanitarian law and that the variance in the definition of what constitutes terrorism at the national level is substantially reduced so that those who fall within Article 1F of the *1951*

60 *Prosecutor v. Ratko Mladic, Case No. IT-09-92-T, Judgement, Volumes III of V, 22 November 2017*, p. 1663. http://www.icty.org/x/cases/mladic/tjug/en/171122-3of5_1.pdf. (accessed February 18, 2018)

Convention relating to the Status of Refugees can be dealt with in a consistent and fair manner.

4.2.3 Part Three

The third section of this collection considers the national dimensions and dynamics of terrorism and exclusion from asylum that features four chapters. The first is Mark Symes's chapter on "Exclusion from Asylum on the Basis of Criminality – the United Kingdom's Response and its Broader International Law Context." This is followed by Barbara Kőhalmi and Anita Nagy-Nádasdi's contribution on Hungary titled, "Asylum-seekers as potential terrorists (?)," and, Nula Frei and Constantin Hruschka, consider the subject of "Caught Between Unworthiness and Exclusion: Asylum Applicants and Refugees Suspected of Terrorism in Swiss Law and Practice." The last chapter in Part Three covers Austria with Julia Kienast's contribution titled, "Forced Migration as a Security Threat: Challenging Criminalization Trends in Austria Under Presumed Links of Asylum and Terrorism."

Mark Symes offers an analysis of exclusion from refugee protection based on complicity in terrorist activities in the case law in the United Kingdom (UK). He points out that it is important to consider the legal environment to be able to understand the history of exclusion. The UK courts and tribunals draw heavily on other national courts and on international criminal law. In addition, the guidance of the UNHCR with respect to the application of the Exclusion Clauses is relevant and important. Here Symes makes reference to the UNHCR's *Guidelines on International Protection: Application of the Exclusion Clauses: Article 1F of the Convention relating to the Status of Refugees,* paragraph 18, that makes reference to "general individual responsibility from the person having committed, or have made a substantial contribution to the commission of the criminal act, in the knowledge that his or her act or omission would facilitate the criminal conduct."[61] The Exclusion Clauses incorporate international criminal law, specifically, within Article 1F(a) and, it is argued, that two strands that are particularly significant are the *Rome Statute* and the decisions of the ad hoc Tribunals that interpreted the pre-existing body of international criminal law. The critical question that has yet to be resolved in international criminal law is what degree of complicity is necessary for criminal liability. The

61 UNHCR, *Guidelines on International Protection: Application of the Exclusion Clauses: Article 1F of the 1951 Refugee Convention relating to the Status of Refugees*, 4 September 2003, p. 6, paragraph 18, https://www.unhcr.org/publications/legal/3f7d48514/guidelines-international-protection-5-application-exclusion-clauses-article.html. (accessed June 1, 2019)

foundational principle of criminal responsibility, it is noted, is personal culpability. Symes further points out the UN Resolutions can also be a source of international law. He states that the series of UN Resolutions that were issued immediately after September 11, 2001, require States to address the incitement, the justification or glorification of terrorist acts, and calls on all "States to deny safe haven to any person who supports, facilitates, participates or attempts to participate in the financing, planning, preparation, or commission of terrorist act."[62] The UN specifically calls on States to punish those who are liable for their intentional participation in terrorism.

The previous test for exclusion under Article 1F relied on the *Ramirez* decision of the Federal Court of Appeal in Canada that stated that mere membership in a "limited and brutal purpose" organization, whose "aims, methods and activities were predominantly terrorist in character, [that] very little more would be necessary" to exclude the applicant.[63] It is observed that *IG Nepal* was likely the high point in this approach that adopted the UNHCR formulation that where there is sufficient proof that the asylum seeker is a member of an international terrorist organization, such as those involved in the September 11, 2001 terrorist attacks, "voluntary membership could be presumed to amount to personal and knowing participation."[64]

In time, this was set aside by the courts that favoured the personal culpability method. This leads Symes to undertake a detailed and thorough analysis of the *JS (Sri Lanka)* judgement of the UK Supreme Court and conclude by noting that the new test established was for a "knowing significant contribution to a criminal purpose." Subsequently, in *Ezokola*, the Supreme Court of Canada ruled that only a voluntary and significant contribution, in the knowledge that their conduct will further the crime and the criminal purpose, would be sufficient to exclude someone under Article 1F. The point was further made that,

> The case law subsequent to *Mbarushimana* had held that conduct that merely *might* contribute to a crime or criminal purpose was insufficient; and the mental element excluded *dolus eventualis* (the awareness of a mere risk of prohibited consequences).[65]

62 UN Security Council Resolution 1368 (12 September 2001); Res/1624 (2005) (14 September 2005); Res/ 2178 (2014) (24 September 2014).

63 *Ramirez v. Canada (Minister of Employment and Immigration)*, 1992 CanLII 8540 (FCA), [1992] 2 F.C. 306.

64 *IG Nepal.*

65 *Prosecutor v. Jean-Pierre Bemba Gombo*, ICC-01/05-01/08-424, Decision Pursuant to Article 61(7)(a) and (b) of the Rome Statute, 15 June 2009 (ICC, Pre-Trial Chamber II), at para. 360.

It is concluded, by noting that even though liability is drawn broadly, it remains the case that guilt by association is not enough to found exclusion. Symes' notes that "the widening of the scope of potential liability is tempered by the requirement that there be an intensity of intention that is stronger than mere recklessness." Nonetheless, it is observed, that the "requirement for procedural rigour in the analysis of who falls for exclusion, combined with the requirement for a distinct level of contribution to the criminal purpose, remains an essential safeguard against overuse of the exclusion clauses."

Barbara Kőhalmi and Anita Nagy-Nádasdi's chapter on Hungary, titled, "Asylum-seekers as potential terrorists (?)," seeks to map out the nexus between asylum and terrorism and how terrorism has shaped the international refugee protection regime. They note that international law recognizes states' rights to security and the asylum-seekers' rights to security or protection from persecution as equal legitimate interests. They are, nonetheless, two competing interests and the right balance must be found through the application and interpretation of appropriate international and European laws. The balancing tests, Kőhalmi and Nagy-Nádasdi argue, generally, "require the comparison of different/opposite interests such as individual (right to protection) and community interests (right to security). States can strike the balance between the rights and restrictions differently, but the boundary of appreciation granted to a State is not unlimited."[66] But, certain human rights can never be derogated from such as the right to life and the right to be free from torture or cruel and unusual treatment or punishment, and derogable rights can only be infringed according to human rights law. What is also indispensable is an independent judiciary to oversee this process and the necessity of ensuring that those whose rights have been infringed will have a right to challenge these decisions in the courts and have an effective remedy. And, finally, that international human rights must be given domestic effect through explicit protection in national legislation.

With respect to terrorism, Kőhalmi and Nagy-Nádasdi, rightly note that there is no comprehensive convention with a universal definition of what constitutes "terrorism." Accordingly, this only adds to the confusion surrounding the legal definition of what constitutes "terrorism." By the same token, they note that asylum also does not have a universally accepted definition and varies from region to region. The situation in Hungary for refugee applicants is that the linkage between terrorism and asylum has been made explicit by politicians and the media. For instance, the Hungarian Government placed a barbed

66 Barbara Kőhalmi and Anita Nagy-Nádasdi, "Asylum-seekers as potential terrorists (?)," p. 3.

wire fence on the Serbian-Hungarian border in an effort to stop illegal border crossing by migrants. At the same time, the *Hungarian Criminal Code* was amended in 2015 to make it illegal to cross the border fence. Anyone violating these provisions of the *Hungarian Criminal Code* would be subject to imprisonment and expulsion. They observe that this is perhaps the classic example of the criminalization of migration or "crimmigration." In September 2015, Hungary declared a state of emergency because of the mass influx of migrants. A declared state of emergency allows the police to enter private homes under suspicion without a warrant, taking real estate into state use, as well as mobile items owned or possessed by other state or municipal agencies, when none of the legally prescribed conditions are met. And, in 2016, the Hungarian Government amended the Fundamental Law to introduce a new type of state order, the "terror emergency situation," that allows for the use of extraordinary measures such as the use of the national army, tightened border controls, curfews, and the control of communications channels, etc., for the protection against terrorist attacks. Furthermore, the Hungarian Government's vigorous controversial billboard campaign opposed to migrants explicitly exemplified its anti-migrant policy stance.

Kőhalmi and Nagy-Nádasdi also note that the Hungarian asylum procedure became a single procedure on August 1, 2015, in which each relevant aspect of the asylum case under consideration, including any national security concerns, are considered by the asylum authority and its partner authorities, including, the Office of Constitutional Protection (OCP). The OCP has eight days to decide whether the asylum applicant is a national security threat. But, given the high abandonment and withdrawal rate for asylum applicants in Hungary, this procedure has proved to be administratively ineffective. Further, it is relevant to point out that the asylum authority can decide whether rejected applicants should be expelled or not.

The authors make reference to a number of interviews they undertook with noted non-governmental asylum authorities in Hungary regarding the nexus between terrorism and asylum. All those who were interviewed did not accept that there was any strong connection between the two terms. Consequently, Kőhalmi and Nagy-Nádasdi conclude, there is no demonstrable link between terrorism and asylum in Hungary, despite the Hungarian Government's hypervigilant policies to deflect refugees from its borders.

Nula Frei and Constantin Hruschka begin with the assertion that the public discourse narrative in Switzerland has not been too much affected by the mixing of "terrorism and asylum." The focus, rather, has been on the prevention of terrorism and the prevention of radicalization. Frei and Hruschka examine in detail the interlinkages between terrorism and asylum. They begin by considering those refugee claimants who fear being persecuted by terrorist groups such as the Islamic States (IS) that is known for targeting Yazidi and Christians in Syria and Iraq or internally displaced females without the protection of a clan or male family member are the target of extremist-terrorist groups like Al-Shabaab in Somalia, among others. They then go on to consider those who are excluded from refugee protection for their involvement in terrorist activities by noting that this very often requires a determination as to whether a person's affiliations and activities are, indeed, terrorist, and to decide whether there is sufficient evidence to conclude that the person was involved in such activities or had contributed in any way to terrorist activities. There are two ways in which a refugee claimant can be excluded from asylum under Swiss law: under Article 1F of the *1951 Convention relating to Refugee Status*; and, for "unworthiness" under Article 53 of the *Asylum Act*, that excludes the person from asylum, but, with the recognition that the person is a refugee. Membership in an organization that has been declared "terrorist" may constitute a criminal offence under Article 260 of the *Swiss Criminal Code*. Frei and Hruschka state that according to the most recent developments in decision practice, "mere membership in an organization labeled as terrorist by the EU may be sufficient to exclude the person concerned from asylum." Under the "unworthiness" provisions of the *Asylum Act*, exclusion from refugee status is much broader than under Article 1F. The consequences of exclusion from refugee status is the person's refugee status claim will be rejected. The Federal Administrative Court (FAC) has the sole jurisdiction to review the judgements of the State Secretariat for Migration (SEM) in the Swiss asylum procedure. The SEM has to conduct the full investigation with regard to the exclusion clause as well as the person's refugee status, on the principle of "inclusion before exclusion," as recommended by UNHCR. Those who are found to be refugees due to a well-founded fear of persecution but are excluded will not be granted a provisional admission as a foreigner.

Frei and Hruschka, lay out in some detail, Article 53 of the *Asylum Act*, that stipulates refugee claimants will not be granted asylum: (a) if they are unworthy of asylum due to serious misconducted; (b) they have violated or endangered Switzerland's internal or external security; (c) they have been made subject to a criminal law expulsion order. The first two of these can be highly relevant for terrorists suspects seeking protection. The point is made that if the refugee is considered to be unworthy of asylum they will be recognized as refugees but will not be granted asylum and will, therefore, be issued an administrative expulsion order. But, because refugees are protected by *non-refoulement* under Article 33(1) of the Refugee Convention and Article 25(2) of the Swiss Federal Constitution (SFC), the expulsion order will not be executed but, rather, replaced by provisional admission.

Frei and Hruschka conclude by stating that Swiss practice is that those who are seen to be "infected" by "terrorism" shall only be granted asylum if they are clear cut "victims of terrorism" or if the person can prove that they have been falsely perceived to be a terrorist. Those who are suspected of terrorism in Switzerland will not be issued a residence permit. The notion of "unworthiness" appears to play a large part in the assessment of whether the person is a "threat to the security of Switzerland." Mere suspicion of terrorist activity may be sufficient to bar a applicant to asylum, if they cannot prove non-involvement in terrorist activities. What Frei and Hruschka call a "purification exercise." They also argue that their analysis indicates the requirements for exclusion have been lowered significantly by the jurisprudence over the last decade. They end by stating that the legislative and judicial trend in Switzerland raises the question whether the "fight" against terrorism is really being advanced by the exclusion of terrorist suspects. It may be having an the reverse effect of radicalizing certain individuals in Switzerland. This leads them to conclude that "deradicalization" programs ought to be considered.

Julia Kienast explores the relationship between terrorism and asylum in Austria. She argues that both of these topics are mystified with many claims but little factual information. The resulting discourse and lack of transparency, she notes, are fertile soil for producing fear that is employed for the purposes of political mobilization. The actual correlation between terrorism and asylum is not seriously reflected upon in Austria. Accordingly, Kienast poses two specific questions: "What are the factual or perceived possible connections of the phenomena of terrorism and asylum? How do they influence Austrian asylum, and wider, migration law?"

In 2015, Austria, like many other European countries, received a mass influx of an estimated 600,000 to 800,000 irregular migrants that caused an overburdening of the reception system with the arrival of some 88,340 asylum applications. With the media's attention focussed on the so-called "asylum crisis" and the polarisation of Austrian society on the issue of migration, politicians immediately seized upon the issues. In the 2017 national elections, the issue of migration and security was still centre stage in the Austrian public's mind. In Austria, like other Western societies since 2001, the fear of terrorism is foremost in mind. Several forms of terrorist activity have been added to the *Austrian Criminal Code*, on several occasions, since 2002. And, there have been a number of prosecutions that have taken place since 2014 and mostly for preparatory acts such as financing terrorist organizations and incitement. Kienast's review and assessment of those forced migrants who are involved in terrorism indicates that the numbers are indeed small.

From the evidence available of those who are most susceptible to radicalization to terrorism in Austria are juveniles and those who are from the Chechen sub-culture. Nevertheless, Kienast further notes that this radicalization profile may change depending on the new demographics of forced migration since 2015. Effectively combatting radicalization efforts in Austria might better be served through integration measures rather than "isolation and stigmatization." There is also the problem of those who cannot be removed from Austrian territory due to their well-founded fear of persecution despite having been rejected from asylum. Their predicament can be, especially, trying given their precarious physical and psychological living conditions.

Kienast also considers various studies that examine the "fear of migration" that includes concerns about increasing crime rates, job shortages, and losing one's "national identity." Studies of security concerns among Austrians have found that 74 percent of citizens have a dread of the "continuous refugee stream." Indeed, Kienast points out that "migration is a heavily prejudiced phenomenon in many regards and, just like terrorism, it has a very 'intimate relationship' with fear." A 2017 IPSOS poll found that 59 percent of Austrians agreed with the statement, "*There are terrorists that are pretending to be refugees who will enter my country to cause violence and destruction.*"

The dramatic increase in the number of irregular migrants travelling through Austria, along with the significant increase in asylum applications in 2014–15, leads Kienast to state that there was a "hysterical" legislative reaction of more than 80 amendments, not counting the underlying provisions of Union Law, to the Austrian asylum system. The three areas that were focused on were accelerated procedures, reduced workload of state agencies and the courts, and trying to reduce the misuse of asylum claims. And, specifically, in 2014 the asylum procedures were re-embedded in the administrative procedure and the Federal Office for Immigration and Asylum (BFA) that was given two tasks: the evaluation of asylum claims; and, the termination of residence. Amongst these legislative changes a new *Integration Act* was passed that required asylum applicants to learn German and to take an "Austrian values course." Further, social benefits were cut at both the federal and state levels. These rapid legislative amendments continue the trend of the "securitization of migration." For instance, persons were excluded from asylum on the mere suspicion of terrorism and an exception to the right of asylum was introduced for persons who "due to substantive reasons" are presumed to be a threat to national security due to "current events" and the threat posed by extremism and terrorism. In addition, the forced return of suspects of terrorism was allowed without exception to residence consolidation being taken into consideration.

Accordingly, Kienast concludes that the securitization of migration is experiencing a strong renaissance in Austria that amounts to a regression of the policies and practices of the 1990s. Moreover, it is argued that the "security narrative" is not a result of the unintentional consequence of two different but equally complex transactional issues, terrorism and asylum, but, rather the purposeful framing of asylum applicants and refugees as a general threat to national security and public order. This deliberately undermines the humanitarian perspective to achieve a political objective, the agenda of securitization of migration. What is being ignored and not pursued is a better understanding of the "root causes" of both terrorism and forced migration in order to develop realistic and sustainable strategies to address these serious concerns now and in the future.

5 Conclusions

From these summaries of the chapters of this edited volume it is evident that the connections between terrorism and asylum is evident across all societies and clearly manifested in international, transnational, and national laws. It is perhaps most evident among those states that were directly impacted by the 2015 refugee crisis in Southern Europe that were located directly in the path of the forced migrants as they made their way through Turkey and Greece and *en route* to Germany and other Northern European states. The impact of these tremendous numbers of forced migrants varied from state to state, but, the association between terrorism and asylum was evident across all states and fully exploited by right-wing political movements and governments to further their own political agendas. Nativism and the fear of the foreigner, the other, ran rampant in these societies and political leaders and legislators were hypervigilant in trying to address the perceived threat that came with this vast flow of humanity, that is, those who were thought to harbour evil intentions, including, terrorism whenever the opportunity might arise.

The exclusion from asylum of those responsible for serious international and national criminality is a built-in feature of the 1951 Refugee Convention, but, was not used extensively by States prior to 9/11. Indeed, it is not a commonly known feature of refugee protection, generally, that those who have committed a serious international or national crime or are guilty of actions that are contrary to the purposes and principles of the United Nations cannot be given refugee protection.

The conceptual and normative dimensions of "terrorism" and "asylum" are confounded, in part, by the lack of a universally accepted definition of what constitutes "terrorism" or, indeed, for that matter what constitutes "asylum." There are different definitions of what is "terrorism" at the national level and there is no Comprehensive Convention on Terrorism at the international level because states cannot agree on what "terrorism" is because some states believe that it would limit or contradict the right to the self-determination of nations or be used against the leaders, civilian and military, of states that are engaged in legitimate armed conflict and warfare. The definition of who is a refugee varies from region to region with definitions that have expanded over time since the 1951 Refugee Convention such as the *1969 OAU Convention*, the *1984 Cartagena Declaration*, the *2011 EU Qualification Directive*. The contested conceptual and normative bases of what constitutes "terrorism" and "asylum" contributes to the conflation of both of these terms. This makes these terms easy prey for those who wish to exploit them for their own use and purpose to advance their own political, economic, and social agendas. The legitimate exclusion of those who are responsible for terrorism is intended to include those who are directly or indirectly responsible for terrorist activities. The perpetrators of terrorism include those who commit the crime through their direct involvement and those who are complicit in the crimes as accessories and aid and abet the crimes through their indirect involvement. Both are equally guilt of the offence of terrorism. What is the extent of the extended liability to terrorism? This has ranged widely amongst states and over time at the international level. Joseph Rikhof has made a persuasive case for the adoption of common standards for extended liability across all levels, international, transnational and national, to ensure that the exclusion clauses are applied uniformly to ensure those who are criminally liable for terrorism are properly excluded from refugee protection. James Simeon equally makes the case for closing the gaps in international and national law with respect to what constitutes terrorism so that there is a common understanding of what constitutes terrorism for the purposes of exclusion from refugee protection as well as for the prosecution of those who are responsible for terrorist actions.

For a number of states, terrorism has had a serious impact on how they perceive forced migrants or refugees. This has been the case for the UK, Hungary, Austria, but, also Australia, the US, and other refugee receiving states. In fact, no states have been left untouched by terrorism, including, Switzerland. In all refugee receiving states, measures have been introduced to limit access to asylum to those suspected of terrorist activities. This is especially the case for both Austria and Hungary. Of course, following 9/11 this would have been expected to be the case. Security measures have taken precedence and the fight to contain, if not defeat terrorism, has made this so. Moreover, terrorism and the threat of terrorism has been employed by political leaders to undertake measures that are likely to have the unintended consequence of radicalizing vulnerable youth who can then be easily manipulated into undertaking terrorist activities. Counter-terrorism measure should focus on protecting the human rights of all those seeking refugee protection rather than to limiting their access to asylum or to integrating fully in their host countries.

What follows then is an in-depth examination and analysis of the relationship between terrorism and asylum. Each of the authors in the accompanying chapters make an important contribution to understanding how these two concepts are interrelated and connected and how one has impacted on the other. We are most grateful for everyone's contribution to this edited volume.

PART 1

Normative Constructions of Exclusion from Asylum for Terrorist Activities

CHAPTER 1

The Construction of a Terrorist under Article 1 of the Convention Relating to the Status of Refugees

Patricia Tuitt

Introduction

All legal systems must contend with the potentially destabilising actions of the "great criminal"[1] whose capacity to challenge the law is the source of the public's "secret admiration."[2] Article 1F of the Refugee Convention[3] is one important means through which this threat to the legal system is managed. The paragraph F supplement to the refugee definition recognises that the revolutionary ambitions of the "great criminal" may come disguised in the form of the exercise of a legal claim to refugee status. It is generally acknowledged that the paragraph seeks to reduce the chances of "such persons hiding behind the cloak of asylum."[4]

Drawing upon the jurisprudence pertaining to Article 1F which has emerged from the UK courts and legislature, this chapter examines whether the treatment of those suspected of terrorist offences[5] is consistent with the legitimate

1 "…one might consider the surprising possibility that the law's interests in a monopoly of violence vis-a-vis individuals is not explained by the intention of preserving legal ends, but, rather, by that of preserving the law itself: that violence, when not in the hands of the law, threatens it not by the ends it may pursue but by its mere existence outside the law. The same may be more drastically suggested if one reflects how often the figure of the 'great criminal', however repellent his ends may have been, has aroused the secret admiration of the public. This cannot result from his deed, but only from the violence to which it bears witness." From: Walter Benjamin "Critique of Violence," in *Walter Benjamin: Reflections, Essays, Aphorisms, Autobiographical Writings*, (New York: Schocken Books), 1995, 281.

2 Ibid, 281.

3 *Convention relating to the Status of Refugees*, Geneva, 28 July 1951. In force 22 April 1954, 1989 UNTS 137.

4 "The refugee defining instruments that preceded the Refugee Convention of 1951 did not include exclusion clauses, but in the aftermath of the Second World War, memories of the misdemeanours of war criminals…combined to call for the exclusion of persons deemed unworthy of international protection," From: Mark Symes and Peter Jorro, *Asylum Law and Practice* (London: Bloomsbury Professional, 2010), 384. See also Chaloka Beyani, Joan Fitzpatrick, Walter Kalin and Monette Zard "Editorial," *IJRL* 12, Special Issue (2000): 2.

5 As has often been remarked, there is no clear definition of terrorism. It has been suggested that "…the following elements can be…terrorist acts: (1) A terrorist act exposes or threatens

© KONINKLIJKE BRILL NV, LEIDEN, 2020 | DOI:10.1163/9789004295995_003

goal of law-preservation. The focus on the UK is justified, in part, because it has adopted a more restrictive approach to perceived terrorist threats when compared with other EU states. In particular, the UK courts do not accept an obligation in Article 1F cases to balance "the threat of persecution if asylum was refused against the gravity of the crime."[6]

Examination of the UK legislation and case law reveals that the UK's response to the threat to its legal system which is posed by those who come within the scope of Article 1F has been effectively to deprive them of all capacity to deploy the law in their defence. This response, arguably, is disproportionate to the threat posed to the stability of the UK legal order. The chapter argues that the disproportionate nature of the UK response is due, in part, to the overtly racial construction of those deemed to have offended the terms of Article 1F. Prakash Shah has demonstrated that the UK legal system has "consistently been favourable to European refugee groups, while it has consistently rejected, or been hostile to, the presence of Asian and African groups."[7]

Frances Webber is one among many writers who have observed that the UK's "national security deportees [are] nearly all Muslim men"[8] – a feature which no doubt owes itself to what Susan Musarrat Akram has written of as the "orientalist" logic underpinning decision-making in asylum claims.[9]

---

to expose persons to danger to their life and physical integrity; (2) The act of violence is directed against an indeterminate group of people or is directed against a category of persons in particular need of protection; and (3) the act is undertaken with a view to constraining a state or its representatives from taking specific actions." From: Walter Kalin and Jorg Kinzlf "Article 1F(b): Freedom Fighters, Terrorists and the Notion of Serious Non-Political Crimes," *IJRL* 12, Special Issue (2000), 75. In the UK context, it is noted that "the House of Lords...described terrorism as a class of offence likely to attract exclusion due to its lack of correlation between means and ends." From: Mark Symes and Peter Jorro, *Asylum Law and Practice* (London: Bloomsbury Professional, 2010), 417.

6 "...in the UK...the court noted that the Secretary of State was required not to act contrary to the 1951 Convention but could find nothing in the Convention to support the view that, in deciding whether a non-political crime was 'serious' and therefore within Article 1F, either the Secretary of State or the IAT was obliged to weigh the threat of persecution if asylum was refused against the gravity of the crime." From: Sibylle Kapferer "Exclusion Clauses in Europe – A Comparative Overview of State Practice in France, Belgium and the United Kingdom," *IJRL* 12, Special Issue (2000): 195–221.

7 Prakash A Shah, *Refugees, Race and the Legal Concept of Asylum in Britain* (London: Cavendish Publishing, 2000), 1.

8 Frances Webber, *Borderline Justice: The Fight for Refugee and Migrant Rights* (London: Pluto Press, 2012), 180.

9 Susan Masarrat Akram (2000) "Orientalism Revisited in Asylum and Refugee Claims," *IJRL* 12, no. 1 12(1), 7–40.

The argument is arranged in three sections. Section one, *Preserving the law against the threat of individual violence*, places the Refugee Convention within the framework established by Walter Benjamin in the 1921 essay "Critique of Violence"[10] concerning how legal systems seek to insulate themselves from the threat posed to their stability by the individual's deployment of natural violence and legal force.[11] Section two. *The UK legal framework on Article 1F*, consists of an analysis of leading UK cases pertaining to Article 1F. This analysis is undertaken in order to demonstrate that the UK legal framework is premised on the idea that certain individuals should be entirely deprived of the capacity to deploy effectively the law in their defence. The third section, *Law, justice and deconstruction* draws upon Jacques Derrida's notion of deconstruction as elaborated in the essay "Force of Law: The 'Mystical Foundations of Authority'"[12] to advance the argument that to deprive individuals of even the hope of achieving justice is a disproportionate response to the threat perceived to be posed by those who fall foul of Article 1F.

I Preserving the Law against the Threat of Individual Violence

Walter Benjamin is by no means the philosopher upon whom those writers concerned to explicate various aspects of the refugee condition would naturally draw. In a recent edited collection on contemporary issues of migration, Thomas Nail provides a sketch of key philosophers/theorists who have placed the migrant as the central figure in political discourse. Whilst Nail attributes to Karl Marx "[t]he first historical expression of the centrality of the migrant,"[13] he acknowledges the enormous influence on scholarly works on immigration, asylum and nationality of the works of Hannah Arendt[14] and Giorgio Agamben[15] especially.

In *The Origins of Totalitarianism,* Hannah Arendt drew upon the position of the stateless refugee to contemplate how and why individuals can be made to

10 Walter Benjamin "Critique of Violence," in *Walter Benjamin: Reflections, Essays, Aphorisms, Autobiographical Writings* (New York: Schocken Books, 1995), 277–300.

11 Ibid, 280–283.

12 Jacques Derrida "Force of, Law: The 'Mystical Foundations of Authority,'" *Cardozo Law Review*, (1990), 919–1045.

13 Thomas Nail "The Political Centrality of the Migrant," in *Critical Perspectives on Migration in the Twenty-First Century*, eds. M. Karakqulaki, L. Southgate and J. Steiner (Bristol: E-International Relations Publishing, 2018), 15–16.

14 Ibid, 18–19.

15 Ibid, 20–23.

exist without the "right to have rights."[16] Arendt's is a framework of analysis which certainly speaks to this account of how those refugees who are deemed to have engaged in, or who are alleged to have planned, terrorist acts are deprived of the capacity to use the law. However, whilst Arendt's analysis of how the stateless refugee exposes the violence of the nation-state form has seldom been surpassed, Walter Benjamin provides a more explicit thesis on the operation of the law in the production of a condition of "rightlessness." To be exact, Walter Benjamin guides us to an understanding of how "rightlessness" is ultimately produced when individuals are denied the ability to use any kind of violence in the achievement of their objectives, including legal violence.

For Walter Benjamin, violence, in principle, can only ever be justified as a means to inaugurate or to preserve law. He arrives at this conclusion by adopting what he describes as a philosophical reading of the history of violence.[17] From this history emerges the "fundamental ... distinction between sanctioned and unsanctioned violence". This distinction is "more precisely, a violence whose ends are based on the presence of a general historical acknowledgement, and one whose ends are not."[18] Thus, it is through acts of violence which have been given "historical acknowledgement" as legitimate that we come to know the law. In short, it is violence which preserves the law against the forces which would threaten its stability. The chief source of the threat to the stability of law is the individual, whose "natural"[19] violence has never been acknowledged as legitimate. This threat of individual violence is curtailed by the measures which the legal system takes to ensure that individual objectives coincide with legal ends. As Benjamin puts it, the "legal system tries to effect, in all areas where individual ends could be usefully pursued by violence, legal ends that can only be realised by legal power."[20] Yet, paradoxically, the legal system is

16 Hannah Arendt, *The Origins of Totalitarianism* (San Diego: Harcourt Brace, 1958), 296.

17 Walter Benjamin "Critique of Violence," in *Walter Benjamin: Reflections, Essays, Aphorisms, Autobiographical Writings* (New York: Schocken Books, 1995), 279.

18 Rudolpho Gasche "On Critique, Hypercriticism and Deconstruction: The Case of Benjamin," *Cardozo Law Review* 12 (1990), 1119.

19 Walter Benjamin "Critique of Violence," in *Walter Benjamin: Reflections, Essays, Aphorisms, Autobiographical Writings* (New York: Schocken Books, 1995), 280. "Yet the distinction in question presupposes another difference, the difference between natural ends, which lack historical acknowledgement, and legal ends which are defined by such sanctioning. The distinction between sanctioned and unsanctioned violence is aimed at replacing all natural ends by legal ends, and thus at monopolizing violence in the name of law" (Rudolpho Gasche, Ibid, 1120).

20 Walter Benjamin "Critique of Violence," in *Walter Benjamin: Reflections, Essays, Aphorisms, Autobiographical Writings* (New York: Schocken Books, 1995), 280.

most threatened by the exercise of those rights which it confers on individuals.[21] This is especially so where the legal system grants individual rights which impose obligations on states rather than on private individuals. In such cases the individual is effectively granted the right to deploy the law in order to "reorder power relations."[22] It is for this reason that the legal system is always poised to declare the individual's use of the legal rights conferred upon him/her an abuse and to limit the scope of their application.

Although operating far away from the philosophical framework which Walter Benjamin erects, Nisha Kapoor demonstrates her ready comprehension of the integral relation between law and violence when she speaks of the "…enforcement of excess levels of state power as legitimate and necessary for policing the exceptional figure of the 'terrorism suspect.'"[23]

The treatment by the state of suspected terrorists therefore poses the question of how the nature and degree of state force "can be legally sanctioned within the parameters of humanitarian frameworks…."[24]

Kapoor argues further that although law occasionally grants a dispensation to individuals enabling them to deploy violence, the "…exceptional moments when violence … can be justified…"[25] never apply to suspected terrorists, for "…there are certain forms of violence … that are automatically disqualified … and which are never legitimate to debate because they are simply 'evil.'"[26]

How might the foregoing be relevant to an analysis of the Refugee Convention regime, and specifically to the definition of refugee under Article 1? First of all, the Refugee Convention, however humanitarian may seem to be its objectives, is an instantiation of a law that is "violent in both its origins and its methods";[27] for even "the best legal sanction in the world is still a kind of violence."[28]

The above notwithstanding, the Refugee Convention is undoubtedly an instance of the kind of legal right that carries a potentially great threat to the stability of a legal system – for it mandates that, in certain clearly defined

21 "By what function violence can with reason seem so threatening to law, and be so feared by it, must be especially evident when its application is still permissible" (Ibid, 281).

22 Carol Smart, *Feminism and the Power of Law* (London and New York: Routledge, 1989), 141.

23 Nisha Kapoor, *Deport Deprive Extradite: 21st Century State Extremism* (London and New York: Verso, 2018), 6.

24 Ibid, 6.

25 Nisha Kapoor, *Deport Deprive Extradite: 21st Century State Extremism* (London and New York: Verso, 2018).

26 Ibid.

27 Louis E. Wolcher, Law's Task: *The Tragic Circle of Law, Justice and Human Suffering* (Ashgate, 2008), 24.

28 Ibid, 27.

circumstances, individuals are legally entitled to withdraw from the sanctioned violence of their state of origin or domicile. Whilst Benjamin conceded that the right of withdrawal from a pre-existing relationship (in our case, a state of origin or domicile from which the refugee wishes to withdraw) in truth, is "not a right to exercise violence, but, rather, to escape from a violence"[29] he foresaw circumstances in which this seeming passive withdrawal would be perceived by the state as a form of aggression, which must be suppressed with force.[30]

Under the Refugee Convention, the right to withdraw from a state is confined to state sanctioned persecution, which includes acts committed by agents of the state. The objective of State persecution must be to nullify an individual's civil and political rights. The exercise of the right to escape from violence must be supported by other states to the extent that they must not, directly or indirectly, connive at returning the individual to the state violence from which he or she seeks legitimately to evade.

The right of an individual to legally challenge legally sanctioned violence carries a deep threat to the preservation of law itself, and for that reason law must render that threat impotent. The potential of the refugee victim of state persecution to exercise the legal right contained in the Refugee Convention in a way that undermines the state monopoly of violence was thus *immediately* curtailed by the construction of a refugee terrorist who poses a threat to the state and, therefore, whose life or freedom could be taken with impunity.[31] Volker Turk readily grasps the ambivalent nature of the Refugee Convention regime when, in the context of the increasing use by states of Article 1F, he poses the question:

> Whose security are we talking about? The security of refugees or the security of states or both? Or is this a false dichotomy in the first place, albeit that it has been quite prominent in the refugee discourses? My proposition is that the concept of security permeates the whole international refugee law framework, both from the perspective of refugee security, as well as from the perspective of national or public security considerations.[32]

29 Walter Benjamin "Critique of Violence," in *Walter Benjamin: Reflections, Essays, Aphorisms, Autobiographical Writings* (New York: Schocken Books, 1995), 281.

30 For further discussion on this point, see Patricia Tuitt "Refugees, Terrorism and Article 1 of the Refugee Convention," in *Terrorism and Asylum*, ed. James C. Simeon (London: Refugee Law Initiative Working Paper Series, 2019), paper 32, 14–16.

31 Ibid, 14.

32 Volker Turk "Opinion: Forced Migration and Security," *IJRL* 15, no. 1 (2003), 113.

The question of whether, in their treatment of those seeking asylum, states have failed to strike the right balance between legitimate self-preservation and humanitarianism has been the theme of several recent publications. In *Europe's Fault-Lines: Racism and the Far Right,* Liz Fekete examines the increasing tendency of European states (the UK included) to "…outsource the punishment, processing and care of asylum-seekers"[33] In Fekete's view, this form of response to the perceived security threat posed by mass migration is "…in keeping with the creation, over at least three decades, of an integrated, transnational system of surveillance and spatial control to slow down, filter, block, contain, warehouse, process and mark out those from the Global South worthy (or unworthy) of the benefits of European civilisation and 'hospitality.'"[34] Susana Ferreira also provides a timely reminder that migration has always been viewed by the state as a potential threat to its security.[35]

Before undertaking further reflection on the implications of the security context in which the Refugee Convention is embedded, a brief summary of the content of the refugee definition is required. It is composed over six paragraphs (A–F) and also contains several sub clauses. Article 1A(2) is the most commonly cited element of the refugee definition. Indeed, it is an element which has, for all intents and purposes, virtually eclipsed all other elements of the Convention which purport to define the refugee. In Article 1A(2) is stated the requirement of alienage; the requirement for proof of state persecution on civil and political grounds, and the mental or psychic condition of the refugee, which the Convention attempts to capture in the notion of a "well-founded fear."

In paragraph (B) is contained a clause which, put at its lowest, privileges European refugees and European refugee producing phenomena. The 1967 Protocol to the Convention[36] formally nullified the geographical limitations to the Refugee Convention of the original paragraph (B) but its effects have not been erased from the field of refugee protection.[37] Paragraphs C–E contain a

33 Liz Fekete, *Europe's Fault Lines: Racism and the Far Right* (London and New York: Verso, 2018), 153.

34 Ibid.

35 Susana Ferriera "From Narratives to Perceptions in the Securitisation of the Migratory Crisis in Europe," in *Critical Perspectives on Migration in the Twenty-First Century*, eds. M. Karakqulaki, L. Southgate and J. Steiner (Bristol: E-International Relations Publishing, 2018), 57–73.

36 *Protocol relating to the Status of Refugees*, adopted in New York on 31 January 1967, entered into force on 4 October 1967. UNTS, vol. 606, 267 [hereinafter referred to as the Protocol to the Refugee Convention].

37 "Another legal obstacle for asylum-seekers is the narrow legal definition of who is a refugee. This was not so much of an issue in the post-Second World War years when there was

number of clauses which set out circumstances in which, despite meeting the requirements of Article 1A(2), the Refugee Convention will cease to apply. In summary, these are instances where an individual whose original victimhood was accepted is deemed no longer to have the need for the protection of a surrogate state. This brings us to the main object of enquiry in this chapter, Article 1F, which writers have been at pains to note is a "fundamental element of the Convention refugee definition,"[38] provides as follows:

> The provisions of this convention shall not apply to any person with respect to who there are serious reasons for considering that:
> (a) He has committed a crime against peace, a war crime, or a crime against humanity, as defined in the international instruments drawn up to make provision in respect of such crimes;
> (b) He has committed a serious non-political crime outside the country of refuge prior to his admission to that country as a refugee;
> (c) He has been guilty of acts contrary to the purposes and principles of the United Nations.

Article 1F not only sets terms that are integral to the refugee definition, it is arguable that it takes precedence over all other elements. Whilst scholars have tended to give primacy to Article 1A (2),[39] this is far from being the practice of the UK courts. When analysing the case of *AS v Sri Lanka* [2013], Gina Clayton

just a trickle of deposed monarchs, ex-dictators and their secret police making their way to Britain. But with the growth of mass travel, mass migration and mass movement of refugees, the refugee definition has become highly contentious. The Home Office and refugee lawyers are engaged in a constant struggle in the courts over the breadth of the definition, the people and the situation it covers. Although 80 percent of the world's refugees (using the word in its ordinary, not legal sense) are women or children fleeing war or violence, most of them are not eligible for refugee status." From: Frances Webber, *Borderline Justice: The Fight for Refugee and Migrant Rights* (London: Pluto Press, 2012), 70.

38 Mark Symes and Peter Jorro, *Asylum Law and Practice* (London: Bloomsbury Professional, 2010), 389.

39 The interpretation of Article 1F which most scholars prefer is exemplified in the Lisbon Expert Round table's Advisory Opinion, which was published in May 2001. In the view of the Lisbon experts, paragraph F's secondary status is such that consideration as to its application should never be considered first. Whilst I do not dispute that paragraph F sets out a principle of exclusion, I suggest that the Lisbon Experts' Opinion is overly influenced by a weak and increasingly discredited binary opposition, which it is doubtful that the courts support when adjudicating on Article 1F cases. For detailed discussion on this point, see Patricia Tuitt "Refugees, Terrorism and Article 1 of the Refugee Convention," in *Terrorism and Asylum*, ed. James C. Simeon (London: Refugee Law Initiative Working Paper Series, 2019), paper 32, 14–16.

highlights the reluctance of the court to accept the suggestion that the issue of exclusion should be separated from consideration of the merits of the asylum claim. In her view, the suggestion was dismissed as artificial. It should be noted that here the court was dealing with a case in which the "evidence for exclusion was substantially the same as that for the asylum claim",[40] but there is evidence elsewhere in UK jurisprudence of a refusal to hold to the distinction between the inclusion and exclusion elements of the refugee definition. For example, in *T6 v Secretary of State for the Home Department* (SSHD) the Special Immigration Appeal Commission (SIAC) set out three legal questions to be decided in respect of the appellant who had sought asylum from Algeria, and who was accused of serious financial criminality.[41] Paragraph 10 of SIAC's judgement makes clear that the court gave primacy to Article 1F over Article 1A(2). The case raised the interesting question of "whether or not offences of dishonesty, however serious, can amount to serious non-political crimes for the purposes of Article 1F(b)."[42] In reaching the conclusion that there is "no ground for limiting the definition to serious offences of violence",[43] the court placed first in the hierarchy of the three questions "which will determine the outcome"[44] the Article 1F exclusion question, and not first the "political context"[45] which would usually be examined under Article 1A(2).

In support of SIAC's approach in the case of *T6 v SSHD*, it must be noted that nowhere in relation to Article 1A(2) is there any mandatory obligation imposed on states. The Refugee Convention only unequivocally places mandatory obligations on states in relation to a finding that a claimant for refugee status falls within the terms of paragraph F. It is not in dispute that where paragraph F applies states are obliged to disapply the Convention and it's protective regime.[46] Equally beyond dispute is the fact that a finding that a person falls

40 For discussion, see Gina Clayton, *Textbook on Immigration and Asylum Law* (Oxford University Press, 2016), 206 & 500.

41 Appeal No. SC/95/2010, 18 February 2011.

42 Ibid, para. 11.

43 Ibid, para. 61.

44 Ibid, para. 10.

45 Ibid, para. 62.

46 "If someone falls within the exclusion clauses of Article 1F, exclusion from refugee status is mandatory. States have no discretion to grant refugee status to those whose actions place them outside of its protection." From: Frances Webber "Exclusion from Refugee Status Under Article 1F of the Convention," (Rights in Exile, http//www.refugeelegalaidinformation.org/exclusion-clause, accessed on 2 July 2018). Symes and Jorro observe that an individual whose case falls within Article 1F "may lose the benefit of the non-refoulement prohibition." From: *Asylum Law and Practice* (London: Bloomsbury Publishing, 2010), 448.

within the scope of Article 1A(2) does not carry the positive right to command asylum.

Despite the quite evident difficulties in drawing a sharp distinction between a "political" and "non-political" crime, a suspicion that a claimant for refugee status has been engaged in terrorist activities would usually bring him/her within the confines of Article 1F(b) of the Refugee Convention.[47] Thus, the case of the alleged terrorist illustrates all too clearly how the law's force can be turned upon the individual in an explicitly self-preserving gesture. As Symes and Jorro note "the consequences of a finding of an association with such crimes are serious, amounting to being declared an international outlaw."[48] Terrorist activity is an instance of those national security cases which displace the non-refoulement principle, and, in spite of the appeal of the idea that the "humanitarian imperative to admit those fleeing persecution should always take precedence over any attempt to screen ... for possible involvement in excludable crimes",[49] the practice in the UK courts would seem rather to prioritise the security of the state over humanitarian considerations. Such is entirely consistent with Walter Benjamin's analysis of the historically settled distinction between sanctioned and unsanctioned violence.

II The UK Legal Framework on Article 1F

The legal framework which governs national security cases in the UK is comprised of the Special Immigration Appeal Commision Act 1997, the Special Immigration Appeal Commission (Procedure Rules) 2003, the latest version of which was published on 28 November 2013, and a repository of case law decided by the Special Immigration Appeals Commission (SIAC). Judgements

---

See also Rene Bruin and Kees Wouters "Terrorism and the Non-Derogability of Non-Refoulement," *IJRL* 15, no.1 (2013).

47 See for discussion, Walter Kalin and Jorg Kinzlf "Article 1F(b): Freedom Fighters, Terrorists and the Notion of Serious Non-Political Crimes," *IJRL* 12, Special Issue (2000), 46–78.

48 Mark Symes and Peter Jorro, *Asylum Law and Practice* (London: Bloomsbury Professional, 2010), 391.

49 "The guiding principle as to 'if' and 'when' to screen has to be one of 'protection'. The exclusion clauses can only be properly understood as a reinforcement of the central purpose of international refugee law – namely the protection of those fleeing persecution or other calamitous events which pose a threat to their freedom, safety and lives. The exclusion clauses also play an important role in ensuring that perpetrators of serious human rights abuses cannot hide behind the cloak of asylum." From: Chaloka Beyani, Joan Fitzpatrick, Walter Kalin and Monette Zard "Editorial," IJRL 12, Special Issue (2000): 3.

of SIAC are available online, but because SIAC deals with security matters, judgements are often very heavily redacted.

Whilst a detailed summary of the legislative framework is beyond the scope of this chapter, sections 5 and 8 of the 1997 Act, in particular, are of direct relevance to the chapter's concerns. In Section 5 we find provisions which enable SIAC to proceed to make determinations "without the appellant being given full particulars of the reasons for the decision which is the subject of the appeal",[50] and which permits the holding of proceedings "in the absence of any person, including the appellant and any legal representative appointed by him."[51] Given the sensitive nature of the matters to be disposed of and the extremely serious consequences for the individuals accused of terrorist offences, the Act sets out very tight timeframes for submission of appeals. In the case of appellants who are within the UK at the time that the grounds of appeal arise, the appeal must be lodged within ten days.[52] For those outside of the UK, a twenty-eight day timeframe is mandated by the legislation.[53]

Aside from the individual SIAC judgements, the full flavour of the SIAC process is better conveyed by the Procedure Rules, and not by the main Act. The Rules establish a paramount duty on the Commission not to disclose information where to do so would be injurious to the public interests.[54] Section 37 of the Rules is of interest because it encompasses the core of what critics see as the secret court process. This provision relates to material relevant to the proceedings which the Secretary of State objects to being disclosed to the appellant or his/her representative on the grounds of national security. In such cases where, following a procedure set out in section 38 of the Rules (the precise details of which do not concern us), the Commission upholds the objection, then the evidence can only be disclosed to a Special Advocate, whose powers and duties are set out between sections 34–36 of the Rules (details of which are also beyond the scope of this chapter). The process of dealing with material deemed sensitive, indicated above, is supplemented by a provision which allows hearings to be held, wholly or partly, in private. To be clear, 'private' in the context of the SIAC process does not connote what would usually be inferred in relation to court hearings – the absence of members of the general public – rather it means that a hearing can take place in the absence of the appellant and his/her legal representative.[55]

50 Special Immigration Appeal Commission Act 1997, s5(3)(a).
51 Ibid, s5(3)(b).
52 Ibid, s8(1)(b)(1).
53 Ibid, s8(1)(b)(2).
54 Special Immigration Appeal Commission (Procedure Rules) 2003, s4.
55 Special Immigration Appeal Commission (Procedure Rules) 2003, s43.

Turning now to the case law of SIAC, Sarah Singer has questioned the extent to which the Commission's decisions are significant in Article 1F cases because of their relatively small number.[56] In terms of the value of this body of jurisprudence, its limitations must be acknowledged.

Ordinary researchers have access only to the open judgements, and, as will be demonstrated shortly, these can be very short on detail indeed. Moreover, the manner in which the substance of the open judgements are recorded can sometimes produce uncertainty over whether or not Article 1F played a part in the decision. The case of *F v Secretary of State for the Home Department* is a case in point. Here, as with some other SIAC decisions, the court appears to have applied the logic of Article 1F without making explicit reference to it or to its underpinning jurisprudence.[57] Of the various judgements available to the public, those marked as being related to deportation decisions are the ones most likely to deal with fact patterns which raise questions of the compatibility of decisions made by the Secretary of State for the Home Department with Article 1F. A sample of these deportation cases have been used to support the argument of this chapter.

The SIAC structure has been subjected to sustained and trenchant criticism. It is accused of being, among other things, a "colonial-style court"[58] with a "… low threshold for convicting terrorism suspects…."[59] For Kapoor "[t]he rationale of national security … underlies the entire judicial process for terrorism suspects…[t]he use of closed procedure trials … where information available to the defendant and/or their lawyer is restricted … means that records of legal arguments, judgements and documents are often only available in part."[60] Frances Webber has described SIAC as:

> …a system where fundamental principles of justice – including the presumption of innocence, equality of arms, the right to know what is said against them – are routinely violated. The secrecy that shrouds the intelligence services have been breached in places, but not for those seeking deportation, exclusion or denial of citizenship on national security grounds. Worse, there does not have to be any specific allegation; it might

56 Sarah Singer, *Terrorism and Exclusion from Refugee Status in the UK: Asylum Seekers Suspected of Serious Criminality* (Brill Nijhoff, 2015), 235.

57 Appeal No. SC/11/2002, 29 October 2003.

58 Nisha Kapoor, *Deport Deprive Extradite: 21st Century State Extremism* (London and New York: Verso, 2018), 16.

59 Ibid, 17.

60 Nisha Kapoor, *Deport Deprive Extradite: 21st Century State Extremism* (London and New York: Verso, 2018), 19–20.

> just be their associations or their reading matter which makes them a 'danger' to national security. And what constitutes such a danger has been stretched beyond imagining.[61]

So, whilst Sarah Singer is correct in cautioning against drawing too many overarching principles from the SIAC judgements, it cannot be denied that the Commission has been involved in some defining case law, such as in *Home Secretary v Rehman*.[62] The extent of its decision-making powers is important for the argument in this chapter concerning the ways in which those asylum-seekers who are suspected of terrorism offences are effectively denied the capacity to deploy the law in their defense. SIAC is entitled to have regard to a wide range of evidence in making its findings of fact. It seems that only evidence obtained through torture is inadmissible. Despite the closed nature of its scrutiny process, SIAC's findings of fact cannot be impugned other than on grounds of perversity.

The problem of access to justice is not one that is lost upon the SIAC judges. For example, in *E v Secretary of State for the Home Department* it was said that "[t]he open material deployed against the Appellant is not at all substantial. The evidence which is relied on against him is largely to be found in the closed material. This has meant that he has been at a real disadvantage in dealing with the case because he is not aware of those with whom he is alleged to be in contact."[63] Despite these expressed concerns, the SIAC went on to dismiss the appeal on the basis of the closed material mainly.[64]

Perhaps in support of Kapoor's argument that the threshold for determining terrorism cases is unacceptably low, SIAC in *D v Secretary of State for the Home Department* supports Kapoor's argument that the threshold for determining terrorism cases is unacceptably low. SIAC was prepared to accept the Secretary of State's determination that the Appellant "was not entitled to the protection of Article 33(1) of the Refugee Convention because Article 1F ... applies to him and his removal from the United Kingdom would be conducive to the public good",[65] despite also finding several flaws in the Secretary of State's investigation of the Appellant's alleged terrorist activities. SIAC found that "[i]t is right to say that the Secretary of State was in error in suggesting that weapons were found at the book shop when D was working there: they were not – they were

61 Frances Webber, *Borderline Justice: The Fight For Refugee and Migrant Rights* (London: Pluto Press, 2012), 180.

62 [2003] AC 153.

63 Appeal No: SC/4/2002, 29 October 2003, para. 2.

64 Ibid, para. 10.

65 Appeal No: SC/6/2002, para. 2.

found … before D started working at the book shop, and, in any event, as weapons they were ineffective."[66] In *Ajouaou and A, B, C and D v Secretary of State for the Home Department*, SIAC noted that "…some Appellants have given evidence … whilst reiterating their objections to the unfairness of the procedures which govern the appeals."[67]

III Law, Justice and Deconstruction

In this final section I advance the argument that even the legitimate goal of law-preservation cannot justify removing from any individual the hope of attaining justice – however far distant that hope might be. Drawing on the writings of Jacques Derrida, I suggest that the treatment of terror suspects within the UK legal system – especially where decisions are made in closed court – has the effect of denying the possibility of justice, for although justice cannot be reducible to law, it cannot be reached other than through the law. Petra Gehring puts the position neatly when she states "one must remain as close as possible to the law even if there is not justice in it."[68]

Niraj Nathani once asserted that "[the] harm refugees fear is much greater than any sanction the immigration regime can offer",[69] but it is to be questioned whether this remains true when, for the state, the question of the security of its legal system collides with its intolerance of racial difference. In cases of alleged terrorist activity, mainly Muslim men are subjected to an orientalist discourse in which "Islam somehow lacks the critical and humanitarian roots of the other faiths, and … the Muslim 'Allah' is a different – and warmongering – God from the Jewish Christian God."[70] This circumstance brings home the reality that the applicant for refugee status is in truth caught between two violent efforts at law-preservation – the sanctioned violence of his state of origin or domicile and the sanctioned violence of the host state, which latter is made manifest in the legal processes which it chooses to adopt.

Even before questions of state security became paramount, "the racial composition of the UK has been uppermost in the minds of policy makers"[71]

66 Ibid, para. 11.

67 Appeal NOs : SC/1/2002, SC/6/2002/SC/7/2002, SC/9/2002, SC/10/2002, para. 117.

68 Petra Gehring "The Jurisprudence of the 'Force of Law,'" in *Derrida and Law*, ed. Pierre Legrand (Ashgate, 2009), 126.

69 Niraj Narwanit (2000) "The Purpose of Asylum," IJRL 12, no. 3, 374.

70 Susan Masarrat Akram (2000) "Orientalism Revisited in Asylum and Refugee Claims," IJRL 12, no. 1, 10.

71 Prakash A Shah, *Refugees, Race and the Legal Concept of Asylum in Britain* (London: Cavendish Publishing, 2000), 7. He notes that "…after the 1960s…notable shifts in the origins

according to Prakash Shah. One dimension of the way in which race has played a part in the shaping of UK immigration law and policy is to place increasing obstacles in the way of "non-Europeans" to use effectively the law in their defense. An "attitude of officials ... adamant against allowing easy recourse to the courts"[72] "shifted to the control of legal advice, a key determinant of litigation in the courts"[73] and also to an "emergence of a politics around 'bogus' advisers ... falsely making asylum claims, or needlessly pursuing appeals and judicial review remedies."[74]

In an article which examines whether adjudication on Article 1F cases is consistent with ideas of procedural justice, Michael Bliss opined that legal processes like those adopted by SIAC creates "great difficulties in procedural fairness terms"[75] but are increasingly being adopted in cases that are deemed to present issues of national security.[76] It is in the absence of what Bliss sees as basic procedural safeguards that terrorist suspects lose the benefit of the Refugee Convention and its protective regime. It is questionable whether adjudicatory bodies such as SIAC operate procedures which assuredly test whether there are "serious reasons to consider" that an applicant has committed acts which fall within the scope of Article 1F.[77] Limited procedural safeguards are compounded by "the monolithic portrayal of Islam in refugee and asylum cases"[78] and, as a consequence, the refugee claimant is effectively deprived of a legal defense. Akram writes of a system that will "silence the voice of the refugee"[79] and thereby "threatens accurate presentation of human rights violations."[80]

of refugees coming to Britain, and a parallel hostility, was already developing against those refugees in practice which was directly linked to their racial background" (117).

72 Ibid, 166.

73 Ibid, 170.

74 Ibid, 189.

75 Michael Bliss (2000) "Serious Reasons for Considering: Minimum Standards of Procedural Fairness in the Application of the Article 1F Exclusion Clauses," *IJRL* 12, Special Issue, 123.

76 "...despite the precarious situation of asylum-seekers, many states provide substantially fewer procedural fairness safeguards in their refugee determination systems than for other administrative proceedings" (Ibid, 97).

77 The "serious reasons for considering" test was outlined in the case of *Al Sirri and DD (Afghanistan v Secretary of State for the Home Department)* [2012] UKSC 54. Here the UK Supreme Court concluded that Article 1F imposed a standard of proof on the Secretary of State for the Home Department that was more exacting than the usual balance of probabilities standard imposed in civil cases.

78 Susan Masarrat Akram (2000) "Orientalism Revisited in Asylum and Refugee Claims," *IJRL* 12, no. 1, 18.

79 Ibid, 18.

80 Ibid, 39.

The case of *Home Secretary v Rehman* [2003][81] provides a particularly stark illustration of the combining of racial hostility and security sensitivity into a particularly forceful mode of law-preservation. Ironically, *Rehman* was a case in which the Special Immigration Appeals Commission (SIAC) was unprepared to accept the Secretary of State's assessment of the threat posed by *Rehman*. The case went to the highest court of appeal, with neither the court of appeal nor the House of Lords being willing to accept that SIAC had the power to substitute its assessment of a risk to national security for the Secretary of State's risk assessment. The House of Lords decision confirms that the interests of state security outweighs the normal processes whereby a tribunal or court of first instance is entitled to make its own assessment of the credibility of a witness – including that of a state witness.

It must be noted that the House of Lord's judgement in *Rehman* has not been received by subsequent SIAC courts with unqualified approval. In *Ekaterina Zatuliveter v Secretary of State for the Home Department* the suggestion that the Secretary of State was better equipped than SIAC to assess security risk was questioned, SIAC stating that "…we believe that we are able to, and do, give more careful and detailed scrutiny to the risk posed by an individual Appellant to national security than the Secretary of State can reasonably be expected to do."[82]

In "Force of Law: The 'Mystical Foundation of Authority'", one of the very few texts in which he explicitly writes about law and legal institutions, Jacques Derrida "sought to foreground the theme of justice"[83] In particular, he poses the question of whether justice exists "outside or beyond the law."[84] He cannot be sure that justice does exist, but he is certain that "if such a thing exists … justice is deconstruction."[85] In the view of Petra Gehring "…Derrida wants to grant law priority as the paradigm of deconstruction…."[86] Thus, only through the practice of law is it possible to attain justice.[87] Gehring states: "it seems that whereas on the one hand Derrida 'deconstructs' legal discourse, that is, decodes the law with respect to what remains unthought, he simultaneously affirms the model of law; it may even be that he adopts it as a certain broken

81 [2003] AC 153.

82 Appeal No: SC/103/2010, 29 November 2011, para. 8.

83 Jacques Derrida "Force of Law: The 'Mystical Foundations of Authority,'" *Cardozo Law Review*, (1990), 7.

84 Ibid, 14.

85 Ibid, 14–15.

86 "…Force de Loi repeatedly stresses this: lawyers' discourse is particularly close to the discourse of deconstruction. Deconstructive …questioning…is…more at home in law schools…than in philosophy departments and much more than in the literature department" (Petra Gehring "The Jurisprudence of the 'Force of Law,'" in *Derrida and Law*, ed. Pierre Legrand (Ashgate, 2009), 127).

87 Ibid, 117–132.

form of justice, as a paradigm of deconstruction itself."[88] If Gehring's reading of Derrida is correct, then the increasing recourse in English criminal and civil law to closed court hearings at which cases are determined on the basis of evidence that has not been subjected to the normal processes of scrutiny is a matter of deep concern. Characteristic of such justice systems is an absence of "…a paper trail in the form of judicial documentation … of state arguments and the ultimate rationalities of judicial decisions."[89] The absent history of a judicial decision attempts to give the lie to Derrida's assertion that the very structure of law is deconstructible. In closed court hearings, the law, as represented in the judicial decision, cannot as readily be the object on which deconstruction is enacted. In other words, judicial decisions and the reasoning behind them cannot as easily be subjected to deconstructive methods, which involve "destabilising" and "complicating."[90]

The Special Immigration Appeal Tribunal regime is one which has exemplified an emerging process which enables, on thin evidentiary justifications, the deportations, extraditions and physical deprivations of those whose citizenship rights are always contingent.[91]

Derrida's text cannot be used as authority to argue that such closed hearings pose a problem for justice because of any particular decision reached, since Derrida refuses to grant justice a tangible or immediately graspable quality. Indeed, he explicitly cautions against any attempt to "speak directly about justice."[92] So, how, if we cannot state that closed court hearings offend because they inevitably reach erroneous decisions, can the form of decision-making which they exemplify pose a problem of justice? If we follow Derrida we are bound to conclude that closed court hearings are troubling because they attempt to conceal the possibility of a justice which exists beyond them, and, by extension, the possibility of a justice that resides beyond the law. The trial then becomes "the locus of state imposed violence."[93] According to Petra Gehring's reading of *Force of Law,* the accessibility of legal institutions – especially open

88 Ibid, 118.

89 Nisha Kapoor, *Deport Deprive Extradite: 21st Century State Extremism* (London and New York: Verso, 2018), 19.

90 Jacques Derrida "Force of Law: The 'Mystical Foundations of Authority,'" *Cardozo Law Review* (1990), 8.

91 See generally, Nisha Kapoor, *Deport Deprive Extradite: 21st Century State Extremism* (London and New York: Verso, 2018).

92 Jacques Derrida "Force of Law: The 'Mystical Foundations of Authority,'" *Cardozo Law Review* (1990), 10.

93 M.M. Slaughter "Comment on Fenues and Heller," *Cardozo Law Review* 12 (1990), 1215. The author goes on to say "this is a legal system that institutionalises relations by which some speak lawfully in the name of others. The others do not speak" (1217).

courts – are indispensable because it is only through the *practice* of law that it is possible to attain justice.[94]

IV Conclusion

Throughout this chapter I have acknowledged that law-preservation is a legitimate objective for which force (violence) can be deployed.[95] Such forceful law-preservation will inevitably seek to reduce the individual's capacity to deploy both natural violence and legal force. However, there are increasing signs that law-preservation is taking the form of measures which seek to strip certain individuals – coming disproportionately from minority races and faiths – of any ability to use law in their defense. The effect of this deprivation is to deny also the possibility that justice might ever be experienced by those individuals, for "…only within law is it possible to take account of the impossibility of justice."[96]

Bibliography

Arendt, Hannah. *The Origins of Totalitarianism.* San Diego, Harcourt Brace, 1958.

Benjamin, Walter. "Critique of Violence." in *Walter Benjamin: Reflections, Essays, Aphorisms, Autobiographical Writings.* New York, Schocken Books, 1995.

Beyani, Chaloka, Fitzpatrick, Joan, Kalin, Walter and Zard, Monette. "Editorial." *IJRL* 12, Special Issue (2000).

Bruin, Rene and Wouters, Kees (2003) "Terrorism and the Non-Derogability of Non-Refoulement." *IJRL* 15, no. 1 (2003).

Bliss, Michael "Serious Reasons for Considering: Minimum Standards of Procedural Fairness in the Application of the Article 1F Exclusion Clauses." *IJRL* 12, Special Issue (2000), 93–132.

94 Petra Gehring "The Jurisprudence of the 'Force of Law,'" in *Derrida and Law*, ed. Pierre Legrand (Ashgate, 2009), 117–132.

95 Louis Wolcher helpfully reminds us that "a decision to recognise law's violent nature is not the same as a decision against legal violence (or even against the suffering it causes); someone who calls the law violent is not necessarily saying that it is evil and should be replaced everywhere by non-violent means of social ordering." From: *Law's Task: The Tragic Circle of Law, Justice and Human Suffering* (Ashgate, 2008), 29.

96 Petra Gehring "The Jurisprudence of the 'Force of Law,'" in *Derrida and Law*, ed. Pierre Legrand (Ashgate, 2009), 122. Gehring goes on to say "For Derrida, the idea of justice corresponds to undecidability in the sense of an 'experience'…this is the thesis…with which Force de Loi directly addresses legal practice, concretely the situation in which judges make judgement" (125).

Clayton, Gina. *Textbook on Immigration and Asylum Law.* Oxford University Press, 2016.

Derrida, Jacques. "Force of Law: The Mystical Foundations of Authority." *Cardozo Law Review* (1990), 919–1045.

Fekete, Liz. *Europe's Fault Lines: Racism and the Far Right.* London and New York, Verso, 2018.

Ferriera, Susanna. "From Narratives to Perceptions in the Securitisation of the Migratory Crisis in Europe." in *Critical Perspectives on Migration in the Twenty-First Century*, eds. Karakqulaki, Mariana, Southgate, Laura and Steiner, Jacob. Bristol: E-International Relations Publishing, 2018, 57–73.

Gasche, Rodolpho "On Critique, Hypercriticism and Deconstruction: The Case of Benjamin." *Cardozo Law Review* 12 (1990), 1115–1132.

Gehring, Petra. "The Jurisprudence of the 'Force of Law'." in *Derrida and Law*, ed. Pierre Legrand, Aldershot, Ashgate, 2009.

Kalin, Walter and Kinzlf, Jorg "Article 1F(b): Freedom Fighters, Terrorists and the Notion of Serious Non-Political Crimes." *IJRL* 12, Special Issue (2000), 46–78.

Kapferer, Sibylle "Exclusion Clauses in Europe – A Comparative Overview of State Practice in France, Belgium and the United Kingdom." *IJRL* 12, Special Issue (2000), 195–221.

Kapoor, Nisha. *Deport Deprive Extradite: 21st Century State Extremism.* London and New York, Verso, 2018.

Masarrat Akram, Susan. "Orientalism Revisited in Asylum and Refugee Claims." *IJRL* 12, no. 1 (2000), 7–40.

Nail, Thomas. "The Political Centrality of the Migrant" in *Critical Perspectives on Migration in the Twenty-First Century*, eds. Karakqulaki, Mariana, Southgate, Laura and Steiner, Jacob. Bristol: E-International Relations Publishing, 2018, 15–27.

Narwani, Niraj "The Purpose of Asylum." *IJRL* 12, no. 3 (2000), 354–379.

Shah, Prakash A. *Refugees, Race and the Legal Concept of Asylum in Britain.* London, Cavendish Publishing, 2000.

Singer, Sarah. *Terrorism and Exclusion from Refugee Status in the UK: Asylum Seekers Suspected of Serious Criminality.* Brill Nijhoff, 2015.

Slaughter, M.M. "Comment on Fenues and Heller." *Cardozo Law Review* 12 (1990), 1215–1217.

Smart, Carol. *Feminism and the Power of Law.* London and New York, Routledge, 1989.

Symes, Mark and Jorro, Peter. *Asylum Law and Practice.* London, Bloomsbury Professional, 2010.

Tuitt, Patricia. "Refugees, Terrorism and Article 1 of the Refugee Convention." in *Terrorism and Asylum*, ed. James C. Simeon, London, Refugee Law Initiative Working Paper Series, 2019, paper 32, 14–16.

Turk, Volker. "Opinion: Forced Migration and Security." *IJRL* 15, no. 1 (2003), 113–125.

Webber, Frances. *Borderline Justice: The Fight for Refugee and Migrant Rights.* London, Pluto Press, 2012.

Wolcher, Louis E. *Law's Task: The Tragic Circle of Law, Justice and Human Suffering.* Aldershot, Ashgate, 2008.

Legislation

Convention Relating to the Status of Refugees, adopted in Geneva on 28 July 1951, entered into force on 22 April 1954. UNTS, vol. 189, p.137.

Protocol Relating to the Status of Refugees, adopted in New York on 31 January 1967, entered into force on 4 October 1967. UNTS, vol. 606, p.267.

Special Immigration Appeal Commission Act 1997.

Special Immigration Appeal Commission (Procedure Rules) 2003.

Cases

Ajouaou and A, B, C and D v SSHD [Appeal NOs : SC/1/2002, SC/6/2002/SC/7/2002, SC/9/2002, SC/10/2002], 29.10.2003.

Al-Sirri and DD (Afghanistan) v SSHD [2012] UKSC 54.

D v SSHD [Appeal No. SC/6/2002], 29.10.2003.

Ekaterina Zatuliveter v SSHD [Appeal No. SC/103/2010], 29.11.2011.

E v SSHD [Appeal No. SC/4/2002], 29.10.2003.

F v SSHD [Appeal No. SC/11/2002], 29.10.2003.

Home Secretary v Rehman [2003] AC 153.

T6 v SSHD [Appeal No. SC/95/2010], 18.2.2011.

Reports

Lisbon Expert Roundtable "*Global Consultations on International Protection.*" UNHCR (2001), http://www.unhcr.org/3b38938a4.pdf (accessed on 2.7.2018), 15–16.

Webber, Frances "*Exclusion from Refugee Status under Article 1F of the Convention.*" Rights in Exile Programme:, http://www.refugeelegalaidinformation.org/exclusion-clause (Accessed on 2.7.2018).

CHAPTER 2

Manufacturing Fear: Examining the Social Component of Anti-immigration Policies within Counter-terrorism Discourse

Selina March

1 A Rising Tide

There is no doubt that the Western world is experiencing a wave of nativist rhetoric and anti-immigration policies, and the plight of displaced people around the world is being swept up in this tide. Although there are a number of factors driving anti-immigration sentiment, trends of securitisation and criminalisation are particularly prevalent, as terrorism and asylum continue to be increasingly intertwined. The linking of terrorism and asylum is a process which has deep historical roots, and, as such, the unlinking of asylum from terrorism is a particularly complex process which starts with examining how these two ideas continue to be entangled. This chapter will focus on this subject by looking at the social component of anti-immigration policies within the context of counter-terrorism discourse, and will analyse the influence of this social component on driving asylum policy.

The social component of the terrorism and asylum link is worth highlighting, because it is this component which I argue ultimately drives the success or failure of restrictive immigration and asylum policies. Without a sort of 'social imperative'– or, political will – restrictive asylum policies would be less palatable to the general public in the face of sympathy towards asylum seekers. In pushing securitisation narratives within counter-terrorism discourse, politicians can degrade any potentially welcoming reaction to asylum seekers in favour of a restrictive response predicated on national security concerns. In other words, a sort of 'zero-sum game' is advanced, pitting the safety of asylum seekers against the safety of a country's own citizens; this, in turn, creates a cultural environment in which restrictive policies are perceived not only as acceptable, but necessary. In advancing such narratives, politicians set themselves up for political success using immigration as a 'hot button' issue to garner votes and justify restrictive policies.

© KONINKLIJKE BRILL NV, LEIDEN, 2020 | DOI:10.1163/9789004295995_004

This analysis focuses primarily on the United States as a case study, as the U.S. has seen a particular rise in anti-immigration sentiment and policy, with immigration taking the spotlight as a driving issue in the 2016 presidential election and beyond. U.S. policies such as the 'travel ban', the 'zero-tolerance policy', and responses to the 'migrant caravan' have all garnered international attention – and, in some cases, condemnation – and the social components at play in the U.S. have significant influence on driving such policies. The Trump administration has built a platform around anti-immigrant sentiment, and the plight of U.S.-bound asylum seekers has been swept up in this rhetoric. Building on the U.S. case study, this chapter will go on to look at the implications of counter-terrorism discourse on asylum more generally, with a particular focus on the social component of securitisation narratives on driving policy.

1.1 *Critical Race Theory*

In looking at the social components driving policy, it is essential to utilise a framework which allows for critical analysis of law and policy. Critical race theory developed as an offshoot of critical legal studies in America in the 1980's, and has since continued to evolve. The central tenet of critical race theory rejects the idea of legal neutrality, asserting that racism is so deeply engrained in American society that a 'colour-blind' analysis of U.S. law only serves to reinforce existing racial hierarchies. Also central to critical race theory is the idea of race as a function of power; critical race theorists "urge recognizing race not as an inherent characteristic of people but instead a product of social practices."[1] Related to this is the concept of evolving 'whiteness' and 'other-ing', which has played a role in U.S. immigration policy; this is explored further below in the review of how targets of nativist immigration policies have shifted over time.

These core tenets of critical race theory make it a useful tool for analysis of U.S. immigration law and policy through examination of the influence of both intentional and unconscious biases. Additionally, its focus on the interplay between cultural and institutional racism makes it an ideal framework for examining the social components which drive and influence policy. When counter-terrorism discourse is advanced in the context of asylum – primarily in the form of securitisation and criminalisation narratives – culturally racist viewpoints are legitimised; this, in turn, provides justification for passing institutionally racist policies. What ensues is a codification cycle in which fears regarding asylum and terrorism are reinforced by the existence of policies which confirm that link – i.e., a self-fulfilling prophecy of sorts. Although critical race

1 The Bridge Project, 2017.

theory is inherently an American framework, these core tenets – rejection of a 'colour-blind' approach, existence of racial hierarchies, and the interplay between cultural and institutional racism – are more generally applicable and appropriate. This is particularly true when it comes to the examination of migration law and policy, which easily falls prey to nativist rhetoric.

2 Case Study: United States

President Trump's campaign flourished under existing biases among the American populace, expertly stoking an ever-more pervasive fear of terrorism and the unknown to ultimately win the presidency. Since coming to power, the Trump administration has continued to employ the same fear-mongering tactics and policy positions that put him in power, and has continuously attempted to push through hard-line anti-immigration policies under the guise of 'making America great again'. Such policies have made the current administration's stance abundantly clear: a 'great' America is one in which immigrants, including refugees, are generally unwelcome. The policies in question – the executive orders entitled "Protecting the Nation from Foreign Terrorist Entry Into the United States,"[2] the 'zero-tolerance policy' enforced by former Attorney General Jeff Sessions, and the administration's response to the 'migrant caravan' at the southern border of the U.S. – have each advanced a narrative characterising immigration and asylum as a national security threat, further codifying nativist sentiment.

It is essential to note that, although Trump serves as the figurehead for current anti-immigration policies, there are a number of social components driving these policies which are no less influential or important. Policy is not created in a vacuum, and the social components under which these policies are created drive the policies themselves, and can greatly influence their potential success or failure. The social components at play include existing biases, insecurities, and fears, and increased social and political polarisation, among many others; these can be generally classed as factors influencing the worldview of the American populace. There are a number of tools which drive this worldview, including the news, political statements, and social media; this is, of course, not an exhaustive list of factors which influence opinion-forming, but these factors, in particular, have received a great deal of attention for their impact on driving this worldview.

2 Executive Order 13769; Executive Order 13780.

This chapter examines how the threat of terrorism has been used to stoke anti-refugee sentiment in the U.S., paving the way for a series of restrictive immigration and asylum policies. This includes a brief discussion on the history of nativism and the securitisation of asylum policy in the U.S. as it relates to contemporary policy. What follows is an analysis informed by critical race theory on how the Trump administration has actively utilised news, social media, and political statements to foster an environment of cultural racism blurring the line between migrants and refugees, criminalising asylum seekers, and linking refugees from Muslim-majority countries with terrorism, in an attempt to codify this bias in the form of anti-immigration policies.

3 Securitisation and Nativism in U.S. Immigration Policy

> ...certainly, nativism played a role in the refusal of the U.S. public to accept Jewish refugees from the Second World War; in public acceptance of Japanese internment camps during the same period; in the continued deportations of Mexican migrants; and in resistance to the resettlement of Vietnamese refugees in the 1970s, to name just a few examples.[3]

It is important to note that, although it may be tempting to claim, the Trump administration's anti-immigrant rhetoric is not new in the context of American history. This is not to say that the current wave of anti-immigrant rhetoric is any less concerning; but, it is essential to go beyond current policy to get a more complete picture of the social components at play today. An in-depth analysis of anti-immigrant rhetoric and policies is beyond the scope of this chapter, but a brief discussion of this history is key to framing the central analysis of the Trump administration's[4] exploitation of existing cultural bias against Muslims, in particular, and immigrants more generally. It is also essential to analyse how the link between refugees and national security has developed over time.

3.1 *Securitisation in Immigration Policy*

U.S. immigration and refugee policy was greatly influenced by the geopolitical context in which it was developed, as was international refugee law. Contemporary international refugee law developed on the heels of World War II, in the

3 Young, 2017, p. 227.

4 It is worth noting that Trump himself, both during his campaign and continuing into his time as President, has a track record of using racist remarks to rally his supporters which, arguably, go beyond cultural and institutional racism into individual racism, and suggest that the beliefs he espouses may be more than simply a political tactic. For more on this, see Hayes, 2018 and Capehart, 2018.

midst of a global movement towards codification of human rights; at the same time, U.S. refugee policy began to develop with a close link to foreign policy relating to the Cold War. Initially, U.S. refugee policy "only allowed refugees from Communist countries or the Middle East,"[5] reflecting a concerted effort to paint the U.S. as a haven for those fleeing oppressive regimes. It was not until the *1980 Refugee Act* that the U.S. began to align its own policies with those laid out in the *1967 Protocol Relating to the Status of Refugees*, to which it was a party. The initial linking of refugee policy with foreign policy concerns set the stage for ongoing securitisation of refugee policy that continues to this day.

A telling example of policy relating to the securitisation and criminalisation of refugee flows is the *1996 Illegal Immigration Reform and Immigrant Responsibility Act* (IIRIRA), which was passed following the 1993 World Trade Center bombing. The IIRIRA introduced a number of security-related immigration measures, many of which "undermine both refugees' access to protection in the United States and U.S. treaty obligations."[6] This sets a major precedent for U.S. actions relating to refugees following acts of terror, and has helped to pave the way for continued links between asylum and national security policy. Interestingly, however, even following the 1993 World Trade Center bombing and the 1996 IIRIRA, "applicants from countries labelled by the U.S. government as state sponsors of terrorism have a consistently high average grant rate, as do applicants from countries with known al-Qaeda activity."[7] As Holmes and Keith point out, this mirrors Cold War-era refugee policy,[8] suggesting a continued attempt on the part of the U.S. to advance foreign policy objectives by establishing a perception as a safe haven for refugees fleeing from terrorism in their own countries, even as it erects barriers to limit the number of refugees resettled in the U.S.

The terrorist attacks on 11 September 2001, and the myriad of policies that followed, represent a turning point in U.S. refugee policy that moves from securitisation of refugee policy, in line with foreign policy objectives, to a criminalisation of refugees as a threat to national security. Three policies are of particular importance in examining refugee policy post-9/11: the *2001 Security Council Resolution 1373*, the *2001 USA-PATRIOT Act*, and the *2005 Real ID Act*. Each of these policies codified a link between terrorism and refugees, on both a national and international level, and grants of asylum to Arabic-speaking applicants and those from a country considered by the U.S. to be a state sponsor

5 Holmes and Keith, 2010, p. 431.
6 Acer and Byrne, 2017, p. 357.
7 Holmes and Keith, 2010, p. 433.
8 Holmes and Keith, 2010, p. 433.

of terrorism sharply declined.[9] In this, there is a concerted move by the U.S. from foreign policy objectives to stand as an alternative to oppressive regimes in the Middle East, to a country unwelcoming and even hostile towards those fleeing such regimes. The institutional link between asylum seekers, particularly from Muslim-majority countries, and terrorism also further enforces existing cultural biases against Muslim immigrants and refugees among the American populace, paving the way for the sort of anti-refugee policies being pursued by the current administration.

3.2 *Nativism in Immigration Policy*

Alongside developments in securitisation and criminalisation in refugee policy, it is important to note how nativism has influenced and shaped such policies over time. As set out below, the U.S. has a long history of nativism far preceding asylum policy, which has strongly influenced immigration policy at large over time. National pride and the concept of what it means to be an American play a large role in U.S. nativism, as do economic insecurity, and, later, fear of terrorism. The result is an evolving idea of 'other-ness' which has shifted over time, taking aim at different subsets of immigrant populations depending on the day-to-day realities of the American populace at any given time.

In the late 1800s and early 1900s, nativist rhetoric was directed against Asian and certain European immigrants, both for their "perceived inability to assimilate"[10] and "because of the labour competition that they represented."[11] Although many of the beliefs associated with immigrants were factually unwarranted, they had a defining influence on policy throughout that time period, leading to strict immigration policies designed to preserve the idea of the American way of life. Throughout this same time period, and into the 1920s, "The increased presence of Mexican migrants in the United States drew out the same xenophobia and nativism that had been directed towards Asians and Europeans";[12] however, there was a lack of immigration policies directed against Mexican migrants, due largely in part to their central role in the U.S. economy.[13] Later, spikes in illegal immigration along the southern border led to a number of policies attempting to control and restrict undocumented migration, which helped to further the nativist narrative of Mexican immigrants as

9 Holmes and Keith, p. 435.
10 Young, 2017, p. 220.
11 Young, 2017, p. 222.
12 Young, 2017, p. 224.
13 Young, 2017, p. 225.

threats to the lifestyle and economic wellbeing of U.S. citizens.[14] These narratives continue to be relevant today, as the administration takes aim at migrants from Central and South America. This clearly illustrates the link between the social and the political, and the selective actions taken by policymakers in relation to nativist rhetoric.

As Young points out, current nativist rhetoric against Muslim immigrants bears a striking resemblance to earlier nativism, pointing out that "Muslim immigrants are perceived by nativists to be inherently dangerous because of their purported links to religious extremists – a fear that echoes historical fears about the potentially dangerous political affiliations of specific immigrant groups during the early twentieth century."[15] Combining this bias with institutionalised links between refugees and terrorists in the U.S. and international policy, it is easy to see how Trump's anti-Muslim rhetoric has struck a chord among portions of the American public. Anti-immigrant rhetoric has become a political strategy for certain politicians in the U.S., one that is likely to garner support among parts of the U.S. electorate; Trump's ascent to the presidency suggests that it is still relevant, and effective. Throughout his campaign and continuing into his time as president, Trump has continuously drummed up support through aggressive anti-immigrant rhetoric. As outlined below, he has expertly played on existing biases and fears to launch himself to political success, and appears to be using the same tactics in his attempt to push through anti-immigration policies, and anti-refugee policies targeting asylum seekers. It is clear that the social and political factors at play today are certainly not new in the context of U.S. history, and Trump is tapping into a resurgence in nativist rhetoric that is a disturbing echo of past nativism to shape his policies.[16]

---

14 Alongside a history of shifting nativist sentiment influenced largely by socioeconomic factors, it is worth noting that U.S. policy regarding immigration from Mexico is also shaped by centuries of history. A detailed overview of Mexico-U.S. relations is beyond the scope of this chapter, but Akers Chacón and Davis (2006) provide a comprehensive history, noting that the U.S. annexation of "nearly half of Mexico's land and three-fourths of her natural resources" in 1848 "found upwards of 125,000 Mexicans crossed by a new border, one that defined them as foreigners in their own ancestral lands."

15 Young, 2017, p. 228.

16 With nativist rhetoric seeing a resurgence not only in the U.S. but in a number of other countries around the world, it is crucial to examine why such movements have been able to gain significant traction domestically and globally. Although it is sometimes suggested that economic downturns can create the political conditions in which nativist politicians and policies thrive, a more holistic view which includes socio-cultural as well as economic factors is more appropriate. For more on this, see Betz, 2018 and Goldstein and Peters, 2014.

4 Manufacturing Fear

> Mob mentality against disenfranchised groups and open hatred never happens overnight, but rather, it's a long and troubling process that starts off with seemingly harmless statements and framing of narratives, and ends with the president of a nation enacting actual policies that begin the process of either banning those groups – or far worse.[17]

There are a number of strategies Trump has employed to cultivate the worldview that refugees constitute a danger to American society; these strategies rely heavily on existing biases, insecurities and fears, and increased social and political polarisation to gain traction and legitimacy on an individual basis. Two of the key strategies that have been used to legitimise this worldview are grouping refugees with other migrants, and norming a factually unwarranted link between refugees from Muslim-majority countries and terrorism. The Trump administration has relied heavily on these strategies, in particular, to influence the worldview of large sections of the American populace in an attempt to manufacture the cultural racism necessary to push through policies banning or significantly curtailing the number of refugees resettled in the U.S. These strategies are particularly influential because they serve to reframe the way refugees are viewed by painting them as people who have not only chosen to leave their country for the U.S., but have also done so with malintent.

4.1 *Refugees as Migrants*

> One might think that refugees would elicit an almost knee-jerk sympathy given the tragic circumstances that drove their migration, but perceptions of refugees are often tied up with geopolitical considerations and domestic political realities.[18]

Grouping refugees with other migrants serves clear social and political purposes. Socially, when refugees are grouped with other migrants, it serves to change "the narrative from one of vulnerable people seeking help and sanctuary to one of people choosing the circumstances of their situation."[19] This creates distance from the sympathy that refugees might typically elicit. Grouping refugees with other migrants also serves to blur the lines between various

17 Khan, 2017.
18 Scribner, 2017, p. 264.
19 Wigglesworth, 2016.

forms of immigration, allowing for a blanket condemnation of immigrants that plays on inherent biases without any associated feelings of guilt. In the context of the U.S., there has been and continues to be a tendency to blame immigration for economic insecurities, and, "While refugees and economic migrants have traditionally been treated separately within Western legal traditions, popular discourse on immigration often conflates the two categories."[20] The result is that refugees are not only viewed unsympathetically, but, along with immigrants generally, as scapegoats for economic insecurities on an individual and a national level.

Discourse on refugees that incorporate this narrative of choice risks seriously undermining the imperative to protect, and helps to make hard-line policies more palatable to the American public. Alongside this narrative of choice, the Trump administration has also repeatedly called into question the legitimacy of asylum seekers from Central and South America. The political implications that arise from this shift in narrative are clear: it is less challenging to pass legislation against a vulnerable group of people, refugees, if the public does not see them as vulnerable. By playing into inherent biases and economic insecurities felt by a portion of the American populace, the Trump campaign and administration garnered support for hard-line anti-immigration policies that include extreme limitations and restrictions on refugees. This strategy has been particularly useful in advancing restrictive asylum policy along the southern border – most notably, the 'zero-tolerance' prosecution policy, and new restrictions on asylum in response to the 'migrant caravan'.[21]

Each of these policies have received international backlash, and each also face domestic social and legal challenges. Particularly, these policies have received criticism for the adverse impact they have had on families – the result of their enforcement has been widespread family separation. However, by advancing a narrative which blurs the lines between asylum seekers and other categories of migrants, the Trump administration has imbued a narrative of choice on migration from Central and South America. This narrative of choice attempts to shift outrage over family separation from the administration and its enforcement mechanisms to the families themselves; by attributing migration along the southern border to choice, it becomes easier to blame parents travelling with children for putting them in the position to be separated in the first place. Additionally, blurring these lines allows for the administration to call into question the legitimacy of asylum seekers at the southern border, which only further undermines access to fair asylum adjudication.

20 Blitz, 2017, p. 394.

21 Gomez, 2018.

4.2 *Refugees as Terrorists*

> At times of high anxiety, political communities tend to become less tolerant, more insular places.[22]

Perhaps one of the most influential strategies that has been used to shift and define the worldview of the American people is the systematic linking of refugees, particularly those from Muslim-majority countries, with terrorism. This is, of course, not a U.S.-specific problem; throughout the Western world, Islamophobia has spread, to the detriment of refugees displaced from the Middle East. There have been concerted efforts on the part of a number of influential people to establish a link between Muslims and terrorism, and even to specifically link refugees to acts of terror. These unwarranted links have even been codified in the realm of international law, notably in Security Council Resolution 1373, which "linked refugee status with acts of terrorism, thus reinforcing a general trend towards the securitisation and criminalisation of refugee flows."[23] Such codification serves only to legitimise the culturally racist belief that Muslims are dangerous, which paves the way for passage of restrictive, bigoted legislation and policy. This link between Muslim immigrants and terrorism has become so commonplace, in fact, that Vice President Pence has used this fear-mongering tactic to justify militarisation of the southern border; he noted, "In the last fiscal year we apprehended more than 10 terrorists or suspected terrorists per day at our southern border from countries that are referred to in the lexicon as 'other than Mexico' – that means from the Middle East region."[24]

The overall result "has been a reconfiguration of refugee policy and a reconnecting of humanitarian and security interests which has enabled a discourse antithetical to the universal right to asylum."[25] In this way, existing bias and preconceived notions influenced policy, which in turn reinforced these beliefs, further legitimising the need for additional institutionally racist policies. Although Trump has not exclusively used these tactics, he has shown himself to be an expert at the type of fear-mongering tactics that paint refugees as potential terrorists. This is a telling example of the interplay between cultural and institutional racism, and is a clear roadmap to how this interplay is being used by the current administration to push through hard-line anti-immigration and anti-refugee policies.

22 Gibney, 2002, p. 42.
23 Ahlborn, 2011, p. 1023.
24 Foley, 2017.
25 Blitz, 2017, p. 381.

4.3 *Refugees as 'others'*

It is important to note that, although the characterisations above – blurring the lines between refugees and other migrants, and linking refugees with terrorism – have had a significant impact on the social components driving migration law and policy in the U.S., there are other trends in the characterisation of refugees and asylum seekers that are worth mentioning. Rhetoric surrounding the 'zero-tolerance policy' and the 'migrant caravan' is riddled with criminalisation and dehumanisation narratives, alongside those mentioned above. These narratives further existing biases and insecurities while simultaneously distancing the general public from the plight of asylum seekers. The continuous and systematic dehumanisation of migrants through the use of terms such as 'aliens' and 'illegals' further enhances processes of 'othering'. The classification of refugees as 'others', in the critical race theory sense, keeps asylum seekers and refugees on the outside of American society as separate entities. In advancing this classification of 'other-ness', an environment of cultural racism is fostered which paves the way for institutionally racist legislation.

5 Spreading the Message

There are a number of factors which influence worldview, and to examine each of them would go far beyond the scope of this chapter. There are, however, a few tools which have been particularly influential in blurring the lines between refugees and migrants, and in advancing the unwarranted link between refugees and terrorism; these include the news, political statements, and social media. These tools are particularly relevant due to the Trump campaign and administration's systematic and methodical use of the news, political statements, and social media to advance a culturally racist narrative of refugees as a threat to the U.S. and its people. Examining the Trump administration's use of the news, political statements, and social media, through the lens of critical race theory, results in a clear picture. There is a concerted effort to advance a cultural narrative that is fearful of and hostile towards refugees, which, in turn, serves to normalise institutionally racist legislation.

5.1 *Refugees in the News*

> We increasingly live in two Americas. And those two Americas have very separate sources of news.[26]

26 Blake, 2017.

It is difficult to find a more telling example of the extreme social and political polarisation in America than the news; far-right and far-left news sources continue to gain traction, and traditionally centrist or neutral news sources continue to move further from the middle in an attempt to maintain viewership. Trump has shown an uncanny ability to exploit this polarisation to his own advantage, raising the profile of far-right news sources, and lambasting left-leaning news sources as 'fake news'. The result is a supporter base that is increasingly reliant on extreme new sources – including notoriously questionable sites such as Breitbart, InfoWars, Gateway Pundit, Conservative Treehouse, and Truthfeeds[27] – and outwardly dismissive of more traditional news sources. Trump's appointment of Steve Bannon, of Breitbart, to his cabinet served to further legitimise these far-right new sources, elevating their profile among his supporters and deepening existing polarisation among the American public. On the other side, by constantly degrading other news sources as 'fake news', Trump seeks to undermine any reporting that does not explicitly support his own agenda. This serves to further enhance social and political polarisation in the U.S., with each side trusting only their own news sources, and dismissing others as illegitimate. Trump has used existing polarisation to further extremist far-right news among his supporters, and diminish any news sources which do not support his agenda; these tactics have served to divide the American public even further, and to pave the way for divisive policy.

With Trump making concerted efforts to elevate far-right news sources, and his supporters becoming increasingly reliant on them, it is essential to note how they have reported on immigration and refugees, and how they have enabled the Trump administration's continued effort to solidify a culturally racist link between refugees and terrorism. In a variety of reports, the site InfoWars continuously places the word refugees in quotation marks, in an apparent move to call into question the legitimacy of their refugee status; this is a departure from international norms, which define an asylum seeker as a person seeking refugee status, and a refugee as a confirmed refugee by definition. After a Swedish report deemed such behaviour as a hateful act in and of itself, the site lambasted the report, claiming "…the Swedish government is now overtly asserting that telling the truth about the 'refugee crisis' is an act of 'hate'. This represents an unprecedented attack on free speech and an Orwellian sign of what's to come."[28] Such reporting illustrates the strategies employed by the Trump campaign and administration to blur the line between refugees and migrants, and to call into question the legitimacy of refugee claims.

27 Blake, 2017.

28 Watson, 2017.

Such sites have also produced an extensive number of articles linking refugees with violence, and linking Islam with terrorism. In a report on the resettlement of refugees from Australia's offshore processing centre on Manus Island to the U.S., Breitbart reports "that unlike what mainstream media reports claim, the refugees are not vulnerable foreign nationals fleeing destruction, but in fact, destructors themselves that could wreak havoc on the U.S. region where they are resettled."[29] Reporting on Trump's "Protecting the Nation from Foreign Terrorist Entry Into the United States" executive order, Breitbart paints opposition to the policy as a "hysterical reaction" and "emotional theater," claiming, "We're being effectively told by the theatrical class to tolerate a certain amount of Islamic terrorism because their feelings would be hurt by the tough measures we need protest (sic) ourselves from a tough enemy."[30] Such reporting serves to link inextricably refugees, particularly those from Muslim-majority countries, with terrorism, further advancing culturally racist narratives. At the same time, these reports play on existing social and political polarisation, and de-legitimise contrasting reports and opinions. It is important to note that, although far-right extremist reports certainly play a significant role in advancing the narrative that refugees, particularly those from Muslim-majority countries, represent a national security threat, more traditional news outlets share part of the blame, as they "gave Trump millions in free airtime to spew his vitriol and bigoted ideas, yet they rarely (if ever) brought on Muslims to counter his lies."[31]

5.2 *Refugees in Political Statements*

Throughout his campaign and continuing into his time as president, Trump has built his political brand on a foundation of anti-immigrant rhetoric. The provisions banning refugees and immigration from certain countries proposed in his series of "Protecting the Nation from Foreign Terrorist Entry Into the United States" executive orders is certainly not a departure, nor is it new. In fact, "Trump first championed his Muslim travel ban in December of 2015 following the San Bernardino attack,"[32] and has continuously invoked the need for a ban following attacks "that involve perpetrators with foreign ties – including…the Pulse nightclub shooting; and the truck attack in New York City."[33] This stance, which is founded on the culturally racist belief that Muslim refugees are

29 Binder, 2017.
30 Hayward, 2017.
31 Khan, 2017.
32 Khan, 2017.
33 Keneally, 2017.

terrorists, became a defining part of Trump's campaign and continues to define his administration, and Trump has effectively used political statements to advance this narrative.

When it comes to political statements, phrasing and choice of words is of the utmost importance; these choices define the message and the narrative, and the political nature of these statements means that the wrong choices can have far-reaching social and political ramifications. Trump himself appeared to acknowledge this point, as he made Obama and Clinton's general refusal to use the phrase 'radical Islamic terror' a sticking point throughout his campaign. Both the Obama administration and the Bush administration refused to use the phrase in order to "make a clear distinction between Islam as a religion built on peaceful precepts and the acts of terrorism carried out by extremists who adhere to radical interpretations of the religion."[34] On the other hand, the Trump campaign did not attempt to maintain this distinction, and sought to inextricably link Muslims with terrorism. In a speech following the 2016 shooting at an Orlando nightclub, Trump used the phrase 'Radical Islam' 16 times; he frames 'Radical Islam' as incompatible with American values, and denounces Clinton's earlier statements calling Muslims a "peaceful and tolerant people… [who] have nothing whatsoever to do with terrorism."[35] In his own comments on Muslim communities, Trump notes, "Our government has been admitting ever-growing numbers, year after year, without any effective plan for our security," and calls on them to "cooperate with law enforcement and turn in the people who they know are bad – and they do know where they are."[36] In this same speech, Trump makes four mentions to refugees, each time linking them with a threat to national security with statements such as: "under the Clinton plan, you'd be admitting hundreds of thousands of refugees from the Middle East with no system to vet them, or to prevent the radicalization of their children," and "We have to stop the tremendous flow of Syrian refugees into the United States – we don't know who they are, they have no documentation, and we don't know what they're planning."[37]

This speech is emblematic of Trump's political statements regarding Islam, terrorism, immigration, and refugees, and his effort to use the threat of terrorism to stoke anti-refugee sentiment. Advancing this cultural racism provides a clear path to institutionalising these racist beliefs, which Trump has attempted to do with his series of 'travel ban' executive orders. The links to this social narrative are clear in the text of the acts, beginning with the title, "Protecting

34 Phelps, 2016.
35 Clinton, 2015.
36 Trump, 2016.
37 Trump, 2016.

the Nation From Foreign Terrorist Entry Into the United States." From the start, the executive orders, each with the same name, frame the immigration restrictions in the context of national security; this inextricably links migrants and refugees from the named countries with terrorism and a threat to national security, aligning with the cultural narrative. On refugees, the executive order states that "…the entry of nationals of Syria as refugees is detrimental to the interests of the United States," and that "…the entry of more than 50,000 refugees in fiscal year 2017 would be detrimental to the interests of the United States."[38] The act also includes a provision requiring the Secretary of Homeland Security to

> …collect and make publicly available within 180 days, and every 180 days thereafter:
>
> (i) information regarding the number of foreign nationals in the United States who have been charged with terrorism-related offenses while in the United States; convicted of terrorism-related offenses while in the United States; or removed from the United States based on terrorism-related activity, affiliation, or material support to a terrorism-related organization, or any other national security reasons since the date of this order or the last reporting period, whichever is later;
>
> (ii) information regarding the number of foreign nationals in the United States who have been radicalized after entry into the United States and engaged in terrorism-related acts, or who have provided material support to terrorism-related organizations in countries that pose a threat to the United States, since the date of this order or the last reporting period, whichever is later;[39]

This provision further links immigrants and refugees with terrorism by advancing a narrative that such reporting is inherently necessary. Executive Order 13780, a revised version of Executive Order 13769 presented under the same name, even further links refugees with terrorism, a likely response to the legal challenges met by the first executive order. In an attempt to prevent further legal challenges, the Trump administration included more context in Executive Order 13780, attempting to justify the need for the provisions outlined. This justification takes aim at refugees a number of times, with statements such as: "Terrorist groups have sought to infiltrate several nations through refugee programs";[40] "…hundreds of persons born abroad have been convicted of

38 Executive Order 13769, p. 8979.

39 Executive Order 13769, p. 8981.

40 Executive Order 13780, p. 13210.

terrorism-related crimes in the United States. They have included not just persons who came here legally on visas but also individuals who first entered the country as refugees";[41] and, "The Attorney General has reported to me that more than 300 persons who entered the United States as refugees are currently the subjects of counterterrorism investigations."[42] The similarities between the sentiments in Trump's campaign speeches and in his legislation make the link between cultural and institutional racism abundantly clear.

5.3 *Refugees in Social Media*

> In the United States, Mr. Trump's tweets were welcomed by a former Ku Klux Klan leader, David Duke, who wrote on Twitter: "Thank God for Trump! That's why we love him!"[43]

The place of social media, particularly Twitter, in Trump's campaign and administration cannot be underestimated; Trump has used it to make headlines, call out world leaders, and even to announce policy. There has also been a great deal of research of the echo chamber effect and hyper-personalisation in social media, and on how these factors influence opinion-forming.[44] This is an issue that continues to live in the spotlight, with speculation and investigations into Russia's use of targeted social media ads, and what role such ads may have played in influencing the results of the 2016 presidential election. With this in mind, it is crucial to examine Trump's continued reliance on Twitter in light of how he has used it to advance culturally racist views against refugees.

Leading up to his campaign and continuing to this day, Trump has used Twitter as a stream of consciousness to present thoughts and opinions on various topics and issues, and as a means for attacking political opponents, media outlets, and, occasionally, members of the general public. While it is easy to dismiss such wide-ranging and half-formed proclamations as random, Trump has, in fact, utilised Twitter in a targeted manner. A recent study analysing Trump's Twitter feed found that his tendency to combine moral ideas such as duty with emotional ideas such as fear, into a moral-emotional idea such as hate, increased their effectiveness.[45] Trump has continuously played into these ideas – a duty to protect American ideals, and a fear of terrorism – in his posts about refugees to gain traction among his supporters. From his personal

41 Executive Order 13780, p. 13212.
42 Executive Order 13780, p. 13212.
43 Baker and Sullivan, 2017.
44 March, 2018.
45 Brady et al., 2016.

Twitter account, @realdonaldtrump, Trump has tweeted about refugees 22 times as of February 2017, with the majority of these tweets occurring from 2015–2017; he has not mentioned refugees from the @potus account.[46] Of these tweets, not a single one has mentioned refugees in a positive light, and the large majority of them link refugees with terrorism and national security threats. During the campaign, Trump frequently tweeted about Clinton's plan for resettling Syrian refugees, stating "ISIS has infiltrated countries all over Europe by posing as refugees"[47] and that it was "Time to get smart and protect America!."[48] Since becoming president, Trump has used tweets about refugees to emphasize the need for passing his executive orders, stating, "Our legal system is broken! '77% of refugees allowed into U.S. since travel reprieve hail from seven suspect countries'. (WT) SO DANGEROUS!."[49] Trump retweeted a series of videos originally posted by Jayda Fransen of Britain First, which were titled "Muslim migrant beats up Dutch boy on crutches!," "Muslim destroys a Statue of Virgin Mary!," and "Islamist mob pushes teenage boy off roof and beats him to death!."[50] This is despite the fact that the videos are unverified, and Britain First has been condemned for its pervasive and often violent anti-Islam rhetoric.[51] In this, it is clear that the Trump campaign and administration has undertaken a concerted effort to link Islam with terrorism, even going so far as to use factually inaccurate sources, in an attempt to codify and institutionalise a culturally racist narrative.[52]

6 Codifying Cultural Racism

> The cultural underpinnings – the pre-political conditions – will continue to shape the context in which specific legislative proposals and administrative actions will be deemed viable, elections will be won and lost, and policies will be shaped that affect the lives of millions, including refugees.[53]

The above analysis provides a clear picture of how Trump has used various tools and strategies to advance the culturally racist narrative that refugees are

46 Trump Twitter Archive, 2017.
47 Trump Twitter Archive, 2017.
48 Trump Twitter Archive, 2017.
49 Trump Twitter Archive, 2017.
50 Baker and Sullivan, 2017.
51 Wright, 2016.
52 Clapper, 2018.
53 Scribner, 2017, p. 279.

terrorists, as well as how advancing such rhetoric paves the way for codification of such racism in the form of policy and legislation. Passing such policies institutionalises the link between refugees and terrorists, lending weight to the cultural bias, which then in turn reinforces the institutional need; in this way, the interplay between cultural and institutional racism becomes a cycle which is difficult to break. This is all in spite of the fact that there is little evidence of any real link between refugees and terrorism, and in spite of the fact that the large majority of terrorist attacks in the U.S. since 2001 have been carried out by U.S. nationals.[54] Rather than rely on facts, the Trump campaign and administration has relied on increased social and political polarisation, and existing fears and biases to stoke anti-refugee sentiment among his supporters. Playing on a generalised fear of terrorism has proven particularly effective, partially due to the fact that terrorism-related fears ranked second and fourth in a 2016 survey of American fears.[55] All of these factors come into play to create an American populace that is increasingly turning towards nativism and away from refugee protection.

Of course, it is important to note that Trump's anti-refugee policies have been met with social, legal, and political challenges. There are certainly sections of the American populace and legislators that are mobilising to prevent such policies from being enacted, and these movements should not be discounted. There are also laws in place at the national and international level which have prevented and could continue to prevent portions of the proposed policies from being passed. The question that remains is what sway these roadblocks hold against the rising tide of nativism and xenophobia among Trump and his supporters. As discussed, the social components at play greatly influence policy, and they can drive the success or failure of Trump's anti-refugee legislation. Cultural racism is a very powerful force, and cultural and institutional racism work to reinforce one another; passing institutionally racist legislation or policy that codifies the culturally racist narrative advanced by the Trump administration would give further weight to that narrative, which would, in turn, reinforce the need for such policies.

The recent decision by the U.S. Supreme Court on the latest version of the Executive Order suggests that cultural racism continues to play a major role in immigration law and policy. In the 5-4 decision, the majority ruled for the Trump administration, noting: "The Proclamation is expressly premised on legitimate purposes…The text says nothing about religion."[56] In the dissent,

54 Schwartz and Kesling, 2017.

55 Anderson, 2017.

56 585 U.S. (2018), p. 34.

Sotomayer strongly condemns the ruling, noting the importance of considering the context in which the policy was developed, and pointing out that the changes made from one Executive Order to the next "cannot conceal an unassailable fact: the words of the President and his advisors create the strong perception that the Proclamation is contaminated by impermissible discriminatory animus against Islam and its followers."[57] The dissent underscores the importance of analysing more than simply the letter of the law, emphasising that a policy can indeed be discriminatory without explicitly reading as such. Although legal and social challenges have been mounted against the ruling, it serves further to codify culturally racist views against Muslim immigrants and asylum seekers. Such codification within the U.S. could potentially have far-reaching outcomes – a movement by the U.S. away from refugee protection could set a devastating precedent, leaving the world's refugees with even less access to needed protection.

7 Looking beyond the Borders

The U.S. case study is a telling example of the influence of securitisation and criminalisation discourse – particularly as it relates to counter-terrorism and national security – on law and policy, and of the social components at play behind restrictive immigration and asylum policies. Although each of the policies detailed in the case study above are facing social and legal challenges, it is crucial to note that the U.S. certainly is not alone in its securitisation of asylum. Narratives linking asylum with terrorism are persistent on a global scale, and appear only to be gathering steam. Codification of culturally racist beliefs can have a widespread impact that extends far beyond the borders of the U.S., as the trend of securitisation of migration is certainly a global one; failure to consider the racial context of immigration policies predicated, on their face, on security concerns allows for discriminatory legislation to be passed under the 'carte blanche' of national security. The overall trend of discriminatory legislation masquerading as necessary security policy is a deeply troubling one that threatens to undermine legal protections for asylum seekers and other migrants on a global scale. It is arguable that, given such trends, current protection policies are not enough to shield migrants from such discriminatory policies.

The implications of narratives and policies linking terrorism and asylum are far- reaching, particularly at a time when there are global efforts to address the

57 585 U.S. (2018), p. 13.

so-called 'crisis' of migrant and refugee flows. Consider, for example, the Global Compact for Safe, Orderly and Regular Migration; the non-binding compact is the result of a global effort to manage migration, but the U.S. – along with Australia, Chile, the Czech Republic, Italy, Hungary, Poland, Latvia, Slovakia, and the Dominican Republic – has refused to sign.[58] Although the deal is non-binding, and its success is not predicated on the full participation of states, the refusal of a number of countries to sign the compact is likely indicative of deeper issues surrounding migration controls. Of particular note in the compact is Objective 17, which is to "Eliminate all forms of discrimination and promote evidence-based public discourse to shape perceptions of migration."[59]

Objective 17 is an interesting, and particularly relevant, inclusion in the compact – and, although it has not been explicitly stated, seems to run counter to the behaviours exhibited by the U.S. and a number of other countries in their advancement of culturally racist securitisation and criminalisation narratives. Counter-terrorism discourse and the need for restrictive immigration and asylum policies for the maintenance of national security has been a cornerstone of U.S. immigration policy both historically and in the current administration; however, as the above analysis has shown, such rhetoric is often predicated on culturally racist beliefs surrounding migration. Objective 17's commitment to "eliminate all forms of discrimination, condemn and counter expressions, acts and manifestations of racism, racial discrimination, violence, xenophobia and related intolerance" targets some of the key strategies the Trump administration has employed to stoke anti-immigration sentiment, including the media and the practice of profiling. As rhetoric linking terrorism and asylum continues to spread, it is unsurprising that a number of countries would not agree to a global compact on migration – particularly one which targets those same narratives being used to advance restrictive policies.

7.1 *Barriers to Enforcement*

Looking beyond global compacts, it is also important to note the barriers faced when attempting to enforce international law against domestic law, because it can certainly be argued that contemporary U.S. immigration policy is in violation of commitments under international law – both treaty and customary. Influence over domestic law is a continual issue in international law due to the primacy of sovereignty in the international system. In such a climate, it is difficult for the international refugee protection regime – whose power is derived from international law on refugee protection – to act as a 'check' on restrictive

58 McVeigh, 2018.

59 GCOM, p. 24.

asylum policies, even when they are in direct violation of those laws. Former U.S. Ambassador to the U.N. Nikki Haley summed up the matter quite succinctly in response to global condemnation of family separation at the southern border, stating, "Neither the United Nations nor anyone else will dictate how the United States upholds its borders."[60]

Securitisation discourse only further exacerbates these challenges, as the invocation of national security has a sort of 'carte blanche' effect in that it is difficult to counter. When states – particularly those with widespread international influence, such as the U.S. – pass restrictive immigration and asylum policies using counter-terrorism discourse, there is little recourse to challenge those domestic laws. Although the legal basis is there, enforcement mechanisms are weakened against assertions of sovereignty and national security. It is also important to note that there may be a lack of political will among other states to challenge such restrictive policies, because a number of other states find these policies more attractive than problematic. As the narrative link between terrorism and asylum continues to grow and to spread, so do restrictive domestic immigration and asylum policies.

7.2 *Addressing Legitimate Threats*

It is important to note that, although much of the rhetoric linking terrorism and asylum is factually baseless, there are legitimate fears and concerns relating to migration and security. This is the primary argument against analyses such as this, and therefore bears addressing. An analysis of whether or not asylum is linked with legitimate security threats is beyond the scope of this chapter, so I will focus instead on the mechanisms in place to address any potential threats in refugee status determination procedures.

Article 1(F) of the 1951 Refugee Convention – often referred to as the 'exclusion clause' – outlines specific circumstances under which a person may be excluded from refugee status:

> F. The provisions of this Convention shall not apply to any person with respect to whom there are serious reasons for considering that:
>
> (a) he has committed a crime against peace, a war crime, or a crime against humanity, as defined in the international instruments drawn up to make provision in respect of such crimes;
> (b) he has committed a serious non-political crime outside the country of refuge prior to his admission to that country as a refugee;

60 Cumming-Bruce, 2018.

(c) he has been guilty of acts contrary to the purposes and principles of the United Nations.[61]

It is clear, given the language of the 'exclusion clause', that any asylum-seeker reasonably suspected of terrorism would be ineligible for asylum per the Refugee Convention. Although there are a number of issues relating to application of Article 1(F), it cannot be argued that an international legal mechanism already exists for protecting the asylum process from abuse by suspected terrorists.

It can, of course, be argued that the system is not fool-proof; this is often where invocation of Article 9 comes into play. Article 9 states:

> Nothing in this Convention shall prevent a Contracting State, in time of war or other grave and exceptional circumstances, from taking provisionally measures which it considers to be essential to the national security in the case of a particular person, pending a determination by the Contracting State that that person is in fact a refugee and that the continuance of such measures is necessary in his case in the interests of national security.[62]

What is crucial to note here is that Article 9 is written to cover "provisionally" cases of "exceptional circumstances" that are "essential to the national security in the case of a particular person."[63] These restrictions on the invocation of this article seem to be designed to prevent abuse or misuse by states of national security to restrict access to asylum. The sweeping restrictive measures currently being advanced by a number of states, particularly the U.S., could not legitimately fall under the provisions of Article 9 because they apply to large groups of people, rather than on a case-by-case basis.

It is clear that, regardless of the legitimacy of security concerns relating to asylum, there are provisions which are already in place to address security concerns on a case-by-case basis. Counter-terrorism narratives relating to asylum procedures tend to allege otherwise in an attempt to provide justification for restrictive measures beyond the scope of what is already provided for in international refugee law. In continuing to advance restrictive asylum policies

61 Convention and Protocol Relating to the Status of Refugees, Article 1(F).

62 Convention and Protocol Relating to the Status of Refugees, Article 9.

63 Convention and Protocol Relating to the Status of Refugees, Article 9.

predicated on national security concerns, states disregard provisions already in place under the guise of a need to protect their own citizens.

7.3 *Implications for Asylum Seekers*

In examining the impact of counter-terrorism discourse on asylum law and policy, it is crucial to consider the potential implications of this interplay between cultural and institutional racism. This chapter has already examined some of these implications in terms of other states, international and domestic law, and on the refugee protection regime more generally; but, it is important to look at the implications of such trends on asylum seekers and refugees themselves. Securitisation and criminalisation narratives have a very real impact on the entire lifecycle of the asylum process – from initial displacement, on through the physical and legal journey of seeking asylum, and continuing forward into resettlement outcomes. A common theme of securitisation narratives is to distance and dehumanise asylum seekers by advancing culturally racist narratives, providing justification for institutionally racist policies that go on to adversely impact asylum outcomes.

As increasingly restrictive asylum policies are advanced under the guise of 'law and order', the already arduous process of seeking asylum becomes only more challenging. By instilling a narrative of choice and malintent, counter-terrorism narratives call into question the legitimacy of asylum applications from the moment they begin; the result is large numbers of asylum seekers being met with increasingly militarised responses on the part of receiving countries, and increasingly hostile responses on the part of receiving communities. In Tijuana, for example, the 'migrant caravan' – vilified almost daily by the Trump administration – has been met with significant hostility by the local community, and with tear gas at the southern border. Protests in Mexico echo many of the sentiments championed in the U.S., with calls of 'Mexico First!' and references to the 'migrant caravan' as an 'invasion' gaining significant traction.[64] Overwhelming hostility – social, political, and legal – at the southern border has led many asylum seekers to 'self-deport' rather than attempt to lodge asylum claims.[65]

This type of hostility is not new, nor is it unique to the U.S. – similar narratives can be found in countries all over the world, whether they are faced with an influx of migrants or not. In such contexts, it is difficult to imagine a 'fair process' of refugee status determination (RSD). While it may be tempting

64 Fredrick, 2018.

65 Da Silva, 2018.

to assert that social components do not have sway over refugee status determination procedures, I would argue that these social conditions do have an adverse impact on fair RSD proceedings. In fact, in the U.S., there have been calls from the Trump administration to suspend domestic and international legal obligations relating to due process for asylum seekers, with President Trump tweeting: "When somebody comes in, we must immediately, with no Judges or Court Cases, bring them back from where they came."[66] Following challenges to the statement, White House Press Secretary Sarah Sanders responded: "Just because you don't see a judge doesn't mean you don't receive due process."[67] In this, we are already seeing securitisation narratives impeding on the right to due process and fair RSD proceedings; considering how many of these sentiments are seeing widespread uptake, it is reasonable to be concerned about the extensive negative implications such rhetoric could have on asylum seekers.

7.4 *Fear as a Political Tactic*

As the analysis of the Trump administration's rhetoric on immigration and asylum has shown, there is extensive use of fear-mongering – particularly, exploitation of the American public's fear of terrorism. Although the long-term effectiveness of such political tactics remains to be seen, in the short-term, such rhetoric has been utilised by the administration to pave the way for restrictive immigration and asylum policies. In laying the groundwork necessary to create conditions under which policies like the 'travel ban' and 'zero-tolerance' are palatable to parts of the American public, the Trump administration has proven to be quite effective at playing off of existing biases and fears; the resulting atmosphere is one in which immigration and asylum are warped into representations of existing insecurities, particularly a fairly pervasive fear of terrorism.

The parallels between this kind of fear-mongering as a political tactic and the way in which fear is utilised in acts of terrorism is worth noting; this is not to say that politicians who engage in anti-immigrant rhetoric under the guise of securitisation are terrorists, but rather that, in both terrorism and this particular brand of counter-terrorism, there is a reliance on fear as a means to a specific political end. In each scenario, generalised fear is exploited to advance a particular narrative – albeit through drastically different tools – in pursuit of political change. This is why it is crucial to critically analyse how the conflation of terrorism and asylum is utilised in political rhetoric, and how fear-mongering plays a role in advancing restrictive policies.

66 Trump Twitter Archive, 2018.

67 Samuels, 2018.

8 Breaking the Cycle

> ...the present refugee crisis represents not a crisis of numbers, but of policy...there is little to suggest that the current "crisis" in terms of refugee numbers and global protection capacity is an insurmountable challenge.[68]

There is a pressing need among world leaders and the international community to address the global 'migrant crisis', and part of this means addressing the social components at play in nativist and anti-refugee sentiment within the U.S., and around the world. With this rhetoric, "By virtue of being escapees from violent conflict and human rights violations...refugees are often construed as carriers of the instability and insecurity that led to their initial departure."[69] Trump and the U.S. alone did not create the culturally racist narrative linking refugees with terrorism, nor is he the only one advancing it. It is essential to examine and understand the origin and context of cultural and institutional racism directed against refugees, and to begin to break down the interplay between these forces. Understanding the history of nativist rhetoric and how it has been used to advance legislation in the past could provide a roadmap for how to avoid codifying racism in the future. International refugee law could stand as one roadblock to passing anti-refugee legislation, but it is limited in many ways, and national laws ultimately stand the best chance of preventing such policies from being enacted.

Amidst the current wave of securitisation and nativism, this analysis placed current rhetoric in a historical context by examining the trends which have helped to shape U.S. immigration policy over time. Through application of critical race theory to the news, social media, and political statements, a number of trends become clear; namely, that there is a concerted effort by the Trump administration to advance narratives blurring the lines between refugees and other migrants and connecting Muslim immigrants with terrorism. These trends underscore the importance of considering the social components which help to shape and determine the success of policy, as there is a strong link between cultural and institutional racism. Although the policy analysed continues to face social and legal challenges within the U.S., the recent U.S. Supreme Court Decision to uphold Executive Order 13780 is indicative of the role cultural racism can play in the codification process, and why it is important to critically examine the context in which laws and policies are developed.

68 Gammeltoft-Hansen & Tan, 2017, p. 45.

69 Gibney, 2002, p. 41.

The key takeaway from analysing the Trump administration and campaign's use of strategies and tools to advance a narrative of refugees as terrorists from a critical race theory perspective is that there are many factors at play that extend far beyond Trump. There is a history of anti-immigration and nativist rhetoric within the U.S., and a precedent of linking refugees with terrorism that extends far beyond American borders. There are a number of existing biases and fears among the American public that are readily used by politicians to advance their own agendas, which has also been seen in other countries. The issues here run much deeper than individual racism on the part of Trump and his supporters, and an understanding of these deeper cultural and institutional narratives is essential to truly comprehend the scale of the problem.

This is illustrative of the dire need for critical analysis of law and policy, because the widespread entanglement of terrorism and asylum allows these securitisation narratives to flourish under the guise of counter-terrorism and national security. This link has been codified in domestic and international law and policy a number of times, perpetuating the cultural and institutional racism cycle in which culturally racist views are justified by institutionally racist policies. Without application of a critical lens to such laws and policies, it is easy to see them simply as relating to national security; however, looking beyond the mere letter of the law and examining the social components at play paints a starkly different picture. This same critical analysis must be turned on the entanglement of terrorism and asylum, which is too quickly becoming a 'given' without question. What emerges from a critical analysis of this link is a long history of securitisation of migration and asylum, a tendency for political opportunists to exploit insecurities relating to migration and asylum, and a concerted effort to further codify this link in both domestic and international law and policy.

Refugees have been swept up in a tide of misdirected fear, anger, and hatred fuelled by misinformation and fear-mongering, and it threatens to undermine international protection commitments if we are not vigilant. The power of social components in driving law and policy cannot be underestimated, and the tools which political opportunists use to manufacture these social components continue to have widespread influence on the general public. Issues such as existing fears, biases, and insecurities and such as extreme political polarisation only serve to exacerbate the impact of securitisation and criminalisation narratives; this enables the creation of culturally racist narratives which become the norm. These narratives justify the creation of institutionally racist immigration and asylum policy, and the cultural and institutional racism cycle continues to reinforce itself in perpetuity.

As this cycle linking terrorism and asylum continues unchecked, the plight of asylum seekers, refugees, and other migrants becomes ever more entangled in counter-terrorism discourse. Even weighed against domestic and international protection mechanisms, the securitisation narrative appears to reign supreme. This is only exacerbated by the widespread nature of these narratives: as more and more countries adopt restrictive migration and asylum policies under the 'carte blanche' of national security, any available enforcement and protection mechanisms for asylum seekers themselves become increasingly weakened. This is particularly concerning in light of contemporary movements to address migrant and refugee flows at a global level, as international agreements are not immune to the social components which are also driving domestic laws and policies on migration. As the global community endeavours to manage migrant and refugee flows, protection narratives need to play a more central role, and securitisation narratives need to be critically analysed. Laws and policies are reflections of the social conditions of their time – and, at a time when securitisation discourse increasingly criminalises asylum seekers, there is a very real threat to the heart of the refugee protection regime.

Bibliography

Acer, Eleanor, and Olga Byrne. "How the Illegal Immigration Reform and Immigrant Responsibility Act of 1996 Has Undermined US Refugee Protection Obligations and Wasted Government Resources." *Journal on Migration and Human Security* 5, no. 2 (2017): 356–378. DOI:10.14240/jmhs.v5i2.88.

Ahlborn, Christiane. "The Normative Erosion of International Refugee Protection through UN Security Council Practice." *Leiden Journal of International Law* 24, no. 04 (2011): 1009–1027. DOI:10.4000/books.iheid.171.

Akers Chacón, J. and Mike Davis. (2006). No One Is Illegal: fighting racism and state violence on the U.S.-Mexico border. Chicago, IL: Haymarket Books.

Anderson, Jenny. "The Psychology of Why 94 Deaths from Terrorism Are Scarier than 301 797 Deaths from Guns." *Quartz*. February 01, 2017. https://qz.com/898207/the-psychology-of-why-americans-are-more-scared-of-terrorism-than-guns-though-guns-are-3210-times-likelier-to-kill-them/.

Baker, Peter, and Eileen Sullivan. "Trump Shares Inflammatory Anti-Muslim Videos, and Britain's Leader Condemns Them." *The New York Times*. October 30, 2017. https://mobile.nytimes.com/2017/11/29/us/politics/trump-anti-muslim-videos-jayda-fransen.html?referer=.

Betz, Hans-Georg. "The Roots of Nativism: Banking on the 'Deplorables'." *Fair Observer*. April 17, 2018. https://www.fairobserver.com/region/north_america/nativism-populism-radical-right-parties-europe-us-news-analysis-11281/. (Accessed January 24, 2019).

Binder, John. "Report: Middle East Refugees to Begin Arriving to U.S. from Australia." Breitbart. October 01, 2017. http://www.breitbart.com/texas/2017/10/01/report-middle-east-refugees-to-begin-arriving-to-us-from-australia/.

Blake, Aaron. "Trump Backers' Alarming Reliance on Hoax and Conspiracy Theory Websites, in 1 Chart." *The Washington Post*. August 22, 2017. https://www.washingtonpost.com/news/the-fix/wp/2017/08/22/trump-backers-disturbing-reliance-on-hoax-and-conspiracy-theory-websites-in-1-chart/?utm_term=.9dca78052f68.

Blitz, Brad. "Another Story: What Public Opinion Data Tell Us About Refugee and Humanitarian Policy." *Journal on Migration and Human Security* 5, no. 2 (2017): 379–400. DOI:10.14240/jmhs.v5i2.89.

Brady, William J., Julian A. Wills, John T. Jost, Joshua A. Tucker, and Jay J. Van Bavel. "Emotion Shapes the Diffusion of Moralized Content in Social Networks." *Proceedings of the National Academy of Sciences* 114, no. 28 (2017): 7313–7318. DOI:10.1073/pnas.1618923114.

Capehart, Jonathan. "Yes, Donald Trump, you are a 'racist'." *The Washington Post*. August 9, 2018. https://www.washingtonpost.com/blogs/post-partisan/wp/2018/08/09/yes-donald-trump-you-are-a-racist/?noredirect=on&utm_term=.1df120ced1fe. (Accessed January 20, 2019).

Clapper, James R. "We've Worked on Stopping Terrorism. Trump's Travel Ban Fuels It." *CNN*. April 23, 2018. https://www.cnn.com/2018/04/23/opinions/trump-travel-ban-fuels-terrorism-clapper-geltzer-olsen/index.html. (Accessed January 5, 2019).

Clinton, Hillary. "Let's Be Clear: Islam Is Not Our Adversary. Muslims Are Peaceful and Tolerant People and Have Nothing Whatsoever to Do with Terrorism." Twitter. November 19, 2015. https://twitter.com/hillaryclinton/status/667371059885301761?lang=en. (Accessed October 28, 2017).

Cumming-Bruce, Nick. "Taking Migrant Children From Parents Is Illegal, U.N. Tells U.S." *The New York Times*. June 05, 2018. https://www.nytimes.com/2018/06/05/world/americas/us-un-migrant-children-families.html. (Accessed June 16, 2018).

Da Silva, Chantal. "Caravan Asylum Seekers Are Signing up to 'Self Deport' over Fears of Border Violence." *Newsweek*. November 27, 2018. https://www.newsweek.com/american-dream-nightmare-caravan-asylum-seekers-are-signing-self-deport-over-1232675. (Accessed December 6, 2018).

"Executive Order 13769: Protecting the Nation from Foreign Terrorist Entry into the United States." The White House. January 27, 2017. https://www.whitehouse.gov/

presidential-actions/executive-order-protecting-nation-foreign-terrorist-entry-united-states/.

"Executive Order 13780: Protecting the Nation from Foreign Terrorist Entry into the United States." The White House. March 6, 2017. https://www.whitehouse.gov/presidential-actions/executive-order-protecting-nation-foreign-terrorist-entry-united-states-2/.

Foley, Elise. "Mike Pence Cites False Statistic On Terrorists At The Southwest Border." *The Huffington Post*. October 23, 2018. https://www.huffingtonpost.com/entry/mike-pence-migrant-caravan-terrorists-border_us_5bcf6d6ae4b0a8f17ef16b2e.

Fredrick, James. "Shouting 'Mexico First', Hundreds In Tijuana March Against Migrant Caravan." NPR. November 19, 2018. https://www.npr.org/2018/11/19/669193788/shouting-mexico-first-hundreds-in-tijuana-march-against-migrant-caravan.

Gammeltoft-Hansen, Thomas, and Nikolas F. Tan. "The End of the Deterrence Paradigm? Future Directions for Global Refugee Policy." *Journal on Migration and Human Security* 5, no. 1 (2017): 28. DOI: 10.14240/jmhs.v5i1.73.

Gibney, Matthew J. "Security and the Ethics of Asylum after 11 September." *Forced Migration Review*, no. 13 (2002): 40–42.

Goldstein, Judith and Margaret E. Peters. "Nativism or Economic Threat: Attitudes Toward Immigrants During the Great Recession." *International Interactions* 40, no. 3 (2014): 376–401. DOI: 10.1080/03050629.2014.899219.

Gomez, Alan. "Homeland Security Focuses on Border Security – Not Processing Asylum Applications from Migrant Caravan." *USA Today*. November 17, 2018. https://www.usatoday.com/story/news/world/2018/11/16/migrant-caravan-asylum-immigration-department-homeland-security-border-dhs-kirstjen-nielsen/2014484002/. (Accessed December 10, 2018).

Hayes, Christal. "Here are 10 times President Trump's comments have been called racist." *USA Today*. August 14, 2018. https://www.usatoday.com/story/news/politics/onpolitics/2018/08/14/times-president-trump-comments-called-racist/985438002/. (Accessed January 20, 2019).

Hayward, John. "Seven Inconvenient Facts About Trump's Refugee Actions." Breitbart. January 30, 2017. http://www.breitbart.com/big-government/2017/01/29/trumps-immigration-pause-sober-defenses-vs-hysterical-criticism/.

Holmes, Jennifer S., and Linda Camp Keith. "Does the Fear of Terrorists Trump the Fear of Persecution in Asylum Outcomes in the Post – September 11 Era?" *PS: Political Science & Politics* 43, no. 03 (2010): 431–436. DOI:10.1017/s1049096510000685.

Keneally, Meghan. "Texas Church Shooting: How Trump's Reactions to Mass Attacks Differ for US-born Suspects like Devin Kelley." *ABC News*. November 07, 2017. http://abcnews.go.com/US/texas-church-shooting-trumps-reaction-mass-attacks-differs/story?id=50962471.

Khan, Nida. "Calculated Anti-Muslim Tweets." *U.S. News & World Report.* November 30, 2017. https://www.usnews.com/opinion/civil-wars/articles/2017-11-30/donald-trump-furthers-islamophobia-by-retweeting-anti-muslim-propaganda.

March, Selina. "New Village, Same Inequalities?: Exploring Global Stratification in Social Media and Its Political Implications." In *The End of the Global?*, edited by Gabriele Piazza, 133–144. London: International Student Journal of Political Economy, 2018. Google Books.

McVeigh, Karen. "UN States Agree Historic Global Deal to Manage Migration Crisis." *The Guardian.* December 10, 2018. https://www.theguardian.com/global-development/2018/dec/10/un-states-agree-historic-global-deal-to-manage-refugee-crisis.

Phelps, Jordyn. "Why President Obama Won't Use the Term 'Radical Islam'." *ABC News.* June 13, 2016. http://abcnews.go.com/Politics/president-obama-term-radical-islam/story?id=39815449.

Sacchetti, Maria, and Nick Miroff. "How Trump Is Building a Border Wall That No One Can See." *The Washington Post.* November 21, 2017. https://www.washingtonpost.com/local/immigration/how-trump-is-building-a-border-wall-no-one-can-see/2017/11/21/83d3b746-cba0-11e7-b0cf-7689a9f2d84e_story.html?utm_term=.7f43e2c5736b#ampshare=https://www.washingtonpost.com/local/immigration/how-trump-is-building-a-border-wall-no-one-can-see/2017/11/21/83d3b746-cba0-11e7-b0cf-7689a9f2d84e_story.html.

Samuels, Brett. "Sanders: 'Just Because You Don't See a Judge Doesn't Mean You Don't Receive Due Process.'" *The Hill.* June 25, 2018. https://thehill.com/homenews/administration/394029-white-house-just-because-you-dont-see-a-judge-doesnt-mean-you-dont.

Schwartz, Felicia, and Ben Kesling. "Countries Under U.S. Entry Ban Aren't Main Sources of Terror Attacks." *The Wall Street Journal.* January 29, 2017. https://www.wsj.com/articles/countries-under-u-s-entry-ban-arent-main-sources-of-terror-attacks-1485708300.

Scribner, Todd. "You Are Not Welcome Here Anymore: Restoring Support for Refugee Resettlement in the Age of Trump." *Journal on Migration and Human Security* 5, no. 2 (2017). DOI:10.14240/jmhs.v5i2.84.

The Bridge Project. "Critical Race Theory." Berkman Klein Center. https://cyber.harvard.edu/bridge/CriticalTheory/critical4.htm.

Trump, President of the United States, et al. v. Hawaii et al, No. 17– 965 (June 26, 2018).

Trump Twitter Archive, <http://www.trumptwitterarchive.com/archive>.

Trump, Donald J. "Donald J. Trump Addresses Terrorism, Immigration, and National Security." Speech, Saint Anselm College, Manchester, NH, June 13, 2016. June 13, 2016.

Watson, Paul Joseph. "Swedish Government Report Says Putting the Word 'Refugees' in Quotation Marks Is 'Hate.'" Alex Jones' InfoWars. November 30, 2017. https://www

.infowars.com/swedish-government-report-says-putting-the-word-refugees-in-quotation-marks-is-hate/.

Wigglesworth, Sam. “Refugees and the Narrative of Choice: Why Language Matters.” *Development In Action* (blog), June 23, 2016. http://www.developmentinaction.org/refugees-and-the-narrative-of-choice-why-language-matters/.

Wright, Paul. “Britain First’s Holy War: Home Office Condemns ‘anti-Muslim Propaganda’ as Petition Calls for Group to Be Banned.” *International Business Times* UK 29, 2016. https://www.ibtimes.co.uk/britain-firsts-holy-war-home-office-condemns-anti-muslim-propaganda-petition-cals-group-1540893. (Accessed November 4, 2017).

Young, Julia G. “Making America 1920 Again? Nativism and US Immigration, Past and Present.” *Journal on Migration and Human Security* 5, no. 1 (2017): 217–235. DOI:10.14240/jmhs.v5i1.81.

CHAPTER 3

Guilt by Association: Contrasting Views on the Fairness of 'secret trials' of 'terrorists'

John R. Campbell

John Rawls'[1] sparked considerable interest in procedural and natural justice which has been taken up by legal scholars and practicing lawyers and jurists, but, it has not been explored comparatively or ethnographically by anthropologists. Laura Nader,[2] a legal anthropologist, has argued that taken for granted phrases such as 'the rule of law' conceal more than they reveal and that anthropologists should question normative assumptions to understand the way that the law may be experienced as a form of 'injustice'. Anthropologists have long recognized that the disciplinary training of lawyers and anthropologists imbues each profession with distinctive paradigms and assumptions.[3] Anthropological research has examined the way that lawyers are trained to think,[4] the very different ways that lawyers/judges and anthropologists approach 'facts',[5] the disjuncture between lawyer and litigant assumptions of fairness[6] and the importance of different 'styles of speaking' in court[7] among other things.

I draw on this literature to examine legal practices and procedures which I observed during the 'secret trial' of a suspected terrorist in which I was instructed as a 'country expert'. By carefully examining legal practice and procedure I examine how lawyers locate liability and arrive at a judgment – guilty or not guilty – in ways that sharply contrast with anthropological methods and

1 John Rawls, *A Theory of Justice* (New York: Oxford University, 1971 [1999]).

2 Laura Nader, 'The words we use: justice, human rights, and the sense of injustice', in K. Clarke & M. Goodale. Eds. *Mirrors of Justice* (New York: Cambridge University Press: N.Y. 2010), 316–331.

3 Kandel, R. 'How lawyers and anthropologists think differently', *Annals of Anthropological Practice* (1992), 1–20.

4 J. Conley, 'Review: Can You Talk like a Lawyer and Still Think like a Human Being? Mertz's the Language of Law School', *Law & Social Inquiry* 34, 4 (2009), 983–2015.

5 A. Good, 'Expert evidence in asylum and human rights appeals: An expert's view', *International Journal of Refugee Law* 16, 3 (2004), 358–380.

6 J. Conley & W. O'Barr, 'Hearing the hidden agenda: The ethnographic investigation of procedure', *Law & Contemporary Problems* 51, 4 (1988), 181–197.

7 J. Conley, J., W. O'Barr & E. Lind, 'The power of language: presentational style in the courtroom', *Duke Law Journal* (1978), 1375–1399.

© KONINKLIJKE BRILL NV, LEIDEN, 2020 | DOI:10.1163/9789004295995_005

training which require one to suspend belief to search for an explanation. In short, I contrast the normative, judgmental approach taken by law with the anthropological requirement of situating a case in a wider social context to understand complex legal processes and the roles played by the state, lawyers, judges and defendants.

In recent years, terrorist attacks have provided legislators with the authority to fundamentally reshape the quality of justice and the work of the law in Europe and North America. This is especially evident in the field of immigration where strategic concerns about national security and terrorism have been used to rewrite law, pass new legislation and reinforce the discretionary power of the executive in ways that would have been unthinkable before 9/11.[8]

Quite apart from the use of counter-terrorism measures in colonial Kenya, Malaysia, and elsewhere, Britain has also used counter-terrorism legislation to ban individuals, prescribe organizations and criminalize behavior in Northern Ireland. This history has informed recent legislation[9] including The Terrorism Act (2000).[10] Indeed the Government continues to enact legislation aimed at enhancing the security of the UK including The Prevention of Terrorism Act (2005)[11] (which introduced control orders), The Terrorism Act (2006)[12] as well as laws which *anticipate* terrorist events such as the 'Terrorism Prevention and Investigation Bill' and the 'Enhanced Terrorism and Investigation Measures Bill'.[13] The latter measures are supposed to be a 'less intrusive system of terrorism and prevention measures' that 'will protect the public from individuals who pose a real terrorist threat' but who cannot be prosecuted or, in the case of nationals suspected of terrorism, cannot be deported.[14] Viewed in their entirety, 'counter-terrorism' legislation has shifted from an attempt to investigate, criminalize and proscribe individuals/organizations operating in the UK to a preemptive, anticipatory attempt to prevent individuals from entering the UK whom the Government suspects may carry out terrorist-related acts.

8 See: E. Brouwer, "Immigration, asylum and terrorism: A changing dynamic. Legal and practical developments in the EU response to the terrorist attacks of 11.09," *European Journal of Migration and Law* 4 (2003), 399–424; and E. Boyle & E. Busse, "Institutional vulnerability and opportunity" Immigration and America's "War on Terror," *Law & Social Enquiry* 31: 4 (2006), 947–974.

9 See: https://www.legislation.gov.uk/all?title=terrorism.

10 See: https://www.legislation.gov.uk/ukpga/2000/11/contents.

11 See: https://www.legislation.gov.uk/ukpga/2005/2/contents.

12 See: https://www.legislation.gov.uk/ukpga/2006/11/contents.

13 https://www.gov.uk/government/publications/enhanced-terrorism-prevention-and-investigation-measures-bill-documents

14 See: http://www.homeoffice.gov.uk/publications/about-us/legislation/tpim-bill/.

In what follows I do not offer a line-by-line reading of legislation nor do I look at the voluminous literature on terror-related litigation. Rather, I adopt an anthropological approach informed by an in-depth examination of the case of one individual who was detained under a control order for six years.[15] This approach requires me to situate the case in a wider legal context to understand the role played by state institutions and key legal actors involved in counter-terrorism hearings. I also seek to understand whether legal procedures are 'fair', how the law affects a person held under a control order/'TPIM notice' and whether such measures contribute to the very thing they seek to prevent.[16]

In most areas of law defendants and their legal representative know the case they will have to answer in court; this is not true in control order/TPIM cases because the 'evidence' relied upon by the Secretary of State for the Home Department (SSHD) is kept secret, i.e., it is not disclosed. Furthermore, under the Prevention of Terrorism Act (2005)[17] – which has been superseded by the Terrorism Prevention and Investigation Measures Act (2011)[18] and the Counter Terrorism and Security Act (2015)[19] – the courts are prevented from adequately reviewing and, if necessary, quashing/setting aside a case and releasing the defendant.

Given the clear temporal, legal and geographic shift reflected in recent terrorist legislation which seeks to anticipate and prevent offences *before* they are committed,[20] it is useful to view this area of law as a hybrid politico-legal field characterized by its own blurred and chameleon-like processes which fuse together criminal law, immigration law and national security considerations. This situation has arisen because, in the face of an expanded perception of

15 The case method in the study of law is a well-known way of examining aspects of a single case from which it is possible to generalize to other cases; see: A.L. Epstein. 'The case method in the field of law', in A.L. Epstein. Ed. *The Craft of Social Anthropology* (Tavistock: London. 1967), 205–230.

16 In *SSHD v AF (no. 3) [2009] UKHL 29*, Lord Hoffman stated that there were 'strong policy considerations that support a rule that a trial procedure can never be fair if a party to it is kept in ignorance of the case against him'. He based his conclusion on two reasons. First, there will be many cases where it is impossible for the court to be confident that disclosure will make no difference. Second, *if individuals are effectively placed under house arrest without being told the gist of the case against them, feelings of resentment will be felt not only by the controlee but also by his family, friends and broader community*' (my emphasis, cited in A. Kavanagh, 'Special advocates, control orders and the right to a. know', *The Modern Law Review* 73, 5 (2010), 841).

17 See: https://www.legislation.gov.uk/ukpga/2005/2/contents.

18 See: http://www.legislation.gov.uk/ukpga/2011/23/contents/enacted.

19 See: http://www.legislation.gov.uk/ukpga/2015/6/contents/enacted.

20 J. McCulloch, 'Pre-Crime and counter-terrorism. Imagining a future crime in the War on Terror', *The British Jo. of Criminology* 49, 5 (2009), 628–645.

threat, legislators tell us that we need to re-calibrate the relation between liberty and security so that security concerns trump individual liberty.[21] This rebalancing can be observed in the way that terrorist legislation increasingly 'targets people on the basis of whom they know and associate with rather than what they have done'[22] which reflects the growing extent to which politicians, rather than the courts, assess 'risk'.

Nowhere is this better seen than in the operation of 'Closed Material Proceedings' (CMP) or 'secret trials'[23] which individuals who are arrested and detained under counter terrorism laws are subjected to. Secret trials, which are distinct from cases in which individuals are publicly tried in a criminal court, have serious implications for a defendant's right to a fair trial including: (a) the right to be tried by an independent and impartial tribunal; (b) the right to have ones' case defended on the basis of established facts and the law; and, (c) the right to know the case against you and the right to respond to that case in an open court.[24]

Central to my task is the need to translate the 'ideology' of law – the language employed by lawyers, the courts and the Home Office (the government department responsible for immigration and passports, drugs policy, counterterrorism and policing) – to reveal the underlying power relations at work. Secret trials need to be understood as an uneven contest whose outcome is influenced by many inter-related factors including: a rapidly changing legislative process; lobbying in Parliament and the House of Lords and efforts by the Home Office to create primary legislation (e.g., to reverse High Court decisions, pursue litigation, overturn policy or case law, and to allow the SSHD to use her executive power to issue new immigration rules and polices).[25]

Secret trials involve actors/institutions which possess differential power and resources – the Home Office, police and prison officials, immigration officials, Special Advocates, the Special Immigration Appeals Commission (SIAC), the Court of Appeal and legally aided lawyers – whose work decides the fate of

21 L. Zedner, 'Securing liberty in the face of terror: Reflections from Criminal Justice', *Jo. of Law & Society* 32, 4 (2005), 507–533.

22 McCulloch, 'Pre-Crime', 628.

23 CMPs operate in 21 different contexts which rely on Special Advocates to ensure that state evidence against a defendant is disclosed where they provide a 'veneer of respectability' to legal proceedings. See: J. Jackson, 'The role of special advocates: Advocacy, due process and the adversarial tradition', *International Jo. of Evidence and Proof* 20, 4 (2016), 345.

24 Graham Hudson & Daniel Alati. 'Behind Closed Doors: Secret Law and the Special Advocate System in Canada', *Queen's Law Journal* 44 (2018): 1: 1–68.

25 J. Campbell, *Bureaucracy, Law and Dystopia in the United Kingdom's Asylum System* (Routledge: NY, 2017), Chapters 2 & 3.

individuals accused of terrorism. Legal appeals against a control order/TPIM are not level politico-legal contests because the Home Office relies on its access to substantially greater 'resources' (including its use of the media) and its ability to rewrite 'the rules of the game' to up the ante and win judicial/political contests.[26]

Regardless of the unevenness of the contest, lawyers and judges uphold an ideology of 'the rule of law' which can loosely be described as flowing from the principles of fairness, equality before the law and human dignity. This principle is actualized by an 'independent judiciary' which, *in theory*, has the right to scrutinize and interpret legislation and to review the decisions of lower courts and state officials.[27] However, this ideology obscures what happens.

Section (i) of this chapter provides a précis of the events leading up to Mr. O2's[28] appeal; it also sets out the restrictions imposed on him by the Home Office. I adopt the pseudonym of 'O2' to emphasize the fact that *suspected* terrorists provide the government with a rationale for its argument that enhanced security arrangements are required to protect the public (i.e., if there are no suspects, there is no oxygen/O2 and, thus, no rationale for the law). I then briefly discuss my involvement in the case and my research methodology. Section (ii) examines at the High Court hearing of O2's appeal against the control order. I focus on the tactics employed by the SSHD. Section (iii) looks at the role played by the judiciary who adjudicate control order appeals. Considering the extensive powers held by the SSHD, as revealed in the case of Mr. O2, I conclude that terrorist legislation has rebalanced the scales of justice in favor of security over individual liberty and that, by anthropological standards, the legal proceedings analyzed in this chapter are unfair.

1 Mr. O2 and the Secretary of State's Allegations

O2 arrived in the UK with his family and claimed asylum in the early 1990s; in 1999 he and his family were granted indefinite leave to remain which permitted them to settle in England. In late 2000, he began to attend mosque and in 2001 he converted from Orthodox Christianity to Islam. In mid-2004, O2 went

---

26 F.G. Bailey, *Stratagems and Spoils. A Social Anthropology of Politics* (Schocken Books: N.Y. 1969).

27 Lord Woolf, 'The rule of law and a change in the constitution', *The Times*, 3 March 2004 at: http://www.timesonline.co.uk/tol/news/article1036741.ece?

28 To protect the identity of the defendant and his family I have stripped all personal information from the text and I have deleted reference material, including court decisions and media coverage which could be used to identify him.

on a camping trip with acquaintances and in 2005, together with a small group of friends, he traveled to Mogadishu, Somalia, to practice '*dawah*'.[29]

While he was in Somalia members of his family were arrested in connection with a failed terrorist attack. However, rather than returning to the UK O2 went to Ethiopia where he remained with his Ethiopian wife until December 2006. On seeking to board a flight to the UK he was arrested, detained and interrogated by the Ethiopian authorities for two weeks. When he was released he flew to London in December 2006 and was detained on arrival. The SSHD initially refused him entry into the UK 'on the grounds that his exclusion was conducive to the public good' and she also cancelled his Indefinite Leave to Remain (ILR). He was arrested and questioned at Paddington Green Police Station, London, by the police and MI5 and four days later he was transferred to prison.

Initially the Home Office objected to O2 being granted bail. In its 'First Open Statement and Objection to Bail'[30] it argued that: (1) he was 'an Islamic extremist who is strongly assessed to have attended a terrorist training camp in Cumbria'; (2) 'he participated in terrorist training in Somalia'; and, (3) given his 'links to an individual assessed to have attempted to carry out terrorist attacks in London, the Security Services assess that there is a real risk that O2 would become involved in attack planning in the UK'. The statement justified a refusal to disclose further information because 'damage could be done by disclosure ... [that] would cause real harm to the work of the Security Service'. The statement continued: 'The general nature of those concerns need little elaboration. They are aimed at both protecting the integrity of security and intelligence operations and at protecting the safety and usefulness of those whose who work for the Security Services and who provide information to it'. As will become evident, the Home Office had little concrete information about O2, but its suspicions created an inordinate hurdle against which O2 and his legal team struggled to secure bail and to challenge the control order in his High Court and subsequent appeals (when some of the allegations were withdrawn).

Nevertheless, O2 was eventually granted bail on stringent conditions (though he was not released from prison until July because secure accommodation could not be found where he could be monitored by the police). In July

29 *Da'wa* or *da'wah* is a religious act/obligation imposed on Muslims. According to H. Wehr, *A Dictionary of Modern Written Arabic* (Arabic-English) (Otto Harassowitz: Wiesbaden. 1979, 365) *da'wa* means: to wither, wilt, fade; but also to spread, get about, circulate, be spread, be disseminated, be or become widespread ... to propagate, make known etc.' There does not appear to be a uniform expectation as to how a Muslim fulfills this obligation.

30 This was a ten-page statement sent to counsel for O2 in early 2007.

2007 his brother-in-law was convicted of involvement in a failed terrorist attack. In August, the SSHD obtained permission to make a control order[31] for O2 (see Table 1, below). At this point, the SSHD re-instated his ILR and withdrew her decision to remove him from the UK.

In April 2008 O2's control order was suddenly modified, and more stringent conditions were imposed on him including a requirement that he move 150

TABLE 1 The principle restrictions placed upon O2 by the SSHD

1. He was required to live at a designated flat.
2. The flat could be searched at any time.
3. He was subject to a curfew from 6:00 pm to 10:00 am.
4. He had to wear an electronic monitoring tag at all times.
5. He was not allowed to leave a designated area (approximately 25 sq. kms).
6. He had to report to the local police station every day.
7. He had to telephone the monitoring company when he first left the flat at the end of a period of curfew, and when he last returned to it before a period of curfew.
8. Only his mother and one brother were permitted to visit him (with the exception of his lawyers or emergency services etc), though he could request the Home Office to permit a named individual to visit.
9. He could not arrange to meet anyone outside the flat apart from his mother and the named brother.
10. He could not attend any pre-arranged meetings or gatherings (unless they were connected with any work he was doing or with any course of study on which he was engaged or with his health or welfare), though he could request the Home Office to permit him to do so.
11. He was not permitted any communication with a named individual.
12. He was not to have access to the internet, though he was permitted to have a fixed telephone line in the flat and to use a mobile.
13. He could visit a mosque of his choosing and take part in prayers, though he could not lead prayers; but he could only visit one mosque for which prior approval had to be obtained. He could request the Home Office to permit him to visit another mosque.

31 For a list of all the restrictions that the SSHD can impose see A. Carlisle (Lord), *Fourth Report of the Independent Reviewer pursuant to Sec. 14(3) of the Prevention of Terrorism Act 2005*. (February). 2009.

miles away from his community and family. While waiting for his appeal, four siblings were charged and convicted under sec. 19 of the Terrorism Act 2000 of failing to inform the police about a possible attack and/or assisting an offender to evade capture.[32] In early July his appeal against the imposition of the control order was heard at the Royal Courts of Justice, London.

2 My Involvement in This Case

In early 2007 I was interviewing an immigration case worker as part of a research project aimed at mapping and analyzing the British asylum system.[33] During the course of the interview, I was asked whether, as a recognized 'country expert',[34] I would be willing to assist a client of the firm who was detained in a high security prison under a terrorist control order.

I agreed to assist and was instructed by the firm to help them understand the circumstances of his detention and treatment by the Ethiopian authorities (which the Home Office had not disclosed information about) and to write an expert report for his hearing at the High Court. I was given access to all correspondence about the case including: legal representations, correspondence with the Home Office, the appellant's asylum application, ten witness statements made by the appellant and material about the criminal trial against members of his family. I also attended the 'open sections' of O2's appeal at which I took verbatim notes of everything that was said during the proceedings. Later I was given a copy of the official transcript of the open sections of O2's appeal which enabled me to cross check my notes. I used my notes and the transcript to undertake a detailed analysis of the way that both legal counsels questioned witnesses and how witnesses and the defendant answered questions during the hearing. It is this analysis which forms the basis of the chapter. In July 2008, at the High Court, I was briefly introduced to O2 (this was the only time we met). Near the end of the appeal I was asked to write a second expert report addressing the Special Advocates 'gist' of information which summarized the evidence that was relied upon in the closed hearing against O2. Finally, I attended O2's first appeal at the English Court of Appeal against the decision by the Home Office to alter his bail/control order conditions.

32 This law was not used at the height of Irish Republican terrorism in the UK.

33 Research was funded by a grant from the UK Economic & Social Research Council entitled "Refugees and the Law: An ethnography of the British asylum system" (RES-062-23-0296). I am indebted to O2 and his legal team for allowing me to follow his case and for giving me access to the transcript of the trial.

34 Good, *Expert Evidence*, 2004.

From this point onward, I followed the case from a growing distance as his subsequent appeals were handled by different legal teams.

3 O2's High Court Appeal, July 2008

Terrorist legislation limits the power of the court to decide whether the SSHD's decision to impose a control order is lawful.[35] This means that the court only has the power to 'review' the SSHDs decision to impose a control order to see whether her decision was 'reasonable' in its assessment of his involvement in 'terrorist-related activity' and whether the SSHD's order was properly made 'to protect the public from a risk of terrorism'. The standard of proof which the court applies is *'reasonable suspicion'.*[36] This very low standard of proof is also used to impose 'anti-social behavior order' (ASBO)[37] against a nuisance neighbor or to assess whether an individual has 'breached the peace' (a civil offence); it requires the court to assess whether the individual poses a *future* risk to the public. In short, the decision to impose a control order *must anticipate whether an individual is likely to pose a threat to national security*. If the court decides that the SSHDs decision was unreasonable it may quash the order; but, the SSHD can reimpose it.[38]

The procedural and evidentiary rules[39] which operate in control order hearings differ substantially from criminal and civil proceedings. In the latter two systems the parties to a hearing are on an equal footing and procedures are in place to ensure that the case is dealt with fairly. However, in CMP hearings the court has a duty to ensure that information about the case is not disclosed to the appellant and his legal team if it 'is contrary to the public interest', i.e., if

35 See the PTA (2005), parts 2, 3, 7 and 10.

36 For example, 'A police officer has "reasonable suspicion" when there exists articulable facts or circumstances which would lead a reasonable person to suspect that a crime has been, is being, or will be committed. At this stage, police may detain the suspect for a brief period and perform a frisk ... Refusing a search does not create reasonable suspicion, although acting nervous and answering questions inconsistently can. For this reason, it is best not to answer questions if you have to lie in order to do so ... As a general rule, reasonable suspicion applies to situations where police have reason to believe you're up to something, but they don't know what it is'. At: http://www.knowmyrights.org/knowledgebase/case-law/probable-cause-reasonable-suspicion.

37 A relatively new offence, see: http://www.homeoffice.gov.uk/anti-social-behaviour/penalties/anti-social-behaviour-orders/.

38 PTA sec. 3 (12–14).

39 See: Statutory Instrument 2003 No. 1034, 'The Special Immigration Appeals Commission (Procedure) Rules, 2003', at: http://www.opsi.gov.uk/si/si2003/20031034.htm.

such information might 'harm' the work of the security services that provide the information.

There are serious questions about the 'mosaic' nature and reliability of the undisclosed information[40] relied on in the closed section of CMP's because it is not 'tested' in open court. To deal with this problem, 'Special Advocates' (SAs) were created. These are government-vetted barristers whose role is to safeguard the human rights of the accused. As Jackson[41] has argued, SA's operate in a structurally difficult position: (1) they can make submissions to the Commission (SIAC) in proceedings which the appellant and his representatives are excluded from; (2) in theory they cross examine witnesses in CMP; and, (c) they can make written submissions to the judge. However (d), SA's do not formally 'act' for the accused nor can the accused person appoint their own SA. Furthermore, '[w]hat is unprecedented ... is the prohibition on any communication between the special advocate and the appellant once the Special Advocate is given sight of the closed material'.[42] In short, once a hearing is about to begin all contact between the SA, the defendant and his lawyer ends.

SAs are supposed to 'test the cogency' of undisclosed material submitted in the closed sections of the hearing to see if it can be disclosed to the appellant without jeopardizing national security. If the court agrees to their request a '*gist*' or 'essence of the case' is released to allow a defendant to respond.[43] However the SA's ability to perform this role is sharply circumscribed by their structural position.[44] SA's are also supposed to assist the appellant by advising on the best possible course of action in view of all the evidence. However, the appellant is not obliged to take their advice. There are, therefore, serious questions about the ability of the SA to perform this dual role.[45]

---

40 Interview with Ian McDonald, barrister at Garden Court Chambers (and former Special Advocate) on 27 November 2007.

41 Jackson, *The role*, 2016, 351-f.

42 Jackson, 'The role', 353.

43 This is referred to as the SA's disclosure role as opposed to his representational role. The state's evidence is based on intelligence which takes a 'mosaic quality' because it is pieced together from various sources including intercept evidence, covert surveillance, agent reports and material taken from the internet. See: A. Kavanagh, 'Special advocates, control orders and the right to know', *The Modern Law Review* 73, 5 (2010), 841–842.

44 In 2004 the role of SA's was sharply criticized because of problems with closed evidence which emerged by accident. The incident led to the resignation of two SAs – one of whom was Ian McDonald – and a Parliamentary enquiry into the operation of SIAC and the use of SAs. See: House of Commons. *The operation of the Special Immigration Appeals Commission (SIAC) and the use of Special Advocates* (Constitutional Affairs Committee. Seventh Report of Session 2004–05. Vol. 1. Report together with formal minutes). 2005.

45 See House of Lords (SSHD v MB [*2007*]) *EWHC 651 (Admin)* on this issue; and A. Sandell, 'Liberty, fairness and the UK control order cases: two steps backward, two steps back', *European Human Rights Law Review* 1 (2008) 120–131.

TABLE 2 The organization of O2's High Court Appeal, Royal Courts of Justice

	Monday	Tuesday	Wednesday	Thursday	Friday
Morning	Procedural Issues	Witness 'T' (cont'd)	Closed Session	Closed Session	Witness B for O2
Afternoon	Witness 'T' for the Security Services	Closed Session	Closed Session	Closed until 3:30 pm Witness 'A' for O2	O2's testimony

Before turning to O2's appeal it is important to observe how his five-day appeal hearing was organized. The appeal began at 10:30 am on a Monday; there was an hour lunch break at about 1 pm; afternoon sessions concluded no later than 5:00 pm. As Table 2 indicates, the duty placed on the court not to disclose information submitted by the Government means that *at least half* of the entire hearing was held in closed session from which O2 and his legal team were excluded.

In examining O2's appeal I focus on key aspects of the case including the power of the SSHD to litigate and orchestrate the appeal in a manner which enhances her power. Clearly, the key task confronting O2's counsel[46] was to discover the basis of the SSHDs case against his client. However, when proceedings opened on Monday morning O2's counsel was forced to make an application in relation to two reports that had been faxed to O2's solicitor late on the preceding Friday. The first report was a police 'interview' with O2 that occurred at the police station where he was required to report on a weekly basis. The interview – in effect a casual conversation – was in the form of a typed summary to which was attached a 'risk assessment'. The assessment stated: 'After careful consideration I would consider O2 *High Risk of causing Serious Harm*'.

His counsel objected to the submission of both reports on the grounds that the information was obtained by deception, that it was served late, that experts

46 In England and Wales, counsel for the defense is normally composed of the instructing solicitor (she interviews her client, takes his evidence, prepares his statements and takes his instructions) who in turn 'instructs' a barrister. It is the barrister's job to advocate on behalf of his/her client before the court (by taking him and his witnesses through their written evidence, cross-examining prosecution witnesses, and making oral and written submissions to the court).

were unable to examine and to comment on it and that counsel had not been able to take instructions from O2 about the interview. The exchange between O2's counsel (X) and counsel for the SSHD (Y) sets out the issues involved:

> X: I ask that it [the report and assessment] be excluded. My position is that O2 has nothing to hide. He has provided eight statements and has indicated his willingness to give oral evidence. The evidence should be adduced fairly.
> Y: One task of the Home Office is in relation to a consideration of the evidence to support the individual and whether it will undermine the case ... The process may produce evidence that may help the Secretary of State [...] that information must be disclosed. [In relation to notes of the interview:] The only challenge could be that they are inaccurate or that disclosure is late [...] The risk assessment is of a different nature. But given that risk assessment is what the court does, it is important for the court to consider it ... It would be inappropriate to rule it out on grounds of evidence.
> X: [...] There are no provisions for this document. Its circumstances are wholly unfair [...] It causes us prejudice...'

The judge read both documents and, following a submission in closed session, ruled the following day that:

> There is no general principle of English law that in civil proceedings ... that evidence obtained by a trick must be excluded to the extent that the admissibility of such evidence involves the exercise of discretion.
>
> I propose to admit the notes of interview in evidence [...] but the weight which should be attached to it will of course have to reflect the circumstances of how he came to be interviewed [...]. As to the risk assessment, I believe I should only take it into account [...] if the officer who wrote it is made available for questioning [...]

At this point Counsel for the SSHD stated that he would not call the police officer to give evidence (this appeared to me to be an attempt by the SSHD to frustrate the appeal).

The Monday session resumed with counsel for the SSHD (Y) addressing the judge about the nature of control order hearings (it was the first control order hearing that the judge had presided over). At 11: 27 am counsel for the SSHD summarized the 'open' evidence against O2. At 12:12 pm a Home Office official was called to give evidence regarding why the SSHD changed the restrictions imposed on O2 and why they refused to vary the restrictions. An hour lunch was followed by a two-hour afternoon session at which 'Witness T' – a member of the security services – gave evidence for the SSHD from behind a curtain.

The ability of O2's counsel to cross examine 'T' was constrained by what the witness was willing to say in open court. However, it soon became clear that his answers, indeed, his willingness to provide information, were shaped by his view of O2. Cross-examination revealed that the witness was, if not hostile, then certainly antagonistic towards O2. Indeed, he refused to comment on a range of questions: (a) on the grounds that the information could not be disclosed; (b) because he assumed that, if relevant legislation had been enacted, that O2 would have been subject to a criminal conviction;[47] and (c) sometimes he did not know the answer (but rather than say this, he refused to comment and had to be specifically asked the reason why he refused to answer).

On Tuesday it emerged that the Security Services' contention was that O2 'may have had a general idea' about the failed attack 'but we accept that he may not have known specifics'. Even so because of the 'extremist company' he kept it was proper that the SSHD should make him the subject of a non-derogating[48] control order. Because the SSHD had refused to disclose whether it was her case that O2 had participated in terrorist training in Somalia, O2's counsel anticipated this allegation and had asked that the SSHD to issue a visa for O2's wife and brother-in-law to travel to the UK from Ethiopia to give evidence. However, the SSHD refused to issue them visas which 'blocked the entry of potentially significant witnesses'. Counsel for the SSHD belatedly conceded that O2 was not alleged to have taken part in terrorist training in Ethiopia.

From Tuesday afternoon through to late Thursday, the court heard evidence in closed session. Open session resumed at 3:30 pm on Thursday to hear evidence from the first of two witnesses called by O2's legal team. After being sworn in on a Koran, counsel for O2 took Witness A, who had been issued a summons requiring him to come to court, through his written statement. The witness – who had met O2 at a camp in England where the SSHD alleged that military training had occurred – was cross examined by counsel for the SSHD in a manner calculated to undermine his testimony. He was asked why he did

---

47 It is important to note that some of the actions attributed to the defendant, and explored during the appeal, were not illegal at the time.

48 The PTA 'creates two types of control order. The first is compatible with Art. 5 of the European Convention on Human Rights and can be made by the Secretary of State; this is called a non-derogating control order. The second type is not compatible with Art. 5 and has to be made by a court on an application by the Secretary of State; this is called a derogating control order' (Sec. 1 of the PTA 2005). The conditions imposed by a non-derogatory control order must not 'unduly restrict' an individual's liberty.

not want to give evidence – the witness had been remanded in prison for 18 months on terrorist charges only to be acquitted – and was accused of covering up what had happened at the camp. This line of questioning led to a heated exchange in which the witness sought to refute allegations that he was a terrorist, only to be confronted by accusations that some of his 'associates' on the camping trip had, subsequently, been deported and/or arrested under terrorist legislation.

Counsel for the Home Office (Q) questioned 'Witness A' about his 'associates' and about what occurred on the trip:

> 'Q. Did you hear anybody talking about extremist activities or extremist views?
> A. You have to define what you mean.
> Q. Well, let me ask this question: did you hear anybody talking about using violence or about the desirability of using violence?
> A. No.
> Q. Sorry, I did not hear that?
> A. No.
> Q. Did you hear anybody talking about jihad?
> A. We all talk about jihad, but you have to understand what jihad is. If you want to say jihad is violence – you have to understand what jihad is and unless you want to explain or I'll explain what jihad is, as far as my knowledge is.
> Q. Well, could you explain to his Lordship what you think jihad is?
> A. Well, jihad[49] is a very simple term in Arab language. It just means to strive, so in other words you can strive to do many things. You can strive to make yourself a better person by being humble, you can strive to – jihadist's strive in many ways, so if people want to try and put the spin on it jihad means holy war, it doesn't mean that at all, because I know that's what's been used in common parlance, that people say jihad is holy war. It's just not. Jihad is just a struggle and the greatest jihad is the struggle with yourself. That's one view of Islam.

49 The concept is not simple. The *Encyclopedia of the Quran* interprets *jihad* as 'struggle, or striving, but often understood both within the Muslim tradition and beyond it as warfare against infidels … The term *jihad* derives from the root j-h-d denoting effort, exhaustion, strain'. Because numerous verses or *sura* have been added to the Koran over time, the term has acquired a number of meanings. For example, it may also refer to (a) combat against one's own desires and weaknesses, (b) perseverance in observing the religious law, (c) seeking religious knowledge, (d) obedience to God and summoning people to worship and so on'.

Q. So can we take it that you would reject the idea of violent jihad?
A. Would I reject it? Well, I mean, it's a fact in Islam that it happens, so I can't reject it. It's a part of Islam, isn't it, so ...
Q. Do you think it is right?
A. Do I think what is right?
Q. Violent jihad?
A. I think that what is written in Islam is right, according to the principles in Islam.
Q. Now, a number of the people who were at the camp in early May 2004 went on to do violent things, did they not?
A. That is what I've heard, yes.
Q. Now that you know that, do you agree with what they did?
A. What, to try and kill innocent people?
Q. Yes.
A. Of course I don't.
Q. Sorry.
A. Of course I don't.
Q. And then there are a number of people, of other people who were in the camp, who have now been convicted in relation to terrorist training, if I can put it broadly. That is right is [it] not?
A. What's right?
Q. That a number of other people who were on the camp have been convicted of terrorist training?
A. Yes, they have been convicted of terrorist training, yeah.
Q. Do you agree with that? Sorry, the providing of terrorist training?
A. No, of course I don't.
Q. But there are a lot of people at this camp who have subsequently gone on to do things that you disagree with, yes?
A. Yes.
Q. But you never heard or saw or suspected anything untoward during the whole of this weekend?
A. No, because nothing untoward happened and the fact of the matter is that nothing untoward happened. You know this very well, nothing untoward happened. You know this very well. You don't need to be trying to nudge nudge, wink wink, you know very well that nothing happened there, and you can tell the court that. You can be honest and upright and tell the court that nothing happened there because you know this; because the reason why you know this is because you've had intelligence reports because they were watching us, so you know nothing ever happened [...]

In fact, counsel for the SSHD was eliding several separate events together when he referred to 'the camp'; the convictions he was referring to arose out of a camping trip that O2 did not attend. The cross examination ended as it had begun, with an accusation which discredited the witness.[50]

Thus, shortly after the above exchange counsel for the SSHD (Y) said:

> Y: Mr. B, I suggest to you that what you have been describing about the May 2004 camp is an attempt to cover up what was happening there.
> WITNESS: Is that your suggestion?
> Y: Yes. What [do] you say to that?
> WITNESS: Well, this is what I say to that: this is your suggestion and your suggestion is based on nothing … because the facts of the matter are – and these are the facts which was explained in Woolwich Crown Court. These are the facts which are on record. Surveillance teams were watching us … They have photographic evidence of us, many, many CDs worth, which I have seen … So your suggestion is just that, a suggestion, because you wish to spin on something just for the benefit of yourself …'

The above exchanges were significant. First counsel deliberately sought to provoke the witness by bringing up the charges made against him under the PTA. This inflamed 'A' who became quite hostile and had the effect of eliciting statements which undermined the value of his testimony. Furthermore, many of counsel's questions were general in nature and did not relate to specific events or to O2 which witness 'A' might reasonably have addressed. Indeed, counsel's questions exploited popular stereotypes about Islam, e.g., jihad as 'violent' and as a justification 'to try and kill innocent people'. Counsel for the SSHD did not seek to obtain new information to assist the court – he sought only to incriminate the witness and reduce the value of his testimony. This tactic was unnecessary because the low standard of proof meant that his testimony could easily be undermined by establishing a 'link' to individuals who had been charged with terrorist offences after the camping trip.

Some information provided in the closed sessions was released on Friday morning in the form of a *'gist'* (a note) which summarized the evidence Witness T had given. The one page *'gist'* (summarized in Table 3) relates to Home Office allegations about O2's visit to Somalia.

---

50 Clearly this type of proceeding is adversarial, as occurs in criminal proceedings, and reflects attempts by counsel for the SSHD to secure a conviction. However, since the SSHD relies on undisclosed, 'secret' evidence, it might well be asked whether they are appropriate in this type of case.

TABLE 3 The 'gist' of witness 'T's evidence

1. 'The Horn of Africa is not a homogeneous area. Somalia, Ethiopia and Eritrea are very different countries, and very conflicted with each other…'.
2. 'Somali's and Ethiopians do not get on. They do not share a common language. Ethiopia does not have the same tribal or clan structure as found in Somalia, so Ethiopians would not fit in. Somalis are generally suspicious of foreigners, anyway'.
3. 'Since the collapse of functioning government in Somalia in 1991, Somalia has been government-less and lawless. It is a militarized society, where everyone has access to weapons. Given the absence of access to clan structures and the linguistic difficulties, a group all composed of foreigners would find it impossible to move around unless they had some form of backing'.
4. 'There are racial/ethnic differences between the countries: Ethiopians look very different from Somalis, and O2 does not look Somali'.
5. To do 'dawah' in Somalia one would have to 'to be sponsored by a mosque or organization' otherwise it would be too dangerous for foreigners.

The disclosure led O2's counsel to instruct me to write a second report addressing the 'gist'. My seven-page report – which discussed the substantial flow of people/refugees moving across the Ethiopia-Somalia border and anthropological data about ethnicity, language and 'racial' differences between Somali's and Ethiopians – was submitted to the court the following Monday.

The proceedings on Friday morning involved a two-hour session in which Witness B, the wife of one of O2's associates who had accompanied him on the trip to Somalia, gave evidence. Counsel for the SSHD questioned her about her husband, his behavior, his associates and why he had gone to Somalia. However, she said that her husband only told her he was going to Somalia the day before he left and that while she knew O2's mother, she did not know him or his siblings. She was unable to provide much information. Counsel for O2 attempted to clarify her evidence but the only relevant facts which emerged from her testimony was that her husband was a devout Muslim and that he did not tell her about his friends, activities or the trip to Somalia.

Friday afternoon was spent taking O2's testimony. This began with his counsel taking him through key issues[51] in his ten statements and ended with

51 The issues were: his last visit to Ethiopia; his visit to Mogadishu; the inability of his family to visit him in northern England where he had been compelled to live because of the control order; his response to an amended statement by the SSHD and his relation to an

questioning him about the statements made in the '*gist*' concerning his activities in Somalia which he sought to refute. During this two-hour period, O2 was repeatedly asked if he had been involved in any (para-)military training, which he denied; he clarified key issues and denied all the allegations made against him by the SSHD.

I turn now to key issues which arose from counsel for the SSHD's three-hour cross-examination of O2 on Friday afternoon. The cross examination consisted of 421 questions and the answers they elicited. Six themes emerged from my analysis of this exchange of which the first (immigration controls in the Horn) and the last (O2's departure from Somalia to Ethiopia) were unimportant (as defined by the small number of questions; fifteen and nine, respectively, and the fact they did not figure in judge's subsequent decision).

Questions are used to obtain evidence and, depending on the jurisdiction and the ability of the lawyer, they can be used to 'control' a witness by discursively compelling him to make an admission and incriminate himself.[52] Questioning in the context of a court room reflects the power of the court over those who are called to give evidence; it is a means of control reserved for those with recognized legal authority.

The first substantive issue pursued concerned O2's 'friends'. Counsel used interrogatives and declaratives – as opposed to open questions allowing the defendant to redefine the question or provide his own answer – to compel O2 to provide affirmative answers[53] which 'linked' him to a number of 'extremists'[54] thereby underlining the 'reasonableness' of the SSHDs decision to impose a control order on him.

'extremist'; his response to questions put to him by the SA; issues in relation to the SSHDs refusal to modify his control orders and recent amendments in a security service statement about him; issues in response to further open material served by the SSHD; finally, his response to the circumstances in which he had been informally interviewed by the police and his comments in the police report.

52 S. Harris, 'Questions as mode of control in magistrate's courts', *International Journal of the Sociology of Language* 49 (1984, 10-f) notes that interrogative questions 'may be built in such a way as to elicit certain preferred answers, and hence create difficulties for witnesses to disagree'. Such questions can only be answered by a simple 'yes' or 'no' and they are used to elicit specific information from a witness to explain their behaviour. It is very difficult for defendants questioned in this way to introduce new topics or to redefine the questions they are asked. See also C. Briggs, *Disorderly Discourse. Narrative, Conflict and Inequality* (University Press: Oxford, 1996).

53 Harris, *Questions as mode*, 10-f.

54 Including his brother-in-law who was later convicted of a terrorist offence. O2 hotly disputed' 'links' to 'Islamic extremists' (including to individuals who were subsequently charged and convicted; some who were charged and acquitted; some who were excluded from the UK; and some whom he disputed that he had any link to).

Questioning also focused on the conviction of members of his family for terrorist-related offences (four questions), before turning to his alleged relationship with convicted 'Islamic extremists' (29 questions). Counsel used disjunctive questions[55] in which O2 was asked about his relationship to individuals named in his witness statements. Among the issues addressed was O2's presence at the house of 'M' who had subsequently been convicted of terrorist-related offences. While O2 was able to explain his presence at M's house, he was compelled to acknowledge that he had socialized with Muslims there. This admission was tied to hear-say evidence[56] from an undercover police officer who had attended similar meetings at M's house, albeit not the meetings attended by O2, that 'jihad'[57] was a subject of discussion.

The focus shifted to the 2004 camping trip (sixty-seven questions). O2 went on the trip at the suggestion of his brother-in-law and they took his six-year old nephew. Was it a social occasion, asked counsel? Was this an opportunity to make new friends? No, said O2, 'it was an opportunity for me to go camping'. Apart from asking him about what occurred during the trip, the nature and tenor of the questions intimated that the campers had planned terrorist attacks and had undergone military training. Indeed, counsel's questions were based on hearsay evidence which derived from the observations of off-duty police officers – in a report written two years after the incident[58] – that some individuals at the camp were 'punished'. Officers described seeing individuals 'dressed identically in black outward-bound fatigue type clothing' who were being shouted at by an 'instructor or leader' who 'controlled the group'. The inference which counsel was asking the Judge to make was that 'punishment' of the kind described must have been 'military' training.

---

55 Disjunctive questions are those which can only be answered by a 'yes' or 'no'.

56 The basic rationale for the rule of excluding hearsay evidence concerns the need to assess the evidence to see 'what, if any, weight can be given to a statement by a person whom the jury have not seen or heard and which has not been subject to any test of reliability by cross-examination' (in 'P. Murphy, *Blackstone's Criminal Practice*. (Oxford University Press: Oxford. 2005), 2425). However, in closed material proceedings there are no rules of evidence other than excluding evidence obtained by torture. In O2's 2010 appeal against his proposed deportation to Ethiopia, SIAC relied on evidence obtained by British security officials about conditions in Ethiopia's secret detention centers where foreign nationals who had been subject to extraordinary rendition had been held SIAC concluded that O2's rights would not be violated if he were returned to Ethiopia.

57 See footnote 49.

58 The admission of hearsay evidence written up two years after the alleged incident would appear to violate the most basic rules of evidence which concern, in this instance, a serious lapse in time between the alleged incident and the writing of a report about the incident. See Rule 602 of the US Federal Rules of Evidence at: https://www.law.cornell.edu/rules/fre/rule_803.

The line of questioning switched to his marriage, his wife's pregnancy (information about which he expressed little knowledge), his trip to Ethiopia in early 2005 and his intention to return to Ethiopia for the birth of his son (one hundred forty-two questions). It was here that Counsel questioned the circumstances surrounding O2's decision to go to Somalia with friends rather than travel to Ethiopia to attend the birth of his son. Didn't he realize how dangerous Somalia was? What was his role in planning the trip to Somalia? Counsel specifically asked him why he had not informed his family about his intention to travel to Somalia. Counsel began by asking O2 whether he perceived that the trip to Somalia might be 'dangerous', an assertion which O2 rejected.

Q. 'You are going to be safe?
A. Yeah.
Q. So there was nothing to worry about from that point of view. So you could tell your mother and your family that you were going to go to Mogadishu, could you not?
A. Are you talking about from the safety point of view or from them...
Q. From any point of view.
A. No, if they were going to prevent me, they'll prevent me from going.
Q. No, there was nothing to prevent you telling them that you were going to Mogadishu?
A. Except that they would tell me not to go, that's the only reason why I didn't tell them.
Q. But they could not have stopped you going?
A. No, they would have told me, look, go to Ethiopia. My mum, she would cry, you know what I'm saying, yeah: "look, I raised you up, your dad used to do this," start crying, you know what I'm saying. You understand? So because of that, yeah, I didn't want to tell them. If I told them they would have talked me out of it.
Q. Well, that would be because your mother was expecting you to go to Ethiopia.
A. Yes, and never heard of me planning go to Somalia [...]'

There followed a brief discussion about another issue before counsel returned to his original line of questioning:

Q. 'So let us see if we can come back ...
A. So the reason why I mentioned Egypt to her, yeah, because previously she knew about Egypt.
Q. Well, your mother's objection was that you were not going to Ethiopia and you were going to be going to somewhere else?

A. Yeah, to Egypt.
Q. Well, her objection was, was it not, that you were not going to Ethiopia and that is where she thought you should be going. That's right, is it not?
A. Yes.
Q. And so it didn't really matter where the other place was, whether it was Egypt or Barbados or Somalia. That is right? You would get the same reaction from her.
A. Yes.
Q. So why did you not say to her, well, actually I am going to Somalia?
A. No, because I'm going to go … like, because, you know, the Egypt thing, she knew that I considered it and stuff like that, yeah, and I told it was for only eight weeks, yeah, and, you know, it's a good opportunity for me to go, basically. I lied to her, you understand, yeah, and that's it. I made up my mind, that's what happened'.

O2 conceded that he had lied to his mother and family about going to Somalia because he went on the spur of the moment. This admission was seized upon by counsel for the SSHD who argued that if the purpose of the trip was really for religious purposes, why 'lie' about it to his family?

At various points counsel deliberately inflamed O2. While both parties were frustrated by their inability to pursue or answer questions, O2's inability to provide clear answers and to provide independent corroboration to support his account undermined his evidence.

The afternoon concluded with O2 being briefly re-examined by his counsel about the camping trip, planning the trip to Somalia and the views of his UK-based Somali friends who discounted any danger of visiting Mogadishu. O2's counsel concluded with questions pertaining to his social isolation which arose from his forced relocation to northern England because of the modified control order.

4 The Work of the Courts

The procedural and evidentiary rules established in the PTA and related terrorist legislation place the Secretary of State and the defendant on a very unequal footing and they require the judge to assess open and closed evidence. Second, given the limited extent to which a Special Advocate can assist an appellant, the onus for ensuring that legal proceedings are conducted fairly falls on the judge who decides on the admissibility of all the evidence. This legislation bears the imprint of three decades of emergency/terrorist legislation aimed at suppressing terrorism in Northern Ireland by single judges (i.e., the 'Diplock Courts'),[59] a fact which must surely explain why the effectiveness of adversarial challenge during the open sessions is so ineffective. If my conclusion is correct, then adversarial challenge by the Special Advocate in the closed sessions must have been practically useless to O2. However, we will never know the effectiveness of the SA because the proceedings were closed (nor is there a published record) and the court only requires sufficient evidence to support the SSHD's suspicion that O2 was associating with 'terrorists'.

In this type of case the Judge must assess whether the SSHD has reasonable grounds for suspecting ('believing' in the case of TPIMs) whether the defendant has been involved in terrorist-related activity (which is not even a balance of probabilities test)[60] and whether s/he is likely to pose a threat to national security. This assessment works by establishing 'links' between a defendant and 'terrorists'.

In a thirty-six-page decision, the judge made it clear that in assessing the closed evidence he required the SSHD either to disclose certain evidence or withdraw it (the SSHD decided not to disclose). He accepted evidence obtained by a trick and all the hearsay evidence as providing a sufficient reason to be skeptical of O2 and of witness A's testimony. Skepticism was, he thought, justified because some of the individuals at the events attended by O2 had subsequently been convicted of terrorist-related activities while others had been excluded from the UK. The judge argued that 'there are a number of reasons to be very skeptical' about O2's account of the trip to Somalia and the groups stated intention of doing 'free-style *dawah*' because Somalia was not a safe place to go.

---

59 B. Dickson, 'Northern Ireland emergency legislation – the wrong medicine?', *Public Law* (Winter, 1992) 592–624.

60 In *Re B* [*2008*] *UKHL 35* Lord Hoffman answered the question of how to decide a case on the balance of probabilities using a mathematical analogy: "If a legal rule requires a fact to be proved (a 'fact in issue'), a judge or jury must decide whether or not it happened. There is no room for a finding that it might have happened. The law operates a binary system in which the only values are 0 and 1. The fact either happened or it did not. If the tribunal is left in doubt, the doubt is resolved by a rule that one party or the other carries the burden of proof. If the party who bears the burden of proof fails to discharge it, a value of 0 is returned and the fact is treated as not having happened. If he does discharge it, a value of 1 is returned and the fact is treated as having happened." At: https://uk.practicallaw.thomsonreuters.com/2-500-6576?transitionType=Default&contextData=(sc.Default)&firstPage=true&bhcp=1. This is a civil law, not a criminal law, standard of proof, which means that more than 50 percent of the evidence must be accepted by the court.

Critically O2's 'reticence with his family' about going to Somalia led the judge to conclude: 'One is entitled to suspect that he concealed the fact that he was going to Somalia in order to hide what he was really intending to do there [...] the justifiable suspicion arises that what he was hiding was the jihadist training which he went to Somalia for'. Furthermore, the absence of any independent evidence concerning his visit to Somalia was damning: '... (T)he fact that he was able to provide a general description of some of the mosques in Mogadishu does not mean that he stayed in them. He could just as easily have visited them to pray while he was in Mogadishu undergoing terrorist training'.

In relation to his links with Islamic extremists, the judge noted that: "This is not so much a case of guilt by association. Rather his connection with so many people associated with extremism makes it much more difficult to treat what might otherwise be normal activities, such as going on a camping trip, as innocent." The judge concluded,

> The many parts of the jigsaw to which the analysis [...] above relates have combined to create a worrying profile of O2. I agree with the assumption underlying the control order, namely that *the evidence* (at any rate the open evidence) *does not justify charges relating to any particular criminal activity being laid against O2*. Any terrorist training which the evidence suggests he would have undergone took place before terrorist training was criminalized. But each of the core features of the Secretary of State's case raises suspicions in themselves to a greater or lesser degree, and when combined together they serve to increase one's misgivings about him. Everyone agrees on the importance of considering both the open and the closed materials together since the latter may have the effect of making the open case less strong than might appear at first sight. But even if such parts of the closed materials as might be regarded as exculpatory are taken into account, *I have concluded that the facts relied upon by the Secretary of State in the open materials* [...] *amount to reasonable grounds for suspecting that O2 has been involved in terrorism-related activity,* as defined in sections 1(1)–1(4) of the Terrorist Act 2000 and section 1(9) of the 2005 Act'. [my emphasis].

O2's counsel appealed against this decision to the Court of Appeal where it was heard in the spring of 2009. It took the Lord Justices less than 30 minutes to dispose of the appeal. Lord Justice W concluded that it could be seen from the determination that 'the judge was putting all the matters together to see if the facts corresponded with the assumptions of the control order that there was a suspicion of evidence of terror related activities'. In relation to the apparent contradiction between the evidence of Witness T and my expert report dealing with the 'gisted'/disclosed information, the Lord Justices noted that the judge had 'considered' both reports so 'what has he [the judge] done wrong?' They allowed an appeal solely on the basis that O2's human rights may have been violated when he was relocated to northern England.[61] The hearing bore all the marks of a 'ritual' in the sense that the Lord Justices, the legal teams for both sides and the SA went through the formality of an appeal knowing that the PTA made it impossible to defend an individual against 'reasonable suspicion' of involvement in terrorist related acts.

In early 2010 the SSHD sought to deport O2 – who had by this time, and out of frustration with being internally exiled, been convicted and prisoned for breaching his control order – to Ethiopia. The SSHD sought to deport him using a newly negotiated 'Memorandum of Understanding'.[62] Her decision triggered an appeal which focused on O2's rights under the European Convention of Human Rights. The Court decided that it was satisfied with the diplomatic assurances that O2 'will not be subjected to treatment' contrary to the ECHR and that the British Government would not be in breach of its obligations under the ECHR. However, O2 remained in prison until 2013 at which time, to end his indefinite incarceration, he asked to be deported.

5 Conclusion

The PTA and associated legislation has given rise to a growing number of appeals challenging the use of secret evidence all of which highlight the courts' limited power to review the SSHD's decisions on control orders. While it has long been known that the decisions made in closed proceedings are subject to 'extra-ordinary weaknesses',[63] the British courts have shown a surprising reluctance to find fault with terrorist legislation.[64] It was not until February 2009

61 The Supreme Court overturned this decision in a subsequent appeal in 2010.

62 Regardless of the fact that Ethiopia had a very poor human rights record, see: 'Letter to the British Foreign Secretary regarding diplomatic assurances (on Ethiopia)' (17/9/2009) at: http://www.hrw.org/news/2009/09/17/letter-british-foreign-secretary-ethiopian-deportation-cases.

63 G. Van Harten, 'Weakness of adjudication in the face of secret evidence', *International Journal of Evidence & Proof* 13 (2009), 3.

64 For a review of a case similar to that of O2, see 'R (AN) v Secretary of State for Justice [2009] EWHC 1921 (Admin), judgment of 28 July 2009'. For a broader review of SIAC procedures see RB (ALGERIA) AND ANOTHER V SECRETARY OF STATE FOR THE HOME DEPARTMENT; OO (JORDAN) V SAME; MT (ALGERIA) V SAME: HL 18 FEB 2009.

when the European Court of Human Rights decided '*A and Others v The United Kingdom*'[65] – a case involving 11 individuals held under control orders – that the British courts were forced to rescind earlier decisions upholding the procedural fairness of hearings which relied on closed evidence.[66]

While the ECHRS ruling forced the SSHD to rethink her policy on the use of secret evidence[67] it did not affect O2 because in his case the court had relied on open material to reach a decision. Even so, reliance on disclosed evidence in the form of a 'gist' is very difficult for appellants to respond to because it requires independent corroborative evidence about events which, by their very nature, are difficult to obtain independent corroboration for. Furthermore, individuals held under a control order/TPIM are barred from seeing their friends and associates, and the latter are naturally reluctant to associate with the individual or provide evidence (as was the case with Witness A).

The Terrorism Prevention & Investigations Measures Act (2011) and associated legislation[68] is much more pre-emptive in nature than earlier counter-terror legislation in that it builds on the Counter-Terrorism and Security Act

65 See ¶220 and passim of http://www.asylumlawdatabase.eu/en/content/ecthr-and-others-v-united-kingdom-application-no-345505-19-february-2009. This case, which involved the lengthy deprivation of liberty, required the SSHD to disclose a core irreducible minimum of the case against a defendant to give meaningful instructions to the SA. The decision saw the SSHD withdraw some control orders rather than disclose even a minimum of information.

66 It is instructive to compare the Canadian Supreme Court's approach to the use of the Art 1F 'exclusion clause' which, until 2013, relied upon similar reasoning to that applied in the British courts with respect to terrorism, namely, that a person found to be 'complicit' in a crime could be excluded from protection. In *Ezokola v Canada* [*2013*] *2 S.C.R* the Supreme Court overturned the existing test and replaced 'the personal and knowing participation test' with a 'contribution-based approached to complicity'. It is now necessary to establish a voluntary, significant and knowing contribution to the organization's crime or criminal purpose. Guilt by association is no longer enough to exclude an individual from the protection of the Refugee Convention (though a lower evidentiary standard is used in Canada than in the UK). See: L. Waldman & W.S. Meighen. 'An Analysis of post-Ezokola and JS Jurisprudence on Exclusion', in I. Atak & J.C. Simeon. Eds. *The Criminalization of Migration: Context and Consequences* (McGill-Queen's University Press: Montreal. 2018), 138–167.

67 See: 'Home Secretary orders review of control orders for terror suspects' (*The Guardian*, 16 September 2009), and 'Terror suspect freed from control order' (*The Independent*, 24 September 2009).

68 Specifically the 'Justice and Security Bill HL (2012–13)' (which provides for closed material procedures in certain civil proceedings and prevents the court from disclosing sensitive information), the 'Enhanced Terrorism Prevention and Investigation Measures Bill' (Cm 8166) allows the SSHD to impose more stringent restrictions on individuals served with a TPIM notice and the 'Human Rights 1998 (Repeal and Substitution Bill) 2011–12' before Parliament.

(2015) by extending 'coercive non-trial-based measures aimed at terrorist suspects generally, but particularly at persons who have gone abroad to support ISIS or who may seek to do so' by creating 'Temporary Exclusion Orders' (TEOs). TEO's are used by the SSHD to prevent British nationals from entering the UK for up to two years (a form of enforced exile) while the individual is investigated. The bill also introduced 'strengthened TPIM measures'.[69] Whereas TPIM notices replaced control orders ostensibly with 'a more focused and less intrusive system of terrorism prevention and investigation measures' (so called 'light-touch measures'), 'enhanced TPIMs' rely on CMPs, SAs and the right to impose conditions which mirror the measures imposed on O2.

What does O2's case allow us to infer about the potential impact of current counter-terrorist legislation? It is clear that the reforms have strengthened the power of the state over the rights of individuals. Notable omissions from the legislation include a refusal to end the state's reliance on intercept 'evidence',[70] continued reliance on Closed Material Proceedings[71] (with their dependence on SA's to ensure fairness in a context in which it is impossible to know if they have fulfilled their responsibility and in which the court has limited power to quash a control/TPIM order), and a failure to amend/repeal other anti-terrorist laws such as Sec. 19 of the Terrorist Act (2000) which was used to convict O2's family.

The new laws do not restrict the power of the SSHD even though The Independent Reviewer of Terrorist Legislation had proposed a scheme that would allow a court to lift restrictions against suspected individuals where 'the Home Secretary had reasonable grounds to believe that a named individual is engaged in terrorist activity **and,** in the view of the Director of Public Prosecutions, a criminal investigation into that individual is therefore justified'.[72] In

69 Whereas individuals with the right of abode in the UK can, eventually, be deported, citizens cannot be deported or stripped of their citizenship; a TEO allows the SSHD time to consider the case against a citizen suspected of terrorism. See: H. Fenwick, 'Responding to the ISIS threat: extending coercive non-trial-based measures in the Counter-Terrorism and Security Act 2015', *International Review of Law, Computers and Technology* 30, 3 (2016), 174–190.

70 Intercept information is not allowed in criminal or civil proceedings but is the basis of accusations and findings in control order/TPIM cases.

71 In the UK it appears that the courts, Parliament *and* citizens are more willing to accept the need for 'secret trials' than is the case elsewhere. What does this acceptance reveal about our society, our fear of others and the need to ensure our 'security' if it comes at the expense of justice?

72 Lord Macdonald, *Review of Counter-Terrorism and Security Powers* (Command paper 8003. London, 2011). Emphasis in the original.

short, the Home Secretary retains the power to impose and sustain measures similar to those O2 experienced.

Given the impact of other legislation and a substantial blurring of boundaries between civil and criminal law, it should be clear that existing legislation undermines the right of individuals to defend themselves against a TPIM notice. Secret trials, with all they entail regarding the erosion of a right to a fair trial, are set to remain an important part of the way in which the government proceeds against individuals who are suspected, but about which little evidence exists, of involvement in terrorism. It should also be remembered that the government withdrew its key claim against O2 that he knew about, and was therefore complicit in, planning a terrorist attack in London. At no point in the open evidence was the argument made, and sustained, that O2 contributed to planning or carrying out the attack.

The SSHD has promised not to 'park' – i.e., fail to progress – cases for more than two years and to attend to the reports of the 'Independent Reviewer of Terrorism Legislation' but, if the experience of the outgoing Reviewer, Lord Carlisle, was anything to go by, the Government finds it easy to ignore unpalatable comments about the impact of restrictions or the length of control order/TPIM notices (see Carlisle 2009).[73]

Were 'O2' able to comment, what might he say? First, he would complain about the many powers of the SSHD – e.g., the ease with which she can remove/reinstate his ILR, the ease with which his case was 'parked' and the consequent social isolation imposed on him and his family, etc. Second, he would draw our attention to the shortcomings of his appeals, notably his inability to know and answer the charges against him, the courts admission of evidence obtained by a trick, its acceptance of hearsay evidence and the fact that he was found 'guilty by association' with individuals which the SSHD deported or arrested.

In relation to the supposedly reduced restrictions that could be imposed under a TPIM notice – i.e., replacement of curfews by 'overnight residence requirements', 'greater access' to communications, greater freedom to associate, freedom to study and work, etc. – I suspect that O2 would see these as superficial changes for two reasons. First, once an individual is placed under a control order no one wishes to be associated with him/her.[74] Secondly, the SSHD

73 At a speech at the Institute of Advanced Law in February 2008 Lord Carlisle referred to the role played by political parties in Parliament who were the force behind the 'pragmatic incrementalism' which was driving the expansion of terrorist legislation which served as an impediment to reviewing and consolidating legislation.

74 As Cerie Bullivant discovered, see: http://www.liberty-human-rights.org.uk/materials/control-orders-case-study-cerie-bullivant.pdf (accessed 11 February 2011). Also see A.

retains her power to impose 'enhanced' restrictions. It seems clear that, from the point of view of suspected individuals placed under them, control orders/TPIM notice are intended to isolate and punish individuals who the SSHD *believes* – but about whose activities there is no clear evidence – may be involved in terrorism-related offences.[75]

To be sure O2's views were evident to his lawyers and, to a more limited extent, to the judges – who are appointed to the Bench following a successful legal career – who presided over his many appeals. It should be clear, however, that by dint of their training lawyers and judges tasked with implementing counter-terrorist laws do not seem to encounter serious ethical difficulties with the roles they are asked to play in control order/TPIM cases, i.e., judging by their willingness to take either or both sides in these legal contests. After all, to appear in the High Court, the Court of Appeal and the Supreme Court to argue or decide 'terrorist' cases represents the pinnacle of a lawyer's career. If they experience discomfort with the CMP and the way in which terror suspects are detained, their frustrations take the form of arguing over 'facts' – based on the binary distinction between 'proved' and 'disproved' – rather than contesting the fairness of legal proceedings which are conducted professionally but which *always* uphold the SSHDs imposition of control orders/TPIM measures. To err on the safe side, which is to say assessing a case on the balance of probabilities that an individual did 'associate' with 'terrorists' is not a problem for lawyers and judges. Advocacy is what lawyers are trained to do in an adversarial system where they act on behalf of their clients. The exception, of course, are Special Advocates who straddle their representational and disclosure roles; however, their ability to perform both roles cannot be assessed which transforms them into chameleons/shape shifters whose professional and ethical responsibilities are poorly defined.

As an anthropologist there is little reason to be sanguine about Closed Material Proceedings because we are taught to see the world differently to lawyers. After having heard all the 'open evidence' it is not evident to me that O2 knew about the terrorist incident which resulted in his lengthy internal exile/detention and the criminal conviction of members of his family. Writing a decade after the case, I find that so little evidence was adduced in his appeal that it is not possible for me to assign unequivocally liability for his behavior or to understand whether the accusations made against him had a basis in fact. Unlike lawyers, it appears to me that the parameters used to define 'the balance of

Carlisle, *Fourth Report of the Independent Reviewer pursuant to Sec. 14(3) of the Prevention of Terrorism Act 2005*. (February). 2009.

75 As Lord Hoffman observed, see footnote 17.

probabilities' to allocate liability for wrong-doing are vague and poorly defined; the legal approach relies on identifying potential 'links' between individuals who are said to associate together. Anthropologists would want to know more about what, if anything occurred at suspected meetings and we would want independent corroboration to assess conflicting accounts. In short, we tend to question normative and accepted views about assumed behavior, etc.

Equally important, anthropologists are taught to step back from specific disputes to see the wider picture. In the context of Closed Material Proceedings this means looking at the role played by powerful institutions and legal actors in organizing, managing and participating in chameleon like political-legal procedures. Furthermore, whereas in law the concept of causality is inseparable from individual responsibility, anthropologists believe that there are likely to be multiple factors[76] explaining (criminal) behavior which are not adequately addressed by a legal process that relies on conflicting, uncorroborated or secret evidence. For anthropologists, a 'fact' cannot be understood as true or false. Facts take their meaning from a moral or social universe which the law, which seeks a simple yes or no to assign liability, is not set up to understand.

In conclusion, anthropology and law operate with different mindsets, assumptions and paradigms such that anthropology – certainly this anthropologist – finds it difficult to have confidence in the ability of Closed Material Proceedings to achieve justice. As Nader has observed, anthropologists attempt to see through legal discourse and legal procedure to lay bare and question concepts such as 'justice' and the 'rule of law' which, in the case of Closed Material Proceedings against an alleged terrorist, reveals a process that is deeply worrying. If it is true to say that law seeks to use its power to enforce, reflect, constitute and legitimize dominant social and power relations, by contrast the role of anthropology is to unsettle, probe and question the certainties which underlay legal practice/procedure and forms of governance which appear to be profoundly unjust.

76 See, for instance: 'Assimilation's Failure, Terrorism's rise' (*The New York Times*, 6 July 2011) which argues that an obsession with radicalisation misses the point about why 'so many young people, who by all accounts are intelligent, articulate and integrated, come to find this violent, reactionary ideology so attractive'. The writer identifies the source of the problem with the failure of 'multiculturalism' and the failure of government to engage directly with ethnic minorities as citizens (to which should be added the impact of racism and discrimination on young Black and ethnic minority residents and citizens).

Acknowledgments

I am grateful to John Jackson and Graham Hudson for their detailed comments on an earlier version of this paper which has been presented and discussed at various conferences and seminars. I would also like to thank James C. Simeon for his detailed comments on the chapter.

References

Bailey, Freddie G. *Stratagems and Spoils. A Social Anthropology of Politics*. Schocken Books: New York, 1969.

Briggs, Charles. *Disorderly Discourse. Narrative, Conflict and Inequality*. Oxford: University Press, 1996.

Brouwer, Evelien. "Immigration, asylum and terrorism: A changing dynamic. Legal and practical developments in the EU response to the terrorist attacks of 11.09," *European Journal of Migration and Law* 4 (2003): 399–424.

Boyle, Elizabeth & Erika Busse. "Institutional vulnerability and opportunity" Immigration and America's "War on Terror," *Law & Social Enquiry* 31, 4 (2006): 947–974.

Campbell , R. John. *Bureaucracy, Law and Dystopia in the United Kingdom's Asylum System*. Routledge: New York, 2017.

Carlisle, Alex (Lord). 2009. *Fourth Report of the Independent Reviewer pursuant to Sec. 14(3) of the Prevention of Terrorism Act 2005*. (February).

Conley, John, William O'Barr & E. Allan Lind. 'The power of language: presentational style in the courtroom', *Duke Law Journal* (1978): 1375–1399.

Conley, John, & William O'Barr. 'Hearing the hidden agenda: The ethnographic investigation of procedure', *Law & Contemporary Problems* 51, 4 (1988): 181–197.

Conley, John. 'Review: Can You Talk like a Lawyer and Still Think like a Human Being? Mertz's the Language of Law School', *Law & Social Inquiry* 34, 4 (2009): 983–2015.

Dickson, Brice. 'Northern Ireland emergency legislation – the wrong medicine?', *Public Law* (Winter, 1992) 592–624.

Epstein, Arnold L. 'The case method in the field of law', in A.L. Epstein. Ed. *The Craft of Social Anthropology*. Tavistock: London. 1967. pp. 205–230.

Fenwick, Helen. 'Responding to the ISIS threat: extending coercive non-trial-based measures in the Counter-Terrorism and Security Act 2015', *Int. Review of Law, Computers and Technology* 30, 3 (2015): 174–190.

Good, Anthony. 2004. 'Expert evidence in asylum and human rights appeals: An expert's view', *Int. Jo. of Refugee Law* 16, 3: 358–380.

Graham Hudson & Daniel Alati. 'Behind Closed Doors: Secret Law and the Special Advocate System in Canada'. *Queen's Law Journal* 44 (2018): 1: 1–68.

Harris, Sandra. 1984. 'Questions as mode of control in magistrate's courts', *Int. Jo. of the Sociology of Language* 49: 5–27.

House of Commons. *The operation of the Special Immigration Appeals Commission (SIAC) and the use of Special Advocates*. Constitutional Affairs Committee. Seventh Report of Session 2004–05. Vol. 1. Report together with formal minutes. (March 2005).

Jackson, John. 'The role of special advocates: Advocacy, due process and the adversarial tradition', *International Jo. of Evidence and Proof* 20, 4 (2016): 343–362.

Kandel, Randy. 'How lawyers and anthropologists think differently', *Annals of Anthropological Practice* (special issue: Double Vision – Anthropologists at Law, 1992). pp. 1–20.

Kavanagh, Aileen. 'Special advocates, control orders and the right to know', *The Modern Law Review* 73, 5 (2010): 836–857.

Macdonald, Lord. *Review of Counter-Terrorism and Security Powers*. Cmd paper 8003. London. 2011.

McCulloch, Jude. 'Pre-Crime and counter-terrorism. Imagining a future crime in the War on Terror', *The British Jo. of Criminology* 49, 5 (2009): 628–645.

Murphy, Peter. *Blackstone's Criminal Practice*. Oxford: Oxford University Press. 2005.

Nader, Laura. 'The words we use: justice, human rights, and the sense of injustice', in *Mirrors of Justice*, K. Clarke & M. Goodale. Eds. Cambridge University Press: N.Y. 2010, 316–331.

Rawls, John. 1971 [1999]. *A Theory of Justice*. University Press: Oxford.

Sandell, Adam. 'Liberty, fairness and the UK control order cases: two steps backward, two steps back', *European Human Rights Law Review* 1 (2008) 120–131.

Van Harten, Gus. 'Weakness of adjudication in the face of secret evidence', *Int. Journal of Evidence & Proof* 13 (2009) 1: 1–27.

Waldman, Lorna & Warda S. Meighen. 'An Analysis of post-*Ezokola* and *JS* Jurisprudence on Exclusion', in I. Atak & J.C. Simeon. Eds. *The Criminalization of Migration. Context and Consequences.* McGill-Queen's University Press: Montreal. 2018. pp. 138–167.

Wehr, Hans. Ed. *A Dictionary of Modern Written Arabic* (Arabic-English). Otto Harassowitz: Wiesbaden. 1979.

Woolf, Lord. 'The rule of law and a change in the constitution' (Squire Centenary Lecture), in *The Times*. (3 March 2004) at: http://www.timesonline.co.uk/tol/news/article1036741.ece?

Zedner, Lucia. 'Securing liberty in the face of terror: Reflections from Criminal Justice', *Journal of Law & Society* 32, 4 (2005): 507–533.

CHAPTER 4

Forced Migration, Diaspora Politics and Extremism: Conceptual, Policy and Operational Implications with a Focus on the United Kingdom

Christopher McDowell

1 Introduction

This chapter argues that the internationalisation of contemporary conflict, in particular, those aspects that relate to forced migration and the failures of refugee protection and integration, create spaces and opportunities for extremist networks to recruit and act among those forcibly displaced and seeking asylum. The chapter identifies four elements of the internationalisation of contemporary conflicts: large-scale population displacement, dispersal, encampment and the refugee journey; the process and experience of settlement and integration in a country of asylum; the diaspora politics that links the conflict to movement and settlement; and lastly, the growing involvement of organised crime in asylum migration. From within these dynamics of contemporary conflict has emerged the aggressive recruitment and radicalization of vulnerable persons, whether asylum seekers or nationals, of a target state to operationalize terrorist tactics and build further support to extremist causes. It is shown that while some areas of the UK Counter Terrorism (CT) policy and strategy articulate and respond to the international and domestic displacement dimensions of such security threats, there remain important gaps in both strategic thinking, and in every day operations. It is proposed that thinking differently about the displacement security threat nexus, and the current response to conflict displacement and asylum settlement, may: first, explain why individuals with an asylum or refugee profile are attracted to extremist narratives and are vulnerable to radicalisation; and second, assist in the development of strategies to avoid radicalisation towards violent extremism among displaced populations. The findings strengthen arguments to improve the legal and humanitarian protections available to people displaced by conflict, and the enhancement of integration strategies for asylum seekers and refugees to avoid marginalisation.

The chapter is based on research conducted in the UK, Europe and Canada by Christopher McDowell, Gemma Collantes Celador and Natasha De Silva between 2016 and 2018, funded by the Centre for Research and Evidence on

© KONINKLIJKE BRILL NV, LEIDEN, 2020 | DOI:10.1163/9789004295995_006

Security Threats (CREST), which examined diaspora refugee politics (McDowell *et al.*, 2018a, b and c). It draws also on commissioned research by the author during the same period on Syrian refugee resettlement in the UK (UNHCR, 2017). The CREST project examined the internationalisation of the Sri Lankan conflict between 1983 and 2009, specifically, Tamil asylum diaspora politics and the strategies of the Liberation Tigers of Tamil Eelam (LTTE) to further its political and military objectives through the mobilisation of Tamil asylum seekers and refugees in western states. The research found that the frequently coercive strategies deployed by the LTTE to build a political support base among overseas Tamils, and to raise funds for the organisation through direct involvement in the asylum journey and assistance in settlement, provided a model for international Jihadist and Salafi networks politically active among Europe-bound migrants and refugees fleeing recent conflicts in the Middle East. The research on Syrian refugee resettlement evaluated the UK Government's resettlement programme for vulnerable refugees identifying opportunities to improve settlement and integration through local authority and voluntary support in housing, education, employment, education and cultural adaptation.

To provide context to the arguments developed about the engagement of refugees in transnational politics, the chapter draws on the diaspora, migration, conflict and refugee studies literature linking that discussion to the literature on extremism and radicalisation. It sets out the main findings of the research in relation to the relationship between the migration experiences of those displaced by conflict and the risks of radicalisation. It then develops the policy implications of the findings for counter terrorism and the prevention of radicalisation in the UK context, and recommends additional research to address gaps in the current knowledge.

2 Diaspora Politics and Extremism

The role of diasporas and diaspora organisations in transnational politics, particularly where politics includes support for violence in pursuit of political aims, tends to be portrayed in two ways. The conflict and economics literature, see for example Collier (2000), argues that diaspora political engagement is more likely to exacerbate conflict where diaspora members see themselves as distanced from the consequences of their actions at home, and where diaspora organisations exploit a sense of social injustice linked to the 'exile condition'. Stronger engagement in conflict is more likely where overseas communities have the resources to contribute, and where an exclusive common identity is sympathetic to demands for national separation and self-determination (Hall and Swain 2007; Collier and Hoeffler 2004; Demmers 2007). According to Collier and Hoeffler (2004:575) the risk of heightened conflict is directly linked to the size of the diaspora and the capacity to raise and donate resources that sustain military activity (Brinkerhoff 2008; Byman et al. 2001; Roth 2015). Better funded and organised diaspora organisations are vital in maintaining the link between the conflict at home and overseas communities providing a platform for action and coalescing demands.

In the migration and refugee studies literature, however, the role of diasporas as peace-makers and agents promoting post-conflict rebuilding is more widely discussed (Baser and Swain, 2008: 11). The literature highlights diaspora members, often working through nongovernmental organisations, lobbying international institutions and host governments to seek political settlements to conflict, and directing aid towards humanitarian and reconstruction programmes (Cochrane, Baser and Swain 2009; Hall and Swain 2007; Hess and Korf 2014; Østergaard-Nielsen 2006). Overseas nationals, many college educated with liberal-cosmopolitan values (Werbner, 2002: 120), return to their countries of origin to take up political positions, or to advise on constitutional, development or transitional justice mechanisms (Hall and Swain 2007: 119; Brun and Van Hear 2012; Hess and Korf 2014; Vimalarajah and Cheran 2010). The transfer of wealth from diasporas via remittances either directly to family, business investment, or through donations to NGOs and charities form a vital flow of funds to repair infrastructure and rebuild social conditions in the homeland (de Haas 2010, Brun and Van Hear 2012).

The oversimplified dichotomy between diasporas as warmongers or peacemakers does not provide a framework to explain why diaspora engagement takes the form it does in any given conflict, or why diaspora members may support violence to achieve ends. Brinkerhoff's (2008) 'identity-mobilisation framework' seeks to understand how degrees of integration in countries of settlement shape political behaviour and suggests that exclusion, or the perception of exclusion among individuals, may lead to destructive rather than constructive contributions. Betts and Jones (2016: 22), drawing on social movement theory developed by Sökefeld (2006) identify the importance of 'animators' either from within or outside diaspora communities who mobilise interests in pursuit of political purposes. This approach is useful in analysing the ways in which power relations can shape political engagement while arguably privileging the role of elites and underplaying the importance of lived migration experience in decision-making.

The CREST research on Sri Lankan diaspora politics that informs this chapter found Koinova's (2010) approach particularly useful in analysing refugee diasporic action, and trends towards radicalism, in relation to the dynamic between events at home, in the place of settlement and the places in between where transnational relations are established and maintained. She rightly observes that periods of intense violence in a conflict at home are likely to be mirrored in the discourse and strategies of diaspora politics, while periods of relative calm allow for democratic reflection and greater consideration of post-conflict arrangements. Following Betts and Jones (2016), Koinova additionally drew on social movement theory to show how forms of mobilisation are shaped by opportunity structures in the homeland and through the relationships established by what she terms 'entrepreneurs' in the country of origin establishing transnational networks of influence, propaganda flow and resource channelling.

The reading of the literature suggests that extremism in the context of transnational diaspora politics cannot be understood through a static, homogenous model of diasporas which are either essentially violent or peaceful. Rather it is necessary to analyse political action through the agency of those involved, identifying structural and contextual factors that include constraints and enablers on action that emerge out of conditions in the countries of settlement as well the stage of conflict.

Refugee studies has been slow to embrace the study of refugees as political agents or actors, however, as Van Hear has noted (2014:177) the implications of forced migration and the flows and exchanges between scattered populations for international politics is forcing itself on to the research agenda as states struggle to agree on policies to respond to refugee movements and their consequences. The concept of diasporas as 'transnational network(s) of dispersed political subjects' (Werbner 2002: 121) connected through socio-political relationships, provides an opportunity to examine the specific politics of 'refugee diasporas' and how the relationships that refugees establish towards their homeland, their place of settlement and their fellow co-nationals shapes political engagement and refugee communities' sense of identity and purpose. It suggests that refugees, for whom the episode of traumatic dispersal and the search for protection is central to their experience, will develop a political orientation that is different to that developed by voluntary migrants. As Wahlbeck has observed, politics provides 'a sense of order, a purpose in the fragmented lives of the refugees' (2002: 226) and 'refugee research needs a conceptual framework in which refugees' specific transnational social relations can be described', and to an extent the concept of diaspora has served such a purpose (2002: 229).

The internationalisation of conflict, it will be argued in this chapter, creates the conditions that influence political mobilisation within diaspora populations, however, as Koinova (2010) has argued, the causality between 'mobilising conditions' and radicalisation or the pursuit of moderate politics is unclear. From their research among Bosnian and Eritrean refugees, Al-Ali, Black and Koser (2001) found that political action is shaped by both a desire to bring about change at home and the capability to do so, and that the agency of the individual is vital in this decision-making. To understand the shift from a desire for change to action it is necessary, as Sökefeld has observed, to focus on political opportunities, mobilising structures, and practices and framings within discourses as explanators for political action (2006:268). Diaspora associations and their elites are central to such mobilisation (McAdam, McCarthy and Zald, 1996; Chaudhary and Guarnizo 2014) because within any community only a small minority are likely to be sufficiently motivated to act, and it requires leaders or 'animators' who can seize specific events, define grievances and claims to legitimise political action through issue-framing (Sökefeld 2006: 270–278; Betts and Jones, 2016).

2.1 *The 'Refugee Experience' and Radicalisation*

The involvement of individuals from a refugee or asylum background in terrorist attacks in Europe since 2005, and particularly since 2016, has raised questions about what, if anything, is specific about refugee diaspora politics, asylum seeking and integration that increases the risk of radicalisation towards violent politics (Abdi 2015; Sude, Stebbins, and Weilant 2015; McDowell et al. 2018c). The terrorism literature lacks generalised theories of radicalisation (Dawson, 2017) but emphasises it as a multifaceted phenomenon with a wide range of contingent factors that are sociological, psychological as well as ideological (Rahimi and Graumans, 2015; Dawson, 2017; Lemon and Heathershaw, 2017; Klausen et al., 2016). Functional models, largely designed by government security agencies, that set out to explain and predict the radicalisation process (Borum 2003; Moghaddam 2005; Silber and Bhatt 2007) identify triggers for radicalisation. Among migrants and refugees, frequently identified triggers include identity crises, social alienation, discrimination or social exclusion, racism, and poverty (Yusoufzai and Emmerling, 2017). As Rahimi and Graumans have observed, 'regardless of the diversity of causes, academic literature as well as governmental strategies have shown a consistent interest in the basic formula that a lack of cultural integration equals an increased threat of radicalisation' (2015: 28), and most of those who have been prosecuted for terrorism, at least in Canada, UK, and US, tend to be citizens, members of the community who were born in those states or who were naturalized over a long period of time. Individuals appear to be "culturally integrated," but, nevertheless, are prone to radicalization.

Within refugee populations it is argued that radicalisation is more likely to occur among friends and relatives where, what Thompson and Bucerius (2017) describe as, 'sentiment pools' exist within those communities and function to mobilise support for the political projects advanced by terrorist networks, or conversely to oppose those projects. Abdi's (2015) research among Somali youth in Minnesota found that programmes to counter isolation and marginalisation may have served to further 'other' the community thus intensifying the 'potential double burden of the lure of gangs and extremist groups as well as contact with institutions and policies that discriminate on the bases of race, religion and class' (2015:575).

A limited but growing literature is examining the radicalisation process at various stages in the refugee journey considering the location of refugees and their physical proximity to a conflict, the pre-existence of militant groups in refugee areas, and the policies and actions of host countries and the international community (Sude, Stebbins and Weilant 2015: 1, 3). Dawson (2017) calls for a similar approach to shift the onus of analysis from the 'why' to the 'how', suggesting the need to consider 'situations', 'contexts' and 'life experiences'.

To this end, research has focused on the 'camp' as a space of exception (Agamben 1998) and one where refugees become political actors, recalling Rygiel's (2011) discussion of the camp as a political space, whereby subjectivities and boundaries of inclusion and exclusion are negotiated and exercised, and where radicalisation processes might emerge in response to those processes. Milton, Spencer and Findley (2013: 637) find that that the conditions of the camp and the ways in which host states treat refugees 'can lead to transnational terrorism as some smaller subset of the refugee population responds against the host state'. Martin-Rayo (2011) highlights conditions within camps that might facilitate radicalisation processes, such as poor education, lack of freedom of movement and work; factors that have also been considered by several policy papers that refer to refugee camps as fertile grounds for recruitment and radicalisation (Koser and Cunningham 2017; Sude, Stebbins and Weilant 2015). Sude, Stebbins and Weilant (2015) imply that lessening the risk of radicalisation goes beyond providing immediate humanitarian assistance, and rather requires a multi-level and long-term approach that provides refugees with viable choices for the future. As Koser and Cunningham (2017) argue, providing psychological and security needs is particularly important because refugees might experience abuse or powerlessness in their place of refuge, and militant groups might exploit the situation to radicalise vulnerable groups (especially youth) 'with narratives of empowerment through violence' (2017: 215).

These ideas strongly resonate with Rygiel's (2011) understanding of subjectivities, and the extent to which a negative perception of one's own subjectivity within a camp (due to abuse, humiliation or powerlessness) could give way to radicalising processes.

3 Research Findings: Sri Lankan Asylum Diaspora and Syrian Refugee Resettlement

The author's research on Sri Lankan asylum diaspora politics, and refugee flight to Europe from the Middle East in the previous two years, builds on the literature reviewed above and extends our understanding of the nexus between conflict-generated forced migration and radicalisation processes.

As previously stated, this chapter argues that the internationalisation of contemporary conflict, which has four main elements:

- the large-scale population displacement, dispersal, encampment and the refugee journey;
- the process and experience of settlement and integration in a country of asylum;
- diaspora politics that links the conflict to movement and settlement and enables interactions between those on the move and political actors;
- and finally, the growing involvement of organised crime in asylum migration in human trafficking, arranging and financing through exploitative loans, passage across borders, travel documentation and coerced employment in places of settlement; ensures that the terrain of conflict extends far beyond a single national territory, and provides new opportunities for extremist actors to politically and economically exploit population movement, encampment and settlement, in order to further strategic and other interests.

McDowell et al. (2018a,b,c) have shown that the direct engagement in displacement and the onward refugee journey by extremist networks creates opportunities to keep a conflict 'alive' among overseas populations. It enables groups to move fighters, recruit among disaffected migrants who are seeking solutions for themselves and their wider families, and importantly, engagement provides a means to raise funds through different forms of smuggling or trafficking and other criminal endeavours. The exploitation of asylum migration and settlement includes the building of networks and dependent relationships with the displaced that may at some later point be 'mobilised' for benign (building a positive sense of community) or malign purposes. Extremist networks, are culturally successful in casting displacement and refugee movements as both humanitarian and political crises that in themselves are framed as outcomes and evidence of western crimes, and therefore an exploitable source of grievance.

Refugee diaspora politics through the displacement cycle – in initial flight, periods in camps, onward movement to countries of asylum and during the settlement and integration phase – plays a critical role in extremism and the process of radicalisation and recruitment. As discussed above, the literature on diaspora politics has tended to employ simplified and limiting framings of diasporas as either violence-prone, 'peace-wrecking actors' or as 'peace-makers' and remittance generating post-conflict rebuilders. Here it is argued that neither of these models are particularly helpful in understanding how diaspora politics, against the backdrop of conflict and extremism when the majority of the members of the diaspora are refugees or asylum seekers, can evolve and shape diaspora political activism. Rather, it is necessary, as Sheffer (2003:45) has argued to identify 'political projects' pursued by transnational actors within diasporas, and the focus on the 'practice' of diasporas and the forms of action that seek to mobilise energies and appeal to loyalties is central to an understanding of the role of diasporas in political mobilisation. Refugee diaspora politics, the research has shown, where the aim is to build support and active engagement in a conflict at home can effectively appeal to nationalist longings, political and religious grievances and the desire to contribute to a cause among those who are removed and geographically distanced from the immediate consequences of conflict. As we can see in the case of overseas Tamil communities, the 'exile-like' condition of refugees in a diaspora, a sense of victimhood coupled with feelings of social injustice elevates support for radical agendas.

The research (McDowell *et al.* 2018b) has found that between the outbreak of the conflict in Sri Lanka in 1983 and the defeat of the LTTE in 2009, the LTTE established an international network of supporting organisations in those countries, such as the UK, Canada, France, Switzerland and Norway, where large populations of Tamil asylum seekers became established eventually securing citizenship. National, regional and locally based organisations and committees were linked to the LTTE's Central Committee in Jaffna via its International Secretariat and structures that included the World Tamil Coordinating Committee (WTCC), the International Federation of Tamils (IFT) and the United Tamil Organisation (UTO). The transnational network coordinated the flow of information and propaganda, organised events and rallies ensuring attendance, created commercial interests through People's Shops and newspapers, and oversaw the collection of financial 'donations' given either voluntarily or involuntarily which were vital to the continuation of the 'struggle' for an independent Tamil homeland.

The LTTE realised soon after the outbreak of the conflict the potential of refugee flight and asylum seeking for the furtherance of their cause. The organisation used the asylum route out of Sri Lanka to pension off fighters who could no longer serve on the front line, it sent abroad political and military figures to establish overseas networks, placing them in key capital cities, and it financed for some the asylum journey. In countries of settlement, the LTTE provided a support network for recently arrived asylum seekers, assisting in asylum claims, housing and finding employment thus building dependent relationships with Tamils abroad that readily translated in to a strong support base that was able to neutralise groups who opposed the Tigers methods towards securing Eelam. The strategy played successfully on overseas Tamils deep concerns for relatives and friends who remained behind in Sri Lanka; in particular the sense of guilt about their safety in the west having escaped the island. The LTTE understood that many overseas Tamils navigating the asylum process and struggling to become established in their new countries needed the kind of social support that the LTTE was able to provide.

There is evidence that international Jihadist and Salafi groups are deploying similar methods to those deployed by the LTTE in the 1980s and 1990s aimed at extending their support base in Europe and to aid recruitment among refugees in transit and in countries of settlement (Clifford and Hughes, 2018). Recent intelligence backed reports from the German Government (Federal Ministry of the Interior, 2018; see also Neumann, 2017:25–28), for example, argue that asylum and refugee movements to the west from the Middle East in 2015 and 2016 covertly included individuals who were members of jihadist groups, and others who were subsequently drawn into extremist networks by recruiters en route or in settlement (the so called *radicalised refugees*). Evidence presented suggests that international Jihadist and Salafist groups recruited among refugees in Lebanon, Jordan and Turkey exploiting the desperation (and destitution) among families seeking a solution beyond the camps or their very poor living conditions outside of camps in Lebanon. Islamic State (IS) and other groups were engaged in the radicalisation of refugees and, it is argued, concealed fighters among refugees to enter European states, and exerted control over individuals once in asylum centres in Europe. Research by McDowell among Syrian refugees in the UK conducted over the same period identified the conditions that create a heightened susceptibility to recruitment and radicalisation. It found that high risk groups for recruitment, among those on the move, were young men (aged 16–30 years) but in particular young people and teenagers who either travelled alone or with relatives. The risk of recruitment, or of simply being drawn to extremist narratives, increased where those accompanying young migrants were themselves previously engaged in extremist politics.

The research found also that, in both Third Country Resettlement Programmes and spontaneous asylum movements, engagement in extremist politics is more likely where there are *opportunities to engage*. Opportunities include the presence of an active, organised and well-resourced diaspora led by strong charismatic and influential leaders. Where diaspora agents operate with few restrictions on their political activities, and are adept at using communications technologies, their ability to mobilise extremist contacts is considerably enhanced. Radicalisation leading to active engagement in extremist politics and preparedness to use violence is more likely where there are low levels of integration and a weak sense of loyalty to and civic membership in their country of asylum settlement. Exclusion, or a perception of exclusion, from the host society can be exacerbated by a poor command of the national language, social marginalisation and an inability to make friends, particularly among the opposite sex in the case of teenage boys, and the lack of qualifications or skills and therefore employment opportunities.

Isolation and disaffection among refugee and asylum-seeking populations may lead individuals to choose exclusive membership of closed groups of co-nationals or co-religionists. Those for whom the legal process is exhausted and asylum claims have been unsuccessful, with the likelihood of removal to their country of origin, going underground and evading the state is a rational option. In such cases, the risks of criminalisation are high where the interests of radical politics and criminal gangs are shared. Asylum seeking in western countries, characterised by a long drawn out legal process, involving restrictions on employment, and with uncertain outcomes engendering mistrust in state officials can create the conditions for a 'drift in to extremism'. The conditions of asylum seekers, poor housing, unemployed or being illegally employed, a breadline existence, and frustrations that arise from the failure to realise the migration dream, shift individuals to the margins of society where extremists provide simple answers to complex problems and offer a sense of belonging and purpose.

3.1 *Migration Histories and Engagement in Extremist Politics*

It is argued here, therefore, that the migration history and experience, and the life stage at which someone migrates, as well as their asylum seeking and integration experiences can make a difference to their engagement in extremist politics; and among asylum seekers and refugees the triggers or risks of pre-arrival-radicalisation, post-arrival-radicalisation, criminality and isolation are amplified. Whilst the evidence derived through media and court reports is quite sparse, it does suggest that the extremist population in the UK includes individuals who apparently integrated well into mainstream society but in to insular groups (co-ethnic/co-religion, closed to outsiders), but also people who never seemed to settle anywhere (geographically, through employment, or via friendship circles).

The main finding of the author's research are that:

- First, for a small minority of migrants who seek asylum, the life stage at which someone migrates is likely to be a factor in their future political development. Recent convictions for terrorist offences in Europe suggest that the extremist population includes people who migrated as children, with their families, and people who migrated as teenagers or young adults – often alone. This raises important questions about the asylum and migration experience for young people, their specific vulnerabilities and exposure to extremist narratives and controlling influences in the country of origin as well as in countries of asylum.
- Second, the extremist population includes people whose relatives (either with them or 'back home') were involved in violent or nonviolent politics; some were or may have been extremists when they arrived.
- Third, a particularly under-researched topic of asylum integration relates to the experiences of asylum seekers whose applications have been turned down but who remain in their country of asylum evading the attention of the authorities, or who are unreturnable. A minority in this population will likely become part of criminal groups and gang membership that may later evolve into or engage in activities that intersect with extremist networks.

The research has therefore identified radicalisation risks associated with the settlement and integration of refugees and asylum seekers in a country of final asylum. However, in the absence of systematic longitudinal studies, the evidence base on the integration trajectories of asylum seekers and resettled refugees in Western countries is weak. The conceptual and theoretical literature on refugee integration is limited to models that fail to address the risks of integration failure or consider the significance of political engagement as a factor in integration. Further research is required in to the process of asylum seeking and the struggles of settlement, with a focus on forms of integration through which emerge sub-cultures of mainly young men who are likely to be disaffected with the state and their host society. Sub-cultures are likely to be marked, as previously observed, by the frequent isolation of individuals, or by the seeking of membership of closed identity groups. The following section considers the implications of these findings for counter terrorism and radicalisation prevention with a focus on the UK.

4 Policy and Operational Challenges

In 2017, there were five major terrorist attacks in the UK in which 35 people died (UK Parliament, 2018). The first attack came on the 22 March, when Khalid Masood drove a car over Westminster Bridge, mounted the pavement and hit pedestrians walking on the bridge. He then entered the grounds of the Palace of Westminster and fatally stabbed a police officer. Five individuals were killed in the attack with many more seriously injured. The second attack took place in the northwest of England on the 22 May, when Salman Abedi detonated an improvised explosive device (IED) in the foyer of Manchester Arena. Twenty-two people were killed, including a number of children and teenagers. Over 100 others were injured. On the 3 June, Khuram Butt, Rachid Redouane and Youssef Zaghba used a van to run over pedestrians on London Bridge, before continuing their attack on foot. Eight people were killed in the attack with many more injured. Later that month, Darren Osborne drove a vehicle into a group of people gathered near an Islamic Centre in Finsbury Park, north London. One person was killed and ten others sustained serious injuries. Lastly, on the 15 September, Ahmed Hassan left an Improvised Explosive Device (IED) on a District line commuter train. The device partially exploded after the train arrived at Parsons Green station. Twenty-three people sustained burn injuries as a result of the partial explosion whilst 28 people suffered crush injuries as crowds surged to leave the train.

Two official reports (Anderson, 2017; UK Parliament, 2018) examined the circumstances of the attacks, reviewed the gathering and handling of intelligence, and provided information on the profiles of the attackers.

The Anderson (2017) Operational Improvement Review sought to draw lessons from nine internal reviews undertaken by the UK domestic intelligence agency, MI5, and Counter Terrorism Police of their responses to the first four of the above attacks (the report was concluded before the Parsons Green attack in September 2017). The Review outlined the migration and refugee histories of the attackers which were described as 'lone actors' or belonging to 'small groups'. The following details were included. Abedi, was born in Libya and came to the UK with his parents who sought and were granted refugee status, subsequently, settling in Manchester where a small Libyan community had recently been established. Abedi's brother was in detention in Libya and subject to an extradition request, Abedi was known to MI5 in the UK. Butt, was born in Pakistan and came to the UK as child asylum seeker with his family, he was granted leave to remain in 2005 and received citizenship in 2010, he was known to MI5 and previously investigated. Redouane, sought asylum in the UK under the false identity of a Libyan national, his asylum request was refused and his appeal rights exhausted. Redouane was reported as an absconder, detained in 2011 but due to the ongoing conflict was released and could not be returned to Libya. Zagbha, had Moroccan and Italian dual citizenship.

The UK Parliament's Intelligence and Security Committee of Parliament Report (2018) examined the circumstances surrounding the Parsons Green attack in September 2017 and described Ahmed Hassan, at the time of the attack, as an 18 year old Iraqi asylum seeker who entered the UK at the age of 15. The teenager arrived in Britain as an 'orphan refugee', previously travelling across Europe and spending time in the so-called 'Jungle' camp at Calais. As an unaccompanied child he was allowed entry to the UK and after being processed through a migrant centre in Kent, was found a home with a foster family in Sunbury on Thames, west of London.

While migration histories, including asylum applications and international connections were included in the descriptions, neither report sought to analyse the significance of these histories or the commonalities between their profiles and the profiles of other attackers elsewhere in the UK and Europe during this period (see McDowell, 2018c, Annex 1).

4.1 *UK Counter Terrorist Strategy*

Informed by the events of 2017, and a number of reviews and investigations in to the circumstances surrounding those attacks, the UK Government revised its national counter terrorism strategy releasing CONTEST in June 2018. The strategy includes a broad analysis of the process of radicalisation with a focus on 'local threats' in 'priority areas' although these areas and specific threats are not disclosed. The strategy reflects much of the terrorism studies literature in arguing that there is no single socio-demographic of a terrorist in the UK and no single pathway or 'conveyor belt' leading to involvement in terrorism. It states that extremists are likely to come from a broad range of backgrounds, becoming involved in different ways for different reasons, and in most cases, it is argued, several factors converge to create the conditions under which radicalisation can occur. The factors, are described as *background* factors, *personal circumstances* that make individuals vulnerable to radicalisation, *initial influences, ideas or experiences* that influence an individual towards supporting a terrorist movement, and a *receptiveness* to an extreme ideology. Beyond broad headings, the strategy does not provide detail on these factors or how they interact.

The strategy includes brief references to the international context explaining that conflict affected and fragile states such as Afghanistan, Libya, Somalia, Syria and Yemen present permissive environments that terrorist groups exploit. It further argues that in these environments terrorists can gain access to weapons and resources, control territory in which they recruit from and oppress local populations, establish training camps and media centres from where they plan for attacks.

4.2 *Prevent and Channel*

The Prevent programme forms an important part of the UK Government's CONTEST and aims to 'safeguard (against) people becoming terrorists or supporting terrorism' whether 'inspired by Islamist or right wing ideologies' (Home Office, 2018b). The programme relies on members of the public, or those working with the public, reporting to the police or local authorities an individual they feel may be susceptible to radicalisation. A large number of referrals are typically made on the basis of observed behaviour including concerning conversations. Each year around one-third of referrals come through the police (although a majority of these are likely to be a result of reports from the public made to the police), one-third through educational institutions, and the remainder from a variety of sources. In 2017/2018, according to the Home Office (2018a), 7,318 individuals were referred, of these 7 percent of the cases were serious enough to be 'escalated' because of CT concerns. Referrals are screened by the police to check that the individual is not already part of, or should be part of, a terrorism investigation. In the largest number of cases (around three quarters of all referrals in 2017/2018), the outcome is that the case is found to not warrant further action, or that the person's vulnerability may be assessed as not linked to radicalisation. In such cases, an onward referral may be made for relevant health, mental health, educational or social support, and the process involves no criminal sanctions or police records.

In those cases, however, where it is deemed that the individual is at risk of radicalisation and would benefit from support to prevent them being drawn in to violent action, the case is referred to the Channel programme which assesses the degree of vulnerability and puts in place a support package in liaison with a range of agencies. Twenty-two per cent of referrals in 2017/2018 were handled through the Channel programme, participation in which is 'voluntary and confidential', and the types of support available include what is termed 'ideological mentoring' as well as support for 'educational, vocational, mental health, and other vulnerabilities'. A Channel panel monitors the progress of an individual in receipt of Channel support, and individuals leave the programme when they are deemed to have no 'further terrorism-related concerns'. Individuals who leave but are deemed still to present a risk of terrorism may be 'managed by the police'.

4.3 *CT Strategy: Conceptual and Operational Gaps*

We have seen that both the Anderson Review (2017) and the UK Parliament's (2018) investigation in to the handling of intelligence considered it relevant to include descriptions of the migration and asylum seeking histories of the perpetrators involved in the 2017 attacks in London and Manchester. However, while the CONTEST strategy identifies specific risk categories, namely prisoners, returning foreign fighters, and undefined 'hard to reach groups', the risks identified in this chapter – and discussed by other European governments in their security reports – which are linked to the internationalisation of conflict, forced migration, integration failure and diaspora politics, are not examined. The Strategy acknowledges that, on the one hand, conflicts overseas provide opportunities for terrorists and it identifies a need for anti-poverty programmes to address the drivers of terrorism in countries such as Nigeria or Somalia, and, on the other, that in the UK 'a successful integration strategy is important to CT'. However, the strategy fails analytically to connect the international and the domestic domains. It presents a fractured picture of geographically discrete problems and solutions – conflict and terrorism in Syria, poverty and terrorism in Nigeria, integration and terrorism in the UK – but overlooks that these phenomena are dynamically connected through those dimensions of the internationalisation of conflict that together create a space for terrorists to recruit and act including in the development of plots, and in which vulnerabilities to radicalisation arise. A displacement background or asylum experience are not included in the list of factors CONTEST identifies that may be relevant to the risk of radicalisation, and the strategy does not set out how the UK's international development, humanitarian and refugee strategies feed into the Prevent, Pursue and Protect activities.

The Prevent and Channel programmes are the most visible public-facing activities emerging out of CONTEST. They are voluntary for participants and, even though there is a statutory obligation for public bodies to show awareness of radicalisation risks, the programmes rely on the engagement of those working in the public service, such as in education, social and health care, and relies also on the cooperation of the public. The UK police, following criticism that Prevent predominantly targets Muslim communities, has sought to gain the trust and confidence of all communities, in order to encourage engagement with the programme. To this end, public information campaigns emphasise the underpinning theory of Prevent that radicalisation is an ideological process, which can be identified and stopped in its tracks, thus, empowering local communities to work with the full range of agencies to provide appropriate support that changes the direction of people's lives away from extremism.

As Dudenhoefer (2017) notes, 'the Prevent strategy is inextricably tied to the notion of vulnerability'. There is a strong presumption within Prevent, and this reflects much of the campaigning literature and imagery produced by refugee support groups, UN agencies and indeed parts of the refugee studies literature, that asylum-seekers and refugees are *a priori* vulnerable. CT policing understands this particular form of vulnerability as one that increases a susceptibility to radicalisation when other conditions are in place. The author has written elsewhere (McDowell, 2013) that it is misguided to ascribe vulnerability to an entire population of people in a blanket way simply on the basis of their legal status as asylum seekers, or based on presumptions about their prior experiences. By doing so, as Dudenhoefer notes, risks stripping people of their agency, portraying them as passive subjects, and may lead to a misunderstanding of the complexities of forced migration and the role of agency, control and choice, as well as to inappropriate or ineffective policy interventions.

The Prevent focus on safeguarding and vulnerability, however, has the positive impact of focusing attention on the conditions of forced displacement, refugee movements, criminality and the challenges of integration that may create an enabling environment for radicalisation to take place. As the UK Parliament's investigation found, in the case of the Parson's Green attack, Ahmed Hassan's vulnerability – as an unaccompanied child asylum seeker from Iraq, who had spent time in camps in the Middle East and many months traveling across Europe with the aim of entering the UK – was identified, and it became the basis of his Prevent referral and a Channel support programme which included 'diversionary activities'. Hassan disclosed in his asylum interview that he had been approached, recruited and trained by Da'esh, however, the Parliamentary Committee investigation found that information was not shared between different parts of the system even within the same government department, and the significance of intelligence supplied did not trigger an investigation. The findings suggest that a safeguarding approach, where the focus is on the individual rather than the context, may preclude attention to security threats that are directly linked to traumatising events, and public safety may not be adequately protected. It further suggests that where extremist groups targeting these same types of people in their efforts to radicalize and use those persons for their terrorist cause, there is a need to develop more proactive programs to protect those vulnerable persons from being recruited and radicalized.

5 Conclusion

This final section of the chapter focuses mainly on gaps in the current knowledge on the risks of radicalisation that leads to terrorism arising out of the internationalisation conflict. The research presented identifies policy and strategic opportunities relating to the drivers and enablers of the terrorism threat in the context of the internationalisation of conflict. In relation to population displacement, encampment and the asylum journey, further research is required to understand the processes through which recruiters and political agents interact with the displaced at different points in the refugee cycle including in countries of first asylum. It is necessary to investigate how extremist attitudes take root and develop in refugee settings (in and out of camps, and in response to the politicisation of humanitarian crises), and to understand the conditions in which they take root (fear and uncertainty, indebtedness, lack of opportunity, unemployment, poor housing conditions, and the lack of legal routes to safety). Research would need to consider the economics of refugee flight, for example, the funding of passage across borders and the securing of travel documents, and to what extent extremist actors are involved in such complex transactions, and in what ways the involvement of organised crime intersects with mobilisation and radicalisation in such transactions?

Staying in touch is vital for people on the move, and access to information and networks is indispensable when identifying options to cross borders and find a place of safety. Connection to mobile networks and the internet are essential but communication takes place in the same spaces where terrorist propaganda and narratives flourish, and in situations where resilience against recruitment is arguably weakest. Research should consider opportunities for preventing such dissemination, or for increasing the resilience of those on the move to radical messages. Such interventions could be part of wider international Prevent type strategies that work with those voluntary, UN and national organisations that assist people on the move, increasing their awareness of the risks of radicalisation. The research that informs this chapter agrees with a recent study which concludes that 'extremist groups … represent transnational movements, and that the role of diaspora networks, migration, and digital connectivity can shape networks of Jihadi recruitment' (Clifford and Hughes, 2018). The organisational structure of extremist networks and their communications, command and recruitment practices, however, are poorly understood, and further research is required to grasp the complexity of these networks.

In relation to asylum and refugee settlement and integration there is a need to think about how integration failure can play out in relation to counter extremism, and to ensure that authorities understand and are alive to signs of failure, particularly among higher risk groups? This requires change in official thinking on refugee and asylum integration, and signals a need for longitudinal studies of the integration trajectories of asylum seekers and refugees in Europe drawing on all available data. It requires also the development of indicators that help build new models of integration that include political engagement and risks of failure. The understanding of integration cannot be geographically bound to a single country. Economic relations and networks that extend across Europe, and elsewhere, among diaspora communities and in the country of conflict are at the heart of refugees' livelihood strategies.

In relation to CT policies the research presented in this chapter has questioned whether current strategies are sufficiently proactive in relation to the situation of asylum seekers and refugees which can often be one of precariousness, with risks of integration failure that have security implications. It is noted that strategies do not sufficiently, analytically or conceptually, link up the international and local context when analysing the sources of threats, and operationally border and entry practices, including asylum interviews, are isolated from the assessment of vulnerability risk.

Bibliography

Abdi, Cawo. 2015. "Disclaimed or Reclaimed? Muslim Refugee Youth and Belonging in the Age of Hyperbolisation." *Journal of Intercultural Studies* 36 (5): 564–578.

Agamben, Giorgio. 1998. *Homo Sacer: Sovereign Power and Bare Life*. Stanford: Stanford University Press.

Al-Ali, Nadje, Richard Black, and Khalid Koser. 2001. "Refugees and transnationalism: The experience of Bosnians and Eritreans in Europe." *Journal of Ethnic and Migration Studies* 27 (4): 615–634.

Anderson, David. 2017. "Attacks in London and Manchester, March-June 2017: Independent Assessment of MI5 and Police Internal Reviews." London.

Baser, Baher and Ashok Swain. 2008. "Diasporas as Peacemakers: third party mediation in homeland conflicts." *International Journal on World Peace* 25 (3): 7–28.

Betts, Alexander and Will Jones. 2016. *Mobilising the diaspora: how refugees challenge authoritarianism*. Cambridge: Cambridge University Press.

Borum, Randy. 2011. "Radicalization into Violent Extremism I: A Review of Social Science Theories." *Journal of Strategic Security. Perspectives on Radicalization and Involvement in Terrorism* 4 (4): 7–36.

Borum, Randy. 2003. "Understanding the Terrorist Mind-Set." *FBI Law Enforcement Bulletin* 72 (7): 7–10.

Brinkerhoff, Jennifer M. 2008. "Diaspora Identity and the Potential for Violence: Toward an Identity-Mobilization Framework." *Identity* 8 (1): 67–88.

Brun, Catherine and Nicholas Van Hear. 2012. "Between the local and the diasporic: the shifting centre of gravity in war-torn Sri Lanka's transnational politics." *Contemporary South Asia* 20 (1): 61–75.

Byman, Daniel, Peter Chalk, Bruce Hoffman, William Rosenau, and David Brannan. 2001. *Trends in Outside Support for Insurgent Movements.* RAND.

Chaudhary, Ali R. and Luis E. Guarnizo. 2016. "Pakistani immigrant organisational spaces in Toronto and New York City." *Journal of Ethnic and Migration Studies* 42 (6): 1013–1035.

Clifford, Bennett and Seamus Hughes. 2018. "United States v. Aws Mohammed Younis al-Jayab: A Case Study on Transnational Prosecutions of Jihadi Foreign Fighter Networks." *CTC Sentinel,* December 2018, 11 (11). https://ctc.usma.edu/united-states-v-aws-mohammed-younis-al-jayab-case-study-transnational-prosecutions-jihadi-foreign-fighter-networks/.

Cochrane, Feargal, Bahar Baser, and Ashok Swain. 2009. "Home Thoughts from Abroad: Diasporas and Peace-Building in Northern Ireland and Sri Lanka." *Studies in Conflict & Terrorism* 32 (8): 681–704.

Collier, Paul. 2000. *Economic causes of civil conflict and their implications for policy.* Washington DC: World Bank.

Collier, Paul and Anke Hoeffler. 2004. "Greed and grievance in civil war." *Oxford Economic Papers* 56 (4): 563–595.

Dawson, Lorne L. 2017. *Sketch of a Social Ecology Model for Explaining Homegrown Terrorist Radicalisation.* ICCT Research Note. The Hague: International Centre for Counter-Terrorism.

de Haas, Hein. 2010. "Migration and Development: A Theoretical Perspective." *International Migration Review* 44 (1): 227–264.

Demmers, Jolle. 2007. "New Wars and Diasporas: Suggestions for Research and Policy." *Peace Conflict & Development: An Interdisciplinary Journal* 11: 1–26. https://www.bradford.ac.uk/social-sciences/peace-conflict-and-development/.

Dudenhoefer, Anne-Lynn. 2017. "Resisting Radicalisation: A Critical Analysis of the UK Prevent Duty." *Journal for De-radicalisation* 14 (Spring 2018). Centre for Criminology, University of Oxford.

Accessed on 16 December, 2018 at: https://www.law.ox.ac.uk/centres-institutes/centre-criminology/blog/2017/09/resisting-radicalisation-critical-analysis-uk.

Federal Ministry of the Interior. 2018. *Constitutional Protection Report 2017,* July 20, Berlin, Germany.

Hall, Jonathan and Ashok Swain. 2007. "Catapulting Conflicts of Propelling Peace: Diasporas and Civil Wars." In *Globalization and Challenges to Building Peace,* edited by Ashok Swain, Ramses Amer, and Joakim Ojendal, 107–120. Cambridge: Cambridge University Press.

Hess, Monica and Benedikt Korf. 2014. "Tamil diaspora and the political spaces of second-generation activism in Switzerland." *Global Networks* 14 (4): 419–437.

Kaldor, Mary. 1999. *New and Old Wars: Organized violence in a Global Era*. Cambridge: Polity Press.

Klausen, Jytte, Selene Campion, Nathan Needle, Giang Nguyen, and Rosanne Libretti. 2016. "Toward a Behavioural Model of 'Homegrown' Radicalization Trajectories." *Studies in Conflict & Terrorism* 39 (1): 67–83.

Koinova, Maria. 2016. "Sustained vs episodic mobilization among conflict-generated diasporas." *International Political Science Review* 37 (4): 500–516.

Koinova, Maria. 2011. "Diasporas and secessionist conflicts: the mobilization of the Armenian, Albanian and Chechen diasporas." *Ethnic and Racial Studies* 34 (2): 333–356.

Koinova, Maria. 2010. "Diasporas and international politics: Utilising the universalistic creed of liberalism for particularistic and nationalist purposes." In *Diaspora and transnationalism: concepts, theories and methods*, edited by Rainer Bauböck, and Thomas Faist, Chapter 8. Imiscoe Research. Amsterdam: Amsterdam University Press.

Koser, Khalid and Amy Cunningham. 2017. "Migration, Violent Extremism and Social Exclusion, in International Organisation for Migration." *World Migration Report 2018*. Geneva: IOM.

Lemon, Edward and John Heathershaw. 2017. "How can we explain radicalisation among Central Asia's migrants?" *Open Democracy*. https://www.opendemocracy.net/od-russia/edward-lemon-john-heathershaw/can-we-explain-radicalisation-among-central-asia-s-migrants (Accessed 06/12/2017).

Martin-Rayo, Francisco. 2011. *Countering radicalization in refugee camps: How education can help defeat AQAP*. Working paper. Cambridge, MA: The Dubai Initiative, Belfer Center for Science and International Affairs, Harvard Kennedy School.

McAdam, Doug, John D. McCarthy, and Mayer N Zald. 1996. *Comparative perspectives of social movements*. Cambridge: Cambridge University Press.

McDowell, Christopher, Valentina Aronica, Gemma Collantes-Celador, and Natasha De Silva. 2018a. "Thematic Report One, Understanding Transnational Diaspora Politics: A Conceptual Discussion." CREST, University of Lancaster https://crestresearch.ac.uk/resources/diaspora-thematic-report-one/.

McDowell, Christopher, Valentina Aronica, Gemma Collantes-Celador, and Natasha De Silva. 2018b. "Thematic Report Two, Forced Migration and the Transnational Politics of Refugees." CREST, University of Lancaster https://crestresearch.ac.uk/resources/diaspora-thematic-report-two/.

McDowell, Christopher, Valentina Aronica, Gemma Collantes-Celador, and Natasha De Silva. 2018c. "Thematic Report Three, Asylum and Security." CREST, University of Lancaster https://crestresearch.ac.uk/resources/diaspora-thematic-report-three/.

McDowell, Christopher. 2017. "Sri Lanka: Diaspora Politics and the End of Violence." *CREST Security Review* Issue 4, After Islamic State. University of Lancaster.

McDowell, Christopher. 2013. "Researching Displacement(s)." In *Researching Refugees and Asylum Seekers: Ethical Considerations,* edited by Block, Karen, Elisha Riggs, and Nick Haslam. Australian Academic Press, Melbourne.

McDowell, Christopher. 1996. *A Tamil Asylum Diaspora: Sri Lankan Migration, Politics and Change in Switzerland* Oxford: Berghahn Books, Series on Forced Migration.

Milton, Daniel, Megan Spencer, and Michael Findley. 2013. "Radicalism of the Hopeless: Refugee Flows and Transnational Terrorism." *International Interactions* 39 (5): 621–645.

Moghaddam, Fathali. 2005. "The Staircase to Terrorism. A Psychological Exploration." *American Psychologist* 60 (2):161–169.

Neumann, Peter, R. 2017. 'Countering Violent Extremism and Radicalisation that Lead to Terrorism: Ideas, Recommendations, and Good Practices from the OSCE Region'. OSCE. September.

Østergaard-Nielsen, Eva. 2006. *Diaspora and Conflict Resolution – Part of the Problem or Part of the Solution?* Danish Institute for International Studies Brief, March.

Østergaard-Nielsen, Eva. 2001. "The Politics of Migrants' Transnational Political Practices." WPTC-01-22. Paper presented to conference on Transnational Migration, Comparative Perspectives at Princeton University, 30 June – 1 July 2001.

Rahimi, Sadeq and Raissa Graumans. 2015. "Reconsidering the Relationship Between Integration and Radicalization." *Journal for Deradicalization* 5: 28–62.

Roth, Amanda. 2015. "The role of diasporas in conflict." *Journal of International Affairs* 68 (2): 289–301.

Rygiel, Kim. 2011. "Bordering solidarities: Migrant activism and the politics of movement and camps at Calais." *Citizenship Studies* 15 (1): 1 19.

Sheffer, Gabriel. 2003. *Diaspora Politics: At Home Abroad.* Cambridge: Cambridge University Press.

Silber, Mitchell D. and Arvin Bhatt. 2007. *Radicalization in the West: The Homegrown Threat.* New York: The New York City Police Department, Intelligence Division.

Sökefeld, Martin. 2006. "Mobilizing in transnational space: a social movement approach to the formation of diaspora." *Global Networks* 6 (3): 265–284.

Sude, Barbara, David Stebbins, and Sarah Weilant. 2015. *Lessening the Risk of Refugee Radicalization.* Perspectives Series. Santa Monica, CA: RAND Corporation.

Thompson, Sara K. and Sandra M. Bucerius. 2017. "Transnational radicalization, diaspora groups, and within-group sentiment pools: Young Tamil and Somali Canadians on the LTTE and al Shabaab." *Terrorism and Political Violence,* Online Version. https://www.tandfonline.com/doi/abs/10.1080/09546553.2016.1264938.

United Kingdom Home Office (2018a), 'UK Government Individuals referred to and supported through the Prevent Programme', April 2017 to March 2018, Statistical bulletin 31/18, 13 December, London. https://www.gov.uk/government/statistics/

individuals-referred-to-and-supported-through-the-prevent-programme-april-2016-to-march-2017.

United Kingdom Home Office (2018b) CONTEST: The United Kingdom's Strategy for Countering Terrorism, June 2018, London https://www.gov.uk/government/publications/counter-terrorism-strategy-contest-2018.

United Kingdom Parliament (2018) The 2017 Attacks: What needs to change? Intelligence and Security Committee of Parliament, HC 1694, London https://drive.google.com/file/d/0B-DemBSSM0_tb2JDcFhORnZ1d0NrbUhzT1Q5QzU5dS1McGU0/view.

UNHCR (2017) 'Towards Integration: Evaluation of the Syrian Vulnerable Persons Resettlement (VPR) Programme', UNHCR, London, November.

Van Hear, Nicholas. 2014. "Refugees, Diasporas, and Transnationalism." In *The Oxford Handbook of Refugee & Forced Migration Studies, edited by* Elena Fiddian-Qasmiyeh, Gil Loescher, Katy Long, and Nando Sigona. Oxford: Oxford University Press.

Vimalarajah, Luxshi and Rudhramoorthy Cheran. (2010) *Empowering Diasporas: The Dynamics of Post-war Transnational Tamil Politics*. Berghof Occasional Paper No 31.

Wahlbeck, Östen. 2002. "The concept of diaspora as an analytical tool in the study of refugee communities." *Journal of Ethnic and Migration Studies* 28 (2): 221–238.

Werbner, Pnina. 2002. "The place which is diaspora: Citizenship, religion and gender in the making of chaordic transnationalism." *Journal of Ethnic and Migration Studies* 28 (1): 119–133.

Yusoufzai, Khouwaga and Franziska Emmerling. 2017. "How identity crisis, relative deprivation, personal characteristics, and empathy contribute to the engagement of Western individuals in Islamist terrorist behaviour." *Journal of Terrorism Research* 8 (1): 68–80.

PART 2

International and Transnational Perspectives on the Crime of Terrorism and Asylum

CHAPTER 5

Complicity in Exclusion for Terrorist Crimes

Joseph Rikhof[1]

1 Introduction

This chapter will discuss the parameters of complicity in exclusion for terrorist crimes. Although a person seeking asylum is entitled to protection under this treaty if he or she has "a well-founded fear of being persecuted for reasons of race, religion, nationality, membership of a particular social group or political opinion,"[2] article 1F sets an exception to this rule by excluding a person if:

(a) he has committed a crime against peace, a war crime, or a crime against humanity, as defined in the international instruments drawn up to make provision in respect of such crimes;
(b) he has committed a serious non-political crime outside the country of refuge prior to his admission to that country as a refugee;
(c) he has been guilty of acts contrary to the purposes and principles of the United Nations.

While it is theoretically possible to pursue persons involved in terrorism under all the headings of the exclusion ground,[3] the practice of states has been to utilize only exclusion grounds (b) and (c) for this purpose.[4] Unlike exclusion ground 1F(a), where the vast majority of exclusion cases are based on complicity, the situation is not so clear cut for 1F(b) and 1F(c) where situations leading to exclusion present a spectrum from personal involvement to complicity in serious crimes, including terrorist activities.

1 Joseph Rikhof is an adjunct professor at the Faculty of Common Law at the University of Ottawa.

2 Refugee Convention, 1951, Art. 1A (2).

3 Certain aspects of underlying offences contained in the draft Comprehensive Convention on International Terrorism as well in the domestic legislation of a number of countries, such as causing death, bodily harm and to property could also be underlying crimes for war crimes or crimes against humanity, provides that the overarching elements for these international crimes are also met, see Joseph Rikhof, *The Criminal Refugee: The Treatment of Asylum Seekers with a Criminal Background in International and Domestic Law* (2012), pages 299 and 303–305.

4 Idem, pages 312, 315–317, 322–323, 328, 330, 332, 335–336, 337–338, 342–343, 352–353, 357–358 and 360–365 (hereinafter Rikhof, *The Criminal Refugee*).

© KONINKLIJKE BRILL NV, LEIDEN, 2020 | DOI:10.1163/9789004295995_007

While as a result of this mix of direct and indirect involvement in terrorist exclusion cases there has been some jurisprudence setting out the parameters of complicity by providing interpretations of the notions of "committed," in 1F(b), and "guilty," in 1F(c), the approach utilized could benefit from further analysis and exploration.

The interplay between articles 1F(a) and 1F(b), regarding extended liability, poses a conceptual dilemma. On one hand, the same word "committed" is used in both provisions, but, on the other hand, exclusion under article 1F(a) includes a specific reference to international instruments (meaning international criminal law or ICL), which is not the case for 1F(b). Since article 1F(b) fulfills a different role than 1F(a), in that it is primarily concerned with individual crimes for which traditional forms of extended liability were envisaged, caution should be exercised in applying forms of liability developed in article 1F(a). Incidentally, while a different word has been used in 1F(c), namely, guilty, virtually the same analysis to find indirect responsibility as used for 1F(a) is also employed for this exclusion provision without further explanation. At times, this is implicit, as in Belgium, where the test of "substantially contributing" is used[5] or where a number of factors are used, as in France[6] while in other countries, such as Canada,[7] this connection is made explicit. Only in the UK is this specific terminology explained by saying that "guilty" does not incorporate a criminal standard but merely means "responsible for."[8]

The contours of complicity for article 1F(b) have been addressed specifically, in general terms, in Australia, Belgium, Canada, Germany, The Netherlands, New Zealand, the UK, and the US. In some instances, it was stated that the same complicity principles that apply to article 1F(a) for the international crimes of genocide, war crimes, and crimes against humanity should also be used for article 1F(b). Germany has employed the words "substantial contribution" to describe the level of involvement required for article 1F(b) activities. In one case, a tribunal in France relied on a number of factors, such as duration and the intensity of the association with a nefarious group, and the manner of disassociation from it, to determine complicity. In Australia, peripheral support functions by crews of ships involved in people smuggling were found not to amount to complicity. An association with a hybrid organization with both a peaceful and a militant faction was considered enough to warrant exclusion

5 See Rikhof, *The Criminal* Refugee, page 353.
6 Idem, page 360–361.
7 Idem, page 358.
8 Idem, page 365.

in the Netherlands and the US, even though in both situations the association was with the peaceful element of the organization.[9]

In order to provide for a more analytical approach for 1F(b) and (c), it would be prudent to look at the national jurisprudence at the highest level in respect to 1F(a) to see what methodology was used to arrive at the appropriate test for complicity. While the *result* of that methodology for 1F(a) might not be the same for 1F(b) and 1F(c), as a result of the inherent limitation pointed out above, the *type* of methodology might yield satisfactory results for the complicity analysis of these exclusion grounds. The methodology for 1F(a) was the most apparent in two Supreme Court cases in the UK and Canada.[10]

This chapter will take a similar approach to 1F(b) and 1F(c) as was done for 1F(a) by the two above decisions in that a number of sources will be examined to determine, what are the broadest parameters developed in those sources and, then, provide a view in how far these parameters can be framed into an overarching theory of complicity for the last two exclusion grounds. However, unlike 1F(a), which only allows ICL as a frame of reference as utilized at both the international and domestic level, 1F(b) and (c) do not contain such a limitation so that other sources will need to be surveyed. The sources in question will be transnational criminal law and domestic criminal law[11] but only in so

9 See Joseph Rikhof, "The Interpretation of Exclusion 1F(b) of the 1951 Refugee Convention Internationally and in Canada," in Idil Atak and James C. Simeon (eds), *The Criminalization of Migration* (2018), pages 175–176.

10 R (on the application of JS) (Sri Lanka) (Respondent) *v* Secretary of State for the Home Department (Appellant), [2010] UKSC 15 (hereinafter JS) and *Ezokola v. Canada (Citizenship and Immigration)*, 2013 SCC 40 (hereinafter *Ezokola*). There has also been a decision by another Supreme Court in the area of complicity in 1F(a), namely *The Attorney-General (Minister of Immigration) v Tamil X and the RSAA*, [2010] NZSC 107 but this case is not as illustrative for purposes of this chapter as its analysis is limited to assessing only one type of complicity in ICL, namely joint criminal enterprise or ICL.

11 The provisions with respect to terrorism in the immigration law at the national level will not be discussed for two reasons. The first reason is that the immigration law of domestic jurisdictions in the area of criminality have many permutations thereby making it difficult to discern patterns, which can be used to reach meaningful conclusions. Secondly, the starting point of this chapter is that it intends to give meaning to 1F(b) from a criminal perspective rather than from an immigration perspective as the former is more relevant to the analysis at hand. For a discussion of the domestic immigration laws in five common law countries in the area of criminality, see Joseph Rikhof, "War Criminals Not Welcome; How Common Law Countries Approach the Phenomenon of International Crimes in the Immigration and Refugee Context," 21 *International Journal of Refugee Law* (2009), pages 453–507. However, it is useful to point out that the relationship between 1F(a) and the immigration inadmissibility for membership in a terrorist organization with respect to membership has been discussed in the recent Canadian jurisprudence where it was said that the *Ezokola* rejection of membership as a heading for complicity would only apply to

far as they pertain to terrorism and with respect to the latter two in selected countries.

While it is quite possible that there will be some overlap between the conclusions arrived at by the two Supreme Court decisions above, there might also be some divergence. As well, the vexing issue of membership as a form of complicity will be examined in some detail, as the above two Supreme Court decisions were of the view that membership should not be a heading for liability in 1F(a), a view also shared so far in the context of 1F(b) in some civil law national jurisdictions[12] as well as by the European Court of Justice (ECJ)[13] but not in common law domestic jurisdictions.[14]

2 Transnational Criminal Law – Introduction

Before examining transnational criminal law (TCL) as a source for complicity in terrorism, it is useful first of all to explain what this sub-area of international law represents and what its relationship is to ICL as well as what the status of terrorism is in both of these areas.

There is a conceptual difference between ICL and TCL. The most accepted approach with respect to ICL is that it refers to conduct that is prohibited under international law itself, and it is international law that provides for individual liability. The enforcement of this area of law manifests itself either directly, when international institutions apply international law, or indirectly, when states bring perpetrators before national courts through the application of extended forms of jurisdiction, primarily universal jurisdiction.[15] The

immigration inadmissibility for international crimes (the equivalency of 1F(a) in immigration law) but not to terrorist or criminal organizations as the latter forms of extended liability are the product of domestic legislation rather than the implementation at the national level of an international treaty; see *Kanagendren v. Canada,* 2015 FCA 86, leave to appeal to SCC dismissed, November 19, 2015, case no. 36508; see also *Moussa v. Canada*, 2015 FC 545; NK v. Canada, 2015 FC 1040; *Mirmahaleh v. Canada*, 2015 FC 1085; *Shanmugarasa v. Canada*, 2016 FC 1374; and Shanmugarasa v. Canada, 2016 FC 1374.

12 Rikhof, *The Criminal Refugee*, pages 323 (France) and 328 (Germany).

13 *Bundesrepublik Deutschland v. B and D*, C-57/09 and C-101/09, European Court of Justice, 9 November 2010, paragraphs 100–105.

14 Rikhof, *The Criminal Refugee*, pages 318 (Canada, but, this was before the *Ezokola* decision), 333 (New Zealand) and 342 (the US).

15 Universal jurisdiction applies in a situation where the crime was not committed in the state wanting to prosecute, nor is the perpetrator or victim a national of that state, but the perpetrator of the crime abroad has subsequently relocated to that state. In some instances, this type of jurisdiction has also been used in circumstances where there is no perpetrator present in the state, but investigations have been undertaken because the crimes are

international crimes which are part of 1F(a), namely aggression, genocide, war crimes, and crimes against humanity, are the foremost examples of crimes that are enforced through both direct and indirect means.[16]

TCL, on the other hand, covers the indirect suppression by international law through domestic criminal law of criminal activities that have actual or potential transboundary effects. Enforcement of transnational law is always indirect, accomplished through prosecution by domestic courts. While ICL can have as its sources in all three forms recognised by general international law, TCL has only treaties as its sources, although these treaties can be international or regional agreements. These so-called suppression treaties have three essential features that distinguish them from international criminal law arrangements and from other international treaties. The first of these aspects is the obligation of states parties to criminalise within their domestic laws the conduct that is the subject matter of the treaties. Second, these treaties oblige states parties to utilise an expanded version of jurisdiction that goes beyond the one usually utilised at the domestic level, namely, territorial[17] or active nationality[18] jurisdiction. They can also include passive nationality[19] jurisdiction; however, the treaties do not go so far as to include universal jurisdiction.

The last and most important feature of these treaties is the fact that they oblige states parties either to prosecute perpetrators of the crimes mentioned in the treaties or to extradite such persons (called the *aut dedere aut judicare* obligation). A number of crimes have had a trajectory from transnational to international crimes. For instance, both genocide and war crimes had their genesis in treaties containing some of the just-mentioned features, namely, the Genocide Convention and the 1949 Geneva Conventions with their 1977 Additional Protocols. There are a number of crimes originating in the transnational sphere which have not been made subject to international jurisdiction, but which have become subject to universal jurisdiction by agreement of the

sufficiently serious that any country is entitled to initiate a prosecution. This is frequently referred to as absolute jurisdiction or universal jurisdiction in absentia, see Terje Einarsen and Joseph Rikhof, *A Theory of Punishable Participation in Universal Crimes* (2018), pages 428–429 (hereinafter Einarsen and Rikhof).

16 Einarsen and Rikhof, page 258.

17 This is the most common type of criminal jurisdiction and is based on the principle of sovereignty, meaning that a state is entitled to prosecute crimes that have taken place within its territory – hence the name territorial jurisdiction, Einarsen and Rikhof, page 428.

18 Active nationality or active personality principle stipulates that a state can prosecute crimes committed by its nationals abroad.

19 Passive personality principle allows a state to prosecute a crime committed abroad in which its national has been a victim.

international community; as such they have become part of international criminal law in a broad sense. The crimes in this category are piracy, torture, slavery, and apartheid.[20]

The status of terrorism in international law has been subject to debate. It is certainly part of TCL as a result of the regulation of a number of aspects of this phenomenon in a wide variety of suppression treaties, which will be discussed below. However, it has also been argued that terrorism has achieved a status, which goes beyond other transnational crimes, in that a large number of states have utilized universal jurisdiction for the crime of terrorism, which would bring it within the realm of ICL. On the other hand, it is still difficult to detect a norm of customary international law in the use of terrorism legislation at the domestic level.[21] For that reason, while terrorism might be an emerging international crime, for the purposes of this chapter, we will still consider it as a transnational crime.

3 Transnational Criminal Law – Forms of Extended Liability

There is a long pedigree in TCL with respect to the formulation of extended liability and it is interesting to see how the number of forms of liability have waxed and waned. The first terrorism treaty, which predates the Second World War (WWII), the 1937 *Terrorism Convention*,[22] had already a broad array of extended liability concepts, namely:

1) Conspiracy to commit any such act;
2) Any incitement to any such act, if successful;
3) Direct public incitement to any acts mentioned under heads (1), (2) or (3) of Article 2, whether the incitement be successful or not;
4) Wilful participation in any such act;
5) Assistance, knowingly given, towards the commission of any such act.[23]

---

20 Einarsen and Rikhof, page 270.

21 Robert J. Currie and Joseph Rikhof, *International & Transnational Criminal Law, 3rd edition.*, 2020, pages 355–361.

22 The Convention for the Prevention and Punishment of Terrorism.

23 Article 3 of the Convention, which refers to acts in article 2, which states:
Acts of terrorism:
(1) Any wilful act causing death or grievous bodily harm or loss of liberty to:
(a) Heads of States, persons exercising the prerogatives of the head of the State, their hereditary or designated successors;
(b) The wives or husbands of the above-mentioned persons.
(c) Persons charged with public functions or holding public positions when the act is directed against them in their public capacity.

After WWII, there have been 12 treaties dealing with aspects of terrorism, which also provide forms of participation in these aspects of terrorism, while there is also a draft treaty, which does the same. The first of these treaties was the *1970 Hague Convention*,[24] which deals with offences committed on aircraft. The circle of perpetrators was considerably smaller than set out in the above convention,[25] namely, only attempt and participating as an accomplice were mentioned.[26] This trend was followed in two other conventions dealing with the same subject matter of aviation terrorism, namely, the *1971 Montreal Convention*[27] and the *1988 Montreal Protocol*,[28] and followed in the *1979 New York Convention*, but, slightly expanded by adding threats in the *1973 New York Convention*[29] and the *1988 Rome Convention*.[30]

A major step forward was reached with the *1994 New York Convention*, which added organizing and ordering to the previous three forms of complicity.[31]

---

(2) Wilful destruction, or damage to, public property or property devoted to a public purpose belonging to or subject to the authority of another High Contracting Party.
(3) Any wilful act calculated to endanger the lives of members of the public.
(4) Any attempt to commit an offence falling within the foregoing provisions of the present article.
(5) The manufacture, obtaining, possession, or supplying of arms, ammunition, explosives or harmful substances with a view to the commission in any country whatsoever of an offence falling within the present article.

Note that another form of extended liability is mentioned in the above article, namely attempt in paragraph 4.

24 The Convention for the Suppression of Unlawful Seizure of Aircraft.

25 Interestingly, the text of the 1948 *Genocide Convention* was quite similar to that of the *Terrorism Convention*, while the parameters of liability of extended liability were the same in ICL until the 1998 Rome Statute of the International Criminal Court, namely, in the Statutes of the International Tribunals of the International Criminal Tribunal for the former Yugoslavia (ICTY), the International Criminal Tribunal for Rwanda (ICTR) and the Extraordinary Chambers in the Courts of Cambodia (ECCC).

26 Article 1(b).

27 The Convention for the Suppression of Unlawful Acts against the Safety of Civil Aviation, article 1(2).

28 The Protocol for the Suppression of Unlawful Acts of Violence at Airports Serving International Civil Aviation, article II(2).

29 The Convention on the Prevention and Punishment of Crimes against Internationally Protected Persons, Including Diplomatic Agents, article 2(1)(c), (d) and (e).

30 Convention for the Suppression of Unlawful Acts against the Safety of Maritime Navigation, articles 2(2) and 3(2).

31 The Convention on the Safety of United Nations and Associated Personnel, article 9(1)(c), (d), and (e).

This was both limited and expanded in the 1997,[32] 1999[33] and *2005 New York Conventions*[34] by eliminating threats (except for the last treaty), changing "ordering" for "directing" and adding common purpose.

The final stage was reached with the text in the *2010 Beijing Convention*[35] and *Protocol*,[36] which consolidated all six aspects of complicity previously used and adding two more, namely, assisting after the fact and conspiracy. As a result, the complete list of forms of complicity in the post WWII terrorism treaties reads as follows:

- attempt
- organizes
- directs
- participates as an accomplice
- assisting after the fact
- conspiracy
- common purpose
- threat.

The *Draft Comprehensive Convention against International Terrorism*, which attempts to move away from a sectoral approach as the title indicates, is a step backwards as it has the same wording as the *2005 New York Convention* with its six forms of extended liability,[37] which is most likely a reflection of the fact that this provision was drafted in 2005 and the negotiations with respect to this treaty have not moved forwarded much since that time; it can be expected that the text will be updated to reflect the most recent developments in this area when the work resumes.

---

32 The International Convention for the Suppression of Terrorist Bombings, article 2(2) and article 2(3); Article 2.3(c) dealing with common purpose inspired Article 25.3(d) of the Rome Statute, which was in turn relied on by the Supreme Court of Canada in the *Ezokola* decision.

33 The International Convention for the Suppression of the Financing of Terrorism, article 2(4).

34 The International Convention for the Suppression of Acts of Nuclear Terrorism, articles 2(2), 2(3) and 2(4).

35 The Convention on the Suppression of Unlawful Acts Relating to International Civil Aviation, articles 1(3), 1(4) and 1(5); articles 1(5)(b) re common purpose is very similar to article 25(3)(d) of the Rome Statute.

36 The Protocol Supplementary to the Convention for the Suppression of Unlawful Seizure of Aircraft, article 1(2), 1(3) and 1(4).

37 See UNDOC A/59/ 894, Appendix II, articles 2(2), 2(3) and 2(4).

4 Transnational Criminal Law – Observations

In order to situate the breadth of the terrorism conventions for the purposes of providing guidance to 1F(b) as opposed to the parameters of ICL in the context of 1F(a), it is useful to first set out the forms of extended liability in ICL. The ICL picture is a bit complicated as forms of liability have seen fluctuations over the years, as a result of which the most recent iteration of such liability as contained in the Rome Statute is not a complete one; for instance, membership, which was part of the post-WWII instruments, and, conspiracy, which was included in the ICTY/ICTR statutes (albeit only for genocide), can no longer be found in the ICC founding document.[38] The Rome Statute sets out the following types of involvement (apart from three forms of perpetration in article 25(3)(a)): ordering, soliciting, inducing,[39] aiding and abetting,[40] common purpose,[41] incitement,[42] attempt[43] and command/superior responsibility.[44]

When comparing this to the listing in the Beijing Treaty (which like all the other terrorism conventions also contains a provision for direct perpetration in the same language as in the Rome Statute, namely, "commits"[45]), both instruments refer to ordering/directing, aiding and abetting/participating as an accomplice, common purpose and attempt. The Rome Statute is broader by also including incitement in limited circumstances[46] as well as soliciting,[47] inducing and command/superior responsibility.[48] On the other hand, the Beijing Treaty includes organizing, assisting after the fact, conspiracy and threat. Of these four latter aspects, it has already been pointed out that conspiracy (in a limited form) was part of the ICTY/ICTR statutes and presumably part of ICL as a whole while accessory after the fact has jurisprudentially made part of aiding and abetting;[49] it is also likely that the notion of organizing could be

38 Re membership in ICL, see Einarsen and Rikhof, pages 418–420.

39 Article 25(3)(b).

40 Article 25(3)(c).

41 Article 25(3)(d).

42 Article 25(3)(e) but only for genocide.

43 Article 25(3)(f).

44 Article 28.

45 Article 1(1).

46 Although incitement was included in the 1937 Terrorism Convention.

47 Although soliciting was included in the 1937 Terrorism Convention.

48 Command/superior responsibility can be found in another TCL treaty, namely, article 6(1)(b) of the International Convention for the Protection of All Persons from Enforced Disappearance.

49 Einarsen and Rikhof, pages 416–417.

included in the ICTY/ICTR concepts of joint criminal enterprise (JCE)[50] or the ICC concept of co-perpetrator or indirect perpetrator in article 25(3)(a).[51] However, uttering threats is not known in ICL at the moment and as such represents a major difference between ICL and TCL.[52]

5 Domestic Criminal Law – Regular Forms of Extended Liability[53]

The methodology used to assess domestic criminal law for the purposes of interpreting 1F(b) is based on the ten countries, which have contributed the most to exclusion and which are the same as mentioned above in the introduction with the addition of Sweden.[54] Secondly, for these countries the regular forms of extended liability will be examined in the legislation followed by special provisions in this area for terrorism.

When examining the general legislation of the ten countries in question,[55] a slightly confusing picture with respect to participation emerges. All the countries entertain various types of liability and the most common forms are known in all jurisdictions. Overall, there appears to be a general attempt at the domestic level to base forms of liability on somewhat similar conceptual notions, at least with respect to some forms of personal liability. However, the precise parameters of liability are often drawn differently in different countries, and at times the language used to express the same type of liability also varies.

50 Idem, pages 389–397.

51 Idem, pages 382–388.

52 Other forms of participation are known in non-terrorism TCL treaties such as cooperation in the Apartheid Convention; association in the 1988 Vienna Narcotics Convention; "preparatory acts and financial operations in connexion" with drug offences in the 1961 and 1971 Drug Trafficking Conventions and the 1972 Drug Trafficking Protocol; and counselling in the 2000 Palermo Convention on organised crime.

53 Most of the legislations discussed below can be found on this website: https://www.legislationline.org/.

54 See Rikhof, *The Criminal Refugee*, page 28; Sweden is added due to the large influx of refugees into that country since 2012, the publication date of the book.

55 Most of the information with respect to these forms of liability are derived from Einarsen and Rikhof, pages 436–437 (The Netherlands), 455 (Germany), 464–465 (Sweden), 469 (France), 471–472 (Belgium), 483–486 (UK), 493–494 (Canada), 497 (US), with concluding comments on pages 499–501. The legislation of Australia and New Zealand was outside the scope of the book but the legislative provisions for these two countries can be found in the Criminal Code Act 1995, sections 11.1–11.5 and 268.115 (Australia) and in the Crimes Act 1961, sections 66–72, 310 as well in the International Crimes and International Criminal Court Act, section 12(1)(a)(vi) (New Zealand).

One notable difference is that the five common law countries in this study – Australia, Canada, New Zealand, the United Kingdom and the United States – tend to use more forms of *inchoate liability*, such as attempt, incitement, and conspiracy, than their five civil law counterparts though it should be noted that attempt is set out in the legislation of all the countries, while incitement can be found in the Netherlands.

Some legislation makes reference to means to *convince a third person* to commit a criminal act, such as threat, abuse of power, deception, use of force, gifts, or promises. This can be found in the Netherlands as part of the perpetration section, while in France it is included under aiding and abetting. In Belgium it comes within the provision dealing with incitement as part of perpetration (although in the French-language version of the Belgian law the word 'provoquer' is used for incitement, the meaning of which is closer to causing or instigating; this is confirmed by the Dutch-language version of the law, which uses the term 'uitgelokt', the same term used in the Netherlands law). In the UK, procuring is generally seen as using deception in this context. It has been postulated, furthermore, in the literature, that in the UK the abuse of power aspect can be considered a form of ordering.

In most common law countries, such as Australia, Canada, New Zealand and the UK, the notion of *common purpose or common intention* is used to delineate forms of group liability where more than one person partakes in the commission of an offence. Australia has also added provisions dealing with joint commission and commission by proxy, the former of which has been developed jurisprudentially in Canada and the UK as part of aiding and abetting.

The definition of *aiding and abetting* also has a number of variants in domestic legislation. In some countries, such as Canada, New Zealand, the United Kingdom, and the United States, this form of participation is set out as a form of liability without further clarification. Other countries have provided some definition with respect to the notion of aiding and abetting, usually by indicating that a person has provided assistance to the commission of the crime. This is the case in Australia, Belgium, France and Germany. Lastly, some countries have added to the general description of aiding and abetting examples of the means, by which the assistance can be accomplished; this is the case in the Netherlands, Belgium and Sweden (as part of the section dealing with preparatory acts). These references can be general in nature, such as providing opportunity, means, or information (the Netherlands); providing instructions or procuring weapons, instruments, or other means (Belgium); or presenting or receiving money or anything else as prepayment or payment for the crime or procuring, constructing, giving, receiving, keeping, conveying, or engaging in any other similar activity with poison, explosive, weapon, picklock, falsification tool, or other such means (Sweden).

The Australian, Canadian, New Zealand and US legislation mention *accessory after the fact* as a form of participation.

Other forms of indirect participation using *persuasion in the preparatory phase*, which resulted in the commission of crime, have been penalised under various expressions, such as inducing, soliciting, counselling, encouraging, and instigation, namely, in Canada, Germany, New Zealand, Sweden, the United Kingdom and the United States.

Command responsibility is known in the Swedish Criminal Code, but in more general language than that used in the Rome Statute, while the US Code lists command responsibility within its iteration of forms of aiding and abetting. In general, some countries have included command responsibility within their criminal codes, such as Australia, but most of the ones discussed in this chapter have implemented the substantive provisions of the Rome Statute, including the command/superior responsibility concepts, in specific legislation, as is the case with the Canada, Germany, Netherlands, New Zealand and the UK. There appear to be different approaches with respect to this notion in Canada and Germany, which treat command/superior responsibility as a distinct offence ('crime'), while the Netherlands and the UK treat it as a form of indirect participation. The former approach extends the parameters of participation, as it allows both regular forms of indirect approaches as well as inchoate offences to be combined with command/superior responsibility as a distinct crime.

With respect to contributions before the execution stage of the crime, such as *conspiracy, further planning and preparation, attempt, and incitement* (as a form of instigation before the execution stage), attempt is known in all countries, while Australia, Canada, New Zealand, and the UK have a general provision regulating conspiracy and incitement. The United States uses these types of liability only in relation to specific crime types. While in theory it would be possible in such countries to have double inchoates by combining, for instance, attempt with conspiracy or incitement with conspiracy, national courts, at least in some cases, have frowned upon drawing the circle of perpetration too wide.[56] The Netherlands also has a provision dealing with conspiracy, but the jurisprudence appears to require that at least one of the co-conspirators commits the crime envisaged in the original agreement, which makes it more akin to some variants of joint criminal enterprise than to a common law – type

56 See for instance in Canada, *R. v. Déry*, 2006 SCC 53, where attempt to conspire to commit an offence was not accepted as a form of lability.

'conspiracy'. In Sweden, the translated provision in the Criminal Code dealing with conspiracy says, "by conspiracy is meant that someone decides on the act in collusion with another as well as that someone undertakes or offers to execute it or seeks to incite another to do so," which appears to also resemble notions of co-perpetration and incitement.

6 Domestic Criminal Law – Special Extended Liability Provisions Related to Terrorism – Overview

There are special provisions with respect to extended liability for terrorism in the legislation in most of the ten countries mentioned above although the exact wording and parameters varies.

Australia: in the Criminal Code Act of 1995 the following forms of extended liability are mentioned:

- threatening to commit offences related to United Nations and associated personnel while intending to compel any other person to do or omit to do an act by making the threat;[57]
- providing or receiving training connected with terrorist acts;[58]
- possessing things connected with terrorist acts;[59]
- collecting or making a document likely to facilitate terrorists acts;[60]
- other acts done in preparation for, or planning, terrorist acts;[61]
- directing the activities of a terrorist organization;[62]
- being a member of a terrorist organization;[63]
- recruiting for a terrorist organization;[64]
- training a terrorist organization or receiving training from a terrorist organization;[65]
- getting funds to, from or for a terrorist organization;[66]

57 Section 71.12.
58 Section 101.2.
59 Section 101.4.
60 Section 101.5.
61 Section 101.6.
62 Section 102.2.
63 Section 102.3.
64 Section 102.4.
65 Section 102.5.
66 Section 102.6.

- providing support to a terrorist organization;[67]
- and associating with a terrorist organization.[68]

Belgium: in the Criminal Code a number of extensions to the regular forms of liability are set out, namely, providing a terrorist group a structured association of more than two persons, established over time and acting in concert to commit terrorist offences;[69] participating in an activity of a terrorist group, including by supplying information or material resources or by any form of funding activity to a terrorist group;[70] being a leader of a terrorist group;[71] and providing material resources, including financial assistance to the commission of a terrorist offence.[72]

Canada: some extensions can be found in the Criminal Code portion dealing with anti-terrorism, which sets out the forms of extended liability for participating in or contributing to,[73] facilitating,[74] leaving Canada to commit an offence related to terrorism,[75] instructing to carry out a terrorist activity,[76] advocating or promoting the commission of a terrorist offence[77] and concealing or harbouring a person involved in terrorism.[78]

France: in its Criminal Code participation in any group formed or association established with a view to the preparation, marked by one or more material actions, of any acts of terrorism;[79] financing a terrorist organisation by providing, collecting or managing funds, securities or property of any kind, or by giving advice for this purpose, intending that such funds, security or property be used, or knowing that they are intended to be used, in whole or in part, for the commission of any of the acts of terrorism, irrespective of whether such an act takes place are made criminal.[80]

67 Section 102.7.
68 Section 102.8.
69 Article 139.
70 Article 140(1).
71 Article 140(2).
72 Article 141.
73 Section 83.18(1), which clarifies these two terms by saying that this means providing, receiving, recruiting, offering, entering or remaining in any country for the benefit of a terrorist group and making oneself available to facilitate or commit a terrorism offence.
74 Section 83.19.
75 Sections 83.181, 83.191 and 83.201–83.202.
76 Sections 82.21–83.22.
77 Section 83.221.
78 Section 83.23.
79 Article 421-2-1.
80 Article 421-2-2.

Germany: in the Criminal Code it is said that a person who forms a terrorist organization or participates as a member of a terrorist organization is punishable.[81]

The Netherlands: in its Criminal Code a number of forms of extended liability related to terrorism are enumerated, namely: obtaining or attempting to obtain for himself or another person means or information for the commission of a terrorist offence or a serious offence for the preparation or facilitation of a terrorist offence, or gaining knowledge or skills for that purpose or imparting this knowledge or these skills to another person;[82] participation in an organisation, which has as its purpose the commission of terrorist offences while founders, directors or managers are specifically included in this category;[83] threats of a terrorist offence.[84]

New Zealand: in the Terrorism Suppression Act 2002 recruiting members of terrorist groups;[85] participation in terrorist groups;[86] and harbouring or concealing terrorists are made punishable.[87]

Sweden: there is an Act on Criminal Responsibility for Terrorist Offences of 2013 but it refers to the regular forms of liability set out in the Criminal Code, which are discussed above.[88]

UK: the UK has the most extensive listing of punishable forms of involvement in terrorist offences in various special legislative documents:

- participating in aspects to the development of nuclear weapons, such as development or production, transfer of such a weapon, engaging in military preparations, or in preparations of a military nature, intending to use, or threaten to use, a nuclear weapon;[89]
- membership in a proscribed terrorist organization;[90]

---

81 Section 129(a).

82 Article 134a.

83 Article 140a.

84 Article 285(3).

85 Section 12.

86 Section 13.

87 Section 13A.

88 Section 4; the Act on Criminal Responsibility for Public Provocation, Recruitment and Training concerning Terrorist Offences and other Particularly Serous Crime of 2010 also contains contains provisions to penalize public provocation, recruitment, training and travel for terrorist purposes while the Act on Criminal Responsibility for the Financing of Particularly Serious Crime in some cases of 2002 makes it criminal to collect, provide or receive funds or other property for terrorist purposes or for travel to carry out such purposes.

89 Section 47(1)(a), (d) and (e), 47(3) and 47(4) of the Anti-Terrorism, Crime and Security Act 2001.

90 Section 11(a) of the Terrorism Act 2000.

- inviting support for such an organization;[91]
- arranging, managing or assisting in arranging or managing a meeting which he knows is
  - (a) to support a proscribed organisation,
  - (b) to further the activities of a proscribed organisation, or
  - (c) to be addressed by a person who belongs or professes to belong to a proscribed organisation;[92]
- addressing a meeting and the purpose of his address is to encourage support for a proscribed organisation or to further its activities;[93]
- using money or other property for the purposes of terrorism;[94]
- entering into or becoming concerned in an arrangement as a result of which money or other property is made available or is to be made available to another for purposes of terrorism;[95]
- entering into or becoming concerned in an arrangement which facilitates the retention or control by or on behalf of another person of terrorist property
  - (a) by concealment,
  - (b) by removal from the jurisdiction,
  - (c) by transfer to nominees, or
  - (d) in any other way;[96]
- providing or receiving instruction or training in the making of certain terrorist weapons or inviting another to receive such instruction or training;[97]
- possession for terrorist purposes;[98]
- collecting of information likely to be useful to a person committing or preparing a terrorist act;[99]
- eliciting, publishing or communicating information about members of armed forces likely to be useful to a person committing or preparing a terrorist act;[100]
- involvement in terrorism-related activity is any one or more of the following forms:
  - (a) the commission, preparation or instigation of acts of terrorism;

91 Section 12(1)(a) of the Terrorism Act 2000.

92 Section 12(2) of the Terrorism Act 2000.

93 Section 12(3) of the Terrorism Act 2000.

94 Section 16 of the Terrorism Act 2000.

95 Section 17 of the Terrorism Act 2000.

96 Section 18 of the Terrorism Act 2000.

97 Section 54(1), (2) and (3) of the Terrorism Act 2000.

98 Section 57(1) of the Terrorism Act 2000.

99 Section 58(1) of the Terrorism Act 2000.

100 Section 58A(1) of the Terrorism Act 2000.

(b) conduct that facilitates the commission, preparation or instigation of such acts, or is intended to do so;
(c) conduct that gives encouragement to the commission, preparation or instigation of such acts, or is intended to do so;
(d) conduct that gives support or assistance to individuals who are known or believed by the individual concerned to be involved in conduct falling within paragraph (a).[101]

US: the United States has set out in its criminal legislation the following forms of extended liability for terrorist offences: harbouring terrorists;[102] material support to terrorists;[103] providing material support or resources to terrorist organizations;[104] providing or collecting funds to terrorism, including an attempt of conspiracy to do;[105] receiving military-type training from a foreign terrorist organization.[106]

7 Domestic Criminal Law – Special Extended Liability Provisions Related to Terrorism – Comparison

To provide a better overview for analytical purposes the above provisions re extended liability for involvement in terrorist offences are organized in a table with the 10 countries along one axis and the forms of liability along the other.

A number of conclusions can be drawn from this table. First of all, as said above, there is considerable variation between the ten countries resulting in a large number of forms of extended liability for terrorist offences; namely, 25 forms for assistance to terrorist offences or individuals involved in such offences (all above the grey bar in the table) and 16 forms of assistance to terrorist organizations, groups or associations (below the grey bar).

Focusing on the individual support portion, some countries, like Canada and the US, emphasize general descriptors of supporting individuals, such as participating, contributing, facilitating and directing (in Canada) or providing material support (in the US); while most other countries prefer to provide

101 Section 14(4) of the Counter-Terrorism and Security Act 2015.

102 Section 803 of the Uniting and Strengthening America by Providing Appropriate Tools Required to Intercept and Obstruct Terrorism (USA Patriot Act) Act of 2001/section 2339 of Title 18, United States Code.

103 Section 805 of Uniting and Strengthening America by Providing Appropriate Tools Required to Intercept and Obstruct Terrorism (USA Patriot Act) Act of 2001/section 2339A of Title 18, United States Code.

104 Section 2339B of Title 18, United States Code.

105 Section 2339C of Title 18, United States Code.

106 Section 2339D of Title 18, United States Code.

TABLE 1 Forms of additional participation in terrorism in 10 countries

	Australia	Belgium	Canada	France	Germany	Netherlands	NZ	Sweden	UK	US
threats	x					x				
preparatory acts	x								x	
leaving the country to commit an offence			x							
advocating or promoting			x							
arranging, managing a meeting										
addressing a meeting									x	
planning	x									
participating			x							
contributing			x							
facilitating			x						x	
directing	x		x							
providing support or assistance									x	x
providing training	x								x	
receiving training	x								x	
gaining knowledge or skills						x				
possessing things	x								x	
obtaining means						x				
obtaining information						x			x	

TABLE 1 Forms of additional participation in terrorism in 10 countries (cont.)

	Australia	Belgium	Canada	France	Germany	Netherlands	NZ	Sweden	UK	US
collecting documents	x									
making documents	x									
providing material resources		x								
providing financial assistance		x								
using money or other property, directly or indirectly									x	
facilitating control of terrorist property									x	
concealing or harbouring a person			x				x		x	x
recruiting for an organization	x						x			
training an organization	x									
receiving training from an organization	x									x
supporting an organization	x									x
inviting support for an organization									x	
financial supporting an organization	x	x		x						x

TABLE 1 Forms of additional participation in terrorism in 10 countries (cont.)

	Australia	Belgium	Canada	France	Germany	Netherlands	NZ	Sweden	UK	US
providing a structured organization		x								
participating in an activity of a group		x								
providing information to a group		x								
providing material resources to a group		x								
being a leader of a group		x				x				
forming an organization					x					
associating with an organization	x									
participation in a group or association				x		x	x			
participating as a member					x					
member of an organization	x								x	

more clarification and describe those interactions in detail. As well, all stages of the commission of a terrorist offences are included, from the preparatory phase (either in general terms, such as preparatory acts or planning in Australia to more specific forms, such as threats in Australia and the Netherlands; advocating or promoting in Canada and Sweden or setting up or speaking at a meeting in the UK), to the execution phase (which will be discussed further below) and even to the post-execution phase such as concealing or harbouring a person as is the case in Canada, New Zealand, the UK and the US.

With respect to the execution phase, the types of support can be grouped in more overarching categories, such as training (both receiving and providing), which is mentioned in the Australian, Dutch, Swedish and US legislation; aspects related to further the ability of an individual to carry out terrorist activities, such as possessing things (Australia and Sweden), obtaining means or information (Netherlands and the UK), collecting or making documents (Australia), and providing material resources (Belgium). And, there are aspects that cover providing financial assistance in general to terrorists organizations, such as in Belgium, using money or other property (the UK), and facilitating control of terrorist property (the UK and Sweden).

With respect to assisting terrorist organizations, again, a number of overarching categories can be detected, such as training activities (both receiving and providing) in Australia and the US; general support for an organization, either in general terms, as in Australia or the UK or more specifically by recruiting for an organization as is done in Australia, participating in an activity of a group (Belgium), providing information or material resources to a group (Belgium); financial support (Australia, Belgium, France and the US); setting up an organization by providing a structured organization (Belgium), forming an organization (The Netherlands) or being a leader (Belgium and The Netherlands); and, lastly, more indirect forms of involvement such as participation in a group (France, The Netherlands and New Zealand), associating with an organization (Belgium); participating as a member (Germany), and being a member (Australia and the UK).

8 Domestic Criminal Law – Special Extended Liability Provisions Related to Terrorism – Observations

In order to determine how far these forms of participation are useful for the interpretation of 1F(b), two questions are relevant at this juncture. The first one is whether the 41 forms of extended liability are unique descriptions or whether they are further clarifications of the general forms of complicity set out the criminal law of these countries and as such do not add much in terms of the conceptual range of these types of liability (an approach taken in Sweden).[107] Secondly, if there are unique forms of liability, which do add to the regular form of liability, are those forms already within the parameters and overarching tests of *JS* and *Ezokola*, which provide an interpretation of the word "committed" in 1F(a), which is also used in 1F(b).[108]

With respect to the first question, as it appears that a number of forms of extended liability are related to the notion of aiding and abetting, a good starting point to ascertain the parameters of this particular form of complicity would be to examine the Taylor case by the Sierra Leone Special Court, which at the trial level indicated in which manner Charles Taylor, as the head of State of Liberia, had aided and abetted the RUF (Revolutionary United Front) rebels in neighbouring Sierra Leone while the appeals chamber provided a comprehensive and historical overview of all the forms of aiding and abetting considered by international criminal law institutions since the Second World War.

The Trial Chamber indicated that the following activities can amount to aiding and abetting: provision of arms and ammunition;[109] provision of military personnel;[110] provision of operational support such as providing communications equipment and training, logistical support and safe havens in the form of a guest house, financial support, medical support, herbalists to bolster confidence of fighters, and security escorts for arms, ammunition, diamonds, drivers, messengers and liaison personnel;[111] and providing advice and direction in military strategy.[112]

The Appeals Chamber said:

> The acts and conduct of those convicted had a substantial effect on the commission of crimes in an infinite variety of ways. An accused's acts and conduct can have a substantial effect by providing weapons and ammunition, vehicles and fuel or personnel, or by standing guard, transporting perpetrators to the crime site, establishing roadblocks, escorting victims to crime sites or falsely encouraging victims to seek refuge at an execution

107 This is not to say that there can be very useful political or even penological reasons to provide some specificity to the general forms of liability but for purposes of this chapter the only focus is on possible legal overlap.

108 A third question of how much support a form of liability, which is not addressed in these two questions, needs at the domestic level to be relevant for the interpretation of 1F(b), which will be discussed below in the conclusion of this chapter.

109 Judgment, *Taylor* (SCSL-03-01-T), Trial Chamber, 18 May 2012, paragraph 6915.

110 Idem, paragraph 6924.

111 Idem, paragraphs 6931–6937.

112 Idem, paragraph. 6950.

> site. Such variety also includes providing financial support to an organisation committing crimes, expelling tenants, dismissing employees, denying victims' refuge or identifying a victim as a member of the targeted group. Senior officials' acts and conduct can have a substantial effect on the commission of crimes by signing decrees, attending meetings and issuing reports, allowing troops to be used to assist and commit crimes, demanding slave labour to satisfy the needs of industries, issuing directives and drafting laws, endorsing official decisions to disarm victim groups, working together with the police, army and paramilitaries to maintain a system of unlawful arrests and detention, or deliberately not providing adequate medical care to detention facilities. In other cases, the acts or conduct of accused persons found to have had a substantial effect on crimes include making a speech to a crowd of listeners encouraging them to commit crimes, implementing a media campaign to arouse hatred against a group or being an approving spectator at the scene of a crime, or by burying bodies, cremating bodies or conserving looted property. The acts and conduct of an accountant, architect or dentist in their respective professional roles can have a substantial effect on the commission of crimes, as can those of prosecutors, judges and religious officials.[113]

As a second preliminary comment regarding the first question is that under ICL the notion of mentioning accessory after the fact, has been recognised as a form of aiding and abetting. The ICTY/ICTR jurisprudence has indicated that participation by adding and abetting may occur before, during or after the act is committed but that if the aiding and abetting occurs after the crime, it must be established that a prior agreement existed between the principal and the person who subsequently aided and abetted in the commission of the crime.[114]

With these two initial comments, it will be possible to assess the forms of extended liability used at the domestic criminal level. Most of the general forms of such liability in assisting individuals as used in Canada and the US would all fall under the heading of aiding and abetting as they all require a substantial contribution in the executory phase of the commission of the crime, which is the hallmark of aiding and abetting in ICL (and which has used this terminology on a number of occasions in the jurisprudence).[115] This is also the case for directing (ordering), which is used in Canada and which is a

113 Judgment, *Taylor* (SCSL-03-01-A), Appeals Chamber, 26 September 2013, paragraph 369.

114 See Einarsen and Rikhof, pages 416–417.

115 See idem, page 413 re facilitating; re the parameters of material support in the US, see Rikhof, *The Criminal Refugee*, page 343.

well-known concepts in ICL.[116] The same can be said for the preparatory acts of planning in Australia[117] and advocating and promoting, which is prohibited in ICL as incitement for genocide if the urged act is not carried[118] out and as instigation if the act is carried out for all crimes;[119] it is also mentioned as form of aiding and abetting by the appeals chamber in the Taylor case.

With respect to the more specific forms of assistance to individuals, forms of financial support have been discussed as forms of aiding and abetting by both the trial chamber and appeals chamber in the Taylor case while providing training was mentioned in the decision of the trial chamber. The latter decision also mentioned logistical support, which could be used to include the various forms of providing assistance to further the ability to carry out nefarious acts. Post-execution activities such as concealing or harbouring a person is a form of accessory after the fact, which is recognized in ICL as indicated above.

As forms of extended liability have been specifically designed or adjusted to hold liable persons operating in groups or other collectivities in ICL, the aspects mentioned above to support groups, such training activities, financial support and providing resources would all be part of ICL as part of the same reasoning in the jurisprudence just mentioned.

Having eliminated a number of forms of extended liability from the range of unique facets of supporting terrorism at the domestic level as these aspects are already known in ICL, there are forms of such liability, which do not occur in ICL, namely, threats (in Australia and The Netherlands) and provisions related to organizations, such as setting up an organization by providing a structured organization (Belgium), forming an organization (The Netherlands) or being a leader (Belgium and The Netherlands); and, lastly, more indirect forms of involvement such as participation in a group (France, The Netherlands and New Zealand), associating with an organization (Belgium); participating as a member (Germany) and being a member (Australia and the UK). While it would be possible to equate some of the aspects of being a leader with superior responsibility in ICL,[120] just being a leader without a connection to the commission of a crime by the members of the terrorist organization would fall outside the parameters of this concept. The same can be said about setting up an organization, which in some circumstances could be part of the legal concepts of JCE and co-perpetration as long there is connection with the eventual commission of crimes. This leaves the types of extended liability

116 See Einarsen and Rikhof, pages 405–406.
117 Idem, pages 375–376.
118 Idem, pages 376–378.
119 Idem, pages 408–409.
120 Idem, pages 400–405.

related to association or membership; while it is outside the parameters of this chapter to examine the national jurisprudence with respect to the notions of participating in a group, participating as a member, and being a member,[121] and as such not, it is feasible to determine whether there are substantial differences between these concepts and their variations in wording, as any of these forms would go beyond the present state of ICL.[122]

In terms of whether the jurisprudence at the national level, with respect to the parameters of ICL in relation to forms of extended liability mentioned in the national criminal legislation, occurs in national exclusion law, a number of these concepts have been reflected in the latter area of law (keeping in mind that mere membership as a head for the liability in 1F(a) crimes is now very much in doubt after the *JS* and *Ezokola* cases in the UK and Canada).[123] Examples of this are findings of complicity when involved in information gathering and sharing;[124] preparation;[125] ordering/directing;[126] financing;[127] planning;[128] advocating;[129] and facilitating.[130]

As can be seen from the analysis above, a number of types of extended liability in national criminal legislation now go beyond the extended liability in refugee law in 1F(a) with the recent contractions in the area of membership.

9 Conclusion

Before addressing the desirable breadth of the notion of "complicity" in 1F(b) and "guilty" in 1F(c) it would be useful to set out the purpose of the former, which to a large extent also applies to the latter. A useful and recent statement to that effect can be found in a 2014 decision of the Supreme Court of Canada, which stated:

> I conclude that Article 1F(*b*) serves one main purpose – to exclude persons who have committed a serious crime. This exclusion is central to the

121 There have been some cases in this regard, see Einarsen and Rikhof, pages 434–435 and 455.

122 Idem, pages 418–420.

123 See the introduction above.

124 See Rikhof, *The Criminal Refugee*, pages 213 (Australia); 216 (Belgium); 224–225 (Canada), 238–239 (Netherlands), 247–249 (NZ) and 258–260 (US).

125 Idem, page 214 (Belgium).

126 Idem, page 215 (Belgium).

127 Idem, pages 235 (Canada), 241 (Netherlands), 249 (NZ), 262 (US).

128 Idem, page 230 (France).

129 Idem, page 231 (France).

130 Idem, pages 239 (Netherlands), 261 (US).

> balance the *Refugee Convention* strikes between helping victims of oppression by allowing them to start new lives in other countries and protecting the interests of receiving countries. Article 1F(*b*) is not directed solely at fugitives and neither is it directed solely at some subset of serious criminals who are undeserving at the time of the refugee application. Rather, in excluding all claimants who have committed serious non-political crimes, Article 1F(*b*) expresses the contracting states' agreement that such persons by definition would be undeserving of refugee protection by reason of their serious criminality. Excluding people who have committed serious crimes may support a number of subsidiary rationales – it may prevent people fleeing from justice; it may prevent dangerous and particularly undeserving people from entering the host country. However, Article 1F(*b*) cannot be confined to any of these subsidiary purposes. Excluding people who have committed crimes in other countries prior to seeking refugee protection may serve other state interests. It may help preserve the integrity and legitimacy of the refugee protection system, and, hence, the necessary public support for its viability. It may deter states from exporting criminals by pardoning them or imposing disproportionately lenient sentences while supporting their departure elsewhere as refugees. Finally, it may allow states to reduce the danger to their society from all serious criminality cases taken together, given the difficult task and potential for error when attempting to determine whether criminals from abroad (on whom they have more limited sources of information than on domestic criminals) are no longer dangerous. Whatever rationales for Article 1F(*b*) may or may not exist, its purpose is clear in excluding persons from protection who previously committed serious crimes abroad.[131]

From this general perspective, some of which also pertain to 1F(a),[132] it would be useful to find a demarcation line between the parameters of 1F(a) and 1F(b), especially, as the same word to connote complicity is used in both provisions, namely, "committed." Given the fact, as stated in the introduction, that 1F(a) contains the inherent limitation that "committed" must relate to ICL, a limitation not found in 1F(b), two conceptual conclusions can be drawn from this juxtaposition. The first one is that "committed" in 1F(b) has the capacity to be

131 *Febles v. Canada (Citizenship and Immigration)*, 2014 SCC 68, paragraphs 35–36.

132 While, in general, it can be said that the overarching objective of 1F(a) is different as it reflects the international approach to find forms of liability to hold collectivities responsible while 1F(b) is related to individual actions, this line has been blurred in the case of terrorist activities, which are often carried out by larger groups of individuals against larger groups of victims akin to 1F(a).

broader than the same term used in 1F(a) and, secondly, that any distinction in terms of meaning should be kept to a minimum given the use of the same word. A solution to this possible dilemma could be that all forms of extended liability applicable to 1F(a) should also be applicable to 1F(b), but, that 1F(b), in addition, can also contain other forms of liability if there is a credible source for such other forms of liability. This would mean that the entire body of ICL in terms of present forms of liability can be imported into 1F(b). Secondly, in terms of credible sources of extended liability for 1F(b), TCL would be a very good candidate. Based on these two observations, it would mean that 1F(b) would contain forms of ICL which are not used in TCL or used sparingly, such as superior responsibility, but also that TCL forms of liability, which do not exist in ICL, are possible; threats come to mind. It bears noting at this juncture that neither ICL (at the present) not TCL allow for membership as an independent form of liability.

However, the inquiry should not stop there. Since 1F(b) is silent as to its sources and since the methodology used in the *JS* and *Ezokola* cases also looked at domestic uses of ICL (albeit in the refugee context), it would also be appropriate to examine domestic criminal laws as they pertain to extended liability for terrorism in this context. This examination resulted in the conclusion above that threats and a number of forms of liability related to membership or association with terrorist organizations have been set out in such domestic legislation. The question then becomes how much of such an occurrence in the domestic legislation is sufficient to make it an appropriate source of interpretation for 1F(b). While it is not the intention here to conduct an exhaustive survey akin to determining customary international law in this area,[133] it is worth noting that of the 10 countries surveyed in this area seven have provisions with respect to membership and association (all except Canada, Sweden and the US). This would provide a powerful argument that forms of membership could be part of 1F(b), especially since Canada and the US, which are not part of these seven countries, already allow this in their immigration law.[134]

133 This was done by the Special Tribunal for Lebanon, Interlocutory Decision on the Applicable Law: Terrorism, Conspiracy, Homicide, Perpetration, Cumulative charging, STL-II-OI/I/AC/RI76bis, Appeals Chamber, 16 February 2011, paragraphs 93–102 when determining the parameters of the crime of terrorism and which assessed the legislation of over 50 countries.

134 See above, footnote 35; this fact would also alleviate a possible argument that allowing for membership in 1F(b) for terrorist activities but not for other criminal acts could result in a two-tier approach and a more complicated analysis as it is unlikely that this form of liability can be expanded to other activities with the exception of possible organized crime (which is already done in Canada, see Rikhof, *The Criminal Refugee*, page 318).

However, it would mean that some civil law countries as well as the ECJ[135] might need to take into account this new development or adjust the reasoning with respect to the prohibition of membership for 1F(b). The fact that only two countries use the notion of threats in their terrorism legislation is of less concern as this form of liability is already known in TCL.

With respect to 1F(c) and the forms of extended liability, the fact that 1F(c) has been seen as residual both in terms of the substantive crimes and extended liability[136] and given the fact that the jurisprudence in the countries under consideration have equated "guilty" with "committed,"[137] there would be no logical reason to have a different approach for this exclusion ground as compared with 1F(b).

135 See above, footnotes 33 and 34. [See the Court of Justice of the European Union (CJEU), https://curia.europa.eu/jcms/jcms/J02_7024/en/. (accessed July 1, 2020)]

136 See Rikhof, *The Criminal Refugee*, pages 367–368.

137 See above, footnotes 5–8.

CHAPTER 6

Counter-Terrorism and the Exclusion of Refugees and Refugee-Citizens from Australia

Peter Billings and Rebecca Ananian-Welsh***

1 Introduction

Successive governments in Australia have securitised migration and particular migrants profiled as risky (especially, protection seekers arriving by boat), which epitomizes the "growing culture of exclusion" from asylum.[1] The "thrust of transnational management of unwanted migration has been to stop migration flows through interception, deterrence and local 'stabilisation' of communities of origin."[2] Accordingly, assorted preventive measures have been adopted, and this "hypergoverance"[3] of borders includes: interdiction and turn-backs at sea for 'irregular' migrants, offshore regional processing arrangements, and extended and indefinite administrative/preventive detention of asylum seekers (including children). Effectively, Australia's 'crimmigration' laws serve to outlaw seeking asylum by boat,[4] provide for a raft of security-based exclusionary provisions upon which to reject felonious and risky asylum seekers, and work to deny protection to refugees who arrived lawfully in Australia. These additional barriers to refugee protection have been erected via immigration laws that have been substantially recast of late, which intentionally depart

* Professor, The University of Queensland, School of Law.

** Senior Lecturer, The University of Queensland, School of Law.

1 Asha Kaushal and Catherine Dauvergne, "The Growing Culture of Exclusion: Trends in Canadian Refugee Exclusions" *International Journal of Refugee Law* 23, no. 1 (2011): 54; and generally, Idil Atak and Francois Crépau, "National Security, Terrorism, and the Securitization of Migration," in *Research Handbook on International Law and Migration*, ed. Vincent Chetail and Céline Bauloz (Massachusetts: Edward Elgar Publishing, 2014).

2 Michael Humphrey, "Migration, Security and Insecurity," *Journal of Intercultural Studies* 34, no. 2 (2013): 178, 185–186.

3 Humphrey, "Migration," 185.

4 See, Alison Gerard and Sharon Pickering "Crimmigration: criminal justice, refugee protection and the securitisation of migration," in *The Routledge Handbook of International Crime and Justice Studies,* ed. Bruce A. Ariggo and Heather Bersot (New York: Routledge, 2013) 587–611; and, Susan Kneebone and Antja Missbach, "The Human Rights Implications of Australian and Indonesian Anti-smuggling Laws" *Int J Migration and Border Studies* 4, (2018): 379.

© KONINKLIJKE BRILL NV, LEIDEN, 2020 | DOI:10.1163/9789004295995_008

from international refugee and human rights law norms and related progressive jurisprudence. Complementing these measures, the Australian government has introduced national security grounds for the revocation of Australian citizenship from dual nationals, thus providing a basis for certain citizens to be rendered alien and subjected to the securitized migration system thus described.

In addition to immigration measures being employed as anti-terror initiatives, since 2001 the Australian government has enacted more counter-terrorism statutes than any other Western democracy, an approach aptly described as one of "hyper-legislation".[5] National anti-terror laws are of staggering scope.[6] They include provisions for banning organisations,[7] preventive[8] and post-sentence detention,[9] control orders,[10] as well as secret detention and compulsory interrogation by Australia's domestic spy agency 'ASIO'.[11] Terrorism offences extend well beyond the commission of terrorist acts[12] to include preparation,[13] support,[14] financing,[15] advocacy,[16] recruitment,[17] and a wide array of terrorist organisation offences.[18] The passage of these laws was eased by Australia's lack of a national bill (or charter) of human rights and a (arguably misleading) political rhetoric of urgency and exceptionalism.[19]

The law and policy approaches canvassed above have been justified on a range of grounds, but national security logic (*qua* terrorism fears) and international criminality (*qua* people smuggling) has featured prominently in political

5 Kent Roach, *The 9/11 Effect* (New York: Cambridge University Press, 2011), 309.

6 George Williams, "A Decade of Australian Anti-Terror Laws," *Melbourne University Law Review* 35, (2011): 1146–1153; George Williams, "The Legal Legacy of the 'War on Terror'," *Macquarie Law Journal* 12, (2013): 7–10.

7 Provided that the Attorney-General is satisfied that the organisation "is directly or indirectly engaged in, preparing, planning, assisting in or fostering the doing of a terrorist act" or "advocates the doing of a terrorist act" (discussed further below): *Criminal Code Act 1995* (Cth) s 102.1(2)(a)–(b).

8 Ibid Div 105.

9 Ibid Div 105A.

10 Ibid Div 104.

11 *i* (Cth), Part III Div 3.

12 *Criminal Code Act 1995* (Cth) s 101.1.

13 Ibid s 101.6.

14 Ibid s 102.7.

15 Ibid Div 103.

16 Ibid s 80.2C.

17 Ibid s 102.4.

18 Ibid Div 102.

19 Rebecca Ananian-Welsh and George Williams, "The New Terrorists: The Normalisation and Spread of Anti-Terror Laws in Australia," *Melbourne University Law Review* 38, (2014): 365–368.

rhetoric. This rhetoric reveals and reflects the prominent place of 'security', including counter-terrorism, in post-9/11 Australia.[20] Consequently, the securitisation of migration (and migrants) has meant that access to asylum in Australia for boat arrivals is categorically denied under contemporary law and policy settings. For other protection seekers arriving in Australia *via* 'regular' legal channels it is increasingly difficult to obtain asylum, maintain residency and secure citizenship. Furthermore, the introduction of several new legislative triggers for citizenship revocation for dual nationals has increased the vulnerability of refugee-citizens to denaturalisation on terrorism-related grounds.

This chapter considers the many points of intersection between Australia's refugee protection and counter-terrorism frameworks. We trace and examine the various tools at the disposal of Australian authorities that facilitate the exclusion of asylum seekers and the expulsion of 'declared' refugees (with lawful residency status or dual citizenship) on adverse security/character grounds. It begins by outlining and scrutinising Australia's punitive, militarised, border security practices which are, in part, justified by a construction of asylum seekers as potential terrorists. It then turns to identifying and analysing the complex, interlacing suite of national security and public order criteria that can support the refusal or cancellation of a protection visa, and we explore the ensuing adverse legal and practical consequences for people. Finally, the chapter outlines Australia's citizenship stripping laws and explains the distinct and deleterious impact those denaturalisation provisions could have on refugees who acquired citizenship by conferral. The primary theme that emerges from this analysis is of exclusion: exclusion from Australian territory, segregation from society, expulsion from community membership, omission of procedural (fair hearing) safeguards and denial of access to (administrative) justice. From approaching Australia's territorial borders by sea, to petitioning for a visa, onto receiving lawful residency status and even enjoying Australian citizenship, refugees may be excluded from Australia's protection on a wide range of security grounds.

2 Border Security

Protection visa claims in Australia are governed by the *Migration Act 1958* (Cth) ('Migration Act'). The *Migration Act* stipulates that asylum seekers without a

20 On the factors shaping Australia's approach to national security see *National Security, Surveillance and Terror: Canada and Australia in Comparative Perspective*, ed. Randy Lippert, et al, (Switzerland: Palgrave Macmillan, 2016).

valid visa have no lawful right to enter Australia, irrespective of whether or not Australia has (or may have) protection obligations in respect of such persons.[21] This provision reflects Australia's aversion to uncontrolled (maritime) migration and symbolises a reluctance to accept the *Refugees Convention*[22] as a *legal* constraint on its sovereign prerogative to exclude asylum seekers at (or beyond) its borders.[23] This political and popular antipathy towards maritime arrivals is at the root of harsh border securitization policies adopted by successive governments towards 'boat people' over several decades. These policies have been justified on a number of bases, with national security featuring prominently.

2.1 *Refugees and National Security – Boat Arrivals*

If asylum seekers journey to Australia by sea they encounter securitised, typically extra-territorial, border controls in the form of maritime interdiction and forced turn-back practices.[24] Should they avoid interdiction,[25] and enter Australia's migration zone by sea unlawfully,[26] they are designated as an "unauthorised maritime arrival" ('UMA').[27] These individuals are "excised from the

21 *Migration Act 1958* (Cth) s 228B.

22 *Convention Relating to the Status of Refugees* (adopted 28 July 1951, entered into force 22 April 1954) 189 UNTS 137; *Protocol Relating to the Status of Refugees* (adopted 31 January 1976, entered into force 4 October 1967) 606 UNTS 267.

23 The Australian government maintains it acts consistently with the *non-refoulement* principle, but purports to give effect to that principle through its policies and practices, not municipal laws. See, also, *CPCF v Minister for Immigration and Border Protection* (2015) 255 CLR 514, 643 [461] (Keane J) adverting to judicial authority that suggests a state's obligations under the *Refugees Convention* are engaged only for those within a state's territory.

24 See, Daniel Ghezelbash, Violetta Moreno-Lax, Natalie Klein and Brian Opeskin, "Securitization of Search and Rescue at Sea: The Response to Boat Migration in the Mediterranean and Offshore Australia," *International and Comparative Law Quarterly* 67, (2018): 315.

25 Few asylum seekers have reached Australian territory since interdiction practices resumed in late 2013. In August 2018 a fishing vessel bearing 'irregular' migrants reached the mainland (the first in four years). They were removed from the mainland and swiftly repatriated to Vietnam (Kristy Sexton McGrath and Brendan Mounter, "Suspected asylum seekers found in Daintree taken to Christmas Island, Minister's office says," *ABC News*, August 28, 2018, https://www.abc.net.au/news/2018-08-28/suspected-asylum-seekers-daintree-christmas-island/10171996, accessed December 8, 2018).

26 *Migration Act 1958* (Cth) s 14 provides that an "unlawful non-citizen" (previously, "illegal entrant") is a person in the migration zone without a valid visa in effect. Travelling to Australia without permission is not criminalised but seeking asylum unauthorised is disrupted and deterred through interdiction and turn-backs/take-backs, and heavy sanctions for people smuggling.

27 Ibid s 5AA.

state" and denied access to asylum in Australia.[28] Specifically, they are statutorily barred from lodging a valid protection visa application. They are subject to accelerated – procedurally suspect and secretive – administrative action known as 'enhanced screening', and are prone to expulsion unless immigration officials believe that Australia's protection obligations might be engaged.[29] In this circumstance the protection seekers are liable to transfer to a third country with which Australia has a bi-lateral agreement, for 'regional processing' purposes and with no prospect of permanent resettlement in Australia.[30] Questions of refugee protection are, subsequently, determined according to the domestic asylum laws and procedures of the third country.

Between October 2001 and November 2003, military interdictions at sea coupled with offshore regional processing of refugees and use of temporary protection visas,[31] were critical aspects of the Howard Government's response to asylum seekers, commonly known as the 'Pacific Solution'. The Howard Government justified these policies by constructing asylum seekers as potential terrorists, which had significant political impact in the wake of the notorious *MV Tampa* affair and 9/11. After a brief hiatus, from 2007–12, regional processing and detention of asylum seekers in designated third countries was resuscitated, followed by maritime interdiction practices in late 2013. Currently, these policies and practices comprise elements of the military-led 'Operation Sovereign Borders'.[32] These government policies are directed at deterring and disrupting irregular migration by sea, and are animated by several purposes,

28 See, Anthea Vogl, "Over the Borderline: A Critical Inquiry into the Geography of Territorial Excision and the Securitisation of the Australian Border" *University of New South Wales Law Journal* 38, no. 1 (2015): 114.

29 See, Maria O'Sullivan, "Interdiction and Screening of Asylum Seekers at Sea: Implications for Asylum Justice," in *States, the Law and Access to Refugee Protection: Fortresses and Fairness* ed. Maria O'Sullivan and Dallal Stevens (Oregon: Hart Publishing, 2017).

30 See, Amy Nethery and Rosa Holman, "Secrecy and human rights abuses in Australia's offshore immigration detention centres," *International Journal of Human Rights* 20, no. 7 (2016):1018; and, Claire Higgins, "The (Un-)sustainability of Australia's Offshore Processing and Settlement Policy", in *Boat Refugees and Migrants at Sea: A Comprehensive Approach* ed. Violeta Moreno-Lax and Efthymios Papastavridis (Leiden: Brill, 2016).

31 See further, Mary Crock and Kate Bones, "Australian Exceptionalism: Temporary Protection and the Rights of Refugees" *Melbourne Journal of International Law* 16, no. 2 (2015): 522; and, Mohammud J Hafeez-Baig, "Putting the 'Protection' in Temporary Protection Visa" *Bond Law Review* 28, no.2 (2016): 115.

32 Another aspect of Operation Sovereign Borders is offshore disruption of people smuggling ventures in transit and source countries, see Helen Davidson, "Almost 300 asylum seekers prevented from sailing to Australia in past year" *The Guardian*, November 12, 2018, https://www.theguardian.com/australia-news/2018/nov/12/hundreds-of-asylum-seekers-disrupted-while-trying-to-sail-to-australia-in-past-year, accessed January 8, 2019.

principally: preventing transnational crime (people smuggling); promoting human security by preventing hazardous journeys on unseaworthy vessels, and; restoring integrity to the immigration system, thereby facilitating an orderly and controlled humanitarian intake.[33]

While political and media discourse since 2009 has, increasingly, associated asylum seekers arriving by boat with organised transnational crime,[34] the alleged terrorist threat posed by asylum seekers (especially Muslims)[35] continues to be promoted by some politicians and media.[36] For example, in 2016 a leaked 'draft' Cabinet document pointed to perceived links between terrorist attacks in Australia and the humanitarian intake (see further below), as a justification for stricter controls over residency and citizenship in order to mitigate threats posed by refugees admitted through the humanitarian resettlement program.[37]

Additionally, in July 2017, then Minister for Immigration, Peter Dutton, intimated that asylum seekers who arrived in Australia by boat without a valid visa or identity documentation should be viewed with suspicion – as a national security risk. Specifically, he said:

> Secure borders, as Europe has learned at great cost, are an important part of national security. It is a concerning fact that a large number of IMAs [irregular maritime arrivals] who could afford to pay the people smugglers to bring them illegally to Australia arrived here without any identification. They needed identity documentation to fly into Indonesia, but disposed of it on the sea journey to Australia. Why?[38]

---

33 Liberal Party of Australia, *Issue 10: Securing Australia's Borders,* https://www.liberal.org.au/our-plan/border-security.

34 Kerstin Lueck, Clemence Due and Martha Augoustinos, "Neoliberalism and nationalism: Representations of asylum seekers in the Australian mainstream news media" *Discourse & Society* 26, no.5 (2015): 608, 616–620.

35 Humphrey, "Migration," 182–185; and, Satvinder Juss, "Detention and Delusion in Australia's Kafkaesque Refugee Law" *Refugee Survey Quarterly* 36, (2017): 146, 151–153.

36 See Fiona H McKay, Samantha L Thomas and R Warwick Blood, "'Any one of these boat people could be a terrorist for all we know!' Media representations and public perceptions of 'boat people' arrivals in Australia" *Journalism* 11, no.5 (2011): 607; and, Kehla Lippi, Fiona Mckay and Hayley McKenzie, "Representations of refugees and asylum seekers during the 2013 federal election" *Journalism* [2017]: 1.

37 David Lipson, "Leaked Government document outlines tougher migration program, increased monitoring of refugees" *ABC News*, February 5, 2016, https://www.abc.net.au/news/2016-02-04/leaked-document-outlines-changes-to-migration/7140952, accessed January 26, 2019.

38 Hon Peter Dutton MP, "Opinion – Operation Sovereign Borders milestone" July 27, 2017 https://minister.homeaffairs.gov.au/peterdutton/Pages/opinion-operation-sovereign-borders-milestone.aspx, accessed 8 January 2019.

Statements of this kind can construct 'moral panics' and fuel latent community fear, which can serve to legitimise popular hostility and prejudice, as well as ground and escalate stringent policies directed towards asylum seekers.[39] Now, almost two decades after 9/11, we are in a better position to assess the association between asylum seekers, refugees and terrorism in Australia. It cannot be claimed with certainty that no refugees who have arrived in Australia 'irregularly' by boat have links to terrorism. However, counter-terrorism scholars have observed that there is no "obvious, compelling evidence" that any terrorist acts have been planned or commissioned by refugees who arrived by boat.[40]

2.2 *Refugees and National Security – Plane Arrivals*

Historically, only a small proportion of all asylum applicants in Australia have arrived, 'irregularly', by boat. Most have arrived by air with a valid visa and, subsequently, lodged protection visa claims. Indeed, flights are now carrying asylum seekers to Australia in record numbers: 27,931 individuals in the 2018–2019 financial year.[41] Duncan Lewis, who served as the Director-General of ASIO from 2014 to 2019, maintained that Australia's refugee and humanitarian program (which includes 'onshore' protection claimants and those refugees arriving on visas *via* Australia's 'offshore' humanitarian program) was not a source of terrorism. Appearing before a parliamentary committee in 2017, Lewis responded to a question about the threats posed by Middle Eastern refugees coming to Australia by stating that he had "absolutely no evidence to suggest that there is a connection between refugees and terrorism."[42] He later added: "We have had tens of thousands of refugees come to Australia over the last

39 Michelle Peterie, "'These Few Small Boats' Representations of Asylum Seekers During Australia's 1977 and 2001 Elections" *Journal of Australian Studies* 40, no.4 (2016): 433, 434.

40 Clarke Jones and Nicola McGarrity, "FactCheck Q&A: have any refugees who came to Australia gone on to be terrorists?" *The Conversation*, November 30, 2015, https://theconversation.com/factcheck-qanda-have-any-refugees-who-came-to-australia-gone-on-to-be-terrorists-51192, accessed December 8, 2018. Also, Catherine Dauvergne, "Irregular Migration, State Sovereignty and the Rule of Law" in *Research Handbook on International Law and Migration*, ed. Chetail and Bauloz, 82, also noting the securitisation of migrants and migration law "even in the absence of any linkage with criminal or terrorist groups or activities."

41 David Crowe, "Stopping the boats masks the migration mess both parties now face," *Brisbane Times*, December 13, 2018, https://www.brisbanetimes.com.au/politics/federal/stopping-the-boats-masks-the-migration-mess-both-parties-now-face-20181213-p50m2b.html?ref=rss&utm_medium=rss&utm_source=rss_feed, accessed 8 January 2019.

42 Legal and Constitutional Affairs Committee, *Estimates*, Senate, May 25, 2017, 191–192.

decade or so and a very few of them have become subjects of interest for ASIO and have been involved in terrorist planning."[43]

Lewis's evidence before the Committee elicited a negative response from a former Prime Minister, Tony Abbott, who claimed:

> We've had three terrorist attacks in Australia and all three of them involved either people claiming to be refugees or the children of refugees, [...] I think that the ASIO director really needs to think again on this issue.[44]

In challenging the Director-General, Abbott was referring to several individuals: Man Haron Monis, Abdul Numan Haider, Farhad Jabar and Saney Aweys. These men had not arrived in Australia by boat. Monis had emigrated by plane, lawfully, on a business visa in 1996, later securing refugee status.[45] He laid siege to the Lindt Café in Sydney in December 2014, which resulted in the deaths of two hostages and Monis himself, who was shot by police. Whether this incident was a 'terrorist' act is contested,[46] but it was used by politicians to stoke popular fears about national security and 'home-grown' radicalised terrorists.

The families of Haider and Jabar had migrated to Australia with visas, as refugees. 18-year-old Haider stabbed two officers from the Joint Counter Terrorism team outside a Melbourne police station in September 2014, before being fatally shot by police.[47] 15-year-old Jabar shot dead NSW Police accountant

---

43 Michael Koziol, "'Absolutely no evidence': ASIO boss shuts down Hanson over refugee terror links," *The Sydney Morning Herald*, May 26, 2017, https://www.smh.com.au/politics/federal/absolutely-no-evidence-asio-boss-shuts-down-hanson-over-refugee-terror-links-20170526-gwdkkl.html, accessed December 8, 2018.

44 Katharine Murphy, "Tony Abbott says ASIO director needs to 'think again' on causes of terrorism," *The Guardian*, May 31, 2017, https://www.theguardian.com/australia-news/2017/may/31/tony-abbott-says-asio-director-needs-to-think-again-on-causes-of-terrorism, accessed 14 January 2019.

45 AAP, "'Mysterious and macabre' Monis revealed," *SBS News*, May 24, 2017 https://www.sbs.com.au/news/mysterious-and-macabre-monis-revealed, accessed 14 January 2019.

46 State Coroner of New South Wales, *Inquest into the deaths arising from the Lindt Café siege: Findings and recommendations* (May 2017) 240. Cf. Russ Scott and Rodger Shanahan, "Man Haron Monis and the Sydney Lindt Café Siege – Not a Terrorist Attack," *Psychiatry, Psychology and Law*, (2018): 32–42.

47 Dan Oakes, "Melbourne shooting: What we know about Abdul Numan Haider, shot dead after stabbing anti-terrorism officers at Endeavour Hills," *ABC News*, September 25, 2014, http://www.abc.net.au/news/2014-09-24/what-we-know-about-abdul-numan-haider/5767044, accessed December 18, 2018.

Curtis Cheng in October 2015.[48] Like Monis, Haider and Jabar claimed their terrorist acts were on behalf of Islamic State ('IS'), though the actual strength of the connections between the individuals and IS were tenuous.[49]

Aweys also arrived as a child in Australia through the offshore humanitarian program, after spending years in an Ethiopian refugee camp. In 2011, he was convicted of conspiracy to do an act in preparation for a terrorist act and sentenced to 18 years imprisonment. Aweys' role in the conspiracy was to call a Somali sheik asking whether it was permissible under Islam to commit a terrorist attack against the Australian army in Australia, a question which was answered in the negative.[50] Commenting on these cases, Lewis explained that, "they were not terrorists because they were refugees they were terrorists because of this warped violent extremist interpretation of Sunni Islam."[51]

The Director-General's conclusions about the lack of a connection between asylum seekers/refugees and terrorism in Australia carry significant weight. Conversely, some may argue that the evidence connecting refugees to terrorism does not exist because Australia's migration laws and policies have been successful in excluding potential terrorists. Nevertheless, the lack of demonstrable connection between a person's asylum seeker/refugee status and their risk to Australian security challenges the resilient counter-terrorism justification for border securitization. Essentially, counter-terrorism emerges as an unconvincing justification for severe extra-territorial border controls, law reforms that delimit Australia's international protection obligations, or more stringent residency and citizenship tests. In short, given that asylum, migration and citizenship systems are very carefully administered, it is hard to imagine a terrorist would voluntarily submit to "robust" screening processes and character/

48 Nick Ralston, "Farhad Jabar captured giving Islamic State salute before Curtis Cheng shooting," *The Sydney Morning Herald*, May 1, 2017, https://www.smh.com.au/national/nsw/farhad-jabar-captured-giving-islamic-state-salute-before-curtis-cheng-shooting-20170501-gvwn36.html, accessed December 18, 2018.

49 Oakes, "Melbourne shooting." For discussion of the links between Monis's actions and IS, see State Coroner of New South Wales, *Inquest*, 233–240.

50 Andrew Lynch, Nicola McGarrity and George Williams, *Inside Australia's Anti-Terrorism Laws and Trials* (Sydney: NewSouth Publishing, 2015), 40.

51 Fergus Hunter, "ASIO Chief Duncan Lewis: Radical Sunni Islam, not refugees, the source of terrorism," *The Sydney Morning Herald*, May 31, 2017, https://www.smh.com.au/politics/federal/asio-chief-duncan-lewis-radical-sunni-islam-not-refugees-the-source-of-terrorism-20170531-gwgsex.html, accessed 18 December 2018.

security checks for the purpose of obtaining either a refugee protection visa, a humanitarian visa, or citizenship.[52]

3 Onshore Refugee Processing: Exclusion on National Security and Community Safety Grounds

For those non-citizens entering Australia lawfully, s 36 of the *Migration Act* provides for a convoluted scheme of exclusive and inclusive conditions, allowing for the rejection of asylum seekers on broad security-related grounds. A non-citizen will be refused a protection visa on the basis of not satisfying mandatory legislative requirements contained in the *Migration Act* or by failing to satisfy public/national interest criteria (including, the 'character test') prescribed in regulations.[53] Specifically, a protection seeker is excludable: (i) on national security grounds (s 36(1B)); (ii) because they present a danger to the community (s 36(1C) and s 36(2C)(b)); and (iii) by failing public/national interest criteria (s. 65; Sch. 2 Migration Regulations).

The exclusionary provisions cited above are additional to, and co-exist with, disqualifying principles that reflect Art 1F *Refugees Convention*. In fact, Art 1F may be viewed as of secondary, and comparatively minor, importance as a foundation for exclusion under Australian migration law. The disqualifying provisions in Art 1F are encased within *both* the codified refugee and complementary protection criteria,[54] enabling the rejection of visa applicants because they have committed egregious crimes, are a threat to community safety and the interests of the receiving State.

The statutory framework, outlined above, for regulating the entry and admission of protection seekers into Australia was substantially reformed in 2014 to represent and reflect the government's understanding of its international

52 Stefanie Balogh, and Joe Kelly, "Paris Attacks: Refugee screening will stop radicals: Dutton" *The Australian*, November 16, 2015, 7 https://www.theaustralian.com.au/national-affairs/immigration/paris-attacks-refugee-screening-will-stop-radicals-peter-dutton/news-story/700d716fcaccb6bb645b03e1a60e63ae, (accessed December 18, 2018). Dutton – (then) Immigration Minister – was responding to concerns raised about the admittance of 12,000 Syrian refugees, pointing to tough vetting processes for offshore refugee and humanitarian entrants including; biometric tests, fingerprinting, vetting applicants with Australia's intelligence partners and detecting fraudulent or forged documentation.

53 If the Minister is satisfied, on reasonable grounds, that exclusionary criteria are met, they are compelled to refuse to grant a protection visa: *Migration Act 1958* s 65.

54 *Migration Act 1958* s 36(2)(a), s 5H(2), s 36(2)(aa) and s 36(2C), respectively. Complementary protection is functionally equivalent to 'subsidiary protection' in Europe (*Council Directive 2011/95/EU*).

obligations towards protection seekers.[55] These reforms were motivated by political concerns that an unduly broad approach was being adopted by the courts to the question of whether, and in what circumstances, protection obligations were owed to non-citizens. The novel scheme is detached from the *Refugees Convention*: legislative references to the *Refugees Convention* were replaced with reference to Australia's "protection obligations" for those who are a "refugee", and the Act re-defines a "refugee".[56] Removing the legislative references to the *Refugees Convention* stemmed from the government's desire to reclaim sovereignty over Australia's legal obligations to protection seekers, and to diminish the progressive influence of foreign courts' interpretations of refugee law.[57] Accordingly, for 'onshore' protection visa applications lodged by eligible non-citizens after 16 December 2014, the *Migration Act* provides for a self-contained framework which articulates the government's own interpretation of its protection obligations.

Arguably, a weakness of the *Migration Act* is that there is nothing governing the order in which particular visa criteria are examined. Therefore, exclusionary criteria – which in certain respects are much broader in scope than their international law counterparts – can be invoked *before* any active consideration of the inclusive refugee/complementary protection criteria.[58] This is important because it means that protection seekers may not be identified as

55 *Migration and Maritime Powers Legislation Amendment (Resolving the Asylum Legacy Caseload) Act 2014* (Cth); and, House of Representatives, *Parliamentary Debates*, September 25, 2014, 10545 (S Morrison).

56 *Migration Act 1958* s 5H, and see s 5J–5LA. Note that the 'complementary protection regime' is also codified in statute: in *Minister for Immigration and Citizenship v MZYYL* (2012) 207 FCR 211, 215 [18] the Court identified the idiosyncratic approach taken in Australia: "The Complementary Protection Regime is a code in the sense that the relevant criteria and obligations are defined in it and it contains its own definitions: [...] Moreover, the Complementary Protection Regime uses definitions and tests different from those referred to in the International Human Rights Treaties and the commentaries on those International Human Rights Treaties."

57 House of Representatives, *Parliamentary Debates*, 25 September 25, 2014, 10545 (S Morrison).

58 *BCR16 v Minister for Immigration and Border Protection* (2017) 448 FCR 456. The government's riposte to *BCR16* was to issue a policy requiring officials to, first, assess whether refugee or complementary protection criteria are met before considering ineligibility criteria. The Immigration Minister is, however, not bound by the policy and may decide a visa applicant is ineligible without recourse to non-refoulement issues (*Ezegbe v Minister for Immigration and Border Protection* [2019] FCR 216 [21]–[24]) although this might give rise to procedural unfairness (*DOB18 v Minister for Home Affairs* [2019] FCAFC 1523 [66], [125] and [167]).

individuals who are owed protection obligations before expansive security and public order exceptions are invoked and removal powers are enlivened. Significantly, the statutory power of removal is no longer conditioned by the *legal* requirement to consider the fundamental *non-refoulement* principle before administrative action is taken. Consequently, the Australian government purports to meet its *non-refoulement* treaty obligations (also a principle of customary international law) through *policy and practice*, and not the rule of law.[59]

3.1 *Exclusion from Protection on National Security Grounds*

A non-citizen, including a 'declared' refugee, is ineligible for a protection visa under s 36(1B) where they have been assessed adversely – that is, as a direct or indirect threat to security – by ASIO. Effectively, the authority to reject decisively a protection seeker's visa claim (or to cancel a protection visa) is vested in security officials, and not those delegated with responsibility for administering protection visa claims. The judiciary have construed the word 'security' very broadly. It appears to have a broader meaning than Art 1F of the *Refugees Convention*.[60] It also appears to subsume the disentitling national security and public order criteria in Arts 32 and 33(2) *Refugees Convention*.[61] Security, within s 4 *Australian Security Intelligence Organisation Act* 1979 (Cth) ('*ASIO Act*'), means (inter alia) "politically motivated violence", and "the protection of Australia's territorial integrity and border integrity from serious threats",[62] and these phrases clearly encompass terrorism offences against the *Criminal Code* and the threat of terrorism intended to achieve a political objective in Australia or elsewhere.[63] Indeed, in *Plaintiff M47/2012 v Director-General of Security*, drawing on Canadian authority,[64] French CJ determined that the scope of

59 *Migration Act 1958* s 197C provides that for the purposes of removal (per s 198) *non-refoulement* obligations are irrelevant. This stems from 2014 reforms that deliberately decoupled the municipal removal power from international *non-refoulement* obligations, in order to negate the impact of HCA decisions that had preserved refugees' rights and frustrated government policies seeking to deter irregular migration.

60 *Plaintiff M47/2012 v Director-General of Security* (2012) 252 CLR 1, 63 [126] (Gummow J). In *Plaintiff M47/2012*, the plaintiff was not excluded from the application of the *Refugees Convention* pursuant to Art 1F, he was found to be a refugee but was the subject of an adverse (ASIO) security assessment.

61 (2012) 252 CLR 1, 48 [71] (French CJ).

62 Within the meaning of the *Australian Security Intelligence Organisation Act 1979* s 4.

63 Ibid s 4; and, *Plaintiff M47/2012* (2012) 252 CLR 1, 53–54 [93] (Gummow J).

64 *Suresh v Canada (Minister for Citizenship and Immigration)* [2002] 1 SCR 3 at 50 [87]: "... we believe courts may now conclude that the support of terrorism abroad raises a possibility of adverse repercussions on Canada's security."

security was broad, and "extended to those concerns which related to Australia's responsibilities to foreign countries in security-related matters."[65] Equally, in *Jaffarie v Director-General of Security*, the Federal Court rejected a limited interpretation of security when determining whether people smuggling constituted a serious threat to Australia's territory and border integrity. The Court observed that a confined meaning "may well hamstring ASIO and its ability to confront the ever-growing threat of terrorism and associated evils."[66]

The *ASIO Act* does not set out the threshold level of risk necessary to support an adverse security assessment, but the High Court of Australia ('HCA') has reasoned that the standard of satisfaction is "no doubt high, because of the seriousness of the finding and of its consequences."[67] Where ASIO determines that a non-citizen is a security risk they may issue an adverse assessment[68] and this triggers adverse administrative action, including visa refusal or cancellation. In this context, the fair administration of justice yields to national security interests; accordingly aspects of procedural fairness are excluded (see below). Furthermore, independent legal oversight is, arguably, ineffectual, with the consequence that people are left frustrated by the process and outcome. Another damaging consequence flowing from an adverse security assessment is that the recipient is vulnerable to prolonged detention pending removal. The maximum period of administrative detention is not prescribed by statute, and indeterminate detention is constitutionally permissible.[69] The period of confinement may be protracted where removal (*qua* deportation) is unachievable due to (inter alia) Australia's international *non-refoulement* obligations, or where third states exhibit reluctance to accept asylum seekers or refugees deemed to be a security threat by Australia.

In the national security context the legislative scheme modifies procedural fairness, insofar as fair hearing requirements are attenuated. For protection seekers (and temporary visa holders) there is no provision for an adverse security assessment to be accompanied by a statement of the grounds and the information relied upon by ASIO.[70] The courts have held that, for reasons of

65 (2012) 252 CLR 1, 46–47 [67].

66 (2014) 226 FCR 505, 525 [65] (Flick and Perram JJ).

67 *Plaintiff M47/2012* (2012) 252 CLR 1, 126 [319] (Heydon J).

68 *ASIO Act 1979* (Cth) s 17(1)(c) and s 37.

69 See, Peter Billings, "Whither Indefinite Immigration Detention: Re-thinking Legal Constraints on the Detention of Non-Citizens," (2015) *University of New South Wales Law Journal* 38, no.4 (2015): 1386.

70 *ASIO Act 1979* (Cth) s 36(b) which excludes the operation of s 37(2). Non-citizens who are not holders of a permanent visa or special purpose visa do not enjoy appeal rights before the AAT.

national security, it may be impossible to disclose the grounds and sensitive information on which administrative action was taken, and that in practical terms the content of the procedural fairness obligation may be reduced to "nothingness."[71] However, recent cases establish that non-citizens may be entitled to sufficient, *general*, information about issues of concern (if not the granular details) so that they can respond meaningfully.[72]

Additionally, the merits of adverse security assessments that ground the rejection of visa applications (and visa cancellations) are unreviewable by the Administrative Appeals Tribunal ('AAT').[73] This contrasts with the statutory review processes generally available where Articles 1F, 32 or 33(2) of the *Refugees Convention* are relied upon to refuse a protection visa.[74] Consequently, the factual and evidentiary bases of ASIO decisions are, essentially, unreviewable. This serious shortcoming is compounded by strictly limited judicial oversight.

In principle, ASIO is subject to the rule of law via judicial review,[75] but in practice litigants must overcome the hurdle of establishing grounds of review when the reasons for an adverse assessment are not disclosed. Further, the Australian courts have consistently exhibited a cautious approach when reviewing executive action in this context, lest their actions harm national security interests and inhibit counter-terrorism initiatives. This deference acknowledges the "practical difficulty faced by a court in evaluating evidence adduced in support of a claim for public interest immunity on grounds of harm to national security."[76] Moreover, judicial deference reflects sensitivity about the separation of powers under the *Australian Constitution*, specifically the

71 *Leghaei v Director-General of Security* (2007) 241 ALR 141, 146–147 [48], [50]-[54] (The Court).

72 *Jaffarie v Director-General of Security* (2014) 226 FCR 505, 536 [113] (Flick and Perram JJ); affirmed in *BSX15 v Minister for Immigration and Border Protection* (2017) 249 FCR 1, 13 [48].

73 *ASIO Act 1979* (Cth) s 36(1); and *Migration Act 1958* (Cth) s 500(4A). The AAT is the peak Commonwealth administrative tribunal, it is an independent body promoting good governance: *Singh* [2017] AATA 850 [19] (Logan J).

74 The *Migration Act 1958 (Cth)* makes provision for merits review against adverse visa decisions based on Art 1F, 32 and 33(2) (and statutory equivalents). However, where the Minister personally chooses to exclude a person because it is in the 'national interest', relying on the *Refugees Convention* Articles (per s 5H or s 36(1C)), there is no independent review. Rather, the Minister is accountable to Parliament (s 502 *Migration Act 1958* (Cth)).

75 A minimum provision of judicial review on the basis of 'jurisdictional error' has been held by the HCA to be constitutionally entrenched: *Plaintiff S157/2002 v Commonwealth* (2003) 211 CLR 476; and *Kirk v Industrial Court of New South Wales* (2010) 239 CLR 531.

76 *Sagar v Sullivan* (2011) 193 FCR 311, 327 [89] (Tracey J).

"necessity of avoiding decision-making on the merits when undertaking judicial review."[77]

Australian laws and procedures that permit the indefinite detention of asylum seekers (and those otherwise satisfying the refugee or complementary protection criteria) who have been subject to an adverse security assessment, breach international human rights laws. Notably, they breach the prohibition on arbitrary detention because: (a) non-citizens endure mandatory detention pending the outcome of health, identity and security checks, as well as the substantive asylum claim, and (b) refugees with adverse security assessments, are vulnerable to prolonged and indefinite detention unless and until either a third country agrees to resettle them or the objective circumstances in the country of origin change and so permit a safe repatriation. In 2013 the UN Human Rights Committee ('HRC') found that the Australian Government's administrative detention of forty-six refugees with adverse security assessments was arbitrary, in breach of Art 9 *ICCPR*, and constituted action contrary to Art 7, which prohibits torture, or cruel, inhuman or degrading treatment or punishment.

The HRC determined that Article 9(1) was violated because the statutory framework governing automatic detention for 'unlawful non-citizens' did not permit an individual assessment of the necessity of detention pre-visa determination. Furthermore, post-visa refusal, Art 9(1) was breached because secretive administrative processes meant refugees were not informed of the reasons for the negative security assessment; therefore, they were unable to mount effectively a legal challenge to their indefinite detention. Additionally, Australia had not utilised any alternative means to detention, or demonstrated that such means would be inadequate or inappropriate in meeting the apprehended security concerns.[78] Moreover, the HRC identified that the wide meaning of 'security', grounding adverse security assessments, was inconsistent with International refugee law operating "as an additional, unilateral ground for excluding refugees which is not authorised under the Refugee Convention."[79]

The HRC established that the arbitrary character of detention, its protracted and/or indefinite duration, combined with the difficult conditions in the detention facilities cumulatively inflicted serious, irreversible psychological

77 Ibid [91].

78 *FKAG v Australia* (UN Doc CCPR/C/108/D/2094/2011) [3.2]-[3.6]; and, *MMM v Australia* (UN Doc CCPR/C/108/D/2136/2012) 20 August 2013). Relatedly, see complaints investigated by the Australian Human Rights Commission: *Immigration detainees with adverse security assessments v Commonwealth of Australia* [2013] AusHRC 64, and *Sri Lankan refugees v Commonwealth of Australia* [2012] AusHRC 56.

79 *FKAG v Australia* [3.7].

harm upon the refugees, and was contrary to both the Art 7 prohibition on torture, or cruel, inhuman or degrading treatment and the Art 10(1) requirement that detainees are treated with humanity and respect for their inherent dignity.[80] The HRC concluded that Australia should release the detainees, apologize to them and offer adequate compensation. The HRC further advocated extensive law reform to eliminate mandatory detention, to introduce periodic independent oversight over the necessity of detention, and facilitate effective judicial review over both the legality of detention and adverse security assessments.[81] The HRC's exhortations have, hitherto, been ignored because the Australian government will not be "lectured to" by the UN.[82]

In summary, there is a want of transparency, procedural fairness and effective legal accountability over adverse security assessments and this heightens the risk of *refoulement* contrary to international laws. A protection/complementary protection visa applicant may receive neither reasons nor a summary of the case to be met, with no access to independent merits review.[83] Obtaining relief via judicial review, without the benefit of reasons and in a context where there is, understandable, judicial deference to the Executive branch, has proven impossible. Thus, the situation for a non-citizen affected by an adverse security assessment has been aptly portrayed as a "legal black hole,"[84] evidently breaching international human rights law and the *Refugees Convention*.

80 Ibid [3.12].

81 Ibid [3.19]–[3.20].

82 Lisa Cox, "Tony Abbott: Australians 'sick of being lectured to' by United Nations, after report finds anti-torture breach" *Sydney Morning Herald*, March 10, 2015, https://www.smh.com.au/politics/federal/tony-abbott-australians-sick-of-being-lectured-to-by-united-nations-after-report-finds-antitorture-breach-20150309-13z3jo.html, accessed December 18, 2018. The then Prime Minister's criticism came after a UN report found Australia's treatment of asylum seekers breached international laws against torture.

83 The creation of an Independent Reviewer of Adverse Security Assessments in 2012 was intended to inject a degree of fairness into the process, but received a lukewarm response: see, Daniel Reynolds, "The Independent Reviewer for Adverse Security Assessments: Comfort but not hope for indefinitely detained refugees," *Australian Journal of Administrative Law* 20, (2013): 199.

84 Ben Saul, "'Fair Shake of the Sauce Bottle": Fairer ASIO security assessments of refugees', *Alternative Law Journal* 37, no. 4 (2012): 221, 222; and, Ben Saul, "Indefinite Security Detention and Refugee Children and Families in Australia," *Australian International Law Journal* 20, (2013): 55.

3.2 *Exclusion from Protection on Security and Community Safety Grounds*

Section 36(1C) was inserted into municipal law in 2014,[85] and provides that a protection visa applicant must not be: a person whom the Minister considers, on reasonable grounds is either: "(a) a danger to Australia's security; or, (b) having been convicted by a final judgment of a particularly serious crime is a danger to the Australian community."[86]

Section 36(1C) is intended to codify Art 33(2) *Refugees Convention*.[87] Paradoxically, Art 33(1) – the cornerstone of refugee protection – is *not* codified in the *Migration Act*. Article 33(2) serves to deny a refugee the benefit of protection from *refoulement* under Art 33(1). It sanctions the *withdrawal* of protection (not refugee status) and, thereby, permits removal of a person whose need for refugee protection has previously been recognised by the State. However, by converting Art 33(2) criteria into s 36, Parliament has stipulated additional substantive grounds on which officials may rely to *refuse* the grant of a protection visa to refugee applicants.[88] Section 36(1C) thereby mistranslates international law in two ways. First, by inserting into municipal law criteria that are directed towards extinguishing the rights of 'declared' refugees, these disentitling criteria can eclipse a person's claim to protection, potentially, prior to a refugee status assessment or consideration of complementary protection needs.[89] Secondly, s 36(1C) is incompatible with human rights law because it qualifies the complementary protection regime via the disentitling terms drawn from Art 33(2) *Refugees Convention*. The deliberate conflation of refugee law with international human rights law is inconsistent with the absolute and

85 *Migration and Maritime Powers Legislation Amendment (Resolving the Asylum Caseload Legacy) Act 2014* Schedule 5, Part Two (commencing 18 April 2015). Exclusion on community protection grounds was a pre-existing aspect of the complementary protection regime per s 36(2C)(b), therefore s 36(1C) is really superfluous for complementary protection purposes.

86 A 'particularly serious crime' includes the commission of (a) a serious Australian offence; or (b) a serious foreign offence: *Migration Act 1958* s 5M.

87 See *DOB18 v Minister for Home Affairs* [2019] FCAFC 63 [48]–[52], [70]–[83] (Logan J) for detailed consideration of the meaning and relationship between Art 33(2) and s 36(1C)(b).

88 Section 36(1C) is directed at circumventing the effect of the decision in *SZOQQ v Minister for Immigration and Citizenship* (2013) 251 CLR 577, where the HCA held, unanimously, that s 91(U) (later repealed) did not translate into the terms of s 36(2) the operation of Art 33(2) of the *Refugees Convention*.

89 A decision to deny a protection seeker a visa, on exclusionary grounds, does not inexorably lead to *refoulement* contrary to international human rights law, but if there is no active consideration of whether they positively engage refugee/complementary protection obligations first, this is a real possibility.

non-derogable nature of *non-refoulement* obligations under international human rights law.[90] Human rights law rejects *refoulement* to serious harm: the *International Covenant on Civil and Political Rights*[91] and the *UN Convention Against Torture*[92] prohibit return to torture, or cruel inhuman or degrading treatment or punishment no matter how dangerous an individual's conduct.[93] By contrast, Art 1 of the *Refugees Convention* denies terrorists the status of refugees and, therefore, disables refugee law's protective regime.

Judicial interpretation of Art 33 (2), and its municipal law equivalent in s 36(1C), is sparse in Australia. Arguably, s 36(1C) is narrower in scope than the grounds for an adverse security assessment by ASIO in s 36(1B) as it is restricted to safeguarding Australia's *domestic* security and community safety. The required state of ministerial satisfaction – "reasonable grounds" – is congruent with the requirement in Art 33 of the *Refugees Convention* that there exist "reasonable grounds for regarding" a refugee as a danger. The danger must be based on an objective assessment of material,[94] which appears to cohere with the test established by the Supreme Court of New Zealand in *Attorney-General v Zaoui (No 2)*.[95]

The first limb – a "danger to Australia's security" – is undefined and so the basis for exclusion from protection is somewhat unclear. Recent judicial authority upon s 36(1C) certifies that "an assessment of whether a person constituted a danger to the community is one of fact and degree," and that the

90 On the lack of harmonization between refugee law and international human rights law, and how this system error results in legal limbo for excludable persons, see Joke Reijven and Joris van Wijk, "Caught in Limbo: How Alleged Perpetrators of International Crimes who Applied for Asylum in the Netherlands are Affected by a Fundamental System Error in International Law," *International Journal of Refugee Law* 26, no.2 (2014): 248.

91 Adopted 16 December *1966, 999 UNTS 171* (entered into force on 23 March 1976).

92 Adopted 10 December *1984, 1465 UNTS 85* (entered into force on 26 June 1987).

93 *Ezegbe v Minister for Immigration and Border Protection* [2019] FCA 216 [7]. The Court noted that a significant feature of these non-refoulement obligations was that "they do not admit of an exception where the person has committed serious criminal offences in the State contemplating deportation." Guy Goodwin-Gill and Jane McAdam, *The Refugee in International Law* (Oxford, 2007) 333; and Geoff Gilbert, "Exclusion under Article 1F since 2001: Two steps backwards and one step forward," in *Research Handbook on International Law and Migration*, ed. Chetail and Bauloz, 524 and 539, noting cases establishing that international human rights law does not allow *refoulement* of a person, no matter what their previous conduct.

94 *Kaddari v MIMA* (2000) 98 FCR 597, [23]-[24].

95 [2006] 1 NZLR 289 [45]. Potentially, a relatively higher level of satisfaction is warranted compared with adverse (ASIO) security assessments (*Plaintiff M47/2012* (2012) 252 CLR 1, 126 [319] (Heydon J)).

concept of "danger" is a present and predictive exercise.[96] Presumably would capture people who promote, incite, organise or engage in terrorism as well as those who have associated with or supported (financially or otherwise) terrorist organisations. Each of these actions constitutes a national security offence under Australian law.[97] The limb might also extend to conduct that marks the individual as a potential extremist, or signifies that they have skills (for instance in bomb-making or insurgency) that place them at risk of involvement in terrorism in Australia.

The second limb relates to those who are "a danger to the community." The word "danger" carries the same meaning as in s 36(1C)(a) and it means "present and serious risk". Dangerousness is not to be subsumed within and is linked to the "particularly serious crime" element,[98] which is characterised as including a refugee convicted by a final judgement of "a serious Australian offence" or, "a serious foreign offence." This element is defined further to include (*inter alia*) violent offences against a person punishable by not less than three years imprisonment.[99] Terrorism and terrorist organisation offences attract serious punishments, usually maximum sentences of life imprisonment, as do other national security offences including: entering a foreign country with the intention of engaging in hostile activity ('foreign incursion'),[100] espionage[101] and presence within a 'declared' overseas area.[102]

If a person is excluded on s 36(1C) grounds they are entitled to seek a review before the AAT. Except that, for reasons of national security, the right to review does not apply where the Minister chooses instead to exercise their personal powers, under s 502 *Migration Act*, to refuse a protection visa and certify a person as an "excluded person." The Minister has the final say, subject to being answerable to parliament,[103] and the limited supervisory jurisdiction of the courts to guard against illegality, (for instance, on the basis of bias, unreasonableness, ulterior purpose or bad faith).

96 *EWG17 v Minister for Immigration and Border Protection* [2018] FCA 1536, [14] (Collier J); and, *DOB18 v Minister for Home Affairs* [2019] FCAFC 63 [74], the concept and meaning of "danger" is the same under either limb of s 36(1C).

97 *Criminal Code Act 1995* Div 101 (Terrorism), Div 102 (Terrorist Organisations).

98 *DOB18 v Minister for the Home Affairs* [2019] FCAFC 63 [48]–[49], [72]–[83] (Logan J). Australian law establishes that there must be separate findings as to a "particularly serious crime" and existence of a "danger to the community".

99 *Migration Act 1958* s 5M and s 5(1), respectively.

100 *Criminal Code Act 1995* s 119.1, stipulating a maximum sentence of life imprisonment.

101 Ibid Div 91, which provides for a complex scheme espionage and espionage-related offences.

102 Ibid s 119.2, stipulating a maximum sentence of ten years imprisonment.

103 *Migration Act 1958* (Cth) s 502(3). The Minister must lodge a notice of the decision before each House of Parliament within fifteen sitting days.

By focusing on the dangerousness of the person, s 36(1C) appears capable of supporting the exclusion of individuals from asylum who have engaged in terrorism related activities, shown signs of supporting such activities, and even those who demonstrate risk factors related to extremism or violent extremism. It is important to remember that these grounds for exclusion may be invoked by the Minister *before* the individual's protection needs have been determined, and that they operate within a broader context of indefinite administrative detention for "unlawful non-citizens."

4 Onshore Refugee Processing: Exclusion from Protection on Art 1F *Refugees Convention* Grounds

The exclusionary grounds explained above, in Part 3, operate in addition to the recognized grounds relating to particular crimes for denying protection under international refugee law. Article 1F of the *Refugees Convention* is re-enacted in ss 36(2)(a), 5H(2) and 36(2C)(a) of the *Migration Act* in respect of both refugee status applicants and complementary protection seekers respectively. Article 1F dis-applies the *Refugees Convention* for those 'undeserving' refugee applicants because they have committed particularly egregious acts, and so it functions to preserve the integrity and legitimacy of the refugee protection system, and hence public support for its viability, along with promoting community safety.[104] Among others, Simeon has observed that: "Terrorists would certainly be persons who could be excluded ... from Convention refugee status and international protection."[105] This is because Art 1F captures those non-citizens with respect to whom there are serious reasons for considering that they have "committed a crime against peace, a war crime, or a crime against humanity" (para (a)), or "a serious non-political crime outside the country of refuge prior to his admission to that country as a refugee" (para (b)), or have "been guilty of acts contrary to the purposes and principles of the United Nations" (para (c)). Moreover, as Simeon identifies, soft law – in the form of UNHCR's guidelines on the exclusion clause – confirms the necessity

104 *Febles v Canada* [2014] 3 SCR 431, 454–455 [35]-[36] (McLachin CJ) (LeBel, Rothstein, Moldaver and Wagner JJ concurring); and, *Minister for Immigration and Multicultural Affairs v Singh* (2002) 209 CLR 533, [94]-[96] (Kirby J). See, Maarten Bolhuis and Joris van Wijk, "Alleged Terrorists and Other Perpetrators of Serious Non-political Crimes: The Application of Article 1F(b) of the Refugee Convention in the Netherlands," *Journal of Refugee Studies* 29, no.1 (2016): 19, 21–23.

105 James C. Simeon, "Complicity and Culpability and the Exclusion of Terrorists from Convention Refugee Status Post-9/11," *Refugee Survey Quarterly* 29, no.4 (2011): 104, 113; and, Gilbert, "Exclusion under Article 1F," for an analysis of leading cases since 2001.

of excluding those who are involved in terrorist activities from Convention refugee status, and confirms that most terrorist activities would appear to be subsumed under Art 1F(b) and (c).[106]

4.1 *State of Satisfaction/Standard of Proof*

There must be "serious reasons for considering" that the protection seeker is excludable under Art 1F. The meaning of this distinctive evidentiary standard was finally settled by the HCA in *FTZK v Minister for Immigration and Border Protection*.[107] Perceiving an international consensus about the required standard of satisfaction (or, standard of proof), the HCA observed that this element requires "strong evidence," and this means more than reasonable suspicion. This requirement is underpinned by "a consciousness of the potentially profound adverse consequences of exclusion from the protection of the Refugees Convention for a person otherwise entitled to that protection."[108] The HCA's interpretation of "serious reasons for considering" in relation to Article 1F, applies with equal force to that same expression as enshrined in domestic law, per s 5H(2)(b) and s 36(2C)(a).

4.2 *Exclusion for the Commission of Serious International Crimes*

There is scant superior court authority on the meaning and application of Art 1F(a) and its codified counterparts[109] in Australia.[110] In *SRYYY*, the Federal Court considered the development of international criminal law,[111] deciding that the definition of international crimes is referable to any international

106 Simeon, "Complicity and Culpability," 115.

107 (2014) 88 ALJR 754. See *ZYVZ v Minister for Immigration, Citizenship, Migrant Services and Multicultural Affairs* [2020] FCA 28 [24]–[25] applying *FTZK* to the present statutory scheme for refugee protection.

108 Ibid, 760 [14] (French CJ and Gageler J), and [80], [83] (Crennan and Bell JJ). The HCA applied the considered approach taken in *Al-Sirri v Secretary of State for the Home Department* [2013] 1 AC 745 [14] (French CJ and Gageler J), and [74]–[75] (Crennan and Bell JJ)). In *Al-Sirri*, the Supreme Court observed that the "reality is that there are unlikely to be sufficiently serious reasons for considering the applicant to be guilty unless the decision-maker can be satisfied on the balance of probabilities that he is." (at [75] (Baroness Hale and Lord Dyson MR)).

109 *Refugees Convention* Art 1F(a), as codified in *Migration Act 1958* s 5H(2)(a), s 36(2C)(a)(i).

110 One notable case is *SZCWP, v Minister for Immigration and Multicultural and Indigenous Affairs* [2006] FCAFC 9 (Gyles and Downes JJ, Wilcox J dissenting) the Federal Court concluded that the applicant – as an active member of a violent Maoist insurgency group in Nepal that had targeted civilians and public officials – was excludable, because he was responsible for (complicit in) international crimes contrary to elements of Articles 7 and 8 of the *Rome Statute of the International Criminal Court*.

111 *SRYYY v Minister for Immigration and Multicultural and Indigenous Affairs* (2005) 147 FCR 1, [19]-[49] (The Court).

instrument (including non-binding instruments) drawn up to make provision in respect of such crimes, as well as to customary international law.[112] The government subsequently prescribed a non-exhaustive list of twelve international instruments defining international crimes, that are relevant for refugee status and complementary protection claims pursuant to the Government's customized legislative scheme.[113] It appears open to decision-makers to select the most appropriate instrument in the circumstances.[114] However, whilst it is conceivable that terrorism and related conduct could fall within the scope of serious international crimes thus defined, both international and domestic law more clearly intend for terrorism to be dealt with under either the non-political crime exclusion or for acts contrary to the purposes and principles of the UN.

4.3 *Exclusion for the Commission of Serious Non-political Crimes*

Article 1F(b), as related to refugee/complementary protection visa applicants under municipal law,[115] operates to exclude from protection those for whom there are "serious reasons for considering that the person/non-citizen has committed a serious non-political crime before entering Australia." This provision has, traditionally, been the most pertinent for immigration officials determining protection visa claims, and been the subject of fairly extensive judicial consideration. *Minister for Immigration and Multicultural Affairs v Singh*[116] was the leading authority before Parliament intervened with its own statutory annotation in 2001.[117] At that particular point in time, Australia had no federal counter-terrorism laws and, therefore, no domestic definition of terrorism to contemplate when determining the scope of Art 1F(b).

The HCA decision in *Singh*, has been hailed as "enlightened,"[118] and the Court's decision is a nuanced response to the complexities arising from cases involving asylum seekers and alleged terrorism. The Court held (by a majority) that whether a crime was committed for political purposes must be assessed after consideration of all the circumstances, and that there was no bright line

112 Ibid, [59]-[67] (The Court). The Statute for the International Tribunal for Rwanda (ICTR) provides for (inter alia) criminal responsibility in respect of 'Acts of terrorism' (*SRYYY* at [35]).

113 Migration Regulations 1994, Reg 2.03B.

114 *SRYYY v Minister for Immigration and Multicultural and Indigenous Affairs* (2005) 147 FCR 1, 26 [73] (The Court).

115 *Migration Act 1958* s 5H(2)(b) and s 36(2C)(a)(ii).

116 (2002) 209 CLR 533.

117 Section 91T *Migration Act 1958* was inserted by the *Migration Legislation Amendment Act (No. 6)*, with effect from 1 October 2001.

118 Satvinder Juss, "Detention and Delusion," 159; and, Satvinder Juss, "Terrorism and the Exclusion of Refugee Status in the UK" *Journal of Conflict & Security* Law 17, no.3 (2012): 465, 467–468 (discussing *Singh*).

dividing political and non-political crime categories. Further, that there should be a close causal link between the criminal act and its alleged political purpose and object, to warrant appropriate characterization as a political act. For the majority, Gleeson CJ observed that, when stating the principles according to which violent crimes committed in another country in different circumstances could be considered political action, the courts had been at pains "to confine the concept of political crime so as to avoid the consequence that all offences committed with a political motivation fall within it."[119] Though terrorist activity *is* typically considered and described as politically motivated violence, Gleeson CJ affirmed that "terrorist activities are not political crimes" for the reasons given by the House of Lords in the important case of *T v Home Secretary*.[120] *T* was a case in which the Court demarcated political and non-political crimes, Lord Lloyd defined a political crime, for Art 1F purposes, thus:

> If (1) it is committed for a political purpose, ..., with the object of overthrowing or subverting or changing the government of a state or inducing it to change its policy; and (2) there is a sufficiently close and direct link between the crime and the alleged political purpose. In determining whether such a link exists, the court will bear in mind the means used to achieve the political end, and will have particular regard to whether the crime was aimed at a military or governmental target, on the one hand, or a civilian target on the other, and in either event whether it was likely to involve the indiscriminate killing or injuring of members of the public.[121]

In *Singh*, Gaudron J was disapproving of the understandable tendency to delimit the notion of non-political crimes by reference to (inter alia) "terrorist activities." Her Honour observed that, "such descriptions are imprecise and may, on that account, involve over-simplification. Moreover, and more to the point, they find no expression in the text of the Convention itself."[122] She continued by explaining that: "Actions which are either unnecessary or disproportionate to the political objectives which are said to justify them are, perhaps, usefully described as 'terrorist' activities."[123] Her Honour added that for Article 1F(b) purposes that description "is not, of itself determinative. The issue is

119 (2002) 209 CLR 533, 543 [16].

120 (2002) 209 CLR 533, 544 [17].

121 *T v Home Secretary* [1996] AC 742, 786–787 (Lord Lloyd of Berwick) (Lord Keith of Kinkel and Lord Browne-Wilkinson, agreeing).

122 (2002) 209 CLR 533, 551 [41].

123 *Minister for Immigration v Singh* (2002) 209 CLR 533, 552 [47].

whether the actions in question were undertaken for a political purpose, in the sense that that purpose was a *significant* purpose" (emphasis supplied).[124]

Kirby J, also in the majority in *Singh*, identified various attempts to characterise conduct that would take a refugee applicant outside of the protection of the *Refugees Convention*, observing:

> Thus if the crime concerned involved an "atrocious act, grossly out of proportion to any genuine political objective," such that it could not reasonably be seen to be advancing a political objective, it might be classified as "non-political." Likewise, the infliction of indiscriminate violence; the "open manifestation of anarchy"; the perpetration of "acts of odious barbarism and vandalism"; the involvement in a "rampage" of crime or sheer acts of terrorism, have all been excluded from the category of "political crime."[125]

Kirby J was sceptical about the utility of such labels; so to avoid an over-simplistic view of the characterisation of crimes he stated that decision-makers should approach the task of characterising criminal conduct mindful that there was no bright line between political and non-political crimes. To be "political" the commission of the crime must be closely linked with the purpose of changing the political environment. Further, he observed that motivations will be relevant considerations but that personal grudges or motivations are not, *per se*, non-political impulses. Additionally, Kirby J found that in deciding whether a crime is "political" or not it may be relevant to consider the weapons and means used; whether the "target" of the crime is a public official or government agent, as distinct from unarmed civilians chosen indiscriminately; and whether the crime is proportionate to the political end propounded.[126]

When the matter of *Singh* was heard by the HCA there was no statutory definition of "non-political crime." Just prior to the HCA delivering its judgement in *Singh*, Parliament moved to countermand "enlightened" court judgments that, purportedly, set the bar too low when determining the degree of political motivation needed in order for a criminal act to fall outside of Art 1F.[127] Therefore, as currently configured, the concept of non-political crime is modified and

124 Ibid. Gleeson CJ also stated that the achievement of the political objective must be the *substantial* purpose of the act at *Minister for Immigration v Singh* (2002) 209 CLR 533, 545 [21]-[22]. Cf. the statutory definition in s 5(1) *Migration Act*.

125 Ibid 569 [111].

126 Ibid 578–579 [141].

127 Migration Legislation Amendment Bill (No.6) 2001, Explanatory Memorandum, [33].

extended by s 5(1) of the *Migration Act*.[128] This stipulates that a "non-political crime" is where a person's motives for committing the crime were *wholly or mainly* non-political in nature. Accordingly, to avoid exclusion a political motivation must be more than a significant factor, it must be the primary motivation. This legislative standard rejects the more nuanced approach taken by the majority in *Singh*,[129] and this stricter requirement appears inconsistent with the *Refugees Convention* absent any indication in that treaty to suggest that the political purpose should be the sole or, even, the overriding purpose of the crime, so long as it is a significant purpose.

For the purposes of the *Migration Act* the particular meaning of Art 1F(b) has been clarified by s 5(1)(a)-(c). These provisions ensure the expression "non-political crime" is understood to encompass terrorism and limits the interpretative discretion of administrative and judicial decision-makers. Specifically, s 5(1) defines non-political crimes to include: (a) offences of a political character that involve an act of violence against a person's life or liberty; (b) extraditable offences (as prescribed in regulations); or (c) an offence that is not a political offence in relation to a (prescribed) country. The *Extradition Act 1988* identifies a broad range of offences that are considered non-political, including offences referred to in a number of specified international instruments.[130]

Beyond extraditable criminality, accepted standards of serious criminality within Australian domestic law have guided decision-makers in the course in determining the gravity of non-political crimes.[131] Recently, administrative decision-makers have used the statutory definitions of a "serious Australian offence" and "serious foreign offence," as benchmarks for indicating what sort of offences may be considered serious enough to warrant exclusion from protection. These definitions include elements relating to violence against the person and serious damage to property, and stipulate that offences be punishable by at least three years imprisonment.[132] As outlined above, this would

128 Inserted by *Migration Amendment (Complementary Protection) Act 2011* (No.121 of 2011). The definition effectively substituted that in s.91T.

129 *Re YYMT and FRFJ* (2010) 115 ALD 590, 663–664 [207] (DP Forgie), construing s 91T.

130 *Extradition Act 1988* s 5(a)-(c) wherein the definition of 'political offence' excludes all offences that involve an act of violence against a person's life or liberty and any offences relevantly prescribed by regulation. The *Extradition Act* was amended by the *Extradition and Mutual Assistance in Criminal Matters Legislation Amendment Act 2012* (Cth).

131 *Dhayakpa v Minister for Immigration and Ethnic Affairs* (1995) 62 FCR 556, and *Ovcharuk v Minister for Immigration and Multicultural Affairs* (1998) 88 FCR 173.

132 *JDSW v Minister for Border Protection* [2017] AATA 2420 [38], [41], [44] (Kendall DP, Boyle DP). See, further *ZYVZ v Minister for Immigration, Citizenship, Migrant Services and Multiculturalism* [2020] FCA 28 [90]–[98] discussing, without resolving, the question of whether people smuggling was a serious crime.

encompass terrorism and terrorist organisation offences under the *Criminal Code*.[133] Administrative decision makers have accepted that the particular circumstances of the commission of the crime need to be taken into account.[134]

Thus, all three branches of government – the parliament through legislation, the executive via regulations and AAT decisions, as well as the judiciary – have ensured that violent and serious offences, such as terrorism, are excluded from the scope of 'political' offences, thereby ensuring that the Art 1F(b) ground of exclusion applies, straightforwardly, to persons engaged in terrorism. Paradoxically, the s 5(1) definition of non-political crime in the *Migration Act 1958* sits awkwardly alongside the legislative definition of terrorism introduced in 2002. A "terrorist act" is defined as an action or threat necessarily undertaken with the intention of advancing a *political*, or religious, or ideological cause, and either coercing or influencing by intimidation a government, or intimidating the public or a section of the public.[135]

Thus, the *non-political* crime exclusion serves to encompass terrorism, despite Australian law defining terrorism by reference to the actor's *political* (or religious or ideological) intent.

4.4 *Exclusion for Acts Contrary to the Purposes of the UN*[136]

As is well known, in the aftermath of the attacks on the World Trade Centre in New York, Security Council Resolution 1373 (2001) was adopted on 28 September 2001.[137] Paragraph 5 of the Resolution, declares:

> that acts, methods, and practices of terrorism are contrary to the purposes and principles of the United Nations and that knowingly financing, planning and inciting terrorist acts are also contrary to the purposes and principles of the United Nations.

In *SRLLL*, the AAT found strong evidence that the refugee applicant committed acts of terrorism by his involvement in the murder of three police officers. Accordingly, the Tribunal considered it reasonable to rely on Security Council Resolution 1373 (2001) "as a statement that terrorist acts are contrary to the

133 *Criminal Code Act 1995* Div 101 and 102.

134 *JDSW v Minister for Border Protection* [2017] AATA 2420 [48].

135 *Criminal Code Act 1995* s 100.1(2). Notably, actions and threats will not qualify as terrorist acts if they are advocacy, protest, dissent or industrial action that is not intended to harm, endanger, or risk the health or safety of others (s 100.1(3)).

136 As codified in the *Migration Act 1958* s 5H(2)(c) and s 36(2C)(a)(iii).

137 Cited in UNHCR, *Background Note on the Application of the Exclusion Clauses: Article 1F of the 1951 Convention relating to the Status of Refugees*, Geneva, 4 September 2003, [49].

purposes and principles of the United Nations, so that the paragraph (c) exclusion" applies.[138] This (apparently, isolated) invocation of Art 1F(c) in Australia sets a lower bar than has subsequently been established in *Al Sirri*, a case in which the UK Supreme Court found that the acts in question had to have adverse international repercussions, and that the correct approach was to interpret Art 1F cautiously and apply it restrictively.[139] Noting the absence of an internationally agreed definition of terrorism, and no Convention binding member states to take action against it, the Supreme Court followed UNHCR guidance, determining that:

> article 1F(c) was only triggered in extreme circumstances by activity which attacked the basis of the international community's coexistence,…; that, since the essence of terrorism was the commission, incitement or threat of serious acts of violence against persons or property for the purpose of intimidation for political ends, such activity could also have international repercussions within the meaning of that guidance; and that whether the test would be met where a person plotted in one state to destabilise conditions in another would depend on the circumstances of the case and whether the resulting acts would have the requisite serious effect on international peace, security and peaceful relations between states.[140]

Read together the sections of the *Migration Act* which reflect Art 1F operate to exclude terrorist offenders. However, this ground of exclusion is rarely invoked in Australia for two reasons. First, there are many alternative grounds for exclusion in the form of adverse security assessments or on community safety grounds (outlined above) and the character test (discussed below). Secondly, there is greater transparency, procedural justice and independent review rights attending Art 1F-based administrative decisions compared with ASIO's adverse security assessments and when ministers make adverse character assessments personally.[141]

138 *SRLLL v Minister for Immigration and Multicultural and Indigenous Affairs* [2002] AATA 795 [59] (Handley DP).

139 *Al-Sirri v Secretary of State for the Home Department* [2012] 3 WLR 1263, 1265.

140 Ibid, [10]-[16], [36]-[40] (Baroness Hale and Lord Dyson MR).

141 A decision to reject a protection seeker under Art 1F (or codified equivalents, per s5H and s 36(2) ('refugee status') and s 36(2C)(a) ('complementary protection regime')), is amenable to merits review by the AAT (unless the Minister acts personally to exclude a person under s 502). On the importance of procedural fairness in Art 1F cases, see Michael Bliss, "'Serious Reasons for Considering': Minimum Standards of Procedural Fairness in the

5 Onshore Refugee Processing: Exclusion on Public Interest Grounds – the 'character test'

One of the public interest criteria a protection visa applicant must satisfy is directed to the character test. The character test serves as a legal foundation for visa *refusal* and visa *cancellation*, permitting the government to exclude protection visa applicants and protection visa holders by reason of their criminal record, past activities, relationships or reputation.[142] As such it presents a very flexible device by which individuals may be excluded from asylum and refugee protection. The circumstances in which a person will not pass the 'character test' are far-reaching,[143] and several elements intersect with the *Refugees Convention*. Accordingly, there is a clear overlap between s 501(6)(d)(v) – the person would "represent a danger to the Australian community or to a segment of that community" – and the basis for expulsion (Art 32) or withdrawal of protection from *refoulement* (Art 33(2)).[144]

Furthermore, the character test permits the refusal or cancellation of a visa on grounds that accord with Art 1F. However, the requisite standard of proof appears too low in light of international law requirements. Specifically, s 501(6)(ba)(iii) provides that a person does not pass the character test if the minister "reasonably suspects" that they have been "involved" in conduct that would constitute international crimes: the crime of genocide, a crime against humanity, a war crime, torture, slavery, or any other crime of serious international concern.[145] By contrast, as noted above, there is an international consensus that the Art 1F evidentiary standard – "serious reasons for considering" – demands more than a reasonable suspicion. Art 1F also stipulates that the individual "has committed" the crimes referred to in art 1F(a)-(b) or "been guilty of" the acts referred to in art 1F(c) which supplies a more exacting standard than the vague legislative reference to involvement.

Application of the Article 1F Exclusion Clauses," *International Journal of Refugee Law* 12, (Supp. Issue) (2000): 92.

142 See, *Migration Act 1958* s 65(1), and Migration Regulations 1994 Sch.2 cl. 866.225 (a) and Sch 4 (Pt.1 Public interest criteria). The character test is set out in the *Migration Act 1958* s 501 and supplies permissive and mandatory grounds for visa refusal/cancellation.

143 The character test was substantially reformed in 2014, these legislative changes broadened the application of the character test (see, Peter Billings, "Getting Rid of Risky Foreigners: Promoting Community Protection at the Expense of Administrative Justice" *Federal Law Review* 47 (no.2), (2019): 231).

144 *M47*, 37 [40] (French CJ), [191] (Hayne J), [380] (Crennan J).

145 Section 501(6)(f) also links with Art 1F, providing that a person does not pass the character test if the person has, in Australia or in a foreign country, been "charged or indicted" with, *inter alia*, genocide, a crime against humanity, or war crime.

Yet the character test goes much further than the enumeration of grounds that purport to 'pick up' international refugee law's exclusionary grounds, and this clearly has the potential to limit a refugee's access to protection visas and durable asylum in Australia. For example, s 501(6)(b) grounds an adverse character assessment where the minister reasonably suspects that the person has been, or is, a member of a criminal group or organisation. It suffices if the person "has been or is a member" of such a group or organisation. Consequently, because mere membership of any group reasonably suspected of any criminal activity is enough, the Minister is not required to further ruminate about whether a person's association with a group or organisation "has a bearing" on the person's character.[146] Therefore, the Minister can refuse or cancel the visa of a person on the basis of a reasonable suspicion of mere membership of the relevant group, without satisfaction (or even reasonable suspicion) that the visa holder has an 'association' with the group, and without forming any positive state of satisfaction as to whether the group is involved in criminal conduct at all.[147] There is a right to appeal an adverse character assessment before the AAT, although this is precluded where decisions are made personally by the Minister in the 'national interest'.

Aspects of the character test align with the approach adopted in Australia's counter-terrorism laws, under which membership of a terrorist organisation is an offence punishable by 10 years imprisonment,[148] and associating with a member of a terrorist organisation on two or more occasions can, in some circumstances, amount to a criminal offence punishable by 3 years imprisonment.[149] Terrorist organisation offences further extend to directing,[150] recruiting,[151] training,[152] funding[153] and supporting[154] these groups, with these

146 *Stevens v Minister for Immigration and Border Protection* [2016] FCA 1280 (2 November 2016) [102] (Charlesworth J). On the breadth of s 501(6)(b) see Parliamentary Joint Committee on Human Rights, *Human rights scrutiny report – Nineteenth Report of the 44th Parliament* (2015) 23.

147 *Stevens* [2016] FCA 1280 (2 November 2016) [128] (Charlesworth J).

148 *Criminal Code Act 1995* (Cth) s 102.3.

149 Ibid s 102.8. The person must intentionally associate with a person he or she knows to be a member of a terrorist organisation, or who promotes or directs the activities of a terrorist organisation; know the relevant organisation is a terrorist organisation; and the association does, and is intended to, support the terrorist organisation. There are a range of exclusions from the association offence, including associations with close family members, and associations to provide aid, humanitarian assistance or legal advice.

150 Ibid s 102.2.

151 Ibid s 102.4.

152 Ibid s 102.5.

153 Ibid s 102.6.

154 Ibid s 102.7.

offences attracting up to 25 years imprisonment if the person knows the group is a terrorist organisation, and up to 15 years if the person is reckless as to this fact. Prosecution for one of these offences would require a full criminal trial and proof beyond reasonable doubt, whereas exclusion on character grounds merely requires a reasonable suspicion on the part of executive officials. However, the policy position is consistent: reprehensible conduct arises from mere association with or membership of a certain group, the person's own intentions and state of mind are a secondary concern.

Crucial to these counter-terrorism provisions is the process by which terrorist organisations are identified. Under s 102.1 of the *Criminal Code (Cth)*, a terrorist organisation is any "organisation that is directly or indirectly engaged in, preparing, planning, assisting in or fostering the doing of a terrorist act". The definition of terrorist act is outlined above. Importantly, this definition has been criticised as being so broad its meaning is unclear.[155] That breadth carries over into the terrorist organisation provisions; however, the key method by which terrorist organisations are identified does not necessarily engage this definition. The *Criminal Code* empowers the executive government to "list" an organisation as a terrorist organisation.[156] At present, 26 organisations are listed terrorist organisations, including a range of Al-Qa'ida and IS-related groups, the Kurdistan Workers' Party (PKK) and Lashkar-e-Tayyiba.[157]

Accordingly, the government is in a position to list a terrorist organisation and then deny a visa application or cancel an existing visa on the basis of a reasonable suspicion that the person is, or has been, a member or associate of the group. Whilst membership and association are criminal offences, the legal and practical consequences of visa refusal for an asylum-seeker or cancellation for a refugee/complementary protection visa holder may be more injurious

155 Parliamentary Joint Committee on Intelligence and Security, Parliament of Australia, *Review of Security and Counter-Terrorism Legislation* (2006), xvii recommendation 10; Security Legislation Review Committee, Parliament of Australia, *Report of the Security Legislation Review Committee* (2006), 10 recommendations 6–8; Council of Australian Governments, *Council of Australian Governments Review of Counter-Terrorism Legislation* (14 May 2013), x; Bret Walker, *Independent National Security Monitor Declassified Annual Report 20th December 2012* (14 May 2013), 128. See also, Special Rapporteur on the Promotion and Protection of Human Rights while Countering Terrorism, *Australia: Study on Human Rights Compliance while Countering Terrorism,* UN Doc A/HRC/4/26/Add.3 (2006), [10]; Nicola McGarrity, '"Testing" Our Counter-Terrorism Laws: The Prosecution of Individuals for Terrorism Offences in Australia' *Criminal Law Journal* 34, (2010): 92, 113–14.

156 *Criminal Code Act 1995* s 102.1.

157 Australian Government, "Australian National Security: Listed Terrorist Organisations," https://www.nationalsecurity.gov.au/listedterroristorganisations/pages/default.aspx, accessed April 16, 2020.

than a defined term of imprisonment. We explore these notions further below in the context of citizenship stripping.

6 The Exclusion of Dual Nationals from Australia

Should an asylum seeker be successful in obtaining a refugee or complementary protection visa, and then proceed to obtain Australian citizenship,[158] they may yet be subject to denaturalisation, detention, removal and barriers to re-entry on national security grounds, *provided* they maintain the nationality of another country. However, in the case of a declared refugee the normal social bonds – of trust, loyalty, protection and assistance – existing between the individual and their country of origin have been severed. As Macklin, observes, "the legal citizenship possessed by a refugee is substantively hollow insofar as membership in a state from which one reasonably apprehends persecution is the cause and not the solution for insecurity."[159] Thus, for a person who obtained a protection visa (as a refugee or beneficiary of complementary protection) and then citizenship in Australia, the revocation of citizenship may leave them effectively stateless, contrary to international law.[160] In such a scenario, it is unlikely they would retain or be granted another protection visa (or any other visa) by Australia and, in most cases, gaining admission to a safe third

158 It should be noted that since June 2014 the processing of certain citizenship applications, seemingly lodged by refugees who were 'irregular maritime arrivals', has been characterised by enhanced scrutiny – seemingly due to 'character' concerns and identity issues. But this has led to administrative drift and unreasonable delays – see *BMF16 v Minister for Border Protection* [2016] FCA 1530. Evidently, checks on identity plays a critical role in mitigating national security risks (Commonwealth Ombudsman, "Delays in processing of applications for Australian Citizenship by conferral" (December 2017) 8).

159 Audrey Macklin, "The Securitisation of Dual Citizenship" in *Dual Citizenship in Global Perspective*, ed. Thomas Faist and Peter Kivisto (London: Palgrave Macmillan, 2007), 43.

160 Article 8 of the 1961 *Convention on the Reduction of Statelessness*, adopted on *30 August 1961, 989 UNTS 175* (entered into force on 13 December 1975) prevents signatory countries from depriving people of their nationality if it would render them stateless. See further; Michelle Foster, Jane McAdam and Davina Wadley, "Part Two: The Prevention and Reduction of Statelessness in Australia – An Ongoing Challenge" *Melbourne University Law Review* 40, (2016): 456, 488–504 where the authors carefully examine (inter alia) the *Allegiance to Australia Act 2015 (Cth)* and its potential usage for rendering persons stateless; and, Guy Goodwin-Gill, *Deprivation of Citizenship Resulting in Statelessness and its Implications in International Law: Opinion*, March, 12, 2014, http://www.kaldorcentre.unsw.edu.au/sites/default/files/gsgg%202-deprivationcitizenshipintlawfinal.pdf, accessed January 17, 2019.

country would be unrealistic.[161] Thus, revocation of Australian citizenship has the potential to place a refugee in 'legal limbo' and carries a significant risk of *refoulement* or prolonged and indefinite administrative detention. These risks are heightened by the novel design of the denaturalisation provisions and by the government's demonstrably flawed approach to assessing accurately a person's dual nationality status.

In December 2015, the Australian Parliament enacted the *Australian Citizenship Amendment (Allegiance to Australia) Act 2016* (Cth) ('AAA') which created three fresh grounds by which the Australian citizenship of dual nationals aged 14 years or over could be revoked. Scholars have expressed reservations about the practical benefit of these citizenship law reforms to national security.[162] The first two grounds for revocation claim to be self-executing whereas the third operates by ministerial discretion.

The first ground of citizenship loss is 'renunciation by conduct'. Renunciation by conduct first requires that the person engage in prescribed conduct, defined by reference to terrorism, foreign incursion and recruitment offences.[163] That conduct must be engaged in with the same intent that applies to acts of terrorism under the *Criminal Code (Cth)*, namely: "advancing a political, religious or ideological cause";[164] "coercing, or influencing by intimidation" a government;[165] or "intimidating the public or a section of the public".[166] Therefore, a dual national who engages in conduct that qualifies as a terrorism offence under Australian law may automatically lose their Australian citizenship. Moreover, a dual national is taken to have satisfied these two grounds if they are a member of, are instructed by, or are cooperating with a listed terrorist organisation.[167]

The second ground for automatic revocation of Australian citizenship for a dual national is if they serve in the armed forces of a country at war with Australia, or fight for or is "in the service of" a listed terrorist organisation.[168] To be caught by this section, the person's actions must have been intentional, not

161 A similar scenario, namely the case of Hirsi Ali, is discussed in Macklin, "Securitisation," 46–47.

162 Pillai and Williams, "Citizenship Stripping," 32–37; and, in a European context, Lucia Zedner, "Citizenship Deprivation, Security and Human Rights" *European Journal of Migration and Law* 18, (2016): 222, 241.

163 *Australian Citizenship Act 2007* (Cth) s 33AA(2).

164 Ibid s 33AA(3)(a).

165 Ibid s 33AA(3)(b)(i).

166 Ibid s 33AA(3)(b)(ii).

167 Ibid s 33AA(4).

168 Ibid s 35.

performed under duress or force, and must not qualify as "neutral and independent humanitarian assistance".[169] The automatic operation of these provisions suggests that a refugee's (severed) relationship with their country of origin will be irrelevant to the initial revocation of Australian citizenship. This issue only comes to the fore if the Minister considers whether to exempt the person from the operation of the provisions (discussed below).

The third avenue of citizenship loss requires that the dual national be convicted of one or more specified terrorism or foreign incursion offences and sentenced to at least six years imprisonment (in a single sentence or cumulatively).[170] Alternatively, a person may be captured by this provision if they were convicted of a relevant offence between December 2005 and December 2015 and were sentenced to a period of at least ten years imprisonment in respect of that conviction.[171] If one of these requirements is met, Australian citizenship may be revoked by exercise of ministerial discretion, provided that the Minister is satisfied that the conduct to which the conviction relates "demonstrates that the person has repudiated their allegiance to Australia" and that revocation is in the public interest.[172] As to the public interest criterion, the Federal Court has recently affirmed that in the visa cancellation context the expression 'national interest' "is, like the expression 'public interest', one of considerable breadth and essentially involves a political question ... entrusted to the Minister."[173]

Upon becoming aware that a person has ceased to be an Australian citizen by operation of the provisions outlined above, the Minister is required to make reasonable attempts to give the non-citizen notice of the revocation.[174] The Minister may, however, determine not to provide this notice in order to protect Australia's national security, defence, international relations or law enforcement operations.[175] The Minister may also decide to exempt a person from the operation of the first two, automatic, avenues of citizenship loss. In exercising this discretionary power the Minister is to have regard to a set of factors which includes the availability of alternative citizenship rights, as well as the rights of

169 Ibid s 35(4).

170 Ibid s 35A(1)(a)-(c).

171 *Australian Citizenship Amendment (Allegiance to Australia) Act 2015* (Cth) s 8(4).

172 *Australian Citizenship Act 2007* s 35A(1)(d)-(e).

173 *Carrascalao v Minister for Immigration and Border Protection* (2017) 252 FCR 352, 390 [156] (The Court), citing *The Pilbara Infrastructure Pty Ltd v Australian Competition Tribunal* (2012) 246 CLR 379, [42] (French CJ, Gummow, Hayne, Heydon, Crennan, Kiefel and Bell JJ).

174 *Australian Citizenship Act 2007* s 33AA(10), s 35(5), s 35A(5).

175 Ibid s 33AA(12), s 35(7), s 35A(7).

the child (if the person is a minor), and the public interest.[176] The exemption power is non-compellable,[177] and it is non-delegable as it is conferred personally on the Minister.[178] Therefore, citizenship revocation may leave a person in possession of their original "substantively hollow" (and insecure) citizenship status and the Minister would be under no obligation to exempt the person from revocation, or even to consider whether to do so.

The claim that the first two grounds of citizenship revocation are "self-executing" has been described as a "legal fiction".[179] To assist the operation of the scheme, the government created a non-statutory executive body, the Citizenship Loss Board, composed of senior departmental secretaries.[180] The Board's terms of reference, composition and mandate are undefined. Its uncertain role and place in the citizenship revocation framework undermines the potential for effective review or oversight of the Board's functions. Pillai and Williams have argued that the lack of a legislative foundation for the Board suggests that it "operates according to its own rules, free from typical administrative law constraints such as the requirement to make decisions reasonably and without bias".[181] The operation of the denaturalisation provisions, including the Minister's roles and that of the Citizenship Loss Board, are shrouded in secrecy. There is no merits review and there is limited scope for judicial review of the operation of the provisions.[182] For instance, in the case of the self-executing provisions there is technically no decision that one could seek to have reviewed.[183]

176 Ibid s 33AA(14)(b), (16), (17) 35(9)(b), (11), (12).

177 Ibid s 33AA(15), s 35(10).

178 Ibid s 33AA (20), s 35(15).

179 Helen Irving, "Bill relies on legal fiction of self-executing law to revoke citizenship," *The Conversation*, August 17, 2017, https://theconversation.com/bill-relies-on-legal-fiction-of-self-executing-law-to-revoke-citizenship-46017. 2015.

180 Sangeetha Pillai and George Williams, "The Utility of Citizenship Stripping Laws in the UK, Canada and Australia," *Melbourne University Law Review* 41, (2018): 874; Jessie Blackbourn, Deniz Kayis and Nicola McGarrity, *Anti-Terrorism Law and Foreign Terrorist Fighters* (New York: Routledge, 2018), 80.

181 Pillai and Williams, "Citizenship Stripping," 874. See also, Blackbourn, McGarrity and Kayis, *Anti-Terrorism Law*, 80. Although there is authority that non-statutory bodies exercising public powers apt to adversely affect individual's interests, are subject to judicial supervision and conventional administrative law principles (see *R v Criminal Injuries Compensation Board ex parte Lain* [1967] 2 QB 864; and *R v Panel on Takeovers and Mergers; Ex parte Datafin Plc* [1987] QB 815).

182 Blackbourn, McGarrity and Kayis, *Anti-Terrorism Law*, 79–80.

183 Ibid 80.

At September 2015, 18 Australians had been identified as potential targets for citizenship revocation.[184] To date, the provisions have been used against twelve individuals, though very little is known about the specific revocations.[185] The first person to be subject to the provisions was notorious foreign terrorist fighter, Khaled Sharrouf, in February 2017.[186] Sharrouf and most of his family have since been killed in Syria. In August 2018 the government revoked the Australian citizenship of five more dual nationals. The only details revealed of these individuals were that they were 'predominantly' from Melbourne and Sydney and sourced their dual nationality 'from a variety of countries'.[187]

Most recently, the government notified Neil Prakash "that his Australian citizenship had ceased due to being in the service of Islamic State".[188] At this time, Prakash – a known IS member and recruiter – was imprisoned in Turkey on serious terrorism charges. He was also subject to a formal extradition request by the Australian Government so he could face an array of further terrorism charges.[189] Whilst Prakash has never held nor applied for refugee/complementary protection status, the revocation of his citizenship is troubling because it demonstrates a lack of rigour on the government's part when assessing a person's dual nationality status. The government's announcement was

184 Ibid 80.

185 The Hon Peter Dutton MP, Media Release, *Neil Prakash stripped of Australian citizenship*, December 29, 2018, https://minister.homeaffairs.gov.au/peterdutton/Pages/Neil-Prakash-stripped-of-Australian-citizenshp.aspx, accessed January 14, 2019.

186 Jane Norman and Caitlyn Gribbin, "Islamic State fighter Khaled Sharrouf becomes first to lose citizenship under anti terror laws," *ABC News*, February 11, 2017, https://www.abc.net.au/news/2017-02-11/islamic-state-fighter-khaled-sharrouf-stripped of citizenship/8262268, accessed January 14, 2019.

187 The Hon Peter Dutton MP, Interview by Neil Mitchell. *Radio 3AW*, August 9, 2018, https://minister.homeaffairs.gov.au/peterdutton/Pages/interview-with-neil-mitchell-radio-3aw.aspx, accessed January 14, 2018.

188 Dutton, *Neil Prakash*.

189 An extradition request was rejected by Turkish courts in mid-2018, before the decision was made to prosecute Prakash under Turkish law: Sean Rubinsztein-Dunlop, "Neil Prakash: Turkish court rejects request to extradite Australian Islamic State terrorist," *ABC News*, July 20, 2018, https://www.abc.net.au/news/2018-07-20/islamic-state-terrorist-neil-prakash-could-be-released-from-jail/10016444, accessed January 17, 2019. And the Australian Government has not confirmed whether a further extradition request exists: David Wroe, "Prakash citizenship revocation could jeopardise extradition chances, says Law Council," *The Sydney Morning Herald*, January 3, 2019, https://www.smh.com.au/politics/federal/prakash-citizenship-revocation-could-jeopardise-extradition-chances-says-law-council-20190103-p50ph6.html, accessed January 17, 2019.

based upon advice from the Citizenship Loss Board to the effect that Prakash was a Fijian citizen.[190] However, Fiji did not allow dual citizenship until 2009, after which Melbourne-born Prakash could only have obtained Fijian citizenship by registering to become Fijian and by living in Fiji for at least three of the five years prior lodging his application.[191] Fiji's director of immigration has expressed his certainty that Prakash is not a Fijian citizen, and claimed that no one from the Fijian Government had been consulted before Prakash's Australian citizenship had been revoked.[192] It appears unlikely that the revocation could stand under current law. Essentially, Prakash may retain his Australian citizenship by virtue of his sole-citizen status. However, if the government had been successful in passing a Bill introduced in December 2018, relaxing the precondition of dual nationality,[193] Prakash would be facing statelessness.

These recent developments give pause for thought. As Foster, McAdam and Wadley observe "neither the legislation itself, nor anything in the background materials, provides guidance as to how the Australian government will verify that a person is a dual national,"[194] and the process relies "on a closed, opaque, internal administrative procedure … at odds with the procedural safeguards adopted in many comparable jurisdictions."[195] That said, the onus to ensure dual nationality would at least require "the government to investigate with the 'competent authority' of the person's presumed other state of nationality as to whether the person is, in fact, a citizen."[196] Prakash was stripped of his Australian citizenship in circumstances where officials were insufficiently attentive to his lack of Fijian nationality. If a similar lack of care attended the stripping of a refugee's Australian citizenship the impact would be serious, placing the person in 'legal limbo' and risking potential *refoulement*, as outlined above.[197] This is in addition to potentially violating international obligations, including those relating to the prevention and prosecution of international criminal conduct.[198] Additionally, it is arguable that the revocation laws are constitutionally

190 The Hon Josh Frydenberg MP, "Doorstop interview, Lorne, Victoria." Interview, January 3, 2019, http://jaf.ministers.treasury.gov.au/transcript/103-2018/, accessed January 17, 2019.

191 David Wroe, "Dutton's citizenship case against terrorist Prakash shredded" *Sydney Morning Herald* 8 January 2019.

192 Ibid.

193 Australian Citizenship Amendment (Strengthening the Citizenship Loss Provisions) Bill 2018 (Cth) cl 1, introducing s 35A(1B).

194 Foster, McAdam and Wadley, "Part Two," 496.

195 Ibid 500.

196 Ibid, 494.

197 On the adverse impacts of citizenship stripping on human rights, see Zedner, "Citizenship Deprivation," 230–231, 236–241.

198 Goodwin-Gill, "Opinion," 1.

suspect in circumstances where a person has no substantive connection to another country,[199] and with refugee status holders there is a presumption that the relationship between the individual and their state of origin is broken.

Denaturalised and without a valid visa, the former Australian could be deported to their country of nationality or held indefinitely in immigration detention pending political efforts to secure their removal to a third country willing to accept them. The AAA was specifically designed with the option of repatriation in mind. Citizenship revocation may only apply to persons who are nationals or citizens of another country.[200] But the AAA makes some allowance for the possibility that removing a refugee to their country of origin or place of habitual residence may be impossible. Ministerial discretions under the AAA (including whether to exempt the person from citizenship loss) are exercised with regard to the person's connection to their country of origin or place of former habitual residence.[201] This reflects a legislative intent that individuals will not be left stateless, in actuality or effect, and could operate to protect former dual nationals from *refoulement*. However, the operation of the provisions does not absolutely preclude this outcome and, as Foster, McAdam and Wadley argue, the provisions contain insufficient safeguards against statelessness as compared to similar provisions in other jurisdictions.[202] The Minister will consider factors such as the capacity for the person to return to their country of nationality and the consequences they would face in doing so, against other, weighty, factors such as Australia's national security, the public interest and the severity of the alleged conduct. Viewed in the broader context of Australia's migration laws, one could expect the government to persist in expelling and excluding the refugee-citizen on the basis of their risk to national security, regardless of the impact on that person's human rights.

Developments suggest that the government is weakening in its resolve that the operation of the AAA will not leave individuals effectively stateless. On 28 November 2018, the government released the Australian Citizenship Amendment (Strengthening the Citizenship Loss Provisions) Bill 2018 (Cth). This Bill would expand the third avenue of citizenship loss in two ways. First, it would extend the range of relevant convictions to include sabotage, espionage and

199 Sangeetha Pillai, "Government's citizenship-stripping plan 'could lead to statelessness and indefinite detention'." SBS *News*, November 26, 2018, https://www.sbs.com.au/news/government-s-citizenship-stripping-plan-could-lead-to-statelessness-and-indefinite-detention, accessed December 18, 2018.

200 *Australian Citizenship Act 2007* s 33AA(1), s 35(1)(a), s 35A(1)(c).

201 Ibid s 33AA(17)(f), s 35(12)(f), s 35A(1)(e)(v).

202 Foster, McAdam and Wadley, "Part Two," 493–494.

foreign interference.[203] Second, the Bill adjusts the threshold for establishing dual nationality, requiring only a state of ministerial *satisfaction* that the person would not be rendered stateless by the act of citizenship revocation.[204] Lowering the threshold risks rendering the person stateless and, in practical terms, sentences them to prolonged and indefinite immigration detention as they await either deportation or re-admission into Australia.[205] In the case of refugees, this further reduces the protection in the Act against deportation and *refoulement*.

To be caught by the AAA, a person has engaged in terrorism-related conduct, been involved with a terrorist organisation, taken up arms against Australia, or been convicted of a terrorism or foreign incursion offence. This type of activity would exclude a person from being granted a visa or conferral of citizenship on adverse character grounds. When a person engages in such conduct after they have obtained Australian citizenship, is citizenship loss an appropriate outcome? In response to this question it should be noted that the operation of these laws is such that refugees stripped of their dual-citizenship status would be vulnerable to harsher outcomes than an Australian national engaged in terrorism subject to the criminal justice system. As Macklin and Zedner argue, denationalisation effectively treats a group of citizens as 'second class citizens', setting different consequences for sole-citizens and dual-citizens who engage in the same conduct.[206] With these factors in mind, citizenship stripping was denounced as "a form of punishment more primitive than torture" by Chief Justice Warren of the US Supreme Court.[207] Macklin has further argued that the consequences of citizenship stripping can effectively amount to a death sentence: "Denationalisation is not only the political analogue to death; it may also be a prelude to it' for instance, "two UK nationals who were stripped of their citizenship while abroad were subsequently executed by US drone strikes".[208] Indeed, former-Australian Khaled Sharrouf met the same fate.[209]

203 Australian Citizenship Amendment (Strengthening the Citizenship Loss Provisions) Bill 2018 (Cth) cl 1, introducing s 35A(1B).

204 Ibid cl 1, introducing s 35A(1)(b).

205 Sangeetha Pillai, "Government's citizenship-stripping plan 'could lead to statelessness and indefinite detention'," SBS *News*, November 26, 2018, https://www.sbs.com.au/news/government-s-citizenship-stripping-plan-could-lead-to-statelessness-and-indefinite-detention.

206 Audrey Macklin, "Citizenship Revocation, the Privilege to Have Rights and the Production of the Alien" *Queen's Law Journal* 40, no. 1 (2014): 48; Zedner, "Citizenship Deprivation," 238.

207 *Trop v Dulles* (1958) 356 US 86.

208 Macklin, "Citizenship Revocation," 8.

209 Zedner, "Citizenship Deprivation," 233.

In summary, the risks associated with citizenship stripping are heightened for any refugee deprived of surrogate protection following denaturalisation. Refugees stripped of their Australian citizenship could be made stateless in practice, with slim prospects of returning to their country of origin safely. The constraint against statelessness, provided by limiting the scope of denaturalisation provisions to dual nationals, has proven an "important limit" on the use of citizenship revocation as a counter-terrorism tool and, Zedner warns, developments that risk statelessness "would appear to create a legal black-hole into which, once people fall, they cannot easily be extracted".[210]

7 Conclusions

This chapter has explained and explored the many connections between national security, terrorism and the securitisation of asylum, refugee status and citizenship. We have shown that the Australian Government's distinctive law and policy approaches toward asylum seekers and refugees are particularly uncompromising. Successive governments have repeatedly redefined and limited their responsibilities to protection seekers under municipal laws, and concentrated broad and effectively unreviewable decision-making power in security officials and politicians, thereby shirking the rule of law. The impulse for stronger, militarised, border controls has been supported by the persistent construction of asylum seekers and refugees (notably Muslims) as potential terrorists. This rhetoric has supplied a justification for extraterritorial border controls – including maritime interdiction and turn backs. The purported connection between asylum seekers/refugees and terrorism has also served to ground the securitisation of immigration and asylum laws, knitting immigration and counter-terrorism closely together in law and policy, and in the minds of the populace. However, expert intelligence officials and scholars alike are clear that there is no evidence to support the link between asylum and terrorism in Australia. The alienation of minority groups and those seeking protection, coupled with a failure to respect basic human rights and the rule of law, not only undermine Australia's domestic and global status but arguably plays into the hands of terrorists and even risks rendering individuals "vulnerable and more susceptible"[211] to radicalisation and recruitment.

Protection seekers are vulnerable to rejection on a wide range of security and community safety grounds. If they have engaged in politically motivated

210 Ibid 242.

211 Ibid, 240.

violence it is likely they will be excluded as a risk to security under the broad terms of s 36(1B) of the *Migration Act*. Alternatively, the Minister for Home Affairs may consider them to be a danger to security or to the community (under s 36(1C)). Anyone captured by these grounds for visa refusal simultaneously attracts the far-reaching 'public interest' focussed 'character test'.

Visa applicants who are rejected on s 36(1)(B) grounds have no access to independent merits review to test the substantive fairness of adverse security decisions. By contrast, those rejected by immigration officials on the basis of s 36(1C) or because they are denied refugee status, per Art 1F (s 5H), or by reason of s 36(2C), may appeal to the AAT. That is, unless the Minister has personally deemed a person excludable because it is in the national interest.[212] Additionally, a refugee whose visa is refused or cancelled on adverse character grounds may appeal to the AAT, subject to that review right being negated by direct ministerial decision-making in the national interest.[213] Administrative injustice and a lack of effective redress mechanisms, coupled with indefinite detention for both adults and children, are all negative facets of the immigration control regime that works crudely to trump due consideration of non-citizen's human rights, including; liberty, dignity, procedural fairness, access to justice, and *non-refoulement*. The findings of the HRC that Australia was in violation of international law by its treatment of asylum seekers with adverse security assessments is particularly damning – as is the lack of a reasoned official response.

The extension of Australia's citizenship stripping provisions, and the subsequent move to lower the threshold for the assessment of dual nationality under these provisions, extend upon the themes of exclusion, concentrated and, effectively, unaccountable political power, and limited recognition of human rights. The scheme provides for refugee-citizens to be reinscribed as non-citizens. As Macklin surmises: "If those deemed threats to national security are not actually alien in law, then they must be alienated by law."[214] This "dubious device fraught with grave risks but of no proven efficacy," underscores that "immigration law as a tool of counterterrorism … targets precisely those who, because their status is already precarious, are most easily subject to draconian and discriminatory laws."[215] Its secretive and largely unreviewable operation can be seen as characteristic of the counterterrorism-immigration aspects of Australian law, and emblematic of the focus on securitisation and exclusion that dominates this space.

212 *Migration Act 1958* s 502.

213 Where the Minister has acted personally under the *Migration Act 1958* s 501(3), there is a form of internal (merits) review called a revocation process, with onward rights to judicial review.

214 Macklin, "Citizenship Revocation," 2.

215 Zedner, "Citizenship Deprivation," 241.

CHAPTER 7

Prosecution and Exclusion for Terrorism in International and National Law

James C. Simeon

1 Introduction

The United Nations has often identified terrorism as a pressing priority and concern for the international community. For instance, in January 2013, the then Secretary-General of the UN, Ban Ki-moon stated at a high-level meeting of the Security Council, "Nothing can justify terrorism – ever."[1] Indeed, as early as 1985 the United Nations General Assembly affirmed that terrorist violence could not be justified under any circumstances.[2] Likewise, in 1999 the UN Security Council issued resolution 1269, binding on its member States, that simply states, "*Condemning* all acts of terrorism, irrespective of motive, wherever and by whomever committed."[3] In fact, the very first point of this UN SC Resolution states:

> 1. *Unequivocally condemns* all acts, methods and practices of terrorism as criminal and unjustifiable, regardless of their motivation, in all their forms and manifestations, wherever and by whomever committed, in particular those which could threaten international peace and security;[4]

At point four the UN SC Resolution goes on to state:

1 United Nations, Meetings Coverage and Press Releases, Security Council, SC/10882, "'Nothing Can Justify Terrorism – Ever', Says Secretary-General, as Security Council Hears from Some 50 Speakers in Day-Long Debate," 15 January 2013, https://www.un.org/press/en/2013/sc10882.doc.htm. (accessed March 15, 2018)

2 United Nations General Assembly, A/RES/40/61, 9th December 1985, 108th plenary meeting, https://www.un.org/documents/ga/res/40/a40r061.htm. (accessed June 30, 2019)

3 United Nations Security Council, Resolution 1269, S/RES/1269, 19 October 1999, 4053rd meeting of the Security Council, https://undocs.org/S/RES/1269(1999). (accessed June 30, 2019) [Emphasis in the original.]

4 Ibid., p. 2., first point. [Emphasis in the original.]

© KONINKLIJKE BRILL NV, LEIDEN, 2020 | DOI:10.1163/9789004295995_009

4. *Calls upon* all States to take, *inter alia*, in the context of such cooperation and coordination, appropriate steps to

– take appropriate measures in conformity with the relevant provisions of national and international law, including international standards of human rights, before granting refugee status, for the purpose of ensuring that the asylum-seeker has not participated in terrorist acts;[5]

Well before 9/11, it is evident, that the UN SC was concerned that terrorists, individuals and their organizations, might be utilizing states' asylum systems to their benefit; that is, either to escape prosecution from terrorist actions or to commit terrorist acts in their host states.

Immediately following 9/11 the UN Security Council adopted Resolution 1373 that was adopted under Chapter VII of the UN Charter and is binding on member states. It requires states to criminalize various acts of terrorism, the suppression and prevention of the financing of terrorism, and the freezing of assets of individuals who are linked to terrorism. However, Resolution 1373 did not define terrorism or mention the need to protect human rights.[6] Manfred Nowak and Anne Charbord, point out that in the rush to adopt counter-terrorism legislation states often did not comply with the requirements of international human rights law.[7]

The UN Security Council has also advanced a "comprehensive approach to terrorism." Following an open debate on this comprehensive approach to terrorism the President of the UN Security Council, at the time, concluded the debate with a statement, "expressing that body's [the United Nations] deep concern over the terrorist threat and its determination to combat it by all means in all its forms and manifestations, in line with the United Nations Charter and international law."[8]

---

5 Ibid., [Emphasis is in the original.]

6 United Nations Security Council, Resolution 1373, S/RES/1373, 28 September 2001, https://undocs.org/S/RES/1373(2001). [accessed June 30, 2019]

7 Manfred Nowak and Anne Charbord, "Key Trends in the Fight Against Terrorism and Key Aspects of International Human Rights Law," in *Using Human Rights to Counter Terrorism*. Eds. Manfred Nowak and Anne Charbord, (Chletenham, UK: Edward Elgar, 2018), p. 19.

8 Supra note 1; United Nations Security Council, S/2013/3, 3 January 2013, Letter dated 1 January 2013 from the Permanent Representative of Pakistan to the United Nations addressed to the Secretary-General, The concept note prepared by the President of the Security Council is found at (*S/2013/3*). See also the United Nations Global Counter-Terrorism Strategy at the United Nations Office of Counter-Terrorism, Counter Terrorism Implementation Task Force, UN Global Counter-Terrorism Strategy, https://www.un.org/counterterrorism/ctitf/en/un-global-counter-terrorism-strategy. (accessed March 16, 2018)

From a legal perspective and in addition to the UN's efforts in this regard, there is no doubt that international humanitarian law has definitively prohibited terrorism. The *1949 Geneva Conventions* and the two *Additional Protocols of 1977* have outlawed terrorism in situations of either international or non-international armed conflict or war. Article 33 of the *Fourth Geneva Convention, Relative to the Protection of Civilians in Times of War*, states, in part, that,

> No protected person may be punished for an offence he or she has not personally committed. Collective penalties and likewise all measures of intimidation or of terrorism are prohibited.[9]

The *Additional Protocol* to the *Geneva Conventions* of the 12 August 1949, *and Related to the Protection of Victims of International Armed Conflicts* (*Protocol I*) states at Article 51(2),

> Article 51 – Protection of the civilian population
>
> 2. The civilian population as such, as well as individual civilians, shall not be the object of attack. Acts or threats of violence the primary purpose of which is to spread terror among the civilian population are prohibited.[10]

Additional Protocol to the *Geneva Conventions* of 1949, and *Related to the Protection of Victims of Non-International Armed Conflicts* (*Protocol II*) states, in no uncertain terms, that,

> Article 4. FUNDAMENTAL GUARANTEES
>
> 1. All persons who do not take a direct part or who have ceased to take part in hostilities, whether or not their liberty has been restricted,

9 The Geneva Conventions of 12 August 1949, *Fourth Geneva Convention Relative to the Protection of Civilians in Times of War of 12 August 1949*, Article 33, p. 162. https://www.icrc.org/eng/assets/files/publications/icrc-002-0173.pdf. (accessed March 14, 2018)

10 United Nations, Treaty Series, Vol. 75, *Protocol Additional to the Geneva Conventions of 12 August 1949 and Related to the Protection of Victims of International Armed Conflicts* (*Protocol I*), adopted 8 June 1977, https://treaties.un.org/doc/Publication/UNTS/Volume%20 1125/volume-1125-I-17513-English.pdf. (March 15, 2018). [Emphasis added]

are entitled to respect for their person, honour and convictions and religious practices. They shall in all circumstances be treated humanely, without any adverse distinction. It is prohibited to order that there shall be no survivors.

2. Without prejudice to the generality of the foregoing, the following acts against the persons referred to in paragraph 1 are and shall remain prohibited at any time and in any place whatsoever:
   (a) violence to the life, health and physical or mental well-being of persons, in particular murder as well as cruel treatment such as torture, mutilation or any form of corporal punishment; …
   (d) Acts of terrorism; …
   (h) threats to commit any of the foregoing acts.[11]

And, Article 13 of *Additional Protocol II* states, as follows:

Article 13. PROTECTION OF THE CIVILIAN POPULATION

2. The civilian population and individual civilians shall enjoy general protection against the dangers arising from military operations. To give effect to this protection, the following rules shall be observed in all circumstances.
3. The civilian population as such, as well as individual civilians, shall not be the object of attack. Acts or threats of violence the primary purpose of which is to spread terror among the civilian population are prohibited.[12]

International criminal law has also criminalized terrorism and can be found in the Statutes of some of the international criminal tribunals, including: the International Criminal Tribunal for Rwanda (ICTR), and the Special Court of Sierra Leone (SCSL). Laura Paredi has noted that, "The crime of 'acts of terrorism' is included among the war crimes list in the Statutes of the ICTR and SCSL. Conversely, the ICTY and ICC Statutes omit any reference to this kind of war

11 United Nations, Treaty Series, Vol. 75, *Protocol Additional to the Geneva Conventions of 12 August 1949 and Related to the Protection of Victims of Non-International Armed Conflicts (Protocol II)*, adopted 8 June 1977, https://treaties.un.org/doc/Publication/UNTS/Volume%201125/volume-1125-I-17513-English.pdf. (March 15, 2018).

12 Ibid.

crime. The omission did not impede the ICTY from establishing its jurisdiction over the crime of terror."[13]

Clearly, international humanitarian law and international criminal law have prohibited and criminalized terrorism in situations of international and non-international armed conflict.

Keeping the foregoing elemental points in mind regarding the UN's efforts to address the growing scourge of terrorism through a comprehensive approach and the prohibition and criminalization of terrorism in international humanitarian and criminal law, it is perhaps prosaic to state that not everyone can be legally recognized as refugees, even if they have a well-founded fear of persecution on one or more of the five grounds: race, religion, nationality, membership in a particular social group and political opinion, and their State is either unwilling or unable to provide adequate protection.[14] All those who are responsible for serious national and international crimes are excluded from refugee protection.[15] This does not imply that they are not protected by the peremptory norm of *non-refoulement*[16] or are ineligible for other forms of international protection of their most fundamental human rights and dignity as persons. It simply means they cannot be recognized legally as refugees and

13 Laura Paredi, *The War Crime of Terror: An Analysis of International Jurisprudence*, International Crimes Database, ICD Brief 11, June 2015, 2, http://www.internationalcrimesdatabase.org/upload/documents/20150610T161554-Laura%20Paredi%20ICD%20Brief_final.pdf. (accessed March 15, 2018) See 6 Article 4(d), *Statute of the International Criminal Tribunal for Rwanda*, adopted by UN Security Council, Res. N. 955, 8 November 1994 and 7 Article 3(d), (h), *Statute of the Special Court for Sierra Leone*, UN Security Council Resolution 1315 (2000), 14 August 2000.

14 *Convention relating to the Status of Refugees*, Geneva, 28 July 1951, in force 22 April 1954, 1989 UNTS 137 and the *Protocol relating to the Status of Refugees*, New York, 31 January 1967, in force 4 October 1967, 19 UNTS 6223, 6257.

15 Article 1F of the *Convention relating to the Status of Refugees* and other international refugee rights instruments such as the UN General Assembly, Declaration on Territorial Asylum, 14 December 1967, A/RES/2312(XXII), see Article 1(2), Article 3(2) and Article 4; *Organization of African Unity* (OAU) *Convention Governing Specific Aspects of Refugee Problems in Africa*, Addis Abbaba, 10 September 1969, in force 10 June 1974, UNTS 14691, see Article 4(f), Article 5; *Cartagena Declaration on Refugees*, Adopted by the Colloquium on the International Protection of Refugees in Central America, Mexico and Panama, Cartagena Des Indias, Colombia, 22 November 1984, Section 3(3).

16 Sir Elihu and Daniel Bethlehem state that '*Non-refoulement* is a concept, which prohibits States from returning a refugee or asylum seeker to territories where there is a risk that his or her life or freedom would be threatened on account of race, religion, nationality, membership of a particular social group, or political opinion'. [Emphasis in the original.] Sir Elihu Lauterpacht and Daniel Bethlehem, 'The scope and content of the principle of *non-refoulement*: Opinion' in *Refugee Protection in International Law*, edited by Erica Feller, Volker Turk, Frances Nicholson, (Cambridge: Cambridge University Press, 2003) 89.

receive the human rights protection that are guaranteed under various international instruments, including, the seminal *1951 Convention relating to the Status of Refugees* and its *1967 Protocol.*

Certain categories of persons are, therefore, excluded from refugee protection due to their serious criminality. Article 1F of the *1951 Convention* identifies three such categories of persons: (1) those who have committed a crime against peace, a war crime or a crime against humanity, as defined by the international instruments that have been drawn up to make provisions for such crimes; (2) those who have committed a serious non-political crime outside the country of refuge prior to their admission in that country as a refugee; (3) those who are guilty of actions that are contrary to the purposes and principles of the United Nations.[17]

What is evident from this categorization of individuals that are ineligible for refugee protection is that they include the most serious national and international crimes. Although, admittedly, "acts contrary to the purposes and principles of the United Nations" appears to be a rather broad, open-ended and expansive provision that could encompass a great deal. There is, nonetheless, general consensus that Article 1F should be applied restrictively and that Article 1F(c), according to the UNHCR, would include "crimes capable of affecting international peace, security and peaceful relations between states would fall within this clause, as would serious and sustained violations of human rights."[18]

Those persons who are liable for serious criminality, of either a national or international nature, 'self-exclude themselves' from refugee protection.[19] If their 'intention' is to cause grave harm to others, through either direct or indirect perpetration, then, they are more likely than not, responsible for producing refugees, on the basis of a well-founded fear of persecution, on one or more of the five Convention grounds. As a consequence, it would be anomalous, indeed, to be providing refugee protection to those who are responsible for persecuting others and for producing refugees.

Those who are involved in terrorist actions or activities would be excluded from refugee protection because they would be responsible for the murder or serious injury of persons and the severe damage or destruction of property in an effort to terrorize a population and in an effort to advance their political

17 *Convention relating to the Status of Refugees*, Geneva, 28 July 1951, in force 22 April 1954, 1989 UNTS 137. Article 1F(a), (b), and (c).

18 *Al-Sirri (Ayslum-Exclusion-Article 1F(c))*, [2016] UKUT 448 (IAC)., paragraph 14, page 8.

19 Those who willful choose to act immorally and to commit a crime must bear the consequences of their immorality and/or criminality. The well-known aphorism, "If you can't do the time, don't do the crime," seems apropos here.

ambitions. Hence, terrorists and their accomplices would be liable for serious criminality and excluded from refugee protection.[20]

Joseph Rikhof notes that most of the discussion and jurisprudence on exclusion and terrorism has been under Articles 1F(b) and (c) of the *1951 Convention relating to the Status of Refugees*.[21] Although this is true of national and international refugee law, it is not the case for international criminal law, particularly, in a war setting or armed conflict, whether international or non-international, that has identified terrorism as not only persecutory, but, as a crime against humanity. This would incorporate terrorist actions and activities under Article 1F(a) as a crime against humanity, if not a war crime. Presumably, in theory, it could also fall within the category of a "crime against peace" or the "crime of aggression," given the type of terrorist attack, its fundamental nature, scope, and the extent of its destructive impact. International criminal law has also identified the "crime of terror" in situations of armed conflict. Consequently, it is important to stress that terrorism has been prohibited under international humanitarian law and criminalized under international criminal law.

This chapter will argue that with the absence of a comprehensive international convention on terrorism, with a universal definition of what constitutes terrorism, and with 19 sectoral international conventions that cover different aspects of terrorism such as hijacking, bombing, hostage taking, etc., and the variance in definitions of what constitutes terrorism across states, leads to a situation that results in gaps and shortcomings in international criminal law, especially, in a non-armed conflict or non-war setting. In addition, a number of jurisdictions have turned to the *1998 Rome Statute*, which established the International Criminal Court (ICC), to define what constitutes serious international crimes such as genocide, war crimes, crimes against humanity, and aggression. However, the *1998 Rome Statute* does not include terrorism within its provisions and it does not fall within the jurisdiction of the ICC. Accordingly, this chapter argues, that these serious gaps and shortcomings in international criminal law, that impact directly on international refugee law, can have a detrimental effect on national refugee status determination systems and for the exclusion of those who are involved in terrorist activities, either directly or indirectly, and seek asylum. There is a potential for these shortcomings in international criminal law and, specifically, within a non-armed conflict situation to benefit inadvertently those it is intended to exclude from refugee protection,

20 Joseph Rikhof, *The Criminal Refugee: The Treatment of Asylum Seekers with a Criminal Background in International and Domestic Law*. (Dordrecht, The Netherlands: Republic of Letters Publishing, 2012).

21 Ibid., p. 307.

even when applied restrictively. Thus, it is argued that these gaps, inconsistencies and deficiencies in international criminal law ought to be addressed by the United Nations and its Agencies and the international community on a priority basis. A failure to do so could potentially lead to the de-legitimizing of the international refugee protection system by the provision of refugee protection to those who ought to be excluded.

The chapter is presented in four parts. The first provides a broad overview of terrorism in international law and underscores the key point that terrorism is accepted as a serious international crime. Secondly, it considers three leading judgements of the International Criminal Tribunal of the Former Yugoslavia (ICTY) that deal with the "crime of terror" and "persecution," which also encompasses "terrorizing civilians," as a crime against humanity.[22] Thirdly, the paper goes on to consider and comparatively analyzes three leading common law Supreme Court judgements on terrorism in Canada, the United Kingdom, and the United States. The conclusions reflect on the current state of international humanitarian and criminal law and its existing gaps and shortcomings and calls on the UN and its Agencies and the international community as a whole to address these gaps and deficiencies on a priority basis, that could otherwise lead to confusion and conflation between terrorism and asylum, as it leaves the current international refugee system potentially in a precarious position vis-à-vis terrorism and the exclusion from refugee protection of those who are involved in terrorist activities.

2 Terrorism and International Law

Terrorism, certainly, is considered to be a serious crime, whether it is fundamentally national or international.[23] And, it can be persecutory if it targets

22 The International Criminal Tribunal of the Former Yugoslavia completed its mandate on 21 December 2017. It was established by UN Security Council Resolution 829 on May 23, 1993. United Nations Mechanism for International Criminal Tribunals. United Nations, International Criminal Tribunal for the Former Yugoslavia, http://www.icty.org/. (accessed March 13, 2018). The work of both the ICTY and the International Criminal Tribunal for Rwanda (ICTR) is being carried on by the Mechanism for International Criminal Tribunals (MICT), http://www.unmict.org/en. (accessed March 13, 2018)

23 Government of Canada, Department of Justice, "About the Anti-terrorism Act," 26 July 2017, http://www.justice.gc.ca/eng/cj-jp/ns-sn/act-loi.html. (accessed February 8, 2018); The Crown Prosecutor's Service (CPS), "Terrorism," (2017), https://www.cps.gov.uk/terrorism. (accessed February 8, 2018); Michael Lawless, "Terrorism: An International Crime?" *Canadian Military Journal*, (2008), Vol. 9, No. 2, pp. 27–39. http://www.journal.forces.gc.ca/v09/n02/05-lawless-eng.asp. (accessed February 8, 2018)

groups deliberately on any of the five grounds of the *1951 Convention*.[24] Assessing the United Nations' efforts in criminalizing terrorism, Michael Lawless states:

> Thus, it is simply not possible to assert that terrorism is not prohibited by the international community, or that terrorism is not an international crime. On the contrary, it is abundantly clear that the UN has deliberated over the course of many years on the topic of terrorism, and the ultimate result of those deliberations has been the creation of a comprehensive prohibition on terrorism as a means of effecting political change, irrespective of any laudatory purpose or change sought by the terrorist.[25]

Indeed, the United Nations has negotiated some 19 conventions and protocols on specific acts of terrorism from the seizure of aircraft, the taking of hostages, to violence at airports, terrorist bombings, terrorist financing, nuclear terrorism, and so on.[26] However, there is no universally accepted definition of the highly contentious and emotive term "terrorism."[27]

Although a comprehensive international convention on terrorism has eluded the United Nations to date, there is a possibility that such a comprehensive convention may be realized in due course.[28] If for no other reason than when

---

24 Canadian Council for Refugees, Comments on Bill C-36, Anti-Terrorism Act, 5 November 2001, http://ccrweb.ca/en/comments-bill-c-36-anti-terrorism-act. (accessed February 8, 2018)

25 Michael Lawless, "Terrorism: An International Crime?" *Canadian Military Journal*, (2008), Vol. 9, No. 2, p.31.

26 United Nations Office of Counter-Terrorism, International Law Instruments, http://www.un.org/en/counterterrorism/legal-instruments.shtml. (accessed February 8, 2018)

27 Anna Maria Brennan, "The Difficulties in Defining Terrorism in International Law," *Human Rights in Ireland*, October 11, 2011, http://humanrights.ie/international-lawinternational-human-rights/the-difficulties-in-defining-terrorism-under-international-law/. (accessed February 12, 2018); Human Rights Voices, UN 101, "There is no UN definition of terrorism," http://www.humanrightsvoices.org/EYEontheUN/un_101/facts/?p=61. (access February 12, 2018); Jean-Marc Sorel, "Some Questions About the Definition of Terrorism and the Fight Against its Financing," *European Journal of International Law*, (2003), Vol. 14, No. 2, pp. 365–378. http://www.ejil.org/pdfs/14/2/420.pdf. (accessed February 12, 2018); Sean Larkin, QC, "Why Can't We Agree on a Definition of Terrorism?" *OpenMind*, December 16, 2013, https://www.bbvaopenmind.com/en/why-cant-we-agree-on-a-definition-of-terrorism/. (accessed February 12, 2018).

28 United Nations, Ad Hoc and Special Committees, Established on the Recommendations of the Sixth Committee, Ad Hoc Committee established by General Assembly resolution 51/210 of the 17 September 1996, Last Updated 22 September 2017, http://legal.un.org/committees/terrorism/. (accessed February 9, 2018); Mahmoud Hmoud, "Negotiating the Draft

those States that hold the view that the use of extreme violence, in the struggle against oppression for the achievement of their right to self-determination, can justify the use of terrorism against its own people, eventually, will come to recognize that such a rationale is totally absurd. Or, those States that oppose a comprehensive convention on terrorism because they are concerned that their military personnel might be charged, tried, and convicted for terrorism in the fulfillment of their military objectives and missions, come to realize that terrorism is already prohibited under international humanitarian law and criminalized under international criminal law.[29] The fact that there has been no agreed universal definition of terrorism does not mean that terrorism is impossible to define.[30] While strongly in favor of a comprehensive international convention on terrorism, Ben Saul, and other legal scholars, are not as sanguine in their views on the achievement of such a comprehensive convention in international law.[31]

If terrorism is a serious international crime, then, it must surely be subject to prosecution under international criminal law. It is worth noting that international criminal law has been defined as "the branch of public international law that deals with direct criminal responsibility of individuals."[32] Robert Cryer has noted that international criminal law can be summed up in the famous statement of the Nuremberg International Military Tribunal (IMT) that,

> ... [i]ndividuals have international duties which transcend the national obligations of obedience imposed by the individual State ... crimes against international law are committed by men, not by abstract entities,

Comprehensive Convention on International Terrorism," *Journal of International Criminal Justice*, 4 (2006), pp. 1031–1043.

29 International Committee of the Red Cross, IHL Database, Customary IHL, Rule 2: Violence Aimed at Spreading Terror Among the Civilian Population, *Rule 2: Acts or threats of violence the primary purpose of which is to spread terror among the civilian population are prohibited.* https://ihl-databases.icrc.org/customary-ihl/eng/docs/v1_rul_rule2. (accessed February 11, 2018)

30 Anthony Richards, "Conceptualizing Terrorism," *Studies in Conflict & Terrorism*, (2014), 37:213–236.

31 Ben Saul, "The Emerging International Law of Terrorism," in *Terrorism*, Ben Saul, ed. (Oxford: Hart Publishing Ltd., 2012); Ben Saul, *Defining Terrorism in International Law.* (Oxford: Oxford University Press, 2006); Alex Conte, *Human Rights in the Prevention and Punishment of Terrorism: Commonwealth Approaches: The United Kingdom, Canada, Australia and New Zealand.* (Berlin Heidelberg: Springer-Verlag, 2010), file:///C:/Users/esouser/Favorites/Downloads/9783642116070-c1.pdf. (accessed March 13, 2018)

32 Robert Cryer, "International Criminal Law," in Malcolm D. Evans, *International Law*, Fourth Edition, Oxford: Oxford University Press, 2014, p. 752.

> and only by punishing individuals who commit such crimes can the provisions of international law be enforced.[33]

It is also important to underscore that for international crimes, the locus of the criminal prohibition is the international legal order but these crimes can also be criminalized in the domestic legal orders as well. Most states have criminalized terrorism within their domestic legal orders and typically within their criminal codes such as Canada and the United States.[34] Indeed, there are differences in how Canada and the United States have defined terrorism, which has raised a number of concerns.[35] In fact, States have defined terrorism in various ways and they have sought to prosecute those individuals who they suspected of being involved in terrorist activities. Various criticisms have been levelled at States for having legislated vague and over-broad definitions of terrorism and the term terrorist. The attendant effect could lead to an "abuse of power" by the State.[36] The way that the term terrorism is defined can have "a vital effect in determining the overall scope and application of anti-terrorism law regime."[37] The legislative basis of how the term terrorism is defined clearly affects how the courts, within a respective jurisdiction, will apply and interpret the term to the factual situation of any case before them.

With respect to international criminal law, there are only four clear examples of international crimes that are called the 'core' international crimes: genocide, war crimes, crimes against humanity, and aggression. These core crimes are found in the *Rome Statute* of the International Criminal Court (ICC).[38]

---

33 Ibid.

34 *Criminal Code* (R.S.C., 1985, c. C 46), Part II.1, See Government of Canada, Justice Laws Website, http://laws-lois.justice.gc.ca/eng/acts/C-46/page-12.html. (accessed February 10, 2018); 18 U.S. Code Chapter 113B – TERRORISM, See Cornell Law School, Legal Information Institute (LII), https://www.law.cornell.edu/uscode/text/18/part-I/chapter-113B. (accessed February 10, 2018)

35 James C. Simeon, "The Evolving Common Law Jurisprudence Combatting the Threat of Terrorism in the United Kingdom, United States, and Canada," Public Law Seminar, Paper 38, LLM Course, Faculty of Law, University of Cambridge, May 1, 2017. (... with the author) and a revised and longer version of this dissertation is published in *Laws* 2019, *8*(1), 5; https://doi.org/10.3390/laws8010005.

36 Keiran Hardy and George Williams, "What is 'terrorism'?: Assessing domestic legal definitions," *UCLA Journal of International Law and Foreign Affairs*, 2011, Vol. 16, p. 83, https://webmail-1.hermes.cam.ac.uk/?_task=mail&_action=get&_mbox=INBOX&_uid=270&_part=2&_frame=1&_extwin=1. (accessed February 10, 2018)

37 Ibid.

38 *Rome Statute of the International Criminal Court*, Text of the Rome Statute circulated as document A/CONF.183/9 of 17 July 1998 and corrected by procès-verbaux of 10 November 1998, 12 July 1999, 30 November 1999, 8 May 2000, 17 January 2001 and 16 January 2002.

Noticeably absent from this list of core international crimes is terrorism. A number of legal scholars have called for terrorism to be included as a 'core' international crime that should come under the jurisdiction of the ICC.[39] Indeed, it was originally intended to include terrorism as one of the most serious international crimes under the ICC's jurisdiction. As Alex Conte has stated,

> It was proposed, within the draft Statute, to include terrorism within the Court's jurisdiction, but the failure of States to agree upon a definition of the term resulted in the crime being removed from the scope of the Court's jurisdiction and subject matter of the constitutive treaty.[40]

As previously noted, there is no universally accepted definition of terrorism; nonetheless, there is a clear prohibition of terrorism in international humanitarian and criminal law, both in terms of customary international and treaty law as well.[41] In addition, despite its highly contentious judgement, the Appeals Chamber of the Special Tribunal of Lebanon issued a landmark ruling that a definition of terrorism has emerged in customary international law that consists of:

> ...[t]he following three key elements: (i) the perpetration of a criminal act (such as murder, kidnapping, hostage-taking, arson, and so on), or

Part 2, Jurisdiction, Admissibility, and Applicable Law, Article 5, Crimes within the jurisdiction of the Court, The Statute entered into force on 1 July 2002, http://legal.un.org/icc/statute/english/rome_statute(e).pdf. (accessed February 10, 2018)

39 Peter J. Wertheim (2003) "Should 'Grave Crimes of International Terrorism' be included in the Jurisdiction of the International Criminal Court?," *Policy and Society*, 22:2, 1–21, DOI: 10.1016/S1449-4035(03)70017-4. https://doi.org/10.1016/S1449-4035(03)70017-4 (accessed February 10, 2018); Juliee Sharma, "The Challenge for the International Criminal Court: Terrorism," Legal Services India, undated, http://www.legalserviceindia.com/article/l247--International-Criminal-Court---Terrorism.html. (accessed February 10, 2018); Aviv Cohen, "Prosecuting Terrorists at the International Criminal Court: Reevaluating an Unused Tool to Combat Terrorism," *Michigan State International Law Review*, 2012, Vol. 20, No. 2, pp. 219–257, https://digitalcommons.law.msu.edu/cgi/viewcontent.cgi?article=1080&context=ilr. (accessed February 11, 2018).

40 Alex Conte, *Human Rights in the Prevention and Punishment of Terrorism: Commonwealth Approaches: The United Kingdom, Canada, Australia and New Zealand.* (Berlin, Heidelberg: Springer-Verlag, 2010), p. 20.

41 International Committee of the Red Cross, *IHL Database, Customary IHL*, Practice Relating to Rule 2: Violence Aimed of Spreading Terror Among the Civilian Population, 1. Treaties; 2. Other Instruments; 3. Military Manuals; 4. National Legislation; 5. National Case Law; 6. Other National Practice; 7. United Nations; 8. Other International Organizations; 9. International Conference; 10. International and Mixed Judicial and Quasi-Judicial Bodies; 11. International Red Cross and Red Crescent Movement; 12. Other. https://ihl-databases.icrc.org/customary-ihl/eng/docs/v2_rul_rule2. (accessed February 11, 2018)

> threatening such an act; (ii) the intent to spread fear among the population (which would generally entail the creation of public danger) or directly or indirectly coerce a national or international authority to take some action, or to refrain from taking it; (iii) when the act involves a transnational element.[42]

Indeed, this judgement was consistent with Presiding Judge Antonio Cassese's previous publications on this very question.[43] The judgement received widespread criticism upon its release.[44] Nonetheless, this judgement has broken new legal ground, no matter how 'radical' and 'unconventional' a judgement at the international level. In the end, this judgement does add credence that there is a growing consensus that there is a commonly accepted definition of terrorism in customary international law. Moreover, it could be argued that it is far from precedential given that the International Criminal Tribunal for the Former Yugoslavia (ICTY) essentially came to the same conclusion in a series of

42 Interlocutory Decision on the Applicable Law: Terrorism, Conspiracy, Homicide, Perpetration, Cumulative Charging, Case No. STL-11-01/I (Feb. 16, 2011), https://www.stl-tsl.org/en/the-cases/stl-11-01/main/filings/orders-and-decisions/appeals-chamber/534-f0936. (accessed February 11, 2018)

43 Antonio Cassese, "The Multifaceted Criminal Notion of Terrorism in International Law," *Journal of International Criminal Justice*, (2006), 4, pp. 933–958. doi:10.1093/jicj/mql074.; Antonio Cassese, "Terrorism as an International Crime," *Enforcing International Law Norms Against Terrorism*, Ed., Andrea Bianchi, and Yasmin Naqvi, (Oxford: Hart Publishing, 2004), pp. 213–226.; Antonio Cassese and Paola Gaeta, *Cassese's International Criminal Law*, 3rd Edition, (Oxford: Oxford University Press, 2013), Chapter 8, Terrorism;

44 Ben Saul, "Legislating from a Radical Hague: The United Nations Special Tribunal for Lebanon Invents an International Crime of Transnational Terrorism," *Leiden Journal of International Law,* 24 (2011), pp. 677–700. https://www.cambridge.org/core/services/aop-cambridge-core/content/view/045D641D5847AD86B2E507B3A5E2CC40/S0922156511000203a.pdf/legislating_from_a_radical_hague_the_united_nations_special_tribunal_for_lebanon_invents_an_international_crime_of_transnational_terrorism.pdf. (accessed February 12, 2018); Saul, Ben, "The Special Tribunal for Lebanon and Terrorism as an International Crime: Reflections on the Judicial Function" (September 6, 2012). *The Ashgate Research Companion to International Criminal Law*, W. Schabas, Y. McDermott, N. Hayes and M. Varaki, eds., Ashgate: Farnham, Forthcoming; Sydney Law School Research Paper No. 12/64. Available at SSRN: https://ssrn.com/abstract=2142324. (accessed February 12, 2018); Almiro Clere, "An Examination of the Special Tribunal for Lebanon's Explosive Declaration of 'Terrorism' at Customary International Law," A dissertation in partial fulfilment of the requirements of the degree of Bachelor of Laws (Honours), University of Otago, October 2012, http://www.otago.ac.nz/law/research/journals/otago043934.pdf. (accessed February 12, 2018); Marko Milanovic, "Special Tribunal for Lebanon Delivers Interlocutory Decision on Applicable Law," EJIL: *Talk!* (February 16, 2011), https://www.ejiltalk.org/special-tribunal-for-lebanon-delivers-interlocutory-decision-on-applicable-law/. (accessed February 12, 2018);

criminal prosecutions of senior military officials following the Bosnian War.[45] This will be dealt with more thoroughly in the next section of the paper dealing with the three ICTY judgements below. But, suffice it to say that the joint Appeals Chamber of the ICTY and ICTR came to the following conclusion in the *Galic* case:

> In light of the foregoing, the Appeals Chamber finds that the prohibition of terror against the civilian population as enshrined in Article 51(2) of Additional Protocol I and Article 13(2) of Additional Protocol II clearly belonged to customary international law from at least the time of its inclusion in those treaties.[46]

3 Leading Cases of the International Criminal Tribunal of the Former Yugoslavia (ICTY) on the Crime of Terrorism

The three cases briefly outlined below illustrate that there is a "crime of terror," as recognized by the United Nation's International Criminal Tribunal of the Former Yugoslavia, in the situation of a war or armed conflict, and, specifically, a non-international armed conflict. The finding is premised on customary international humanitarian law or the laws or customs of war. This is a crucial ruling that emerged in several major cases before the ICTY that included the following: *2001 Krstic, 2006 Galic*, and *2017 Mladic*. The criminal prosecution of these three perpetrators of the most serious international crimes by these former senior military officers, that included the crime of terror and persecution

45 John R. Lampe, "Bosnian Conflict, European History, 1992–1995," *Encyclopedia Britannica*, undated, https://www.britannica.com/event/Bosnian-conflict. (accessed February 19, 2018); Robert Cryer, "Prosecutor v. Galic and the War Crime of Terror Bombing," *Israel Defense Forces Law Review*, (2005–2006) Vol. 2, pp. 75–102; Marlies Glasius, "Terror, Terrorizing, Terrorism: Instilling Fear as a Crime in the Cases of Radovan Karadzic and Charles Taylor," in *Narratives of Law and Justice in the International Courtrooms, Former Yugoslavia and Beyond*, edited by Dubravka Zarkov and Marlies Glasius (New York: Springer International Publishing, 2014), pp. 45–61; Roberta Arnold, "Terrorism, War Crimes and the International Criminal Court," in *Research Handbook on International Law and Terrorism*, edited by Ben Saul, (Cheltenham: Edward Elgar Publishing Ltd., 2014), pp. 282–297. Laura Paredi, *The War Crime of Terror: An Analysis of International Jurisprudence*, International Crimes Database, ICD Brief 11, June 2015, pp. 4–5. http://www.internationalcrimesdatabase.org/upload/documents/20150610T161554-Laura%20Paredi%20ICD%20Brief_final.pdf. (accessed March 15, 2018)

46 *Prosecutor v. Stanislave Galic*, Case No. IT-98-29-A, Appeals Chamber, Judgement, 30 November 2006, paragraph 90.

that encompasses, terrorizing civilians, marked a significant step forward with respect to terrorism in international criminal law.

3.1 *Prosecutor v. Radislav Krstic, Case No. IT-98-33-T, Judgement, 2 August 2001*

Radislav Krstic was Chief of Staff/Deputy Commander of the Drina Corps of the Bosnian Serb Army (VRS). He was appointed Commander of the Drina Corps on 13 July 1995. Krstic was indicted by the ICTY on one count of genocide, one count of complicity to commit genocide, and five counts of crimes against humanity, including, persecution (Count 6), and four counts of violations of the laws or customs of war.[47] He was the first person convicted by the ICTY for genocide and was initially sentenced to 46 years in prison, but, on appeal the sentence was reduced to 35 years on the lesser charge of aiding and abetting genocide. Krstic was indicted for his part in the murder of 8,000 Bosniak prisoners of war and civilians in the Srebrenica massacre in Europe's worst atrocity since World War II.[48]

Under the Prosecutor's Amended Indictment, Krstic was charged with persecution on the sixth count that included the following:

> 30 Beginning on 11 July 1995 and continuing through 1 November 1995, RADISLAV KRSTIC committed, planned, instigated, ordered, or otherwise aided and abetted the planning, preparation, or execution of a crime against humanity, that is, the persecutions of Bosnian Muslim civilians on political, racial, or religious grounds, in Srebrenica and its surroundings.
>
> 31 The crime of persecutions was perpetrated, executed, and carried out by or through the following means:
>
> a) the murder of thousands of Bosnian Muslim civilians, including men, women, children, and elderly persons;
>
> b) the cruel and inhumane treatment of Bosnian Muslim civilians, including severe beatings;
>
> c) *the terrorising of Bosnian Muslim civilians;*
>
> d) the destruction of personal property of Bosnian Muslims; and,

---

47 United Nations, International Criminal Tribunal for the Former Yugoslavia, Case Information Sheet, Radislav Krstic (T98-33), undated, http://www.icty.org/x/cases/krstic/cis/en/cis_krstic_en.pdf. (accessed February 18, 2018)

48 R. Jeffrey Smith, "Srebrenica Massacre, Bosnian History 1995," *Encyclopedia Britannica*, https://www.britannica.com/event/Srebrenica-massacre. (accessed February 18, 2018)

e) the deportation or forcible transfer of Bosnian Muslims from the Srebrenica enclave.

By these acts or omissions, and the acts and omissions described in paragraphs 4, 6, 7, 11, and 22 through 26, RADISLAV KRSTIC committed:

COUNT 6: Persecutions on political, racial and religious grounds, a CRIME AGAINST HUMANITY, punishable under Articles 5(h), and 7(1) and 7(3) of the Statute of the Tribunal.[49]

Within the "crime of persecutions," it is evident, as emphasized, that the "terrorising of civilians" is included as part of this crime. At paragraph 534 of the Trial Chamber's judgement, it is noted that the crime of persecutions was defined, and more significantly, it was identified as a crime against humanity and one of the core international crimes that it could prosecute persons who were responsible for such crimes. Wherein it states:

> ...bearing in mind that the crime of persecutions has been defined, in the *Kupre{ki}* Judgement, as "the gross or blatant denial, on discriminatory grounds, of a fundamental right, laid down in international customary or treaty law, reaching the same level of gravity as the other acts prohibited in Article 5."[50]

And, at paragraphs 536 and 537, the Trial Chamber goes on to state:

> 536 The Trial Chamber has previously determined that a widespread and systematic attack was launched against the Bosnian Muslim population of Srebrenica from 11 July onwards, by reason of their belonging to the Bosnian Muslim group.
>
> 537 The humanitarian crisis in Poto~ari, the burning of homes in Srebrenica and Poto~ari, the terrorisation of Bosnian Muslim civilians, the murder of thousands of Bosnian Muslim civilians, in Poto~ari or in carefully orchestrated mass scale executions, and the forcible transfer of the women, children and elderly out of the territory controlled by the Bosnian Serbs, constitute persecutory acts.[51]

49 *The Prosecutor of the Tribunal Against Radislav Krstic, Amended Indictment, Case No. IT-99-33,* [Emphasis added] http://www.icty.org/x/cases/krstic/ind/en/krs-1ai991027e.pdf . (accessed February 18, 2018)

50 *Prosecutor v. Radislav Krstic, Case No. IT-98-33-T, Judgement 2 August 2001*, paragraph 534, http://www.icty.org/x/cases/krstic/tjug/en/krs-tj010802e.pdf. (accessed February 18, 2018)

51 Ibid., paragraphs 536 and 537.

The Trial Chamber then went on to conclude that the crime of persecution was committed in the enclave of Srebrenica. However, the key point that needs to be stressed here is that the crime of persecution includes acts of terrorism against a civilian population.

3.2 *Prosecutor v. Stanislav Galic, Case No. IT-98-29-A, Judgement, 30 November 2006*

Stanislav Galic was a Bosnian Serb commander of the Sarajevo-Romanija Corps of the Army of Republika Srpska (VRS) during the Bosnia and Herzegovian War. He served in this capacity from 7 September 1992 to 10 August 1994.[52] The "Siege of Sarajevo" was one of the longest in the modern history of warfare and lasted for close to four years, 5 April 1992 to 29 February 1996.[53] The International Criminal Tribunal of the Former Yugoslavia indicted Galic for individual responsibility on a list of charges that included murder, inhuman acts other than murder, crimes against humanity, unlawfully inflicting terror upon civilians, attacks on civilians and violations of the laws and customs of war.[54] According to the indictment, "The attacks on Sarajevo civilians were often unrelated to military actions and were designed to keep the inhabitants in a constant state of terror."[55]

Galic was indicted specifically for the "Infliction of Terror," that stated, in part, that he had "conducted a protracted campaign of shelling and sniping upon the civilian population thereby inflicting terror and mental suffering upon its civilian population."[56]

> By his acts and omissions, STANISLAV GALIC is responsible for:
>
> COUNT 1: Violations of the Laws or Customs of War (unlawfully inflicting terror upon civilians as set forth in Article 51 of Additional Protocol I and Article 13 of Additional Protocol II to the Geneva Conventions of 1949) punishable under Article 3 of the Statute of the Tribunal.[57]

52 *Prosecutor v. Stanislav Galic, Case No. IT-98-29-A, Judgement, 30 November 2006*, http://www.icty.org/x/cases/galic/tjug/en/gal-tj031205e.pdf. (accessed February 17, 2017)

53 BBC News Europe, "Sarajevo 1992–1995: Looking back after 20 years," 10 April 2012, http://www.bbc.co.uk/news/world-europe-17617775. (accessed February 18, 2018)

54 The Prosecutor of the Tribunal Against Stanislav Galic, Dragomir Milosevic, *Indictment*, Case No. 98-29-I, undated, http://www.icty.org/x/cases/galic/ind/en/gal-ii011102e.pdf. (accessed February 17, 2018)

55 Ibid., p. 2, paragraph 4(b).

56 Ibid., p. 4, Charges, Count 1 (Infliction of Terror).

57 Ibid.

After assessing the evidence presented on the charge of the "infliction of terror," the ICTY came to the decision that, "The Accused knew or should have known that this was so. Terror as a crime within international humanitarian law was made effective in this case by treaty law. The Tribunal has jurisdiction *ratione materiae* by way of Article 3 of the Statute."[58]

Following his appeal, the ICTY Appeal Chamber increased Galic's sentence to life imprisonment.[59] Laura Paredi has noted that, "In 2003, Stanislav Galic, commander of the Bosnian Serb forces, became the first person to be convicted for the spreading of terror among the civilian population and, in particular, the first case in which terror was considered as an autonomous war crime."[60]

3.3 *Prosecutor v. Ratko Mladic, Case No. IT-09-92-T, Judgement, Volumes I to V, 22 November 2017*

Ratko Mladic was the Chief of Staff of the Army of the Republika Srpska during the Bosnian War of 1992–1995. The media frequently labelled him as the "Butcher of Bosnia." He was indicted for the following international crimes: genocide; crimes against humanity, and violations of the laws and customs of war.[61] But, more to the point, Mladic was also indicted, specifically, for "13. b. Crimes Committed to Spread Terror among the Civilian Population of Sarajevo through a Campaign of Sniping and Shelling."[62] Paragraph 14 of the indictment states that,

> 14 Between 12 May 1992 and November 1995, Ratko MLADIC participated in a joint criminal enterprise to establish and carry out a campaign of sniping and shelling against the civilian population of Sarajevo, the primary purpose of which was to spread terror among the civilian

---

58 *Prosecutor v. Stanislav Galic, Case No. IT-98-29-A, Judgement, 30 November 2006,* paragraph 138, http://www.icty.org/x/cases/galic/tjug/en/gal-tj031205e.pdf. (accessed February 17, 2017)

59 *Prosecutor v. Stanislav Galic, Case No. IT-98-29-A, Appeals Chamber, Judgement, 30 November 2006,* paragraph 48, http://www.icty.org/x/cases/galic/acjug/en/gal-acjud061130.pdf . (accessed February 17, 2018)

60 Laura Paredi, *The War Crime of Terror: An Analysis of International Jurisprudence*, International Crimes Database, ICD Brief 11, June 2015, p. 1. http://www.internationalcrimesdatabase.org/upload/documents/20150610T161554-Laura%20Paredi%20ICD%20Brief_final .pdf. (accessed March 15, 2018), See *Prosecutor v. Stanislav Galic*, Case No. IT-98-29-T, Trial Chamber, Judgement, 5 December 2003.

61 *The Prosecutor v. Ratko Mladic, Prosecution Submission of the Fourth Amended Indictment and Schedules of Incidents, Case No. IT-09-92-PT, 16 December 2011*, p. 1,http://www.icty .org/x/cases/mladic/ind/en/111216.pdf. (accessed February 18, 2018)

62 Ibid., p. 9.

population. This joint criminal enterprise existed between April 1992 and November 1995. The objective of this criminal enterprise involved the commission of the crimes of terror, unlawful attacks on civilians, and murder charged in this indictment.[63]

Further, under Count 3, Persecutions, paragraph 59 (e), he was indicted for:

(e) the terrorising and abuse of Bosnian Muslims of Srebrenica in Poto~ari and the beating of men and boys of Srebrenica prior to their execution, as cruel or inhumane treatment;[64]

In addition, on Counts 9 and 10, he was indicted for "Terror, Unlawful Acts."[65] At paragraph 75 of the indictment it states:

(75) Ratko MLADIC committed in concert with others, planned, instigated, ordered, and/or aided and abetted the crimes of terror and unlawful attacks on civilians. In addition, Ratko MLADIC knew or had reason to know that his subordinates were committing the crimes of terror and unlawful attacks on civilians or had done so. Ratko MLADIC failed to take the necessary and reasonable measures to prevent such acts or to punish the perpetrators thereof.[66]

The judgement of the Trial Chamber at paragraph 3186 states that the crime of terror requires proof of the following three elements:

a) acts or threats of violence directed against the civilian population or individual civilians not taking direct part in hostilities causing the victims to suffer grave consequences;
b) the offender willfully made the civilian population or individual civilians not taking direct part in hostilities the object of those acts or threats of violence; and

63 Ibid.
64 Ibid., p. 26.
65 Ibid., p. 33.
66 Ibid., pp. 33–34. Under Count 9, Ratko Mladic, was criminally responsible for "Acts of Violence the Primary Purpose of which is to Spread Terror among the Civilian Population, a VIOLATION OF THE LAWS OR CUSTOMS OF WAR, punishable under Articles 3, and 7(1) and 7(3) of the Statute;" (p. 35)

c) the above acts or threats of violence were committed with the primary purpose of spreading terror among the civilian population.[67]

On the basis of the exhaustive evidence presented in this case, the Trial Chamber ruled that acts examined "constituted the crime of terror as a violation of the laws and customs of war."[68] Ratko Mladic was also convicted of the crime of genocide[69] and sentenced to life imprisonment.

3.4 *A Comparative Analysis of These Three Leading ICTY Cases*

It is evident that all three ICTY cases deal with atrocity crimes: genocide, crimes against humanity and war crimes, involving the Siege of Sarajevo and the Srebrenica Massacre during the Bosnian War, 1992–1995. The three cases involve senior commanders in the Army Republika Srpska: former Chiefs of Staff of the VRS; and, senior Bosnian Serbian Commanders. All three cases invoke the charge of the crime of terrorism or persecution, which encompasses terrorizing a civilian population during an armed conflict, whether international or non-international. The strong implication or the implicit assumption throughout these three cases is that the "crime of terror" and/or the persecutory acts of "terrorizing civilians" are crimes against humanity.

The crime of terror was found among the violations of the laws or customs of war and is part and parcel of international humanitarian law. Moreover, the ICTY has defined the crime of terror with three elements: acts or threats of violence are directed to a civilian population that results in grave consequences; the perpetrators willfully targeted the civilian population; and, the primary intention of the acts or threats of violence are to spread terror among the civilian population. The ICTY has also identified and incorporated "terrorizing civilians" as a persecutory crime that falls within Article 5 of the ICTY statute as crimes against humanity.

The ICTY has set a precedent by criminalizing terrorism in situations of armed conflict, whether international or non-international. It has also defined the three essential elements that must be met for the crime of terror to be made out. Furthermore, it has also incorporated terrorism as part of the "persecutions on political, racial and religious grounds" as crimes against humanity. It seems reasonable to assume that these three judgements will have an impact on the international crime of terrorism and the future judgements and

67 *Prosecutor v. Ratko Mladic, Case No. IT-09-92-T, Judgement, Volumes III of V*, 22 November 2017, p. 1663. http://www.icty.org/x/cases/mladic/tjug/en/171122-3of5_1.pdf. (accessed February 18, 2018)

68 Ibid., paragraph 3206, p. 1672

69 Ibid., paragraph 3555, p. 1808.

jurisprudence of international criminal courts and tribunals as well as national courts.

4 Leading Supreme Court Judgements on Terrorism in the UK, US, and Canada

A study and consideration of three leading "terrorism" cases in the UK, US, and Canada is instructive on how the jurisprudence on terrorism is developing within these leading common law jurisdictions. The three cases selected are all common law Supreme Court judgements; one from each of the three States, and, include: the well-known Canadian *2002 Suresh* judgement; the UK, *2010 JS (Sri Lanka)* case; the US, *2010 Holder v. Humanitarian Law Project* judgement. These three cases will be briefly outlined and comparatively analyzed below.

4.1 *2002 Suresh v. Canada (Minister of Citizenship and Immigration)*

This was one of the first terrorism cases dealt with by the Supreme Court of Canada following the tragic 9/11 terrorist attacks in the United States. Manickavasagam Suresh, a Sri Lankan Tamil, arrived in Canada in 1990 and was recognized as a Convention refugee in 1991. In 1995 he was detained by the authorities based on the opinion of the Canadian Security Intelligence Service, on the grounds that he was a fundraiser and member of the Liberation Tigers of Tamil Eelam (LTTE), an organization known to be engaged in terrorist activities. The government started proceedings to deport him and he challenged the order for his deportation on various grounds of substance and procedure.

On September 17, 1997, the Minister notified Suresh that she was considering issuing an opinion that would declare him a danger to Canada under section 53(1)(b) of the *Immigration Act*. This section allows the Minister to deport a refugee on security grounds even where a refugee's "life or freedom" would be threatened upon return. On January 6, 1998, the Minister issued an opinion that Suresh constituted a danger to the security of Canada and should be deported pursuant to section 53(1)(b).

> The appellant applied for judicial review, alleging that: (1) the Minister's decision was unreasonable; (2) the procedures under the Act were unfair; and (3) the Act infringed ss. 7, 2(b) and 2(d) of the Canadian Charter of Rights and Freedoms. The application for judicial review was dismissed on all grounds. The Federal Court of Appeal upheld that decision.[70]

70 *Suresh v. Canada (Minister of Citizenship and Immigration)*, [2002] 1 S.C.R. 3, 2002 SCC 1, pp. 4–5. https://scc-csc.lexum.com/scc-csc/scc-csc/en/item/1937/index.do?r=AAAAAQAJVGVycm9yaXNtAQ. (accessed February 16, 2018)

The case raised a number of important questions that the SCC had to resolve, including: "the standard to be applied in reviewing a ministerial decision to deport; whether the Charter precludes deportation to a country where the refugee faces torture or death; whether deportation on the basis of mere membership in an alleged terrorist organization unjustifiably infringes the Charter rights of free expression and free association; whether "terrorism" and "danger to the security of Canada" are unconstitutionally vague; and whether the deportation scheme contains adequate procedural safeguards to ensure that refugees are not expelled to a risk of torture or death."[71]

The Court was acutely aware of the importance and relevance of its judgement at that historic moment in time, in the aftermath of 9/11, and underscored the now famous paragraph three of the judgement that summarized the enormous difficulty in deciding a case of this nature given the situation in the world at that time,

> The issues engage concerns and values fundamental to Canada and indeed the world. On the one hand stands the manifest evil of terrorism and the random and arbitrary taking of innocent lives, rippling out in an ever-widening spiral of loss and fear. Governments, expressing the will of the governed, need the legal tools to effectively meet this challenge. On the other hand stands the need to ensure that those legal tools do not undermine values that are fundamental to our democratic society – liberty, the rule of law, and the principles of fundamental justice – values that lie at the heart of the Canadian constitutional order and the international instruments that Canada has signed. In the end, it would be a Pyrrhic victory if terrorism were defeated at the cost of sacrificing our commitment to those values. Parliament's challenge is to draft laws that effectively combat terrorism and conform to the requirements of our Constitution and our international commitments.[72]

The Court considered the *International Convention for the Suppression of the Financing of Terrorism*, GA Res. 54/109, December 9, 1999, and found its definition of terrorism adequate. This Convention approaches the definitional problem of terrorism in two ways: first, through a functional definition under Article 2(1)(a) that utilizes the definitions of terrorism that are found in nine treaties that cover a range of terrorist activities such as aircraft hijackings, terrorist bombings, and so on; and, second, it supplements the offence-based list with a stipulative definition of terrorism found in Article 2(1)(b).

71 Ibid., p. 12.

72 Ibid., pp. 12–13.

> Any other act intended to cause death or serious bodily injury to a civilian, or to any other person not taking an active part in the hostilities in a situation of armed conflict, when the purpose of such act, by its nature or context, is to intimidate a population, or to compel a government or an international organization to do or to abstain from doing any act.[73]

The Court argued that this definition catches the essence of what the world understands to be terrorism. It concluded that this definition is sufficiently certain under the *Immigration Act* to be workable, fair and constitutional.

In summary, the SCC ruled that deporting a refugee back to his country of nationality to face torture would generally violate Section 7 of the *Canadian Charter of Rights and Freedoms*. If the *Immigration Act* is properly applied, then, it conforms to the Charter. The SCC rejected the arguments that the terms "danger to the security of Canada" and "terrorism" are unconstitutionally vague and that ss. 19 and 53(1)(b) of the Act violate the Charter guarantees of free expression and free association, and concluded the *Immigration Act's* impugned procedures, properly followed, are constitutional.[74]

The SCC further noted that Suresh had made a *prima facie* case that he would face a substantial risk of torture if he was returned to Sri Lanka and that his hearing did not provide the procedural safeguards required to protect his right not to be sent back to a risk of torture or death. Accordingly, the SCC came to the judgement that Suresh was entitled to a new deportation hearing under the *Immigration Act*, R.S.C., 1985, c. I-2.[75]

4.2 *2010 JS (Sri Lanka)*

Very briefly, the facts of this case are that the respondent in *JS* (*Sri Lanka*) was a Sri Lankan Tamil who was a member of the LTTE, one of the fiercest, most ruthless, and feared liberation organizations in the world before its defeat in 2009.[76] The respondent joined the LTTE when he was 10 years old in 1992.[77] The next

---

73 Ibid., pp. 54.

74 Ibid., p. 13.

75 Ibid., p. 11.

76 United States, Central Intelligence Agency, *The World Factbook*, Sri Lanka, Terrorism, https://www.cia.gov/library/publications/the-world-factbook/geos/ce.html. (accessed February 12, 2018); The FBI, Federal Bureau of Investigation, "Taming the Tamil Tigers: From here in the US," 01/10/08, https://archives.fbi.gov/archives/news/stories/2008/january/tamil_tigers011008. (accessed February 12, 2018)

77 It is important and relevant to point out that the recruitment and enlistment of child soldiers is a war crime, in and of itself. United Nations, Office of the Special Representative of the Secretary-General for Children and Armed Conflict, Child Recruitment and Use, undated, https://childrenandarmedconflict.un.org/effects-of-conflict/six-grave-violations/child-soldiers/. (accessed February 19, 2018)

year he joined the Intelligence Division of the LTTE and held various positions within the organization.

The respondent came to the UK in 2007 and claimed asylum and was excluded from refugee protection on the basis of Article 1F(a). The UK Secretary of State's decision was based on the authority of *Gurung [2002] UKIAT 04870* (starred).[78] In essence, it was asserted that voluntary membership in an extremist organization amounted to *"personal and knowing participation"* or at least acquiescence to complicity in the crimes in question.

The reasoning of the Secretary of State was that given the respondent's voluntary membership and command responsibility in an organization that was responsible for war crimes and crimes against humanity indicated that there were serious reasons for considering he was fully aware and understood the methods of the LTTE.[79]

The respondent's appeal to the UK Immigration and Appeal Tribunal was denied and on subsequent appeal to the UK Court of Appeal the Secretary of State's decision was overturned and the case made its way, eventually, to the UK Supreme Court (SC).[80]

In essence, the *ratio decidendi* in the UK SC's judgement was that the Court did not accept that either the LTTE or its Intelligence Division could be said to be "predominantly terrorist in character." Hence, on this alone there could not be any question of "personal and knowing participation" or "complicity" in war crimes or crimes against humanity.

It was further noted that the *Gurung* decision could no longer be held in the same high regard. Moreover, it was no longer helpful to characterize organizations as exclusively engaged in terrorist activities. It is preferable to focus on at least seven determining factors:

- the nature and size of the organization and the part of it that the person was most directly concerned;
- whether and, if so, by whom the organization was proscribed;
- how the person came to be recruited;
- the length of time the person remained in the organization and what, if any, opportunities the person had to leave;

78 *R (on the application of JS) (Sri Lanka) (Respondent) v Secretary of State for the Home Department (Appellant)* [2010] UKSC 15, On appeal from: [2009] EWCA Civ 364, p. 3. https://www.supremecourt.uk/cases/docs/uksc-2009-0121-judgment.pdf. (accessed February 13, 2018)

79 Ibid.

80 *Regina (JS (Sri Lanka)) v. Secretary of State for the Home Department* ([2009] EWCA Civ 364), England, Court of Appeal 30 April 2009.

- the person's position, rank, standing and influence within the organization;
- the person's knowledge of the organization's war crimes activities;
- the person's personal involvement and role in the organization including particularly whatever contribution the person made to the commission of any war crimes.[81]

In the words of Lord Brown, "I would hold the accused disqualified under article 1F if there are serious reasons for considering him voluntarily to have *contributed in a significant way* to the organization *to pursue its purpose of committing war crimes, aware that his assistance will in fact further that purpose*."[82]

In his concurring reasons, Lord Hope observed, even more emphatically, that it is a mistake to find there is complicity when "the organization was or has become one whose aims, methods and activities are predominantly terrorist in character 'very little more will be necessary.'"[83] He then goes on to opine:

> But it is a dangerous doctrine. It leads people to think, as the Secretary of State did in this case, that voluntary membership of such a group gives rise to a presumption of personal and knowing participation, or at least acquiescence, amounting to complicity; para 34. It diverts attention from a close examination of the facts and the need for a carefully reasoned decision as to precisely why the person concerned is excluded from protection under the Convention.[84]

The UK SC unanimously dismissed the appeal but varied the order such that the Secretary of State would follow the judgement of the UK SC and not the Court of Appeal in the redetermination of the respondent's asylum application.

What is of great interest in this UK SC judgement was that the LTTE was not predominantly terrorist in nature, including the Intelligence Division of the LTTE, and that in its judgement the *1998 Rome Statute* of the ICC should be the basis of international criminal law for the purposes of deciding whether a person should be excluded under Article 1F(a) of the *1951 Convention relating to the Status of Refugees*. As noted previously, there is no universally accepted definition of terrorism and the *1998 Rome Statute* of the ICC does not incorporate terrorism within its jurisdiction. Moreover, it is also relevant to point out that

---

81 *R (on the application of JS) (Sri Lanka) (Respondent) v Secretary of State for the Home Department (Appellant)* [2010] UKSC 15, On appeal from: [2009] EWCA Civ 364, paragraph 30.

82 Ibid., paragraph 38. [Emphasis added]

83 Ibid., paragraph 44.

84 Ibid.

most jurisdictions in the world, including the UK, have listed the LTTE as a terrorist organization.[85] While exclusion here was based on Article 1F(a) that deals with crimes against peace, war crimes and crimes against humanity, it is evident that at all instances in the court system the question was whether the LTTE was a terrorist organization and what degree of involvement within an organization that engages in terrorist activity can lead to exclusion from refugee protection. For the UK SC it had to be a voluntary and significant contribution. But, it is evident that the UK SC did not find that the LTTE was predominantly a terrorist organization, as listed by the UK government, for the purposes of exclusion under Article 1F(a).

4.3 *2010 Holder v. Humanitarian Law Project*

In 1997 the US Secretary of State designated the Kurdistan Workers' Party, the Partiya Karkeran Kurdistan or PKK, and the LTTE, and 28 other organizations, as foreign terrorist organizations.

The plaintiffs filed a law suit in the US Federal Court in 1998 challenging the constitutionality of the material-support statute, §2339B, on the grounds that they wanted "to provide support for the humanitarian and political activities of the PKK and the LTTE in the form of monetary contributions, other tangible aid, legal training, and political advocacy,"[86] but they were prohibited in doing so for fear of prosecution under §2339B. The plaintiffs claimed that the statute was unconstitutional because it violated their rights under the First Amendment, freedom of speech and freedom of association, by criminalizing their material provision of support to the PKK and LTTE without requiring the Government to prove that the plaintiffs had a specific intend to further the unlawful ends of these organizations. The plaintiffs also argued that the statute was too vague and, hence, unconstitutional.[87]

Ultimately, on the question of material support, the US Supreme Court states, that it is meant to "promote peaceable, lawful conduct ... can [in fact] further terrorism by foreign groups in multiple ways."[88] The point was made that such "support frees up other resources within the organization that may be put to violent ends."[89] It can also add legitimacy to foreign terrorist groups that

85 United Kingdom, Home Office, *Proscribed Terrorist Organizations*, 12 July 2013, updated 22 December 2017, https://www.gov.uk/government/uploads/system/uploads/attachment_data/file/670599/20171222_Proscription.pdf. (accessed February 14, 2018). At page 15 it notes that LTTE have been proscribed since March 2001.

86 *Holder v. Humanitarian Law Project*, *561* U.S. 1 (2010), 130 S.Ct. 2705, p. 4, https://www.supremecourt.gov/opinions/09pdf/08-1498.pdf. (accessed February 14, 2018).

87 Ibid., 5.

88 Ibid., 25.

89 Ibid.

"makes it easier for those groups to persist, to recruit members, and to raise funds – all of which facilitate more terrorist attacks."[90] Further, the evidence presented indicates that "terrorist groups systematically conceal their activities behind charitable, social, and political fronts."[91] Moreover, there is evidence that indicates that the PKK and the LTTE, especially, have not respected the line between humanitarian and violent activities.

> Providing material support in any form would also undermine cooperative international efforts to prevent terrorism and strain the United States' relationships with its allies, including those that are defending themselves against violent insurgencies waged by foreign terrorist groups.[92]

The US Supreme Court also considered the foreign policy implications and the international counter-terrorism efforts of the material-support statute and stated that providing foreign terrorist groups with material support in any form also furthers terrorism by straining the United States' relationships with its allies and undermining cooperative efforts between nations to prevent terrorist attacks.[93]

The Supreme Court ruled that, "We hold that, in regulating the particular forms of support that plaintiffs seek to provide to foreign terrorist organizations, Congress has pursued that objective consistent with the limitations of the First and Fifth Amendments."[94]

4.4 *Comparative Analysis of These Three Supreme Court Judgements*

One of the most obvious points of comparison in these three judgements is that they all deal with applicants from Sri Lanka. Not surprisingly, at least in part, due to the fact that the Sri Lankan civil war lasted for decades, from 1983 to 2009.[95] And, this civil war produced thousands upon thousands of refugees during those years.[96]

---

90 Ibid.

91 Ibid.

92 Ibid., 5.

93 Ibid., p. 27.

94 Ibid., p. 36.

95 BBC News, Sri Lanka Profile – Timeline, http://www.bbc.co.uk/news/world-south-asia-12004081. (accessed February 16, 2018); "The Sri Lankan Civil War," *ThoughtCo*, https://www.thoughtco.com/the-sri-lankan-civil-war-195086. (accessed February 16, 2018)

96 Connecting with Emigrants: A Global Profile of Diasporas. Key Statistics of Diasporas from Sri Lanka, OECD Publishing, 26 July 2012, http://www.keepeek.com/Digital-Asset-Management/oecd/social-issues-migration-health/connecting-with-emigrants/key-statistics-on-diaspora-from-sri-lanka_9789264177949-graph30-en#.WodPfYPwbIU.

It is interesting to note that in all three cases the Supreme Courts upheld, for the most part, their respective governments' legislation that were all challenged on human rights grounds. In the *Suresh* judgement, the Supreme Court of Canada ordered a new deportation hearing for the applicant but also found that the impugned legislation did not violate of the *Canadian Charter of Rights and Freedoms*. Indeed, they left open the possibility that persons who were properly determined to be a "danger to Canada" could be sent back, in exceptional circumstances, to a risk of torture and even death, despite being determined to be Convention refugees. This was truly an exceptional ruling that incurred widespread international criticism of the Canadian Supreme Court's judgement in *Suresh*. However, if the appellant's support of and activities for the LTTE were known prior to his refugee hearing, assuming he was actively supporting the LTTE for years, then, the issue of exclusion under Article 1F would certainly have been raised and he may well have been excluded from refugee protection.

The UK Supreme Court in *JS* (*Sri Lanka*) did not accept that the LTTE was "predominantly a terrorist" organization and that in order to exclude a refugee applicant it was necessary to establish that they had made a "voluntary" and "significant contribution" to a terrorist action or activities. The key was establishing the personal liability of the refugee applicant in an act or acts of terrorism. Membership in a terrorist organization was insufficient to establish complicity in war crimes or crimes against humanity. And, in the US Supreme Court's decision in *Holder v. Humanitarian Law Project* the material-support bar was found to be constitutional and did not infringe on either First or Fifth Amendment rights. Any material support to a terrorist organization would be sufficient to bar any applicant from refugee protection in the United States. This appears to be a far lower standard for barring someone from refugee protection than "voluntary" and "significant contribution."

The judgement that was perhaps the most exceptional among the three appears to be the *JS* (*Sri Lanka*) case of the UK Supreme Court. It set a new standard for excluding refugee applicants under Article 1F(a), it now must be shown that the refugee applicant made a "voluntary and significant contribution" to a war crime or a crime against humanity in order to be excluded from refugee protection. This is a far higher standard for excluding someone from

(accessed February 16, 2018), There were 433,200 Sri Lankan emigrants living in OECD countries in 2005/2006.

refugee protection than the US material-support bar.[97] The US material-support bar is undoubtedly one of the lowest standards for barring anyone from refugee protection.

5 Conclusions

From the review of terrorism and international law today and the foregoing presentation and the comparative analysis of some of leading jurisprudence of the Supreme Courts in Canada, UK, and the US and at the former ICTY, it is clear that the terrorism is recognized as a serious international crime in both national and international criminal law and is prohibited in international humanitarian law. The ICTY had identified the "crime of terror," within international and non-international armed conflicts to be based not only on treaties but also in customary international law and, in addition, it has interpreted "terrorising civilians" as persecution and a crime against humanity. Indeed, among the three ICTY cases presented here, *Krstic, Galic,* and *Mladic,* all were convicted for the crime of terror and/or terrorizing civilians. There is no doubt whatsoever that terrorism is prohibited in situations of armed conflict, under both international humanitarian and criminal law.

Despite there being no universally accepted definition of what constitutes terrorism and the absence of an comprehensive international convention on terrorism, there is little doubt that given the repeated resolutions of the UN Security Council, the declarations of the UN General Assembly, and the 19 sectoral conventions negotiated under the auspices of the UN on different aspects of terrorism that terrorism, irrespective of whatever laudatory goals it may claim to espouse, is prohibited clearly in international criminal law.

The same holds true at the domestic level where terrorism has been criminalized within national legislation, typically, within the countries' criminal codes. While there may be a lack of consistency in terms of how terrorism is defined at the national level, there is no question as to it being a serious crime that can incur serious penalties upon conviction.

Those who apply for asylum and have been involved in terrorist activities will be excluded from refugee protection. What is anomalous for the UK and Canada is that their respective Supreme Courts have adopted the *1998 Rome*

97 The recent Canadian Supreme Court judgement in *2013 Ezokola* adopts the UK *JS* (*Sri Lanka*) standard of "voluntary, significant and knowing contribution." *Ezokola v. Canada* (*Citizenship and Immigration*) 2013 SCC 40.

Statute of the International Criminal Court for defining what constitutes serious international crimes for the purposes of exclusion under Article 1F of the *1951 Convention relating to the Status of Refugees*, when the *1998 Rome Statute*, in fact, does not include terrorism that is now recognized as one of the most serious international crimes. Albeit, some would argue that it could fall under one or more of the four core international crimes: war crime, crime against humanity, genocide or even aggression. Although there are efforts underway to do so, this has yet to occur and appears to be some way off. Accordingly, the courts will have to rely on other international instruments and the ongoing development and interpretation of international humanitarian and criminal law to define what constitutes terrorism. The lack of a universal definition of terrorism and the multiple sectoral conventions that are available contribute to the existing confusion surrounding the legal definition and understanding of what constitutes terrorism. These obvious gaps and shortcomings in international humanitarian and criminal law and the divergencies at the State level will likely continue to contribute to the confusion and conflation between terrorism and asylum.[98]

The logical next step is to address these gaps and shortcomings in international criminal law as it has a clear and evident impact on international refugee law, especially, as it affects those who are culpable for terrorist activities.[99] These gaps and deficiencies in international criminal law and the lack of a comprehensive international convention on terrorism, potentially, can generate injustices in how the persons who claim refuge can be excluded from refugee protection for their serious criminality. This is evident especially in the majority of the instances of those who are excluded from refugee protection on the grounds of being complicit in serious international crimes.[100] These apparent gaps and shortcomings in international criminal law have a direct impact on the application of exclusion within the refugee status determination

98 James C. Simeon, "Terrorism and Asylum: Unravelling the Myths," RLI *Blog on Refugee Law and Forced Migration*, Refugee Law Initiative, School of Advanced Study, University of London, January 25, 2018, https://rli.blogs.sas.ac.uk/2018/01/25/terrorism-and-asylum-unravelling-the-myths/. (accessed February 19, 2018)

99 James C. Simeon and Sarah Singer, "Armed Conflict, Terrorism and Asylum: Global Solutions for Global Problems?" RLI *Blog on Refugee Law and Forced Migration*, Refugee Law Initiative, School of Advanced Study, University of London, November 1, 2017, https://rli.blogs.sas.ac.uk/2017/11/01/armed-conflict-terrorism-and-asylum-global-solutions-for-global-problems/. (accessed February 19, 2018)

100 James C. Simeon, "Complicity and Exclusion in International Refugee Law," RLI *Blog on Refugee Law and Forced Migration*, Refugee Law Initiative, School of Advanced Study, University of London, March 12, 2018, https://rli.blogs.sas.ac.uk/2018/03/15/complicity-and-exclusion-in-international-refugee-law/. (accessed March 17, 2018)

systems of States and the UNHCR, through its mandate or statutory refugee status determination system, on the international refugee protection system as a refuge for those responsible for serious criminality. If anything can delegitimize international refugee law and its system of asylum this surely can and, accordingly, addressing these gaps and deficiencies in international criminal law dealing with terrorism should be made a priority of the UN, the UNHCR, and all States in their efforts to counter the growing threat of terrorism.[101]

---

101 James C. Simeon and Elies van Sliedregt, "New Wars, Ever Escalating Crises, and Exclusion," RLI *Blog on Refugee Law and Forced Migration*, Refugee Law Initiative, School of Advanced Study, University of London, April 9, 2019, https://rli.blogs.sas.ac.uk/2019/04/09/new-wars-ever-escalating-crises-and-exclusion/. (accessed June 27, 2019)

PART 3

The National Dimensions and Dynamics of Terrorism and Exclusion from Asylum

CHAPTER 8

Exclusion from Refugee Status on the Basis of Criminality – The United Kingdom's Response and Its Broader International Law Context

Mark Symes

1 Introduction

Not every asylum seeker enjoys the protection of the *1951 Refugee Convention*. It makes specific provision for exclusion from refugee status for those associated with serious criminality, at both domestic and international levels, and for acts contrary to the purposes and principles of the UN. There are few species of criminality more serious than offences classified as terrorism.

This chapter traces the doctrine of exclusion for participation, first setting the scene in the broad context of international law and other relevant legal sources, before going on to trace the development of exclusion for participation in the UK context.

Article 1F states that the provisions of the *1951 Refugee Convention* "shall not apply to any person with respect to whom there are serious reasons for considering" that:

a) he has committed a crime against peace, a war crime or a crime against humanity, as defined in the international instruments drawn up to make provision in respect of such crimes;
b) he has committed a serious non-political crime outside the country of refuge prior to his admission to that country as a refugee;
c) he has been guilty of acts contrary to the purposes and principles of the United Nations.

The language of the *1951 Refugee Convention* is clear: commission of serious non-political crimes and international crimes can attract exclusion; so too can being "guilty" of acts contrary to the UN's mission. Not only the principal offenders but also their accomplices are excluded. This article reviews the development in the UK of the principles governing the ambit of the exclusion for participation in relevant misdemeanours.

The bare text of the Convention gives little guide to the scope of exclusion for participation in criminality. However, the reference to the international instruments addressing international criminality plainly imports the principles

© KONINKLIJKE BRILL NV, LEIDEN, 2020 DOI:10.1163/9789004295995_010 developed in the case law that interprets those provisions, given the need to afford a dynamic interpretation to the *1951 Refugee Convention* which takes account of the development of the surrounding legal framework.[1]

2 Relevant Materials – The Legal Environment

Although this chapter's primary purpose is to analyse the development of exclusion for complicity in the case law of the United Kingdom, it is important to identify some authorities from the surrounding legal environment in order to put that history in context. The domestic response of the UK courts and tribunals has drawn very heavily upon the jurisprudence of other national courts and on international criminal law, and so too must any writer seeking to track its path.

UNHCR is the organisation with responsibility for the Refugee Convention's international implementation, and so Guidance from that organisation, such as that on the *Application of the Exclusion Clauses: Article 1F* is always important. It states:

> 18. For exclusion to be justified, individual responsibility must be established in relation to a crime covered by Article 1F. … In general individual responsibility flows from the person having committed, or made a substantial contribution to the commission of the criminal act, in the knowledge that his or her act or omission would facilitate the criminal conduct. The individual need not physically have committed the criminal act in question. Instigating, aiding and abetting and participating in a joint criminal enterprise can suffice.[2]

This passage has taken centre stage in the analysis by judges of the ambit of exclusion for participation in crimes UNHCR reiterated their view that physical involvement in criminal acts was not required in a letter they wrote during the *JS (Sri Lanka)*[3] proceedings in 2009,[4] stating that individual responsibility for

1 *IG Nepal* [2002] UKIAT 04870 §109.

2 Paragraph 18 of the UNHCR *Guidelines on International Protection: Application of the Exclusion Clauses: Article 1F of the 1951 Convention relating to the Status of Refugees*. https://www.unhcr.org/publications/legal/3f7d48514/guidelines-international-protection-5-application-exclusion-clauses-article.html. (accessed June 1, 2019)

3 That is, the litigation leading to the governing UK authority, *JS (Sri Lanka), R (on the application of) v Secretary of State for the Home Department* [2010] UKSC 15 §33.

4 Letter from Roland Schilling of UNHCR to the parties following the Court of Appeal's judgment in *JS (Sri Lanka)* (8 December 2009).

excludable acts may be presumed where there was voluntary membership of a group whose activities involved indiscriminate killings or injury of the civilian population, or acts of torture, including control of the organisation's funds or otherwise "substantially assisting" the organisation to function effectively in pursuit of such aims. Nevertheless, UNHCR acknowledged that due regard still had to be given to the nature of the acts allegedly committed, and to the personal responsibility and involvement of the applicant.

The Convention being a living instrument, it must incorporate not just international law as extant in the early 1950s, but also subsequent developments. The instruments detailing the modern understanding of individual criminal responsibility culminate in the Rome statute,[5] as usefully summarised by Lord Brown in *JS Sri Lanka*, who draws attention to the symmetry between Article 25 thereof and a modern regional transposition of the Refugee Convention, that is found in Article 12 of the Qualification Directive,[6] thus:

> Paragraph (b) encompasses those who order, solicit or induce (in the language of article 12(3) of the Directive, "instigate") the commission of the crime; paragraph (c) those who aid, abet, or otherwise assist in its commission (including providing the means for this); paragraph (d) those who in any other way intentionally contribute to its commission (paras (c) and (d) together equating, in the language of article 12(3) of the Directive, to "otherwise participat[ing]" in the commission of the crime).[7]

International criminal law, then, is an obvious source of instruction. Two strands of particular significance are the provisions of the Rome Statute, and the decisions of the ad hoc Tribunals interpreting the pre-existing body of international criminal law. The former defines various forms of liability both as principal and accessory. The latter discusses a species of liability of particular interest to the consideration of complicity, the concept of joint enterprise liability, particularly in the landmark decision of *Tadic*. Notably this is treated as a form of liability committed by *principals* rather than mere *accomplices*, but it

5 Rome Statute of the International Criminal Court. The Statute of the International Criminal Tribunal for the former Yugoslavia at Article 7 states: "1. A person who planned, instigated, ordered, committed or otherwise aided and abetted in the planning, preparation or execution of crime referred to in articles 2 – 5 of the present Statute, shall be individually responsible for the crime." Lord Brown in *JS* (*Sri Lanka*) §9 described it as "the most comprehensive and authoritative statement of international thinking on the principles that govern liability for the most serious international crimes."

6 Directive 2004/83.

7 *JS* (*Sri Lanka*), *R* (*on the application of*) *v Secretary of State for the Home Department* [2010] UKSC 15 §33.

covers sufficiently similar terrain as to merit attention. Given that UK law has not developed any specific thinking on joint enterprise liability, analysis of the principles can await another day.

Article 30 of the Rome Statute, addressing the requisite *Mental element*, is also relevant. It provides that the material elements of the crime must be committed with both intent (i.e., that they intend to engage in the conduct, with the intent to bring about the consequence that followed or knowing that the said consequence would ordinarily follow) and knowledge (i.e., awareness of the existing circumstances or that a particular consequence will ordinarily follow).

However, neither the Rome Statute nor its legal ancestors such as the London Charter of the International Military Tribunal answer the critical question as to the *degree* of complicity that attracts criminal liability. Thus, the Canadian Federal Court of Appeal has noted that whilst it was clear that leaders, organisers, instigators and accomplices participating in the formulation or execution of a common plan or conspiracy to commit relevant crimes were responsible for all acts performed by any persons in that plan's execution, it remained unclear as to the extent of participation that would be necessary to attract liability as an accomplice.[8]

This is important, because the provisions of international criminal law acknowledge and affirm one foundational principle:

> The basic assumption must be that in international law as much as in national systems, the foundation of criminal responsibility is the principle of personal culpability: nobody may be held criminally responsible for acts or transactions in which he has not personally engaged or in some other way participated (*nulla poena sine culpa*).[9]

One decision of the international criminal courts that merits particular attention is that of *Tadic*.[10] The Appeals Chamber cited the Report of the Secretary-General on the establishment of the International Tribunal, which set out that office's belief "that all persons who participate in the planning, preparation or execution of serious violations of international humanitarian law in the former Yugoslavia are individually responsible for such violations."[11] This encouraged

8 McGuigan JA in *Ramirez v Canada (Minister of Employment and Immigration)* (1992) 89 DLR (4th) 173 citing Article 6 of the London Charter.

9 The ICTY in *Tadic* (appeals chamber judgment of 15 July 1999) §96.

10 *Prosecutor v Tadic*, 15 July 1999, (1999) 9 IHRR 1051.

11 Ibid.

the Appeals Chamber to conclude that a broad approach to participation in international crime was appropriate:

> Thus, all those who have engaged in serious violations of international humanitarian law, whatever the manner in which they may have perpetrated, or participated in the perpetration of those violations, must be brought to justice. If this is so, it is fair to conclude that the Statute does not confine itself to providing for jurisdiction over those persons who plan, instigate, order, physically perpetrate a crime or otherwise aid and abet in its planning, preparation or execution. The Statute does not stop there. It does not exclude those modes of participating in the commission of crimes which occur where several persons having a common purpose embark on criminal activity that is then carried out either jointly or by some members of this plurality of persons. Whoever contributes to the commission of crimes by the group of persons or some members of the group, in execution of a common criminal purpose, may be held to be criminally liable, subject to certain conditions.[12]

The rationale for this broad approach was identified in *Tadic* as arising from the object and purpose of the ICTY's Statute, but also from the very nature of the international criminality at which that Statute was aimed: for the relevant "manifestations of collective criminality [were] ... crimes ... often carried out by groups of individuals acting in pursuance of a common criminal design." In this context the participation and contribution of other members was vital, and accordingly attracted the same moral gravity.[13] Thus *Tadic* concluded that "international criminal responsibility embraces actions perpetrated by a collectivity of persons in furtherance of a common criminal design."

Tadic went on to review the post-Second World War jurisprudence on war crimes addressing common criminal purpose, finding therein three distinct categories of collective criminality.[14] Firstly there was the regular joint enterprise case where all the co-defendants have the same criminal intent and each played a part in executing the crime. Here each individual fixed with criminal responsibility must have voluntarily participated in one aspect of the common design, which might include the provision of material assistance to the activities

12 Ibid.

13 The Canadian Supreme Court noted in *Ezokola v. Canada (Citizenship and Immigration)* [2013] 2 SCR 678 §5 that "party liability plays a much greater role in the commission of those crimes recognized as some of the most serious in the international legal order."

14 *Tadic* §196.

of others, with the intention to achieve this result. Secondly, there were the so-called "concentration camp" cases where all those in authority who participate in enforcing the repressive system fell to be regarded as co-perpetrators of the war crime of ill-treatment (as the ICTY itself acknowledged, these were "really a variant of the first category"). Thirdly, there were those cases where the principal offender commits an offence outside the common design but where the defendant foresaw and both knowingly and willingly took the risk of its occurrence (Lord Brown was to later style this as the standard basis for secondary liability for joint enterprise criminality under domestic law).[15] Academic commentators have suggested that this third class of liability, JCE III, will not be taken up by the International Criminal Court.[16]

The ICTY then went on to address the elements of these crimes. The *actus reus* for each of the three categories of collective criminality just identified was that a plurality of persons, whether or not organised within any particular administrative structure, were connected to a common plan, design or purpose which amounted to or involved the commission of a crime provided for in the ICTY Statute:[17]

> (iii) Participation of the accused in the common design involving the perpetration of one of the crimes provided for in the Statute … need not involve commission of a specific crime under one of those provisions (for example, murder, extermination, torture, rape, etc.) but may take the form of assistance in, or contribution to, the execution of the common plan or purpose.

As to the requisite *mens rea*:[18]

> By contrast, the mens rea element differs according to the category of common design under consideration. With regard to the first category, what is required is the intent to perpetrate a certain crime (this being the shared intent on the part of all co-perpetrators). With regard to the second category (which, as noted above, is really a variant of the first), personal knowledge of the system of ill-treatment is required (whether proved by express testimony or a matter of reasonable inference from the

15 In *JS*.

16 See those cited in *Ezokola* fn66: van Sliedregt, at p. 101; Lafontaine, at p. 238; A. Cassese, "The Proper Limits of Individual Responsibility under the Doctrine of Joint Criminal Enterprise" (2007), 5 J.I.C.J. 109, at p. 132; Manacorda and Meloni, at p. 176.

17 *Tadic* §227.

18 *Tadic* §228.

accused's position of authority),[19] as well as the intent to further this common concerted system of ill-treatment.

The mental element for the third category of cases required participation in the "common purpose" *via*:[20]

(i) the intention to take part in a joint criminal enterprise and to further – individually and jointly – the criminal purposes of that enterprise; and

(ii) the foreseeability of the possible commission by other members of the group of offences that do not constitute the object of the common criminal purpose.

As already indicated, it is of course the Rome Statute rather than the instruments establishing the *ad hoc* Tribunals such as the ICTY which represents the present high watermark of international criminal law, but as the former has received close attention from the decisions of national supreme courts, I will reserve reference to it until later.

UN resolutions are a further potential source of international law. Directly after the attack on the World Trade Centre on 11 September 2001, the UN Security Council issued a resolution which called for "those responsible for aiding, supporting or harbouring the perpetrators, organisers and sponsors of these acts will be held accountable."[21] Later resolutions went onto expressly condemn the incitement of terrorist acts[22] and to express concern over the increased use of communications technology for the purposes of radicalisation.[23] The Court of Appeal of England and Wales has noted that this series of Resolutions, which emphasise the obligations of States to address the "*incitement ... justification or glorification ... of terrorist acts*" and calls upon States to "*deny safe haven ... any person who supports, facilitates, participates or attempts to participate in the financing, planning, preparation or commission of terrorist acts,*" tends to suggest that liability for exclusion may, in the eyes of the international community as embodied by the United Nations, be broader than that suggested by UNHCR in their Guidelines originating in September 2003.[24]

19 cf Linden JA in *Sivakumar v. Canada (Minister of Employment and Immigration)* (CA.) [1994] 1 C.F. 433: "the closer one is to a position of leadership or command within an organization, the easier it will be to draw an inference of awareness of the crimes and participation in the plan to commit the crimes."

20 *Tadic* §220.

21 UN Security Council Resolution 1368 (12 September 2001).

22 Res/1624 (2005) (14 September 2005).

23 Res/ 2178 (2014) (24 September 2014).

24 Irwin LJ in *Youssef v Secretary of State for the Home Department* [2018] EWCA Civ 933 §62–63, referring to the series of UN Resolutions cited in the last 3 footnotes post-dating the

UK law has since October 2006 been subject to the Qualification Directive[25] which forms part of the European Union's Common European Asylum System. This instrument defines the inclusion and exclusion of third country nationals from refugee status by reference to very similar terminology as used by the Refugee Convention. The Directive makes express reference to the notion of complicity: for the exclusion regimes expressly "applies to persons who instigate or otherwise participate in the commission of the crimes or acts mentioned therein."[26] As noted by Lord Brown, this provision "does not, of course, enlarge the application of article 1F; it merely gives expression to what is already well understood in international law."[27]

There are other aspects of EU law that bear on complicity in terrorism. The legislation[28] addressing "Offences relating to a terrorist group" provides that Member States must take the necessary measures to ensure that intentional participation in terrorism is punished,

> including by supplying information or material resources, or by funding its activities in any way, with knowledge of the fact that such participation will contribute to the criminal activities of the terrorist group.

Indeed, an EU Common Position[29] contains an annex that specifies particular "persons, groups and entities involved in terrorist acts."

The UK's approach to the Refugee Convention is also subject to legislative activity. Section 54 of the Immigration, Asylum and Nationality Act 2006 states that when Article 1F(c) is construed and applied, acts contrary to purposes and principles of the UN include acts of committing, preparing, or instigating terrorism, whether or not they amount to an actual or inchoate offence, and acts encouraging others in those same activities. Several Judges have noted that legislation of this nature must be construed having regard to the broader legal context in which it arises: thus section 54 must take account of the single autonomous meaning for which decision makers must generally strive in order to ensure consistency of approach internationally when construing the Refugee

---

UNHCR Guidelines on International Protection: *Application of the Exclusion Clauses: Article 1F of the 1951 Convention relating to the Status of Refugees* (4 September 2003).

25 Directive 2004/83.

26 Directive 2004/83 Article 12(3).

27 *JS (Sri Lanka), R (on the application of) v Secretary of State for the Home Department* [2010] UKSC 15 §33.

28 Paragraph 2 of Article 2 of Framework Decision 2002/475 (OJ 2002 L 164, p. 3).

29 Common Position 2001/931/CFSP on the application of specific measures to combat terrorism (OJ 2001 L 344, p. 93).

Convention,[30] as well as being read subject to the provision governing the same legal issue in European Union law, i.e., Article 12 of the Qualification Directive.[31]

One point stands out from this initial survey. Both the UNHCR, and the ICTY in *Tadic,* take the view that it is necessary to mark the special status of some forms of offending, such that a broader form of participation is recognised than that commonly found in criminal law elsewhere. Thus, UNHCR countenance individual responsibility arising from the making of a *substantial contribution* to a criminal act *via* actions falling short of instigating, aiding and abetting; *Tadic* notes that the ICTY statute extends beyond planning, ordering, aiding and abetting, into the territory where persons contribute to a common purpose by which they and others together embark on a criminal course.

3 History of Complicity in UK Law

3.1 *The First Steps in UK Law*

Most if not all of the UK cases concern involvement with the activities of an organisation. This issue, given significant impetus by a UNHCR position paper produced shortly after events in the USA in September 2001,[32] is the nature of the organisation which attracts potential exclusion. To what extent is the bare fact of membership a matter which may lead to exclusion?

Some early UK decisions took the view that if the organisation was of a "limited, brutal purpose"[33] or "one or has become one whose aims, methods and activities are predominantly terrorist in character, very little more will be necessary" to conclude that exclusion is appropriate.[34] Thus one view was that an individual excluded on account of association with such an organisation had no complaint:

> ...it is no use his asserting that he does not support its policy or methods. If he does not endorse a central policy of the party he should not be a

30 Irwin LJ in *Youssef v Secretary of State for the Home Department* [2018] EWCA Civ 933 §54.

31 Lady Hale and Lord Dyson in *Al- Sirri v Secretary of State for the Home Department* [2012] UKSC 54 §36.

32 *Addressing Security Concerns without Undermining Refugee Protection: UNHCR's Perspective,* at paragraph §18; first issued in 2001.

33 Drawing here on *Ramirez v. Canada (Minister of Employment and Immigration)* (1992) 2 F.C. 306 which had previously recognised the notion of an organisation that has a "limited, brutal purpose."

34 *IG Nepal* §105;

> member of it: in any event his membership and contribution to the life of the party is indirect support for its violent acts.[35]

Such an approach was thought essential in order to address the nature of modern terrorism: because any involvement in such groups must encompass "those who provide the latter with the physical, logistical support that enables modern, terrorist groups to operate."[36] Even these decisions recognised limitations on this doctrine of exclusion by association. Firstly there was the question of the voluntary nature of such activities; secondly there was the requirement for actual knowledge of the excludable activities; thirdly there was the issue of the extent to which any such organisation was fragmented, its nature and that of the society in which it operated.[37] The highpoint of this doctrine came with the decision in *IG Nepal* which was followed and approved[38] for a period. There the Tribunal posited a continuum as a decision making aid, with at one end organisations endorsing pro-democratic aims and embracing human rights that briefly conducted an armed struggle against a dictatorial government, and at the other, authoritarian-regime supporting organisations which chose civilian targets in the course of operations that were predominantly terrorist and abhorred human rights norms.[39]

The UT in *IG Nepal* also adopted[40] a formulation suggested by the UNHCR that where there is sufficient proof that an asylum seeker belongs to an extremist international terrorist group, such as those involved in the 11 September [2001] attacks, voluntary membership

> could be presumed to amount to personal and knowing participation,[41] or at least acquiescence amounting to complicity in the crimes in question.

However, although this view held sway for a significant period, senior courts came to disapprove it, on the basis that it represented an unnecessary

35 *Ozer* (10922, May 1994).

36 *IG Nepal* §10 citing *McMullen v INS* 685F 2d 1312 (9th Cir 1981).

37 *IG Nepal* §108, 110.

38 For example, by the Court of Appeal in *MH (Syria) v Secretary of State for the Home Department* [2009] EWCA Civ 226.

39 *IG Nepal* §113.

40 §105.

41 Linden JA in *Sivakumar v. Canada (Minister of Employment and Immigration)* (CA.)[1994] 1 C.F. 433 stated that "association with a person or organization responsible for international crimes may constitute complicity if there is personal and knowing participation or toleration of the crimes."

distraction from the true question that confronted decision makers: i.e., personal culpability. The vehicle for the resolution of the true question to determine complicity was the appeal of the Sri Lankan asylum seeker in the *JS* litigation.

3.2 *The UK's General Approach to Exclusion for Complicity: The JS Litigation (and its Echoes Elsewhere)*

JS was a Sri Lankan Tamil. In 1992, aged 10, he became a member of the Liberation Tigers of Tamil Eelam ("LTTE"), joining the LTTE's Intelligence Division a year later. Aged 16 he took on the role of team leader of a nine-man combat unit, and at 17 became the leader of a 45-man platoon, on each occasion engaging in military operations against the Sri Lankan army. At 18 he was appointed to lead a mobile unit responsible for transporting military equipment and other members of the Intelligence Division through jungles to a point where armed members of the Division could be sent in plain clothes to Colombo. He continued to do this for some three years from September 2000, save for around ten weeks when he was appointed one of the chief security guards to the Intelligence Division's leader, whom he accompanied as a trusted aide on visits to the LTTE District Leader, and other prominent LTTE members. From early 2004 to September 2006 he served as second in command of the combat unit of the Intelligence Division. In October 2006 he was sent incognito (in plain clothes and under an assumed name) to Colombo to await further instructions. Soon afterwards he learned that his presence in Colombo had been discovered and arrangements were made for him to leave the country.

JS had been refused asylum by the UK Home Office in circumstances which precluded a statutory right of appeal; accordingly he challenged the decision by way of judicial review. The Administrative Court judge who first considered his case concluded that he had held significant roles in the LTTE including positions of responsibility in the intelligence service.

The case first received a significant appellate judgment at Court of Appeal level.[42] There Toulson LJ was troubled by the phrase "or at least acquiescence amounting to complicity in the crimes in question" in the UNHCR formulation approved by the IAT in *IG Nepal*. As he put it, "acquiescence is a slippery word" which risked opening the gate to a finding of guilt by association alone.

In Toulson LJ's view, the international criminal statutes could have been expected to have defined the attribution of criminal responsibility by omission, by clearly defining the circumstances that might give rise to that situation, had they intended to create such liability. Indeed, where the notion of criminal

42 *JS (Sri Lanka), R (on the application of) v Secretary of State for the Home Department* [2009] EWCA Civ 364.

omission was addressed in the Rome statute, this was done in express terms, as where a commander might be criminally responsible for crimes committed by forces under his effective command as a result of his failure to exercise proper control over such forces where the commander "should have known that the forces were committing or about to commit such crimes."[43]

The continuum approach identified in *IG Nepal* was found wanting for three reasons. Firstly, the examples given at the two ends of the spectrum were too subjective: the UK's own colonial history demonstrated how it was that value judgments as to whether individuals were terrorists or freedom fighters might change over time. Secondly, the nature of an organisation's long-term aims was too remote from the question of criminality to be a relevant consideration. Thirdly, the continuum approach took the decision maker's eye off the critical question of whether both the *actus reus* and the *mens rea* for committing an international crime were present.

Toulson LJ for the Court of Appeal concluded in *JS*

> that in order for there to be joint enterprise liability:
> 1. there has to have been a common design which amounted to or involved the commission of a crime provided for in the statute;
> 2. the defendant must have participated in the furtherance of the joint criminal purpose in a way that made a significant contribution to the crime's commission; and
> 3. that the participation must have been with the intention of furthering the perpetration of one of the crimes provided for in the statute.

Toulson LJ then applied this test to JS's circumstances. He found that his position as bodyguard showed that he was trusted by those in authority, but that neither this factor nor his command responsibility for a combat unit provided any positive reason to think he was guilty of international crimes. The Secretary of State had wrongly concentrated on the nature of the organisation upon which a presumption of exclusion was formulated, rather than considering whether there was evidence affording serious reason for considering that he was party to that design, that he had participated in a way that made a significant contribution to the commission of such crimes and that he had done so with the intention of furthering the perpetration of such crimes.

The case then proceeded to the Supreme Court. Three of the Judges gave full judgments, all to the same effect. Lord Brown reviewed the central provisions

43 Rome Statute, Article 28.

from the Rome Statute and the case law on them. He also noted the decision of *Tadic*, finding its three-fold classification of joint criminal enterprise cases unhelpful in the *JS* scenario, because the crimes in question did not fall outside the intended activities of the LTTE, ruling out the third class of case, and noting that (as had *Tadic* itself) that its second category was but a sub-class of the first. The question that confronted the Supreme Court was the application of *Tadic*'s "first category" to the case at hand.

An ICTY authority that got nearer the point was that of *Brdjanin*.[44] There the Tribunal stated that whilst it was unnecessary for any part of the *actus reus* to have been committed by the accused, they must have participated in furthering the common purpose at the enterprise's core: though "not every type of conduct would amount to a significant enough contribution to the crime for this to create criminal liability ... JCE [joint criminal enterprise] is not an open-ended concept that permits convictions based on guilt by association."

The Supreme Court was particularly impressed with a decision from the German Federal Administrative Court, *BVerwG*, which had stated:[45]

> ...the person seeking protection need not have committed the serious non-political crime himself, but he must be personally responsible for it. This must in general be assumed if a person has committed the crime personally, or made a substantial contribution to its commission, in the knowledge that his or her act or omission would facilitate the criminal conduct (see Paragraph 18 of the UNHCR Guidelines). Thus this principle covers not only active terrorists and participants in the criminal sense, but also persons who perform advance acts in support of terrorist activities.

Drawing on these authorities, the Supreme Court went on to give the quietus to the continuum approach of *IG Nepal*, stating that presumptions arising from the nature of the organisation, rebuttable or otherwise, might well lead a decision maker into error. Of course, voluntary active membership of an organisation that solely pursued its objectives by terrorism would most likely justify a conclusion of complicity in criminal activities that would warrant exclusion, but nevertheless this was only one factor amongst several. The objectives of the organisation were irrelevant to determining guilt for war crimes.[46]

44 *Prosecutor v Brdjanin* (unreported) 3 April 2007, the ICTY Appeals Chamber, particularly §427–428.

45 The German Federal Administrative Court in *BVerwG* (10C 48.07; 14 October 2008).

46 *Accord* Lord Hope in *JS* (*Sri Lanka*) §44–46, and Lord Kerr §57–58.

Lord Brown proceeded to adumbrate this list of potentially relevant considerations[47] (Lord Kerr alongside him emphasised[48] that no list would necessarily capture all the relevant considerations; thus a decision maker should "concentrate on the actual role played by the particular person, taking all material aspects of that role into account so as to decide whether the required degree of participation is established"):

(i) the nature and (potentially of some importance) the size of the organisation and particularly that part of it with which the asylum-seeker was himself most directly concerned,
(ii) whether and, if so, by whom the organisation was proscribed,
(iii) how the asylum-seeker came to be recruited,
(iv) the length of time he remained in the organisation and what, if any, opportunities he had to leave it,
(v) his position, rank, standing and influence in the organisation,
(vi) his knowledge of the organisation's war crimes activities, and
(vii) his own personal involvement and role in the organisation including particularly whatever contribution he made towards the commission of war crimes.

Lord Brown noted that the conception of joint enterprise criminal liability enshrined in the international instruments was significantly wider than any such notion found in domestic criminal law. The extent of individual responsibility for such complicity was captured by the making of a "substantial contribution" (the phrase used by UNHCR in their Guidelines on International Protection and by the German authority of *BVerwG*). The formulation of the Court of Appeal had been too narrowly drawn, and in so doing had produced a test very much akin to that required to secure a conviction under domestic law. The relevant mental element was required, by way of intention, although as shown by Article 30 of the Rome Statute, this would be established where a person was aware that a particular consequence would follow from their actions.

All this led Lord Brown to conclude[49] that

> I would hold an accused disqualified under article 1F if there are serious reasons for considering him voluntarily to have contributed in a significant way to the organisation's ability to pursue its purpose of committing war crimes, aware that his assistance will in fact further that purpose.

47 *Ibid* §30.
48 *Ibid* §55.
49 *Ibid* §38.

Lord Hope agreed with Lord Brown's conclusion,[50] noting that Toulson LJ in the Court of Appeal had used the word "participation," itself not found in the language of the Rome Statute. Lord Kerr also agreed, though noting[51] the contents of an *amicus curiae* brief[52] which had argued that the participation should be such as "allowed the institution to function" or that it allowed "the crimes to be perpetrated" or that it was "an indispensable cog." Lord Kerr added[53] that the degree of participation had to be such as to go beyond "mere passivity or continued involvement in the organisation after acquiring knowledge" of the criminality in question.

Lord Brown considered that on the evidence before her the Secretary of State was amply entitled to conclude that the LTTE, in general, and the Intelligence Division, in particular, were guilty of such widespread criminal acts and atrocities, the most obvious perhaps being suicide bombings, attacks upon civilians, assassinations, kidnappings and the forcible recruitment of children. Whereas the Court of Appeal had concentrated on JS's command of a combat unit and his role as a bodyguard, a more formidable case for exclusion arose from the three years when he led a mobile unit transporting military equipment (possibly including explosives) and personnel through the jungle so that members of the Intelligence Division could go armed in plain clothes to Columbo. Those observations aside, it was unnecessary for the Supreme Court to finally resolve the exclusion question for itself, as that was a matter for the primary administrative decision maker, now the appropriate legal test had been clarified.

In conclusion, then, we can see that the Supreme Court has drawn liability for exclusion a little more broadly than did UNHCR in their landmark Guidelines on International Protection from 2003.[54] Those Guidelines sought a knowing "*substantial contribution* to the commission of *the criminal act*"; whereas *JS (Sri Lanka)* authorises exclusion for a significant contribution to the criminal purpose, which does not necessarily require contemplation of any particular crime.

We might note that another senior national court has cautioned against too readily excluding asylum seekers due to "mere association or passive

50 *Ibid* §49.

51 *Ibid* §56.

52 Amicus Curiae Brief of Professor Antonio Cassese and members of the Journal of International Criminal Justice on Joint Criminal Enterprise Doctrine" (for Case File No 001/18-07-2007-ECCC-OCIJ) (2009) 20 CLF 289.

53 *JS (Sri Lanka)* §56.

54 Fn 22 above.

acquiescence." Thus the Canadian Supreme Court in *Ezokola v Canada*[55] confronted this question, as certified by the court below as suitable for appellate consideration:

> complicity by association in crimes against humanity [can] be established by the fact that the refugee claimant was a senior public servant in a government that committed such crimes, along with the fact that the refugee claimant was aware of these crimes and remained in his position without denouncing them?

The Federal Court of Appeal had found that exclusion for complicity by way of "personal and knowing participation" might arise where a senior official remained in position without protest, continuing to defend the interests of his or her government while being aware of the crimes in question. The Supreme Court thought differently, rejecting a guilt-by-association approach to complicity when addressing general participation in a group's criminal activity, and emphasising that "even the broadest modes of commission[56] require a link between the individual and the crime or criminal purpose of a group."[57] It examined the widest form of complicity found in the *Rome Statute* (i.e., Article 25(3)(d)), which it summarised as representing a "broad residual mode of commission," one which did not require any essential contribution to the crime in question, drawing attention to the decision of Pre-Trial Chamber I in *Mbarushimana*[58] which had concluded that here only a *significant*, rather than an *essential* or *substantial* one, would suffice.

Ezokola notes that the broad phrase delineating liability for *assistance* in "every other way" in 23(d) represented a broadening out of the species of co-perpetration that might be caught, but not necessarily a quantitative one. Thus *Mbarushimana*[59] had noted that merely public knowledge of a group's criminality could not have been intended to attract criminal liability for everyone in

55 *Ezokola v. Canada (Citizenship and Immigration)* [2013] 2 SCR 678. For a specialist account of Canadian jurisprudence see The Application and Interpretation of International Humanitarian Law and International Criminal Law in the Exclusion of those Refugee Claimants who have Committed War Crimes and/or Crimes Against Humanity in Canada (James C Simeon; *International Journal of Refugee Law*, Volume 27, Issue 1, 1 March 2015, Pages 75–106)

56 Being common purpose liability under art. 25(3)(d) of the Rome Statute and joint criminal enterprise developed in the jurisprudence of the ad hoc Tribunals including the ICTY.

57 *Ibid* §53.

58 *Mbarushimana* ICC-01/04-01/10-514, Judgment on the Prosecutor's Appeal against the Decision on the Confirmation of Charges, 30 May 2012 (ICC, Appeals Chamber).

59 *Mbarushimana* §277.

the surrounding community who somehow contributed to their activities. The all-important leap from intent to commit a particular crime to willing participation in a broader purpose was explained thus in *Mbarushimana*:[60]

> Since knowledge of the group's criminal intentions is sufficient for criminal responsibility, it is therefore not required for the contributor to have the intent to commit any specific crime and not necessary for him or her to satisfy the mental element of the crimes charged.

However, the Pre-Trial Chamber in *Mbarushimana* went on to explain that whilst there needed to be no specific intention to commit a particular crime, the scope of potential liability was narrowed by the requirement that there be a link stronger than mere recklessness. The case law subsequent to *Mbarushimana* had held that conduct that merely *might* contribute to a crime or criminal purpose was insufficient; and the mental element excluded *dolus eventualis* (the awareness of a mere risk of prohibited consequences).[61]

These considerations led the Supreme Court in *Ezokola* to conclude that there must be a link between the accused's conduct and the criminal conduct of the group such that it can be stated with confidence that the relevant individual knowingly (or, at the very least, recklessly) contributed in a significant way to the crime or criminal purpose of a group. It therefore found that the decision of the Federal Court of Appeal below had drawn the boundary unduly widely in stating that a senior official who had remained in position without protest whilst aware of their government's criminal actions might be excluded from refugee status. To do so would risk pressuring high-ranking officials to feel compelled to abandon their legitimate duties during times of conflict and national instability in order to maintain their ability to claim asylum, and would breach the international criminal law norms demanding personal culpable conduct as the foundation of criminal liability and effectively penalising an individual for an omission when they were not under any legal duty to act. Thus only a voluntary and significant contribution, in the knowledge that their conduct will further the crime or criminal purpose, should suffice for exclusion.[62]

---

60 *Mbarushimana* §289.

61 *Prosecutor v. Jean-Pierre Bemba Gombo*, ICC-01/05-01/08-424, Decision Pursuant to Article 61(7)(a) and (b) of the Rome Statute, 15 June 2009 (ICC, Pre-Trial Chamber II), at para. 360.

62 *Ezokola* §68, 92.

We see similar thinking in the jurisprudence of the international courts themselves: thus the Trial Chamber in *Krajisnik*[63] was criticised for finding that the joint criminal enterprise included a "rank and file consist[ing] of local politicians, military and police commanders, paramilitary leaders, and others," an impermissibly vague formulation: the parties belonging to the joint criminal enterprise must be identified, which whilst not necessarily requiring the identification of every person by name, nevertheless demanded a greater degree of precision than this.

3.3 *Subsequent Developments: Specific Exclusion Scenarios in UK Law*

The UK courts have looked at other issues surrounding complicity and exclusion. In *MH (Syria)*[64] the Court of Appeal looked at the situation of a junior recruit to the PKK who had joined following the death of two of her brothers on active service for the group, and who was given 3 months training in first aid and became an assistant nurse in a hospital in the camp. The Tribunal had found that she was excluded because she had been a voluntary member of the PKK with personal knowledge of their activities, including illegal military operations, and she supported their military infrastructure by nursing the wounded and other duties; she served for some years before asking to resign. Whilst she had never been a fighter she had contributed to the PKK by other means.

The Court of Appeal disagreed, noting that nurses and other medical personnel enjoy a special status and protection under international humanitarian law. This was a relevant factor, though would not be conclusive in all cases: one could envisage even a nurse engaging in some action, such as deliberately treating an injured suicide bomber with the intention that he or she should carry out a further bombing mission, such as to have grave difficulty in resisting exclusion. On the facts here, MH had been only involved in relatively minor acts of support, in a context where she had joined the organisation during her childhood in circumstances that might not have been fully voluntary, and the PKK was not an organisation solely involved in acts of terrorism.

A distinct line of thinking addresses involvement with armed groups, typically fighting against the security forces of the national authorities. Both the early decisions of the Tribunal[65] and the last word on the subject from the

63 The Appeals Chamber in *Prosecutor v Krajisnik* (IT-00-39-A; 17 March 2009) §157.

64 *MH (Syria) v Secretary of State for the Home Department* [2009] EWCA Civ 226.

65 *PK v Secretary for State for the Home Department* [2004] UKIAT 00089; *Pushparajah v Secretary of State for the Home Department* (UKAIT AA/000124/2007, 18 January 2008); *Arokiyanathan v Secretary of State for the Home Department* (UKAIT AA/09777/2006, 24 June 2008).

Court of Appeal[66] agree that simply being a foot soldier involved in conducting military operations will not suffice to found exclusion. Stanley Burnton LJ in *KJ (Sri Lanka)* explained that a foot soldier who simply agreed with an organisation's political objectives but had not participated in its terrorist activities had not committed acts contrary to the purposes and principles of the United Nations. He added that the higher they were in the chain of command, the more likely it would be that an inference could be drawn that they had participated sufficiently to warrant exclusion.

As mentioned already, UK law is (for now) subject to the European Union's legal order, and the Common Position mentioned above[67] contains an annex that specifies particular "persons, groups and entities involved in terrorist acts." Inevitably the construction of that provision would raise issues akin to those that concerned the courts in the *JS* litigation. This duly came to pass with the Reference to the CJEU in *B*.[68] There two asylum seekers had been involved in terrorist groups thus proscribed, one having taken part in armed guerrilla warfare in the Turkish mountains against the Turkish state for Dev Sol (now DHKP/C), and whilst imprisoned having killed a suspected informant, and one who had been a senior official and guerrilla fighter with the PKK.

One of the questions that confronted the CJEU was whether bare membership of these proscribed organisations would found exclusion. The Court's answer was in the negative, noting that the language of the EU Directive (reflecting the Refugee Convention itself) "he … has committed" (a serious non-political crime) or that "he … has been guilty" (of acts contrary to the UN purposes and principles) themselves mandated an individualised fact-sensitive assessment. Furthermore, that list was part of a regime that lay outside of the framework set out by the Qualification Directive (indeed, Advocate General Mengozzi raised the issue of whether any such list could "provide an accurate reflection of the frequently complex reality of the organisations or groups listed," as well as the need to take account of the fact that the asylum seekers in question had left the groups in question prior to their designation as "terrorist").[69]

Nevertheless, such membership was part of the factual background against which the asylum claim had to be determined. The CJEU concluded an exclusion finding could be made only where

66 *KJ (Sri Lanka) v Secretary State for the Home Department* [2009] EWCA Civ 292.

67 Above fn 27.

68 *B (Area of Freedom, Security and Justice)* [2010] EUECJ C-57/09.

69 Advocate General Mengozzi in *B (Area of Freedom, Security and Justice)* [2010] EUECJ C-57/09 §73.

> it must be possible to attribute to the person concerned – regard being had to the standard of proof required under Article 12(2) – a share of the responsibility for the acts committed by the organisation in question while that person was a member.

That enquiry necessitated assessment of the true role played of the asylum seeker in the perpetration of the acts in question, his organisational position, the extent of the knowledge he had, or was deemed to have, of its activities, any pressure to which he was exposed, or other factors likely to have influenced his conduct.[70] A person who occupied a prominent position could be *presumed* to have individual responsibility for the relevant acts, but nevertheless an individualised factual assessment was still essential if that starting point was reached.

The principles laid down by the higher courts have been applied by the UK Upper Tribunal in practice.

In *MT Zimbabwe*,[71] a police detective in Zimbabwe was found to have participated in two incidents of torture, being present at the scene in a position of authority; during one of the incidents she was taking notes but was found to be fully aware that her colleagues were inflicting ill treatment on a detainee, and indeed she herself had threatened him with drowning by being thrown into a river whilst he was blindfolded. The Upper Tribunal concluded that she had thus facilitated commission of the crime of torture in a significant way, on this occasion with specific intent to contribute substantially to it; her role assisted the common purpose of leaving the victim in fear for his life. At a later incident she was present and was fully aware that the beating being visited on the victim by the officers present, including herself, amounted to serious harm. The Upper Tribunal held it was incontrovertible that her actions during this incident had a substantial effect on the commission of the crime of torture which took place, and thus that her participation in this incident amounted to the aiding and abetting of a crime against humanity.

In *SK Zimbabwe*[72] an asylum seeker was found to have been a voluntary (though reluctant) member of the Zanu-PF youth militia in Zimbabwe. She

70 Advocate General Mengozzi *Ibid* §77–79 gave a more detailed list of the potential criteria, encompassing physical and psychological constraints which might have contributed towards the subjective aspect of their conduct, and "the nature, structure, organisation, activities and methods of the group concerned, as well as the political, economic and social context in which it was operating."

71 *MT (Article 1F (a) – aiding and abetting) Zimbabwe* [2012] UKUT 15 (IAC).

72 *SK (Article 1F(a) exclusion) Zimbabwe* [2010] UKUT 327 (IAC).

had participated in two invasions of white-owned farms where property was burned and farm workers beaten severely.

The Tribunal noted that much of the discussion and decision in *JS* as to the "substantial contribution" doctrine related to the basis for a wider criminal responsibility based on the wider forms of participation identified in the *Rome Statute*, rather than to what is required for international responsibility on a joint enterprise basis. Personal responsibility for international crimes could arise *via* direct participation, but also *via* lesser forms of participation so long as a substantial contribution had been made. Joint enterprise did not itself require a substantial contribution; because joint enterprise liability meant one was a principal offender, not a mere contributor. The lesser form of participatory culpability might be found where the involvement was more indirect to the actual use of force.

The Tribunal concluded that the appellant was excluded for joint enterprise criminality. She had been a voluntary active participant in mob violence constituting inhumane acts causing great suffering or serious injury. This was sufficient for the purposes of exclusion.

One point that deserves attention is the fact that the three limbs of exclusion address distinct scenarios. The first concentrates on international crimes, the second on domestic criminality with a non-political dimension, and the third on "acts" rather than crimes. A particular terrorist act may fall within more than one of these three categories: thus European Union law holds, in *B*,[73] that terrorist acts characterised by violence towards civilians (notwithstanding an ostensibly political objective) can constitute both a serious non-political crime and an act contrary to UN purposes and principles (relying on UN Resolutions[74] to so conclude), UNHCR have noted that it may often be the case that Articles 1F(a) and (b) will apply to the same fact pattern, whether or not Article 1F(c) is also in play.[75]

However, whilst some such acts may potentially fall within each of the three categories, one can nevertheless hypothesise offences characterised as "terrorism" that fall within only one. In such a case any variation of the test for complicity might well be determinative of an applicant's liability.

Commentators have noted trends in the European jurisprudence tending to apply the same standards derived from international criminal law that have been considered appropriate for assessing *acts contrary to UN purposes and*

73 *B (Area of Freedom, Security and Justice)* [2010] EUECJ C-57/09.

74 Resolutions 1373 (2001) and 1377 (2001) of the UN Security Council.

75 Paragraph 17 of the UNHCR Guidelines on International Protection: *Application of the Exclusion Clauses: Article 1F of the 1951 Convention relating to the Status of Refugees.*

principles;[76] and "even purely logistical acts of support of sufficient importance may fulfil the conditions of Article 12(2)(c) in conjunction with Article 12(3)."[77] The Court of Appeal has found that the principles giving rise to liability *via* participation in criminal acts either as a principal or on the basis of secondary liability in criminal law should not govern exclusion for *acts* rather than crimes, however.[78]

There is national level authority that excludable participation in *serious non-political crimes* "may also arise through planning, ordering, soliciting, instigating, or otherwise inducing the commission of a crime by another person, or by making a contribution to the commission of an excludable act by others through aiding and abetting or on the basis of participation in a joint criminal enterprise/common purpose liability."[79]

The Court of Appeal in *Youssef*[80] looked at two cases, one applicant being alleged to have been involved directly with acts contrary to UN purposes and principles, though the case of the other, Mr Youssef, turned on issues of complicity. One issue that arose was whether the elements of individual responsibility were the same under all three limbs of Article 1F.

Youssef himself was said to have published many sermons and other material on the internet glorifying Al Qaeda. It was argued on his behalf that there was a critical difference between international and domestic criminal law as to the necessity for an actual criminal offence to have been committed pursuant to such encouragement: whereas domestic law would impose liability for inchoate offences, international law as embodied by Article 25 of the *Rome Statute* required that the related criminal offence had actually taken place, or at least been attempted. The distinction was thrown into relief by the express step taken in the *Rome Statute* to criminalise "direct and public incitement" of genocide,[81] a step that had not been considered appropriate vis-á-vis other international crimes.

---

76 *Exclusion: Articles 12 and 17 Qualification Directive (2011/95/EU) A Judicial Analysis* (European Asylum Support Office, January 2016) pp. 30–31.

77 Federal Administrative Court (Germany), judgment of 7 July 2011, 10 C 26.10, DE:BverwG: 2011:070711U10C26.10.0, BverwGE 140, p. 114, para. 28; cited in EASO *Judicial Analysis* above, in its text to fn 150.

78 *MH (Syria) v Secretary of State for the Home Department* [2009] EWCA Civ 226 §30.

79 UNHCR Guidelines on international Protection no 5, fn. 69, para. 18.

80 *El-Sayed El-Sebai Youssef v Secretary of State for the Home Department* [2018] EWCA Civ 933.

81 Rome Statute, Article 4(3)(c).

The Court in *Youssef* concluded[82] that Article 1F(c) should not be limited in this way. There might well be good reasons for different requirements for establishing responsibility under the different limbs of Article 1F, particularly given that 1F(c) targeted "*acts*" rather than "*crimes.*"[83] The decision to treat genocide in a particular way under the jurisdiction of the international criminal court might be relevant to Article 1F(a) liability, but could not directly affect the ambit of "acts" contrary to UN purposes and principles. The Supreme Court in *JS* had been addressing the ambit of Article 1F(a) rather than 1F(c).

Nevertheless, there were limitations implicit within Article 1F(c): the encouragement in question would have to reach a certain level of severity in order to threaten the international legal order as required by the true construction of Article 1F(c), and so it could be imagined that an immature youth who posted pro-jihad messages online might well not have committed actions of sufficient gravity, albeit that such activities on a large scale might qualify.[84]

3.4 *The Burden and Standard of Proof*

Issues of burden and standard of proof are important in determining exclusion from refugee status. It is readily apparent that it is the party asserting exclusion who bears the burden of proof. In general, one that could reasonably say that there is effectively an evidential burden on the national authorities to point to evidence allegedly raising exclusion issues: for if there is no material drawn to the court's attention that calls for exclusion, then it is difficult to see that the matter is on the judicial agenda. However, if there is material on the face of the court file, as where the Applicant's own account mentions some excludable action, then it would seem appropriate for the issue to be raised. Otherwise, given that the refugee definition includes the exclusion question, an individual who in truth does not qualify might wrongly receive status.

The standard of proof is the tool by which decision makers determine the facts to which the law is applied. The test posed by the Refugee Convention is whether there are "*serious reasons for considering*" the relevant crime or act to have been committed. The Supreme Court[85] has explained that this form of words strongly suggests that there is a higher test for exclusion than would be

82 Irwin LJ in *Youssef* §68–75.

83 UNHCR did not differentiate between the test for complicity when proposing their umbrella test of "*substantial contribution*" in their Guidance *Application of the Exclusion Clauses* (4 September 2003).

84 Irwin LJ in *Youssef* §82–86.

85 *Al- Sirri v Secretary of State for the Home Department* [2012] UKSC 54 §75.

intimated by an expression such as "*reasonable grounds for suspecting.*" The term "*considering*" approximated more to a degree of certainty expressed by "*believing*" than to lesser degrees of confidence such as "*suspecting.*"[86] Other judges have indicated that the words of the Convention itself, "*serious reasons for considering,*" cannot be improved upon.[87]

A related aspect of the procedure for assessing exclusion is the need for the clauses to "*be interpreted restrictively and used cautiously*";[88] a mantra echoed by European Union context, identifying the need for a "*particularly cautious*" approach, as a CJEU Advocate General put it.[89]

4 Conclusions

The foregoing review of the UK's approach and the broader context in which it arises aims to demonstrate the broad trends in judicial thinking in relation to the assessment of exclusion claims where issues of complicity arise.

The UK's judges have drawn on international criminal law in several contexts. Firstly, we can see that the three distinct categories of collective criminality identified in *Tadic* were of limited utility as an aid to construing exclusion law, because refugee cases would generally fall within the first category: i.e., there would be some degree of shared criminal intent in which each participant contributed towards the completion of a common design. Secondly, we see that international criminal law *has* been found useful in delineating the strength of the contribution that is required to found exclusion, for example *via* reliance on *Brdjanin* for the proposition the conduct in question must reach a certain level of *significance* to warrant exclusion. This latter extrapolation runs in parallel with the Canadian approach in *Ezokola* which had found support in *Mbarushimana* for the proposition that a *significant* contribution could found exclusion for complicity.

It can be seen that over the period over which these cases have been examined, there has been a broadening out of the scope of exclusion. However, this has not been a decision based on construction of the Refugee Convention or policy considerations identified by domestic courts. Rather it represents

86 *Accord* the Canadian Supreme Court in *Ezokola* §101–102.

87 *IG Nepal* §95; Sedley LJ in *Yasser Al-Sirri v Secretary of State for the Home Department* [2009] EWCA Civ 222 §33.

88 Lord Brown in *JS* (*Sri Lanka*) [2010] UKSC 15 §2.

89 Advocate General Mengozzi in *B* (*Area of Freedom, Security and Justice*) [2010] EUECJ C-57/09, citing para 4 of the conclusions of UNHCR's Global consultations on International Protection (3–4 May 2001).

judicial endorsement on the applicability of the interpretation of international criminal law concepts in the context of refugee status determination. Essentially, the same extension of liability that was recognised in international criminal law by decisions such as *Mbarushimana* has been followed in domestic refugee status interpretation.

The scope of liability for terrorism was identified as necessarily wide in the series of UN Resolutions cited above,[90] which stressed that aiding and supporting, and participation and even attempted participation was necessarily stigmatised as sufficiently close association with the principal perpetrators to attract accomplice liability. In so doing, the UN acted consistently with the steps already taken by the ICTY in *Tadic* which had contemplated criminal liability attaching to those who had acted together with a common criminal purpose even where the accomplices might not have been aware of the precise crime that was ultimately to be committed. Thus, the Supreme Court's decision in *JS* (*Sri Lanka*), with the imposition of the relevant level of responsibility for having substantially or significantly contributed to a common criminal purpose albeit not any particular crime, can legitimately be seen as the inevitable refugee law corollary of steps taken much earlier by various actors, ranging from international criminal law judges to international bodies.

Nevertheless, whilst liability is broadly drawn, it remains the case that guilt by association is not enough to found exclusion. Thus, both the UK courts, in the *JS* litigation, and the Canadian court in *Ezokola* emphasised that decision makers must identify that both the *actus reus* and *mens rea* aspects for participation in the common criminal purpose is present. Mere association may well support an inference of connivance in that purpose, but it is no replacement for a principled analysis of the relevant criminal law ingredients. UNHCR's 2003 Guidelines[91] may well have contributed to the confusion, with their reference to potential exclusion for remaining part of a government responsible for being engaged in excludable activities, and to a presumption of individual responsibility due to membership of a particularly violent groups. Both of those statements risk undue focus on association rather than identifying the ingredients of criminality.

This point aside, the review of the UK case law and its broader environment reveals a series of restrictions on the scope of exclusion for participation.

Firstly, there is the question of the standard of proof: there must be *serious* reasons for *considering* (connoting a degree of certainty more akin to belief

90 Text to Fns 19–21.

91 UNHCR Guidelines on International Protection: *Application of the Exclusion Clauses: Article 1F of the 1951 Convention relating to the Status of Refugees* (4 September 2003).

than lesser forms of confidence) that the relevant degree of association with the criminal purpose is established, bearing in mind that the burden of proof is on the state asserting exclusion. A cautious and restrictive approach is required.

Secondly, there must be a degree of association that is "*significant*" or "*substantial*" (though not *essential*), the words used respectively by UNHCR in their International Protection Guidelines and the Supreme Courts in *JS* and *Ezokola*. As it was put by the Court of Appeal in *Youssef*, in the context of encouraging acts contrary to UN purposes and principles, the complicity must be of a certain severity to attract the necessary moral gravity.

Thirdly, as noted by the Pre-Trial Chamber in *Mbarushimana*, whilst a contribution to a common criminal purpose albeit not a particular crime is sufficient to found exclusion, the ensuing widening of the scope of potential liability is tempered by the requirement that there be an intensity of intention that is stronger than mere recklessness.

We can conclude, then, that whilst the authorities and legal sources unite in finding that the scope for exclusion under the Refugee Convention for misconduct, including that which is terrorist in nature, has widened in recent years, nevertheless the requirement for procedural rigour in the analysis of who falls for exclusion, combined with the requirement for a distinct level of contribution to the criminal purpose, remains an essential safeguard against overuse of the exclusion clauses.

CHAPTER 9

Asylum-seekers as Potential Terrorists (?)

Barbara Kőhalmi and Anita Nagy-Nádasdi

1 Introduction

This chapter intends to map the nexus between asylum and terrorism. We examine how the age of terrorism shapes the international protection regime today. As a starting point, we analyse how human rights and the security interests of the state clash in the case of the terror threat. Serious concerns may arise in connection with *bona fide* asylum-seekers who may be the victims of public prejudice and restrictive legislative or administrative measures of anti-terrorism policies. Thus, international terrorism may result in criminalising asylum-seekers and refugees.

This chapter aims to confirm that there is no demonstrable link between seeking asylum and terrorism. International law recognizes both states' right to security and asylum-seekers' right to protection as equal legitimate interests that should not be considered as competing interests. The right balance between the two interests should be found through the interpretation and implementation of binding international and European law. Besides analysing the relevant international legal framework, we examine concrete national practices in order to demonstrate the impact of anti-terrorism measures on national asylum systems.

In response to the recent migration flows, States reconsidered security issues related to receiving asylum seekers from conflict zones, in spite of the fact, that most asylum seekers arriving in Europe do not pose a terrorist threat and most terrorist attacks in Europe do not involve any asylum seekers. From the 194 publicly disclosed Islamist terror plots or acts of violence between January 2014 and December 2017 only 16 % involved refugees or asylum seekers. Since January 2014, 44 refugees or asylum seekers have been involved in 32 attacks in Europe. Most refugee and asylum-seeker plotters were radicalized prior to their entry to Europe however, radicalization after arrival has increased since fall 2016.[1]

1 "We are thankful for the valuable comments of James C. Simeon and Petra Bárd. We also wish to thank those migration experts who shared their views on the topic/issue: Ágnes Ambrus, Vivien Vadasi, Péter Tálas, Zoltán Somogyvári." Robin Simcox, "The Asylum–Terror Nexus: How Europe

© KONINKLIJKE BRILL NV, LEIDEN, 2020 | DOI:10.1163/9789004295995_011

The relationship between migration and terrorism has been widely discussed recently. Some argue that migration policies and national security crosscut in many areas and suggest that more migration into a country is very likely to generate security risks. However, they also warn against establishing too close links between migration and insecurity. While others use the perceived link between migration and terrorism to legitimize the implementation and enforcement of stricter migration legislation and controls that leads to the "securitization" of migration. The United Nations Security Council Resolution 1373[2] also confirms this when encouraging states to "prevent the movement of terrorists or terrorist groups by effective border controls and controls on issuance of identity papers and travel documents, and through measures for preventing counterfeiting, forgery or fraudulent use of identity papers and travel documents."[3] Bove and Böhmelt argue that immigrants are an important vehicle for the diffusion of terrorism from one country to another, however, emphasize that immigration *per se* is unlikely positively to affect terrorism, more migration generally is associated with a lower number of terrorist attacks.[4]

After discussing the legal concept of terrorism, international protection, and the basic principles of international human rights law we demonstrate how the terror threat affected the legislation and the concept of asylum in Hungary since 2015. In spite of the criticism, government focuses only on the security issues of the refugee regime and foremost the protection of nationals from asylum-seekers. Besides the legal analysis, we also conduct quantitative research among counter-terrorism experts, civil servants, civil organizations who work with immigrants who are perceived to pose national security risks due to assumed terrorist activity in order to confirm our hypothesis.

2 International Context

2.1 *Right to Security versus Right to Protection*

Security is privileged over values in various political philosophies giving an important role to the state being the protector of the physical security of people and property. According to classical social contractarians, the dangerousness of life is in the "state of nature" and by "signing" a social contract people

Should Respond," The Heritage Foundation: Backgrounder No. 3314, June 18, 2018, 1–2. https://www.heritage.org/terrorism/report/the-asylum-terror-nexus-how-europe-should-respond.

2 UN Security Council, Security Council resolution 1373 (2001) [on threats to international peace and security caused by terrorist acts], 28 September 2001, S/RES/1373 (2001) para 2 (g).

3 Vincenzo Bove and Tobias Böhmelt, *"Does Immigration Induce Terrorism?,"* Journal of Politics (October 2015): 6–7.

4 Bove and Böhmelt, *"Does Immigration Induce Terrorism?,"* 25.

voluntarily renounce a certain part of their individual freedom in exchange for their security and protection provided by a legitimate political authority and, as a result, providing security becomes a primary obligation of the state since that is what individuals have contracted for in submitting to a state authority.[5] The communitarian idea also privileges security over individual privacy. Additionally, given the inherently limited nature of privacy, also an argument for the primacy of security over privacy, people tend to want more security rather more privacy.[6]

The right to equality and protection against discrimination are fundamental elements of international human rights law. Nevertheless, international law also recognizes that certain rights may be limited by proportional and justified national security measures. There is no doubt that the highly complex forms of threats to national security require States to take effective measures to defend themselves, but states cannot be permitted to take any measure they like in the name of this fight.[7] National security should not be used as a convenient excuse to violate individual rights as these rights define the nation, therefore, if we destroy these human rights, even with good intentions, we destroy the essence of the nation. Consequently, when ensuring that people can live their everyday lives with only little concern about national security threats, we should achieve that goal without any serious violation of individual rights.[8]

International human rights law needs to strike the right balance between opposing rights claimed. As regards the balancing test, there are exact provisions in multilateral human rights treaties (e.g. European Convention on Human Rights (ECHR)[9] or the International Covenant on Civil and Political Rights (ICCPR)[10]). These balancing tests generally require comparison of different/opposite interests such as individual (right to protection) and community interests (right to security). States can strike the balance between the rights and

5 David Boucher and Paul Kelly eds, *The Social Contract From Hobbes to Rawls.* (London: Routledge 1994), 2–10.

6 Jennifer A. Chandler, "Personal Privacy versus National Security: Clarifying and Reframing the Trade-off" in Kerr, Lucock and Steeves, eds. *On the Identity Trail: Anonymity, Privacy and Identity in a Networked Society*, Oxford Univ. Press, 2009, pp. 121–138.

7 Council of Europe, *National Security and European Case-law,* (2013) p. 4. https://rm.coe.int/168067d214. (last accessed: 19 April 2020).

8 José Berumen's views on individual rights and national security on Prezi, vol. XCIII, no. 311 9/12/2015 https://prezi.com/xjfkmbdoaebs/individual-rights-vs-national-security/ (last accessed: 19 September 2017).

9 Council of Europe, *European Convention for the Protection of Human Rights and Fundamental Freedoms, as amended by Protocols Nos. 11 and 14,* 4 November 1950, *CETS 005*.

10 UN General Assembly, *International Covenant on Civil and Political Rights*, 16 December 1966, United Nations, Treaty Series, vol. 999, p. 171.

restrictions differently, but the boundary of appreciation granted to a State is not unlimited.[11] In this regard, accountability is indispensable in a real democracy so as to protect national interests and public security as well as to prevent the abuse of powers by the State authorities.[12] In this context, the accountability for human rights protection is special as national security authorities have to operate under constraints as regards the disclosure of sensitive and confidential information, therefore human rights may be placed at particular risk. Nonetheless, national security agencies have to create an accountability framework that reflects human rights principles.[13]

Justice John von Doussa QC argues that there are six key principles for building a human rights approach in national security measures. Firstly, governments should not violate non-derogable human rights. International human rights law provides some margins of appreciation to enable governments to balance national security interests and human rights and to recognise that sometimes it is necessary to limit individual rights to protect national security. Nevertheless, this balancing exercise is not unlimited. Certain rights such as the right to life or the right to be free from torture or cruel inhuman and degrading treatment cannot be suspended in any circumstances. Secondly, derogable rights may only be infringed in accordance with human rights law as international human rights law provides the possibility for states to take necessary measures which limit the derogation of human rights in special circumstances. Thirdly, the respect for an independent judiciary in overseeing these measures is indispensable, together with establishing a regular, independent review, of the operation as the fourth element. The fifth principle is to ensure that those who are subjected to these measures may challenge the validity of decisions, so when a right of an individual is violated as a result of the abuse of powers, the individual should have access to an effective remedy. And, last but not least, domestic effect should be given to international human rights law by introducing explicit protection for human rights in national legislation.[14]

---

11 Alif Ahmed, "Individual Protection versus National Security: A Balancing Test Concerning the Principle of Non-refoulement," 21 *International Organization of Scientific Research – Journal of Humanities and Social Science* 21, no. 5, Version. 5 (May 2016): 31–32.

12 R. Whitaker and S. Farson, "Accountability in and for National Security", 15 *IRPP Choices*, v (2009): 8. http://irpp.org/wp-content/uploads/assets/research/security-and-democracy/accountability-in-and-for-national-security/vol15n09.pdf (last accessed: 20 September 2017).

13 Pearl Eliadis, "National Security and Human Rights" Canadian Human Rights Commissioner (2011) http://publications.gc.ca/site/fra/415996/publication.html 5–6.

14 John von Doussa QC: "Incorporating Human Rights Principles into National Security Measures," speech held as the president of the Human Rights and Equal Opportunities Commission at International Conference on Terrorism, Human Security and Development:

To sum up, international human rights law recognizes states' interest to security as well as asylum-seekers' right to protection as equal legitimate interests. National security interest and duty to provide protection for asylum-seekers and refugees are 'complementary and mutually reinforcing'.[15] The fair balance between the two interests should be found through the implementation and interpretation of binding international legal instruments.

2.2 *The Absence of a Comprehensive and Universal Definition of 'terrorism'*

At the international level, the United Nations, has not adopted a comprehensive definition of terrorism yet as there is no consensus on what constitutes 'terrorism'. There are existing international legal instruments that set out only certain acts and its core elements to be terrorism.

Terrorism is commonly referred to as acts of violence that target civilians in the pursuit of political or ideological aims. The UN Security Council referred to terrorism as "criminal acts, including against civilians, committed with the intent to cause death or serious bodily injury, or taking of hostages, with the purpose of provoking a state of terror in the general public or in a group of persons or particular persons, intimidate a population or compel a Government or an international organization to do or to abstain from doing any act."[16] According to the UN General Assembly's Declaration on Measures to Eliminate International Terrorism, terrorism includes "criminal acts intended or calculated to provoke a state of terror in the general public, a group of persons or particular persons for political purposes' and that such acts are in any circumstances unjustifiable, whatever the considerations of a political, philosophical, ideological, racial, ethnic, religious or other nature that may be invoked to justify them."[17]

The General Assembly is still working on the adoption of this comprehensive convention against terrorism, which would complement the existing sectoral

Human Rights Perspectives, City University of Hong Kong, October 16–17, 2017 https://www.humanrights.gov.au/news/speeches/incorporating-human-rights-principles-national-security-measures (last accessed: 25 December 2018).

15 J.C. Murillo, "The Legitimate Security Interests of the State and International Refugee Protection," 6, no.10, *Sur. Revista Internacional de Direitos Humanos* (June 2009) http://dx.doi.org/10.1590/S1806-64452009000100007.

16 UN Security Council, Security Council Resolution 1566 (2004) [concerning threats to international peace and security caused by terrorism], 8 October 2004, S/RES/1566 (2004) point 3.

17 UN General Assembly, Measures to eliminate international terrorism: resolution / adopted by the General Assembly, 17 February 1995, A/RES/49/60 point 1.3.

anti-terrorism regulations. Article 2 of the draft contains a definition of terrorism as follows 'unlawfully and intentionally' causing, attempting or threatening to cause: '(a) death or serious bodily injury to any person; or (b) serious damage to public or private property, including a place of public use, a State or government facility, a public transportation system, an infrastructure facility or the environment; or (c) damage to property, places, facilities, or systems (...), resulting or likely to result in major economic loss, when the purpose of the conduct, by its nature or context, is to intimidate a population, or to compel a Government or an international organization to do or abstain from doing any act'. Unfortunately, the negotiations of the Comprehensive Terrorism Convention are deadlocked due to the disagreement among the Member States over the definition of terrorism.

In spite of the lack of widely accepted definition of terrorism the UN Security Council accepted UNSC Res 1373 (28 September 2001) has had 'an impact on the substantive content of international protection' and on those 'aspects of the rule of law that require procedural standards of justice and the separation of executive and judicial functions are at risk'.[18]

Respect for international law is also a barrier in exercising sovereign rights in the name of protection of the state. "Significantly, however, and in terms which many governments tend not to mention, the Security Council also insists that States – measures to combat terrorism should be in accordance with their obligations under international law – and that any such measures should comply with all their obligations, in particular under international human rights law, refugee law and humanitarian law. In this, the Security Council continues a tradition going back to 1999, and in which it has followed the lead established earlier by the General Assembly."[19] However, for example, in the case of Hungary, these obligations are embedded in the Hungarian Fundamental Law in rather a general way and the dualist system weighs down the practical application of these obligations. Besides the requirement for transition of international norms the hierarchy of the legal system does not support the extensive knowledge and application of international law.

The major powers influencing the international system have an increasing concern for immigrants and asylum seekers, especially after the emergence of the phenomenon of terrorism and the exploitation by the terrorist groups of the humanitarian nature of immigration to infiltrate these countries in order

18 Guy S Goodwin-Gill, "Forced Migration: Refugees, Rights and Security," in *Forced Migration, Human Rights and Security*, ed. Jane McAdam (London: Hart Publishing, 2008), p. 6, https://doi.org/http://dx.doi.org/10.5040/9781472564283.ch-001. (last accessed 8 June 2019)

19 Goodwill-Gil, "Forced Migration" 2.

to carry out acts of violence and influence the public security and the prevailing order.

To determine whether the applicant for asylum represents a serious threat to national security or public order, the Immigration and Asylum Office (IAO) shall request the National Intelligence Agency of Hungary (Alkotmányvédelmi Hivatal) or the Counter Terrorism Centre (Terrorelhárítási Központ – TEK) to provide an expert opinion. Since 2017 the majority of the applications have been decided in the transit zones at the border. The ECRE report notes, however, as set out in Art 71/A(8) of the Asylum Act, these authorities are not involved in asylum status determination in border procedures (ECRE, 2018:117).[20]

According to Schmid terrorism refers to a political communication strategy for psychological mass manipulation whereby unarmed civilians (and non-combatants such as prisoners) are deliberately victimised in order to impress third parties (e.g., intimidate, coerce or otherwise influence a government or a section of society or international public opinion), with the help of portrayals of demonstrative violence in front of audiences and/or for coverage in mass or social media. Terrorism from non-state actors is often a strategy of provocation aiming at societal polarisation and conflict escalation while state or regime terrorism serves the purpose of repression and social control. Terrorism as psychological warfare is also an irregular and illegal tactic in armed conflict where it can be used by one or both sides.[21] The lack of definition causes a measure of confusion and unhelpful ambiguity,[22] and in the light of this it is quite understandable why we need to distinguish between legal, political, and the everyday approach to the word.

2.3 *Right to Asylum*

The right to asylum is historically rooted in an ancient juridical concept according to which a person persecuted by his/her own country may be protected by another sovereign authority, for example, a state or a church. Later, the right of sanctuarium was first codified by King Ethelbert of Kent considering the right of sanctuary as being inviolable and under royal protection which emerged into the right to asylum in its contemporary meaning.[23] In Prakash

20 Daniel Gyollai, "Hungary Country Report" in *Global Migration Consequences and Responses* eds Veronica Federico and Ginevra Cerrina Feroni, *Migration Governance Legal and Policy Framework Working Papers* 2018/13 https://www.crs.uu.se/respond/ (last accessed 21 April 2020) 315.

21 Alex P. Schmid, *The Routledge Handbook of Terrorism Research* (London: Routledge, 2011) pp. 86–87.

22 Richard English: *What is terrorism?* (New York: Oxford University Press 2009) p. 3.

23 S. Prakash Sinha, *Asylum and international law*, (The Hague; Martinus Nijhoff Publishers, 1971), 14.

Sinha's view "the basis of asylum was found in the sovereignty of the city or state, instead of the religious sanctity of the places of refuge."[24]

In spite of its deep historical roots, the term 'asylum' does not have a clear and universally accepted definition.[25] Nevertheless, when discussing 'asylum' as a right, scholars are able to list concrete elements of that right, more concretely that imply certain specific manifestations of state conduct such as (i) to admit a person to its territory; (ii) to allow the person to stay there; (iii) to refrain from expelling the person; (iv) to refrain from extraditing the person; and, (v) to refrain from prosecuting, punishing, or otherwise restricting his or her liberty.[26]

In his book on territorial asylum, Professor Grahl-Madsen developed a three-faced concept of the right of asylum according to which three distinct "rights" constitute the right of asylum, namely, the right of the state to grant asylum, the right of an individual to seek asylum, and, the right of an individual to be granted asylum.[27] The right of a state to grant asylum is recognized in international law deriving from the principle of state sovereignty. As a general rule, every sovereign state has exclusive control over its territory, consequently, it has the exclusive right to grant or deny asylum to persons residing on its territory. According to Professor Hersch Lauterpacht, this right is one that every state has under international law.[28] Consequently, one may conclude that traditionally the right of asylum has been understood as the right of a state to grant asylum, rather than the right of an individual to seek asylum.[29] Based on the principle that "a State may not claim to own its nationals or residents" the second element of the right of asylum is the right of an individual to seek asylum, namely, to leave his country of residence to seek asylum.[30] This right is enshrined as a binding obligation in international law and it is also part of customary international law.[31] Thus, the right to leave one's own country in pursuit of asylum is enforceable in certain situations,

24 Sinha, "Asylum and international law," 15.

25 Atle Grahl-Madsen, *Territorial Asylum* (Stockholm: Almqvist & Wiksell International, 1980), 50.

26 Tom Clark, "Human Rights and Expulsion: Giving Content to the Concept of Asylum," *International Journal of Refugee Law*, Volume 4, Issue 2 (April 1992): 189–190., https://doi.org/10.1093/ijrl/4.2.189.

27 Grahl-Madsen, *Territorial Asylum,* 2.

28 Hersch Lauterpacht, "The Universal Declaration of Human Rights," *British Yearbook of International Law* (1948): 354, 373.

29 Grahl-Madsen, *Territorial Asylum,* 2.

30 Grahl-Madsen, *Territorial Asylum,* 2., 26.

31 See Article 13 (2) of the Universal Declaration of Human Rights, Article 12 (2) of the International Covenant on Civil and Political Rights, Article 2 (2) of the Protocol No. 4 to the ECHR.

however, as it is not a qualified right, a valid state interest in prosecuting the asylum-seeking individual may overrule the right to seek and enjoy asylum in accordance with valid extradition treaties.[32] In connection with the right of an individual to be granted asylum it has to be emphasized that under international law an individual has no right to asylum enforceable *vis-á-vis* the state of refuge.[33] Article 14 (1) of the Universal Declaration of Human Rights[34] states that "everyone has the right to seek and to enjoy in other countries asylum from persecution." Sinha argues that Article 14 (1) provides the individual "the right to seek and to enjoy asylum, but not to be granted asylum."[35] In Lauterpacht's view Article 14 (1) gives "a right 'to seek' asylum, without any assurance that the seeking will be successful."[36]

The 1951 Geneva Convention sets out the criteria for eligibility for asylum more precisely; according to this, a refugee is a person "who is outside their own country's territory or place of habitual residence in case of stateless persons owing to well-founded fear of persecution on one or more of the protected grounds: race, nationality, religion, political opinion and belonging in any particular social group and is unable or, owing to such fear, is unwilling to avail himself of the protection of the country of nationality or habitual residence and as a result of such events, is unable or, owing to such fear, is unwilling to return to it."[37] In cases where people are not eligible for asylum, they can be removed from the territory of the state.

Today, the idea of global protection becomes a part of the customary international law. Rendering victims of persecution to their persecutor is a violation of the non-refoulement principle.[38]

2.4 *Non-refoulement and National Security*

The principle of non-refoulement is a fundamental basis of international refugee law as well as customary international law and it is understood as the duty of a state not to return a person to a place of persecution.[39] The principle of non-refoulement signifies an inherent conflict with state sovereignty as it

32 Felice Morgenstern, "The Right of Asylum," *British Yearbook of International Law* (1949): 331–335.

33 Morgenstern, "The Right of Asylum," 335.

34 UN General Assembly, "Universal Declaration of Human Rights," 10 December 1948, 217 A (III).

35 Sinha, "Asylum and international law," 90.

36 Lauterpacht, "The Universal Declaration of Human Rights," 373.

37 Article 1A (2) of the ECHR.

38 Ahmed, "Individual Protection versus National Security," 31–32.

39 UN High Commissioner for Refugees (UNHCR): The Principle of Non-Refoulement as a Norm of Customary International Law, Response to the Questions Posed to UNHCR by the Federal Constitutional Court of the Federal Republic of Germany in Cases 2 BvR 1938/93,

infringes on a state's right to exercise control over its own borders and those who reside within them. In legal proceedings immediately following World War II, non-refoulement was considered as a distinct right, which could be abridged under certain circumstances.[40]

The duty of non-refoulement was first imposed in Article 3(2) of the Convention relating to the International Status of Refugees[41] stating that "each of the Contracting Parties undertakes, in all cases, not to return refugees across the frontiers of their country of origin."

Article 33 (1) of the 1951 Geneva Convention provides that no refugee should be returned to any country where his or her life or freedom would be threatened on account of his race, religion, nationality, membership of a particular social group or political opinion from which no derogation is allowed. Article 42 (1) of the Convention enlists Article 33 as one of the articles to which a state may not make reservations. However, it has to be noted that the Convention only binds the states that are parties to it and/or its Protocol and States have the duty of non-refoulement that is applicable only with respect to persons determined to be refugees under the Convention and it does not provide the right of admission for the purpose of seeking asylum.[42]

The Convention Against Torture and Other Cruel, Inhuman or Degrading Treatment or Punishment[43] also contains the principle of non-refoulement. Article 3(1) stipulates that "no State Party shall expel, return ('refouler') or extradite a person to another State where there are substantial grounds for believing that he would be in danger of being subjected to torture." When comparing the two non-refoulement provisions a difference between their scope can be identified. While the 1951 Refugee Convention only protects those determined to be refugees under its provisions, the Convention Against Torture defines a more general personal remit by extending its protection against

2 BvR 1953/93, 2 BvR 1954/93, 31 January 1994, http://www.refworld.org/docid/437b6db64.html (last accessed: 23 September 2017).

40 Vijay Padmanabhan, "To Transfer or not to Transfer: Identifying and Protecting Relevant Human Rights Interests in Non-Refoulement," *Fordham Law Review* 80, no. 1, Rev. 73 (2011): 73–123.

41 League of Nations, *Convention Relating to the International Status of Refugees*, 28 October 1933, League of Nations, Treaty Series Vol. CLIX No. 3663.

42 Grahl-Madsen, *Territorial Asylum*, 40.

43 UN General Assembly, Convention Against Torture and Other Cruel, Inhuman or Degrading Treatment or Punishment, 10 December 1984, United Nations, Treaty Series, vol. 1465, 85.

refoulement to any person who would be in danger of being subjected to torture that may have a significant impact in practice.[44]

The terror attacks committed by perpetrators with migratory background have shifted the focus to migration and transforming it to a global concern. In this context, States' international obligation to protect refugees meets States' internal security interests, thus, making it a highly complex issue where applying the balancing test is inevitable.[45] In case of conflict between individual rights and national security interest there are two possible scenarios to resolve this conflict. Protection needs of an individual may get priority based on concrete international instruments imposing obligation on states with regard to the non-refoulement principle or as a part of customary international law.[46] Furthermore, there are judicial decisions that support the approach according to which individual protection would get priority,[47] though there are judicial decisions that gave priority to national security under the doctrine of bias and uncertainty.[48]

The ECtHR also gradually established its position on this matter.[49] In general, the ECtHR States are required to strike the right balance between their obligation to protect national security and their obligation to respect human rights laid down the Convention. When examining whether national security measures comply with the Convention, the ECtHR examines very cautiously the particular circumstances of the case.

2.5 *Exclusion from International Protection*

The 1951 Geneva Convention is the first international treaty on asylum that contains provision about criminals. According to the *travaux préparatoires,* the drafters wanted to ensure that criminals who committed crimes against humanity, war crimes or acted against the aims of United Nations' Purposes and

44 Roman Boed, "The state of the right of asylum in international law," *Duke Journal of Comparative & International Law* 5 (1994): 21–22.

45 Arif Ahmed, "Individual Protection versus National Security," 31.

46 See also the ICCPR, The Organization of African Unity Convention Governing the Specific Aspects of Refugee problems in Africa (OAU Convention), ECHR, Charter of Fundamental Rights of the European Union, American Convention on Human Rights, The Third and Fourth Geneva Conventions of 1949.

47 See *Soering v United Kingdom* (1989) 11 EHRR 439; *Chahal v. United Kingdom* (1997) 23 EHRR 413.

48 *Suresh v. Canada (Minister of Citizenship and Immigration),* 2002 SCC 1, [2002] 1 S.C.R. 3

49 Some ECtHR cases on arbitrary detention: case of Nolan and K. v. Russia, Application no. 2512/04, Case of Mikolenko v. Estonia, Application no. 10664/05, Case of Louled Massoud v. Malta, Application no. 24340/08, Case of Amie and others v. Bulgaria, Application no. 58149/08, Case of Suso Musa v Malta, Application no. 42337/12.

Principles may not avoid their punishment under the umbrella of refugee protection. Article 1F is an exhaustive list of reasons with a wide range of interpretation.[50] When the State Party applies Article 1F in a case, the well-based suspicion about the commitment of such crimes is enough with a thorough examination of all circumstances of the case concerned. Only by the applicant's place in the treaty can it be interpreted that the use of exclusion clauses invokes the proportionality test; that is, first that the authority shall ensure that the applicant is fit to conditions of recognition, otherwise, certain people would be deprived of their right to the examination of their claim. This can lead to the criminalization of applicants.

Thus, Article 1F of the 1951 Geneva Convention provides the possibility to States to exclude certain asylum-seekers and refugees from refugee status. By establishing the system of exclusion clauses, States had sought to achieve two legitimate goals. On the one hand, to protect refugee status from abuse by prohibiting its grant in undeserving cases and, on the other hand, to ensure that those who had committed grave crimes in World War II, other serious non-political crimes or who were guilty of acts contrary to the purposes and principles of the United Nations be punished. Nevertheless, due to the fact that the application of Article 1F imposes limitation on its humanitarian provisions, it should be interpreted restrictively and be applied only in particular and legally well-based circumstances.[51]

Article 1F (a) states that 'the provisions of this Convention shall not apply to any person with respect to whom there are serious reasons for considering that he has committed a crime against peace, a war crime, or a crime against humanity, as defined in the international instruments drawn up to make provision in respect of such crimes'.

In the European context, the Common European Asylum System (CEAS) is the legal framework that EU Member States created in order to apply shared competences in the area of asylum prescribed in the Article 3 and 4 of the Treaty of European Union. The CEAS is a collection of secondary legislation in the field of asylum, and as such all Member Stated implemented its provisions. In our context, the recast Qualification Directive[52] and the recast Asylum

50 UNHCR Handbook pp. 147–148.

51 Geoff Gilbert, *"Current Issues in the Application of the exclusion clauses,"* UNHCR as a background paper for an expert roundtable discussion on exclusion organised as part of the Global Consultations on International Protection in the context of the 50th anniversary of the 1951 Convention relating to the Status of Refugees, 2. http://www.unhcr.org/uk/419dba514.pdf (last accessed: 26 December 2018).

52 Article 4 of Directive 2011/95/EU of the European Parliament and of the Council of 13 December 2011 on standards for the qualification of third-country nationals or stateless

Procedures Directive[53] are those that define the possibility and procedure of exclusion of applicants based on national security concerns. As of 2010 the European Court of Justice (hereinafter: ECJ or Court) has gradually crystallizing its jurisprudence concerning exclusion from international protection based on security concerns linking EU's asylum law and anti-terrorism law.[54] The ECJ analysed the previous Qualification Directive,[55] in particular its exclusion clause, in light of the Geneva Convention. ECJ also examines the relationship between the application of the Qualification Directive and EU legislation on the fight against terrorism.

Both the Qualification Directive and its recast version reflect Article 1F of the Geneva Convention by providing that a person should be excluded from eligibility for refugee status for acts contrary to the principles and purposes of the United Nations including acts of terrorism, as well as those who instigate or otherwise participate in the commission of these acts.

The Court dealt with these questions for the first time in the *B and D* case ruling that the fact that a person had been a member of an organisation which is on the list of the Common Position 2001/931/CFSP on the application of specific measures to combat terrorism and that person has actively supported the armed struggle waged by that organisation did not automatically constitute a serious reason for considering that the person has committed 'a serious non-political crime' or 'acts contrary to the purposes and principles of the United Nations'. If there are serious reasons for considering that a person has committed such a crime or has been guilty of such acts is conditional on an individual assessment of the facts, with a view to determining whether the acts committed by the organisation concerned meet the necessary conditions and whether individual responsibility for carrying out those acts can be attributed to the person concerned. In addition, the Court also held that the exclusion from refugee status does not depend on the person concerned representing a

persons as beneficiaries of international protection, for a uniform status for refugees or for persons eligible for subsidiary protection, and for the content of the protection granted *OJ L 337, 20.12.2011, p. 9–26.*

53 Article 23 of Directive 2013/32/EU of the European Parliament and of the Council of 26 June 2013 on common procedures for granting and withdrawing international protection, *OJ L 180, 29.6.2013, p. 60–95.*

54 Joined Cases C-57/09 and C-101/09 *Bundesrepublik Deutschland v B and D*, EU:C:2010:661; Case C-373/13 *H.T. v Land Baden-Württemberg*, EU:C:2015:413; Case C-573/14 Commissaire général aux réfugiés et aux apatrides v Mostafa Lounani, EU:C:2017:71.

55 Council Directive 2004/83/EC of 29 April 2004 on Minimum Standards for the Qualification and Status of Third Country Nationals or Stateless Persons as Refugees or as Persons Who Otherwise Need International Protection and the Content of the Protection Granted, *OJ L 304/12, 30.9.2004, p. 12–23.*

present danger to the host Member State and it is not conditional on an assessment of proportionality in relation to the particular case. Moreover, Member States may grant protection under their national law to a person who is excluded from refugee status provided that this other kind of protection cannot be in confusion with refugee status.

Later in the *H.T.* case, the Court also held that the fact that a person was a member of an organisation which is on the list of the Common Position 2001/931/CFSP due to its involvement in terrorist acts, does not automatically constitute a serious reason for exclusion from international protection, exclusion is not conditional on the person concerned representing a present danger to the host Member State or on an assessment of proportionality. Additionally, the Court ruled that a residence permit, once granted to a refugee may be revoked either there are compelling reasons of national security or public order within the meaning of that provision, or there are reasons to apply the derogation from the principle of non-refoulement. Supporting a terrorist organisation included on the list may constitute one of the 'compelling reasons of national security or public order'. The competent authorities are obliged to carry out an individual assessment of the specific facts concerning the acts of both the organisation and the person concerned.

As a continuation, in the *Lounani* case the Court examined the act constituting a terrorist act when implementing the exclusion clause in Article 12 of the Qualification Directive. According to the Court, Article 12 (2)(c) is not limited to direct terrorist acts extending its scope to various other activities associated with terrorism and terrorist organisations, hence, to those offences listed in Article 1 of the Framework Decision on Combating Terrorism.[56] Consequently, membership and participation in the running and activities of a terrorist organisation, forgery of documents and facilitating travel of foreign fighters could fall within the scope of the exclusion clause in spite of the fact that there is no direct link between activities of the person concerned and specific acts of terrorism. Additionally, the Court reaffirmed again the necessity of an individual assessment in such cases.

In contrast, the Hungarian legislation did not provide room for wide individual assessment because it states that a foreign national shall be excluded if he/she shall be punished five or more years according to the Hungarian law.[57]

56 Framework Decision 2002/475/JHA on combating terrorism [2002] OJ L 164/3.

57 Hungarian Helsinki Committee "A magyar jogállamiság mellett állt ki az európai bíróság" 18 September 2018., https://www.helsinki.hu/a-magyar-jogallamisag-mellett-allt-ki-az-europai-birosag/ and also case of CJEU- C-369/17, *Shinjan Ahmed v Bevándorlási és Állampolgársági Hivatal*.

3 Restrictive Migration Policies – An International Outlook

By immigration control mechanisms, States may decide who can enter their territory. On the one hand, border regulations may serve as an effective tool to filter out potential terrorists who intend to take advantage of migration channels. It can manifest in screening immigrants and specific nationalities are not permitted to enter based on national security consideration. On the other hand, States may permit only highly skilled or wealthy foreigners to enter their territory by which States may reduce the number of potential terrorists. States may also regulate entry by controlling access to their labour markets and may ban recruitment of certain nationalities under national security considerations. States' regulations may limit family reunification or in using quotas. As regards the asylum systems, States can impose restrictive measures such as allowing only a small number of refugees and asylum seekers especially among those who come from populations suspected of engaging in terrorist activities. Last, but not least, accurate law enforcement mechanisms are necessary for immigration control to filter out potential foreign terrorists.[58]

The current national practice of the United States is a good example for restrictive immigration policy where immigration regulation has often been linked to issues of national security. The Immigration and Nationality Act (INA)[59] is grounded on national security interests excluding aliens who may be entering the country to engage in such activities as espionage, sabotage, or other activities that are inherently prejudicial to the public interest. INA rejects the admission of those aliens who have ever advocated for or been affiliated with any organization that has supported certain anti-governmental political views, such as communism or anarchy. It also provided for excluding of aliens posing a threat to the nation's security. The INA also excludes some category of persons from protection even if they otherwise meet the requirements of refugee status setting out various exceptions that prevent otherwise qualified applicants from being granted asylum including persecution of others, particularly serious crimes, serious non-political crimes, and danger to the security of the United States. The new wave of immigration reforms relating to national security came after 9/11. As a response to the terrorist attacks, the adoption of the PATRIOT Act[60] and the REAL ID Act[61] reformulated and

58 Choi, Seung-Whan, "Does Restrictive Immigration Policy Reduce Terrorism in Western Democracies?" *Perspectives on Terrorism* 12, no. 4 (2018): 14–25.

59 United States: Immigration and Nationality Act (last amended March 2010) [United States of America], 27 June 1952.

60 Uniting and Strengthening America by Providing Appropriate Tools Required to Intercept and Obstruct Terrorism Act of 2001, Public law, 107–156 · Statutes at Large, 115 Stat. 272.

61 Real ID Act of 2005, Pub.L. 109–13, 119 Stat. 302.

modified immigration law concerning terrorism that were based on security-driven considerations.

During his presidential campaign, President Donald Trump has long claimed that terrorists are using the U.S. refugee resettlement program to enter the country. One of his first measures as a President was to enact Executive Order 13769,[62] titled, Protecting the Nation from Foreign Terrorist Entry into the United States, (it is often referred as the 'Muslim ban' or the "travel ban"). It was in effect from 27 January 2017 until 16 March 2017 lowering the number of refugees to be admitted into the United States in 2017 to 50,000, suspended the U.S. Refugee Admissions Program (USRAP) for 120 days, suspended the entry of Syrian refugees indefinitely, directed some cabinet secretaries to suspend entry of those whose countries do not meet adjudication standards under U.S. immigration law for 90 days, and, included exceptions on a case-by-case basis. Homeland Security listed these countries as Iran, Iraq, Libya, Somalia, Sudan, Syria, and Yemen. Revoking and replacing Executive Order 13769, Executive Order 13780,[63] titled, Protecting the Nation from Foreign Terrorist Entry into the United States, entered into force on March 6, 2017, limiting traveling to the U.S. from certain countries, and barring entry for all refugees who do not possess either a visa or valid travel documents.

So far, President Trump has issued three different orders targeting terrorist travel. The first enlisted Iraq, Iran, Somalia, Sudan, Syria, Libya, and Yemen (see above). The second removed Iraq, and the third removed Sudan and added North Korea, Chad, and Venezuela. Iran and Syria where state sponsors of terrorism; Libya, Yemen, Chad, and Somalia where extensive terrorist activities inside their borders took place.[64] "This exercise shows the inherent difficulty with blanket discrimination based on national origin. Even if the executive order was perfectly aligned with past incidents, the fact that it is dealing with

62 Executive Order Protecting the Nation from Foreign Terrorist Entry into the United States by President Donald J. Trump, 27 January 2017 https://www.whitehouse.gov/presidential-actions/executive-order-protecting-nation-foreign-terrorist-entry-united-states/ (last accessed: 2 June 2019).

63 Executive Order Protecting The Nation From Foreign Terrorist Entry Into The United States by President Donald J. Trump, 6 March 2017 https://www.whitehouse.gov/presidential-actions/executive-order-protecting-nation-foreign-terrorist-entry-united-states-2/ (last accessed: 2 June 2019).

64 Hans A. von Spakovsky "Restrictions on Travel from Terrorist Safe Havens Are Not a 'Muslim Ban'" *The Heritage Foundation,* 30 April 2018, https://www.heritage.org/immigration/commentary/restrictions-travel-terrorist-safe-havens-are-not-muslim-ban (last accessed: 2 June 2019).

such rare, low probability and low-risk events inevitably means that the past will be a poor predictor of the future."[65]

As a part of protective measures a series of walls and fences along the Mexico–United States border was constructed aimed at preventing illegal crossings from Mexico into the United States. The barrier is not a continuous one, but a group of short physical walls, secured with a system of sensors and cameras. By signing the Border Security and Immigration Enforcement Improvements Executive Order 13767,[66] the Trump Administration commenced to extend the border wall.

Despite the anti-immigrant political rhetoric and restrictive immigration measures the statistics show that only four asylum seekers, only 0.0006 percent of the 700,522 admitted to the US between 1975 and 2015, later turned out to be terrorists. For every terrorist who was granted asylum, 175,131 non-terrorist asylum seekers were admitted. In total, asylum seekers caused four fatalities, or one for every 175,131 admitted. And most importantly, no asylum seekers were involved with 9/11.[67] The average chance of dying in an attack by a foreign-born terrorist on U.S. soil was 1 in 3,609,709 a year.[68]

4 The Hungarian Case

Hungary became a country of emigration with changing intensity but the overall number of people living abroad has been constantly increasing. Neither the Central Statistical Office, however, nor other authorities publish data on the emigration of Hungarian citizens. Based on aggregate mirror statistics of 2017, the number of Hungarians resident in other EU Member States is about 600,000.[69]

The number of legal immigrants to Hungary has been steady for years. Among them are those who entered in an irregular, or as it is popular in

65 David Bier "New Travel Ban Would Not Have Prevented the Entry of Any Terrorists Since 9/11." *Cato Institute* 25 September 2017, https://www.cato.org/blog/new-travel-ban-wouldve-prevented-entry-no-terrorists-911 (last accessed: 2 June 2019).

66 Executive Order: Border Security and Immigration Enforcement Improvements by President Donald J. Trump, 25 January 2017, https://www.whitehouse.gov/presidential-actions/executive-order-border-security-immigration-enforcement-improvements/ (last accessed 9 June 2019).

67 Alex Nowrasteh, *"Terrorism and Immigration: A Risk Analysis"* CATO Institute Policy Analysis No. 798. September 13, 2016. p. 14. https://www.cato.org/publications/policy-analysis/terrorism-immigration-risk-analysis.

68 Nowrasteh, "Terrorism and Immigration" p. 17.

69 Gyollai, "Hungary Country Report" 287.

Hungary to say, in an illegal way. Those who have sought asylum in Hungary, due to life threatening situations, hit a record in 2015 with more than 380,000 registrations. Only 17,715 asylum application were registered. Due to the high absconding rate of asylum-seekers who left Hungary, most of these asylum cases ceased without decision on the merits.[70] The number of applicants decreased drastically after the building of fence on the Serbian-Hungarian border. Besides the physical border there was a legal one that had the message that refugees are not welcomed. The Criminal Code alongside immigration and asylum law was changed several times and linked the concept of terrorism to immigrants. The politicians and the media repeated the same messages on billboards, on questionnaires of national consultations, and, on the referendum that was held in 2016.

4.1 *Legislative Amendments in 2015*

Hungary was and is a transit country in spite of the CEAS regulations and its obligations. There are different calculations, but we share its conclusions: the substantive evaluations of the applications are left to another EU Member State – unless the person simply remains in the EU without authorization.[71] Behind the current refugee protection crisis, there might be a more structural one. The border police were integrated into the general police forces in 2010 that created systematic problems in the control of immigration according to scientific research studies on this field.[72]

As a response to the mass influx of migrants, the Hungarian Government technically closed the Hungarian-Serbian border by a barb-wired fence in order to stop illegal border-crossing of migrants.[73] A fence deters, and if, nevertheless, one wishes to cross it, then it becomes a tool of obstructing access to protection.[74] Although the EU asylum legislation contradicts the usage of these obstacles because it hampers the right to access to the territory. However, from a national security point of view, it was praised as the solution to be

70 Further data available at the webpage of Office of Immigration and Asylum http://www.bmbah.hu/index.php?option=com_k2&view=item&layout=item&id=492&Itemid=1259&lang=en (last accessed 28 December 2018).

71 Boldizsár Nagy, "Hungarian Asylum Law and Policy in 2015–2016: Securitization Instead of Loyal Cooperation" in: Special Issue Constitutional Dimensions of the Refugee Crisis' *German Law Journal,* 17, 6 (2016.) 1033–1081. DOI: https://doi.org/10.1017/S2071832200021581.

72 Balázs Laufer, "A migráció rendvédelmi és nemzetbiztonsági kihívásai" (PhD dissertation, National Public Service University, 2013) DOI: 10.17625/NKE.2013.021.

73 See in Governmental Decision No. 1401/2015. (VI. 17.) on certain governmental measures to handle the exceptional migration pressure.

74 Nagy, "Hungarian Asylum Law and Policy in 2015–2016" 1061.

followed by the EU Member States to protect EU external borders and as the most effective way to fight against terrorism.[75]

Simultaneously, the Hungarian Criminal Code[76] was also amended by the Act CXL of 2015. It entered into force on the 15 September 2015, introducing the following criminal acts: the unlawful crossing of the border fence (Section 352/A); vandalism of the border fence (Section 352/B); and, obstruction of construction works on the border fence (Section 352/C).[77] The introduction of these criminal acts greatly contributed to the amendment of the expulsion regulations in case of perpetrators of these acts where an executable term of imprisonment should be imposed and expulsion may not be omitted.[78] The ban from the whole Schengen area for entering the territory of Hungary irregularly is a punishment in a broad sense, accompanying the expulsion order served on those asylum seekers who are returnable to a safe third country and/ or who were subject to a formal criminal procedure for having crossed the fence irregularly.[79]

Those who crossed the border fence illegally and were caught on the scene and arrested, applied for asylum just after they were sentenced. As a result, the execution of the sentence is suspended for the duration of asylum determination procedure. This phenomenon was reported by UNHCR as malpractice but that did not lead to any change in the legislation.[80]

According to the relevant statistics, between September 2015 and June 2016, a total number of 2898 persons were charged, 9 persons were detained, 18 house arrests were ordered, 2753 persons were sentenced to expulsion, 3 cases

75 Miklós Böröcz, "A migrciós válság terrorkockázata" *Terror&Elhárítás*, 6,1 (2016) HU ISSN 2064-0374.

76 Act C of 2012 on the Criminal Code.

77 The illegal crossing of the 175 km long fence was made a criminal act by introducing Articles 352 A, B, and C into the Criminal Code. A maximum of three years imprisonment threatens all who cross the fence illegally (Article 352A). Under Article 352B, damaging of the fence is a separate crime with a maximum penalty of five years imprisonment. Even obstructing the construction of the fence was made a separate crime. (Article 352 C). Crossing the international border where no fence has been erected remains a minor offence.

78 Sándor Madai "A „tömeges bevándorlás okozta válsághelyzet" kezelésének büntető anyagi jogi eszközei hazánkban." In ed Zoltán Hautzinger *A migráció bűnügyi hatásai,* Budapest: Magyar Rendészettudományi Társaság Migrációs Tagozat (2016) 246.

79 Nagy "Hungarian Asylum Law and Policy in 2015–2016"1065.

80 UN High Commissioner for Refugees (UNHCR), *Hungary as a country of asylum. Observations on restrictive legal measures and subsequent practice implemented between July 2015 and March 2016,* May 2016, <http://www.refworld.org/docid/57319d514.html> (last accessed 31 January 2018).

ended by cassation, 1 case ended with executed imprisonment, others sentenced from 3 months up to 1 year 6 months imprisonment.[81]

The above-mentioned changes clearly reflects the 'crimmigration' phenomenon when immigration is not regarded as part of the civil or administrative law but the criminal law, thus, those persons become the perpetrators who did not commit any other crime and are punished solely because they circumvented immigration rules and border controls. This kind of attitude becomes significant in Hungary as established border controls and large-scale application of exclusions based on the assumption that foreigners may, indeed, be criminals or may have committed entry-related crimes, including human smuggling.[82]

The Act LXXX of 2007 on asylum was also amended September 2015 by introducing the state of emergency due to mass influx of migrants that may be ordered by the Government on recommendation of the minister of interior.[83] The special state of emergency introduces in two counties for the first time and later was extended to four more counties close to the Serbian border and by March 2016 to the whole territory of the country. The state of emergency can be initiated by the chief of police and the general director of immigration and asylum authority and their requests are confidential for 10 years.[84] This, so called 'crisis situation caused by mass migration' is not a special state order and may be ordered if the daily number of asylum application is higher than 500 or there are more than 1000 people in the transit zones. Besides these objective cases it can be ordered if the public order, security or public health of a city is in danger. The crisis situation caused by mass migration entitles the police to enter private homes under suspicion without a warrant, taking real estate into state use, as well as mobile items owned or possessed by other state or municipal agencies, when none of the legally prescribed conditions are met probably only serve the securitizing intent.[85]

The rules of expulsion have also changed in the *Criminal Code*. As of 15 September 2015, an additional requirement namely 'legally staying on the territory of Hungary' was added to the respect for family life.[86] This means that

81 According to the response of State Attorney General to the Parliament in 2016.

82 Nagy, "Hungarian Asylum Law and Policy in 2015–2016" 1044.

83 Madai, "A tömeges bevándorlás okozta válsághelyzet" 247.

84 Press Helsinki "Féléves a törvényellenes országos válsághelyzet" *HelsinkiFigyelő* (9 September 2016) http://helsinkifigyelo.blog.hu/2016/09/09/feleves_a_torvenyellenes_orszagos_valsaghelyzet (last accessed 29 April 2020).

85 Nagy, "Hungarian Asylum Law and Policy in 2015–2016" 1061.

86 Article 59 (4) Expulsion may only be imposed upon a person sentenced to a term of imprisonment of ten years or more: (a) who has been residing in the territory of Hungary legitimately for not less than ten years; or, (b) who is lawfully residing in the territory of

illegal migrants may be expelled regardless of their right to respect for family life.[87] Moreover, expulsion may not be omitted if an executable term of imprisonment is imposed for an unlawful crossing of a border barrier, vandalism of a border barrier or obstruction of construction works on a border barrier. If expulsion is ordered for a specific term, it shall be double of the term of imprisonment, but at least two years. Permanent expulsion may be imposed upon a person who was sentenced to a term of imprisonment of ten years or more, and presence of the perpetrator in the country is assessed as posing a potential and considerable risk to public safety taking into account the severity of the criminal offense, the nature of the act and the connections of the perpetrator.[88]

The immigration authority is responsible for ordering the expulsion of third country nationals (hereinafter: TCNs). There is little evidence demonstrating that a return decision was issued for a national security interest.[89]

Currently, TCNs staying irregularly on the territory of the Member States are faced with the increasing phenomenon of the criminalisation of irregular entry or stay sanctioned with criminal penalties such as fines, house confinement or imprisonment. The relation between immigration law and criminal law as well as national penal measures (imposed as a punishment for illegal migration) compatibility with the Return Directive and EU Charter has been reported. This prolific jurisprudence has been the result of national courts addressing preliminary references to the ECJ concerning the imprisonment of TCNs in return procedures for the crime of irregular entry or stay.[90]

4.2 *Legislative Amendments in 2016*

In order to manage the migration crisis as well as to cope with the new type of security challenges, the Hungarian Government also initiated the amendment

Hungary and whose right to family union would be injured; provided that the presence of the perpetrator in the country is assessed as posing a potential and considerable risk to public safety.

87 Madai, "A tömeges bevándorlás okozta válsághelyzet" 254–255.

88 Madai, "A „tömeges bevándorlás okozta válsághelyzet" 254, and Hungarian Criminal Code Articles 60. 2a and 60.3.

89 Boldizsár Nagy "National Synthesis Report – Hungary Report on the Hungarian Court Cases Implementing the Return Directive (2008/115/EC)," sections 13–15.

90 Madalina Moraru and Géraldine Renaudiere, *"European Synthesis Report on the Judicial Implementation of Chapter IV of the Return Directive – Pre-Removal Detention,"* REDIAL RR 2016/05, (San Domenico di Fiesole (FI): European University Institute) 2016, 8.

of the Fundamental Law introducing a new special state order. A terror threat could not be referred under any previous special legal order regimes as they were established to handle classical inter-state challenges, therefore, a new kind of special legal order has been introduced, the so-called "terror emergency situation." Terror emergency situation may be ordered by the two-thirds majority of the members of the Hungarian Parliament if a terror attack or related significant and direct risk has occurred. In case of a terror emergency situation, extraordinary measures (e.g., extraordinary use of the national army, tightening border control regardless of international standards and conventions, ordering a curfew, enhanced control of communication channels, etc.)[91] may be taken derogating from the normal operation of the state established by the Fundamental Law in order to prevent any terror attack and to protect citizens.[92]

After the radical change in national migration policy in 2015, the country-wide billboard campaigns in 2015,[93] the national questionnaire on migration[94] in 2016 and the referendum on 2 October 2016[95] and the attempted 7th amendment of the Fundamental Law in fall of 2016, by wintertime, the Hungarian Constitutional Court (hereinafter: CC) declared in its decision No. 22/2016. (XII.6.) AB that Hungary's constitutional identity is rooted in its 'historical constitution'. Consequently, constitutional identity cannot be waived by way of an international treaty – Hungary can only be deprived of its constitutional

91 Act CXIII of 2011 on National Defense.

92 Dániel Kuli, "Nyolcadik utas a terrorista" *Ars Boni* (23 November 2016) <http://arsboni.hu/nyolcadik-utas-terrorista/> (last accessed 4 December 2017).

93 The billboards carried one of the three messages of the campaign: 'If you come to Hungary, you must respect our laws'; 'If you come to Hungary, you must respect our culture'; and, finally, 'If you come to Hungary, you must not take the jobs of the Hungarians'. In a clear indication of their intended audience, all of the billboards were in Hungarian. In September, a new set of the billboards and advertisements in print and online media appeared, referring back to the 'results' of the national consultation, with the following text: 'The people have decided: The country must be defended'.

94 The questionnaire included leading questions such as: 'Do you think that Hungary could be the target of an act of terror in the next few years?' and 'Do you agree with the view that migrants illegally crossing the Hungarian border should be returned to their own countries within the shortest possible time?' It also asked whether, in contrast to Brussels's lenient policy, the government should introduce more stringent regulations and whether the citizen was in support of more stringent regulations, including that 'migrants illegally crossing the Hungarian border could be taken'. see: Nagy, "Hungarian Asylum Law and Policy in 2015–2016" 1053–1054.

95 The Government website translated the questions as 'Do you agree that the European Union should have the power to impose the compulsory relocation of non-Hungarian citizens to Hungary without the consent of the National Assembly of Hungary?'

identity through the final termination of its sovereignty, its independent statehood. Therefore, the protection of constitutional identity shall remain the duty of the CC as long as Hungary is a sovereign State.[96] The background of the decision is a constitutional complaint concerning the legality of the relocation decision of the European Council.[97] The complaint assumed that its implementation might constitute a collective expulsion of TCNs that would be an infringement not only of Article XIV of the Fundamental Law prohibiting collective expulsion of aliens but also of international law in general.[98] Nevertheless, the CC did not rule over this question because of the Article E of the Fundamental Law but applied the complaint to interpret the constitutional identity.

Nevertheless, the idea of constitutional identity is not a new one[99] but its use in the Hungarian CC was not frequent, and the linkage between the refugee protection crisis and the emerging idea was concerning.[100]

By these steps, the Government and Parliament intentionally replaced the figure of the refugee in need of protection with the (imagined) illegal migrant, who arrives in an unlawful manner and only has sinister intentions, against whom Hungary has to be defended.[101]

4.3 *Legislative Amendments in 2017*

On 23 March 2017 a new amendment of the asylum legislation came into force. Since that time all asylum-seekers are placed in the transit zone, except those unaccompanied children who are under age 14. The *Ilias and Ilias v. Hungary* case in 2016 was the cornerstone of the debate whether the transit zones are detention places or not. The Government did not accept the decision of ECtHR and turned to the Grand Chamber. The so-called '8 km rule,' applicable to the whole territory of the country, means that the apprehended illegal migrant, who asked for asylum, requires the responsible authority to accompany the applicant back to Serbia.

96 22/2016 (XII. 9.) CC decision <http://public.mkab.hu/dev/dontesek.nsf/0/1361AFA3CEA26B84C1257F10005DD958?OpenDocument&english> (last accessed 21 April 2020).

97 Council Decision (EU) 2015/1601 of 22 September 2015 establishing provisional measures in the area of international protection for the benefit of Italy and Greece.

98 Anita Nagy-Nádasdi and Barbara Kőhalmi, "Hungarian Constitutional Identity and the ECJ Decision on Refugee Quota" http://verfassungsblog.de/hungarian-constitutional-identity-and-the-ecj-decision-on-refugee-quota/ (last accessed 30 December 2017).

99 R.D. Kelemen and Laurent Pech "Why autocrats love constitutional identity and constitutional pluralism" Reconnect *Working Papers* No. 2 2018 p. 9 https://reconnect-europe.eu/wp-content/uploads/2018/10/RECONNECT-WorkingPaper2-Kelemen-Pech-LP-KO.pdf.

100 Kelemen and Pech "Why autocrats love" p. 9.

101 Nagy, "Hungarian Asylum Law and Policy in 2015–2016" 1057.

The accordance of these legislative changes with international and European law is highly questionable. But, the Hungarian Government's use of migration as a key component in it political program, therefore, they are tending to challenge the current understanding of international legislation in every forum.

4.4 *Legislative Changes in 2018*

The changes of migration legislation did not link only to the Act on Asylum or the immigration statuses but interlinked with the election campaign of the governing party that themed around stopping migration. As a frequent intentional misunderstanding the term migrant was used but what everybody understood they were; that is, those who crossed the border illegally and then asked for asylum. Migrants are even those wealthy foreign citizens who bought state bonds and have received a permanent residence permit. Furthermore, the government expressed, mainly at international forums, that they follow their international obligations and provide sanctuary for those who flee from persecution. But, somehow the two groups of people, those asylum-seekers who cross the border illegally and those who are called migrants are never one the same.

After the election 2018, that provided a two-thirds majority to the government, the Fundamental Law was amended for the seventh time. As a result, some new expressions appeared in the constitution such as alien population and their settlement which caused constitutional instability regarding interpretation.[102] Moreover, the concept safe third country was codified in the constitution that narrowed further the right to asylum.[103]

Also, new crimes were proposed in the *Hungarian Criminal Code* such as assistance to illegal immigration and the organisation of illegal immigration.

On November 6, the Minister of Interior submitted the new amendement No. T/3366 of the Asylum Act that changes controlling competencies of asylum and immigration authorities in order to prevent and to investigate the abuses in the system of residency of foreign citizens. It also made it more complicated for third country nationals' resident in Hungary as family members.

4.5 *National Security Considerations in the Hungarian Asylum Procedure*

First of all, it has to be noted that we should take into account not only legal but political and sociological perspectives in order to describe the situation

102 One critic of the amendment by the NGO: https://menedek.hu/sites/default/files/media/document/2018/06/05/menedek_eszrevetel.pdf (last accessed 19 April 2020).

103 Article XIV (4) of the Fundamental Law.

properly, as Boldizsár Nagy uses non-legal disciplines in his study to describe these events, not just because "migration lawyers, including refugee lawyers, rarely bother with locating their research beyond the positivist-comparatists jurisprudential space, but, otherwise, these changes could not be understandable."[104] Nevertheless, in this chapter, we only discuss legislative changes.

During the negotiations of the recast Qualification Directive[105] (QDII) the contradiction between the Geneva Convention and QDII regarding exclusion, based on national security issues, was discussed and some of the national experts argued that there is no contradiction between the two instruments. The Geneva Convention is an international treaty that can be interpreted differently. From a reading of Articles 32 and 33 it is clear that the goal of the treaty is not to protect those who pose a threat to the security of a country. This teleological interpretation is supported by the practical interpretation, too.[106] On the other hand, the wording of the QDII states that exclusion is only a possibility that was not implemented into the national legislation.

As result, those who posed a threat to national security could not be recognised by the state as beneficiary of international protection. However, it may happen. Nevertheless, the practice of the Hungarian authorities remained unchanged and the opinion of the national security agency is still regarded as expert opinion and as such has a binding effect on the asylum agency, according to general administrative law.[107] Therefore, if the national security agency signalled its concern, the applicant was rejected. Nevertheless, the judicial branch did not share this interpretation of the legislation because the national security agency could not have the authority to decide over the recognition but only to provide the information if the person concerned is posing a threat to the national security or not.[108] If the answer was positive, this could not be an

104 Nagy, "Hungarian Asylum Law and Policy in 2015–2016" 1040.

105 Council of the European Union, Directive 2011/95/EU of the European Parliament and of the Council of 13 December 2011 on standards for the qualification of third-country nationals or stateless persons as beneficiaries of international protection, for a uniform status for refugees or for persons eligible for subsidiary protection, and for the content of the protection granted (recast), 20 December 2011, OJ L. 337/9–337/26; 20.12.2011.

106 Árpád Szép "A nemzetbiztonsági szempont erősödése a menedékjogi törvényben" (The emerging national security notion in the ct on Asylum Law) In ed Zoltán Hautzinger *A migráció bűnügyi hatásai,* (Budapest: Magyar Rendészettudományi Társaság Migrációs Tagozat) 2016, 304.

107 Szép, "A nemzetbiztonsági szempont erősödése"309.

108 Szép, "A nemzetbiztonsági szempont" 305.

obstacle to the asylum procedure.[109] The UNHCR expressed its concern during the drafting process of QDII because the new wording changed the time of the acts committed from application to issuance of residence permit and it is against the declarative approach of the recognition of the agency.[110]

What does national security interest mean in the Hungarian legal framework? The Act CXXV of 1995 on the national security services defines national interest as to ensure of the autonomy of Hungary and protection of the legal order such as among others[111] the detection and prevention of terrorist acts, illicit arms and drug trafficking and the illegal trafficking of internationally controlled products and technologies.

The main areas where we identified legislative changes of the asylum system in relation to national security or national interest are the following: detention of asylum-seekers, issuance of travel documents, shortening the duration of the procedure by introducing a single procedure and an accelerated procedure, as well as the application of Geneva Convention 1F(c).

Firstly, major legislative amendments linking the asylum regime to security interests were introduced in 2013. It did not only reflect the second phase of the CEAS but have also tried to further improve the national asylum system while preventing possible abuses. The national regulation is in coherence with the UNHCR guidelines[112] on detention: the detention may only be ordered on

109 This approach of the judicial branch shows resemblance with the current ECJ preliminary judgement in C-473/16, F. case when the expert opinion cannot be the sole reason of rejection.

110 UN High Commissioner for Refugees (UNHCR), UNHCR Annotated Comments on the EC Council Directive 2004/83/EC of 29 April 2004 on Minimum Standards for the Qualification and Status of Third Country Nationals or Stateless Persons as Refugees or as Persons Who Otherwise Need International Protection and the Content of the Protection Granted (OJ L 304/12 of 30.9.2004), 27 January 2005, 27. <http://www.refworld.org/docid/4200d8354.html> (last accessed 31 January 2018).

111 Article 74 'the detection of attempts to attack the country's independence and territorial integrity; the discovery and elimination of disguised aspirations that hurt or threaten the political, economic, national defence interests of the country; the discovery and elimination of disguised aspirations that hurt or threaten the political, economic, defence interests of the country, the acquisition of information on foreign countries or of foreign origin required for governmental decisions; detecting and eliminating disguised efforts to change the legal order of the country to ensure the exercise of basic human rights, to represent democratization based on multiparty system and to alter or disturb the operation of legitimate institutions;'

112 UNHCR Guidelines on the Applicable Criteria and Standards relating to the Detention of Asylum-Seekers and Alternatives to Detention. (2012) 'Governments may need to detain a particular individual who presents a threat to national security. Even though determining what constitutes a national security threat lies primarily within the domain of the government, the measures taken (such as detention) need to comply with the standards in these

the basis of an individual assessment and the full consideration of alternative options. The detention of asylum seekers must be exceptional (a measure of last resort) and has to be proportionate to the objectives to be achieved. As a consequence, as of July 2013 a person seeking asylum may be and frequently is detained if his/her entitlement to stay is exclusively based on the submission of an application for recognition where if it is necessary for the protection of national security or public order.[113] Detention can be maintained during the court proceedings as well as it was advised by the group of the judicial experts on asylum next to the Supreme Court of Hungary, the Curia.[114] However, national security risk in itself is not sufficient for ordering detention as it also requires any other basis laid down in Article 5 of the ECHR. Typically, the lawful arrest or detention of a person is to prevent his/her affecting an unauthorised entry into the country or of a person against whom action is being taken with a view to deportation or extradition.[115] The widely used tool of detention was raised repeatedly by critics, but, the tendency to employ it did not stop.[116]

Secondly, according to the relevant provisions of the Asylum Act the issuance of travel documents for persons granted refugee or subsidiary protection status may be denied based on national security reasons.[117] It is justified by the fact that the person concerned may constitute a national security threat only upon travelling abroad and the national security concerns may arise after

Guidelines, in particular that the detention is necessary, proportionate to the threat, non-discriminatory, and subject to judicial oversight'. [39] http://www.unhcr.org/publications/legal/505b10ee9/unhcr-detention-guidelines.html (last accessed 19 April 2020).

113 Article 31/A 1. d. of Act LXXX of 2007 on Asylum Law.

114 The summary of the judicial and legal expert group stated the necessity and prolongation of the detention cannot be affected by the fact that judicial part has commenced. The detention can be prolonged even though the administrative procedure has already finished. 64. (translated by the authors) <http://kuria-birosag.hu/hu/joggyak_csop/menekultugyi-joggyakorlat-elemzo-csoport-osszefoglalo-velemenye> (last accessed 20 January 2018).

115 Szép, "A nemzetbiztonsági szempont erősödése" 307.

116 UNHCR in 2012 expressed concern about the serious challenges asylum seekers face in accessing protection in Hungary. It noted that 'Since April 2010, asylum detention has become the rule rather than the exception', mentioned that the practice between 2008 and 2010 was unlawful and continued to criticize the regime after 2010 for lack of effective remedies, unpredictability, and the lack of legitimate aims in many cases. UN High Commissioner for Refugees (UNHCR), Hungary as a country of asylum. Observations on the situation of asylum-seekers and refugees in Hungary, 24 April 2012, https://www.refworld.org/docid/4f9167db2.html (last accessed 10 June 2019).

117 Section 10 paragraph 3 point (a) in Act LXXX of 2007 on Asylum.

recognition and, therefore, the person may apply for a travel document during the withdrawal procedure.[118]

Thirdly, as of 1 August 2015, the asylum procedure has become a single procedure in which each relevant aspect of the case, including national security concerns, is considered by the asylum authority and its partner authorities (e.g., CCT and Office of Constitutional Protection (hereinafter: OCP)). The OCP is involved in each asylum case and has to decide on whether the person concerned constitutes a risk to national security within 8 days. The amendment of the previous Act on Administrative Procedures[119] ceased the possibility to extend the procedural time of the OCP in asylum cases and as a result, the OCP had to give an expert opinion within 8 days in thousands of cases. Besides the relatively short deadline, the lack of personal interviews was another factor that has negative impact on the asylum procedure. As a result, their procedure started to run separately and in parallel with the asylum procedure. They might not know about the details of identity or any relevant information that the applicant revealed during the interview. Some have even suggested turning back to the old regime that applied before 2008, when the OCP examined the cases only after the asylum interviews finished.[120] The high rate of absconding made the request for their expert opinion ineffective. The CCT also provides expert opinion on the migration-terrorism nexus in accordance with its regulations.

Fourthly, the application of an asylum-seeker may be decided in an accelerated procedure where the applicant may pose a threat to Hungary's national security for a serious reason.[121] This provision may limit the applicants' procedural rights as they have a short time-limit to demonstrate their well-founded reasons applying for asylum that ultimately might have a negative impact on their case. By this amendment, the debate over the weight of expert opinion is decisive on the issue whether the claimant poses a risk to national security. If so, it can be the reason to reject the claim. This amendment was part of the transposition package of the Article 14.4-5 of the recast QD II,[122] which does

118 Szép, "A nemzetbiztonsági szempont erősödése" 300.

119 Act CXL of 2004 on the general rules of administrative proceedings and services, not in force since 1 January 2018.

120 Szép, "A nemzetbiztonsági szempont erősödése" 309–310.

121 Article 51.7 (j) in Act LXXX of 2007 on Asylum.

122 Article 14. 4. 'Member States may revoke, end or refuse to renew the status granted to a refugee by a governmental, administrative, judicial or quasi-judicial body, when: (a) there are reasonable grounds for regarding him or her as a danger to the security of the Member State in which he or she is present; (b) he or she, having been convicted by a final judgment of a particularly serious crime, constitutes a danger to the community of that Member State'. 5. In situations described in paragraph 4, Member States may decide not to grant status to a refugee, where such a decision has not yet been taken'.

not oblige States to reject these applicants, but certainly opens that possibility to choose less favourable options. But certainly, it raises the question of compliance with Article 1F of the Geneva Convention. Accelerated procedure is to be finished within 15 days. Courts have 8 days to decide on these appeals. The appeal does not have suspensive effect thus rejected applicants could be removed from the country before the first judicial hearing.

Fifthly, legislative changes also made clear that refugee status may not be granted to those foreigners whose stay in Hungary poses a risk to national security. And, for practical reasons, the amendment of the Asylum Act declared that in the application of Article 1F(c) of the Geneva Convention, the following, in particular, shall be contrary to the purposes and principles of the United Nations acts of terrorism, financing terrorism, and incitement to these acts.[123]

The act of terrorism may be defined variously in different legal systems, but, in general, it contains common elements such as danger against people with the use of objects and of force and targets an undefined group of people or a certain group of vulnerable people or state or representatives of the state in order to compel them for a certain aim. In light of this broad term, Article 1F(b) can be used if, as UNHCR guideline suggests, the test of proportionality and causality could be applied, the perpetrator is personally responsible for the result and the action happened outside the country of asylum before the application.

The serious non-political act, from a legal point of view, may be interpreted as a terrorist activity but, in general, political aims, motivations are also significant elements of the definition. The political action needs to have a close and causal relationship between the political will and the result of such action and, *a contrario*, we may assume the non-political act is the one when one of these elements are missing. The extradition treaties may shed light on the political actions and provides help to understand non-political actions. Furthermore, the *travaux prépartoires* of Article 1F suggests that only those persons who can be excluded from protection can be extradited, but, this suggestion does not appear in the text of the treaty.

Finally, as of August 2015, in its decision rejecting international protection, the asylum authority may also decide on the expulsion of those persons who are not entitled to stay on the territory of Hungary. This provision has a negative impact on the asylum-seekers as they do not have any independent procedure and remedy against the decision and the duration of the right to stay on the territory is significantly decreased. Nevertheless, it is not contrary to the international or European law, but, the need for this amendment is rooted in a

123 Szép, "A nemzetbiztonsági szempont erősödése" 310.

duplicate system. Previously, the asylum authority only examined whether the expulsion of a rejected applicant is in line with the principle of non-refoulement and confirmed if the applicant can be expelled. The immigration authority decided on the question of expulsion. Now, the asylum authority can state if that person has to be expelled.[124]

4.6 *Experiences from the Field: How Hungarian Experts Evaluate the Situation?*

In this part, we evaluate the experts' opinions based on half structured interviews[125] that we have conducted with national experts on the field of migration, asylum and terrorism[126] in order to explore how terrorism and asylum law are interconnected in the practice and gather experiences directly from the field.

Methodologically, we intended to map how Hungarian experts see the connection between the two fields. We focused on their choice of wording, the aspects they underlined in each question. Certainly, there are issues, expressions that have several layers of meaning, but we tried to summarize them separately. By doing this evaluation we would like to capture how they think of their field of expertise, under this new and heavy political pressure.

---

124 Árpád Szép, "A 2015-ös migrációs válságra adott menedékjogi válaszok. Jogszabály-módosítással a tömeges beáramlás ellen?" in: *Magyarország és a 2015-ös európai migrációs válság Tanulmányok* ed: Péter Tálas and József Balla (Budapest: Dialóg Campus) 2017, ISBN 978-615-5376-63-4.

125 The fixed questions were the following: 1. What is your opinion about the legislative changes proclaimed since 2015? 2. What is your general opinion? 3. What sort of cases do you know? 4. Do you see the potential risk that terrorists may come with asylum-seekers? 5. Since the stricter regulations how has the procedure of the Centre of Counter-Terrorism and Constitution Protection Office changed? 6. Do you see the coupling of the migration and terrorism as a political tool? 7. Does the frequent stereotype that "Muslim is Terrorist" exist beyond the political scene and does it have any grounding? 8. What sort of international examples do you know for the coupling of these two phenomenon? And, what example do you know of from France, Germany, Italy, USA, about cases when the applicant was rejected due to national security reasons? 9. What is terrorism? 10. How typical is radicalisation in Hungary?

126 We tried to connect with governmental authorities on the field, but it was unsuccessful due to the high media attention on the topic. Our interviewees were Péter Tálas, scientist from the field on national security; Ágnes Ambrus, who worked as a national expert on asylum at UNHCR in Hungary for 25 years; Vivien Vadasi, who was JHA counsellor for 8 years and now is working for Menedék Association, a non-governmental organisation on migration as a legal counsellor; Zoltán Somogyvári, who is a legal advisor at a non-governmental organisation, Hungarian Helsinki Committee for 7 years where he provides free legal assitance for asylum seekers.

Having regard to the fact that there is not a widely accepted definition of terrorism, we did not agree upon a definition at the beginning of the interviews. In their response to later questions the experts defined the notion but its content differs depending on the viewpoints of each interviewee. We have selected our interviewees according to different areas in connection with our topic (migration and asylum experts from the government, NGOs, UNHCR, as well as a security studies' expert from the academe) so that we can guarantee a comprehensive description of migration and terrorism in Hungary.

The main findings based on the research interviews are the following.

All legal experts agree that the legislative changes made between 2015 and 2018 have made the national asylum system more rigorous, even to the extent that it has reached the point where it ceases to exist in the form as it was before 2015. This process has already started much earlier, but, it has been overemphasized by the media since 2015. Only a few people receive international protection and the state of emergency situation is still proclaimed. Ironically, the exceptional order was introduced when the real mass migration was over. The current regulations tightened up even more the legislation, as Vadasi, pointed out. Ambrus argued that the changes polarized the system between human rights and security, it became 'unbalanced'. The pressing issue of emigration of Hungarian intellectuals highlights the concern of who will rebuild the checks and balances in the legal system. Somogyvári highlighted that the government sabotages the system through the legislation introduced in Parliament and keeping up the special state orders with Governmental Decrees.

The general situation of refugees and NGOs is of concern in several ways. As Vadasi pointed out, the governmental measures have a clear message for refugees: you are not welcome. They are in a half legal situation and their realistic next step is to leave the country and to live illegally in another European country. Somogyvári mentioned the hate campaign against migrants made it hard to integrate them into the society.

In Tálas's view, the strong connection between migration and terrorism is not supported by evidence in Europe. Several national studies support[127] Tálas's argument that there were only a few terror plots in which the perpetrator

127 Andrea Ambrus "A tömeges migráció és az iszlamista terrorizmus közti kapcsolat az Európai Unióban" *Nemzet és biztonság,* 6(2017) 105–124. http://www.nemzetesbiztonsag.hu/cikkek/neb_2017_06_08_ambrus_andrea_-_a_tomeges_migracio_es_az_iszlamista_terrorizmus_kozti_kapcsolat_az_euban.pdf p. 121.

arrived with the flow of the recent migration crisis. In general, those persons who pose a risk to national security do not receive refugee or subsidiary protection status under EU law; however, they fall under the scope of the principle of non-refoulement and temporary protection granted to them. Vadasi pointed out that they know only a few cases in which an asylum-seeker was rejected on the ground of posing risk on national security. In one of the recent cases, the applicant was rejected several times but, finally, he received temporary protection. However, during several judicial hearings the reason why he posed a threat to national security is still not known by the applicant.[128] Ironically, the fact that he poses a risk to national security is widely known thanks to the administrative circumstances. From a legal point of view, the fact that he does not know why he poses a risk to national security may constrain his fundamental human right to effective remedy.

Another example mentioned by Somogyvári was Alekszij Tourobarov's asylum application case. He is a Russian politician who fled the country due to the criminal charges, as a consequence of his political activity. He applied for asylum in Hungary, then in the Czech Republic and in Hungary again. During the process of his second application in Hungary, the Constitution Protection Office raised the notion that he posed a risk to national security that led to the rejection of his application. The court ceased the decision and rendered a new process from the asylum authority. In its decision, the judge specifically emphasized that the expert opinion of the CPO could not amount to the rejection of the applicant only after he had the chance to know about it. Also, he cited the regulation of Fundamental Law as an effective remedy that may hinder, due to the non-consistent reasoning that did not refer the expert opinion, in merit due to its confidentiality.[129] In the last 20 years, there were international arrest warrants towards some of the Russian asylum-seekers, as Ambrus recalled it, but sadly they were given back to Russia in a quick manner. As she described, the terrorist activity rather arose in relation with East-European applicants before 2015.

The Geneva Convention and CEAS entails a bouquet of rights to integration into the host society and it does not stop at the point when the person gets status and how. Sadly, terrorist related exclusion follows the migrants. As

128 This is an ongoing case at the time of writing. The applicant did not accept the temporary protection that is based on the non-refoulement principle and provides a year long residence permit and limited access to the labour market. He applied again for refugee or beneficiary of subsidiary protection status.

129 The decision of Judge Balázs Sipos is accessible in Hungarian https://www.helsinki.hu/wp-content/uploads/torubarov_2_itelet.pdf. (last accessed 10 June 2019).

Vadasi indicated that the terrorism as a problem may arise when a refugee intends to open a bank account. Some branches of banks did not consider them as quasi nationals; however, the legislation provides a wide range of social and political rights to persons recognised as a refugee or beneficiaries of international protection and with regard to opening a bank account they do not face any restriction. In spite of this some banks did not consider this basic point and reject their request to open a bank account based on the fact that they originate from countries which are on the list of money laundering for terrorist organisations.

With regard to the issue of the potential risk that terrorists may channel themselves among asylum-seekers, Somogyvári argues, that there is a risk if there is a lack of monitoring and checks, and the need for safety and security of citizens makes it understandable to detain certain asylum-seekers, but only if their detention is necessary, proportionate and not arbitrary. As EU law allows member states to conduct border procedures within four weeks in case of non-vulnerable applicants that should be enough for the necessary security checks. However, if asylum seekers are detained during the border procedure – as they are in Hungary – they must be given an individualized detention order against which they have the right to seek an effective legal remedy.

What makes the whole national security checks controversial is that there are foreigners who got residence status for buying state bonds and some of them actually posing a risk to national security. Tálas pointed out that it is not likely that terrorists use the channels of migrants did, i.e., walking, shipping or paying smugglers. The assets of a terrorist group are far too precious to risk his/her identity or security through such a perilous journey. If they used this way of arrival it would be only to raise the level of fear among the host countries' nationals from foreigners. The data shows that there are plenty of applicants for committing terrorist activity among citizens with a migratory background.

Most of the interviewees did not have experience with how the stricter regulation of the procedure of the Counter Terrorism Centre and the Constitution Protection Office appeared in the practice. As Somogyvári said, in general, the practice of the state regarding rejection due to national security risks is an infringement of EU law as the Hungarian authorities are not sharing their assessment with the asylum seeker. Therefore, the applicant does not have any idea why she/he is considered a threat to national security, which seriously violates the principle of the equality of arms and thereby her/his right to an effective legal remedy.

As regards the lead migration and terrorism slogan, all interviewees pointed out that the hypothetical linkage between terrorists and asylum-seekers is weak and indirect. Even though all of them are working in the field of migration or national security, from 7 years up to 25 years, they did not experience the threat that terrorist organisations systematically use migration flows to attack European countries. According to the experts, this is the more expensive way to create fear among the citizens compared to using other forms of migration as most of them are highlighted. In spite of this most Hungarians fear migrants since the country wide billboard campaign started in 2015. None of the experts confirmed that the linkage between terrorism and migration is strong. On the contrary, there are some surveys that support the hypothesis that the fewest number of terrorists are among refugees. Somogyvári agreed with this assertion, but only a very low percentage of the applicants pose a risk to national security and the communication of the government has exaggerated their number. He emphasised that the issue is a hot topic on the political agenda and loses complexity due to the high populist attention.

Regarding the stereotypes concerning migrants, Somogyvári called attention to the recent changes of the German political agenda: recently a conservative Bavarian politician had stated human rights and not Christian rights should be protected and provided to all. All of our respondents pointed out that there is racist based terrorist attack against Hungarians of Roma ethnic origins but these were not classified as an act of terrorism but rather as hate crimes. Ambrus pointed out that the stereotype is over controlled in Hungary. She has long experience of mediation and travelled and worked in several countries where Muslim minorities live. In North Ossetia where more than 60 ethnicities live these stereotypes are non-existent. In comparison with neighbouring countries in the Balkans, where the level of nationalism was high, the level of hate does not give room for other types of hate. In Mostar, Bosnia, there is a university for every nation, as a sign of the level of segregation or of reconciliation. As we can see, Hungary is on the same road as this phenomenon.

As regards the potential radicalization of asylum seekers, Vadasi highlighted that some people among the asylum-seekers are open to radicalisation theoretically, but, they did not meet any of these people. The general attitude towards migrants shifted since 2015 in Hungary, as Somogyvári also pointed out. He added that the greater concern is that the majority of the population is going through a type of radicalisation. He mentioned the attitude of some border guards, policemen who are more aggressive may raise the level of fear in asylum-seekers who want to live in Hungary. The UNHCR has registered these incidents several times and has asked for investigations but an official procedure was started in very few cases. There was one case where a policeman received a fine because he kneeled on the face of an asylum-seeker.

Tálas has pointed out regarding the definition of terror and terrorism that it always needs an audience, the attention of the media is one of its key elements.

Also, something always has to happen with the terrorist group in the news otherwise they will lose their audience.

5 Conclusion

After 9/11, the recent refugee crisis in Europe has again drawn attention to the relationship between migration and terrorism. States apply different policy models for managing the national security threat in the migration context. Certain migration policies are introduced as general security measures while others are designed as a response to terrorist activities in other countries as well. States have the prerogative to decide who can enter their territory, thus border regulations may serve as an effective tool to filter out potential terrorists who intend to take advantage of migration channels. Despite this there is no demonstrable link between seeking asylum and terrorism, certain States have introduced strict control measures and other policies that have negative impact on asylum-seekers. In the current political environment, it seems impossible but international protection and national security interests should be seen as complementary and not conflicting values.

Through the detailed analysis of the Hungarian case, it is demonstrated how national security interests prevail over the human rights of asylum-seekers. As a response to the current refugee crisis, national security considerations have gradually been incorporated in the asylum legislation in order to lower the risk of abusing the migration flows by potential terrorists and not in border regulations. This choice of the type of legislation itself indicates a certain level of fear of refugees and that they pose a potential risk to the well being of nationals.

As terrorism does not have a commonly agreed definition, the use of the term is a double edged sword. There may be a fear that there is a risk to misuse of asylum procedures by people or organisations which may intend to commit acts of terrorism, but, the data does not support this in the case of Hungary. Therefore, using the term raises the level of xenophobia and the expectation and fear that some incident may happen as it already happened earlier.[130] There were other asylum-seekers who posed a threat, according to the CPO, due to their terrorist activity but it happened in silence. As the asylum-seekers' numbers dropped since 2015, the risk of terror attack committed by asylum-seekers or refugees reduced. It is a matter of time while the 'audience waits'.

130 Barbara Kőhalmi and Anita Rozália Nagy-Nádasdi Rozália "The fight against terrorism and the need for international protection: the Hungarian solution," *Refugee Law Initiative Working Paper Series* (2019): 44, https://sas-space.sas.ac.uk/9204/. (accessed June 13, 2019).

But the of question that terrorism itself as well as counter-terrorism measures both have a huge negative impact on asylum-seekers' rights to international protection starting from the access to territory and ending with living in a rather hostile community.

Terrorism means an intimidation with purpose[131] and the way it is used in the media and in legislation as well as in law enforcement mechanisms may raise negative stereotypes about migrants and asylum-seekers as potential terrorists, even though the data does not support it. Therefore, using the term has to have another reason. As the perpetrator of Brighton bombing, Patrick Megee, pointed out, that 'terrorism' has become a non-explanation designed to perpetuate injustice, repression, and many gross asymmetries of power,"[132] and, this is a quite a common sense and current description of the term.

131 Primoratz 'What is terrorism' in English "Terrorism," 5.

132 English, "Terrorism," 3.

CHAPTER 10

Caught between Unworthiness and Exclusion: Asylum Applicants and Refugees Suspected of Terrorism in Swiss Law and Practice

Nula Frei and Constantin Hruschka

1 Introduction

In October 2016, the then Director of the Swiss Federal Intelligence Service (FIS – Nachrichtendienst des Bundes) reported that the asylum procedure is not a major way of entry to Switzerland chosen by terrorist subjects, but that there are individual cases where jihadists have been identified among refugees and asylum seekers.[1] The public discourse narrative in Switzerland has until now not been too much "infected" with the mixing of terrorism and asylum, as observed in other states. The discussions about terrorism have – with some exceptions – been very much about national strategies to prevent terrorist activities (2015 National Strategy against Terrorism[2]) and radicalization (2017 National Action Plan against Radicalization[3]).

This article examines these aspects of the interlinkage between terrorism and asylum. It starts with a brief description of Swiss practice regarding persecution by terrorist groups; (2) and then goes on to an analysis of the law and practice concerning terrorist suspects seeking asylum in Switzerland; (3) it then analyzes in detail the different legal consequences of a suspicion of terrorism in asylum procedures. Thereafter, (4) the consequences of a decision excluding the person from being granted asylum are examined, in order to shed more light on the situation of terrorist subjects who cannot be deported from Switzerland. Finally, some current legal and political developments will be discussed (5) before presenting our concluding remarks (6).

1 See the report by Markus Seiler: *Nachrichtendienst-Chef: « Der IS hat in der Schweiz an Glanz verloren »,* in: Berner Zeitung of 15 October 2016, www.bernerzeitung.-ch/schweiz/standard/der-is-hat-in-der-schweiz-an-glanz-verloren/story/16954575.

2 Dated 18 September 2015, Swiss Federal Gazette (SFG) 2015 7487.

3 Swiss Security Network, *National Action Plan to Prevent and Counter Radicalisation and Violent Extremism* of 4 December 2017, available at: https://www.ejpd.admin.ch/dam/data/ejpd/aktuell/news/2017/2017-12-04/171204-nap-e.pdf.

© KONINKLIJKE BRILL NV, LEIDEN, 2020 | DOI:10.1163/9789004295995_012

2 Persons Persecuted by Terrorist Groups

There are a number of precedent setting cases where asylum-seekers claim that they are at risk of being persecuted by terrorist groups. Specifically, the rise of the IS in *Syria* and *Iraq* has led to a new set of cases of asylum-seekers invoking persecution by the IS. Generally, Swiss practice considers membership in a certain group that is targeted by IS – especially Yazidi[4] and Christians[5] – as a risk-increasing factor to be taken into account when assessing the well-founded fear of being persecuted. With regard to the Yazidi, the Swiss Federal Adminstrative Court[6] (FAC) has recognized a situation of collective persecution in the Iraqi province of Ninawa.[7] "Collective (group based) persecution" is a concept in Swiss refugee law, according to which, if such a situation exists, the mere membership of that collectively persecuted group is enough to give rise to a well-founded fear of being persecuted. Members of that group do not have to demonstrate an additional individualized risk. The FAC has also recognized a situation of collective persecution of Christians in the IS-dominated areas in the south of Syria.[8]

The targeting of certain groups by extremist and terrorist militia has also been at the core of the analysis in cases concerning female applicants from *Somalia.* There, the FAC repeatedly held that internally displaced women who do not benefit of the protection of a clan and/or a male family member are a particular target of terrorist-extremist groups such as Al-Shabaab. The FAC has accordingly recognized their refugee status in several cases.[9]

Persecution by terrorist groups being non-state persecution, the question of state protection arises. In the case of the Hazara in *Pakistan,* an ethnic group that is regularly targeted by religious extremists, the Swiss Federal Administrative Court came to the conclusion that the Pakistani State and its security forces are not able to protect the Hazara from extremist religious violence, since the State itself is often the victim of violent attacks and therefore prioritizes to defend itself rather than to protect religious minorities.[10]

4 FAC, D-3302/2014 of 8 September 2015; FAC D-4600/2014 of 29 November 2016.

5 FAC, E-7028/2014 of 6 December 2016; D-1495/2015 of 21 March 2016; D-5337/2014 of 27 October 2016; D-5884/2015 of 13 April 2017.

6 The Federal Administrative Court is the only judicial instance deciding on the provision of protection in the Swiss asylum procedure.

7 FAC, D-4600/2014 of 29 November 2016, para. 6.2.4.

8 FAC, E-7028/2014 of 6 December 2016.

9 FAC, E-7228/2013 of 8 May 2014, para. 3.3 and 3.4; Law Reports of the Swiss FAC (ATAF) 2014/27.

10 ATAF 2014/32 of 25 November 2014, para. 6.10.

In a leading case from 2011 concerning *Afghanistan*, the Federal Administrative Court ruled that the security situation in Afghanistan is extremely bad. The Afghan State is not able to protect its citizens against violence by terrorist groups (mainly the Taliban), insurgents and criminal networks.[11] An internal flight alternative may exist in Kabul, but it is available only under very strict conditions. In particular, the person concerned needs a reliable social network at the new place (i.e. relatives or friends).[12] Members of "high risk groups", such as persons who cooperate with international forces are, according to the FAC, particularly vulnerable because extremist and terrorist groups consider Muslims working for what they consider to be "faithless occupiers" to be traitors who must be severely punished.[13]

As a conclusion it can be held that persecution by terrorist groups may lead to refugee status in Swiss practice, especially if the person applying for the recognition of refugee status is a member of an ethnic minority that is specifically targeted by terrorist and extremist groups. However, the availability of state protection is often seen as available (for example Kabul being perceived as a place where internal protection may be found).[14]

3 Terrorist Suspects Seeking International Protection

The following paragraphs turn the focus away from terrorists as persecutors, on to terrorist suspects as persecuted individuals. It should first be noted that there have been only a few "clear" cases of terrorists in the Swiss asylum procedure, i.e., where it was known beyond doubt that the person concerned had committed terrorist acts. In practice, it is therefore very often necessary to determine, in the first place, if the activities and affiliations of the person concerned are to be considered "terrorist" and, secondly, if there is enough evidence to conclude that the person is actually involved in such activities or had otherwise contributed (e.g., by way of material or financial support) to those activities.

In the Swiss asylum procedure a person may be granted either asylum under the Asylum Act (AA)[15] or a temporary suspension of the removal called "provisional admission" under the Federal Act on Foreign Nationals and Integration

11 ATAF 2011/7, para. 9.7.4.

12 ATAF 2011/7, para. 9.9.2.

13 FAC, E-2802/2014 of 15 January 2015, para. 5.3.3.

14 FAC, D-5800/2016 of 23 October 2017.

15 Law Number 142.31 of the Classified Compilation of Swiss Federal Laws, to be found under https://www.admin.ch/gov/en/start/federal-law/classified-compilation.html.

(FNIA).[16] The decision is taken by the federal asylum authority, the State Secretariat for Migration (SEM). However, the granting of the residence status falls within the competency of the cantonal migration authorities. These authorities are bound by the asylum decision of the SEM. If an asylum applicant is suspected to be a terrorist, the SEM will consult with the Swiss Federal Intelligence Service (FIS) in order to assess the (likely) degree of involvement of the person in terrorist activities as this may have implications for the protection decision.

Under Swiss asylum law, there are two possibilities to exclude terrorist suspects from receiving international protection, both (currently) lead to a similar result. The first possibility is the exclusion of a terroist suspect under Article 1 F 1951 Convention, in these cases the person will be excluded from asylum and from refugee protection, and the second is the exclusion from asylum for "unworthiness" under Article 53 Asylum Act, leading to an exclusion from asylum, but to a recognition of the person as refugee. On the residence side, in both cases the person is – in principle – entitled to a provisional admission as he or she is protected from refoulement under Article 25 (3) of the Swiss Federal Constitution (SFC)[17] and under international human rights law. However, persons excluded under Article 53 AA are entitled to the rights of refugees under Articles 2–34 of the 1951 Convention, while persons excluded under Article 1F are not considered to be refugees.

Under the Swiss Criminal Code (SCC)[18] mere membership in an organization that has been declared to be a terrorist organization may constitute a criminal offence according to Article 260th SCC. Currently, Switzerland has only declared (and prohibited) Al Qaeda and IS/Daesh (and related organizations) as terrorist organizations. For other organizations, it has to be decided on a case by case basis, whether these organization are "terrorist organizations" and whether the individual is responsible for acts committed by these organizations. The majority of asylum cases where terrorism played a role for the protection decision concerned "freedom fighters." According to a new development in the decision practice, the mere membership in an organization labeled as terrorist by the EU may be sufficient to exclude the person concerned from asylum (see below 3.2). Initially, the decision of unworthiness of protection within the scope of what is today Article 53 AA was the same as for the exclusion clauses under Article 1F Refugee Convention. However, over

16 See Article 3 and 44 AA and Article 83pp FNIA. Law Number 142.20 of the Classified Compilation of Swiss Federal Laws.

17 Law Number 101 of the Classified Compilation of Swiss Federal Laws.

18 Law Number 311.0 of the Classified Compilation of Swiss Federal Laws.

time, the term "unworthiness" under the AA became broader and started in practice also to comprise acts that do not justify the exclusion from refugee status.[19] In practice, the assessment starts with an analysis whether the person is individually responsible for a terrorist act and may therefore by excluded from refugee status (3.1). If this is not the case the potential exclusion from asylum for unworthiness will be assessed (3.2). If the person had already been granted protection a revocation of status may be at stake (3.3).

3.1 *Exclusion from Refugee Status (Article 1F Refugee Convention)*

First and foremost, when a person suspected of being associated to or a member of a terrorist group applies for international protection, the exclusion clauses under Article 1F of the Refugee Convention may be applicable. Switzerland has ratified the 1951 Convention, but did not transpose the exclusion clauses into national law. Consequently, decisions regarding exclusion from refugee status are based directly on Article 1F of the Convention.[20]

To our knowledge, no asylum seeker falling into the group of concern – persons associated with terrorism or terrorist organizations – has been excluded from refugee status based on Article 1F in Switzerland[21]. However, there are a few cases before the Federal Administrative Court[22] where exclusion under Article 1F was negotiated. These cases concerned persons who were engaged in liberation movements and associated with organizations that did not pursue their goals with purely pacific means and engaged *inter alia* in armed fighting and have also committed acts against civilian targets. In these cases, the Federal Administrative Court assumes that such organizations are not to be regarded exclusively as terrorist organizations, but at the same time cannot be regarded solely as a party to a civil war if the choice of their means leads to considerable human rights violations.[23]

In line with the character of the exclusion clauses, the FAC admits that because of the grave consequences of exclusion decisions, the provisions have to

19 See for a description and the consequences of this development, JICRA (Decisions of the Asylum Appeals Commission) 1996/18, 177 ff. The Asylum Appeals Commission was replaced in 2007 by the Swiss Federal Administrative Court.

20 See e.g. JICRA 2006/29; ATAF 2010/43, 2010/44 and 2013/36.

21 Since the decisions of the first instance, the State Secretariat for Migration, are not public, cases that are not appealed against can go unnoticed.

22 Which is – as a rule – the only judicial instance in asylum matters in Switzerland as appeals to the Federal Court (the highest Court in Switzerland) in cases involving an assessment of the protection needs are excluded.

23 FAC, D-4291/2012 of 26 July 2013, para. 5.2.1 ff.

be applied restrictively.[24] Moreover, the standard of proof for the exclusion from refugee status is directly derived from the Refugee Convention looking at serious reasons for considering that (at least) one of the exclusion criteria applies. In practice, this means that it cannot be inferred merely on the basis of the rank and function of the person concerned, that he or she has participated in an act covered by the exclusion clause. To justify exclusion, the specific activity of this person or the organisational unit in which this function was exercised needs to be assessed and thoroughly investigated.[25] The SEM has to carry out a complete investigation not only with regard to the exclusion clause, but in particular on the question of the fulfilment of the complainant's refugee status, in accordance with the principle of "inclusion before exclusion".[26] If this is not the case, the Court may refer the case back to the SEM for further investigation.

The consequences of exclusion from refugee status in Switzerland are that the person's asylum claim will be rejected. The person is not recognized as a refugee, will not be granted asylum and will receive an administrative expulsion order. However, since the person fulfils the inclusion clauses of Article 1A(2) and the risk of being persecuted is equivalent, according to the jurisprudence, to the risk of a violation of Article 3 ECHR and Article 25 (3) SFC, the deportation will be suspended because of the risk of refoulement. The expulsion order will thus not be executed and the person will be granted a so-called provisional admission as a foreigner (Article 83(3) FNIA). The consequences of this (non-)status will be elaborated in more detail below.[27] It is a less favourable status than asylum, especially regarding family reunion, access to labour market, social aid, freedom of movement, and integration.

In the assessment of the exclusion clauses of the 1951 Convention the FAC generally complies with the relevant case law of the Federal Court in extradition cases[28] as well as with the relevant UNHCR Guidelines[29] and primarily considers the type of crime involved and the purpose of the offence. When assessing the applicability of Article 1F(b) of the 1951 Convention the question arises whether the committed offence was "non-political." To assume that it

24 See e.g. ATAF 2013/36, para. 5.2.1, which refers to the relevant section in the 1979 UNHCR Handbook.

25 See ATAF 2013/36, para. 5.3 and 5.4.

26 See ATAF 2013/36, para. 5.5.

27 See below, 4.

28 See in particular ATF (Law Reports of the Swiss Federal Supreme Court) 106 Ib 297 of 11 July 1980.

29 See UNHCR, Guidelines Article 1F (2003) that are regularly cited by the FAC, see e.g. JICRA 2006/29 and ATAF 2013/36.

was a political offence, there must be a close and direct causal connection between the crime committed and the alleged political purpose and aim of the crime. The political element of the offence should outweigh the non-political element. Serious crimes directed against life and limb can only be described as political offences if the offence was the only means of safeguarding the elementary interests at stake and achieving the set political goal.[30] Military operations in the context of internal armed conflicts and insurrections generally fulfil the requirements for the attribution of political character and the killing of a human being in the context of a civil war or an open armed conflict may appear to be an appropriate means.[31] However, if the means used are disproportionate, the political nature of the acts can be denied and therefore lead to an exclusion decision under Article 1F(b) Refugee Convention.

One of the precedent setting cases concerned an applicant who had been an active member of the *Liberation Tigers of Tamil Eelam* (LTTE).[32] He had inter alia served as a soldier and later as a vice-commander of a unit of 40 to 100 LTTE fighters, who had been actively involved in various armed confrontations with the Sri Lankan army, in which he also fired at soldiers and was himself injured several times, in some cases severely. He was also responsible for the training of his subordinates.[33] The Federal Administrative Court considered it proven that during his "career" with the LTTE, the applicant had identified with its objectives and approach. The Court therefore assumed that he accepted and approved the strategy of the military wing of the LTTE to use force and even supported it militantly. The Court therefore had to assess whether his acts fell under the exclusion clause of "serious non-political crimes" according to Article 1F(b) Refugee Convention. It considered that the applicant was responsible for acts of violence in the context of armed conflicts between the LTTE and the Sri Lankan army, that he had killed and injured members of the Sri Lankan army or was responsible for the commission of such acts by the combatants subordinated to him. However, the Court did not see any indications that he was directly or indirectly involved in attacks on the civilian population. Assuming that the complainant's actions took place with regard to the LTTE's objective of achieving autonomy for the Tamil-dominated areas in the north and east of Sri Lanka, the Court found that his actions had a political

30 ATAF 2011/29, para. 8.3.3.1.

31 ATF 106 Ib 307 of 11 July 1980, para. 3c; Walter Kälin/Jörg Künzli, Article 1F[b]: Freedom Fighters, Terrorists and the Notion of Serious Non-Political Crimes, *International Journal of Refugee Law*, 2000/12, Special Supplementary Issue on Exclusion, p. 67.

32 ATAF 2011/29.

33 ATAF 2011/29.

background, personal or economic motives not being apparent.[34] In view of these considerations and taking into account the fact that the exclusion clauses should be applied restrictively, the Court classified the acts of the complainant as political offences.[35] The applicant was recognized as a refugee. He was, however, subsequently excluded from asylum under Article 53 Asylum Act due to unworthiness.[36]

Another case concerned a Pakistani citizen from the Balochistan Province who had been a member of the insurgent *Baloch Republican Party* (BRP), inter alia as a district president, central committee member and vice president. In Pakistan, he had been accused of treason and the assassination of members of the state security forces.[37] The SEM found that there were serious grounds for imputing responsibility for serious non-political crimes within the meaning of Article 1F(b) Refugee Convention, because he had in the past held a leadership function not only with the Baloch Republican Party (BRP), but also with the Baloch Republican Army (BRA), which had been responsible for the killing of numerous politicians and civilians as well as for many other serious non-political crimes. However, the State Secretariat also came to the conclusion that in view of various circumstances – in particular the complainant's withdrawal from the BRP in 2014, his detachment from the personal environment concerned and the associated critical examination of the BRP's and the BRA's actions, as well as the fact that the complainant's life was marked by tragic family blows and numerous deprivations – the application of the exclusion clause proved to be disproportionate and was therefore not activated.[38]

The threshold for the application of the exclusion clause of Article 1F(b) is generally quite high in Swiss practice.[39] The two cases mentioned here demonstrate that this is also the case for persons who are associated with groups that can be defined at least partly as terrorist. The practice of the Court suggests that acts of warfare such as the killing of soldiers, executed in the context of a freedom fight or struggle for self-determination, can be seen as political and will, therefore, not fall under the exclusion clause of Article 1F(b) Refugee convention. If the acts are, however, directed against civilian targets (such as killing of politicians or civilians), they will be considered as terrorist and hence a serious non-political crime. Moreover, since the Swiss practice follows the view

34 ATAF 2011/29, para. 8.3.3.2.
35 ATAF 2011/29, para. 8.3.3.2.
36 See below, 3.2.
37 FAC, D-4172/2018 of 6 August 2018.
38 FAC, D-4172/2018, para. 5.4.1.
39 See, Frei, in: OSAR (ed.) Handbuch zum Asyl- und Wegweisungsverfahren, 2nd ed. 2015, p. 210 ff.

that Article 1F(b), other than 1F(a) and (c), contains an element of proportionality, the fact that applicants have withdrawn from the terrorist organization and distanced themselves from the ideology of the organization can lead to the exclusion clause not being applied out of proportionality considerations.

In sum, the exclusion clauses under Article 1F are rarely ever applied and to our knowledge have never been applied to a person involved in a terrorist group. This can be due to the fact that – to the knowledge of the authors – no "high profile terrorists" have ever applied for asylum in Switzerland. Another reason might be that the practical consequences of the exclusion from asylum under Article 53 AA are generally the same as those of exclusion under Article 1F, whereas the threshold for exclusion is much lower under the national provision, as will be shown in the following section.

3.2 *Exclusion from Asylum and/or Provisional Admission*

If a person is not excluded from refugee status, their actions can still lead to exclusion from asylum under national law. Asylum is the legal status that is granted to persons who qualify as refugees in Switzerland. According to Article 49 AA, asylum is granted if the person qualifies as refugee and if there are no grounds for excluding the person from asylum. The most relevant ground for exclusion from asylum is "unworthiness": According to Article 53 AA, refugees shall not be granted asylum if (a) they are unworthy of asylum due to serious misconduct; (b) they have violated or endanger Switzerland's internal or external security; or (c) they have been subject to a (criminal-law) expulsion order.

If a refugee is considered unworthy of asylum within the meaning of one of the alternatives of Article 53 AA, they will be recognized as refugees but will not be granted asylum and will therefore receive an (administrative) expulsion order. However, as refugees are protected from refoulement in Article 33(1) Refugee Convention and Article 25(2) SFC, the expulsion order will not be executed and will instead be replaced by a provisional admission.

The first two alternatives of unworthiness under Article 53 AA, namely, serious misconduct (a) and a violation or danger to Switzerland's internal or external security (b) can both be relevant in the context of terrorist suspects seeking protection. The alternative (c), applicants who have received a criminal-law expulsion order, is less important in practice because it presupposes that the person has already been long enough in Switzerland to be subject to a full criminal procedure. We will thus focus on the first two alternatives and describe their application in practice in the following paragraphs.

To date, the practice in relation to terrorist suspects was mainly centered on paragraph (a) of Article 53, serious misconduct, which will be described in paragraph 3.2.1 below. However, in a recent judgement of 25 September 2018,[40] the Court has, for the first time, applied paragraph (b) in a case concerning a person supposedly involved with a terrorist organization (see below, 3.2.2.).

3.2.1 "Serious misconduct"

"Serious misconduct" is defined as any act that corresponds to the abstract definition of a "felony" under Article 10(2) SCC.[41] "Felonies" are offences that are punishable by more than three years of imprisonment (in contrast to misdemeanors, which are offences that are punishable by custodial sentences not exceeding three years or a monetary penalty).

For the application of the exclusion clause under Article 53(a) AA, it is irrelevant whether the reprehensible act has a political character or not.[42] "Serious misconduct" thus also covers offences that would *not* constitute a serious crime within the meaning of Article 1F(b) Refugee Convention, either because they do not reach the threshold of a serious crime or because they are of a political nature.

The standard of proof for the application of Article 53(a) AA is the same as for Article 1F Refugee Convention: No strict proof is required for criminal offences that are committed abroad and/or before the asylum application, "serious reasons for considering" that the person concerned is guilty of a criminal offence within the meaning of the above provisions are sufficient.[43]

Different constellations can be identified that may be related to terrorism:

- First of all, many acts of a terrorist nature are defined as felonies according to the Swiss Criminal Code, such as homicide (Art. 111), murder (Art. 112), assault (Art. 122), false imprisonment and abduction (Art. 183), hostage taking (Art. 185), causing an explosion (Art. 223), manufacturing of explosives (Art. 226), criminal damage to electrical installations, hydraulic or protective structures (Art. 228), endangering public safety with weapons (Art. 260^{quater}), high treason (Art. 265), subversive propaganda (Art. 275bis) and many more. A person who has committed such acts (abroad or in Switzerland) may therefore be excluded from asylum according to Article 53(a) AA. However, cases of persons having directly

40 See for a review and commentary: Frehner/Hruschka, Asylgewährung als moralischer Akt? in: Asyl 1/19, p. 43 ff.

41 JICRA 1993/8 para. 6 p. 49 ff., JICRA 1996/18 para. 5–7 p. 173 ff., JICRA 1993 No. 8 para. 6 p. 49 ff., JICRA 1996/5–7 p. 173 ff., JICRA 1993/8 para. 6 p. 49 ff., JICRA 2002/9.

42 JICRA 2002/9 para. 7b p. 79 s.

43 See Message of the Federal Council on the Asylum Act, BBl (Swiss Federal Gazette) 1996 II 73.

committed such terrorist attacks are, as already mentioned, not known in the Swiss asylum practice until now.

- Much more frequently cases may occur where the asylum-seeking person is associated with a terrorist group, be it as member, sympathizer or supporter. However, only two organizations are prohibited in Switzerland because of their terrorist nature: Al-Qaeda and the Islamic State as well as all cover and successor groups to those two organizations. According to the Federal Act on the Proscription of the Groups « Al-Qaeda » and « Islamic State » and Associated Organisations from 12 December 2014,[44] any person who participates in one of those groups, supports them in human resources or material terms, organises propaganda, recruits for them or promotes their activities in any other way is liable to a custodial sentence not exceeding five years or to a monetary penalty.[45]
- For other organizations that are not legally banned, it has to be decided on a case-by-case analysis whether the organization may be considered terrorist or not. The Swiss Criminal Code defines membership or support to a criminal organization as a felony as well. According to Article 260ter Criminal Code, any person who participates in an organisation, the structure and personal composition of which is kept secret and which pursues the objective of committing crimes of violence or securing a financial gain by criminal means, and any person who supports such an organisation in its criminal activities, is liable to a custodial sentence not exceeding five years or to a monetary penalty. The participation or support without proof of the individual contribution to a concrete offence is sufficient. Organizations within the meaning of Article 260ter of the Criminal Code are not only mafia-like crime syndicates but also terrorist groups. On the other hand, extremist parties (in principle), opposition political groups and organisations that struggle for political power in their home country by appropriate means or fight for freedom against dictatorial regimes are not covered by the definition of Article 260.ter[46] According to the case-law of the Federal Court, support or participation in the

44 Federal Act of 12 December 2014 on the Proscription of the Groups "Al-Qaeda" and "Islamic State" and Associated Organisations, Law Number 122 of the Classified Compilation of Swiss Federal Laws.

45 Article 2(1) of the Federal Act of 12 December 2014 on the Proscription of the Groups "Al-Qaeda" and "Islamic State" and Associated Organisations.

46 ATF 130 II 337, para. 6 p. 344 f., ATF 131 II 235 para. 2.12 p. 240 ff., ATF 133 IV 58 para. 5 p. 63 ff.

> organization is required, which means functional integration into the organization. Mere sympathy or passive membership is not sufficient.[47]

If it can thus be established that a refugee is a member of a terrorist organization, in view of the existing threat of criminal sanctions, this would per se constitute a serious misconduct which would lead to the exclusion of asylum according to Art. 53(a) Asylum Act. As indicated above, a criminal conviction is not necessary, "serious reasons to consider" that the person's membership fulfils the criteria of Article 260ter Criminal Code would be enough. According to the case law, mere membership in a terrorist organisation is sufficient to justify unworthiness for asylum. An individual contribution to a crime would then no longer have to be examined.[48]

To our knowledge, no cases exist where a person has been excluded from asylum under Article 53(a) Asylum Act based on mere membership in a terrorist organization (see, however, Article 53(b) and new case-law, below 3.2.2.). In cases concerning an applicant who had been member of the TKP/ML (Communist Party of Turkey/Marxist–Leninist), the Federal Administrative Court came to the conclusion that the Party itself could not be considered a terrorist organization.[49] It justified its conclusion with the fact that the organization does not figure on the so called EU terrorist list[50] and neither the Swiss Federal Office of Police (fedpol) nor the German "Verfassungsschutz" (the German Intelligence Agency) generally consider the TKP/ML to be a terrorist organization. Furthermore, the party is not prohibited in Switzerland. Although the party can be classified as an extremist and sometimes violent movement, it can, in view of the Federal Administrative Court, not be equated with a terrorist group. Exclusion from asylum based on mere membership with the TKP/ML was therefore not seen as appropriate.[51]

If the organization is not itself prohibited or considered terrorist as a whole, the individual responsibility of the applicant must be assessed. According to the case-law, it is necessary to determine the applicant's individual

47 ATF 133 IV 58 p. 74.

48 JICRA 2002/9, para. 7c; FAC E-3603/2006 of 14 August 2009, para. 5.3.

49 See FAC, E-3602/2006 of 28 July 2008 and FAC, D-6464/2006 of 26 February 2009.

50 Council Common Position 2001/931/CFSP of 27 December 2001 on the application of specific measures to combat terrorism. The Annex to this Decision contains a list of persons, groups and entities to which Articles 2, 3 and 4 of Common Position 2001/931/CFSP apply. It is regularly updated (approximately every six months) the latest available update at time of writing was: Council Decision (CFSP) 2018/1084 of 30 July 2018 updating the list of persons, groups and entities subject to Articles 2, 3 and 4 of Common Position 2001/931/CFSP on the application of specific measures to combat terrorism, and repealing Decision (CFSP) 2018/475.

51 FAC, D-3525/2006 of 9 July 2009, para. 5.3.3.

contribution to the offence, as well as the seriousness of the offence, the motives of the offender and any justification or defenses. In the case mentioned above concerning involvement in the TKP/ML, the FAC gave indications which elements need to be assessed inter alia: the concrete role that the applicant had or still has in the organization, the tasks he was involved in and the competences which were assigned to him, his hierarchical position, with whom he had contact, from whom he received orders or to whom he issued such orders and how communication took place within and outside the organization.[52] Furthermore, the principle of proportionality must be respected: The time passed since the offence, the offender's age at that time and any change in living conditions must be weighed against the consequences of exclusion from asylum.[53]

In the case mentioned above concerning an ex-member of the LTTE, vice-commander of a unit of 40 to 100 LTTE fighters, who had also been responsible for the training of his subordinates,[54] the FAC did not find enough indications for the applicability of the exclusion clauses of Article 1F(b) Refugee Convention, but it did conclude from the facts that the applicant had provided support to the LTTE's violent organization over a comparatively long period of time "to an extent not to be underestimated." In addition, in the opinion of the Court, it could be assumed that the applicant did indeed identify with the LTTE's aims and procedures. In the view of the Court, there were thus sufficient indications of "serious misconduct" in the sense of Article 53(a) Asylum Act.[55] Furthermore, the Court did not find the exclusion from asylum altogether disproportionate, especially since the applicant was allowed to remain in Switzerland (as a provisionally admitted refugee) and therefore the consequences of exclusion were not as serious (as if the person had been excluded from refugee status).[56]

However, it is generally necessary that the person concerned has individual responsibility for the offence. This is not the case if the applicant merely provides support to an organization considered terrorist, without acting as an accomplice or aiding and abetting in a concrete crime. For example, in a case concerning a sympathizer of the LTTE, the applicant had stated that he was not a member of the LTTE, but merely hid weapons and carried out spying activities for the LTTE on corresponding instructions. The FAC ruled that, even

52 FAC, D-3560/2006 of 9 July 2009, para. 5.3.

53 See e.g. Hruschka, in: Spescha et.al (eds.), Kommentar Migrationsrecht, 5th ed. 2019, Article 53 N 6.

54 See above, 3.1.

55 ATAF 2011/29, para. 9.3.

56 ATAF 2011/29, para. 9.4.

though it could not be ruled out that the assistance made a contribution to achieving the objectives of the LTTE, it was not known in what context and whether the weapons hidden by the complainant were used. The same applied to his support services in the form of the procurement of information and material such as batteries. Since the complainant did not take part in combat operations and deliberately decided against membership of the LTTE, i.e., against participation in the armed struggle, it would lead too far to assume a general responsibility of the applicant for acts of the LTTE. Even taking into account the fact that acts committed abroad do not require strict proof according to Article 53(a) Asylum Act, no participation of the applicant in any act of the LTTE could be assessed as a significant contribution, in the sense of a crime, was evident from the files.[57]

Another case concerned a couple who were both members of the Kurdistan Workers' Party (PKK). The PKK has not been declared as a terrorist organization in Switzerland; and, in contrast to the practice of various German courts, mere PKK membership has not yet led to a conviction in Switzerland on the basis of Art. 260ter Criminal Code. The Federal Administrative Court has stated that there was no doubt that the PKK is responsible for a large number of terrorist acts inside and outside Turkey, but that it is also beyond doubt that its political motivation, and to some extent its warfare, correspond to that of a conflict party of a civil war. It is therefore neither appropriate to define all acts of the PKK as acts of war with the consequence that they cannot serve as grounds for exclusion from asylum, nor would it be appropriate to base exclusion of asylum solely on the basis of membership in the PKK.[58]

While the husband stated that he had actively participated in combat as a fighter for the PKK, the wife brought forward that she never actively participated in hostilities, but merely kept watch behind the front. On occasions, she participated in the mine clearance of strategically important areas. Even though she claimed that none of the mines ever exploded because they were defective, the Court concluded that she, like her husband, had clearly participated in military activities aimed at taking enemy combatants out of action and accepting the killing and injury of civilians. The fact that she was promoted several times, also indicated, in view of the Court, that she played an important role in the military hierarchy. In sum, the Court considered that both applicants took part in hostilities as PKK fighters and committed acts of violence themselves. Both also took part in PKK congresses as delegates, which

57 FAC, D-7471/2014 of 1 March 2018, para. 5.3.2.

58 See JICRA 2002/9, para. 7c; FAC D-11/2008 of 9 July 2009, para. 6.2; cited in ATAF 2011/10, para. 6.1.

underlines their agreement at the time with PKK activities, including military ones. Though they had in the meantime resigned from the PKK, the Court was of the view that they had not fundamentally distanced themselves from or condemned the PKK's acts of violence; their resignations from the party were essentially based on personal disappointment with the party and certain statements by Abdullah Öcalan and not on insight into the reprehensibility of the military means used in the fight for the rights of the Kurds. It therefore found both applicants to be unworthy of asylum due to serious misconduct.[59]

3.2.2 Violation of or Danger to Switzerland's Internal or External Security

The second alternative under Art. 53 AA provides for unworthiness to be granted asylum if the person violated or threatens Switzerland's internal or external security. The terms internal and external security of Switzerland are indeterminate legal terms ("unbestimmte Rechtsbegriffe") and must therefore be interpreted by the courts. The terms used in Art. 53 AA are also used in Art. 63 para. 2 AA with regard to the possibility to revoke asylum and are thus generally interpreted consistently. For the latter definition, the FAC holds that it is, *inter alia* due to the internationalisation of security dimensions, difficult to distinguish strictly the terms from one another.[60] In the relevant provision of the Swiss Constitution (Article 121 (2) SFC) the differentiation between internal and external security was waived in the 1998 revision process in favour of the formulation "security of the country". According to the FAC, "security" has to be seen as any "threat to the primacy of state power in the military or political sphere; one must think of the concrete threat posed by terrorism, violent extremism, the forbidden intelligence service, organized crime as well as actions and aspirations that seriously endanger Switzerland's foreign relations or aim at a violent change in the state order".[61] Since these facts are often sufficient to justify the existence of a reason for exclusion pursuant to Article 53(a) AA, Article 53(b) AA rarely played a role in practice until recently. However, a precedent setting case of September 2018 may have the potential to alter this approach.[62]

The case concerned a person that had been identified as a member of Komalên Ciwan (a youth organization of the PKK). He had been participating at

59 ATAF 2011/10, para. 6.2.

60 ATAF 2013/23, para. 3.2.

61 ATAF 2018 VI/5, para. 3.4 referring to Swiss Federal Gazette 1996 II 1, p. 72.

62 ATAF 2018 VI/5.

peaceful protesting activities in Switzerland and the Netherlands. The Swiss Intelligence Service (FIS) had the suspicion that he was involved in terrorist activities, however, there have been no proven criminal offences involved. In its judgment, the FAC confirmed the asylum exclusion decided by the SEM even though the applicant had not committed any offence that would lead to criminal liability and had stated that he had not been involved in further activities with the PKK and its youth organizations. The FAC held that the evidence was sufficient to exclude the applicant from asylum as he was not able to prove that he has not been part ot activities furthering terrorist goals. This approach alters the relationship between the different alternatives contained in Article 53 AA. The extensive interpretation of the term "endangerment of the internal or external security of Switzerland" contained in the judgement means that Article 53(b) AA becomes a quasi catch-all clause for security related concerns in asylum decision making. The Court explicitly opens up the definition of "endangerment of the security of Switzerland" to all actions that could impair Switzerland's policy of neutrality. It thereby equals the neutrality interests to Switzerland's security and explicitly emphasises that the interest in protecting good relations with all states, regardless of their political organisation, can (and must) be considered as a state interest in the context of the grounds for asylum exclusion.[63] This interpretation of the scope of "security of Switzerland" also differs considerably from the term used internationally and under European law to describe a threat to internal security or order that justifies expulsion.[64]

As mentioned above, the consequence of asylum exclusion is that the person concerned will, even though recognized as a refugee, not be granted asylum and will receive a "provisional admission" instead. The same consequence arises from the application of the exclusion clauses in Article 1F of the Refugee Convention, with the only difference that in the former case, persons provisionally admitted as refugees are also entitled to the bundle of refugee rights from the Convention, while in the second case they do not.

3.3 *Revocation of Status*

While the measures described above concern the granting of protection in an asylum procedure, there are also cases where the person had already received protection in an asylum procedure and becomes a suspect of terrorist acts. In these cases there are several possibilites for migration authorities to revoke the

63 FAC, E-2412/2014 of 25 September 2018, para. 3.6.1.

64 See on this the review of the decision by Frehner/Hruschka in: Asyl 1/2019, p. 43.

status of a person who is associated with terrorist crimes: revocation of refugee status, revocation of asylum, expulsion (and subsequent extinction of status).

A *revocation of refugee status* is normally not possible simply because a person poses a threat to the host country. The precondition for the revocation of refugee status is the existence of an exclusion ground under the 1951 Convention. In some cases, also, other reasons to end refugee protection may apply. For example, there have been cases of terrorist suspects who have travelled as "foreign fighters" to their home countries, where the Swiss authorities have applied the cessation clause of Article 1C(1) Refugee Convention. In a case that was treated by the Cantonal Administrative Court of Basel-Stadt, a young man, son of Iraqi refugees, had been under observation by the FIS, because of his contacts to several known (and convicted) Iraqi nationals active in the context of the Islamic State. The young man was seen as a threat to Switzerland's internal and external security. The State Secretariat for Migration revoked his refugee status because he had travelled back to Iraq and had been issued an Iraqi passport.[65] Also, in a publicly discussed case of a "hate preacher" from Biel (he was acting as an imam and had allegedly incited hatred and called for violence against non-muslims), the authorities did revoke his refugee status because he had travelled to his home country (Libya) at least twelve times within four years.[66]

When revocation of refugee status is not possible, *asylum may still be revoked*, according to Article 63(3) of the Asylum Act, if the refugee has violated or represents a threat to Switzerland's internal or external security or has committed a particularly serious criminal offence. Revocation of asylum does not affect the status as a refugee. In practice, a revocation of asylum will regularly lead to a provisional admission of the person concerned. In essence, such revocations constitute a "downgrade" of the person's status from asylum to provisional admission. The most emblematic and publically discussed case where revocation of asylum was applied in the context of terrorism concerned the case of a young man, son of recognized Palestinian refugees from Jordan, who had travelled *inter alia* to Kenya to (allegedly) join the Al-Shabaab militia and later on to Syria, where he (allegedly) joined the Al-Nusra Front and was eventually killed in in Iraq.[67] The case became publicly known in 2012 when he was arrested by the Kenyan authorities and accused of involvement in terrorist

65 Court of Appeal of Basel-Land, VD.2016.162 of 12 August 2016.

66 FAC, D-4877/2017 of 19 September 2017.

67 https://www.bielertagblatt.ch/nachrichten/biel/terrorist-aus-biel-soll-gefallen-sein.; https://www.srf.ch/news/schweiz/bieler-gymnasiast-beim-is-dschihadisten-mutter-enthuellt-terrorplan-in-der-schweiz.

activities. Shortly after, the FIS requested the SEM to revoke the asylum decision, because it disposed of information that he had travelled to a Jihadist region as a voluntary combatant and therefore constituted a considerable threat to the external and internal security of Switzerland. The SEM followed the request of the FIS. Subsequently, the Federal Office of Police (fedpol) imposed an entry ban on him.[68] The main differences in revocation cases under Article 63(2) AA to first asylum decisions concern evidentiary issues. If a status is to be revoked, the burden of proof is on the SEM.[69] No formal proof is needed, but a substantial suspicion has to be established and mere speculations do not suffice to justify an exclusion decision.[70] The FAC made it clear in another case that from a material point of view the necessary threat to the internal or external security of Switzerland is the same for protection and for revocation decisions. The revocation is "dependent on the unworthiness of protection in the sense of Article 53 AA", but this unworthiness needs to be qualified to justify a revocation of the asylum status and the principle of proportionality also needs to be adhered to.[71] However, there are no cases that we were able to track where it was found that an exclusion from the asylum status would be disproportionate. The proportionality assessment in these cases often refers to the fact that the person will not be deported and will receive a provisional admission.

There is also the possibility that an expulsion order by fedpol pursuant to Article 68 FNIA may end the asylum status. If the expulsion order is issued for security reasons there is no independent appeals body, only an internal appeal at the Federal Department for Police and Justice (EJPD) is possible.[72] In such cases the person will regularly also be subject to status revocation. However, an execution of the deportation order would be a violation of Article 3 ECHR and is usually suspended in practice.[73]

4 Consequences of Exclusion

As shown above, a person who is suspected to be a "terrorist" (i.e., being member of a terrorist organization or having him- or herself committed acts of a terrorist nature) will usually – if the inclusion criteria for refugee status or

68 See ATAF 2013/23.

69 ATAF 2013/23, para. 3.3 citing JICRA 2006/29, para 4.1 and 4.3 as well as ATAF 2011/11, para. 6.

70 Ibid.

71 See FAC, D-3858/2017 of 17 October 2017, para. 5.1.

72 See FAC, F-1116/2018 of 28 May 2018.

73 See Federal Supreme Court, 2C-584/2018 of 9 July 2018.

human rights law refoulement protection are applicable – be granted a provisional admission.

4.1 *Non-status*

Provisional admissions are regulated by Article 83 pp. FNIA. The provisional admission is only a substitute measure due to the (legal or practical) impossibility of deportation. It is therefore no legal status, and persons with a provisional admission are, according to the law, still obliged to leave Switzerland.[74] Consequently, if a person with a provisional admission leaves Switzerland the provisional admission ceases. Persons admitted provisionally by the SEM are assigned to one canton. They receive a renewable document (confirmation of their presence and legal status) by their canton of residence for a maximum of twelve months. It will be extended after twelve months if the reasons for the provisional admission still persist. In order to move to another canton, an application to the Federal State Secretariat for Migration is necessary. According to Article 85(4) FNIA, the decision on the change of canton can only be contested on the ground that it violates the principle of family unity, any other grounds for challenging a negative decision on change of canton is excluded.

Within the canton, persons temporarily admitted are normally free to choose their place of residence. If they depend on social aid, the cantonal authorities can oblige them to live in collective centers (usually centers where asylum applicants are accommodated as well). However, this restriction is not possible for refugees who are temporarily admitted, since they benefit from freedom of movement under Article 26 Refugee Convention.[75] Since 1 January 2019, persons provisionally admitted as foreigners are allowed to work if certain conditions are met. There is no need for application for a work permit (any more), but the employer has to report to the authorities the salary, the activity and the place of work (Article 85a FNIA). Already, since 2016, there are no restrictions regarding priority (of other groups) on the labour market (see Article 85(6) FNIA).

Family reunion is restricted for all persons with a provisional admission. The most relevant restrictions are financial and time-wise: only three years

74 This "non-status" is one of the main arguments for a reform of the provisional admission in a process, which was (re-)launched through a report on the provisional admission by the SEM in October 2016 (available at: https://www.sem.admin.ch/sem/fr/home/aktuell/news/2016/ref_2016-10-14.html) and which is still debated and assessed by the Swiss parliament. "Terrorists" are one of the "groups" mentioned that would need to be excluded from a residence permit even if provisional admissions would in future lead to a legal residence status.

75 See also ATAF 2012/2, para. 5.

after the admission can an application for family reunification be introduced (Article 85(7) FLF) and the conditions to grant family reunification essentially depend on whether the person who is already in Switzerland has suitable housing available (i.e., big enough to host the family) and the family will not depend on social aid. This applies for both foreigners and refugees who are provisionally admitted, because the Refugee Convention does not contain a binding provision regarding the right to family unity.[76]

Social aid is granted differently for foreigners and refugees provisionally admitted. Provisionally admitted foreigners receive the same form and amount of social aid like asylum seekers. This means that the level of support is less than the level offered to persons resident in Switzerland and support is – by law – normally to be provided in the form of benefits in kind. On the other hand, provisionally admitted refugees benefit from a right to equal treatment within the "group" of refugees (Article 3 of the 1951 Convention) and with nationals regarding social security (Article 24 of the 1951 Convention). They therefore receive the same social aid as refugees with asylum, which is essentially the same one as for Swiss nationals.

In sum, the legal status of persons with a provisional admission is considerably less "attractive" than the one for persons with asylum or foreigners in general. The freedom of movement is restricted, social aid is lower, family reunification is constrained. However, the recent removal of some of the legal and practical obstacles to access the labour market may make it more likely for a provisionally admitted person to become independent of social aid. Despite this development, integration possibilities are seriously hampered by this status, as also, e.g., with regard to taxes, travel outside Switzerland and practical access to housing as well as to necessities of daily life. It is indicative for the "status" of these persons that official statistics do not count them within the permanent resident population (unlike refugees and all other persons holding a longer-term residence permit).

4.2 *(No) Durable Solution*

Furthermore, for persons having received a provisional admission as a consequence of being a terrorist (suspect), it is practically impossible to receive a durable residence permit under the so-called hardship clause (Article 84(5) FNIA) as the granting of such a residence permit is *inter alia* dependent on "social integration." Social integration is seen not to have materialized if a

76 ATAF 2017 VII/4.

person is supporting a terrorist group in any manner whatsoever (other reasons comprise a non-negligable criminal record and the "denial of integration").[77]

The practical impossibility to receive a residence permit also has consequences on the chances of further integration of the person including the (im) possibility of naturalization. Terrorist suspects face obstacles both with regard to the formal and the material criteria for naturalization under the Federal Act on Nationalization (FLN), which as a rule will permanently hinder their access to Swiss citizenship.

Already, the formal criteria of Article 9 FLN may with difficulty be fulfilled by a terrorist suspect as *inter alia* a minimum of ten years of residence with a residence permit, and the holding of a permanent residence permit (the so-called "permit C"), are required for naturalization, which is, as shown above, almost impossible for persons excluded from refugee status and/or asylum due to an affiliation with terrorism.

On the substantive side, Article 11 FLN enumerates three material conditions for naturalization: The applicant must be successfully integrated, be familiar with the "Swiss way of life" and must not pose a danger to Switzerland's internal or external security. It is evident that the element of posing a danger to Switzerland's internal or external security is, as a rule, hindering the access to a C-permit and to naturalization, if the person was excluded from asylum. Moreover, a candidate for naturalization is required to commit to the democratic institutions of the country. Applicants whose attitude does not unequivocally exclude violence as a means of political conflict may on this ground be excluded from naturalization.[78]

These criteria were, for example, contested in the case of a young American citizen, who had applied for Swiss citizenship.[79] Although not a case related to asylum, it illustrates well the criteria mentioned above. The applicant has been in contact with several persons who played an active role in the violent *extremist scene in Northern Ireland,* most of them IRA activists. He had established contacts with them at solidarity events and social forums in Italy and Northern Ireland. While the SEM at first instance concluded that the information provided by the federal intelligence service FIS was enough to conclude that he constituted a threat to Switzerland's internal or external security, the FAC came to a different conclusion. After having established that the potential danger posed by the IRA and their supporters to Switzerland's internal or external security today appears to be minimal, if any, and the mere fact of being a member

77 See on the general requirements, Bolzli, in: Spescha et al. (eds.) Kommentar Migrationsrecht, 5th edition 2019, Article 84 para. 10 ff.

78 See FAC, C-2946/2008 of 21 June 2011 and ATAF 2013/34.

79 See FAC, C-2946/2008 of 21 June 2011.

or sympathizer of this group does not in itself constitute a threat, the Court observed that the contacts of the applicant with persons from the IRA were loose and superficial, of a rather collegial nature. In its decision the FAC held that the applicant had been able to credibly demonstrate that his motives had a social character and that he firmly believed in non-violence.[80] Moreover, the Court pointed out that anti-capitalist views overlapping with ideas of left-wing extremist groups are not hindering naturalization as long as they are pursued and implemented by legal (peaceful) means. It stressed that the only decisive factor is the possible threat to internal security, which has to be at least individualized and realistic.

Another case concerned a couple from Sri Lanka that had applied for naturalization. In their case, the federal intelligence service had come to the conclusion that the couple were long-time activists of the LTTE. The husband was managing director of a jewelry store in Switzerland, and the authorities were of the view that he supported the LTTE financially with the help of his wife in that they executed cash transfers from Europe to Sri Lanka, using their jewelry company as a cover. The Court emphasized that persons who apply for citizenship do not have to deny their cultural identity which is also protected by fundamental rights. Accordingly, a commitment such as that for the Tamil cause in principle is no obstacle to naturalization, as long as such activities are non-violent and do not affect Switzerland's security interests. However, the applicants were not able to overturn the suspicion that they contributed to the financing of the LTTE's activities by enabling a steady flow of money from Switzerland to the war zone. This indirect support was not to be classified as insignificant in the Court's view, because the money collected for the LTTE, during the civil war, in Switzerland contained a potential for conflict and violence within the Tamil diaspora that should not be underestimated and there were indications that the applicants continued to organise cash transports to Sri Lanka even after the military defeat of the LTTE. Even though the LTTE has been destroyed militarily and currently posed only a low risk for the security of Switzerland and the money transfers served mainly humanitarian purposes, it could, in the Court's view, not be ruled out that the LTTE or a successor organisation could resume armed combat. The "informal" cash transports to Sri Lanka were therefore still problematic with regard to the internal or external security of Switzerland, which led to the court confirming the exclusion from naturalization.[81]

80 FAC, C-2946/2008 of 21 June 2011.

81 ATAF 2015/1, para. 6.3.6.

In another case from the LTTE environment, the court came to a different conclusion as no money transfer was involved. The applicant for citizenship had been working as the headmaster of an association called TESS, which had set itself the task of offering courses in the Tamil language and culture. No political or economic objectives or purposes were pursued. Because of his commitment, the first instance authority suspected the applicant of being directly involved in the LTTE's activities. The Court, however, saw those concerns to be of a theoretical nature. The FIS did not claim that he actually exerted influence or otherwise attempted to propagandise within the TESS and the applicant was not accused of concrete acts that would be illegitimate in a democratic state. Thus, the FAC concluded that the information in question did not constitute sufficient grounds for the assumption that the applicant posed a relevant threat to the internal or external security of Switzerland.[82]

Finally, according to the practice, a threat to internal or external security of Switzerland can also arise from persons who, due to their association with extremist organizations, pose a threat to the good relations of Switzerland with other States. As emphasized in the case-law, there is the possibility to refuse to grant authorization to naturalization when the candidate poses a threat to Switzerland's international relations. This will be the case, for example, if a person has been active in or for organisations whose activities are likely to destabilise the political situation in one State and its neighbouring territories and, as a result, is capable to jeopardise the good relations between Switzerland and third States. This is justified with the argument that Switzerland's security situation also depends, to a significant extent, on the quality of its relations with third countries, with international cooperation being of crucial importance.[83] According to administrative practice, it is sufficient that concrete evidence raises fears of such a threat, without it being necessary that the latter has already occurred.[84]

This standard had, for example, been applied in the case of an Algerian citizen who not only had a commitment within the Algerian opposition, but also maintained relations with an Islamist organization (the Islamic Salvation Front, ISF), and was even considered a terrorist by the authorities of his home country, which refused to renew his national passport.[85] The first instance authority and subsequently also the Federal Administrative Court were of the

82 ATAF 2013/34, para. 7.3.2.

83 Gutzwiller, Droit de la nationalité et fédéralisme en Suisse, Geneva 2008, p. 233 and 241; TFE 129 II 193.

84 See Uebersax et al., Ausländerrecht, Basel 2009, Chap. 12.

85 FAC, C-1124/2006 of 21 August 2009, para. 5.

view that since he was to be considered as a "persona non grata" in Algeria because of his political actions, his naturalization would irritate the authorities of that State and, consequently, damage the quality of relations between Switzerland and Algeria.

4.3 *Revocations*

The consequences of a revocation of the asylum or refugee status are as a rule only relevant if the person does not yet hold a permanent residence permit (C permit). Such a C permit may only be revoked pursuant to Article 63(1)(b) FLF, "if the foreign national has seriously violated or represents a threat to public security and order in Switzerland or abroad or represents a threat to internal or external security." In all other cases the revocation will lead to a revocation or an expiry of the residence permit. In these cases, the above-mentioned consequences apply as these persons will only be provisionally admitted in Switzerland.

5 Current Political and Legal Developments

Probably the most important legal development outside the asylum area affecting the status of terrorist subjects was the entry into force of the provisions related to the popular initiative for the expulsion of criminal foreigners. After the adoption of this initiative in a referendum in November 2010[86] the Swiss legislature (legislature) has added to the SCC provisions regulating the expulsion of "criminal foreigners." An expulsion order has to be ordered as a penalty by the competent Criminal Court if a person who is not a Swiss national is convicted for an offence featuring on the list of Article 66a SCC. Article 66a (1) (l) states that "acts preparatory to the commission of an offence (Art. 260bis para. 1 and 3), participation in or support for a criminal organisation (Art. 260ter), endangering public safety with weapons (Art. 260quater), financing terrorism (Art. 260quinquies)" are among the crimes that will lead to a compulsory expulsion order if the hardship clause does not apply.[87] If an expulsion order under Article 66a SCC is becoming final and the non-refoulement obligation applies, the executing of the expulsion order "may" be deferred by the competent cantonal authority pursuant to Article 66d SCC. In such a case, asylum may not be granted (Article 53(c) AA) or – if already granted – ceases

86 See Official Records (Amtliche Sammlung) 2011, 1199.

87 See on this Hruschka/Zurbrügg, in: Niggli/Wiprächtiger (eds.), BSK-Strafrecht I, 4th Edition 2018, Article 66a.

(Article 64(1)(e) AA). A provisional admission may also not be granted or ceases (Article 83(9) FNIA), which means that the person is protected from refoulement, but will not have access to the labour market or to any other integration measures. He or she will only – upon request – have access to so-called emergency aid (Nothilfe) pursuant to Article 12 SFC. If in need of accommodation the person will – after having served the sentence – be obliged to live in an assigned center. This consequence applies to all non-Swiss persons subject to a criminal conviction pursuant to Article 66a (1) SCC, so it is not specifically aimed at terrorist subjects in the asylum procedure, but might have an important effect on the respective persons.[88]

More specifically related to terrorism and as a reaction to the rise in the terrorist threat, in line with other European states' measures, Switzerland has intensified its efforts to counter terrorism. What can be observed is a tendency to increase preventive measures and thus enlarge the competences of police and intelligence services. In 2017, the Swiss Security Network, which consists of the Confederation, the cantons (the respective cantonal justice and police authorities, the education authorities, the social services) and the Communes have drawn up a National Action Plan to Prevent and Counter Terrorism.[89] The Action Plan is methodologically based on the United Nations plan of action[90] and comprises measures in four areas: Knowledge and expertise, cooperation and coordination, prevention of extremist ideologies and extremist groups, disengagement and reintegration and international cooperation. In December 2017, the Federal Council additionally proposed a new law containing police measures to prevent and combat terrorism.[91] The police should be given more possibilities to deal with so-called "endangerers" outside of criminal proceedings. The new "Federal Act on Police Measures to Combat Terrorism (PMT)" supplements the National Action Plan (NAP) where its preventive measures are not sufficient, namely at the beginning of radicalisation, but also after a prison sentence. Measures proposed comprise reporting obligations, an exit

88 See on the effects of a non-executable expulsion order: Ibid., Vor Art. 66a-d, N 86pp.

89 See above footnote 3.

90 United Nations (2015). Action Plan to Prevent Violent Extremism of 24 December 2015 (A/70/674). The UN Secretary General's Plan of Action cites the following push and pull factors: 1. Lack of socio-economic opportunities; 2. Marginalisation and discrimination; 3. Poor governance, violations of human rights and of the rule of law; 4. Prolonged and unresolved conflicts; 5. Radicalisation in prisons; 6. Individual background and motivations; 7. Collective grievances and victimisation; 8. Distortion and misuse of beliefs, political ideologies and ethnic and cultural differences; 9. Leadership and social networks, including new communication media.

91 See for details the documents and the press release by the EJPD of 8 December 2017, available at: https://www.ejpd.admin.ch/ejpd/de/home/aktuell/news/2017/2017-12-080.html.

ban, but also preventive detention. Further legal amendments are also foreseen. In asylum procedures this has no consequences as such, but the overall direction is also impacting on the asylum decision making in cases of terrorist suspects.

Consequently, the 2015 National Strategy against Terrorism and the 2017 National Action Plan against Radicalization contain only a few connections to the asylum area mainly related to training and awareness raising of staff and on potential network partners within the asylum area. The main feature regarding the fight against terrorism is the tracking of terrorists in Switzerland coordinated by the Task Force TeTra (**Te**rrorist **Tra**cking).[92] This tracking also contains one element of involvement of the FIS into individual asylum procedures that might have a security related aspect,[93] which has *inter alia* led to a permanent background check of Syrian asylum seekers by the FIS. All these measures are reported within the strategy under the goal of "Prevention." No asylum specific measures are foreseen in the three other areas (Repression, Protection and Crisis Preparedness).

Moreover, in the context of recent terrorist attacks with an Islamic background in France, Belgium and Germany, and because of the intermediate rise of the "Islamic State" and various (Swiss) citizens travelling to the combat zones abroad, in Switzerland, as in many other countries, a discussion has emerged relating to persons radicalized in Switzerland and the possibility to prevent such radicalization. The Annual Report of the federal National Intelligence Service (FIS) for 2018 stresses that jihadist-motivated radicalisation is currently regarded as the main threat to Switzerland's security.[94]

The most emblematic and probably most publicly discussed case in Switzerland concerned the young man who was the son of recognized Palestinian refugees from Jordan and who had travelled abroad *inter alia* to Kenya and Syria and was reported to have died in Iraq.[95] More recently, the cases of five Iraqi nationals that have been convicted for supporting IS/Daesh have led to a

92 Swiss Security Network, *National Action Plan to Prevent and Counter Radicalisation and Violent Extremism* of 4 December 2017, p. 5.

93 See SFG 2015 7487, 7493.

94 FIS, Switzerland's Security – Situation Report 2018 of the Federal Intelligence Service, 2018, available at: https://www.newsd.admin.ch/newsd/message/attachments/52216.pdf, p. 20.

95 Staub, Terrorist aus Biel soll gefallen sein, in: Bieler Tagblatt of 29 March 2016, available at: https://www.bielertagblatt.ch/nachrichten/biel/terrorist-aus-biel-soll-gefallen-sein.

parliamentary debate on the scope of the principle of non-refoulement. The persons had seen their asylum status revoked, but a return to Iraq would put them at the risk of being subject to torture or inhuman or degrading treatment prohibited under Article 25(3) SFC.[96] In this context, the Swiss parliament voted in favour of a motion asking for an amendment of the procedure regarding these cases giving Article 33(2) of the 1951 Convention precedence over Article 25(3) SFC[97], meaning that the protection from refoulement would not (anymore) apply to "terrorists."

Finally, what is worth mentioning is an ongoing discussion about the possibility to *revoke citizenship* of persons posing a (terrorist) threat to Switzerland. Since Swiss nationals can not be expelled (Article 25(1) SFC) and they have an unconditional right to enter Switzerland (even after participating in foreign combat), expulsion would be dependent on a prior revocation of citizenship. Both the old and the new Federal Act on Swiss Citizenship (SCA) foresee a possibility for the federal authorities to revoke citizenship of a person who holds dual nationality, if their conduct is seriously detrimental to the interests or the reputation of Switzerland (Article 42 SCA). During almost 63 years of existence, this Article had never been applied. Only recent developments (civil wars in Syria and Iraq and "jihad travelers" with Swiss citizenship) probably led to the rediscovery of this Article by federal authorities in a publicly discussed case concerning an Italian-Swiss dual citizen – a presumed jihadist from Winterthur who had joined the terrorist organization "Islamic State" as a mercenary and who is said to have died in the meantime.[98] This led several members of parliament to call for expatriation of jihadist mercenaries.[99] Those parliamentary interventions were all rejected, and the presumed jihadist from Winterthur had (reportedly) died before his citizenship could be revoked by the authorities. However, the legislature reacted to the discussions as well as to the criticism voiced by the doctrine[100] and clarified the conditions for revocation

96 Gyr, Die Unauschaffbaren, in: NZZ, 6 July 2018, available at: https://www.nzz.ch/schweiz/die-unausschaffbaren-ld.1400737.

97 See Motion 16.3982 (by Fabio Regazzi of the Christian Peoples Party), which was approved by both chambers of the national parliament (details available at: https://www.parlament.ch/de/ratsbetrieb/suche-curia-vista/geschaeft?AffairId=20163982).

98 Tiefenthal, Ausbürgerung terroristischer Kämpfer, in: AJP 2017, 73, 81.

99 Motion Romano (14.3705), Aberkennung des Schweizer Bürgerrechtes bei Dschihadisten mit Doppelbürgerschaft; Parlamentarische Initiative (14.450) betreffend den Entzug des Schweizer Bürgerrechts für Söldner» von Nationalrat Toni Brunner (SVP) am 26. September 2014.

100 See Achermann, Kurzgutachten zum Entzug des Bürger-rechts nach Artikel 48 BüG, p. 19, available at https://www.woz.ch/sites/woz.ch/files/text/download/kurzgutachten_achermann_entzug_burgerrecht_juli15.pdf.

of citizenship by amending Article 30 of the Ordinance on Naturalization. This provision specifies which conduct can be seen as seriously detrimental to the interests or the reputation of Switzerland and therefore lead to revocation of citizenship. The possibility remains ambiguous. First of all, it is doubtful if expatriation would really solve the problem or if it simply transfers the "problem" to another State.[101] Furthermore, following the principle of prevention of statelessness, according to Article 42 SCA only persons with dual citizenship can be expatriated. While laudable in principle, this exception and the corresponding fact that terrorists without dual citizenship can not be expatriated raises the question whether the discussion on the revocation of citizenship really addresses the issue or if it is not rather of a symbolic nature.

6 Conclusion: Caught between Unworthiness and Exclusion

The Swiss practice regarding terrorism and asylum is very much guided by the idea that persons potentially "infected" by "terrorism" should only be granted asylum if they are either clear cut "victims of terrorism" or if the person is able to prove that he or she has falsely been seen as a terroist suspect. The jurisprudence developed standards that in practice lead to the exclusion of terrorist suspects from the possibility to be provided with a residence permit in Switzerland.

Whereas exclusion from refugee status is rare in the Swiss practice, exclusion from asylum (and hence from the possibility to be granted a residence permit) has been the rule for persons "unworthy of asylum" pursuant to Article 53 AA. The notion of "unworthiness" has developed over time in jurisprudence and in the political debate. The current developments show that access of terrorist suspects to protection and integration in Switzerland starting with an asylum procedure is very much dependent on the question whether the person is assessed as a "threat for the security of Switzerland." The standards for the meaning of this notion have been defined in jurisprudence and ever more situations have been identified where such a threat was confirmed. In the latest judgement of 2018, the former minimum requirement that a criminal law offense was necessary to exclude a person from asylum was lifted and the FAC accepted an exclusion from asylum of a person that had not committed any

101 Swiss Official Bulletin of Parliamentary Discussions 2016 S 505 f. (Votum Andrea Caroni), available at https://www.parlament.ch/en/ratsbetrieb/amtliches-bulletin.

criminal offense but was seen by the FIS as a terrorist subject merely because he seemed to be associated with a youth group of the PKK.

If the FIS reports a potential threat to the "security of Switzerland" the standard of proof is in practice reversed and the person will need to prove in his or her asylum case (above 3.2 and 3.3) or in the regularization or naturalization proceedings that he or she is not involved in acts endangering the security of Switzerland. Consequently, if the FIS has a suspicion that a security threat may be possible, only a "purification exercise" prevents the exclusion from protection and integration. "Purification" consists of the proof of non-involvement in terrorist activities.

If there are no such allegations by the FIS, the legal standard for exclusion is different and the burden of proof remains mainly on the authorities. Authorities need to demonstrate that there are "concrete incidents or reproachable actions with minimal potential for danger and relevance to the present." "General assumptions or theoretical possibilities of influencing by virtue of one's professional position" are not enough to justify the application of an exclusion clause in the asylum or integration proceedings.[102]

The adequacy of the (exclusion) measure is rarely assessed even though Article 36 of the Swiss Constitution would be required to assess the proportionality of such measures.[103] In practice, this means that speculations ("Mutmassungen") are often enough to justify an exclusion decision, which was especially apparent in the case regarding potential LTTE financing (above, 4.2). The court stated that it is sufficient to exclude the couple from naturalization as "it could not be ruled out that" the financing provided has contributed to violence in Sri Lanka.[104]

Such exclusion decisions seem to be justified by the unworthiness of protection of the person suspected to be a terrorist. The assessment is in practice very much dependent on the assessment of the FIS. If this is the case, neither material protection nor further integration of the person are likely to be granted.

The practical measures and decisions analysed in this contribution suggest that the standards outlined by the national strategies against terrorism are not always upheld. The strategy sets out that the fight against terrorism should take

102 See on this especially ATAF 2013/34, para. 7.3.2.

103 See on Article 53(b), Frehner/Hruschka, p. 46 and more generally on the principle of proportionality in Swiss and international law: Kälin/Künzli, Das Verhältnismässigkeitsprinzip als Bestandteil des zwingenden Völkerrechts? In: Jusletter 23 June 2014. The authors suggest that the principle of proportionality is part of *ius cogens*.

104 ATAF 2015/1.

place within the framework of the Federal Constitution, Public International Law, as well as of Fundamental and Human Rights Law and be coupled with a balancing act between freedom and security.[105]

In the political arena, the developments are similar and have led in 2016 to the implementation of measures aiming at the expulsion of terrorist subjects (Article 66a SCC) as well as in 2018/19 to a decision by the Swiss parliament to ask the legislators to propose a provision that suspends the principle of non-refoulement for terrorists.

Our analysis shows that the requirements for exclusion decisions have been significanlty lowered in the jurisprudence over the last decades. Exclusion from asylum also seems to be used in situations were a criminal conviction is not likely to happen for evidentiary reasons in order to secure that the person is not granted a residence permit.

The practical consequences of such exclusion decisions are problematic as they will often lead to situations where not only asylum or a residence permit or naturalization is denied, but the person may not have access to the labour market or Swiss society at large even if no criminal offence has been committed and an actual departure or deportation is not likely to happen. Under these circumstances, there are higher chances that the persons will feel excluded and potentially stay in the community of other persons facing the same challenges or sharing similar beliefs. This is, as a recent report on prevention of radicalization by the Federal Department (Ministry) of Defence, Civil Protection and Sports[106] and the 2018 report of the Federal Intelligence Service, FIS, show, the main ground for recruitment for radical ideas in Switzerland. The question thus arises whether the "fight" against terrorism by excluding terrorist suspects from protection and integration is not rather having the adverse effect of further contributing to the radicalization of certain individuals in Switzerland. Especially measures to "punish" terrorism suspects where there is no real criminal case have the potential to foster radicalization and might therefore be counter-productive.

In this context, the notion of internal/external security is applied somewhat inconsistently and it seems that authorities use it as a "catchall clause" to "punish" persons they deem unworthy of protection. From a legal perspective, the concept of internal/external is vague and not defined by "hard" criteria. It should be borne in mind that "terrorism" alone is not sufficient for exclusion

105 See Strategy against Terrorism, SFG 2015 7487.

106 Sicherheitsverbund Schweiz, Präventionsmassnahmen zur Verhinderung von Radikalisierung. Eine Bestandsaufnahme in der Schweiz, July 2016, available at: https://www.newsd.admin.ch/newsd/message/attachments/44716.pdf.

(from refugee status or asylum), because the individual contribution of the person concerned must be considered. This would lead to an approach – also suggested by research and governmental studies – that is less repressive, more focused on integration. To ensure more effective prevention of radicalization, the conducting of de-radicalization programmes should be considered.

CHAPTER 11

Forced Migrants as a Security Threat: Challenging Criminalization Trends in Austria under Presumed Links of Asylum and Terrorism

Julia Kienast

1 Introduction[1]

Terrorism and asylum have become two of the most controversial political issues of the recent decades.[2] Both topics are mystified in a space of many claims and little facts, as reliable information is hardly accessible or verifiable for the ordinary citizen. Furthermore, the estimation of real risks is usually difficult for the individual. This lack of transparency has become a fertile soil for generating emotion – especially fear.[3] In consequence, both subjects are frequently misused for the purpose of political mobilisation.[4] This commonality has one unfortunate result: A vague correlation becomes established between the two

---

1 This book chapter is based on a former version published in the Working Paper Series of the Refugee Law Initiative. See Julia Kienast, 'An Introduction to the Common Security Narrative of Terrorism and Asylum and Its Influence on Austrian Migration Law', in *Terrorism and Asylum*, vol. 33, Working Paper Series (London: Refugee Law Initiative, University of London, 2019), 17–31, https://sas-space.sas.ac.uk/9204/.

2 For example, according to Fritz Plasser and Franz Sommer, *Wahlen im Schatten der Flüchtlingskrise: Parteien, Wähler und Koalitionen im Umbruch*, Schriftenreihe des Zentrums für angewandte Politikforschung, Band 33 (Wien: Facultas, 2018), 87 f in July 2017, 61 percent of the Austrian population had serious concerns about the arrival of asylum applicants and refugees. 62 percent were concerned about "radical Islamism" and 38 percent about terrorist attacks.

3 Compare Ruth Wodak, *The Politics of Fear: What Right-Wing Populist Discourses Mean* (London: Sage, 2015), 4, for the relations of right-wing populism and fear. With regard to the enormous role fear has occupied in everyday life David L. Altheide, *Creating Fear: News and the Construction of Crisis*, Social Problems and Social Issues (New York: Aldine de Gruyter, 2002), 3, states: 'Fear begins with things we fear, but over time, with enough repetition and expanded use, it becomes a way of looking at life'.

4 Plasser and Sommer, *Wahlen im Schatten der Flüchtlingskrise*, 89 f, describe how Sebastian Kurz used the political method of 're-framing' consequently in the 2017 elections to the Austrian National Assembly. By linking migration and integration concerns causally with other themes, such as school and labour market politics, he managed to expand his perceived area of competence for the voter. He, thereby, joined and reinforced the crisis-interpretations of the ongoing discourse on migration and asylum matters.

© KONINKLIJKE BRILL NV, LEIDEN, 2020 | DOI:10.1163/9789004295995_013

issues, sometimes even by the mere act of putting both terms into one sentence or paragraph repeatedly.[5] The actual correlation between terrorism and asylum, however, remains inadequately reflected upon in Austria.

The following chapter examines this vague link more closely to contribute to its demystification by looking at current numbers and tracing the claims back to their origins. It asks: What are the factual or perceived possible connections of the phenomena of terrorism and asylum? How do they influence Austrian asylum, and wider, migration law? For this purpose, next to several basic facts and figures about the Austrian situation, the second section reviews possible commonalities of terrorism and asylum. The third section sets out how both issues are accompanied by a strong fear of security loss and, thereby, feed into the 'security narrative'. The last section recalls how the mystification of the link plays into the securitisation trend of Austrian migration law and how this dynamic developed historically. Furthermore, several of the recent legal amendments will be reviewed in this regard. The topic of securitisation is evidently not new and not limited to Austria or to migration issues alone.[6] However, Austria has experienced migration from many perspectives – it has produced refugees and it has received refugees. Insofar, it makes for a suitable study example.[7] Therefore, basic information about the Austrian perspective on the phenomenon shall be made accessible to readers outside the German speaking community as well.

The chapter is largely based on literature research in the fields of law, sociology, communication and political sciences as well as on research on past and present amendments of Austrian migration law.[8] It takes into account relevant figures as provided by the Austrian government. It is, however, not based on an independent empirical study of terrorism cases with the involvement of forced migrants in Austria, since no significant amount of jurisprudence on the subject exists or is publicly available at present.[9] Yet, several recent studies

5 Altheide, *Creating Fear*, 83.

6 Compare, e.g., Elspeth Guild and Anneliese Baldaccini, eds., *Terrorism and the Foreigner: A Decade of Tension around the Rule of Law in Europe* (Boston: Brill Nijhoff, 2007) with similar studies on the securitisation phenomenon in the UK, Germany, France, the Netherlands, and Italy.

7 Magdalena Pöschl, 'Migration Und Mobilität', Gutachten für den 19. Österreichischen Juristentag, 2015, 7 f.

8 Hence, the author takes a socio-legal approach. See, e.g., Fiona Cownie and Anthony Bradney, 'Socio-Legal Studies: A Challenge to the Doctrinal Approach', in *Research Methods in Law*, ed. Dawn Watkins and Mandy Burton (London and New York: Routledge, Taylor & Francis Group, 2013), 35–54.

9 The research of cases for the present study was finalised on 1 February 2019.

on radicalisation in Austria and beyond were taken into account insofar as they discuss typologies of perpetrators and can elucidate the public figures.[10]

Although irregular migrants, refugees and asylum applicants commonly form the core of the group targeted by the aforementioned rhetoric, the persons referred to are usually not explicitly specified and several terms used interchangeably in public discourse. Often, they are simply summarised under the term 'migrants'.[11] This chapter reflects this notion by using the terms of the respective source of information where possible or the term that describes the relevant group best. It will refrain from using the term 'refugees' for the general group as the author upholds the definition of this term by the Convention relating to the Status of Refugees[12] and, hence, it would fall short of describing the broader group of persons affected by the studied phenomenon. Therefore, the most commonly used terms will be 'asylum applicants' (meaning persons who seek to apply for asylum or have already lodged an application), 'forced migrants' (referring to both asylum applicants and recognised refugees) or 'irregular migrants' (pointing to their entrance into the territory without prior allowance regardless of a subsequent asylum procedure) in opposition to 'voluntary/labour/regular migration'. The term 'displaced persons', similar to forced migrants, refers to persons who had to leave their home, but takes a broader, global or macro-level perspective, as it is independent of a subsequent act of migration and does not take a European or national viewpoint.

2 Facts, Figures & Correlations

With respect to Austria, three conceivable links between the issues of terrorism and asylum exist: terrorism by right-wing radicals against asylum applicants,

10 In this regard, more specific research on the correlation of forced migration and the radicalisation potential should be encouraged to provide deeper insights for the purpose of informing state policies. Such research might provide counter-arguments to some dangerous claims and put actual incidents in perspective to the amount of asylum applications received. The hope persists that, once fact-based information will be communicated appropriately, the discourse might take a turn towards a more substantial and solution-oriented direction. Compare, e.g., Alex Nowrasteh, 'Terrorism and Immigration – A Risk Analysis', Policy Analysis (CATO Institute, 13 September 2016), https://www.cato.org/sites/cato.org/files/pubs/pdf/pa798_2.pdf.

11 Compare Ruth Wodak, 'Mediation between Discourse and Society: Assessing Cognitive Approaches in CDA', *Discourse Studies* 8, no. 1 (1 February 2006), 186.

12 Art 1 Convention relating to the Status of Refugees (adopted 28 July 1951, entered into force 22 April 1954) 189 UNTS 137 (Geneva Refugee Convention – GRC).

terrorism as a cause for displacement, and the possible involvement of forced migrants in terrorism. This section will begin with a brief outline of the Austrian facts and figures on asylum and terrorism and, afterwards, examine each of these three possible links separately. Although the first two issues are of equal importance and remain underreported, the focus remains on the third possibility, since it is the most relevant in relation to the securitisation of migration law.

In 2015, Austria was one of the EU Member States most affected by the movement of irregular migrants.[13] The arrival of 88,340 asylum applications – and an estimated 600,000–800,000 people crossing the country to reach other destinations[14] – led to a temporary overburdening of the reception system in this Central European country with a population of about 8.5 million.[15] The dramatic scenes of stranded people waiting for trains and searching for shelter received great attention by the media and citizens that came with good and bad consequences. On the one hand, it generated strong solidarity and engagement of civil society.[16] But, on the other hand, the situation was received with scepticism by other parts of society and Austrian politicians quickly recognised the potential of this polarised attention.[17]

13 See, e.g., 'Countries Under the Most Strain in the European Migration Crisis', *The New York Times*, 22 December 2015, sec. World, https://www.nytimes.com/interactive/2015/08/28/world/europe/countries-under-strain-from-european-migration-crisis.html; Eurostat, 'Asylum and First Time Asylum Applicants – Annual Aggregated Data (Rounded) (Tps00191)', Eurostat – Your key to European statistics, accessed 19 April 2020 https://ec.europa.eu/eurostat/tgm/table.do?tab=table&init=1&language=en&pcode=tps00191&plugin=1.

14 See, e.g., 'Ein Jahr danach' (Austrian Red Cross, 2016), https://www.roteskreuz.at/site/ein-jahr-danach/, accessed 19 April 2020; Rainer Nowak, Thomas Prior, and Christian Ultsch, *Flucht: Wie der Staat die Kontrolle verlor* (Vienna Graz Klagenfurt: Molden, 2017).

15 'Asylstatistik 2016' (Bundesministerium für Inneres, Sektion III – Recht, 2016), https://www.bmi.gv.at/301/Statistiken/files/Jahresstatistiken/Jahresstatistik_Asyl_2016.pdf, accessed 19 April 2020. How the arrival of this many forced migrants in 2015 played out in Austria is well portrayed in Wolfgang Gratz, *Das Management der Flüchtlingskrise: Never Let a Good Crisis Go to Waste* (Vienna: NWV, 2016).

16 See, e.g., the initiative 'Train of hope', which received a human rights award for its commitments during this time: 'Train of Hope – Flüchtlingshilfe', Train of Hope, accessed 19 April 2020, http://www.trainofhope.at/_www_/; Andrew Standen-Raz, 'Scenes of Vienna: Boarding the Train of Hope', *Metropole* (blog), 31 October 2015, https://metropole.at/scenes-of-vienna-boarding-the-train-of-hope/; see also 'Vienna – 150.000 People Standing in Solidarity with Refugees in Europe', *Solidar* (blog), 10 May 2015, http://www.solidar.org/en/news/vienna-150-000-people-standing-in-solidarity-with-refugees-in-europe.

17 Whereas the Austrian Freedom Party (FPÖ) has always engaged in aggressive rhetoric against migrants, the rhetoric of the Austrian People's Party (ÖVP) shows a strong shift to the right from this moment on. Even the Austrian Socialist Party (SPÖ) joined the right-wing populist chorus increasingly. Edith Meinhart, 'Im Wendekreis des Stacheldrahts', *profil.at*,

Two years later, the numbers had normalised,[18] but the picture stuck. The political campaigns for the 2017 election to the Austrian National Assembly were still strongly dominated by the topic of migration, especially in the context of security issues.[19] The general 'security fear' in view of migration is complemented by the fact that Austria is equally affected by the fear of violent extremist terrorism[20] that has befallen Western societies since 2001.[21]

This fear clearly contradicts present figures. In fact, Austria is not affected much by terrorism compared to other European countries.[22] Yet, several forms

20 October 2017, https://www.profil.at/oesterreich/fluechtlingskrise-nationalratswahl-8383004; Plasser and Sommer, *Wahlen im Schatten der Flüchtlingskrise*, 71; Nowak, Prior, and Ultsch, *Flucht*, 157.

18 In 2016, the applications decreased by almost 50 percent to 42,285 and another 40 percent to 24,296 applications in 2017. See 'Asylstatistik Dezember 2017' (Bundesministerium für Inneres, Sektion III – Recht, 2017), https://www.bmi.gv.at/301/Statistiken/files/Jahresstatistiken/Asyl-Jahresstatistik_2017.pdf; in 2014 Austria received 28.064 applications 'Asylstatistik 2016', 4.

19 The leading party candidates used more than 2.5 hours on the topic of migration and asylum in national TV discussions – more time than on any other topic such as tax and labour policy, for example. 'Medienanalyse TV-Wahlkampf: 2,5h Sprechzeit für Migrationsthemen', *OTS.at*, 12 October 2017, https://www.ots.at/presseaussendung/OTS_20171012_OTS0199/medienanalyse-tv-wahlkampf-25h-sprechzeit-fuer-migrationsthemen-grafik; Meinhart, 'Im Wendekreis des Stacheldrahts'; 'Themen, die die Wahl entscheiden: Migration vor Sozialem', *DiePresse.Com*, 12 October 2017, https://diepresse.com/home/innenpolitik/nationalratswahl/5301717/Umfrage_Themen-die-die-Wahl-entscheiden_Migration-vor-Sozialem. This phenomenon, when the topic dominating the political discussion dictates the criteria for the election, is called 'priming-effect' in communicative science according to Plasser and Sommer, *Wahlen im Schatten der Flüchtlingskrise*, 55.

20 For the choice of wording see, e.g., Richard Stengel, 'Opinion | Why Saying "Radical Islamic Terrorism" Isn't Enough', *The New York Times*, 13 February 2017, https://www.nytimes.com/2017/02/13/opinion/why-saying-radical-islamic-terrorism-isnt-enough.html.

21 Anneliese Baldaccini, 'Introduction', in *Terrorism and the Foreigner: A Decade of Tension around the Rule of Law in Europe*, ed. Elspeth Guild and Anneliese Baldaccini (Boston: Brill Nijhoff, 2007), xiv. Ivan Krastev, *After Europe* (Philadelphia: University of Pennsylvania Press, 2017), 41, agrees that the 'refugee crisis' has influenced European politics by provoking a moral panic with a fear of 'Islamic terrorism and a general anxiety over the unfamiliar' at its core. For a study on how the fear of terrorism developed in the U.S.A. see David L. Altheide, 'Terrorism and the Politics of Fear', *Cultural Studies ↔ Critical Methodologies* 6, no. 4 (November 2006), 415–39.

22 See visualization at 'GTD World Map: 45 Years of Terrorism', Global Terrorism Database, 2016, https://www.start.umd.edu/gtd/images/START_GlobalTerrorismDatabase_TerroristAttacksConcentrationIntensityMap_45Years.png; see further 'Global Terrorism Index 2017' (Institute for Economics and Peace, 2017), 10 ff, http://visionofhumanity.org/app/uploads/2017/11/Global-Terrorism-Index-2017.pdf.

of terrorist activities have been added into new sections of the criminal code since 2002 and adapted several times since. The criminal offenses rank from the participation in a terrorist organisation in § 278b *Austrian Criminal Code* (StGB) to the prohibition of the incitement or approval of terrorist crimes in § 282a StGB.[23] The purpose of their introduction was to conform to international and European agreements for combatting terrorism and to create a legal basis for preventive anti-terrorism measures at the earliest stage.[24] Yet, the convictions under these criminal offenses remain few: in 2014, there were only 2 convictions, 21 occurred in 2015, 43 in 2016 and 29 in 2017. Most of them did not concern actual terrorist attacks on Austrian soil, but preparatory acts (such as financing of organisations and incitement), an participation in a terrorist organisation or terrorist criminal offenses in other states such as Syria (i.e., 'foreign-fighters').[25]

2.1 *Right-wing Radicalism Directed against Asylum Applicants*

The public fear of radicalisation is mostly directed at foreigners, especially irregular migrants.[26] However, right-wing radicalism is actually the more serious concern in terms of numbers. Radicalism targeting migrants has drastically increased in the recent years.[27] In 2015, the Austrian security authorities registered a rise by 54.1 percent in right-wing extremist, xenophobic/racist, Islamophobic and anti-Semitic criminal acts. In comparison, 2014 the increase was 2.3 percent. In 2016, this worrisome trend continued with an increase by further

---

23 See § 278b-d Strafgesetzbuch (StGB) [*Criminal Code*] introduced by BGBl 2002/134; § 278e StGB introduced by BGBl 2010/108; § 278f StGB introduced by BGBl I 2011/103; § 282a StGB introduced by BGBl I 2011/103.

24 See ErläutRV 1166 BlgNR 21. GP for the reform of the Austrian criminal code in 2002; and ErläutRV 674 BlgNR 24. GP for the reform in 2010.

25 According to 'Statistik-Austria' the convictions are as follows. In 2014: one conviction for the participation in a terrorist organisation (§ 278b StGB), one conviction for the incitement of terrorist offenses (§ 282a StGB); in 2015: 17 convictions under § 278b StGB, one conviction for the instruction of terrorist offenses (§ 278f StGB), three convictions under § 282a StGB; in 2016: 33 convictions under § 278b StGB, two convictions for terrorist criminal offenses (§ 278c StGB), one conviction for the education for terrorist purposes (§ 278e StGB), seven convictions under § 282a StGB; in 2017: 22 convictions under § 278b StGB, one conviction for the financing of terrorism (§ 278d StGB), two conviction under § 278e StGB, four convictions under § 282a StGB; http://statcube.at/statistik.at/ext/statcube/jsf/tableView/tableView.xhtml accessed 19 April 2020.

26 See also Baldaccini, 'Introduction', xiv.

27 That this development affects several OECD members was shown in 'Global Terrorism Index 2017', 57.

13.6 percent. Only in 2017, the numbers began to decrease again by 19 percent.[28] In some cases, these offenses even reached the severity of terrorist acts as defined by the Global Terrorism Database (GTD).[29]

Although according to the Austrian Federal Office for Constitutional Protection and Terrorism Prevention (BVT) this trend is one of the largest concerns in the field of radicalism, it seems to be underrepresented in the public discourse. On the contrary, the circumstance that these right-wing radical incidents increased so dramatically in 2015 – when migration and asylum had been the most discussed topics for months – indicates a connection between the number of incidents and the fear of migration, fostered by public opinion and media.[30]

2.2 *Terrorism as a Root-Cause of Displacement*

The public discourse further fails to acknowledge the background of many forced migrants. Most of the persons applying for asylum in Austria are from Afghanistan, Syria, Iraq and Pakistan. Also Nigeria, Somalia and Morocco are amongst the most frequent countries of origin.[31] A similar distribution has been pictured in the statistics for many years already and several spikes in the distribution of the last decade mirror the occurrences in these countries. For instance, Syrian applicants more than doubled from 2010 to 2011 and in every year since.[32]

---

28 'Verfassungsschutzbericht 2017' (Vienna: Bundesministerium für Inneres, Bundesamt für Verfassungsschutz und Terrorismusbekämpfung (BVT), 2017), 25, https://bvt.bmi.gv at/401/files/Verfassungsschutzbericht2017.pdf; 'Verfassungsschutzbericht 2016' (Vienna: BVT, 2016), 12, https://bvt.bmi.gv.at/401/files/Verfassungsschutzbericht2016.pdf; 'Verfassungsschutzbericht 2015' (Vienna: BVT, 2015), 12, https://bvt.bmi.gv.at/401/files/Verfassungsschutzbericht2015.pdf; 'Verfassungsschutzbericht 2014' (Vienna: BVT, 2014), 17, https://bvt.bmi.gv.at/401/files/VerfassungsschutzberichtfuerdasJahr2014.pdf.

29 'GTD Search Results', Global Terrorism Database, accessed 19 April 2020, https://www.start.umd.edu/gtd/search/Results.aspx?page=1&casualties_type=&casualties_max=&country=15&count=100&expanded=yes&charttype=line&chart=overtime&ob=GTDID&od=desc#results-table. The line between radical right-wing violence against asylum applicants and terrorism is blurry as no official definition of the term exists; for the definitions used by GTD see 'Data Collection Methodology', Global Terrorism Database, accessed 19 April 2020, http://www.start.umd.edu/gtd/using-gtd/. Compare examples in Section 2.3 of this chapter.

30 The increase in right-wing radicalism becomes intensified by right-wing populism that points out scapegoats of society and politics built on fear according to Wodak, *The Politics of Fear*, 2. See similar assessment in 'Verfassungsschutzbericht 2017', 53.

31 See 'Asylstatistik 2016'.

32 Asylum applications of Syrian nationals to Austria: 2006: 88; 2007: 166; 2008: 140; 2009: 279; 2010: 194; 2011: 422; 2012: 915; 2013: 1.991; 2014: 7.730; 2015: 25.563. Numbers are mostly

Evidently, the root-causes of people displacement as well as paths of migration are manifold and it would go beyond the purpose and scope of this book chapter to discuss all of them.[33] However, it is generally known that groups listed as internationally banned terrorist organisations tyrannise several of the mentioned states of origin and, in some, these groups have acclaimed power over large territories. The rule of Al-Qaida and the Taliban in Afghanistan and parts of Pakistan, the rule of Daesh and its associates in parts of Syria and Iraq, and the dominance of Al Shabab in Somalia and Boko Haram in Nigeria are some obvious examples.[34]

That is not to say that every asylum applicant from these countries is persecuted by terrorist organisations *per se*. A persecution in the sense of the Geneva Refugee Convention would require, i.e., the individual to be personally persecuted for 'reasons of race, religion, nationality, membership of a particular social group or political opinion'.[35] The exact interpretation of the scope of these terms remains an on-going task of judicature. However, many asylum applicants are found to be personally persecuted by terrorist organisations and some have received protection in the past due to this reason and because their state of origin was not capable of protecting them.[36] But also those, who are not found to be personally persecuted, still may suffer the consequences of a life under a radical regime or other influences of terrorist organisations reaching from instability and a lack of freedom to (civil) war.[37]

Hence, it becomes evident that terrorism is, indeed, one of the underlying reasons for many asylum applications in Austria, as these people flee from radical activities in their home countries and the instability that follows. At the same time, people in an unstable environment might be more prone to join terrorist organisations and so the instability perpetuates itself.[38] In this setting,

accessible in the public asylum statistics of the Ministry of Interior 'Asylstatistik [2005–2015]' (Bundesministerium für Inneres), http://www.bmi.gv.at/Downloads/start.aspx, or were communicated via e-mail after enquiry to the ministry.

33 For an overview of persons, methods and routes of 'illegal' migration to Austria see, e.g., Andreas Schloenhardt, ed., *Schlepperkriminalität in Österreich* (Vienna: NWV, 2017).

34 See 'Global Terrorism Index 2017', 15 ff; for concrete information about the security situation in the mentioned countries see, e.g., European Asylum Support Office (EASO), 'Country Reports', accessed 19 April 2020, https://www.easo.europa.eu/information-analysis/country-origin-information/country-reports.

35 Art 1 Geneva Refugee Convention.

36 See, e.g., decisions by the Austrian Administrative Court concerning Algeria in VwGH 19.06.2001, 200/01/0170, 0171; VwGH 12.03.2002, 99/01/0205.

37 See 'Global Terrorism Index 2017', 62.

38 See, e.g., Jerrold M. Post, Keven G. Ruby and Eric D. Shaw, 'The Radical Group in Context: 2. Identification of Critical Elements in the Analysis of Risk for Terrorism by Radical

'terrorism' (i.e., radicalisation) and 'asylum' (i.e., displacement) seem to be two sides of the same coin, which would both benefit from the stabilisation of the respective region. Taking care of the root-causes of forced displacement, therefore, equals effective terrorism prevention in several ways.

2.3 *Forced Migrants' Involvement in Terrorism*

In light of this knowledge, the common allegation that forced migrants could be involved in terrorism seems even more destructive. The claims are twofold: first, the fear exists that terrorists could arrive in the Schengen zone amongst the irregular migrants.[39] Second, it seems possible that their vulnerable situation makes them an easy prey to radicalisation.[40] It should not be concluded that these fears are utterly unreasonable and that the perceived threats should not be taken seriously. However, in view of the severity of the claims and their political consequences – not only for the individuals accused, but commonly

---

Group Type' (2002) 25 *Studies in Conflict & Terrorism* 101, 113 who found that '[…] two variables, 1.1 Historically Rooted Culture of Violence, and 1.2 Current Communal Conflict [are] of high significance nearly across the board for the four major terrorist group categories […]'; see further Magnus Ranstorp, 'The Root Causes of Violent Extremism' (Radicalisation Awareness Network (RAN) 2016) Issue Paper 3, https://ec.europa.eu/home-affairs/sites/homeaffairs/files/what-we-do/networks/radicalisation_awareness_network/ran-papers/docs/issue_paper_root-causes_jan2016_en.pdf accessed 19 April 2020 who describes radicalisation '[…] as a kaleidoscope of factors, creating infinite individual combinations. There are some basic primary colours which create complex interlocking combinations: (1) individual socio-psychological factors; (2) social factors; (3) political factors; (4) ideological and religious dimensions; (5) the role of culture and identity issues; (6) trauma and other trigger mechanisms; and three other factors that are a motor for radicalisation: (7) group dynamics; (8) radicalisers/groomers; and (9) the role of social media. It is the combined interplay of some of these factors that causes violent extremism'. Barbara Sude, David Stebbins and Sarah Weilant, 'Lessening the Risk of Refugee Radicalization' (RAND Corporation 2015) 4 f, https://www.rand.org/pubs/perspectives/PE166.html accessed 19 April 2020.

39 Compare Baldaccini, 'Introduction', xviii, xxi.

40 So for instance, Christina Schori-Liang, 'Leaderless Jihad in a Leaderless World: The Future of Terror' in 'Global Terrorism Index 2017', 88, 90 f; see many studies on general root-causes of radicalisation, e.g. Post, Ruby, and Shaw, 'The Radical Group in Context'; 'Handbook on the Management of Violent Extremist Prisoners and the Prevention of Radicalization to Violence in Prisons', Criminal Justice Handbook Series (New York: United Nations Office on Drugs and Crime (UNODC), October 2016), 58 ff, http://www.unodc.org/pdf/criminal_justice/Handbook_on_VEPs.pdf; Ranstorp, 'The Root Causes of Violent Extremism'. These studies are not specified on the radicalisation of forced migrants. However, forced migrants usually have a great risk of exposure to some of the key factors, such as conflict, traumatisation and victimisation, stigmatisation and marginalisation. This exposure depends to a large part on the reception conditions in host countries; see Sude, Stebbins, and Weilant, 'Lessening the Risk of Refugee Radicalization', 4 f.

for all asylum applicants and migrants – such concerns should not be voiced in an inconsiderate manner and without validation.

The GTD registered only three terrorist attacks between 2014 and 2016 on Austrian soil. Two of them are attributed to unknown perpetrator groups. However, both were directed against asylum reception centres and, hence, likely were right-wing motivated. The third was an attack on a Turkish institution by the Kurdistan Workers' Party (PKK).[41] None of them involved an asylum applicant or refugee on the side of perpetrators.[42]

Generally, convictions for other terrorist crimes remain few in Austria (2014: 2; 2015: 21; 2016: 43; 2017: 29).[43] The government does not publish statistics on the motives and profiles of perpetrators of terrorist offenses or on the involvement of forced migrants in particular. However, Austria reported 26 convictions for terrorist offences in 2016 to Eurojust, of which 26 were considered 'jihadist terrorism'.[44] Austria further reported 'several cases of individuals suspected of terrorism among the migrants staying in, or travelling through, its territory'[45] without further specification of their profiles. In general, information about these few convictions that would allow assessing forced migrants' involvement is to a large part not publicly accessible. In criminal proceedings, only the jurisprudence of the last instance is published on principle. Administrative proceedings could give information about cases, in which the right to

41 'GTD Search Results' (n 22); for more details on the incidents see further 'Austrian Asylum Center Hit by Molotov Cocktail' *The Express Tribune* (28 November 2016) https://tribune.com.pk/story/1246669/austrian-asylum-center-hit-molotov-cocktail/ accessed 19 April 2020 'Brandstiftung bei Unterkunft für Flüchtlinge in Oberösterreich' *derStandard.at* (1 June 2016) http://derstandard.at/2000037998380/Neugebautes-Fluechtlingsheim-in-Oberoesterreich-abgebrannt accessed 19 April 2020. The GTD results, relying on news reports for its data collection, show one more terrorist attack in Austria in 2017. However, the perpetrator was later acquitted of terrorism, but instead convicted for murder and sentenced to a life sentence in a facility for dangerously disturbed prisoners. See 'Lebenslang Für Doppelmord an Linzer Ehepaar', *DerStandard.At*, 18 June 2018, https://derstandard.at/2000081819827/Lebenslang-fuer-Doppelmord-an-Linzer-Ehepaar.

42 A study in the U.S.A. found an immensely small risk emanating from forced migrants as well; Nowrasteh, 'Terrorism and Immigration – A Risk Analysis'.

43 Compare FN 25.

44 'Terrorism Situation and Trend Report 2017' (Europol, 2017), 51 f, https://www.europol.europa.eu/sites/default/files/documents/tesat2017_0.pdf. Austria further reported 2 convictions in 2014 and 29 convictions in 2015. These numbers do not match the figures published by 'Statistik Austria' see FN 25. The reasons thereof could not be retraced from the TE-SAT report. Compare similar statements in 'Terrorism Situation and Trend Report 2018' (Europol, 2018), 28, https://www.europol.europa.eu/sites/default/files/documents/tesat_2018_1.pdf.

45 Ibid 14.

asylum or other protection was denied or revoked based on involvement in terrorist activities. Yet, they are only accessible in the second instance in front of the Federal Administrative Court. The administrative decisions of the Austrian Federal Office for Immigration and Asylum (BFA), the first instance of asylum proceedings, are not published.[46]

Of the accessible cases, only few show a conviction of forced migrants for terrorism. The search within the jurisprudence of the Austrian Federal Administrative Court matched 22 cases. Almost all of these available cases concerned appeals to the Federal Administrative Court from citizens of the Russian Federation with Chechen ethnicity, whose asylum claims were rejected or their protection revoked after being convicted under § 278b StGB, for the participation in a terrorist organisation. Among these cases are at least two groups (of five and three persons), who attempted to leave Austria together to join the "jihad" in Syria.[47] The results further contain two administrative proceedings against Syrian citizens convicted of terrorist crimes and three criminal proceedings against citizens from respectively Syria, Iraq and Afghanistan.

The provisional findings obtained from the explorative inspection of these published cases confirm the results of recent empirical studies conducted on radicalisation in Austria. The study of *Hofinger* and *Schmidinger*, for example, revealed clearly that the general radicalisation potential is very narrowly distributed amongst two demographic groups: juvenile and Chechen subculture.[48] These findings are supported by further studies on radicalisation in Austria.[49] The Chechen group, so far, constitutes the only group of forced

46 The research on relevant jurisprudence was conducted on the government website for the publication of jurisdiction https://www.ris.bka.gv.at/Judikatur/ accessed 19 April 2020. The search (a) within convictions of the Austrian Criminal Courts for terrorist acts under §§ 278b-d and § 282a StGB matched three results and (b) within jurisdiction of the Austrian Federal Administrative Court, the Austrian Supreme Administrative Court and the Austrian Constitutional Court matched 22 cases. The different results can i.a. be explained by the access to a case depending on the instance of decision-making.

47 See, e.g., BVwG 31.01.2018, W211 1428789-2 (VwGH 16.04.2017, Ra 2017/19/0016), BVwG 11.01.2018, W140 2167860-3; see also the most recent judgment as reported by Manfred Seeh, 'Milde Urteile im Terrorprozess: Anklage erwägt Berufung', *DiePresse.com*, 15 February 2018, https://diepresse.com/home/panorama/oesterreich/5372459/Milde-Urteile-im-Terrorprozess_Anklage-erwaegt-Berufung.

48 Veronika Hofinger and Thomas Schmidinger, 'Endbericht zur Begleitforschung: Deradikalisierung im Gefängnis' (Institute for the Sociology of Law and Criminology 2017) 4 https://www.irks.at/publikationen/studien/2017/deradikalisierung-im-gef%C3%A4ngnis.html accessed 19 April 2020.

49 See, e.g., interview with Ramazan Demir in Jakob Tschachler, Agnes Steinberger, and ACUNS Liaison Office Vienna, eds., *(De)Radikalisierung von Jugendlichen Phänomene, Akteure,und Lösungen.* (Vienna: NWV, 2018), 95; Ednan Aslan and Evrim Ersan Akkılıç,

migrants in Austria of which several individuals have been confirmedly involved in terrorism. Most of them arrived to Austria in the 2000s fleeing the second Chechen war and seem to be coined by a strong resentment against the Russian government. Partially for this reason, they join the jihad without strong religious ideology but based on a common enemy, as Russia supports the Syrian government in the on-going armed conflict.[50] The study by *Hofinger* and *Schmidinger* also suggests that eight cases of Syrian and Iraqi asylum applicants are currently under trial.[51] Hence, it is possible that future research in Austria will reveal different results changed by the new demographics of forced migration since 2015.[52]

Conclusively, most cases above concern persons from one very specific group of forced migrants and seem to have only little explanatory power on a general level. The combination of a small total amount of cases and its irregular distribution of nationality renders the sample unpromising to achieve significant general assertions on potential threats emanating from the very heterogenic group of forced migrants. Furthermore, as long as future convictions do not extremely exceed the present figures, these cases stand in very small relation to the number of asylum applications.[53]

'Islamistische Radikalisierung – Biografische Verläufe im Kontext der religiösen Sozialisation und des radikalen Milieus' (Vienna: Asyl-, Migrations- und Integrationsfonds (AMIF), 2017), http://iits.univie.ac.at/fileadmin/user_upload/p_iits/Pictures_colleagues/radikalisierung_2017_07_19_onlineversion_einzelseiten.pdf.

50 For the situation of Chechens in Austria, their reasons for radicalisation (amongst them 'collective grievances and victimization') and how the revocation of their protection contradicts de-radicalisation efforts see Hofinger and Schmidinger (n 40) 21 ff, 38 ff, 141 ff.

51 See particularly FN 20 in Hofinger and Schmidinger, 40 ff. The study further states that three suspects of the attacks in Paris on 13 November 2015 and in Brussels on 22 March 2016 had been in Austrian prisons before their extradition to France, but these cases were inaccessible for scientific research (42 f).

52 During the revision of this publication, the results already changed drastically from 11 matches in administrative proceedings at the beginning of 2018 to 22 matches at the end of the year. On 14 December 2018, the search within convictions of the Austrian Criminal Courts for terrorist acts under §§ 278b-d and § 282a StGB matched three results with asylum applicants from Iraq, Syria and Afghanistan, whereas at the beginning of the year the search matched no results. However, the demographics remained similar: 20 of the 22 administrative proceedings concerned members of the Chechen community.

53 Compare the analysis in Nowrasteh, 'Terrorism and Immigration – A Risk Analysis', 1 stating that '[…] the chance of an American being murdered in a terrorist attack caused by a refugee is 1 in 3.64 billion per year while the chance of being murdered in an attack committed by an illegal immigrant is an astronomical 1 in 10.9 billion per year. By contrast, the chance of being murdered by a tourist on a B visa, the most common tourist visa, is 1 in 3.9 million per year.'; for dynamics of fear spreading and scapegoating typical for (right-wing) populism see Wodak, *The Politics of Fear*, 12.

Eventually, empirical analysis can only inform about the estimation of a risk based on past terrorist incidents undertaken by forced migrants. Whether the respective number is actually sufficient to justify national security concerns against a whole group, instead of an individual assessment, and whether the prognosis of a national security threat can allow derogations from basic rights are then, first and foremost, legal and, ultimately, political questions.[54] For the legal scholar, the answers are to be found in existing human rights provision and the principle of proportionality.[55] The same is true for the questions, whether convictions of terrorism should entail different consequences for the individual from those of other serious crimes. This difficult weighing of interests occupies the minds of many legal scholars.[56]

On a practical level, radicalisation amongst forced migrants on Austrian territory might be met best by preventive measures offering them an adequate future perspective and integration, instead of isolation and stigmatisation. Such actions are clearly indicated by research, but remain political decisions as well.[57] A severe problem in this regard remains the irregular migration status, which the revocation of protection often leads to, when the individual cannot be returned, in spite of a conviction of terrorism.[58] In these cases, the person is rendered even more stigmatised and excluded from society, and forced into precarious physical and psychological living conditions. All of which are

54 This is especially true in times, where representatives of government explicitly state that they do not see themselves bound by (constitutional) law as Austrian Minister of Interior, Herbert Kickl; Maximilian Steinbeis, 'Minister of Civil Resistance', *Verfassungsblog* (blog), 26 January 2019, https://verfassungsblog.de/minister-of-civil-resistance/.

55 Baldaccini, 'Introduction', xv f.

56 See, e.g., other authors in this book. See further Jens Vedsted-Hansen, 'The European Convention on Human Rights, Counter-Terrorism, and Refugee Protection', *Refugee Survey Quarterly* 29, no. 4 (2010): 189–206; James C. Simeon, 'Complicity and Culpability and the Exclusion of Terrorists From Convention Refugee Status Post-9/11', *Refugee Survey Quarterly* 29, no. 4 (2010): 104–37.

57 Compare Stijn Sieckelinck and Amy-Jane Gielen, 'Protective and Promotive Factors Building Resilience against Violent Radicalisation', Issue Paper (Radicalisation Awareness Network (RAN), April 2018), 6 f, https://ec.europa.eu/home-affairs/sites/homeaffairs/files/what-we-do/networks/radicalisation_awareness_network/ran-papers/docs/ran_paper_protective_factors_042018_en.pdf.

58 See, e.g., one of the administrative cases against a Syrian citizen, BVwG 12.09.2018, W214 2194515-1. For the dimensions of irregular status issues see, e.g., Kevin Hinterberger, 'Die Mehrebenendimension Aufenthaltsrechtlicher Irregularität. Konzeptionelle Überlegungen zum Auftreten Irregulärer Migration in der EU (The Multi-Level Dimension of Residential Irregularity. Conceptional Observations on the Appearance of Irregular Migration in the EU)' in Daniel Thym and Tobias Klarmann (eds), *Unionsbürgerschaft und Migration im aktuellen Europarecht* (Nomos 2017) https://papers.ssrn.com/abstract=2946865 accessed 19 April 2020.

observed to have negative effects on radicalisation.[59] Hence, security concerns usually do not get solved by the revocation of protection, but are at best geographically shifted.[60]

3 The Common Security Narrative

As demonstrated, the evidence for concerns exists, but remains small. No asylum applicant or refugee has been convicted at this point of time for the attempt of a terrorist act on Austrian soil. Only a few and specific forced migrants that we may be aware of have radicalised here and attempted to join the jihad elsewhere.[61] Hence, the threat that forced migrants will participate in terrorist acts appears low with regards to, both, the probability of attacks in general and the relation of convicted forced migrants to the overall numbers of arrivals. Yet, a widespread security fear persists in the public and it seems to have roots in the fear of terrorism, on the one hand, and the fear of migration, on the other hand.[62] Both of these fears will be introduced briefly in the following paragraphs.

After the terrorist attacks on September 11th 2001, the media landscape changed severely in terms of form, frequency, and the manner of reporting. Several psychological studies were conducted to show the influence of media output on the public and politics since then.[63] As Altheide pointed out, media coverage linking the topics of terrorism, fear and victimisation increased enormously after 2001.[64] This study also demonstrated that with time the frequent use of the word 'terrorism' increases fear by the 'association of words with

59 See Hofinger and Schmidinger, 'Endbericht zur Begleitforschung: Deradikalisierung im Gefängnis', 141 ff.

60 See further Elisabeth Kath, 'Abschiebung von Schutzbedürftigen bei Straffälligkeit und Terrorismusverdacht', in *40 Jahre 'Deutscher Herbst': Neue Überlegungen zu Sicherheit und Recht – Tagungsband zum JuWissDay 2017 in Köln*, ed. Tobias Brings-Wiesen and Frederik Ferreau, Schriften der Jungen Wissenschaft im Öffentlichen Recht (Nomos, 2018), 250.

61 The dark figures might be high here, since this crime is clandestine by nature.

62 Plasser and Sommer, *Wahlen Im Schatten Der Flüchtlingskrise*, 52.

63 See, e.g., Altheide, 'Terrorism and the Politics of Fear', 423 ff; Sonia Suchday, Amina Benkhoukha, and Anthony F. Santoro, 'Globalization and Media: A Mediator between Terrorism and Fear: A Post-9/11 Perspective', in *Psychology of Fear, Crime, and the Media: International Perspectives*, ed. Derek Chadee, Researching Social Psychology (New York: Routledge, Taylor & Francis Group, 2016); Jennifer S. Lerner et al., 'Effects of Fear and Anger on Perceived Risks of Terrorism: A National Field Experiment', *Psychological Science* 14, no. 2 (2003), 144–50.

64 Altheide, 'Terrorism and the Politics of Fear', 426.

certain problems and issues'.[65] Furthermore, a field experiment on the influence of emotions on risk judgment showed that the emotion of fear perpetuates pessimism in the U.S. In the study, respondents estimated their personal probability to be hurt in a terror attack at 20 percent and that of the average American at 48 percent.[66] Also Austrians seem overly pessimistic about the proximity of terror attacks. According to a study in 2016, 10 percent are certain that a future attack in Austria is unavoidable; another 38 percent believe terror attacks might occur in Austria.[67]

Similar to terrorism, (forced) migration has been a hot topic for the media for a long time and increasingly since 2015.[68] This topic has a very high potential to generate fear in the public. In a historical legal study, *Pöschl* identified six specific fears of migration that reoccur consistently.[69] Amongst them persists the fear of security loss, which is connected with the fear of terrorism. But, as many other authors have noted, the fear of migration further includes concerns of rising crime rates, of job shortage or simply of losing "national identity."[70] In the aforementioned study on security perception of Austrians, 74 percent stated to dread the 'continuous refugee stream'.[71] At the same time, Austria is one of the countries where the attitude of citizens towards immigration grew increasingly negative in the recent years, as studies by *The European Social Survey* in 2014 and 2016 indicate.[72] Evidently, migration is a heavily

65 Ibid 419.

66 Lerner et al., 'Effects of Fear and Anger on Perceived Risks of Terrorism', 148, 150.

67 'Österreicher haben Angst vor Terror', *DiePresse.com*, 10 August 2016, https://diepresse.com/home/panorama/oesterreich/5066874/Oesterreicher-haben-Angst-vor-Terror.

68 Plasser and Sommer, *Wahlen im Schatten der Flüchtlingskrise*, 140 ff.

69 Pöschl, 'Migration Und Mobilität', 9 ff. These include: (1) The fear of poverty (social perspective); (2) The fear of infiltration by outer enemies (foreign-policy perspective); (3) The fear of security loss (security perspective), (4) The fear of foreign diseases or the exploitation of the health system (health perspective); (5) Financial fears (economic perspective); and (6) the fear of 'otherness' (cultural perspective). For similar observations in Germany see Jürgen Bast, *Aufenthaltsrecht und Migrationssteuerung*, Jus Publicum 207 (Tübingen: Mohr Siebeck, 2011).

70 Wodak, *The Politics of Fear*, 7. Krastev, *After Europe*, 40 ff calls this the 'moral panic' of Europe. These analyses were confirmed by studies on voter behaviour in Austria; see Plasser and Sommer, *Wahlen Im Schatten Der Flüchtlingskrise*, 61.

71 'Österreicher haben Angst vor Terror'.

72 James Dennison and Andrew Geddes, 'OP-ED: Are Europeans Turning against Asylum Seekers and Refugees?', *European Council on Refugees and Exiles* (ECRE) (blog), 17 November 2017, https://www.ecre.org/op-ed-are-europeans-turning-against-asylum-seekers-and-refugees/.

prejudiced phenomenon in many regards and, just like terrorism, it has a very 'intimate relationship'[73] to fear.

Austria is not alone with this issue and the phenomenon of 'security fear' in the context of migration is nothing new.[74] What is new is the current socio-historical context and that, next to the fear of other criminal acts and the disturbance of public order, terrorist acts committed by refugees now form one further aspect of this fear. According to a survey by *IPSOS* conducted in 2017, the fear that terrorist 'moles' could find their way into the country by hiding amongst the refugee masses is persistent in many countries around the world – mostly amongst persons with conservative value orientation. The study revealed that 59 percent of the questioned persons agreed to the statement: '*There are terrorists pretending to be refugees who will enter my country to cause violence and destruction*'.[75]

The mingling of these two top media concerns with so many commonalities on a conceptual level should not come as a surprise.[76] Despite the few incidents of suspicion against forced migrants and the even fewer incidents, where these suspicions turned out to be factually founded, the news of asylum applicants participating in terrorism are spread rapidly. In addition, the disseminated information is often overly simplified and, therefore, misleading.[77] A great abundance of examples exists to illustrate this kind of fear spreading and emotional rhetoric. Especially various newspaper headlines contain statements like '*Three Asylum Applicants Arrested for Participation in Terror Militia*', '*Terror: Lifelong Arrest for Asylum Seeker*' etc.[78]

73 For the 'intimate relationship' of fear and terrorism see Suchday, Benkhoukha, and Santoro, 'Globalization and Media: A Mediator between Terrorism and Fear: A Post-9/11 Perspective', 98 ff.

74 Pöschl, 'Migration Und Mobilität', 9 ff.

75 IPSOS, 'Global Views on Immigration and the Refugee Crisis' (IPSOS, September 2017), 22, 24, https://www.ipsos.com/sites/default/files/ct/news/documents/2017-09/ipsos-global-advisor-immigration-refugee-crisis-slides_0.pdf; see also Dennison and Geddes, 'OP-ED: Are Europeans Turning against Asylum Seekers and Refugees?'

76 Unfortunately, the convolution of the terms 'terrorism' and 'asylum' often occurs in the form of claims that forced migrants might participate in terrorism and neglects other possible correlations and interdependencies. See, e.g., the preface of the Minister of Interior in 'Verfassungsschutzbericht 2017', 5.

77 Wodak, *The Politics of Fear*, 12.

78 See, e.g., 'Salzburg: Asylwerber wegen Terror-Verdachts Festgenommen', *Kleinezeitung.At*, 24 January 2017, http://www.kleinezeitung.at/oesterreich/5159067/; 'Terror: Lebenslange Haft Für Asylwerber (27)', *Krone.At*, 24 July 2017, http://www.krone.at/580173; 'Drei Asylwerber wegen Beteiligung an Terrormiliz Verhaftet', *DiePresse.Com*, 17 June 2016, https://diepresse.com/home/panorama/oesterreich/5023240/Drei-Asylwerber-wegen-Beteiligung-an-Terrormiliz-verhaftet.

Although the media often are blamed for controlling the news circle in a negative way and for creating images that deflect reality for their own gain, which to a certain degree they do,[79] media are in a tricky situation. *Wodak* states with regard to right-wing populism:

> […] the media are forced into a 'no-win' situation: if they do not report a scandalous racist remark or insinuation […], they might be perceived as endorsing it. If they do write about it, they explicitly reproduce the prejudicial utterance, thereby further disseminating it. If they critically interview the politician, they give him/her more face time and an opportunity for perpetrator–victim reversal. This triggers a predictable dynamic which allows right-wing populist parties to set the agenda and distract the media (and the public) from other important news.[80]

Furthermore, terrorists and governments alike can benefit from this side effect of free media reporting on terrorism. For terrorists, it is a declared goal to create fear and hysteria in the public. This is only possible, when information about an attack circulates and receives attention. The Austrian population seems to respond well to these triggers: 57 percent wish for more state agency to prevent the country from terrorist attacks.[81]

At this point, politicians and governments can use the emotionally charged audience.[82] For instance, the former Austrian Minister of Interior, who called himself the 'Security Minister', warned about terrorism in social media and took a strong stand against the 'unlimited and uncontrolled' reception of refugees.[83] The Austrian Freedom Party (FPÖ) explicitly posed an interpellation in Parliament with 51 questions under the heading '*Security instead of Islamisation and Asylum Chaos*'.[84] The explanatory notes of several government proposals

79 Plasser and Sommer, *Wahlen im Schatten der Flüchtlingskrise*.

80 Wodak, *The Politics of Fear*, 19.

81 'Österreicher haben Angst vor Terror'. The highest competence to undertake preventive measures against terrorist attacks and to stop the 'inrush' of forced migrants was ascribed to the Austrian People's Party (ÖVP), who consequently won the elections to the National Assembly in 2017. See Plasser and Sommer, *Wahlen im Schatten der Flüchtlingskrise*, 88 f.

82 Plasser and Sommer, *Wahlen im Schatten der Flüchtlingskrise*, 86; Nils Coleman, 'From Gulf War to Gulf War – Years of Security Concern in Immigration and Asylum Policies at European Level', in *Terrorism and the Foreigner: A Decade of Tension around the Rule of Law in Europe*, ed. Elspeth Guild and Anneliese Baldaccini (Boston: Brill Nijhoff, 2007), 83 f.

83 See, e.g., 'SPÖ nimmt Innenminister Sobotka ins Visier' (*vol.at*) http://www.vol.at/spoe-nimmt-innenminister-sobotka-ins-visier/5179444 accessed 19 April 2020.

84 Interpellation by Heinz-Christian Strache (2979/J 25. GP) https://www.parlament.gv.at/PAKT/VHG/XXV/J/J_02979/fname_371688.pdf accessed 19 April 2020.

include arguments on increased security needs in a globalised world and sometimes even mention security threats, including terrorism, by migrants and refugees without further explanation. In the last year, such sentences became less in explanatory notes of legislative proposals and the government is now limiting itself to presuming a general threat to national security and public order emanating from migrants. However, other documents produced by the ministries contain similar wording and undefined presumptions, not to mention the media appearances of some members of government.[85] In general, migration was a constant topic in the recent election campaigns and often was spoken about in convolution with vague security concerns.[86]

The generated fear creates public support for otherwise unpopular security measures touching upon individual rights.[87] A common populist tool is the imagery of a 'crisis' that must be handled and managed by the state, giving the population a sense of protection and control by the government.[88] It is important to note that politicians are one frequent source for the media and can thereby actively frame the public discourse. Moreover, by setting a certain issue

85 Compare e.g., phrases like 'the prevention of terrorism in a globalised world' in ErläutRV 763 BlGNR 25. GP 1 or 'quicker and more adequate possibilities of reaction to threats like terrorism in the migration and asylum law' in Vorblatt RV 582 BlgNR 25. GP 1. or the generally vague wording in ErläutRV 582 BlgNR 25. GP4 (Translated from German by the author.). Also, the wish of the former Minister of Interior, Herbert Kickl, that the police reports the citizenship of foreign perpetrators and sexual or especially violent crimes "proactively" to the press is one example of this governance strategy; see Vanessa Gaigg et al., 'Wie die Polizei die Wahrnehmung von Kriminalität beeinflusst', *DerStandard.At*, 5 January 2019, https://derstandard.at/2000094927194/Wie-die-Polizei-die-Wahrnehmung-von-Kriminalitaet-beeinflusst.

86 Plasser and Sommer, *Wahlen im Schatten der Flüchtlingskrise*, 149; see, e.g., Thomas Mayer, 'Doskozil und Kurz: "Darf keine illegale Migration nach Europa geben"', *DerStandard.At*, 8 September 2017, http://derstandard.at/2000063809822/Kurz-Doskozil-ist-Partner-fuer-restriktive-Migrationspolitik.

87 See Altheide, 'Terrorism and the Politics of Fear', 417, 426 ff; Wodak, *The Politics of Fear*, 5; Suchday, Benkhoukha, and Santoro, 'Globalization and Media: A Mediator between Terrorism and Fear: A Post-9/11 Perspective', 107 ff. The first explicit strike against individual rights was voiced by Minister of Interior, Herbert Kickl, in an interview on national TV, where he described the ECHR as an 'strange thing from the 50s' preventing him to use the 'fire hose' to 'to put out the fire' (in reference to Austria's migration situation) that he deems necessary to challenge and to be resistant against; Steinbeis, 'Minister of Civil Resistance'.

88 Plasser and Sommer, *Wahlen im Schatten der Flüchtlingskrise*, 86 f. In election campaigns, the opposition frequently uses this tool as well, either to deny the competence of the governing politicians or to emphasise their own competence to handle the crisis. But also in government this tools proves useful to politicians; see Petra Stuiber, 'FPÖ: Meister Der Angstmache', *DerStandard.At*, 23 January 2019, https://derstandard.at/2000096935007/FPOe-Meister-der-Angstmache.

on their agenda, creating legislation and specialised institutions, state actors can influence how certain topics will be portrayed.[89] Just like in terrorism, the chimera of a 'migration crisis' allows politicians to benefit from the public support created by fear and perceived loss of control, as set out above. Additionally, the social process of 'othering' plays an important role in this area for allowing the unequal treatment of migrants due to the reduction of solidarity.[90]

The Austrian Federal Office for Constitutional Protection and Terrorism Prevention (BVT) recognises this problem in its annual report. It holds that it is mostly EU citizens involved in the armed conflict ('foreign-fighters'), who pose a concern for the stabilisation of Syria and Iraq and who might spread radicalisation to Europe, and states that the greatest potential for radicalisation generally exists for juveniles, not asylum applicants.[91] The report, moreover, warns that single incidents and suspicions might further increase right-wing radicalisation in Austria, which it also acknowledges to pose a severe threat for the public order.[92] Subsequently, the report admits that the public discourse on migration was framed by recent terrorist attacks in Europe and, consequently, the topics of migration movements and terrorism became conflated. However, in the very next sentence the report points out that the BVT receives regular hints of terrorists hiding amongst the transiting refugees without giving further explanation.[93] Another chapter repeats this statement and informs that several Syrian and Iraqi suspects are currently under pre-trial detention. The

89 Tom Cockcroft, 'Late Modernity, Risk and the Construction of Fear of Crime', in *Crime, Media and Fear of Crime*, ed. Gorazd Meško et al. (Ljubljana: Tipografija, 2009), 19 f; Altheide, 'Terrorism and the Politics of Fear', 418 ff, 432 ff; Mike Berry, Inaki Garcia-Blanco, and Kerry Moore, 'Press Coverage of the Refugee and Migrant Crisis in the EU: A Content Analysis of Five European Countries' (Report prepared for the United Nations High Commission for Refugees (UNHCR), December 2015), 7 ff, https://www.unhcr.org/56bb369c9.pdf.

90 See Altheide, 'Terrorism and the Politics of Fear', 419 f; for the social process of 'othering' and how it is regulating discourse see Michael Schwalbe et al., 'Generic Processes in the Reproduction of Inequality: An Interactionist Analysis', *Social Forces* 79, no. 2 (December 2000): 434 ff.

91 'Verfassungsschutzbericht 2016', 23 f; compare also 'Who Were the Paris Attackers?', *BBC News*, 27 April 2016, sec. Europe, http://www.bbc.com/news/world-europe-34832512.

92 'Verfassungsschutzbericht 2016', 24.

93 'Unter dem Eindruck der Anschläge in Europa wurden bzw. werden im öffentlichen Diskurs die aktuellen Migrations- und Flüchtlingsbewegungen in Zusammenhang mit dem „Extremismus bzw. Terrorismus" thematisiert bzw. miteinander vermischt. Dem BVT liegen mehrere Hinweise vor, die darauf hindeuten, dass es unter den hier aufhältigen oder durchreisenden Migranten Sympathisanten bzw. Mitglieder dschihadistischer Gruppen oder Personen aus Syrien oder dem Irak gibt, die wegen Straftaten bzgl. Terrorismus verdächtig sind'. ibid.

motives of terrorists to travel with the refugee stream are acclaimed to be a demonstration of power and spreading fear and mistrust against refugees.[94] Hence, the report serves as an illustrative example for the contradictory behaviour of state institutions towards the issue. It seems that experts have achieved a certain degree of sensitivity for this frequent convolution in the public sector. Yet, state actors still enmesh themselves in the same problem by issuing vague statements without giving evidence or clear information.

4 Securitisation Trends in Austrian Migration Law

4.1 *The Beginnings of Austrian Migration Regulation and Rising Security Concerns*

In Austria, the regulation of migration already began in the Early Modern Age, when migration was first and foremost a social issue. In the early 18th century, the Habsburg Monarchy received migrants and refugees from the Ottoman Empire. This occasion remains the first known countrywide, systemic regulation of the entrance, travel and residence of migrants in Europe. Despite the strict border regime of the Habsburg Monarchy – mainly owed to epidemic plagues and customs – these persons were predominantly seen as a welcome economic opportunity.[95] Yet, next to this 'health and economic perspective', a 'cultural perspective' played a role as well. For instance, Jewish and Osman migrants were reportedly perceived with mistrust and their loyalty was under doubt.[96] In contrast, the Monarchy admitted refugees fleeing the French Revolution, but here the only precondition was that they could provide for themselves.[97] Although this example illustrates the social and economic perspective again, it also points out the different treatment of both groups. The reason

94 Ibid 35.

95 Jovan Pešalj, 'The Mobility Control of the Ottoman Migrants in the Habsburg Monarchy in the Second Half of the Eighteenth Century', in *Encounters in Europe's Southeast: The Habsburg Empire and the Orthodox World in the Eighteenth and Nineteenth Centuries*, ed. Harald Heppner and Eva Posch, vol. 5, The Eighteenth Century And The Habsburg Monarchy. International Series (Bochum: Winkler, 2012).

96 Jürgen Streihammer, 'Als Die Habsburger Europas Erste Moderne Grenze Zogen' *DiePresse.com* (16 September 2016) https://diepresse.com/home/zeitgeschichte/5083388/Als-die-Habsburger-Europas-erste-moderne-Grenze-zogen accessed 19 April 2020.

97 Friedemann Pestel, 'Französische Revolutionsmigration Nach 1789', *Europäische Geschichte Online* (EGO) (blog), 24 February 2017, MN 20 f, http://www.ieg-ego.eu/pestelf-2017-de.

seems to be that the cultural perspective did not pose a great issue for the French refugees, due to the common socialisation.

After World War I and II, many displaced persons sought refuge in Austria. The actual number is unclear to this day. Amongst them were Jews, war prisoners, forcibly recruited workers from Russia, France, Italy and Poland as well as many forced migrants from Poland and Romania and about one million displaced ethnic Germans.[98] After 1945, Austria hosted more than two million forced migrants, many of which arrived during one of four large displacement crises: The first occurred in 1956, when 180,000 persons fled Hungary (following their 114,000 fellow compatriots, who had already arrived after WWII). Austria, in search for its new geopolitical role, granted the Hungarians asylum without further procedure.[99] The next group of 162,000 Czechs and Slovaks fleeing the Warsaw Pact troops came in 1968. Another twelve years later, 150,000 Poles arrived to Austria, of which about 30,000 applied for asylum.[100]

Until then, forced migrants and their need for solidarity from the Austrian society were tolerably accepted.[101] Moreover, until the 1970s Austria was rather seen as a country of emigration, of transit and of first response for the displaced, who would soon return to their homes.[102] Apart from that, migration was primarily perceived as the temporary reception of foreign workers [*Gastarbeiter*]. After many Austrians had migrated to neighbouring countries in the 1960s, the national industry required foreign workers to fill the employment gap. For this purpose, bilateral agreements with Spain, Yugoslavia and Turkey were introduced that simplified the reception of these workers under the

98 Pöschl, 'Migration Und Mobilität', 29 ff; see also Michael Jandl and Albert Kraler, 'Austria: A Country of Immigration?', *Migration Policy Institute* (blog), 1 March 2003, https://www.migrationpolicy.org/article/austria-country-immigration.

99 Brigitta Zierer, 'Willkommene Ungarnflüchtlinge 1956?', in *Asylland Wider Willen: Flüchtlinge in Österreich Im Europäischen Kontext Seit 1914*, ed. Gernot Heiss and Oliver Rathkolb, Veröffentlichungen des Ludwig-Boltzmann-Institutes für Geschichte und Gesellschaft, Bd. 25 (Wien: J & V Edition, 1995), 163.

100 Jandl and Kraler, 'Austria: A Country of Immigration?'; UNHCR Austria, 'Asylum Country with Tradition', accessed 19 April 2020, http://www.unis.unvienna.org/documents/unis/25vic/25years_vic_unhcr.pdf.

101 Pöschl, 'Migration Und Mobilität', 144.

102 Susanne Mauthner-Weber, 'Was man von bisherigen Flucht-Bewegungen lernen kann' *kurier.at* (17 October 2016) https://kurier.at/wissen/konferenz-ueber-migration-und-integration-was-man-von-bisherigen-flucht-bewegungen-lernen-kann/225.697.239 accessed 19 April 2020.

precondition that it would remain temporary.[103] The fact that many of these workers eventually happened to migrate permanently was neglected for a long time. Consequently, Austria failed to provide a sophisticated policy on the issue, but instead let the labour market regulate it. This led to an accumulation of non-integrated migrants that, with the oil crisis and the ensuing decline of economic prosperity in the 1970s, prepared the ground for the fundamental change of migration policies.[104]

From 1975 onwards, it was no longer deemed sufficient to consider migration merely from an economic perspective. For the first time, public security and public order was to be considered also in the permission of labour forces.[105] Despite this, regulation still remained with the Ministry of Social Administration and the social partners.[106] Most political 'refugees' from Turkey after the military coup of 1980 and from Poland after the violent suppression of the democratic movement in 1981 found their way to Austria by way of labour migration, since it was still easier than applying for asylum.[107] Hence, the policy shift was not substantial yet. But the security perspective gained continuously in importance and with that the executive's role in curbing the immigration flow.

4.2 *1990s: The Securitisation Shift*

The mind-set completely changed with the breakup of communist regimes in Eastern Europe, the fall of the Iron Curtain and the immigration increase it caused for Austria in the 1990s. In the aftermath of the Balkan armed conflicts, more than 100,000 persons from Croatia, Bosnia and the Kosovo arrived to Austria.[108]

103 Agreement between Austria and Spain on the recruitment of Spanish workers and their employment in Austria as introduced by BGBl 1962/193 and amended by BGBl 1969/26; agreement between Austria and Turkey on the recruitment of Turkish workers and their employment in Austria as introduced by BGBl 1964/164; agreement between Austria and the Federal Republic of Yugoslavia on the employment of Yugoslavian employees in Austria as introduced by BGBl 1966/42. Pöschl, 'Migration Und Mobilität', 33.

104 Pöschl, 34, 38; Johan Wets, 'The Turkish Community in Austria and Belgium: The Challenge of Integration', *Turkish Studies* 7, no. 1 (March 2006): 87.

105 See §§ 13, 14 Ausländerbeschäftigungsgesetz (AuslBG) [*Foreigner Employment Act*] 1975 as introduced by BGBl 1975/218.

106 § 35 AuslBG 1975.

107 Pöschl, 'Migration Und Mobilität', 41; Wets, 'The Turkish Community in Austria and Belgium', 87; Paul Lewis, 'Austria Braces for Flood of New Polish Refugees', *The New York Times*, 24 December 1981, http://www.nytimes.com/1981/12/24/world/austria-braces-for-flood-of-new-polish-refugees.html.

108 UNHCR Austria, 'Asylum Country with Tradition'; Pöschl, 'Migration Und Mobilität', 61.

In 1991, as part of a large reform of migration law, the existing provision was replaced by a new Asylum Act[109] in order to adapt to the 'sudden influx of asylum claims' and 'Austria's new geopolitical role'.[110] The legislative material to this amendment points out several interesting parallels to the situation nowadays: First, a sudden increase of asylum applications occurred, as they more than tripled within 5 years from 1985 (6,724) to 1990 (22,798).[111] This is also true for the years 2014 (28,064) to 2015 (88,340).[112] Second, the social rejection of refugees from the Balkans – similar to that of the Ottoman migrants in the 18th century – suggests that one underlying issue might have been the perceived 'otherness' of the arriving society.[113] This could also be acclaimed for the current refugees, who primarily come from the Middle East or Africa.[114] Third, political and economic factors are evident as well. The economy was declining and the topic of migration was on the top of domestic politics as right-wing populism was flourishing. For instance, the Austrian populist Freedom Party (FPÖ) ran a petition against migration called 'Austria First'[115] and demanded 'zero immigration'.[116] The proposal of the new *Asylum Act* also claimed that the asylum seekers were not refugees in accordance with the definition of the Geneva Refugee Convention, but migrants in search for a better economic situation [*Wirtschaftsflüchtlinge*], and suggested that they were abusing the asylum system for a temporary residence in Austria by staying at least for the time of the asylum procedure until their claim would be denied. Hence, a great reform of the Austrian Asylum system would be necessary.[117]

In consequence, the paradigm shifted from employment policy to security policy and, symptomatically, was taken from the hands of the social partners and the Ministry of Employment put into the hands of the Ministry of Interior.[118] The reform involved, amongst others: the creation of a specialised Federal Asylum Agency; the acceleration of proceedings – for example, in obviously founded or non-founded cases, the authorities had to proceed without

109 Bundesgesetz über die Gewährung von Asyl (Asylgesetz – AsylG) [*Asylum Act*] 1991 as introduced by BGBl 1992/8.

110 The reasoning for the introduction of a new Asylum Act 1991in RV 270 BlgNR 18. GP 8; see also AB 328 BlgNR 18. GP; see Jandl and Kraler, 'Austria: A Country of Immigration?'

111 RV 270 BlgNR 18. GP 10.

112 'Asylstatistik 2016', 4.

113 Compare Krastev, *After Europe*, 40 ff.

114 Ibid 5.

115 Pöschl, 'Migration Und Mobilität', 144 ff.

116 Jandl and Kraler, 'Austria: A Country of Immigration?'

117 RV 270 BlgNR 18. GP 10.

118 Johannes Peyrl, Thomas Neugschwendtner, and Christian Schmaus, *Fremdenrecht*, 2017, 35 ff.

further investigation after the first hearing;[119] and a great extension of the immigration police's competences, i.e., push-backs at the border, custody pending deportation up to six months, deportation without procedure when caught within seven days of illegal entrance (with no suspensive effect of remedy after entering illegally) and the allowance to enter houses.[120] In this way most migrants, who were caught entering the Austrian territory illegally, were deported within one or two weeks after their entrance.[121] In this context, the fight against migrant smuggling was emphasised: sanctions were raised and even smuggling without any financial benefits for the perpetrator became penalised.[122] Furthermore, data collection and exchange was introduced for certain suspicious foreigners and asylum applicants.[123] At the time, the only instance to prevent the legislature from departing too much from a humanitarian course was the Austrian Constitutional Court.[124]

Despite these restrictions on the right to asylum, Austria also introduced a new legal instrument to deal with mass migration: § 12 of the new *Residence Act* allowed for the government to enact a regulation on the reception of whole groups of aliens fleeing from armed conflict, which it made use of for the reception of Bosnians from 1993 until 1997.[125] This instrument is comparable to the Temporary Protection Directive (TPD) of the EU, which was also developed in the face of the Balkan crises and the masses of displaced persons they caused.[126] It can only be presumed that this efficient instrument was later

119 See § 17 AsylG 1991, BGBl 1992/8.

120 §§ 17 para 2, 18, 27 para 3, 35, 41, 47, 50 Fremdengesetz (FrG) [*Alien Act*] BGBl 1992/838; see the reasoning for the introduction of the Alien Act 1992 in RV 692 BlgNR 18. GP; see also AB 869 BlgNR 18. GP.

121 Ulrike Davy, 'Die Neuordnung des österreichischen Asylrechts' (1993) 2 Zeitschrift für Ausländerrecht und Ausländerpolitik 70, 71 f; see §§ 17 para 2, 18, 27 para 3, 35 FrG 1992.

122 §§ 80 ff FrG 1992; RV 692 BlgNR 18. GP 60.

123 §§ 72 ff FrG 1992; § 15 AsylG 1991.

124 See Pöschl, 'Migration Und Mobilität', 64 f.

125 § 12 Aufenthaltsgesetz (AufenthaltG) [*Residence Act*] 1993 BGBl 1992/466; see further regulation of the Austrian government on the number of admissions under the Residence Act, BGBl 1993/402 and the regulations of the Austrian government on the admission of displaced citizens of Bosnia-Herzegovina, BGBl 1994/368, BGBl 1994/1038, BGBl 1995/389, BGBl 1996/299 and BGBl II 1997/215.

126 Directive 2001/55/EC of July 2001 on minimum standards for giving temporary protection in the event of a mass influx of displaced persons and on measures promoting a balance of efforts between Member States in receiving such persons and bearing the consequences thereof [2001] OJ L212/12 (Temporary Protection Directive – TPD); for an in-depth analysis of the TPD and the obstacles to its implementation see Hanne Beirens et al., 'Study on the Temporary Protection Directive – Final Report', Study for the Directorate-General for Migration and Home Affairs of the European Commission, January 2016,

dropped for similar reasons as the TPD, in particular, the concern of creating a 'pull factor'.[127]

Hereafter, the many relevant provisions that altogether form the Austrian asylum system have been amended and altered more than 80 times, not counting the underlying provisions of Union law.[128] Most of them can be summarised under the goals of accelerating procedures, reducing the workload of state agencies and courts and reducing the 'misuse' of asylum claims. Instead, these apparent hysterical reactions in the legislation put further burden on the already exhausted legal professionals of administrative offices, courts, law firms and NGOs, which constantly have to adapt to ever-new provisions and deal with great backlogs causing delays in procedures. But, also for the applicants the legal situation became increasingly non-transparent and, thereby, undercuts legal certainty. Furthermore, the provisions of the Austrian asylum procedure contain many differences compared to the ordinary administrative procedure – the necessity of which is not always evident.[129]

Out of these many amendments, two are especially worth noting in this study: In 2005 another comprehensive reform of the Austrian migration law was undertaken, which introduced several provisions into the new *Aliens Act* with explicit reference to terrorism as a reason to refuse visas or issue exclusion orders for example.[130] This amendment must be viewed in context of the generally emerging terrorism awareness at that time. It illustrates how the issues of terrorism and forced migration became also legally intertwined. In 2014, during an overall reform of the Austrian administrative procedure, the asylum procedure became re-embedded in the ordinary administrative procedure. However, the new Austrian Federal Office for Immigration and Asylum (BFA) was now given two contradicting tasks: the evaluation of asylum claims and the termination of residence. This implies a danger that humanitarian concerns will be viewed from the security perspective of the immigration police and that their decisions will not be taken from an entirely objective point, as the single administrative body will find itself on the fence of two differing

---

https://op.europa.eu/en/publication-detail/-/publication/1c753fe9-9aab-11e6-868c-01aa75ed71a1.

127 See Beirens et al., 33.

128 For a more detailed listing of relevant provisions see Franz Merli, 'Das Asylrecht als Experimentierfeld: Einführung', in *Das Asylrecht als Experimentierfeld: Eine Analyse seiner Besonderheiten aus vergleichender Sicht*, ed. Franz Merli and Magdalena Pöschl (Wien: MANZ, 2017), 2 ff.

129 Pöschl, 'Migration Und Mobilität', 62 f.

130 RV 925 BlgNR 22. GP.

obligations.[131] Also, many of the particularities of the asylum procedures remained in spite of the reform.

4.3 Status Quo: *Enhanced Securitisation since 2015*

As aforementioned, from 2014 to 2015 asylum applications approximately tripled from 28,064 to 88,340.[132] Given the flooded media, amongst other fertilisers, this put the Austrian nation in a condition that could be described as 'polarised shock'. As ordinary citizens and politicians became drawn into a highly emotional debate over the right answer to the 'refugee crisis', legislation was not beyond the situation as well. The frequency of amendments increased dramatically, as a consequence: Since 2015, the *Asylum Act* was amended seven times,[133] the *Alien Police Act* eight times,[134] the procedural law 14 times,[135] the *Residence Act* nine times[136] and the *Citizenship Act* four times.[137] In the same time, in total eleven amendments of the *Security Police Act*[138] and the *Border Control Act*[139] took place. Furthermore, a *State Police Protection Act*[140] was introduced to assign advanced investigation competences to the police for the

131 Pöschl, 'Migration Und Mobilität', 65. Moreover, the government has announced plans to move the legal consultation of asylum applicants into the authority of the BFA as well. This caused a wave of protest in Austria. See Julia Kotal, 'Grundrecht auf faires Verfahren bedroht. Wir fordern: unabhängige Rechtsberatung für Asylsuchende!', Menschenwürde Österreich, 16 May 2018, https://www.mwoc.at/offener brief/.

132 'Asylstatistik 2016', 4.

133 Asylgesetz (AsylG) [*Asylum Act*] 2005 BGBl I 2005/100 as amended by BGBl I 2015/70, BGBl I 2016/10, BGBl I 2016/24, BGBl I 2017/68, BGBl I 2017/84, BGBl I 2017/145 and BGBl I 2018/56.

134 Fremdenpolizeigesetz (FPG) [*Alien Police Act*] 2005 BGBl I 2005/100 as amended by BGBl I 2015/70, BGBl I 2015/121, BGBl I 2016/24, BGBl I 2017/68, BGBl I 2017/84, BGBl I 2017/145, BGBl I 2018/32 and BGBl I 2018/56.

135 BFA-Einrichtungsgesetz (BFA-G) BGBl I 2012/87 as amended by BGBl I 2015/70 and BGBl I 2018/56; BFA-Verfahrensgesetz (BFA-VG) BGBl I 2012/87 as amended by BGBl I 2015/41, BGBl I 2015/70, BGBl I 2015/84, BGBl I 2016/16, BGBl I 2016/24, BGBl I 2016/25, BGBl I 2017/17, BGBl I 2017/84, BGBl I 2017/140, BGBl I 2017/145, BGBl I 2018/32 and BGBl I 2018/56.

136 Niederlassungs- und Aufenthaltsgesetz (NAG) [*Residence Act*] BGBl 2005/100 as amended by BGBl I 2015/70, BGBl I 2015/119, BGBl I 2015/122, BGBl I 2017/68, BGBl I 2017/84, BGBl I 2017/145, BGBl I 2018/32, BGBl I 2018/56 and BGBl I 2019/14.

137 Staatsbürgerschaftsgesetz (StbG) [*Citizenship Act*] BGBl 1985/311 as amended by BGBl I 2017/39, BGBl I 2017/68, BGBl I 2018/32 and BGBl I 2018/56.

138 Sicherheitspolizeigesetz (SPG) [*Security Police Act*] BGBl 1991/566 as amended by BGBl I 2016/5, BGBl I 2016/61, BGBl I 2017/130, BGBl I 2018/29, BGBl I 2018/55 and BGBl I 2018/56.

139 Grenzkontrollgesetz (GreKoG) [*Border Control Act*] BGBl 1996/435 as amended by BGBl I 2016/25, BGBl I 2017/84, BGBl I 2017/45, BGBl I 2018/32 and BGBl I 2018/93.

140 Polizeiliches Staatsschutzgesetz (PStSG) [*State Police Protection Act*] as introduced by BGBl I 2016/5.

purpose of state protection against terrorism, amongst others. This indicates that both fields of law, migration law and security law, were similarly affected by the great 'security lack' narrative as described above. Also, on the social level the law noticeably changed: a new *Integration Act* was introduced obliging asylum applicants to learn German and undertake 'Austrian value courses'.[141] Furthermore, social benefits were cut on the federal as well as on the state level with several further amendments.[142] Most of these alterations occurred within two main reforms in 2015 and again in 2017. Further amendments are to be expected.[143]

Substantially, these amendments continued the trend of securitisation. So did the last great reform that entered into force on November 1st, 2017:[144] To facilitate the acceleration of procedures, a revocation of the right to asylum will be able to begin not only after a criminal conviction, but already in earlier stages of the procedure, and should be completed within one month. This harsh acceleration, in contradiction of the principle *in dubio pro reo*, was justified on the base of security considerations.[145] Also, a notification of the date of forced return is not obligatory anymore and, if the person was informed, remedies now do not have suspensive effect.[146] These amendments are comprehensible from the pragmatic point of view of governing authorities. However, they have severe consequences for the concerned individuals, who are taken out of their homes unexpectedly without chance to make any preparations and experience strong interferences of their personal rights.[147]

141 §§ 4, 5 Integrationsgesetz [*Integration Act*] BGBl I 2017/68 as amended by BGBl I 2017/86 and BGBl I 2018/37.

142 Bundesgrundversorgungsgesetz 2005 (GVG-Bund) [*Federal Reception Act*] BGBl 1991/405 as amended by BGBl I 2015/70, BGBl I 2017/84 and BGBl 2017/145; for the state level see e.g. NÖ Grundversorgungsgesetz (GVG-NÖ) [*Lower Austrian Reception Act*] LGBl 9240-0 as amended by LGBl 2015/80 and LGBl 2017/63; NÖ Mindestsicherungsgesetz [*Lower Austrian Basic Care Act*] LGBl 9205-0 as amended by LGBl 2015/71, LGBl 2015/96, LGBl 2016/24, LGBl 2016/103, LGBl 2017/63 and LGBl 2018/12.

143 Another amendment was again suggested in May 2018; see Fremdenrechtsänderungsgesetz (FrÄG) [*Migration Law Amendment Act*] 2018 proposed by 38/ME 26. GP and entered into force in June 2018 with BGBl I 2018/56. This reform continued the trend exemplified by the 2017 amendments.

144 FrÄG I + II 2017 proposed by 279/ME and 2285/A 25. GP and made known by BGBl I 2017/84 and BGBl I 2017/145; the subsequent list of amendments is by no means exhaustive, but rather exemplary.

145 § 7 para 2, 27 para 3 AsylG; see 279/ME Erläut 25. GP 2.

146 § 12a para 3/2 AsylG; see 279/ME Erläut 25. GP 28.

147 See Caritas, 'Stellungnahme zum FrÄG I 2017 (27/SN-279/ME 25. GP)' 9 https://www.parlament.gv.at/PAKT/VHG/XXV/SNME/SNME_08637/index.shtml accessed 19 April 2020; Katharina Beclin, 'Stellungnahme zum FrÄG I 2017 (41/SN-279/ME 25. GP)' 4

Further, the competencies of the immigration police were extended. For instance, custody pending deportation now can take up to 18 months in extreme cases and will in practice affect more persons than before.[148] House searches are permitted under less strict conditions; for example, whole asylum centres could be searched, if there was only one suspect (of illegal migration, e.g.) residing.[149] Moreover, coercive powers were conferred upon private security personnel in asylum reception centres without concrete description of the conditions thereof.[150]

In addition, sanctions for migrant smuggling were increased. In the case of illegal entrance, stay or neglecting the obligation to exit – which, in fact, happens with every denied asylum application – a fine up to € 15,000 (or six weeks of custody) could be imposed. This fine is 15 times higher than before; an increase that seems disproportionate. Further, the administrative offence of 'false statement in front of security authorities' was introduced.[151] Data collection and distribution was expanded.[152] As stated above, social support for persons whose asylum claim was denied became abolished, thereby endangering many to become homeless. The latter seems self-defeating, even from the perspective of public interest. If these individuals become homeless or cease to reside in state facilities, they will become more difficult to locate as a consequence and, hence, the provision rather contradicts public order.[153]

These amendments received a harsh critique from NGOs taking care of asylum applicants, scholars, UNHCR and the Austrian Data Protection Agency amongst others. Many of these statements accused the government in very clear words of setting populist measures in contradiction, not only of human rights obligations, but also in contradiction to what would be useful and appropriate to achieve the goal of preventing security gaps.[154] Without discussing the amendments in every detail, it can be stated that the government resorted

https://www.parlament.gv.at/PAKT/VHG/XXV/SNME/SNME_08743/index.shtml accessed 19 April 2020.

148 § 7 para 2 AslyG; see 279/ME Erläut 25. GP 28.

149 § 35a ff FPG; see 279/ME Erläut 25. GP 11.

150 § 9 para 3a GVG-Bund; see 279/ME Erläut 25. GP 32.

151 § 120 FPG; see 279/ME Erläut 25. GP 26 ff; see also critically Katharina Beclin, 'Stellungnahme zum FrÄG I 2017 (41/SN-279/ME 25. GP)' 3 https://www.parlament.gv.at/PAKT/VHG/XXV/SNME/SNME_08743/index.shtml accessed 19 April 2020.

152 §§ 34 ff NAG; see 279/ME Erläut 25. GP 9.

153 § 2 para 7 GVG-Bund; see the expert opinion on the first migration law amendment in 2017: Caritas, 'Stellungnahme Zum FrÄG I 2017 (27/SN-279/ME 25. GP)', 16.

154 See e.g. Caritas, 2; all expert opinions [Stellungnahmen] on the FrÄG I 2017 are available in German at https://www.parlament.gv.at/PAKT/VHG/XXV/ME/ME_00279/index.shtml accessed 19 April 2020.

to the very tendencies and instruments of securitisation already developed in the 1990s: Acceleration, detention, returns/deportation, data collection, extension of police competencies, establishing control by closing borders and fighting migrant smuggling.

Notably, in many of the listed amendments, security threats due to migration were proclaimed to be tackled. In some materials, terrorism and migration were explicitly or vaguely convoluted. For instance, phrases like 'the prevention of terrorism in a globalised world'[155] or 'quicker and more adequate possibilities of reaction to threats like terrorism in the migration and asylum law'[156] found their way into government bills. The latter referred to the possible exclusion of persons who are mere *suspects* of terrorism from travel documents and the non-suspensive effect of their remedies.[157] In particular, an exception to the right to asylum was introduced for persons who are – due to 'substantial reasons' – presumed to threaten national security with reference to 'current events' and the threat posed by extremism and terrorism. Additionally, with reference to terrorism, forced return of *suspects* became allowed without taking exceptions due to residence consolidation into regard.[158]

The similarities of the 1991/92 and 2015/17 amendments point out that, currently, migration law experiences a regression to a similar state as when the security narrative directed policies for the first time. Such a development, however, would signify a negation of the humanitarian progress of the last two decades that has been achieved in a joint effort by stakeholders in Austria and Europe. In particular, EU legislation has been a strong impetus for Austrian migration law in the sense that it tends to fulfil the minimum standards prescribed by EU secondary law.[159] Despite some digressions, the influence of

155 ErläutRV 763 BlGNR 25. GP 1.

156 Vorblatt RV 582 BlgNR 25. GP 1.

157 Ibid.

158 ErläutRV 582 BlgNR 25. GP 4, 11 in implementation of Art 14 para 4 lit a of European Parliament and Council Directive 2011/95/EU of 13 December 2011 on standards for the qualification of third country nationals or stateless persons as beneficiaries of international protection, for a uniform status for refugees or for persons eligible for subsidiary protection, and for the content of the protection granted (recast) [2011] OJ L337/9.

159 Although, in some instances, it tries to undercut them as well: for example, Austrian law imposes the obligation on vulnerable groups of asylum applicants to hand medical reports to the Austrian authorities contradicting the meaning of Article 21 Reception Directive. Compare § 15 AsylG and Art 15 European Parliament and Council Directive 2013/33/EU of 26 June 2013 laying down standards for the reception of applicants for international protection (recast) [2013] OJ L 180/96. Furthermore, the restriction of asylum applicants' access to the labour market does not correspond to Article 15 Reception Directive; see, e.g., AB 1599 BlgNR 25. GP discussing resolution proposal 740/A(E) 25. GP.

European law and the judicature of both European courts is undeniable. It safeguards certain standards, which the Austrian constitution alone (for lack of codification of social rights and restriction of many basic rights to Austrian citizens) could not guarantee.

5 Conclusion

The trend of securitisation is currently experiencing a strong renaissance in Austria. For migration law this implies a regression to policies and instruments of the 1990s. The rights of asylum applicants get restricted based on vague hints at a security deficit that are not supported by facts.

This kind of rhetoric incites security fear and perpetuates the security narrative. The fear of terrorism is only one of several aspects within the general security concern towards irregular migration. This concern also includes the fear of criminal acts committed by migrants and the general disturbance of public order. However, terrorism has proven to be a very strong rhetorical instrument and the frequent mentioning of the words 'terror' and 'migration' within one sentence, when the topic of state security arises, has far reaching effects on the psychological state of the population.[160] Also, migration law is not the only field that gets drawn into the trend of securitisation. Security generally became one of the highest values in the Western 'post heroic' society. Advocates of privacy rights, the right to fair trial and the right to assembly find themselves in a defensive position as well.[161]

Asylum applicants are individuals, who by Austria's ratification of several international treaties and human rights conventions have been granted subjective rights. Most of these provisions contain exceptions, which allow for a restriction of these rights in the public interest, especially in the interest of national security and public order – insofar as they remain proportional.[162] Hence, to justify further restrictions on forced migrants' rights it seems to be morally, politically and legally necessary to take on this security perspective. The claim has become that forced migrants constitute a threat, which the

160 Altheide, *Creating Fear*, 3, 83 ff.

161 See Ralph Janik, 'Den Ausnahmezustand (Neu) Denken: Zwischen Prävention und "Extremen Notfall"', in *Recht Und Krise*, ed. Manuel Aigner et al. (Jan Sramek, 2017), 29.

162 See, e.g., art 15 Convention for the Protection of Human Rights and Fundamental Freedoms (European Convention on Human Rights, as amended); or art 4 International Covenant on Civil and Political Rights (adopted 16 December 1966, entered into force 23 March 1976) 999 UNTS 171 (ICCPR).

state, its institutions and the population must reasonably and justifiably be defended against.[163]

In consequence of this narrative, not only specific provisions are introduced to tackle convicts or suspects of terrorism. Instead, the whole migration law becomes more rigorous and the rights of forced migrants restricted. Furthermore, migration related offenses, making forced migration a crime *per se*, are developed.[164] In some cases, the restriction of suspected asylum applicants' rights go even further than those in criminal procedures (e.g., detention, house searches), although the potential acts only form administrative offenses. Eventually, the already taken measures did not prevent Austrian voters from demanding for an even stricter asylum and migration regime.[165] Hence, these provisions must be questioned, not only in regard to their legal proportionality and necessity, but also their efficiency in reaching the declared goal of giving Austrians a stronger sense of security.[166]

Keeping this in mind, it becomes clear that the security narrative is not merely an unintentional result of the confusion of two different, but equally complex, transnational issues: terrorism and asylum – intertwined primarily by common root-causes.[167] More likely, it seems to be a purposeful framing of asylum applicants and refugees as a general threat to national security and public order, undermining the humanitarian perspective in order to achieve a certain political agenda. This agenda of securitisation not only scapegoats vulnerable human beings, but it also neglects expert opinions calling for a better understanding of the root-causes of terrorism and forced migration in order to develop sustainable strategies for the future.

163 Wodak, *The Politics of Fear*, 5.

164 For this topic commonly known under the term 'crimmigration' see e.g. Maartje van der Woude, Vanessa Barker, and Joanne van der Leun, 'Crimmigration in Europe', *European Journal of Criminology* 14, no. 1 (2017): 3–6; César Cuauhtémoc García Hernández, 'What Is Crimmigration Law?', *Insights on Law & Society*, 2017, http://www.antoniocasella.eu/nume/Crimmigration.law_spring17.pdf.

165 Plasser and Sommer, *Wahlen Im Schatten Der Flüchtlingskrise*, 52 f.

166 Caritas, 'Stellungnahme Zum FrÄG I 2017 (27/SN-279/ME 25. GP)', 3; Beclin, 'Stellungnahme Zum FrÄG I 2017 (41/SN-279/ME 25. GP)'.

167 See above in Section 2 (2).

CONCLUSION

Concluding Thoughts and Reflections on Terrorism, Asylum and Exclusion from International Protection

James C. Simeon

1 Introduction

The dual subject matter of this edited volume is far from an easy one. It covers two of the most pressing international public policy issues and concerns of our time: terrorism and asylum. The eleven original contributions of this edited volume provide an in depth examination of these two phenomenon that are the cause and consequence of so much pain, suffering, and misery in the world today. It is hoped that this edited collection will shed some further light on how these two phenomena have impacted all of our lives and, most importantly, that it will contribute to a better understanding of how these two phenomena may be similar or different and, indeed, how they function, so, that they may be able to be addressed effectively and, ultimately, resolved for the benefit of all.

These conclusions are intended to bring together some of the key points of the major contributions offered by the contributing authors to this volume. Together, the chapters in this collection provide a thorough and in depth review of the current situation and circumstances of how terrorism and asylum have been associated and interact, in and across a number of jurisdictions as well as internationally, in the world today. The chapter commences with a review and consideration of the varying legal definitions of terrorism and asylum that are extant globally. The salient point being that there is no universally accepted legal definition of terrorism. Likewise, there are different legal definitions for who is a refugee.

The similarities and the difference with respect to these two terms is reviewed, analyzed and considered as factors that have led to the conflation and confusion arising from the use of these two terms. What is notable is that these two terms have presently a common antecedent in non-international protracted armed conflict. From here the chapter moves on to consider terrorism and asylum in international criminal law. The various recent efforts of the United Nations and the international community in combatting the global terrorist threat are considered here. In addition, the challenges with respect

© KONINKLIJKE BRILL NV, LEIDEN, 2020 | DOI:10.1163/9789004295995_014

to determining whether an asylum applicant ought to be excluded from refugee protection on the basis of their alleged involvement in terrorist activities are also considered.

The chapter then then moves on to provide a brief review and consideration of some of the key findings and conclusions of each of the contributing chapters to the volume. Accordingly, this leads to five recommendations based on the key findings and conclusions of each of the contributing chapters on terrorism and asylum. While the recommendations are neither novel nor contentious they do reinforce the necessity for the international community to come together to resolve some of the long standing issues and concerns respecting these major preoccupations -- terrorism and asylum -- of the 21st Century and, especially, following the events of the world's worst terrorist attack to date, September 11, 2001.

These conclusions end with a call for states, regional organizations, the United Nations and other international organizations, along with a vibrant and supporting civil movement to come together in a renewed effort to address one of the major causes of both of these ever escalating phenomena of terrorism and asylum, protracted armed conflict. The five measures offered here are mere steps along the way in the more pressing commitment and effort to deal directly with the crux of the problem as opposed to its symptoms.

2 Varying Legal Definitions of Terrorism and Asylum

Two of the most contentious and most difficult terms to achieve a consensus on have been the legal definitions of terrorism and asylum. The legal definitions of terrorism and asylum are far from set and vary from continent to continent and from state to state. There is no universally accepted legal definition of what constitutes terrorism[1] and, likewise, the legal definition of who is a

1 United Nations, Meetings, Coverage, and Press Releases, "Fight Against International Terrorism Impeded by Stalemate on Comprehensive Convention, Sixth Committee Hears as Seventy-Third Session Begins," 3 October 2018, GA/L/3566, https://www.un.org/press/en/2018/gal3566.doc.htm. (accessed July 22, 2019); United Nations, General Assembly, Seventy-first session, Agenda item 108, 20 December 2016, "Resolution adopted by the General Assembly on 13 December 2016, 71/151 Measures to eliminate international terrorism," paragraph 24. https://undocs.org/en/A/RES/71/151. (accessed July 22, 2019); Jean-Marc Sorel, "Some Questions About the Definition of Terrorism and Fight Against its Financing," *European Journal of International Law*, (2003), Vol. 14, No. 2, 365-378. http://www.ejil.org/pdfs/14/2/420.pdf (accessed May 25, 2020); Government of Canada, Department of Justice, "Memorializing the Victims of Terrorism, Definitions of Terrorism and the Canadian Context," Date modified: 2015-01-07, https://www.justice.gc.ca/eng/rp-pr/cj-jp/victim/rr09_6/p3.html (accessed May 25, 2020)

refugee varies from one region to another.[2] Naturally, this results in wide policy and legal discrepancies in determining who is a terrorist and who is a refugee from one region to another and from one state to another. It also has serious implications for counter-terrorism strategies and measures on an international, transnational, and national scale.

The international community has yet to settle on a universal legal definition of terrorism. This is largely due to the division among member states of the United Nations on the basis of the concern that 'nations' have a fundamental right to self-determination and any definition of terrorism cannot infringe on this right. This applies to those peoples who are struggling under foreign occupation, colonial rule, or alien domination. There is also disagreement on whether it ought to include State sponsored terrorism, that covers States' political leaders and their senior military officials and armed groups under their control. States are not agreed whether the definition of terrorism captures State actors who are engaged in terrorist activities, outside the bounds of international humanitarian law, while seemingly preforming their legitimate duties as members of their armed forces.[3] However, neither of these concerns merits not reaching an agreement on what ought to be the legal definition of "terrorism." It has been noted that reaching an agreement on a common definition of what constitutes terrorism "would be a step towards universal cooperation in the prevention of terrorism."[4] Specifically, not having a universal definition for terrorism, clearly limits achieving cooperation on the basis of "transnational counter-terrorism" efforts.[5] It is also argued that a clear definition of terrorism is needed to help plan counter-terrorist measures at the national level, especially, amongst law enforcement agencies and the military.[6]

2 James C. Simeon, "Protecting Refugee Rights: International Refugee Law and the UNHCR," in *The Institutions of Human Rights: Developments and Practices*, eds. Gordon DiGiacomo and Susan L. Kang. (Toronto: University of Toronto Press, 2019), pp. 108–133. Vanessa Holzer, "The 1951 Refugee Convention and the Protection of People Fleeing Armed Conflict and Other Situations of Violence," Legal and Protection Policy, Research Series, Division of International Protection, UNHCR, September 2012, https://www.refworld.org/pdfid/50474f062.pdfhttps://www.refworld.org/pdfid/50474f062.pdf. (accessed May 25, 2012)

3 James C. Simeon, "Exposing Terrorism's False Association with Asylum," Canadian Association for Refugees and Forced Migration Studies, *Winter Newsletter 2018*, Issue 9, pp. 13–19, http://carfms.org/wp-content/uploads/2018/01/CARFMS-newsletter-winter-2018.pdf. (accessed July 23, 2019)

4 Gregor Bruce, "Definition of Terrorism: Social and Political Effects," *Journal of Military and Veterans' Health*, Vol. 21, No. 2, May 2013, pp. 26–30. https://jmvh.org/article/definition of-terrorism-social-and-political-effects/. (accessed July 23, 2019)

5 Ibid.; p. 27.

6 Ibid., p. 29.

By the same token, it is perhaps appropriate to ask, "Why does it seem that in the general public's mind, in the media at-large, and, within government at all levels, national, transnational and international, the words "terrorism" and "asylum" are all too often associated?[7] Why is there an apparent association between these two terms beyond the most obvious: a visceral 'fear' of the unknown, and, the proverbial "other," of the stranger in our midst? Or, is it that both terms are rooted, at their very core, in extreme violence, one as an instrument to advance political, religious, racial, ideological or social causes, and the other to escape from these same instrumentalities that threaten people's lives, liberty, and their security?

Can this fear also stem from the fact that mixed migratory flows not only include those who are *bona fide* refugees, but, also those who may harbor ill intentions, such as terrorists, against their putative host societies?[8] Indeed, the US State Department, Bureau of Counterterrorism and Countering Violent Extremism, *Country Reports on Terrorism 2016*, states that, "ISIS sought to exploit refugee and migrant flows to disguise the travel of its operatives, causing alarm but resulting in increased vigilance in many of the destination countries."[9] The

7 Witness the media's and the Canadian Government's response to the marine arrivals at Canada's East and West Coasts: Scott D. Watson, "Manufacturing Threats: Asylum Seekers as Threats or Refugees," *Journal of International Law and International Relations*, Vol. 3, No. 1, 2007, pp. 95–118; Alex Neve and Tiisetso Russell, "Hysteria and Discrimination: Canada's Harsh Response to Refugees and Migrants who Arrive by Sea," *University of New Brunswick Law Journal*, Vol. 62, 2011, pp. 37–45; Chelsea Han, *Smuggled Migrant or Migrant Smuggler: Erosion of Sea-Borne Asylum Seekers' Access to Refugee Protection in Canada* (2014). Paper submitted in partial fulfilment of the requirements for the Degree of Master of Science by course work in Refugee and Forced Migration Studies at the University of Oxford, 2014; Criminal Justice, Borders and Citizenship Research Paper No. 2565439. Available at SSRN: https://ssrn.com/abstract=2565439 or http://dx.doi.org/10.2139/ssrn.2565439. (accessed May 25, 2020)

8 Rowan Scarborough, "Islamic State finds success infiltrating its terrorists in refugee flows to the West," *The Washington Post*, January 29, 2017, http://www.washingtontimes.com/news/2017/jan/29/isis-finds-success-infiltrating-terrorists-into-re/. (accessed October 30, 2017); Alan Yuhas, "NATO Commander: ISIS 'spreading like cancer' among refugees," *theguardian*, 1 March 2016, https://www.theguardian.com/world/2016/mar/01/refugees-isis-nato-commander-terrorists. (accessed October 30, 2017); Marc Thiessen, "How ISIS smuggles terrorists among Syrian refugees," *Newsweek*, 27 April 2016, http://www.newsweek.com/how-isis-smuggles-terrorists-among-syrian-refugees-453039. (accessed October 30, 2017); Robin Simcox, "Terror is alive and well in the United Kingdom," *The Hill*, November 7, 2018, https://thehill.com/opinion/national-security/396553-terror-is-alive-and-well-in-the-united-kingdom. (accessed July 23, 2019)

9 US State Department, Bureau of Counterterrorism and Countering Violent Extremism, *Country Reports on Terrorism 2016*, Chapter 1, Strategic Assessment, https://www.state.gov/j/ct/rls/crt/2016/272228.htm. (accessed October 30, 2017); For an in depth analysis of the situation in Europe see, Robin Simcox, "The Asylum-Terror Nexus: How Europe Should Respond," *Backgrounder*, The Heritage Foundation, No. 3314, June 18, 2018, https://www.heritage.org/sites/default/files/2018-06/BG3314.pdf. (accessed July 23, 2019)

Country Reports on Terrorism 2017 make reference to a number of countries that arrested refugees on the suspicion of involvement in terrorist activities. The 2017 report on Greece, for instance, makes reference to,

> The porous nature of Greece's borders remained a concern, particularly given the challenge the refugee and migration crisis presents in Greece. Six of the individuals responsible for the 2016 attacks in Paris and Brussels passed through Greece. Greece worked with the U.S. Department of Homeland Security (DHS) to improve its screening of immigrants, asylum seekers, and refugees entering Greece. Personnel from the Hellenic National Police (HNP) and the Hellenic Coast Guard participated in DHS-sponsored training related to border screening, interdictions, and investigations in May. The FBI trained HNP officers on counterterrorism analysis in August and December.[10]

The official position of the US government appears to be that terrorists are exploiting their victims' efforts to seek asylum abroad from where they can continue their activities.[11]

It is critical to be able to examine and to analyze calmly and rationally how these two terms have been conflated in the media, within government policy circles, and in the public's mind to be able to call out this false association of these two highly emotive terms in order to be able to formulate an effective evidence based approach to resolve both of these seemingly rapidly escalating international, transnational, and national concerns.[12] At the heart of both of these global issues is the driver behind them, protracted armed conflict, that is, ongoing civil wars or non-international armed conflicts that are the root cause for both. In the end, it is, in fact, the international community's failure to be able to resolve protracted armed conflict that needs to be urgently addressed.[13]

10 US State Department, Bureau of Counterterrorism and Countering Violent Extremism, *Country Reports on Terrorism 2017*, Chapter 1, Country Reports Europe, Greece, Legislation, Law Enforcement, Border Security, https://www.state.gov/reports/country-reports-on-terrorism-2017/. (accessed July 24, 2019)

11 For a broader and more balanced perspective see Jeff Crisp, "Refugees: The Trojan Horse of Terrorism?" *openDemocracy: free thinking for the world*, June 5, 2017, https://www.opendemocracy.net/can-europe-make-it/jeff-crisp/refugees-trojan-horse-of-terrorism. (accessed November 2, 2017)

12 United Nations, *Global Issues Overview*, http://www.un.org/en/sections/issues-depth/global-issues-overview/. (accessed October 31, 2017) Wherein Peace and Security and Refugees are listed as two of the 18 global issues facing the world.

13 Robert Malley, "10 Conflicts to Watch in 2019," *FP, Foreign Policy*, December 28, 2018, https://foreignpolicy.com/2018/12/28/10-conflicts-to-watch-in-2019-yemen-syria-afghanistan-south-sudan-venezuela-ukraine-nigeria-cameroon-iran-israel-saudi-arabia-united-states-china-kurds-ypg/. (accessed July 25, 2019)

Undoubtedly, what these two diametrically opposed terms share in common is the powerful primal emotion, "fear," that, as we all know, can induce physical and psychological changes that can, in turn, bring about changes in behavior. In fact, terrorism has been called, "A strategic war against our minds... and, most importantly, an overwhelming feeling of vulnerability."[14] The primary goal of terrorists is to leave everyone in a state of "constant fear."[15] This is captured in the way that "terrorism" has been defined by States at the national level and by the United Nations and international courts at the international level. In the *Canadian Criminal Code*, Part II.1, Terrorism, Section 83.01(1), for instance, it states that "*terrorist activity*" means, in part, an "act or omission, in or outside Canada"[16] that is intended to intimidate or compel a person, a government, a domestic or international organization to do or refrain from doing any act.[17] Likewise, "fear" is central to the notion of asylum as evident from the *1951 Convention relating to the Status of Refugees* (*1951 Convention*) which defines a refugee, in part, as a person with a "well-founded fear of being persecuted for reasons of race, religion, nationality, membership in a particular social group or political opinion."[18] The one utilizes fear to "terrorize" a population, while the other flees a "well-founded 'fear' of being persecuted."[19]

14 Sandee LeMotte, "The psychology and neuroscience of terrorism," *CNN*, 15 July 2016, http://edition.cnn.com/2016/03/25/health/brain-and-terrorist-attack/index.html. (accessed July 24, 2019) See the embedded video, "The Psychology of Terror."

15 Ibid.

16 Government of Canada, Justice Laws Website, *Criminal Code* (R.S.C., 1985, c. C-46), http://laws-lois.justice.gc.ca/eng/acts/C-46/page-12.html#h-25. (accessed October 29, 2017)

17 Ibid., Section 83.01(1) states, in part, as follows:
act or omission, in or outside Canada,
(i) that is committed,
(A) in whole or in part for a political, religious or ideological purpose, objective, or cause, and
(B) in whole or in part with the intention of intimidating the public, or a segment of the public, with regard to its security, including its economic security, or compelling a person, a government or a domestic or an international organization to do or to refrain from doing any act, whether the public or the person, government or organization is inside or outside Canada.

18 *Convention relating to the Status of Refugees* (adopted 28 July 1951, entered into force 22 April 1954) 189 *UNTS* 137. See Article 1A(2).

19 Persecution is the infliction of the worse type of hardship or human rights violation possible. The UNHCR in its *Handbook and Guidelines on Procedures and Criteria for Determining Refugee Status Under the 1951 Convention and the 1967 Protocol Relating to the Status of Refugees*, Reissued Geneva, 2011, at paragraph 51, describes persecution in the following way:

There is no universally accepted definition of "persecution," and various attempts to formulate such a definition have met with little success. From Article 33 of the 1951

Terrorism is a term that seemingly defies any agreed universal definition. In Anthony Richards' well-known book, *Conceptualizing Terrorism*, he summarizes this definitional dilemma as follows:

> Defining terrorism has thus been a controversial endeavour that has perplexed both academics and policymakers. The political, subjective, and pejorative use of the term has rendered any prospect of achieving a universally agreed definition as remote indeed, and, as such, continuing deliberation over the meaning of terrorism is often seen as a stale and redundant exercise.[20]

Indeed, Anthony Richards and other commentators have noted that this definitional failure, across States and at the international level, has serious consequences that "undermines attempts to generate international cooperation against terrorism and can lead to unilateral and (even if unwittingly) counterproductive strategies. Indeed, some have suggested that the failure to define the concept is itself a cause of terrorism."[21]

Ben Saul, in his seminal work, *Defining Terrorism in International Law*, states,

> Terrorism should be defined and criminalized because it seriously undermines fundamental human rights, jeopardizes the state and peaceful politics, and may threaten international peace and security. Definition would also help to distinguish political from private violence, eliminating the overreach of the many 'sectoral' anti-terrorism treaties.[22]

The main point is that despite repeated attempts by the international community, for at least the last century, it has failed to define and to criminalize terrorism per se in international law.[23] Most recently, the UN's Ad Hoc

Convention, it may be inferred that a threat to life or freedom on account of race, religion, nationality, political opinion or membership of a particular social group is always persecution. Other serious violations of human rights – for the same reasons – would also constitute persecution. http://www.unhcr.org/3d58e13b4.pdf. (accessed November 2, 2017)

20 Anthony Richards, *Conceptualizing Terrorism*, (Oxford: Oxford University Press, 2015), p. 6.

21 Ibid, p. 4.

22 Ben Saul, *Defining Terrorism in International Law*. (Oxford: Oxford University Press, 2008), Oxford Scholarship Online, 2010, Abstract, http://www.oxfordscholarship.com/view/10.1093/acprof:oso/9780199535477.001.0001/acprof-9780199535477. (accessed October 31, 2017)

23 Ibid.

Committee established to negotiate a draft comprehensive convention on international terrorism reached an impasse on a number of issues, including:

> … "between acts of terrorism and the legitimate struggle of peoples under foreign occupation and colonial or alien domination in the exercise of their right to self-determination, as endorsed in General Assembly resolution 46/51 and other related United Nations documents" and whether it should include "the notion of State terrorism, including acts committed by the military forces of a State … that … should include, activities of individuals in command of the armed forces of a State or in control of armed groups in situations where these activities are not governed by international humanitarian law." [24]

While these negotiations continue, concern has been expressed that to be able to move forward Member States need "to be willing to show flexibility and demonstrate the necessary political will."[25]

If there is disagreement and a lack of consensus on how to define "terrorism," the same also can be said for the term "asylum," and those who seek it, "asylees" or "refugees." While the *1951 Convention* and its *1967 Protocol* together provide a legal definition of who is a refugee, it has been criticized as being far too narrow.[26] First, it is important to note that out of the 193 member States of the United Nations, there are only 148 State parties to the *1951 Convention* and

24 United Nations, Report of the Ad Hoc Committee established by General Assembly resolution 51/210 of 17 December 1996, Sixteenth Session (8 to 12 April 2013), A/68/37*, General Assembly Official Records, Sixty-Eight Session Supplement No. 37, paragraph 23, http://legal.un.org/docs/index.asp?symbol=A/68/37. (Accessed November 11, 2017)

25 United Nations General Assembly Seventy-First Session, Official Record, Sixth Committee, A/C.6/71 SR/31, 2 December 2016, Agenda item 108: Measures to eliminate international terrorism (continued), paragraph 39. http://undocs.org/A/C.6/71/SR.31. (accessed November 11, 2017)

26 For instance, see Adrienne Millbank, Social Policy Group, 5 September 2000, "The Problem with the 1951 Refugee Convention," Parliament of Australia, https://www.aph.gov.au/About_Parliament/Parliamentary_Departments/Parliamentary_Library/pubs/rp/rp0001/01RP05. (accessed October 29, 2017); William Thomas Worster, "The Evolving Definition of the Refugee in Contemporary International Law," *Berkeley Journal of International Law*, Vol. 30, No. 1, 2012, http://scholarship.law.berkeley.edu/cgi/viewcontent.cgi?article=1428&context=bjil. (accessed October 29, 2017); IRIN, "Has the Refugee Convention outlived its usefulness?" Johannesburg, 26 March 2012, http://www.irinnews.org/analysis/2012/03/26/has-refugee-convention-outlived-its-usefulness. (accessed October 29, 2017)

its *1967 Protocol*.[27] About one quarter of the States in the world are not State Parties to these key international human rights instruments that define, "Who is a refugee?" There are, in addition, at least four regional refugee rights instruments with broader definitions of 'who is a refugee'; including: *1966 Bangkok Principles; 1969 OAU Convention; 1984 Cartagena Declaration;* and, the *2011 EU Qualifications Directive*.[28] It is sufficient to note here that the *1984 Cartagena Declaration*, which builds on the *1969 OAU Convention*, is the most expansive definition of 'who is a refugee'. The *2011 EU Qualifications Directive* incorporates the provision of subsidiary protection for those who do not qualify for refugee status. 'Who is a refugee', then, will vary depending on where in the world a person is claiming refugee status. These legal definitions of 'who is a refugee' is not what is commonly understood to be a refugee; that is, as frequently used by the media or in everyday conversation.[29] Consequently, even on this basis, it is evident to see that there is no universal definition of who is a refugee, legally or in common parlance.

If the terms "terrorism" and "asylum" do not have a universal legal meaning then this can cause, obviously, anomalous situations where someone can meet the legal definition of "terrorist" or "refugee" in one country but not another. The ambiguity this generates for a common understanding of these two terms can create confusion as well as injustices. A fundamental principle in law is to

27 UNHCR, United Nations High Commissioner for Refugees, State Parties to the 1951 Convention relating to the Status of Refugees and 1967 Protocol, April 2015, http://www.unhcr.org/uk/protection/basic/3b73b0d63/states-parties-1951-convention-its-1967-protocol.html. (accessed October 29, 2017)

28 Asian-African Legal Consultative Organization (AALCO), *Bangkok Principles on the Status and Treatment of Refugees*, 31 December 1966; Organization of African Unity (OAU), *Convention Governing the Specific Aspects of Refugee Problems in Africa* (OAU Convention), 10 September 1969, 1001 UNTS 45; *Cartagena Declaration on Refugees, Colloquium on the International Protection of Refugees in Central America, Mexico and Panama*, 22 November 1984; European Union: Council of the European Union, *Directive 2011/95/EU of the European Parliament and the Council of 13 December 2011 on standards for the qualification of third-country nationals or stateless persons as beneficiaries of international protection, for a uniform status for refugees or for persons eligible for subsidiary protection, and the content of protection granted* (*recast*), 20 December 2011, OJL 337/9-337/26; 20.12.2011, 2011/95/EU. See also Asylum Information Database, *aida*, Useful Documents and Links, EU Legislation, http://www.asylumineurope.org/useful-documents-and-links. (accessed October 30, 2017)

29 Sharon Stanton Russell, "Refugees: Risks and Challenges Worldwide," *MPI, Migration Policy Institute*, November 1, 2002, https://www.migrationpolicy.org/article/refugees-risks-and-challenges-worldwide. (accessed October 29, 2017); Jill Goldenziel, "Five myths of refugees and migrants," *The Washington Post*, 25 September 2015, https://www.washingtonpost.com/opinions/five-myths-about-refugees/2015/09/25/ecd8a9d6-6149-11e5-b38e-06883aacba64_story.html?utm_term=.7f05405881bf. (accessed October 29, 2017)

"treat like cases alike." Because of the lack of a universal definition, then, this appears to be clearly absent from these two concepts.

It is important to underscore that we are in a period of escalating numbers of forced migrants. The UNHCR's annual 2018 *Global Trends* report found that there are 70.8 million people who were forcibly displaced at the end of 2018.[30] It noted that war, violence and persecution had uprooted more people than at any time in the seven-decade history of the UNHCR. The UNHCR spokesperson, Adrian Edwards, stated a year earlier that, "UNHCR's Global Trends report shows an average of one person was displaced ever two seconds in 2017, with developing countries most effected."[31] Edwards goes on to state that:

> Sadly, solutions remained in short supply. Wars and conflict continued to be the major drivers, with little visible progress towards peace. About 5 million people were able to return to their homes in 2017, with most returning from internal displacement. Among these were people returning under duress, or to fragile contexts.[32]

The top ten countries of origin for the world's refugees came from Syria, Afghanistan, South Sudan, Somalia, Sudan, Democratic Republic of Congo, Central African Republic, Myanmar, Eritrea, Burundi.[33] All of these countries have been wracked by protracted armed conflict. In fact, only five countries accounted for 67 percent or more than two-thirds of the world's refugees: Syria (6.7 million), Afghanistan (2.7 million), South Sudan (2.3 million), Myanmar (1.1 million) and Somalia (0.9 million).[34] The correlation between protracted armed conflict and forced displacement is blatantly obvious. The most telling and sad, if not most shocking, statistic in the *2018 Global Trends* report is that

30 UNHCR, The UN' Refugee Agency, *Global Trends: Forced Displacement in 2018*, Geneva: United Nations High Commissioner of Refugees, 2019, p. 3, file:///C:/Users/esouser/Documents/UNHCR/Global%20Trends%20in%20Forced%20Displacement%202018.pdf. (accessed July 22, 2019); UNHCR, *Figures at a Glance*, Statistical Yearbook, undated, https://www.unhcr.org/figures-at-a-glance.html. (accessed July 22, 2019)

31 Adrian Edwards, "Forced Displacement at Record 68.5 million," UNHCR, 19 June 2018, https://www.unhcr.org/news/stories/2018/6/5b222c494/forced-displacement-record-685-million.html. (accessed July 22, 2019)

32 Ibid.

33 UNHCR, The UN's Refugee Agency, *Global Trends, Forced Displacement in 2018*, UNHCR 2019, p. 15, (July 22, 2019) file:///C:/Users/esouser/Documents/UNHCR/Global%20Trends%20in%20Forced%20Displacement%202018.pdf. (accessed July 22, 2019)

34 Ibid. In fact the top three countries, Syria, Afghanistan, and South Sudan, made the top ten lists of conflicts to watch in 2019. Robert Malley, "10 Conflicts to Watch in 2019," *FP, Foreign Policy*, December 28, 2018, https://foreignpolicy.com/2018/12/28/10-conflicts-to-watch-in-2019-yemen-syria-afghanistan-south-sudan-venezuela-ukraine-nigeria-cameroon-iran-israel-saudi-arabia-united-states-china-kurds-ypg/. (accessed July 25, 2019)

half of the world's refugees are children.[35] But, what is much less obvious and, just as significant, is that there is also a correlation between terrorism and protracted armed conflict.

It is important and relevant first to acknowledge that "terrorism" is a global phenomenon. START, the National Consortium for the Study of Terrorism and Responses to Terrorism, in its Background Report, *Overview: Terrorism 2016*, indicates that there were terrorist attacks in some 108 countries.[36] No continent, save Antarctica, is left unspared. From its Global Terrorism Database, START reports that 13,400 terrorist attacks took place that resulted in more than 34,000 deaths, including, 11,600 perpetrator deaths.[37] It further notes that the terrorist attacks were geographically concentrated with the vast majority of attacks (87%) and deaths (97%) occurred in the Middle East and North Africa, South Asia and Sub-Sahara Africa.[38] These are precisely the regions of the world where most of the protracted armed conflicts are located. The report points out that,

> In 2016, the Islamic State of Iraq and the Levant (ISIL) remained the deadliest terrorist organization in the world, with its "core" operatives carrying out more than 1,400 attacks that resulted in more than 11,700 total deaths, including more than 4,400 perpetrator deaths. This represents a 19 percent increase in total attacks and a 39 percent increase in total deaths between 2015 and 2016. ISIL remained capable of gaining the allegiance of established and emerging perpetrator organizations around the world, and continued to inspire unaffiliated individual perpetrators who acted with little or no contact with ISIL operatives.[39]

35 Ibid. The report notes that, "Children below 18 years of age constituted about half of the refugee population in 2018, up from 41 percent in 2009 but similar to the previous few years."

36 START, National Consortium for the Study of Terrorism and Responses to Terrorism, Background Report, *Overview: Terrorism in 2016*, August 2017, University of Maryland, 2017, p. 1. https://www.start.umd.edu/pubs/START_GTD_OverviewTerrorism2016_August2017.pdf. (accessed July 25, 2019)

37 Ibid.

38 Ibid.

39 Ibid., p. 2. The figures for 2017 are similar but lower with only 10,900 terrorist attacks around the world, killing 26,400 people, including 8,075 perpetrators and 18,488 victims. The geographic concentration is the same. The report states that:

> Terrorist violence remained heavily concentrated in certain locations and coincided with other types of political violence. More than half of all attacks took place in four countries: Iraq (23%), Afghanistan (13%), India (9%), and Pakistan (7%). More than half of all deaths took place in three countries: Iraq (24%), Afghanistan (23%), and Syria (8%).

The above statistics clearly demonstrate the high correlation between terrorism and protracted armed conflict and persecution. Hence, both terrorism and refugees are sourced in those areas across the globe that are plagued by protracted armed conflict. Is there, then, some sort of 'guilt by association', that is to say, that refugees who come from protracted armed conflict situations, where most of the terrorism takes place, are "tarred with the same brush," as it were? Because protracted armed conflict produces both extreme violence in the form of terrorism as well as forced displacement confusion may arise in relation to the two. The fact that the perpetrators of terrorism may be exploiting their victims may further obfuscate matters in the public's mind. False associations may be generated, and the two concepts become conflated. Fran Cetti has argued that,

> As terrorism, crime, and asylum become entangled together with the narrative of national security, this analytical framework can then be applied indiscriminately to all those categorized as 'alien' or 'illegal'.[40]

This false association must be denounced in the strongest terms and manner possible. And, as it has been forcibly stated, "Conflating refugees with terrorists is irrational. It is not logical. Worse still, it is dangerous."[41]

Part of the difficulty may stem from the well-known fact that those who flee persecution often must resort to illegal means to exit their countries and to travel to a safe haven outside their own country of nationality. Those fleeing persecution may have to resort to smugglers to leave their own countries and to travel to other countries to claim asylum. However, it is important to point out that such *bona fide* asylum seekers cannot be punished for their illegal means for leaving their country of nationality or former habitual residence to seek asylum abroad. Article 31 of the *1951 Convention* prohibits Contracting States from imposing penalties on asylum seekers illegal entry or presence in

START, National Consortium for the Study of Terrorism and the Responses to Terrorism, Background Report, *Global Terrorism 2017*, August 2018, University of Maryland, 2018, p. 2, https://www.start.umd.edu/pubs/START_GTD_Overview2017_July2018.pdf. (accessed July 25, 2019)

40 Fran Cetti, "Asylum and the discourse of terror: the European 'security state,'" in *Discourses and Practices of Terrorism: Interrogating Terror*, edited by David Brecher, Mark Devenney, and Aaron Winter, (London: Routledge, 2010), p. 60.

41 Joint Statement of UNHCR Representative in Cyprus, Mr. Damtew Dessalegne, and the Commissioner of Administration and Human Rights, Ms. Eliza Savvidou, "Do not conflate refugees with terrorists," UNHCR and 1991 Ombudsman. Undated, http://www.unhcr.org.cy/fileadmin/user_upload/JointStatementUNHCR-OmbudswomanFINAL2.pdf. (accessed November 2, 2017)

their host State.[42] This essential point is often overlooked with respect to asylum seekers by elements of the general public who consider their presence as unlawful. This is highly inaccurate and a clear misconception.

And, it is absolutely crucial to make it abundantly clear that no one involved with "terrorism," in any way, can be determined to be a refugee.

Persons involved in terrorist activities would be excluded from Convention refugee status under Article 1F.[43] Accordingly, terrorists cannot use and abuse the asylum system as a cover for their nefarious surreptitious death dealing activities. The essential point being here that terrorists who contribute to the production of refugees cannot be the beneficiaries of a system designed to provide protection for their victims.[44] It is also important to emphasize that asylum systems are among the most closely scrutinized and assessed making it extremely difficult for criminals to penetrate.[45]

Exposing terrorism's false association with asylum is the first essential step to address the underlying cause of both, protracted armed conflict. But it is imperative that terrorism and asylum not be falsely associated. This is an

---

42 *Convention relating to the Status of Refugees* (adopted 28 July *1951*, entered into force 22 April 1954) 189 *UNTS* 137, Article 31(1) states:

> 1. The Contracting States shall not impose penalties, on account of their illegal entry or presence, on refugees who, coming directly from a territory where their life or freedom was threatened in the sense of article 1, enter or are present in their territory without authorization, provided they present themselves without delay to the authorities and show good cause for their illegal entry or presence.

43 *Convention relating to the Status of Refugees* (adopted 28 July *1951*, entered into force 22 April 1954) 189 *UNTS* 137. Article 1F states as follows:

> F. The provisions of this Convention shall not apply to any person with respect to whom there are serious reasons for considering that:
>
> (a) he has committed a crime against peace, a war crime, or a crime against humanity, as defined in the international instruments drawn up to make provision in respect of such crimes;
>
> (b) he has committed a serious non-political crime outside the country of refuge prior to his admission to that country as a refugee;
>
> (c) he has been guilty of acts contrary to the purposes and principles of the United Nations.

Sarah Singer, "The War on Terror and Refugee Law," in Satvinder Singh Juss, ed., *The Research Handbook on International Refugee Law*. (Cheltenham, UK: Edward Elgar Publishing, 2019), pp. 374–389.

44 James C. Simeon, "The Moral and Legal Philosophical Justifications of Article 1F Exclusion from Convention Refugee Status," Presented at the 2019 IVR World Congress, Special Workshop 56, Migration Philosophy, University of Lucerne, Thursday, July 11, 2019. (With the author.)

45 For instance, see the US refugee screening process at The White House, President Barack Obama, Amy Pope, "Infographic: The Screening Process for Refugee Entry into the United States," https://obamawhitehouse.archives.gov/blog/2015/11/20/infographic-screening-process-refugee-entry-united-states. (accessed October 31, 2017)

extremely difficult and sensitive subject area that needs to be studied, analyzed, and assessed in greater detail so that both terrorism and asylum can be properly understood and addressed. Perhaps it is not an exaggeration to assert that our failure to resolve protracted armed conflict has now reached the point that it poses an existential risk to humanity.[46]

2.1 *Terrorism and Asylum and International Criminal Law*

There is no doubt whatsoever that any type of terrorism is a serious international crime.[47] Terrorism that targets individuals and groups deliberately on any of the five grounds of the *1951 Convention* can be persecutory and can be the basis for a claim for refugee protection.[48] The United Nations has undertaken a great deal of work trying to address the problem of international terrorism. Since 9/11, it has passed a number of General Assembly resolutions and a number of binding Security Council resolutions in an effort to try to criminalize terrorism at the national and international levels and clearly establish that terrorism can never be sanctioned or resorted to no matter what the cause.[49] It is worth quoting paragraphs 4 and 10 of United Nations General Assembly Resolution 72/123 of 7 December 2017, "Measures to eliminate international terrorism," in their entirety that state:

> 4. Reiterates that criminal acts intended or calculated to provoke a state of terror in the general public, a group of persons or particular persons for political purposes are in any circumstances unjustifiable, whatever the considerations of a political, philosophical, ideological, racial, ethnic, religious or other nature that may be invoked to justify them;[50]

---

46 Nick Bostrom, "Existential Risks: Analyzing Human Extinction Scenarios and Related Hazards," *Journal of Evolution and Technology*, Vol. 9, No. 1 (2002), https://nickbostrom.com/existential/risks.html. (accessed October 31, 2017)

47 Government of Canada, Department of Justice, "About the Anti-terrorism Act," 26 July 2017, http://www.justice.gc.ca/eng/cj-jp/ns-sn/act-loi.html. (accessed February 8, 2018); The Crown Prosecutor's Service (CPS), "Terrorism," (2017), https://www.cps.gov.uk/terrorism. (accessed February 8, 2018); Michael Lawless, "Terrorism: An International Crime?" *Canadian Military Journal*, (2008), Vol. 9, No. 2, pp. 27–39. http://www.journal.forces.gc.ca/v09/n02/05-lawless-eng.asp. (accessed February 8, 2018)

48 Canadian Council for Refugees, Comments on Bill C-36, Anti-Terrorism Act, 5 November 2001, http://ccrweb.ca/en/comments-bill-c-36-anti-terrorism-act. (accessed February 8, 2018)

49 United Nations General Assembly, A/RES 72/123, 18 December 2017, Resolution adopted by the General Assembly on 7 December 2017, Measures to eliminate international terrorism, https://www.un.org/en/ga/search/view_doc.asp?symbol=A/RES/72/123. (accessed July 25, 2019) states, for instance, "*Reaffirming* that no terrorist act can be justified in any circumstances," and, "*Noting* the importance of continuing to strive towards achieving a world free of terrorism."

50 Ibid.

> 10. Emphasizes the need for States to cooperate resolutely against international terrorism by taking speedy and effective measures to eliminate this scourge, and in this regard calls upon all States, in accordance with their obligations under applicable international law and the Charter, to deny safe haven and bring to justice or, where appropriate, extradite, on the basis of the principle of extradite or prosecute, the perpetrators of terrorist acts or any person who supports, facilitates or participates or attempts to participate in the financing, planning or preparation of terrorist acts;[51]

And, in September 2006, the United Nations General Assembly adopted the *Global Counter-Terrorism Strategy*.[52] It is composed for four pillars: "1. Addressing the conditions conducive to the spread of terrorism; 2. Measures to prevent and combat terrorism; 3. Measures to build states' capacity to prevent and combat terrorism and to strengthen the role of the United Nations system in that regard; 4. Measures to ensure respect for human rights for all and the rule of law as the fundamental basis for the fight against terrorism."[53] It also includes a Plan of Action.[54] The Plan of Action outlines measures to address the conditions that are conducive to the spread of terrorism that includes "prolonged unresolved conflicts,"[55] the number one cause, as noted previously, of all those who are seeking asylum in the world today.

The United Nations also established an Office of Counter-Terrorism in June 2017.[56] It is led by an Under-Secretary General who is tasked to provide strategic leadership to the United Nations counter-terrorism efforts.[57] In addition, there is also a Terrorism Prevention Branch within the United Nations Office of Drugs and Crime in Vienna.[58] This UN Branch provides key legal counter-terrorism technical assistance to member States.[59] For instance, it provides

51 Ibid.

52 United Nations, Office of Counter-Terrorism, *UN Global Counter-Terrorism Strategy*, https://www.un.org/counterterrorism/ctitf/en/un-global-counter-terrorism-strategy. (accessed July 26, 2019)

53 Ibid.

54 Ibid., Annex, Plan of Action, https://www.un.org/counterterrorism/ctitf/en/un-global-counter-terrorism-strategy#plan. (accessed July 26, 2019)

55 Ibid.

56 United Nations, Office of Counter-Terrorism, https://www.un.org/en/counterterrorism/. (accessed July 26, 2019)

57 Ibid.

58 United Nations Office on Drugs and Crime, "Office of Drugs and Crime, Terrorism Prevention," https://www.unodc.org/unodc/en/terrorism/index.html. (accessed July 26, 2019)

59 Ibid.

States, upon request, "with the ratification, legislative incorporation and implementation of the universal legal framework against terrorism." The common universal legal framework against terrorism includes:

> ...the 19 universal legal instruments against terrorism along with the relevant United Nations Security Council Resolutions. The implementation of these conventions, protocols and resolutions is informed by the guidance provided by the UN Global Counter-Terrorism Strategy along with United Nations General Assembly Resolutions.[60]

Indeed, as pointed out, the United Nations has negotiated some 19 conventions and protocols on specific acts of terrorism from the seizure of aircraft, the taking of hostages, to violence at airports, terrorist bombings, terrorist financing, nuclear terrorism, and so on.[61] But, despite its best efforts to date there is still no universally accepted definition of this highly emotive and politically laden term, "terrorism."[62]

Although a comprehensive international convention on terrorism has eluded the United Nations to date, this does not mean that such a comprehensive convention can not be realized eventually.[63] The right to self-determination for peoples or nations does not include, if it ever did, the right to use extreme violence, including terrorism, to achieve its goal of autonomy. Terrorism is stunningly anathema to democracy, and everything that democracy is premised

60 Ibid.

61 United Nations Office of Counter-Terrorism, International Law Instruments, http://www.un.org/en/counterterrorism/legal-instruments.shtml. (accessed February 8, 2018)

62 Anna Maria Brennan, "The Difficulties in Defining Terrorism in International Law," *Human Rights in Ireland*, October 11, 2011, http://humanrights.ie/international-lawinternational-human-rights/the-difficulties-in-defining-terrorism-under-international-law/. (accessed February 12, 2018); Human Rights Voices, UN 101, "There is no UN definition of terrorism," http://www.humanrightsvoices.org/EYEontheUN/un_101/facts/?p=61. (access February 12, 2018); Jean-Marc Sorel, "Some Questions About the Definition of Terrorism and the Fight Against its Financing," *European Journal of International Law*, (2003), Vol. 14, No. 2, pp. 365–378. http://www.ejil.org/pdfs/14/2/420.pdf. (accessed February 12, 2018); Sean Larkin, QC, "Why Can't We Agree on a Definition of Terrorism?" *OpenMind*, December 16, 2013, https://www.bbvaopenmind.com/en/why-cant-we-agree-on-a-definition-of-terrorism/. (accessed February 12, 2018)

63 United Nations, Ad Hoc and Special Committees, Established on the Recommendations of the Sixth Committee, Ad Hoc Committee established by General Assembly resolution 51/210 of the 17 September 1996, Last Updated 22 September 2017, http://legal.un.org/committees/terrorism/. (accessed February 9, 2018); Mahmoud Hmoud, "Negotiating the Draft Comprehensive Convention on International Terrorism," *Journal of International Criminal Justice*, 4 (2006), pp. 1031–1043.

on such as the rule of law, freedom of speech and press, and other means of communication, free and fair elections, protection of the rights of minorities, freedom of assembly and association, and so on. In short, all the most core and fundamental human rights that everyone possesses, by virtue of their human dignity as sentient beings, and that they should enjoy fully. State sovereignty does not include the right, if it ever did, to use extreme violence, including terrorism, to achieve its goal of maintaining its legitimate control over a given people and territory through its monopoly on the legitimate exercise of force. Accordingly, this excludes the use of such things as persecution, torture, cruel and unusual treatment and punishment, extreme violence and terrorism. Indeed, it could be argued that the United Nations' doctrine of the Responsibility to Protect (R2P), endorsed and ratified by all UN member states, clearly contradicts the notion that state sovereignty is all encompassing.[64] Each individual state has a responsibility to protect its populations from genocide, war crimes, ethnic cleansing, and crimes against humanity.[65] And, the international community, through the United Nations, has the responsibility to use diplomatic, humanitarian, and other peaceful means to protect populations from genocide, war crimes, ethnic cleansing and crimes against humanity.[66] To assert that any comprehensive convention on terrorism would somehow limit the right of a peoples' to self-determination or would be an unnecessary infringement on state sovereignty or could lead to unwarranted charges against the military personnel of States, in the normal course of the fulfilment of their legitimate duties, are extremely specious arguments indeed.

Many States oppose a comprehensive international convention on terrorism because they are concerned that their political leaders and/or military personnel might be charged, tried, and convicted for terrorism in the fulfilment of their legitimate military objectives and missions. First, it is important to point out that terrorism is already prohibited under international humanitarian law and international criminal law.[67] Workable definitions of terrorism are already accepted at the national and international levels. Generally, the international

64 United Nations Office on Genocide Prevention and the Responsibility to Protect, *Responsibility to Protect*, undated, https://www.un.org/en/genocideprevention/about-responsibility-to-protect.shtml. (accessed July 31, 2019)

65 Ibid.

66 Ibid.

67 International Committee of the Red Cross, IHL Database, Customary IHL, Rule 2: Violence Aimed at Spreading Terror Among the Civilian Population, *Rule 2: Acts or threats of violence the primary purpose of which is to spread terror among the civilian population are prohibited.* https://ihl-databases.icrc.org/customary-ihl/eng/docs/v1_rul_rule2. (accessed February 11, 2018)

legal scholarly community is overwhelmingly in favour of a comprehensive international convention on terrorism.[68]

Terrorism is a serious international crime that is subject to prosecution under national and international criminal law. Most States have criminalized terrorism within their domestic legal orders, but States have defined terrorism in various ways. States have prosecuted individuals who they suspected of being involved in terrorist activities. Various criticisms have been levelled at States for having legislated vague and over-broad definitions of terrorism and the term terrorist. One of the attendant effects of this is that it could lead to an "abuse of power" by the State.[69] The way that the term terrorism is defined can have "a vital effect in determining the overall scope and application of an anti-terrorism law regime."[70] The legislative basis of how the term terrorism is defined clearly affects how the courts, in a respective jurisdiction, will apply and interpret the term to the factual situation of any case before them.

With respect to international criminal law, only four are called the 'core' international crimes: genocide, war crimes, crimes against humanity, and aggression. These core crimes are defined in the *Rome Statute* of the International Criminal Court (ICC).[71] What is missing from this list of core international crimes is terrorism. Legal scholars have called for terrorism to be included as a 'core' international crime that would fall under the jurisdiction of the ICC.[72]

68 Ben Saul, "The Emerging International Law of Terrorism," in *Terrorism*, Ben Saul, ed. (Oxford: Hart Publishing Ltd., 2012); Ben Saul, *Defining Terrorism in International Law.* (Oxford: Oxford University Press, 2006);

69 Keiran Hardy and George Williams, "What is 'terrorism'?: Assessing domestic legal definitions," UCLA *Journal of International Law and Foreign Affairs*, 2011, Vol. 16, p. 83, https://webmail-1.hermes.cam.ac.uk/?_task=mail&_action=get&_mbox=INBOX&_uid=270&_part=2&_frame=1&_extwin=1. (accessed February 10, 2018)

70 Ibid.

71 *Rome Statute of the International Criminal Court*, The text of the Rome Statute circulated as document A/CONF.183/9 of 17 July 1998 and corrected by procès-verbaux of 10 November 1998, 12 July 1999, 30 November 1999, 8 May 2000, 17 January 2001 and 16 January 2002. Part 2, Jurisdiction, Admissibility, and Applicable Law, Article 5, Crimes within the jurisdiction of the Court, The Statute entered into force on 1 July 2002, http://legal.un.org/icc/statute/english/rome_statute(e).pdf. (accessed February 10, 2018)

72 Peter J. Wertheim (2003) "Should 'Grave Crimes of International Terrorism' be included in the Jurisdiction of the International Criminal Court?," *Policy and Society*, 22:2, 1–21, DOI: 10.1016/S1449-4035(03)70017-4. https://doi.org/10.1016/S1449-4035(03)70017-4 (accessed February 10, 2018); Juliee Sharma, "The Challenge for the International Criminal Court: Terrorism," Legal Services India, undated, http://www.legalserviceindia.com/article/l247--International-Criminal-Court---Terrorism.html. (accessed February 10, 2018); Aviv Cohen, "Prosecuting Terrorists at the International Criminal Court: Reevaluating an Unused Tool to Combat Terrorism," *Michigan State International Law Review*, 2012, Vol. 20, No. 2,

Even though there is no universally accepted definition of terrorism there is a clear prohibition of terrorism in International Humanitarian Law, both in customary international law and within treaty law.[73] The Appeals Chamber of the Special Tribunal of Lebanon issued a landmark ruling that a definition of terrorism has emerged in customary international law that consists of three key elements: (i) the perpetration of a criminal act (such as murder, kidnapping, hostage-taking, arson, and so on), or threatening such an act; (ii) the intent to spread fear among the population (which would generally entail the creation of public danger) or directly or indirectly coerce a national or international authority to take some action, or to refrain from taking it; (iii) when the act involves a transnational element.[74] In fact, this Special Tribunal of Lebanon Appeals Chamber judgement was consistent with Presiding Judge Antonio Cassese's previous scholarly publications.[75] Nonetheless, the judgement received widespread criticism upon its release.[76] What cannot be denied,

---

pp. 219–257, https://digitalcommons.law.msu.edu/cgi/viewcontent.cgi?article=1080&context=ilr. (accessed February 11, 2018)

73 International Committee of the Red Cross, *IHL Database, Customary IHL*, Practice Related to Rule 2: Violence Aimed of Spreading Terror Among the Civilian Population, 1. Treaties; 2. Other Instruments; 3. Military Manuals; 4. National Legislation; 5. National Case Law; 6. Other National Practice; 7. United Nations; 8. Other International Organizations; 9. International Conference; 10. International and Mixed Judicial and Quasi-Judicial Bodies; 11. International Red Cross and Red Crescent Movement; 12. Other. https://ihl-databases.icrc.org/customary-ihl/eng/docs/v2_rul_rule2. (accessed February 11, 2018)

74 Interlocutory Decision on the Applicable Law: Terrorism, Conspiracy, Homicide, Perpetration, Cumulative Charging, Case No. STL-11-01/I (Feb. 16, 2011), https://www.stl-tsl.org/en/the-cases/stl-11-01/main/filings/orders-and-decisions/appeals-chamber/534-f0936. (accessed February 11, 2018)

75 Antonio Cassese, "The Multifaceted Criminal Notion of Terrorism in International Law," *Journal of International Criminal Justice*, (2006), 4, pp. 933–958, doi:10.1093/jicj/mql074.; Antonio Cassese, "Terrorism as an International Crime," *Enforcing International Law Norms Against Terrorism*, Ed., Andrea Bianchi, and Yasmin Naqvi, (Oxford: Hart Publishing, 2004), pp. 213–226.; Antonio Cassese and Paola Gaeta, *Cassese's International Criminal Law*, 3rd Edition, (Oxford: Oxford University Press, 2013), Chapter 8, Terrorism;

76 Ben Saul, "Legislating from a Radical Hague: The United Nations Special Tribunal for Lebanon Invents an International Crime of Transnational Terrorism," *Leiden Journal of International Law*, 24 (2011), pp. 677–700. https://www.cambridge.org/core/services/aop-cambridge-core/content/view/045D641D5847AD86B2E507B3A5E2CC40/S092215651100020 3a.pdf/legislating_from_a_radical_hague_the_united_nations_special_tribunal_for_lebanon_invents_an_international_crime_of_transnational_terrorism.pdf. (accessed February 12, 2018); Saul, Ben, "The Special Tribunal for Lebanon and Terrorism as an International Crime: Reflections on the Judicial Function" (September 6, 2012). *The Ashgate Research Companion to International Criminal Law*, W. Schabas, Y. McDermott, N. Hayes and M. Varaki, eds., Ashgate: Farnham, Forthcoming; Sydney Law School Research Paper No. 12/64. Available at SSRN: https://ssrn.com/abstract=2142324. (accessed February

however, is that this judgement has broken new legal ground, no matter how 'radical' and 'unconventional' a judgement at the international level. The judgement adds further credence that there is a growing consensus that there is a commonly accepted definition of terrorism in customary international law. Moreover, it could be argued that it is far from precedential given that the International Criminal Tribunal for the Former Yugoslavia (ICTY), essentially, came to the same judgement in a series of criminal prosecutions of senior military officials following the Bosnian War.[77]

Given the unprecedented number of forcibly displaced persons in the world, at 70.8 million,[78] and the overwhelming majority, over two-thirds,[79] fleeing conflict zones, it is reasonable to assume that the exclusion provisions of the *1951 Convention relating to the Status of Refugees*,[80] Article 1F, those who would be subject to exclusion for serious international crimes, is likely to be more relevant than not in claims for asylum.

Asylum claims that involve exclusion tend to be more complex and difficult to decide than the average asylum claims. For instance, in Canada they are adversarial hearings rather than the typical non-adversarial hearings and these

12, 2018); Almiro Clere, "An Examination of the Special Tribunal for Lebanon's Explosive Declaration of 'Terrorism' at Customary International Law," A dissertation in partial fulfilment of the requirements of the degree of Bachelor of Laws (Honours), University of Otago, October 2012, http://www.otago.ac.nz/law/research/journals/otago043934.pdf. (accessed February 12, 2018); Marko Milanovic, "Special Tribunal for Lebanon Delivers Interlocutory Decision on Applicable Law," EJIL: *Talk!* (February 16, 2011), https://www.ejiltalk.org/special-tribunal-for-lebanon-delivers-interlocutory-decision-on-applicable-law/. (accessed February 12, 2018);

77 John R. Lampe, "Bosnian Conflict, European History, 1992–1995," *Encyclopedia Britannica*, undated, https://www.britannica.com/event/Bosnian-conflict. (accessed February 19, 2018); Robert Cryer, "Prosecutor v. Galic and the War Crime of Terror Bombing," *Israel Defense Forces Law Review*, Vol. 2, pp. 75–102; Marlies Glasius, "Terror, Terrorizing, Terrorism: Instilling Fear as a Crime in the Cases of Radovan Karadzic and Charles Taylor," in *Narratives of Law and Justice in the International Courtrooms, Former Yugoslavia and Beyond*, edited by Dubravka Zarkov and Marlies Glasius (New York: Springer International Publishing, 2014), pp. 45–61; Roberta Arnold, "Terrorism, War Crimes and the International Criminal Court," in *Research Handbook on International Law and Terrorism*, edited by Ben Saul, (Cheltenham: Edward Elgar Publishing Ltd., 2014), pp. 282–297.

78 UNHCR, The UN' Refugee Agency, *Global Trends: Forced Displacement in 2018*, Geneva: United Nations High Commissioner of Refugees, 2019, p. 2, https://www.unhcr.org/5d08d7ee7.pdf. (accessed July 27, 2019); UNHCR, *Figures at a Glance*, Statistical Yearbook, undated, https://www.unhcr.org/figures-at-a-glance.html. (accessed July 27, 2019)

79 Ibid., p. 3.

80 *Convention relating to the Status of Refugees*, (28 July 1951 in force 22 April 1954) 1989 UNTS 137 and the *Protocol related to the Status of Refugees*, (31 January 1967, in force 4 October 1967) 19 UNTS 6223, 6257.

kinds of refugee cases require the intervention of a Ministerial representative, from the Canadian Border Services Agency (CBSA), and, the onus is on the Minister to make out the case for exclusion from refugee status.[81] Clearly, refugee claims that involve exclusion issues involve a greater commitment of time and resources to hear and to conclude. They are more difficult cases to decide because they involve knowledge of international criminal and humanitarian law as well as refugee law. And, at least in Canada, where these types of claims require adversarial proceedings, it requires an experienced decision-maker who is capable of handling difficult and, potentially, contentious hearings. Accordingly, these types of cases are triaged as complex cases that typically can take an entire hearing day, if not more, to conclude.[82]

It is also important to note that the vast majority of those who are excluded from refugee protection are excluded on the basis of being complicit in serious criminality; that is, as accomplices, as opposed to being the direct perpetrators.[83] Accordingly, this further implies that the decision-makers who are deciding these types of asylum claims are familiar with accomplice liability and how this ought to be applied when deciding whether an applicant should be excluded or not from refugee protection.

Those asylum applicants that are fleeing extreme violence in the form of not only protracted armed conflict or political extremism in the form of totalitarian states and authoritarian dictatorships are likely to be coming from countries that are also experiencing terrorist activities, either from the oppressor State and/or extremist groups. Terrorism can be perpetrated in both times of peace and in times of war.[84] But, from the statistics available on terrorism

81 Government of Canada, Justice Laws Website, Refugee Protection Division Rules (SOR/2012-256), Exclusion, Integrity Issues, Inadmissibility and Ineligibility, http://www.laws-lois.justice.gc.ca/eng/regulations/SOR-2012-256/page-4.html#h-18 (accessed April 19, 2018); Immigration and Refugee Board of Canada, Legal and Policy References, Legal References, Chapter 11, Article 1F, http://www.irb-cisr.gc.ca/Eng/BoaCom/references/LegJur/Pages/RefDef11.aspx. (accessed April 19, 2018)

82 Exclusion cases at the Immigration and Refugee Board of Canada are scheduled for two member hearings. Ordinary cases are scheduled with one member. Immigration and Refugee Board of Canada, Case Management Principles, https://irb-cisr.gc.ca/en/legal-policy/procedures/Pages/CasPrincip.aspx. (accessed July 27, 2019);

83 Joseph Rikhof, "The Exclusion Clauses in Refugee Law," in Satvinder Singh Juss, ed., *Research Handbook on International Refugee Law*, (Cheltenham, UK: Edward Elgar Publishing, 2019), pp. 390–402.

84 Council of Europe, "War and Terrorism," Compass: Manuel for Human Rights Education for Young People, undated, https://www.coe.int/en/web/compass/war-and-terrorism. (accessed May 7, 2018); Micah Zenko, "Bush and Obama Fought a Failed 'War on Terror.' It's Trump's Turn," Opinion, *The New York Times*, August 25, 2017, https://www.nytimes.com/2017/08/25/opinion/trump-afghanistan-war-on-terror.html. (accessed May 7, 2018)

events it is clear that terrorism overwhelmingly takes place in the same geographic locations where protracted armed conflict is also taking place. This adds a further complicating dimension to exclusion for those refugee applicants who come from the top source countries for refugees. It also suggests that those who are assigned to decide these types of 'complex' refugee claims must have a very sophisticated and detailed understanding of the country conditions in these geographic locations and the activities of the oppressor State as well as various extremist groups and their activities.

The exclusion of those who are involved in terrorist activities requires a knowledge and understanding of international criminal law and international humanitarian law, and what constitutes terrorism both nationally and internationally.

2.2 *Major Findings from The Contributions of This Volume*

Part 1 of this collection deals with the normative basis of the exclusion from asylum for terrorist activities. It deals with the salience of the Exclusion Clauses in international refugee law and its practical application within national asylum systems. The exclusion of the "refugee terrorist" element in the functioning of any asylum system is a manifest element of the very basis of the law itself that is premised on the sanctioned use of violence. US society is premised, it is often argued, on racist lines, and US President Donald J. Trump is only its current figurehead, that has been manifest throughout the history of the United States of America. Since 9/11 and the predominance of national security concerns, because of the fear of the terrorist threat, has provided a ready platform for politicians to introduce policies restraining forced migrants from particular Muslim countries. Counter-terrorism measures and strategies have gone from investigative, criminalization, and prescriptive to being, now, preemptive, anticipatory, and preventative. While extremist elements have sought to exploit asylum systems to harbor former armed combatants and to continue to radicalize vulnerable persons from within, through the machinations of diaspora politics that are led by political operatives and associational elites.

Patricia Tuitt concentrates on the law as the exercise of sanctioned and unsanctioned violence, the construction and the exclusion of the "terrorist refugee," and the use of "secret trials" through the Special Immigration Appeals Commission (SIAC), that deals with the appeals of persons who are deported from the UK by the Home Secretary on the grounds that the person is a national security threat. Tuitt sees the Exclusion Clauses of the *1951 Refugee Convention* as important and essential as the Inclusion Clauses and argues that the current asylum system in the UK leaves much to be desired.

Salina March addresses the underlining cultural and institutional narrative of America society, that is fractured by racism, with US President Donald J. Trump as its current figurehead. Applying critical race theory, nativism, and the overriding consideration of national security and the threat of terrorism, following 9/11, demonstrates how these are exploited by politicians through populism to advance a particular political agenda that includes limiting asylum from selected Muslim countries. Unravelling of the complex interrelationship between terrorism and asylum in American society reveals, in part, the dominance of a hierarchical racialized society based on affluence, social privilege and economic control.

John R. Campbell takes into consideration how 9/11 has resulted in the prevalence of national security, due to the overwhelming preoccupation with the threat of terrorism, that has allowed legislatures to pass laws that would not have been possible otherwise.[85] He focusses specifically on the Special Immigration Appeals Commission and how it functions in a case that he was directly involved in. SIAC is premised on the Special Advocate who represents the appellant at the Commission. The Special Advocate, who has been first vetted by the UK Secret Service, has access to "secret evidence" on which the trail is based but that is not disclosed to appellant, on national security grounds. The standard of proof for upholding the Home Secretary's decision to deport is a "reasonable suspicion" of the appellant being involved in terrorist related acts, a rather low threshold, indeed. Campbell notes that counter-terrorism measures have shifted from investigation, criminalization, and prescription to preemptive, anticipatory and preventative strategies.

Christopher McDowell's chapter deals with the aggressive recruitment and the radicalization of vulnerable persons and points out that extremist elements are exploiting the spaces created by the failures of the refugee protection and integration systems of host societies. He begins his analysis with the salient point that the "internationalization of contemporary conflict" has at least four elements: (1) large scale populations displacement; (2) resettlement and integration within host societies; (3) diaspora politics that links the movement and settlement of people; and, (4) the growing organized criminality in migration. McDowell demonstrates the critical role that diasporic associations and their elites play in the mobilization of their communities by seizing on specific events, the framing of issues and defining of grievances, and, their claims to legitimate action. Furthermore, the "internationalization of contemporary

85 For the impact of 9/11 or its lack thereof on the asylum systems in the US and Canada see Obiora Chenedu Okafor, *Refugee Law after 9/11: Sanctuary and Security in Canada and the United States*. (Vancouver: UBC Press, 2020).

conflict" incorporates the use of the asylum systems for retired combatants and their engagement in diaspora politics, the raising of necessary financial resources to advance their cause, and, ongoing radicalization of vulnerable persons, especially, disaffected youth, between 16–30 years of age.

The "internationalization of conflict" highlights the significance and relevance of how "diaspora politics" serve as a functional conduit of resources and support for protracted armed conflicts within countries of origin. This magnifies the highly complex interrelationship between terrorism and asylum and the pivotal role of the Exclusion Clauses in diminishing the impact of importing seemingly endless foreign armed conflicts to their resettlement communities within their host societies. Accordingly, counterterrorism measures can only be truly effective if they seek to address the tactics and strategies that are employed within the political diaspora that continually supports and seeks to advance the armed struggle within the homeland.

Part 2 of the collection analyzes the terrorism and asylum dimensions along the international, transnational, and national perspectives of the crime of terrorism with four chapters that cover the following critical points. Firstly, a mapping of the contours of exclusion from refugee protection based on complicity in terrorist crimes indicates that all forms of extended liability ought to apply to Article 1F of the *1951 Refugee Convention*. Secondly, that politicians seemingly rely on the association between terrorism and asylum, no matter how tenuous, to justify the securitization of immigration and refugee law, policy, and practice. As an example, Australia rarely uses the Exclusion Clauses because it has a wide array of other ways by which it can exclude asylum seekers. Thirdly, it is relevant and important to note that there is a "crime of terrorism" and a crime of the "infliction of terrorism" under international humanitarian law. And, fourthly, there is no question that there should be an international comprehensive convention on terrorism that clearly and legally defines the term. This would ensure greater consistency in judicial decision-making on matters dealing with terrorism in international criminal, humanitarian, and refugee law.

Joseph Rikhof's contribution is interested in mapping the contours of exclusion from refugee protection for complicity in terrorist crimes. His chapter considers ten Western liberal democracies: Australia; Belgium; Canada; France; Germany; The Netherlands; New Zealand; Sweden; UK; and USA, and how extended liability operates in each of their criminal law jurisdictions. He finds that there is a wide variation in the use of extended liability for involvement in terrorist offences: 25 forms of assistance to terrorist offences for individuals; and, 16 forms of assistance to terrorist offences for organizations, groups or associations. Rikhof points out that the forms of extended liability in national criminal law is wider than is found in international refugee law. He concludes by calling for the application of all forms of extended criminal liability to Article 1F of the *1951 Refugee Convention*. This implies the extension of both international criminal law and transnational humanitarian law to all subsections of Article 1F.

Peter Billings and Rebecca Ananian-Welsh examine the relationship between asylum and terrorism in Australia and, essentially, conclude that it is the justification the Government presents for the securitization of immigration and asylum laws in Australia. They also outline how the 2001 to 2003 "Pacific Solution," that was premised on interdiction at sea, offshore processing, and, temporary protection visas, gave way to "Operation Sovereign Borders" in 2013 that is also based on maritime interdiction and offshore processing, but, is now bolstered with the detention of asylum seekers, It is important to point out that the indefinite detention of migrants is constitutional in Australia. "Operation Sovereign Borders" is intended to disrupt and deter irregular migration, specifically, people smuggling, and try to affect an orderly and controlled humanitarian intake of forced migrants. What is most interesting is that the "Exclusion Clauses" are rarely used in Australia, given the many alternative ways of excluding someone such as an adverse security assessment or the character test. Moreover, membership in a terrorist organization is subject to a ten-year imprisonment, while directing, recruiting, training, funding, or supporting a terrorist organization is subject to a 25-year imprisonment. All told, Australia is far from a welcoming place for asylum seekers.

James C. Simeon notes that there is absolutely no doubt that "terrorism" is a serious international crime and that the "crime of terrorism" and the "infliction of terrorism" are criminal offences in international humanitarian law or the laws of war and international criminal law. Indeed, there is a "crime of persecution" that includes terrorizing civilians. The very first case where "terrorism" was determined to be an autonomous war crime was the *2006 Galic* case of the International Criminal Court of the Former Yugoslavia. Indeed, it is evident that even though there is no universally accepted definition of what constitutes terrorism it is still nonetheless banned, both, in terms of customary international law and treaty law. The *2001 Krstic* case, the *2006 Galic* case, and, the *2017 Mladic* case clearly established that there is a "crime of terrorism," both in international humanitarian law and in customary international law, and that the "crime of terrorism" is also encompassed within "persecution." All of those perpetrators of terrorism, Krstic, Gallic, and Mladic, were convicted and sentenced for the commission of the "crime of terrorism" and the "infliction of terrorism." Likewise, in the three Supreme Court judgements of *2002 Suresh* in Canada, *2010 JS (Sri Lanka)* in the UK, and the *2010 Holder v. Humanitarian Law*

Project, in the US, upheld their Government's impugned legislation. In the case of *Suresh*, the Supreme Court of Canada, stated that a person found to be a refugee could be returned to their country of nationality to face persecution, in exceptional circumstances, if they were deemed to be a national security risk. This would be a clear and blatant breach of the customary law principle of *non-refoulement*. It also came to the judgment that "terrorism" is not a constitutionally vague term and accepted the definition of terrorism found in the *International Convention for the Suppression of the Financing of Terrorism*.[86] In *JS (Sri Lanka)*, the UK Supreme Court ruled that for personal liability for exclusion from refugee protection the appellant had to have made a "voluntary" and "significant contribution" to the serious international crime of terrorism. And, in the US Supreme Court's *Holder v. Humanitarian Law Project* judgement, they ruled that the material support bar was constitutional and did not infringe on the *US Bill of Rights*. Nonetheless, a universal comprehensive definition of what constitutes terrorism needs to be approved to limit the differences in the definition of terrorism and to help ensure the consistent application of Article 1F exclusion from Convention refugee status across states.

One must be mindful of the fact that there is a "crime of terrorism" and the "infliction of terrorism" and that the "crime of persecution" includes 'terrorizing civilians'. Thus, terrorism can be clearly persecutory and serve as a basis for a claim for refugee protection. It can also serve as a basis for exclusion from refugee protection as well. This indicates clearly that all forms extended criminal liability ought to be applied to all subsections of Article 1F of the *1951 Refugee Convention*. But, more to the point, this makes it imperative that the very first priority ought to be an International Comprehensive Convention on Terrorism that defines what it is in precise legal terms.

Part 3 of the collection addresses the important topic of the national dimensions and dynamics of terrorism and exclusion from asylum. Given the variation in the application and interpretation of States Parties to the *1951 Refugee Convention* and its *1967 Protocol*, and the lack of a universally accepted definition of terrorism and States' different definitions of what constitutes terrorism, it is important to consider how the relationship between terrorism and asylum operates and is played out at the State level and how the Exclusion Clauses, with respect to terrorism, are applied within and across States. While the United Nations insists that those who are involved in terrorism must be criminally

86 *Suresh v. Canada (Minister of Citizenship and Immigration)*, [2002] 1 S.C.R. 3, 2002 SCC 1, paragraph 98; For an interesting legal analysis of this judgment see Audrey Macklin, "Mr. Suresh and the Evil Twin," *Refuge: Canada's Journal on Refugees*, (2002), Vol. 20, No. 4, pp. 15–22.

prosecuted, individual superior courts across jurisdictions continuously refine what the standard of proof ought to be for personal culpability for intentional participation in terrorism. If "voluntary, knowing and significant contribution" is the new standard of proof for exclusion from refugee protection, then, what amounts to a "significant contribution?" Terrorism and asylum are too often manipulated by States to advance other political agendas such as "securitization" and the use of blatant anti-refugee public policy discourses to mobilize their populist support base. In Switzerland, the *Asylum Act* at Article 53 allows for a determination as to whether a refugee applicant is "unworthy" of Convention refugee status. Further, membership in a terrorist organization can constitute a criminal offence under the *Swiss Criminal Code.* Combatting radicalization to extremism and to terrorism can perhaps best be achieved through effective integration policies and practices rather than through "isolation and stigmatization."

Mark Symes reminds us that international criminal law has yet to establish what degree of complicity in terrorist activity is necessary for criminal liability. However, the United Nations has made it clear that States must punish those who are liable for their intentional participation in terrorism. The UK Supreme Court in *JS* (*Sri Lanka*) decided that personal culpability was established when there was a "knowing significant contribution to a criminal purpose." The Supreme Court of Canada determined, in *Ezokola,* that it must be a "voluntary and significant contribution, on the knowledge that their conduct will further the crime or criminal purpose." The point raised is then, what constitutes a "significant contribution" to this crime or criminal purpose? While this will vary with the facts of each case and their circumstances one thing is for sure, it cannot be mere guilt by association, even when it is membership in a "limited brutal purpose organization." What further could be added here, as the *Ramirez* judgement insists? Perhaps it is the applicant's knowledge and understanding that they are part of an organization that is directly involved in crimes against humanity? Symes suggests that it is "the requirement of the intensity of intention that is stronger than mere recklessness."

Barbara Kőhalmi and Anita Nagy-Nádasdi analyze the situation in Hungary during the so-called, "Refugee Crisis in the Mediterranean Sea." They ask the question: "How has terrorism shaped the International Refugee Protection Regime?" Kőhalmi and Nagy-Nádasdi point out that there are at least two legitimate competing interests and rights at stake: the State's rights to maintain the security of its citizens; and, the refugees' rights to seek asylum or protection from persecution. How these two legitimate competing rights are balanced will vary from State to State but the balanced achieved must be within the margin of appreciation granted to States. Of course, some human rights are non-derogable, for instance, the right to life, the prohibition against torture, and so on, and, should never be balanced or diminished. The association between terrorism and asylum has been drawn upon by Hungarian politicians and the media. This has politicized and polarized the situation in Hungary, and, has led politicians to construct a barbed wired fence along the Serbian-Hungarian border and they have made it a criminal code offence to cross this barbed wire fence illegally. Based on interviews with a number of non-governmental asylum authorities in Hungary, Kőhalmi and Nagy-Nádasdi concluded, that there is no demonstrable link between terrorism and asylum in Hungary, despite the Hungarian Government's anti-asylum public policies that play on the unfolded fears of the public.

Nula Frei and Constantin Hruschka examine the terrorism and asylum nexus in Switzerland and note that the focus here is on the prevention of terrorism and radicalization. They analyze asylum cases where the applicant's fear of terrorist groups, like the Islamic State (IS) in Syria and Iraq and Al-Shabaab in Somalia. They also analyze asylum cases where the applicants are excluded for their involvement in terrorist activities under either Article 1F or Article 53, "unworthiness," of the Swiss *Asylum Act*. Membership in a terrorist organization may constitute a criminal offence under Article 260 of the *Swiss Criminal Code*. Those applicants who are found to have a well-founded fear of persecution, but, are excluded will not be granted a provisional admission as a foreigner. Those applicants who are found unworthy of asylum will not be determined to be refugees but will be allowed to remain in Switzerland if they have a well-founded fear of being persecuted should they return to their country of nationality or former habitual residence. The notion of "unworthiness" appears to play a large part in the determination of whether the person is a "threat to the security of Switzerland."

In Julia Kienast's examination of the relationship between terrorism and asylum in Austria, she refers to the 2017 national election where terrorism and asylum were center stage and ever present in the public mind. Kienast considers the number of asylum applicants who were excluded from refugee protection in Austria and, indeed, there were a few. There is also an examination of those who were radicalized in Austria. Kienast argues that effectively combatting radicalization efforts in Austria might be better served through integration measures rather than "isolation and stigmatization." Kienast also considers research on the "fear of migration" and finds that 74 percent of Austrians have a dread of the "continuous refugee stream." Reference is also made of a poll that revealed that 59 percent of Austrians agreed with the statement that, "*There are terrorists that are pretending to be refugees who will enter my country to cause violence and destruction*." The securitization of migration is making a major come back in Austria, according to Kienast. Rather than considering the "root causes" of both terrorism and asylum, the public agenda of the "securitization of migration" is being wilfully pursued.

The "securitization of migration" has been premised on the association of terrorism and asylum, even though there is no demonstrable linkage between the two. A number of jurisdictions have criminalized membership in a terrorist organization and additional bars have been added such as a character test or an "unworthiness" test for those who have been associated with terrorist organizations in some way. In other jurisdictions, membership within an organization that is involved with terrorist activities is insufficient to exclude the applicant for refugee protection unless something more is added. The suggestion that where there is a strong intention with respect to affiliation with a terrorist organization, that is more than mere recklessness, then this should be sufficient for the purposes of exclusion from refugee protection.

2.3 *Recommendations for Effectively Combatting Terrorism While Protecting the Right to Access Asylum*

Five measures for combatting terrorism while protecting the right to access asylum are offered here that arise from the work presented in the chapters of this edited volume. They are distilled and refined from the contributions of the authors of this edited collection. Each chapter offers its own perspective and insights on the subject of terrorism and asylum. However, they are all premised on the fundamental point that unless the predominate "root cause" of both terrorism and forced migration are left unaddressed then the problems attendant to terrorism and asylum will continue to plague States, the UN, and other international and regional organizations, and the international community as a whole. The overriding "root cause" is, of course, protracted armed conflict of a non-international nature or intrastate conflict or civil war. Authoritarian political oppression is also a factor, but, not to the same degree as protracted armed conflict and, of course, occasionally, the two overlap and are interrelated. Organized extreme violence in any form, outside that sanctioned by the United Nations Security Council, needs to be eradicated, for without peace and security nothing is really genuinely possible.

As indicated previously, terrorism can often serve as the catalyst for forced displacement in an armed conflict or war setting or under the throes of an oppressor state. Terrorized civilians will not remain in a war zone, it stands to reason, when their lives are at risk on a daily basis. As is often noted, this may be a deliberate strategy on the part of the armed combatants in order to gain both a tactical and/or strategic advantage in the midst of the armed conflict, whether in the heat of a battle or as a overall military strategy over the course of the armed conflict.[87] The population of a specific town, city or region is deliberately targeted in order to forcibly displace them from the area. While this may be a breach of the laws of war and be either a war crime and/or a crime against humanity, often very little can be done while the armed conflict is raging, and people are forced to flee their homes in order to survive. It is often not until the conflict has ended will perpetrators be investigated, charged, and prosecuted for their deliberate violations of international humanitarian and criminal law. This all takes time and it could be years before the perpetrators could be brought to justice for their crimes. However, this does little for all those who are caught in the middle of the armed conflict and are being used as pawns in the protracted armed conflict and whose human rights are being severely violated. There have been calls for the criminalization of mass force displacement in these types of circumstances.[88] This type of measure is intended to serve as a deterrent to armed combatants not to use people as "weapons of mass migration" in any armed conflict.

Ending the "scourge of war," the overall purpose of the United Nations, would do much to end many of today's most serious international crimes such as war crimes, genocide, crimes against humanity, and aggression. It would also do much to end terrorism and the need for asylum, as the principal cause of forced displacement in the world today that is due to, principally, protracted armed conflict. While the UN has been tasked for bringing lasting peace to the world, it is up to all of us to play our part if we hope to achieve this most marvelous goal. All of us must pledge to do so and to work toward achieving this goal that will, in all likelihood, take generations to bring about.[89]

87 Kelly M. Greenhill, *Weapons of Mass Migration: Forced Displacement, Coercion, and Foreign Policy*. (Ithaca: Cornell University Press, 2010); James C. Simeon, "Terrorism and Asylum: Unravelling the Myths," *RLI Blog on Refugee Law and Forced Migration*, January 2, 2018, https://rli.blogs.sas.ac.uk/2018/01/25/terrorism-and-asylum-unravelling-the-myths/. (accessed July 31, 2019)

88 James C. Simeon, "Enhancing Refugee Protection Through the Criminalization of 'Mass Forced Displacement'," *RLI Blog on Refugee Law and Forced Migration*, August 2, 2018, https://rli.blogs.sas.ac.uk/2018/08/02/enhancing-refugee-protection-through-the-criminalization-of-mass-forced-displacement/. (accessed July 31, 2019); Phil Orchard, "Making States Accountable for Deliberate Forced Displacement," WRC Research Paper No. 17, June 25, 2019, https://www.cigionline.org/publications/making-states-accountable-deliberate-forced-displacement. (accessed May 30, 2020)

89 Tom Clark and James C. Simeon, "War, Armed Conflict, and Refugees: The United Nations Endless Battle for Peace," *Refugee Survey Quarterly*, Volume 35, No. 3, September 2016, pp. 35–70. https://academic.oup.com/rsq/article/35/3/35/1752850. (accessed July 31, 2019); James C. Simeon, "Endless Wars and the Ever Escalating 'Global' Refugee Crisis," *CARFMS Blog*, August 18, 2016, http://carfms.org/endless-wars-and-the-ever-escalating-global-refugee-crisis/. (accessed July 31, 2019)

But, what further can be done in the immediate and short-term to address the problem of terrorism and forced displacement or asylum? The following five essential measures are offered for your perusal and consideration that have been distilled from findings of this volume.

1. ***It is imperative that the very first priority ought to be a Comprehensive Convention on Terrorism that defines what "terrorism" is in precise legal terms.***

Without a doubt, the fact that there is no commonly accepted universal definition of what terrorism is contributes to the lack of consistency of any counter-terrorism measures on a transnational and international bases. The variation in the definition across states is problematic because it undermines a fundamental legal principle, "like cases, must be treated alike." With the wide variations in the legal definition of who is a terrorist this does not ensure that "like cases are treated alike" or that there are consistent results for those who are responsible for the commission of these serious international crimes. An International Comprehensive Convention on Terrorism will help to ensure that there is greater consistency in prosecuting perpetrators for these serious international crimes.

2. ***All forms of extended criminal liability ought to be applied to all subsections of Article 1F of the 1951 Refugee Convention.***

Those who are complicit in the crime of terrorism are as responsible for the crime as those who were the direct perpetrators. This is a fundamental principle of any criminal law system. The accessories to a crime are as guilty as those who perpetrated the crime directly. All forms of extended liability need to be applied to all subsections of Article 1F. Joseph Rikhof's study of all the forms of extended criminal liability in ten Western liberal democracies and exclusion from asylum on the basis of terrorism activities demonstrates that international criminal law has now exceeded international refugee law with respect to extended liability. What would be required to make things operate in a more principled and consistent manner for terrorism exclusion cases is to ensure that all forms of extended liability are applied to the three subsections of Article 1F; that is, (a), (b), and (c).

3. ***For those jurisdictions where membership in a terrorist organization is not criminalized there is the suggestion that where there is a strong intention with respect to affiliation with a terrorist organization, that is more than mere recklessness, then this should be sufficient for the purposes of exclusion from refugee protection.***

Mere membership in a terrorist organization is no longer sufficient for exclusion under Article 1F in a number of jurisdictions. Assuming the organization that the asylum seeker is associated with is actively involved in terrorist activities, then, what further would be needed to determine that they ought to be excluded from refugee protection? The suggestion that Mark Symes proposes is admirable. In those circumstances, when the asylum seeker has expressed a strong intention with respect to their association with a terrorist organization, that is beyond mere recklessness, then, the asylum seeker has gone beyond mere membership to an expression of their willing affiliation and support for an organization, whose principles and purposes are fundamentally terrorist in nature, then, this ought to be sufficient for exclusion under Article 1F.

4. ***Counterterrorism measures can only be truly effective if they seek to address the tactics and strategies that are employed within the political diaspora that continually supports and seeks to advance the armed struggle within the homeland.***

To be truly effective counterterrorism measures must take into consideration the "internationalization of conflict." This includes the principal cause of forced displacement in the world today, protracted non-international armed conflict, and all of its attendant effects: the flight and journey; resettlement, adjustment, and integration in the new host society; diaspora politics; and, ultimately contributing to the new host society as a fully functional member/citizen. Overseas protracted armed conflicts may rely heavily on their diaspora for resources and support in their armed struggle to achieve their political goal, often to have their own independent state recognized by the world community. Funding the war effort at home may involve voluntary donations or even tax levies, amongst other things, from the members of their own community abroad. Not being aware of the diaspora community's efforts and activities in their respective host society could seriously undermine the effectiveness of any counterterrorism measures.

5. ***Those who are excluded from refugee protection on the basis of their involvement in terrorist activities ought to be prosecuted for their crime of terrorism, whenever the evidence warrants it.***

Terrorism is a serious international crime and the United Nations has called on its member states to prosecute all those who are responsible for such crimes. Those who are excluded from refugee protection because of their involvement in terrorism should be prosecuted where the evidence fully warrants it. A finding of guilty in a criminal prosecution is quite different from a determination that the person should be excluded from refugee protection under Article 1F. However, if there is sufficient evidence to reach a guilty verdict in a criminal prosecution then the state ought to proceed on that basis and hope for a conviction. This is absolutely essential if we are to end impunity for serious international crimes, but, even more importantly, if we are to bring an end to the use of terrorism to advance any political cause.

Taken together these five recommendations would be a good start to ending the blight of terrorism as well as ensuring that asylum is sufficiently distinguished from terrorism that the two are not mistaken or conflated in any pernicious ways. A precise universal legal definition for both terms would be a worthy goal to try to achieve in the near-term future. The international community, regional organizations, and states must come together on this, with the strong and forceful support of national and international coalitions of citizens from around the world, to assist in making this happen.[90]

90 World Refugee Council, *A Call To Action, Transforming the Global Refugee System.* (Waterloo: Centre for International Governance Innovation, 2019), Chapter Ten, Taking These Ideas Forward, https://www.worldrefugeecouncil.org/sites/default/files/documents/WRC_Call_to_Action.pdf. (accessed May 30, 2020)

Index

Printed in the United States
By Bookmasters